The Omaha Language and the Omaha Way

The Omaha Language and the Omaha Way

An Introduction to Omaha Language and Culture

Umóⁿhoⁿ Language and Culture Center,
Umóⁿhoⁿ Nation Public School, Macy, Nebraska:
Vida Woodull Stabler, Marcella Woodhull Cayou,
Donna Morris Parker, Patricia Phillips, Rufus
White, and Bryan James Gordon

and

Omaha Language Instruction Team, University
of Nebraska–Lincoln: Mark Awakuni-Swetland,
Alberta Grant Canby, Emmaline Walker Sanchez,
Rory Larson, Arlene Walker, Delores Black,
Aubrey Streit Krug, and Loren H. Frerichs

UNIVERSITY OF NEBRASKA PRESS | LINCOLN AND LONDON

Material in lesson 4.11 is from "Traditional Umóⁿhoⁿ Foods"
published by the Carl T. Curtis Health Education Center
(CTCHEC) with support from the Health Promotion and
Education Program at the Nebraska Department of Health; used
by permission of the CTCHEC. Introductory material included
here also appears in Mark Awakuni-Swetland, *Dance Lodges of the
Omaha People* (Lincoln: University of Nebraska Press, 2008).

RECOVERING
LANGUAGES & LITERACIES
OF THE AMERICAS

This book is published as part of the Recovering Languages and
Literacies of the Americas initiative. Recovering
Languages and Literacies is generously supported by
the Andrew W. Mellon Foundation.

Library of Congress Cataloging-in-Publication Data
Names: Awakuni-Swetland, Mark J., author. | Stabler, Vida
Woodhull, author. | Larson, Rory, author. | Streit Krug, Aubrey,
author. | University of Nebraska–Lincoln, sponsor.
Title: Umóⁿhoⁿ Íye-tʰe, Umóⁿhoⁿ Úshkoⁿ-tʰe : The Omaha
Language and the Omaha Way : An Introduction to Omaha
Language and Culture by Umóⁿhoⁿ Language and Culture
Center, Umóⁿhoⁿ Nation Public School, Macy, Nebraska:
Vida Woodhull Stabler, Marcella Woodhull Cayou, Donna
Morris Parker, Patricia Phillips, Rufus White, and Bryan James
Gordon, and Omaha Language Instruction Team, University
of Nebraska–Lincoln: Mark Awakuni-Swetland, Alberta Grant
Canby, Emmaline Walker Sanchez, Rory Larson, Arlene Walker,
Delores Black, Aubrey Streit Krug, Loren H. Frerichs.
Description: Lincoln; University of Nebraska Press, [2018] |
Includes bibliographical references. |
Identifiers: LCCN 2017030472 (print)
LCCN 2017047713 (ebook)
ISBN 9781496204936 (pdf)
ISBN 9780803211476 (cloth: alk. paper)
ISBN 9781496200440 (pbk.: alk. paper)
Subjects: LCSH: Omaha language—History.
Classification: LCC PM2071.A9 (ebook) |
LCC PM2071.A9 A9 2018 (print) | DDC 497/.5253—dc23
LC record available at https://lccn.loc.gov/2017030472

This work is offered in the memory of all of our Umóⁿhoⁿ Elders who have left us but remain in spirit to guide our journey.

This work is presented to our Umóⁿhoⁿ children and grandchildren — now and in the future — that they might respect, cherish, and care for the Omaha language and culture.

IN OUR MEMORY

Alberta Grant Canby
Uzhóⁿgeagthiⁿ, Tesíⁿde Waʔú
1930–2007

IN THEIR WORDS

Marcella Woodhull Cayou
Thátawesa, Thátada Waʔú
1937–2010
Donna Marie Morris Parker
Úʔiwathe, Hóⁿga Waʔú
1939–2011

This work is also in remembrance of Elders who taught culture at Umóⁿhoⁿ Nation Public School (Macy Public School) in the past.

1970S

John Turner & Suzette La Flesche Turner
Clyde Sheridan Jr. & Lillian Sheridan

1980S

Nellie (Enóⁿdabe) Canby Morris
Mary Clay
Wilson Wolfe & Gertrude Esau Wolfe
Coolidge Stabler
Clifford Wolfe Sr. & Bertha McCauley Wolfe
Valentine "Ty" Parker Jr. & Winifred Parker

EARLY 1990S

Oliver Cayou & Marcella Cayou
Mary Lieb Mitchell
Thurman Cook
Lawrence Cook
Morgan Lovejoy
Lillian Dixon Wolfe

1995 TO PRESENT

Donna Marie Morris Parker
Alice Freemont Saunsoci
Susan Freemont
Winona Mitchell (Háwate) Caramony
Rufus White
Octa Mitchell Keen
Blanche Robinson Harvey
Grace Walker Freemont
Dorothy Miller Montez
Elmer Blackbird & Nancy Miller Blackbird
Edna Cook
Pat Phillips

Excuse us if someone's name was mistakenly omitted from the preceding list acknowledging past Elder culture teachers at Umóⁿhoⁿ Nation Public School (Macy Public School). The names were compiled with good intentions. —Vida Woodhull Stabler

ILLUSTRATORS

Miya Kobayashi: figures 10–16
Barbara Salvatore: figures 33–102, 104–210
Jacob Smith: figures 5–9, 17, 18, 103

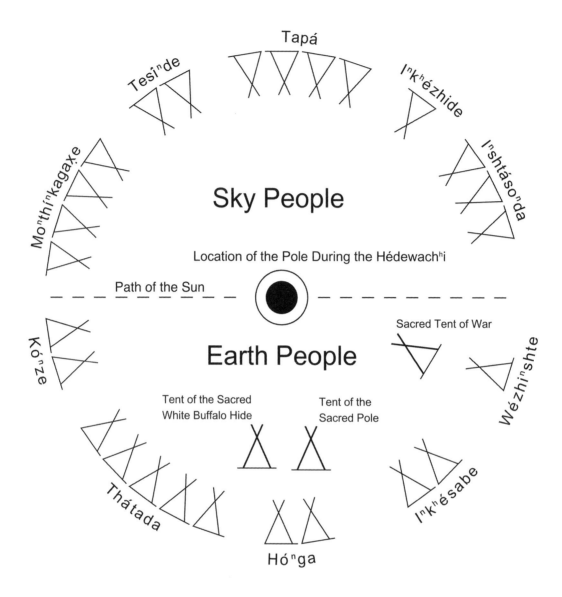

Tapá

Tesíⁿde

Iⁿkʰézhide

Moⁿthíⁿkagax̣e

Iⁿshtásoⁿda

Sky People

Location of the Pole During the Hédewachʰi

Path of the Sun

Sacred Tent of War

Earth People

Wézhiⁿshte

Kóⁿze

Tent of the Sacred
White Buffalo Hide

Tent of the
Sacred Pole

Thátada

Iⁿkʰésabe

Hóⁿga

FIG. 1. The Clans, Húthuga. In 2017 an Umóⁿhoⁿ Elder translated húthuga to mean: "All have a voice." See the introduction and lesson 4.11.

CONTENTS

ACKNOWLEDGMENTS

Oⁿthíthahoⁿ, "WE THANK YOU ALL"

In gratitude to the following Elders and people who wholeheartedly supported and encouraged the efforts of the Umóⁿhoⁿ Language and Culture Center's/UNPS Umóⁿhoⁿ Iye tʰe Umóⁿhoⁿ Ushkoⁿ tʰe textbook:

Umóⁿhoⁿ Elders Marcella Woodhull Cayou and Donna Morris Parker;

The children, grandchildren, and family members of Marcella Woodhull Cayou;

The children, grandchildren, and family members of Donna Morris Parker;

Umóⁿhoⁿ Nation Public School Student Senate, 2006;

Umóⁿhoⁿ Nation Public School District 16 Board of Education;

Administration, Umóⁿhoⁿ Nation Public School 2006–Present;

Umóⁿhoⁿ Tribal Council Omaha Tribe of Nebraska;

Title VI Parent Advisory Committee: Oliver Evan and Lavette Saunsoci, Libby Webster, and Students and Teachers of UNPS;

Title VI/ULCC Program at Umóⁿhoⁿ Nation Public School: our team and our relatives, Rufus White, Pat Phillips, Erwin Morris, Bryan James Gordon, Vida Woodhull Stabler.

Also

Octa Keen, for your guidance and teachings;

Umóⁿhoⁿ reservation community, too numerous to mention;

University of Nebraska–Lincoln and all who made our textbook possible;

Úthixide, Nephew Mark Awakuni-Swetland . . . for the love you showed for our Umóⁿhoⁿ Ways and the care you took to document. Your documentation will continue to help us as we continue to take back and practice what is ours. Many of us knew the relationships you had with our Elders and they shared their knowledge with you. In turn, you always shared when appropriate. You asked for permission from the Elders and our leadership before you acted. You showed that kind of respect.

Oⁿthíthahoⁿ. Tiúzhi oⁿgúta-ama, Oⁿthíthahoⁿ. "Our families, we thank you."

Our people say . . . Wóⁿgithe, thaékithai-a. Washkóⁿi-a. Moⁿthiⁿi, thaékithai-a: "All of you, pity one another. Try hard. In your daily walk of life, pity one another." Umóⁿhoⁿ words to live by . . .

—Vida Woodhull Stabler
with the ULCC at UNPS

WE GIVE THANKS

We thank Donna Awakuni-Swetland, wife of Mark Awakuni-Swetland, and their sons, Micah and Keali'i, for permission to publish Wagōⁿze Ūthixịde's work and for the trust they have placed in us.

We thank all of the Elders and speakers who have so generously shared their Omaha ways.

We thank the participants in Omaha language classes at the University of Nebraska–Lincoln; even after finishing the class, many former students have stayed in touch and volunteered their time and help.

We thank the faculty and staff of the UNL Institute for Ethnic Studies and the Department of Anthropology, especially Professor LuAnn Wandsnider, for their teachings and constant support.

We thank our colleagues in the Siouan and Caddoan Languages Conference and the Dhegiha Language Conference, whose dedication to language preservation and revitalization has enriched our work.

We thank our reviewers for their thorough and helpful suggestions.

We thank the editorial and design staff of the University of Nebraska Press, especially Matt Bokovoy, for their patience and commitment. We thank the Andrew W. Mellon Foundation's Recovering Languages and Literacies of the Americas Initiative for supporting our publication with the press.

We thank all of our families and relatives.

—UNL Omaha Language
Instruction Team

PREFACE

Wôⁿgithe thatʰí i tʰe ūdoⁿ. Welcome! It is good that you all are here.

We have completed this textbook, part of Mark Awakuni-Swetland's life's work, following his death in 2015. We honor him, Wagōⁿze Ūthixide, as a teacher, scholar, community member, and relative.

Awakuni-Swetland taught Omaha language classes at the University of Nebraska–Lincoln (UNL) from 2000 to 2013. Working with the Omaha Elder Elizabeth Stabler, he published the first Omaha dictionary ever produced as a book, the *Umóⁿhoⁿ Iye of Elizabeth Stabler* (1977, with a revised edition in 1991). He digitized the slip files of the late nineteenth-century anthropologist James Owen Dorsey in order to create the Omaha and Ponca Digital Dictionary (http://omahaponca.unl.edu/), a project funded by an NSF-NEH Endangered Languages grant and made possible by the work of a team of collaborators, including Catherine Rudin at Wayne State College, the UNL Center for Digital Research in the Humanities, and student workers.

Awakuni-Swetland initiated the project to write and publish an Omaha textbook in 2006. He again assembled a team of people, bringing together UNL teachers, Elder speakers, and the Umóⁿhoⁿ Language and Culture Center (ULCC) at Umóⁿhoⁿ Nation Public School in Macy, Nebraska. The team agreed that the ULCC would hold the textbook's copyright and receive all royalties, and everyone involved became contributing authors.

In 2013, when Awakuni-Swetland was faced with the return of a recurring illness, he once more brought people together. Several more of his students accepted his invitation to join the team he asked to complete the textbook. As a team of contributing editors and authors, we have compiled and arranged the introduction and cultural lessons Awakuni-Swetland authored; revised and finalized the lessons developed through the UNL language courses; updated and enhanced the lessons created through the ULCC; and incorporated the illustrations that Awakuni-Swetland solicited and contracted while he was preparing the textbook.

The structure and organization of the textbook have changed over time. From the project's beginning, though, the textbook has consistently aimed to (1) teach both Omaha culture and language, and (2) reflect generous collaboration between UNL and the ULCC. Working with the accumulated wisdom and knowledge Awakuni-Swetland left in our trust, we have organized the textbook to show these Omaha values of balance and integration. We shaped the contents into two parts, each of which complements the other—just as the Earth and Sky do.

Out of respect, and in order to retain his unique voice in writing, we have refrained from making substantial edits to Awakuni-Swetland's introduction. We believe this introduction was composed circa 2006; the ethnohistorical narrative it includes tells of the Omaha up to about the end of the twentieth century. Contemporary readers may wonder about the Omaha in the twenty-first century, or about the number of Omaha speakers and students now. We leave such topics and questions for others to address. Our purpose in completing this textbook has been to honor the work that has been done in service of future generations.

Our departments have been blessed to work with beautifully fluent speakers, relatives who have lived and continue to live the language with every fiber of their very beings as Umóⁿhoⁿ níkkashiⁿga, Omaha people. Any shortcomings in the textbook will reflect the fact that the elicitations, ways of thinking, and ways of writing and editing the printed words come through those of us influenced by the dominant society. On behalf of Awakuni-Swetland, we accept responsibility for any errors that may appear in spite of our team's best efforts. Please contact the Umóⁿhoⁿ Language and Culture Center at Umóⁿhoⁿ Nation Public School with corrections or questions.

GUIDE FOR READERS

This textbook provides a diverse body of materials about Omaha language and culture for a diverse set of audiences. Following the introduction, the material generally increases in complexity through its two parts. However, the volume as a whole is not designed to be read front to back. Readers may instead choose where to begin and how to proceed based on their interests and goals. For example:

Readers new to Omaha culture may wish to start with the historical background segment "The Omaha People" in the book's introduction and the practical cultural lessons in part 2, chapter 9.

Community members and adult language learners may wish to start with the "Writing System Quick Sheet" in chapter 1 and the "Situation Quick Sheets" in chapter 2.

Parents and caregivers of children may wish to start with the "Games: Úshkade" in chapter 3.

Teachers of elementary and secondary students may wish to start with the seasonal lessons in chapters 4–7.

College students and professional linguists may wish to start with the grammatical lessons in part 2, beginning in chapter 10.

Readers looking for a translation of a specific word may wish to reference the glossaries, provided both in Macy Standard Orthography in chapter 8 and in University of Nebraska–Lincoln Orthography in chapter 21.

Finally, we suggest that whenever in their learning process students and teachers find themselves in need of strength and inspiration, they consult the closing "Words of Encouragement" at the back of the book.

CONTRIBUTORS

The Umóⁿhoⁿ language instructors, Elder speakers, and team members who worked on this textbook were asked to share their thoughts about the project and any other things they might wish to contribute.

UMÓⁿHOⁿ LANGUAGE AND CULTURE CENTER, UMÓⁿHOⁿ NATION PUBLIC SCHOOL

Vida Woodhull Stabler, ULCC Documentary Recorder, Director and Certified Teacher

I was fortunate to have my Mothers near me when I was around six years old. The Woodhull women took part in helping to raise one another's children. Mom Gerine would go home to Macy to visit her eldest sister. It was in Macy, while watching Mom Minnie Woodhull Parker, that I first saw our traditional Umóⁿhoⁿ ways in full force. Along with many other women, she was butchering hogs for a feast. I will always remember that sight. There were numerous trips back to Macy where we kids were piled in the back seat. We even made it back to the dog races to sell racing programs to buy popcorn and pop.

There was little Umóⁿhoⁿ language spoken to us kids while growing up. Umóⁿhoⁿ words were mingled with English. In hindsight, it was because my Mothers (the two youngest Woodhull sisters) married outside the tribe. It was when the six Woodhull sisters were together that

PHOTO 1. ULCC team (*left to right*): Donna Morris Parker, Vida Woodhull Stabler, and Marcella Woodhull Cayou at the Umóⁿhoⁿ Language and Culture Center, 2008. Photo by Mark Awakuni-Swetland.

we heard fluent Umóⁿhoⁿ spoken. Even then, I thought it was wonderful to hear. There were two brothers too, Elmer and George Woodhull.

Our family carries with us a song that was sung to all our babies. I sang this song to my daughters, Mihusa and Rosette, and I now sing that same song to my own grandchildren Ruby and Dorion. While they are on their baby boards, I hum them to sleep while I rock them back and forth across my knees, or rub their backs as they lie on their bellies. I believe through song, language can be taught to our young ones.

I was raised in the urban area of Omaha around the other Umóⁿhoⁿ people who moved to Omaha during the relocation period. We lived around the 16th Street area along with the other Umóⁿhoⁿ people who moved there to find work.

The people my age and older all remember Hobo Park and 16th Street. This area and its people were my influence during my young years.

I attended boarding schools—St. Augustine's Indian Mission was one—as well as other Catholic Schools. I graduated from Central High in 1976. I married and moved back to our reservation. I remember the first time I went to the Tribal Building. I heard multiple sideline conversations in Umóⁿhoⁿ taking place by those who worked there or lived in our community— another lasting impression. My adult life has been here on our reservation with our people.

Education was taught to me in a meaningful way at the Nebraska Indian Community College at Macy. Umóⁿhoⁿ traditional knowledge was embraced, and as students we were encouraged to include aspects of our culture in all assignments. I also attended Wayne State College and Oklahoma City University.

In 1997 I began work as the Indian Education Program Director at the Umóⁿhoⁿ Nation Public School (UNPS). It was here that I became a student to relatives Marcella Woodhull Cayou, Donna Morris Parker, and Susan Freemont. I am the scribe who documented their words. I am blessed to have worked with them over the past sixteen years. My biggest challenge at Umóⁿhoⁿ Nation Public School has been my own limited knowledge of our language. As an adult learner, I learn and teach at the same time, but the joy is always in working with Elders and the students. Aunt Marcella and Grandma Donna were like mothers to me; with kind voices and patience they nurtured all whom they taught.

The passing of our Elders has caused much change. We must find our way and keep going. For our team of committed people, it is a labor of love to develop materials to teach language and culture to our children. This textbook is important because of the valued information the Elders shared with us. It is lucrative in word and those words feed our spirits.

Our school continues to grow, to expand and value the Umóⁿhoⁿ knowledge of our community and our people. This textbook, *Umóⁿhoⁿ Íye-tʰe, Umóⁿhoⁿ Úshkoⁿ-tʰe*, contains the printed words of two Umóⁿhoⁿ women who truly loved their cultural ways. It is their voices that make it of great importance to us. What is within is a sampling of the work they left for our Umóⁿhoⁿ people. Our textbook is designed to be easy to use. One will need to learn to read Umóⁿhoⁿ in order to make full use of this tool. We come from intelligent, resourceful people and we will continue to go against the current— as we always have. We have a strong history, and we will design a future where Umóⁿhoⁿ continues to be spoken. Our textbook was made with our Umóⁿhoⁿ people in our hearts and minds.

SPEECH BY HIⁿXPEWIⁿ
(VIDA'S OMAHA NAME)

Translations: Donna Morris Parker; elicitations/transcriptions: Vida Woodhull Stabler

Koⁿhá, óⁿbathe íⁿchʰoⁿ itháe kóⁿbtha.
"Grandmother, today . . . now I want to say something."

Úthitʰoⁿ wiwita-tʰe uágtha kóⁿbtha.
"I want to tell about my work."

Éthe wiwita nóⁿ-ma egóⁿ-ma wathítʰoⁿ zhawágigthe.
"I'm working with my Elder relatives."

Umóⁿhoⁿ íye-tʰé oⁿgíkoⁿza.
  "They teach me the Umóⁿhoⁿ
    language."

Zhiⁿgá-ama oⁿwóⁿshkoⁿ-xti Umóⁿhoⁿ
  íye-tʰe thipʰí oⁿwóⁿgikóⁿtha.
  "We try hard, we want our children to
    speak Umóⁿhoⁿ."

Umóⁿhoⁿ íye-tʰe oⁿgísithe shóⁿshoⁿ
  oⁿgóⁿtha, uxpáth-óⁿgithe oⁿgúthi'aga.
  "We want to remember always to talk
    Umóⁿhoⁿ Íye. We don't want to lose it."

Éthe oⁿgúta-ama áhigi Umóⁿhoⁿ íye
  thipʰí oⁿwóⁿgikoⁿtha.
  "We want many of our relatives to learn
    to speak Umóⁿhoⁿ Íye."

Íⁿchʰoⁿ, Umóⁿhoⁿ íye-tʰe thipʰí góⁿthai-a!
  "Now, please try to learn Umóⁿhoⁿ Íye!"

Wóⁿgithe wíbthahoⁿ, iⁿdádoⁿ égipʰe-tʰe
  óⁿthanoⁿʼoⁿ.
  "I want to thank all of you for listening
    to me."

Gánoⁿ ígipʰe.
  "I'm done speaking."

For my mother, Eunice Pauline Woodhull, Thátawesa; my father, Manuel Castro; my daughters, Mihusa and Rosette Stabler; and my grandchildren, Ruby Stabler and Dorion George.

Marcella Woodhull Cayou, ULCC
Umóⁿhoⁿ Language Instructor

  Ebé bthíⁿ-tʰe uwíbtha-tamiⁿkʰe.
  "I will tell you who I am."

Iⁿdádi wiwíta-akʰa izházhe-tʰe George
  Woodhull Jr.
  "My father's name is George Woodhull Jr."

Íⁿnoⁿha wiwíta-akʰa izházhe-tʰe Rachel
  Johnson.
  "My mother's name is Rachel Johnson."

Itígoⁿ wiwíta-akʰa izházhe-tʰe George
  Woodhull Sr.
  "My grandfather's name is George
    Woodhull Sr."

Ikóⁿ wiwíta-akʰa izházhe-tʰe Fannie
  Frost Woodhull.
  "My grandmother's name is Fannie
    Frost Woodhull."

Tóⁿwoⁿgthoⁿ wiwíta-tʰe Thátada.
  "My clan is Thatada."

Wazhíⁿga móⁿtʰanoⁿha wéatʰa-mazhi.
  "I cannot touch wild birds."

Witígoⁿ wiwíta-akʰa izházhe-tʰe
  Scott Johnson.
  "My grandfather's name is Scott
    Johnson."

Iⁿshtásoⁿda niáshiⁿga thíⁿ.
  "He is a Thunder clan person."

Wíkoⁿ wiwíta-akʰa izházhe-tʰe Maggie
  Mitchell Johnson.
  "My grandmother's name is Maggie
    Mitchell Johnson."

Tóⁿwoⁿgthoⁿ etái-tʰe Iⁿkʰésabe.
  "She was in the Black Shoulder
    Buffalo clan."

I was born at the Winnebago Indian Health Service Hospital in 1937. My parents were George Woodhull Jr. and Rachel Johnson. My mother's parents were Maggie Mitchell and Scott Johnson. My father's parents were Fannie Frost and George Woodhull Sr.

We stayed with my grandfather Scott, south of Macy near Decatur. My grandparents had a home there. Grandpa Ed Mitchell lived nearby and had a single-room log cabin. We used wood stove heat. There was well water with a pump to fill a nearby tank for use. My grandmother would home-can vegetables in the summertime. There were not too many kids. Grandpa made a large garden. He dug a cellar for the potatoes. We had tomatoes and string beans. He did not have a steady job but worked for a neighbor as a farmer's helper, fixing fence, and feeding hogs and cows.

We hauled water from the well using big cans. Dad plowed his own garden with his horses. We had one old horse and one lazy young horse. The old horse would get after the lazy one.

Grandpa Ed Mitchell traveled to town daily to buy tobacco and meat. He liked beef ribs and soup. We did all of our cooking on a wood stove, which was better than modern stoves.

The house was close to the timber. We would go down bottom with Grandma to collect raspberries and gooseberries for canning and to store in the cellar for winter pies. We could fill our buckets up right away. After supper we would clean them. Sometimes she would not cook them completely, just enough to put them in jars. Then she would cook them again when opening the jar. Gooseberries were for pies. Raspberries were for pies and desserts after supper.

I was accustomed to being an only child. There was always somebody there (in the house). My grandpa was a gambler and liked to play cards. Grandma liked handgames. People in the countryside with large living rooms often held handgames. Grandma would go there to play. Bonehead George Mitchell had a large place to play. We would do this on holidays. People would cook chickens potluck, not buy two hundred dollars' worth of meat like today. Whole chickens cost maybe 29–39 cents apiece. Somebody would get five chickens and that would be enough for a handgame.

People helped make those things in those days; it seemed easy. Today people only seem to help their own. My childhood friends included Mary Louise Grant, my step-father's sister. She lived down bottom. She'd come home with me and stay with us. Others came over to stay, too. They would help around the house and stay with us. It was common to have extended family members staying with us.

I met my future husband when he was in the service. He was seven years older than me. His girlfriend introduced me to him. She still doesn't like me today. Living out in the countryside was better than how we are gathered together today. You could have animals. We had a dog named Jiggs. He would come meet us as we rode the wagon home down bottom. He would bark at us all the way home. It did not bother the horses. Grandma would always feed him when we got home. Maybe that is why he would never stray far from home. We were married in 1952. We had four girls and three boys. Our children are Orville Cayou, Janice Cayou Sherman, Oliver Cayou Jr., Vanessa Cayou Parker, Debra M. Cayou, Francine Cayou, and Scott A. Cayou Sr.

My grandmother on my mother's side lived a long time, as did her mother. Now that Oliver is gone I miss them, too. Orville is the first-born son. He was born in 1953, when I was seventeen years old. We were living in Omaha at the time. Grandma Margaret and Grandma Jeanette and others would come and check on us. They would put Orville on the baby board and help take care of him. Other relatives living nearby would also check on us and the baby. He was small, but then many of our family on one side were small. On the other side many were taller and larger.

Oliver worked at United States Cold Storage in South Omaha. Orville was eight or ten years old. Then we had Janice, Junior, and Vanessa. Oliver said he did not want to raise his children in the city. He said let's just go home, and he would find something there. So we returned to Macy. Orville had already started school in Omaha.

Oliver went to work in Arlington, Nebraska, at a nursery digging trees. A lot of Omaha people worked over there. A truck would take them or he would take his own car. He applied to the Indian Health Services and the Roads Department. Both places offered him a job. He chose to work at the IHS Hospital. He retired after thirty-three years — around 1994.

Oliver and I always liked handgames. We would go way down south of Macy to play. We didn't know we were going to get a Native American Church staff. We used to be visited by Mormons when we lived down bottom (east of Macy). Several of our children went to school through the Mormons. They went all over, staying with different families. They learned a lot. They learned how to be responsible.

I started working at Macy school after Scotty, the youngest, started school. They had a cook's job open. I applied but did not get it. Instead I became a teacher's aide, paying three dollars an hour. I worked with a lot of teachers who are all gone now. Betty Hightree is still around. I worked over twelve years. I also worked with a lot of children and would help the teachers if the students gave them a hard time. The children often made one teacher cry. Once, when the teacher left the room crying, I stood up to the students and corrected them about being mean. When the teacher came back they all stood up and said they were sorry. I guess they paid attention to me that time. — Marcella Woodhull Cayou, as told to Vida Woodhull Stabler

Tápuska-kʰe-di umóⁿthiⁿkʰa áhigi
wabthítʰoⁿ.
"I've worked in the school for many years."

Umóⁿthiⁿkʰa gthéboⁿ noⁿba-shte
wabthítʰoⁿ.
"I've even worked twenty years."

Grades, classrooms ázhi-thoⁿthoⁿ
wabthítʰoⁿ.
"I've worked different grades and
classrooms."

Pahóⁿga-tʰe-di íⁿchʰoⁿ Umóⁿhoⁿ Íye
Tí-kʰe-di wabthítʰoⁿ.
"Just now I'm working for the first time
in the Umóⁿhoⁿ Language and Cultural
Center."

Donna Morris Parker, Hóⁿga waʼu,
ULCC *Umóⁿhoⁿ Language Instructor*

Iⁿdádoⁿ shkáxe-tʰe thipʰi gáxa.
"Whatever you do, do it right."

Thipʰí-xchi gatʰégoⁿ wémoⁿxa.
"Ask in the right way."

One day, relative Vida came to my home. She described this job here and what she was doing and how she needed help to teach the children. I wanted to come but I was taking care of my husband, who was ill at the time. I said I would consider it later on. Later on came soon when my husband passed away.

Vida still wanted me to come in and help teach Umóⁿhoⁿ íye, the Omaha language. I talked to my girls about it, and they told me to "go for it." They thought it would help take my mind off being lonely.

I began working in the Umóⁿhoⁿ Language and Culture Center on August 10, 2004. I enjoy what I am doing, working with Vida, the students, and my sister Marcella Woodhull Cayou. I'm doing this because I don't want us to lose our language. That is what it is all about. There is Marcella, Grandma Sue Freemont is the oldest, and Rufus White. They are all very good at teaching the language. I like working here. I have been working with the high school. Occasionally I work with the younger elementary students too. I have been helping to document the language in both written and audio recordings.

I hope the textbook we are writing will help my children to speak Omaha. They understand the language but do not speak it fluently. That is what I would like for my children. I still talk Indian to them. I hope everybody learns to do that with this book. If not, Umóⁿhoⁿ íye ta akʰa, Umóⁿhoⁿ íye, the Omaha language, will be gone. It needs to go down to the next generation.

Note: Grandma Donna's children are Carla Parker, Reanea Ethel Parker, Lawrence Parker Jr., Brenda Parker, Anthony Parker, and Jeremy Parker. She loved her children, grandchildren, relatives, Umóⁿhoⁿ language, and ways. She believed, "Before you act, you must get permission to do things. Take time to consider things before you act." As a Hoⁿga wa'u, she was taught to promote her beliefs and language—so that our language would survive. —Brenda Parker

Patricia Phillips, Wagóⁿze, ULCC
Umóⁿhoⁿ Language Instructor

She was born on March 14, 1942, and given the name Patricia Phillips. Her Umóⁿhoⁿ izhazhe is Wétoⁿne. She is of the Thatada tepa itazhi clan.

Her schooling began at home with Great Grandmother Lucy Mitchell Saunsoci, who raised her. She grew up north of Macy out in the country on her grandmother's land. The Umóⁿhoⁿ language is her first language. She never heard English as a child until she went to school.

She and her four siblings were raised in a very sheltered environment, where Umóⁿhoⁿ was the only language she heard. When I asked her to describe what it was like living out in the country, she replied with a look of pure joy, "The timbers was our playground and the streams our swimming pool." She made her toys from materials in nature.

She went to elementary school at Macy Day School. This was where she first heard English. She started to understand English at the age of twelve. Macy Day School was filled with Umóⁿhoⁿ-speaking children. Macy Day School burned down, and some children were sent to Winnebago or Flandreau Indian School. She graduated twelfth grade from Flandreau.

In later years she went to the Nebraska Indian Community College, continuing on at Wayne State College with the career ladders project. Today she enjoys teaching culture to the children at the Umó^{n}ho^n Nation Public School, where she has taught for eight years. She continues to learn our language. She believes the biggest challenge to teaching our language is the lack of language use within our homes and community.

"The best time to start to teach our language is when the child is young. At a young age, the child has no fear to try to speak. They know how to have fun with our language and they're not afraid to make mistakes."—Written on behalf of Pat Phillips by Vida Woodhull Stabler

Rufus White, Shúde Giná, ULCC
Umó^{n}ho^n Language Instructor

Rufus White, Elder traditional singer of the Umó^{n}ho^n Tribe, was groomed from birth to be a singer. He was born on October 25, 1939, in Macy, Nebraska to Theodore and Emily White. He married Maxine Turner, and together they raised grandchildren within their traditional home.

His uncles taught him to sing the traditional songs of the Umó^{n}ho^n people. His voice and cultural knowledge are known and deeply respected by all.

Today Mr. White teaches the Umó^{n}ho^n language to adult teachers and young relatives at Umó^{n}ho^n Nation Public School. He also integrates traditional stories and games into the language classroom. He continues to raise his grandchildren.—Vida Woodhull Stabler

Bryan James Gordon, ULCC *Instructional, Technical, and Linguistic Support Staff*

Ebé bthí^n t^{h}e uwíbtha tami^{n}k^{h}e. Umó^{n}ho^n bthí^n mazhi. Jú bthí^n. Iyéska bthí^n.
"I'm going to tell you who I am. I'm not Umó^{n}ho^n. I'm Jewish. I'm a linguist."

Izházhe wiwíta t^{h}e Bryan James Gordon. Umó^{n}ho^n Táp'ska k^{h}e di wabthít^{h}o^n no^{n}mó^n.
"My name is Bryan James Gordon. I work at Umó^{n}ho^n Nation Public School."

Education built on the knowledge and culture in our communities is a needed healing way, and language is part of its foundation. I came here at Wik^{h}áge Vida's invitation so I could help build toward this healing way. The university world where most linguistics lives is not where this work is done. I am grateful to be working for the Umó^{n}ho^n Language and Culture Center here at the school, because the work I have been blessed to contribute to here can be of help to my own éawathe. I especially appreciate the opportunities I have had to repatriate Umó^{n}ho^n knowledge back to this community and share linguistic skills to make the work of past linguists accessible and useful, and hope I will continue to be able to offer these things into the future.

Wó^{n}githe wíbthaho^n,
מודה אני לפניכם, לכו לשלום ולרפואה שלמה
modé aní l'fanékhem, l'khú l'shalóm v'lir'fu'á sh'lemá.
"I give thanks to you all, walk toward peace and full healing."

OMAHA LANGUAGE INSTRUCTION TEAM, UNIVERSITY OF NEBRASKA-LINCOLN

Mark Awakuni-Swetland, Wagṓⁿze Ūthiχide,
UNL *Omaha Language Instructor*

My name is Mark Awakuni-Swetland. Umóⁿhoⁿ izházhe wiwítta tʰe Ūthiχide. I was born into a white family in Lincoln, Nebraska. I do not know where or when the interest in Native American cultures originated in my elementary school days. In 1971 I attended the opening night of Omaha language classes at the Lincoln Indian Center. The teacher was Omaha Elder Elizabeth Saunsoci Stabler. With that chance encounter I began walking the path to becoming a better human being through learning the Omaha language. Elizabeth and her husband Charles opened the door to their home and the Omaha culture—welcoming me with patience, kindness, and humor. In 1977, with the approval of tribal leaders and clan Elders, we formally exchanged terms of relationship at a feast at Macy, Nebraska. Charlie and Elizabeth Stabler accepted me into their family as a grandson, and Grandpa Charlie gave me a name from his Iⁿkʰésabe-Wathígizhe clan.

Grandma Elizabeth Stabler was using as her teaching guide an original 1911 edition of *The Omaha Tribe* by Alice C. Fletcher and Francis La Flesche, the Twenty-Seventh Annual Report of the Bureau of American Ethnology. Students were not given a pronunciation guide of any sort, or instruction in syntax (sentence word order), grammar (rules of language), or how to write (orthography system). I realized years later that Grandma Elizabeth probably assumed that we students were functionally literate in English and able to read and take notes. Unfortunately the class enrollment dwindled. The class was eventually canceled by the Indian Center.

When that happened, Grandma asked me if I intended to carry on learning Omaha. I assured her that I was committed to learning it, even if I was her only student. We decided to continue working and moved our class to her home at 18th and G Streets. Sometime during that first winter the idea of putting together a dictionary emerged. I cannot recall who brought up the idea first. We agreed that it might be a helpful tool, since the Fletcher and La Flesche word lists were limited. The work stretched for six years, culminating with the publication of 488 copies of *Umoⁿhoⁿ Iye of Elizabeth Stabler* in 1977.

In 1988 I was offered a job as a culture program coordinator at Macy Public School. John Mangan, music teacher, itinerant printer, and my "elder brother," had found himself pressed into service as the director of the school's Culture Program. He convinced the administration that he needed an assistant for the spring semester. My job was to make sure the four Elders arrived each day, discuss with them what they would each be teaching in their respective twenty-minute classes for K–6 grade students, and develop language and culture activities for various grades and groups of children. There were no preexisting curriculum materials, lesson plans, or textbooks available.

The opportunity to reprint the English-Omaha dictionary was developed. The school allocated some of its federal funding to purchase materials to reprint three hundred copies of *Umoⁿhoⁿ Iye*. John Mangan and I pooled our beer money and covered the cost of an additional three hundred copies, with a different colored cover, for public sale and distribution. The original 1977 edition was reprinted unchanged in 1991 as *Umoⁿhoⁿ iye of Elizabeth Stabler: A Vocabulary of the Omaha Language with an Omaha to English Lexicon*. The public copies were quickly distributed to an increasingly interested Omaha community. The most common comment from people acquiring the dictionary in the 1990s was that they wanted a copy so that their children could learn the language. In other words, the dictionary was to be the teacher of the next generation!

In 1999 I was invited to apply for a faculty position at the University of Nebraska–Lincoln. It was a proposed joint appointment in the Department of Anthropology and the Institute for Ethnic Studies (Native American Studies Program). My primary job was to develop a series of Native language courses. I solicited input from the Omaha community in Lincoln, Omaha, and Macy. With the encouragement of several Omaha Tribal Council members and the Senior Citizens at Macy, I set out to teach the Omaha language.

Not being a fluent native speaker, I turned to my Elder relatives living in Lincoln for help. My Aunt Alberta Grant Canby and my Daughter Emmaline Walker Sanchez agreed to assist me as best they could. We began organizing lessons while lacking any curriculum materials beyond Grandma Elizabeth Stabler's out-of-print dictionary. The first UNL Omaha language class began in the fall of 2000. Rory Larson was one of the first students. He came to the class with a deep understanding of multiple languages and a keen interest in the working of languages (lin-

PHOTO 2. Mark Awakuni-Swetland at the University of Nebraska–Lincoln, 2010. Photo © 2016, The Board of Regents of the University of Nebraska. All rights reserved.

guistics). He quickly became indispensable to the class as mentor, colleague, and friend. He earned the admiration and respect of the Elder speakers (see following three profiles).

When I was hospitalized for a semester the next year, I asked my Omaha language student Tamara Levi to fill in as my teaching assistant. She rose to the occasion and did a stellar job. Her classmates rallied together. They completed a complex group project started the first year of compiling a bilingual booklet of Omaha recipes. Rory provided invaluable assistance to her as they struggled through the course.

It became evident in following years that the UNL class needed a textbook. We had formed a close, collaborative relationship with the Umóⁿhoⁿ Language and Culture Center at

Umóⁿhoⁿ Nation Public School. It was clear that they as well as the wider Omaha community could benefit from a textbook. However, the ULCC lacked the time and resources to muster such a project.

I wrote for a small grant from UNL to start developing the textbook. I received support from the Research Council Layman Fund. Additional funds from the Department of Anthropology and the Institute for Ethnic Studies supported our efforts. We put aside offering Omaha for the 2006–2007 academic year to devote our energies to the project. Rory, now a member of the UNL teaching team, and other UNL team members met with ULCC team members to work on eliciting language materials. My Aunt Vida Stabler offered to share the ULCC electronic files of Omaha language lessons.

The result is this volume. I am not an Indian in the legal sense. Generally speaking, I am not recognized as a member of the tribe by the ever-changing Omaha Tribal Council. I am not a fluent speaker. Nonetheless, I am Charlie and Elizabeth Stabler's grandson. I remain awed and humbled by all that their relationship means to me. Grandma started me on this lifelong path through the language. I recognize that her gift to me has come with some responsibilities on my part. What Grandma and Grandpa shared with me requires that I give it back to the next generation. I feel that I have not strayed too far from her path. This volume, and Omaha related work that I have done, are given to the community that they might benefit from Grandma's teachings. I can still hear her voice over my shoulder as she encourages me to speak, and act, in the proper Omaha way. I pray that all Omaha people can experience the same connection to the past, while responsibly carrying it forward to the future.

Shénoⁿ. Ahó!

Alberta Grant Canby, UNL
Omaha Language Instructor

I was born at the Winnebago Hospital in 1930. My parents were Mr. and Mrs. George M. Grant. We lived east of Macy on the Missouri River bottomlands. While dad was having our house built we lived across the creek from my grandparents in a tent. We made it through the cold winter. When the house was finished we moved east and lived there.

Dad was a farmer. I learned how to milk the cow. Dad showed me how to do it. My brother Chubby and I would go after our horses that were allowed to graze in the fields north of home. I watched Dad harness the horses. The first time I put the harness on backwards, but I kept trying until I learned. Today I probably could not even lift a harness.

I would try anything and everything. I hauled water in heavy cream cans from the neighbor's well. My brother and I would go to the timber to haul wood. I helped cut wood and carry it into the house.

Dad worked at the school as a bus driver. Mom would be cooking supper in time for him to arrive home. She would tell me to set the dishes and have everything ready when he got home. I did the same with my husband when he was working. My mother said that they were out all day working with only a little lunch. They were going to be hungry by the time they get home. That is what I taught my girls to do. Today my girls are teaching it to my granddaughters.

If Dad needed clothes washed, something fetched, or something done he would ask me to do it. I was glad that I learned how to do it. I miss him since he passed away because I feel there are a lot of things I haven't learned. If I don't know something I go to the Elders. Mom and Dad started me talking Omaha, but then as I grew up they used English. They would say a few words in Omaha to us and joked with us when we did not know the meaning. Today, sometimes when I don't know a word in the Omaha language, I go and ask them.

There were ten children, but we lost the next to last boy. He was sickly. Mom could hardly do anything. She could not set him down or he would cry. I would help her by following my mom's instructions to cook and do different things in the home. I'm glad she taught me those skills. My grandchildren compliment my cooking today. Maybe there was more I could have learned from my parents.

I left the reservation when I was twenty. I met Bill Canby and followed him to Lincoln. Today they want me to come back to Macy. But I am too accustomed to living here. I'd rather stay with my children in Lincoln.

When we first got together we thought we were in love. We stayed with Clyde and Lillian (Saunsoci) Sheridan Jr. about one year until Wilma was born. I told Bill I did not want to be living with another family while raising my own. I did not have any dishes or cooking utensils, so I used paper plates. My Aunt Mary Grant loaned me a coffee pot, skillet, and kettle. I returned them as soon as we got our own stuff. I continued to use paper plates.

I had Wilma. We had a little place in the back of a house on First Street. A little two-bedroom house. We lived there three years until Gary was born. It was enough for our family. There was a place to keep my brother Donald and sister Gladys. I didn't think I would ever have any kids. When I did I was so proud. Bill was so proud. He would get paid every week and he would buy Wilma clothes. Lillian told him not to do that since she would outgrow them so quickly. But we kept doing that. Grandma Saunsoci was so proud of Bill getting married. Wilma was her first grandchild from Bill. She furnished everything for the baby. At that time we used cloth diapers. I was so thankful for the help.

We got a stroller, but it broke down. Aunt Mabel bought a buggy when Gary was born. One time I walked up town from First Street along the tracks. George F. Grant and his wife lived on Second Street. His wife saw me carrying the two children in my arms because they were too lazy to walk. She told her husband that I must be a very strong woman to be packing two babies. Wilma was a big baby. Grandma Saunsoci would get after me for carrying her when Gary was the baby.

Elaine was born seven years later. Uncle Joe La Flesche said he felt sorry for Elaine because she thought she would always be the baby. But she came to learn to take care of her baby brother Greg when he was born seven years later.

All of my children were put on a cradleboard. Grandma Saunsoci said to wait until the navel stump fell off. She said tie their legs together so they don't get bowlegged. Greg was the last one to use it. Usually you keep the board in the family. You are not supposed to get rid of it. I gave the board to Duane Canby's daughter Sharon. I don't know what happened to that board.

Grandma Saunsoci said to put the navel

stump away. I have the three older ones, but Greg's fell off in the hospital and I don't know what they did with it. But I have Wilma's, Gary's, and Elaine's.

I am in the Tesíⁿde (Buffalo Tail) clan through my father's side. All my children are named into Bill's Kéiⁿ Turtle clan. Grandma Saunsoci named the three oldest children. My mom named Greg. She had to ask the Turtle clan people for a name. Turtle clan families include the Edwards and Canbys.

I first worked at St. Elizabeth Hospital laundry at its old location on South Street. My sister Gladys also worked there. My first three children were born there. I worked there three years. It became hard to get a ride in the mornings. I left there and got a job at Bryan Hospital where Greg was born. I was working there in the insurance records office. I worked until Greg was almost two.

I quit working at Bryan and worked making Russell Stover candy until it closed, about nine years later. I went to work at Paramount Laundry as a presser for twelve years. I retired from there. I felt that I had to compromise with all of the workers, regardless of race, in order to get the job done. Someone asked me if I felt people acted prejudiced toward me. I said I did not notice, but if I did I would tell them about it.

I went to the hospital with pneumonia. That's when they found out I was borderline diabetic. I could not get my sugars down, so they put me on pills. In the last five years they put me on insulin. At first I refused to take insulin because my mom was diabetic. She used insulin and it didn't seem to do her any good. She lost her eyesight and both of her legs. So that is why I refused.

Finally I gave up and took it. It brought my sugar down at first, but since I lost Bill it is going back up. It was doing real good for awhile. Now the sugars are going up again.

I am depressed these days. They say I should talk to someone. I was with Bill for forty-eight years. I lost him. Now I'm struggling alone with my family. Sometimes I feel like packing up and moving back to Macy. Then I think about my grandchildren here. I think it is slowly working itself out.

Today I am working at the Urban Indian Health Clinic. I could not stand staying at home without money. Bill passed away with a little retirement. The Lincoln Indian Center found me a job at Urban Health and I have been there six years. I have to keep working to keep myself from starving. It seems like that is what's keeping me going. I don't feel so old, even though I have arthritis in my back. The job does not require too much bending. My knees give me troubles when climbing stairs.

When my dad was getting the Native American Church staff, we were told not to run around the house. We could sit in the car. Henry Phillips, Naomi Phillips Grant's dad, told us not to run around the car or we would get hurt. Sure enough, I was running around the car and hit a spoke on the bumper. It cut my leg and peeled back the skin. I didn't go to the doctor. I put mercurochrome on it and it healed. Maybe it was a reminder to behave around that staff.

I tell my kids not to run around the house due to the staff that I have in the home. I tell the kids always to keep the dishes cleaned up. Other practices that I have been taught include always cleaning up the stove, covering and putting away leftovers, not sweeping floors and picking up the dirt after sundown, cleaning up the dishes and wiping the table, not to leave crumbs on the table or floor. Especially if you have a staff in your care. Dad and others were always telling me about these things. I think they planned for me to have that staff in my home.

Even though I have retired, I am working at Urban Indian Health and am now working at UNL as a visiting scholar with the Omaha language class. I have tried to help in the development of curriculum materials for teaching at the college level and also providing materials that go back to Macy. I am proud to be an Omaha. A full-blooded Omaha—and yet still I don't know the meaning of some of the Omaha words. What an Indian, huh?

Note: This narrative is drawn from a UNPS Oral History video project filmed in Lincoln on November 5, 2000. Alberta Grant Canby departed this world in March 2007 after a long struggle with cancer and diabetes. She is sorely missed. In 2000 she was the first of two Omaha Elders in Lincoln to accept a request by Mark Awakuni-Swetland to assist in developing and teaching the Omaha language courses. She was always a strong advocate of Omaha language and cultural ways. She treated all the students as her own children, mentoring the students and instructors in every possible way. As her health declined in the later years, she continued to make every effort to come into the classroom. She would always tell us that she was just a student herself, and that she did not want to fall behind in her studies. —UNL Omaha Language Instruction Team

Emmaline Walker Sanchez, UNL
Omaha Language Instructor

My name is Emmaline Walker Sanchez. I was born on the Omaha Reservation, on the Paul and Bert Fremont homestead. My father was Thomas Carson Walker. My mother was Cecelia Fremont Walker. I have two sisters, Arlene Mary Walker (the youngest) and Florence Grant Walker (the eldest). I have two brothers, Bert Carson Walker and Edwin Walker.

I am the mother of seven children, six sons and one daughter: Daniel B. Sanchez Jr., Stacey Lynn Sanchez Stabler, Jason William Christopher Sanchez, Eric Shane Sanchez, Duane Dallas Sanchez, Thomas Kevin Sanchez, and the youngest, Kerry Lee Sanchez. I now have ten grandchildren: Kyle, Tristen, and Braden Stabler are Stacey's children; Albert, Allie, and Taya Sanchez are Kerry's children; Jared and Sala Sanchez are Jason's children; Thomas Sanchez is Thomas's son; and I have another grandchild on the way from Duane.

Four of my children are in military service: Dan Jr. (army), Stacey (army), Eric Shane (army), and Jason (marines). Dan Jr., Jason, Stacey, Shane, and Tommy have completed their master's degrees. Duane and Kerry Lee have completed their undergraduate degrees. Dan Jr. also holds a medical degree and is working on his law degree.

My first language is the Omaha language. My father taught my sister Florence and me to speak English. I grew up on a farm, and I think I was about nine or ten years old when we got our first car. Before that we rode in a wagon pulled by our trusted friends Bill and Dolly. We did not have much, but we were a happy family.

PHOTO 3. UNL team (*clockwise from top*): Rory Larson, Aubrey Streit Krug, Arlene Walker, Emmaline Walker Sanchez, and Barbara Salvatore at the Dhegiha Language Conference, 2016.

I am now an orphan. I lost my mother, father, and sister Florence, the one we called "Jeanie." Many of my children are out in the world. I am blessed to have them only a telephone call away, but I miss my loved ones.

I hope to help the Omaha language get off the ground and get printed. I feel I have accomplished something. Even if I am gone my work will remain so that my current and future grandchildren can read this book and cherish our language. My work is for them.

Rory Larson, Wagáx̌thoⁿ, UNL Omaha Language Assistant Instructor

All of my life I have been fascinated with the evolution of complex systems over time, whether the development from egg to tadpole to frog, the succession of fauna from one geological period to the next, or the historical changes undergone by human societies. As a young adult I became interested in learning human languages. At first this was to achieve a practical skill, or to dabble in comparative linguistics and glottochronology. The more I learned, however, the more I came to appreciate Goethe's remark along the lines of: "Every time I learn a new language, I gain a new soul." I feel that the importance of knowing a language to understanding the cultural history, and the very thought patterns of the people who have spoken that language, can scarcely be underestimated.

Today the once rich linguistic heritage of the world is rapidly disappearing, submerged by English and other international languages. Of the several thousand languages spoken in the world in modern times, we will soon be down to a few hundred. Of the perhaps three hundred Native American languages spoken in the United States, almost all will be gone as first languages a generation from now. Each language lost is the loss of a conceptual universe and all its history.

My studies of Omaha came about somewhat circumstantially. As with many other white people, my fascination and love for things Indian is probably rooted in the romance of the wilderness and a racial longing for a more natural and humane, pre-urban/commercial/industrial society. I first turned serious attention to the history and languages of American Indians in the late 1980s and took two years of Lakʰota that was offered at the University of Nebraska–Lincoln about 1993–95 by Dr. James Gibson and native speaker Ann Keller.

In the fall of 2000 I enrolled in the new Omaha language class that was being offered by Mark Awakuni-Swetland with the help of native speakers Alberta Canby and Emmaline Sanchez. At first I expected to spend no more than the two-year series in the class, as there were unlimited other areas that I wanted to explore as well. But the new and unformed nature of the class encouraged me to shape my own course of study and to contribute actively to the curriculum almost from the beginning. Then in the second year a life-threatening health crisis for the instructor put me and one other graduate student in the remarkable position of teaching the same class we were taking! The other student moved on, but I was hooked, and Mark generously allowed me to continue to attend as an informal co-instructor.

From then on I was included in Mark's weekly meetings with the speakers, where he served us supper and we did cultural and linguistic research. Alberta and Emmaline supported me with warmth and humor and helped me complete my master's thesis in anthropology. Early on Mark pointed me to the Siouanist list, a discussion forum for linguists interested in Siouan languages, run by his "elder brother" John Koontz, who, along with Bob Rankin and others, diverted considerable efforts over the years to mentoring me and arguing with me electronically. I became very close to all these

people, and I feel I owe them a debt to pass on what I have learned from them.

When Mark was granted a contract in late 2005 or early 2006 to write this textbook in coordination with Vida Woodhull Stabler of the Umóⁿhoⁿ Language and Culture Center at Umóⁿhoⁿ Nation Public School in Macy, I asked if I could help with the project and was accepted. I started with an outline for twelve chapters over two semesters and began writing lessons in a discussion format as a linguistic guide to the teacher and to whoever would be writing the finished textbook. Somehow, over the course of the first year of writing, this guide became considered the textbook itself for the UNL side. Then, about May of 2007, with five chapters completed, early feedback indicated that it was a bit verbose and lacking in examples, exercises, and summary bullet points. We decided to rewrite it all to achieve a more student-friendly BOXed ("Broken Out with eXamples") version; I unexpectedly got that job, while Mark did the cultural material. So I spent the summer and fall racing the first-year students to get them their daily lessons, complete with nicely formatted sample sentences, bullet points, vocabulary, exercises, and suggested games, while trying to stave off the demands of the rather strict instructor of a third-year Japanese course I was trying to take simultaneously. In our fourth cohort (2007–2008) we had just three very bright and very dependable students that year, for whom we generally maintained a schedule of a lesson a day. The class went well and the students learned rapidly, but by early November it became apparent that we weren't going to make it through chapter 6 if we wanted to have any time at all for cultural lessons. We decided to cut off the semester with chapter 5. Burnout occurred in the middle of the following semester, as we struggled with a chapter 6 that would not end. We left it there, and used those six chapters, only half of the projected textbook, as our instructional core for the next two cohorts as well.

In December 2013 Mark's leukemia recurred for the third and final time. He was given five months to live but decided to shoot for two years and continued to work on his many projects. In August 2014 he arranged a special class for former students Loren Frerichs, Aubrey Streit Krug, Kat Krutak, and me to finish the textbook. Optimistic as always, he wanted us to have it done that semester so that he could see it finished before he was put underground. He almost immediately handed the project off to us and passed away in February 2015. His departmental chair, LuAnn Wandsnider, kindly stepped in to shepherd the project and has kept us supplied with everything we have needed ever since.

Two years later, ten years after it began, Mark's Omaha textbook project is finally coming to completion. I have written grammar lessons, and Aubrey wrote the sentences for several chapters. She and I have worked, dined, and laughed for many evenings with our speakers Emmaline Walker Sanchez (Ttesóⁿwiⁿ) and her sister Arlene Walker (Mísebe), to confirm that these lessons and sentences and those for later chapters are acceptable, or to correct them if they are not. LuAnn has seen to it that our speakers are compensated for their expertise.

Early on, Loren researched styles and nonspacing Unicode characters for us, since which our Omaha orthography has become almost a pleasure to type. He and Aubrey took charge of gathering in and sorting out the myriad possibly relevant files and folder trees from Mark's computers. Loren has been a rock of support and mordant good advice throughout, generously sharing his office, his phone, and his computer expertise. Aubrey has become our organizational genius, designing the book as a whole, interfacing with our many collaborators, and keeping us all on track. She stepped in early on to become our liaison with the University of Nebraska Press. She organized the files left over in Mark's office and kept us in contact with UNPS. She also took charge of tracking down illustrations and illustrators Mark had commissioned, working with Barbara Salvatore, another of Mark's vastly talented and devoted former students, who has contributed hundreds of beautiful original drawings to adorn the vocabularies. For my part, I marvel at my teammates and frequently entertain the thought that with them on my side, I could hardly lose a war.

Arlene Walker, UNL Omaha Language Instructor

Hello! My name is Arlene Mary Walker. I am the youngest child of Thomas C. Walker and Cecelia Walker. I am a graduate of the Omaha Nation High School. I have six children: four girls (LeAnne, Tosanna, Elise, and Angel), and two boys (Troy and Thomas). I have eighteen grandchildren and two great-grandchildren.

My daughter LeAnne Walker Curiel's children are Keonah Brown, Yajara Walker, Czerina Castillo, Alicia Rios, and Orlando Carriaga Jr. From Keonah I have a great-grandbaby named Lanaya Taylor and another great-grandson on the way. My daughter Tosanna Walker's children are Serena, Isabella, Ismael, and Mario Izaguirre. My daughter Elise Mallory's children are Zylena Ramirez, Adrionna Arlene Ramirez, Ernesto Mallory, and Angel Luna Mallory. My son Troy Mallory's children are Demarrio Whiteface, Abel Mallory, and Ava Mallory. Finally, my son Thomas Mallory's children are Anastacia and Mehladie Mallory.

I grew up knowing the Omaha language. I used to be teased as a "*Big* Indian" because I spoke Indian with English. In later years I was always proud that I could understand all my Elders. I spoke English back to them because I was afraid to talk Omaha for fear of messing up the pronunciation. But now I am happy and proud to be able to offer some knowledge to our young people. I hope they learn and use the Omaha language, to keep it up and not let it be forgotten.

I am but an Omaha tribal member. I hope people will grasp our language and keep it going. Thank you.

Delores Black, UNL Omaha Language Instructor

The reason I wanted to help with this book project was because I do not want our Omaha language to be lost or forgotten. I want our culture and customs to be carried on by our upcoming generations, so they will not be lost and forgotten. Our Omaha tribe may not be large, but we cherish our ways and our language. I would like our future generations to carry them on.

Aubrey Streit Krug, UNL Omaha Language Instruction Team Member

My great-grandparents immigrated to the Great Plains from Germany in the late nineteenth century. I grew up in the small town of Tipton in north-central Kansas, where my family still farms and ranches, not far from Waconda Lake. When I came to graduate school at the University of Nebraska–Lincoln to study the literature and ecology of the Great Plains, my advisor Fran Kaye suggested that I also study a Great Plains language. So in the fall of 2011 I joined what would be the last cohort of the two-year accelerated Omaha language program taught by Mark Awakuni-Swetland, Wagōⁿze Ūthixide. From Wagōⁿze, the Elder teachers, and the classroom community I was reminded of the importance of listening, speaking clearly, being generous, and having a sense of humor. I learned first-hand how language and culture are interrelated with each other and with place: for instance, I now see the lake and the Wakkóⁿda Springs underneath it in a new way. In the fall of 2014 Wagōⁿze invited me to join his team of people working to complete this textbook. By then I was the mother of my own little boy, Bob. Observing my own child learn to speak has helped me to understand more about how vital it is for Omaha children to be able to learn and speak their own language. I am grateful for everything that Omaha people have taught me, and I hope this textbook can play a part in helping Omaha people teach many future generations of Omaha children.

Loren H. Frerichs, UNL Omaha
Language Instruction Team Member

I grew up on a dairy farm on the edge of the south table near Ogallala, Nebraska, where my father was born and my parents still live.

I have always enjoyed learning—particularly science. Even though I am the son of a school teacher, I was never great at school. I started college as an engineering student but never finished. I got a full-time computer job at the university with the goal of finishing any degree part time (I'm still working on it). Trying to take Spanish and German to fulfill the language requirement, I struggled with the daily quizzes because of spelling. I was fascinated with how much insight into English I gained from "failing" language classes. When I was diagnosed with dyslexia, it finally explained my school issues. Understanding that I learn differently has made school and life easier.

I got to know Rory Larson over many hours helping him knit a chainmail shirt. Rory claimed that Umóⁿhoⁿ was purely an oral language (I guess this book helps change that), so my dyslexia would not get in the way. On this advice I joined the 2002–2004 cohort of Omaha language learners led by Mark Awakuni-Swetland. Along with the language production and grammar I really enjoyed Mark's mix of history, culture, and particularly material production.

As I worked through the class I struggled with handwriting this (or any) language and kept looking for a better way to type Umóⁿhoⁿ. I campaigned to use International Phonic Society symbols via common Unicode-compliant fonts because custom fonts did not display on the web. I feel honored that some of the online study resources I made to help me with my homework helped inspire the 2008 Omaha and Ponca Digital Dictionary and garner a grant for work on its development as an online resource.

One day on campus Mark approached me and asked if I would join a 2014 class with the goal of finishing the textbook. I responded that I didn't think I knew enough to contribute, but Mark told me I had contributed a lot and had talents to add to the team. I am proud to have had my life enhanced by knowing Mark and the Umóⁿhoⁿ community. I hope future language learners use this book as a tool to enhance their learning experience and follow Mark's example of continual learning outside the classroom.

ILLUSTRATORS

Miya Kobayashi

Mark was my uncle. He, along with my Aunty Donna and two cousins, would visit my family, driving from Nebraska to Colorado and back again. When they arrived at our house my aunty would always say that there wasn't any room in their trunk because of the rocks and sand or roadkill he found along the way. He was always on the go, even when he was sick.

I graduated from the University of Northern Colorado with a bachelor's degree in graphic design. I'm really glad I was able to work on this project with Uncle Mark. He was visiting during the holidays when he asked me to illustrate certain topics he wanted to cover in this textbook. It was a great way to get to know him better and understand what he was passionate about. He would describe each scene and the significance behind it, and the more scenes I drew, the more I realized how important this textbook was to him. I am thankful that so many people came together to help him complete it so that future generations can carry on the Omaha language and culture.

Barbara Salvatore

I received my bachelor of fine arts in drawing and painting from the School of Visual Arts in New York City. As a writer and illustrator, my interest in the Omaha and Ponca languages began as research for my character *Big Horse Woman.* My historical-fiction novel series features a Ponca woman and a German woman, *Magghie,* who ultimately share plant healing knowledge and work together to save the seeds of medicine plants in the face of sweeping cultural and historical changes.

My study of the language eventually led to my position as Ponca language educator for the Ponca Tribe of Nebraska in 2014, working with youth ages 5–18 throughout Nebraska. My work continues, using storytelling, visual art, and theater to rekindle interest in and study of the language, for present and future generations.

Jacob Smith, Iⁿshta Móⁿze

Jacob Smith is an enrolled member of the Umóⁿhoⁿ Tribe of Nebraska. He is the son of Barb Stabler and Harold Smith and grandson to Charles Stabler and Elizabeth Saunsoci Stabler. Jacob's art is heavily influenced by the culture of his Umóⁿhoⁿ relatives in the Lincoln area. He told me his art reflects our people engaged in very specific cultural practices that he witnessed while growing up.

Jacob expressed that he felt the textbook project is important and wanted to help. He makes his home in Lincoln with his wife and two daughters. — Vida Woodhull Stabler

INTRODUCTION

Mark Awakuni-Swetland, Wagōⁿze Ūthixide

Aho, Éwithai wôⁿgithe! I greet all of my relatives! Thank you for your interest in the Omaha language and culture. Today the condition of the Omaha language is critical. Community members of all ages regularly voice their interest in reinvigorating and maintaining the Omaha language. Sadly, some community members have internalized mainstream social attitudes that regularly belittle the importance of our language.

In 1994 an Omaha Language Preservation Project grant proposal prepared by the Omaha Tribe stated that about 2,000 of the 5,227 tribal members lived on the reservation, with less than 1 percent of the total enrollment identified as fluent speakers. The tribal government reported that less than seventy elderly speakers of the language remained. Of the seventy speakers, thirty Elders were said to use the language on a daily basis in the Macy area.[1] In the passing years since that report many of our Elders have departed to the spirit world.

Since the 1970s the transmission of Omaha language and culture has been delegated almost exclusively to the local K-12 public school at Macy. In the mid-1990s the Umóⁿhoⁿ Language and Culture Center (ULCC) was created in the school to strengthen Native language and culture revitalization efforts. Vida Woodhull Stabler, a State of Nebraska–certified teacher, became the director of the ULCC. She has worked tirelessly to gather together willing Elder speakers to document and teach Omaha language and culture. The ULCC team provides classes at various grade levels while simultaneously crafting lessons, recording and analyzing the language, coaching active and passive speakers in the mechanics of teaching, and being accessible to the wider community as a language and culture resource.

ORIGIN STORY OF THE UNL OMAHA LANGUAGE CLASS

I initiated this textbook project as the Omaha language instructor at the University of Nebraska–Lincoln (UNL). To understand the motivations for this volume, and the connection to the ULCC language efforts, I must first tell you a little history about the Omaha language classes at UNL. In 1999 I was asked to join the University of Nebraska faculty and develop a Native language presence on campus. Because of my positive experiences in the Omaha community I chose to devote myself to promoting the Omaha language. In 2000 the first Omaha language class convened at UNL. The Department of Anthropology is the home for the class, and it is co-sponsored by the Institute for Ethnic Studies and the Native American Studies program. Classes began in spite of the lack of teaching materials. Unlike other college-level language courses, we did not have a grammar, readers, audio reinforcements, or an in-print dictionary.

The first six UNL years consisted of creating daily lessons on the fly that introduced basic rules of grammar and targeted usual language domains (e.g., colors, numbers, verb patterns, commands, etc.). Ongoing student feedback was critical to the creation and refinement of lessons. Such refinements, augmentations, and boiling-downs have proceeded sporadically as time permits. Students participate in immersion exercises, games, one-on-one recitation, and group work. Elder speakers work with the students individually and as a group to monitor pronunciation, offer translations and interpretations, provide cultural context, and encourage the class to excel.

UNL language instruction is interspersed with lessons on points of Omaha history and contemporary cultural practices. When Omaha Elder Howard Wolf visited an early UNL class, he illustrated the connection of language and culture. Pointing to the back of his hand and then his palm, he said, "One side is the Omaha language, the other is the Omaha culture. You cannot learn about one without learning about the other."

To help students achieve this broader knowledge they must collect a small library of Omaha texts. In a modestly rank-ordered list these include:

Dorsey, *Omaha Sociology*, 1884, and *The Ƈegiha Language*, 1890

Mead, *The Changing Culture of an Indian Tribe*, 1932

La Flesche, *The Middle Five*, 1900

Boughter, *Betraying the Omaha Nation, 1790–1916*, 1998

Ridington and Hastings, *Blessing for a Long Time*, 1997

Scherer, *Imperfect Victories*, 1999

Welsch, *Omaha Tribal Myths and Trickster Tales*, 1981

Wishart, *An Unspeakable Sadness*, 1994

Stabler and Swetland, *Umoⁿhoⁿ iye of Elizabeth Stabler*, 1977, 1991

For full publication details, see the bibliography at the end of this introduction.

UNL students are encouraged to attend local Native social functions as observant participants. Essay writing promotes critical thinking about their experiences at handgames, war dances, gourd dances, and feasts. With the support of the UNL Elder speakers and instructor, students develop an entry-level knowledge of contemporary Omaha cultural values and behaviors. They regularly report a welcoming experience with members of the Lincoln Indian Club.

From its inception, the UNL program has worked to remedy the lack of language teaching materials. These efforts benefit both the UNL program and the ULCC at Macy. Early on a collaborative relationship was established between our two programs working to share ideas, speaker resources, and materials. Day-long field trips to the Omaha Reservation provide UNL students the opportunity to interact with community members and become familiar with the Omaha landscape. Elder speakers at the ULCC frequently work with UNL students to refine translations of UNL-produced Omaha materials.

Weekend cookouts at my home provided the setting for the first students to work with the UNL Elder speakers to learn how to cook a selection of Omaha foods. The first group (2000–2002) wrote instructions for cooking in the Omaha language and produced a collection of common Omaha recipes. Elder speakers at the ULCC double-checked the translations. Later students have been using these bilingual recipes as an Omaha reader. The recipes with audio files are available at the UNL Omaha class website (see UNL Omaha Language Class 2002).

The second UNL group (2002–2004) produced a draft bilingual instruction booklet on how to assemble a tipi. This was based upon their experiences setting up and dismantling a fourteen-foot tipi several times during the Omaha classes. They worked out a step-by-step descriptive text (see UNL Omaha Language Class 2007). This group also worked with "Two Faces and the Twin Brothers," a popular nineteenth-century bedtime story from the Dorsey texts. They re-transcribed Dorsey's orthography into what we came to call the *Macy Standard Orthography* (MSO) used at the ULCC. I decided to change the nineteenth-century narrated style of storytelling to a more active voice and reader's theater style, hoping it would be more attractive to younger readers. Elder speakers at the ULCC double-checked the Two Faces translations (see UNL Omaha Language Class 2006). The "new-old" story was printed and is now used by current students, along with the tipi instruction text, both serving as additional Omaha readers.

The third group (2004–2006) was challenged to master the Two Faces story and produce an accompanying audio component. Each student selected one or more characters from the story. They all took turns going into a UNL digi-tal recording studio to record their parts. The spouse of a student provided background music based on song notations in the original Dorsey story. A student digital engineer mixed the voice tracks with the music and added sound effects. The resulting CD now accompanies the text version and also resides on the UNL Omaha class website (UNL Omaha Language Class 2006).

By this time it became evident that the UNL language class would benefit from a systematic collection of grammar lessons.

I applied for funding from UNL to develop an entry-level Omaha language and culture textbook. In 2006 I received support from the UNL Research Council Layman Fund to compensate UNL and ULCC Elder speakers for translation work. Additional funding came from the Department of Anthropology, Institute for Ethnic Studies, and the Native American Studies program at UNL, and the ULCC program at Umóⁿhoⁿ Nation Public School. ULCC Director Vida Woodhull Stabler made all of her program's digital lesson plans available for this project. She assisted with coordinating workspace and meetings with ULCC team members at Macy who were dedicated to the textbook work.

This volume is a collaborative effort of a committed group of Elder Omaha speakers and students at the ULCC and UNL. It is presented to the community of language learners with the wish that we will all pick up and carry the Omaha language and culture forward for future generations. It is designed to be accessible to middle school and high school language classes as well as to undergraduate college students and adult learners in the Omaha community. The ULCC and UNL speakers and instructors have tried diligently to offer clear and correct Omaha language materials. Please bring any errors or oversights to our attention.

Wíbthahoⁿ.

I thank you.

NOTE TO INSTRUCTORS AND STUDENTS

Let us begin our journey together. First and foremost, we want to speak the Omaha language as often as possible. For generations Omaha has been learned as a first language in the same manner in which any first language is acquired—within the home and among family and community. Today, Omaha language is learned as a second language through instruction centered in a school environment.

In keeping with Omaha protocols, a culturally appropriate classroom arrangement would be an open circle of student desks or chairs. The instructor(s) and native speakers sit on the west side of the class room facing east. The room should contain an assortment of teaching aids, such as a chalk board or other large-scale writing surface (flip chart, white board), an overhead projector with screen, and wall space for mounting pictures and objects related to Omaha language and culture.

In this textbook we do not attempt to reproduce all the background cultural and historical materials that a well-prepared instructor would want. We draw heavily from a selection of foundational books that remain in print or are available as reprints. See the list of primary source documents mentioned earlier and the expanded list in the bibliography at the end of this introduction. Out-of-print books may be available through the inter-library loan system at the local library. Instructors and self-guided students are encouraged to acquire copies of these and other relevant works for ready reference.

Some Thoughts about Teaching

The Omaha people maintain a strong awareness regarding *proprietary knowledge, gendered knowledge,* and *gendered behavior* (for definitions of the italicized words, see the Key Concepts at the end of this introduction). This results in the expectation that certain types of knowledge, and the behaviors associated with acting upon or transmitting that knowledge, are either male-only or female-only. Waʾú ūshkoⁿ (woman's customs/ways) include knowledge of childbirth and care giving, housekeeping and culinary skills, ethnobotanical resources, and kinship maintenance. Nú ūshkoⁿ (man's customs/ways) include ritual knowledge and performance, ethnozoological resources, internal and external defense of the community, leadership, and public speaking.

The person being asked for certain types of knowledge or skills should be the socially recognized *appropriate authority* and gender. As well, the person asking for the knowledge should be of the appropriate gender. Speech is marked by male and female speakers. Of particular interest are the gendered ways of marking a command, marking emphatic statements, differences in some terms of relationship, and unitary utterances. This having been said, the majority of Omaha knowledge and skills are in the hands of the community members, from the youngest to the eldest. Because of our daily engagement with Omaha knowledge, language, cultural beliefs, history, and behaviors, the urban and reservation Omaha communities remain dynamic and productive.

The lessons in this textbook are written to reflect the teaching environments at both Macy and Lincoln. At UNL at the time of writing this includes a non-fluent male instructor, non-fluent male assistant instructor, and one or more fluent female native speakers. At the ULCC in Macy there is a non-fluent female instructor with one or more fluent Elder females and males. The lessons offered here should be modified and embellished to meet the language abilities and goals of both the teachers and students.

Public school teachers are encouraged to craft lessons that meet the goals of foreign language instruction developed by the State of Nebraska Department of Education.[2]

The lesson plans are built around an ideal fifty-minute class period. The actual rate of progress for each group of students will be unique and is expected to vary from day to day. Every class day should begin with a brief immersion activity. Speaking and listening activities can be built around a routine of greetings, introductions, personal naming, reports on the current weather, and related domains. Each activity can be presented in the simplest form, followed by increasing complexity as students master the language. By the middle of the semester the robust form of each activity can be rotated on a daily basis. Immersion, repetition, and excitement on the part of teachers and students are keys to mastering language skills.

The day's language or culture lesson follows the opening immersion exercise. Teachers can pick from a selection of topics in each chapter. It is recommended that students read the day's grammatical or cultural materials before class

so that the valuable class time can be devoted to answering questions and discussion of the topic. Longer lessons can be divided and taught in sequence on the following days. The lessons are delivered in English.

After the lesson has been delivered the class returns to the Omaha language and engages in another immersion activity that reflects the day's lesson topic or some related seasonal or cultural activity. The class ends with a homework assignment, assessment, or reading exercise.

The Omaha language materials from Macy (part 1 of this book) are presented in the writing system currently used by the ULCC at Umóⁿhoⁿ Nation Public School. It is an active system that is still being revised in some minor areas. The names of the Elder contributors for each lesson are included wherever possible. The Omaha language materials from the UNL Omaha language team (part 2 of this book) are presented in a slightly modified Macy writing system. Our experience in teaching at the university has been to notice that students regularly over-aspirate tense stops /p/, /t/, and /k/. UNL applies the Siouan linguist's representation of /pp/, /tt/, and /kk/ for the stand-alone unaspirated tense stops. The ULCC writing system does not distinguish between the harsh /x̌/ and the more muted /x/. UNL makes these and other minor distinctions as an aid for proper pronunciation, a goal often requested by our Elder speakers. The UNL system is definitely not the Omaha community standard. The writing system used at the ULCC is considered by the UNL program as "the" *Macy Standard Orthography* (MSO). The UNL system can be thought of as the Macy Standard with training wheels for early learners. Students at UNL use the UNL system to aid in appropriate pronunciation. Students and instructors elsewhere can choose which system best fits their teaching and learning expectations.

Students should always be encouraged to pronounce the Omaha words properly. Students should speak loudly enough to be heard by all classmates and instructors. Encourage students to take pride in speaking the language. In formal speech making, Omaha language prosody (pacing) is slower than mainstream English. The slower pacing allows for careful pronunciation and can give more weight to the meaning of the words.

Immersion

It is useful to "announce" the start of Omaha language immersion activities regularly to help students focus on staying in the target language. One way to announce the activity is to say: Ttígaxe ongátha-tta-i, "We ought to go make-believe." "Make-believe" refers to the game of "making a house" or the pretend scenario that will be enacted. It does not mean that the Omaha language is a "pretend" language. Another way to announce the activity is to say: Umóⁿhoⁿ íe oⁿthóⁿthe-tta-i-tʰe, "We ought to speak Omaha."

THE OMAHA PEOPLE: UMÓⁿHOⁿ NÍKKASHIⁿGA AMA

The *Omaha* remain a much studied but little understood people. Their strategic location and socioeconomic influence on the Middle Missouri River fur trade brought them to the attention of early military and scientific expeditions.[3]

After the Omaha signed the 1854 treaty and moved to the *reservation* they were subjected to intense ethnographic examination. The first researcher on the scene was James Owen Dorsey.[4] He was followed by Alice Cunningham Fletcher, who published and spoke widely on the Omaha, both alone and in partnership with Francis La Flesche.[5]

Much of the early federal Indian policy was formulated and influenced by Omaha actions and reactions to Americanizing and civilizing efforts of missionaries, government agents, and a group of Christian zealots who called themselves "Friends of the Indian." The Omaha reactions to such efforts played a critical role in shaping land *allotment* practices, land leasing policies, and how the Indian Claims Commission crafted compromise settlements for other Native claimants. In spite of generations of intense *assimilation* efforts by outsiders, the Omaha remain socially and culturally distinct from mainstream society.

The following sketch places the Omaha in an ethnographic context. It is not meant to reduplicate the stories of Omaha history and culture already in print; nor is it intended to be a comprehensive account. It is drawn from a more detailed contemporary description prepared by this writer for the Human Resources Area Files *Encyclopedia of World Cultures Supplement*.[6] This ethnohistorical account draws heavily from Fletcher and La Flesche's 1911 *The Omaha Tribe*. Their late nineteenth- and early twentieth-century writings present a homogenized view of Omaha history and cultural practices. Most contemporary Omaha people seem to prefer this interpretation of a unified, relatively contention-free society as part of their imme-

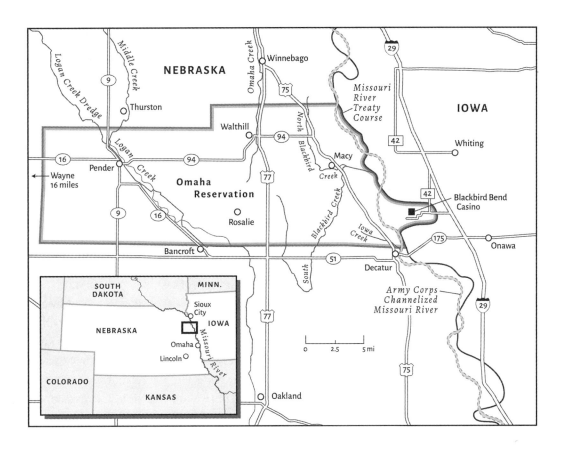

MAP 1. Location map of the Omaha Reservation. Area shown is the 1854 reservation after two congressional acts transferring northern lands to the Ho-Chunks (Winnebagos). As told by oral histories, the Omahas helped the Winnebagos by allowing them to recuperate on Omaha land, and the federal government brokered the Winnebagos' move by in turn promising trade goods to the Omahas. As decided by the Supreme Court (*Nebraska et al. vs. Parker et al.*, March 22, 2016), allotments and land sales after this time did not diminish sovereign Umóⁿhoⁿ jurisdiction.

diate history. Political and economic developments in the late twentieth and early twenty-first centuries suggest that the Omaha continue to struggle with the dynamics of factionalism.

The Omaha are headquartered in and around the northeastern Nebraska town of Macy on a portion of their ancestral lands retained under an 1854 *treaty*. In the 1990s the much-reduced reservation still includes farmable Missouri River bottomlands to the east, bordered by steep bluffs and fertile rolling upland prairie extending west to Logan Creek. Records from prior to 1800 indicate an Omaha population of more than two thousand people. A smallpox *epidemic* in 1800–1801 reduced the number by more than half, but high birth rate and productive *subsistence practices* permitted a return to earlier numbers by the 1820s. The Omaha suffered years of displacement and famine that again reduced their numbers, to fewer than eight hundred by the 1850s. Indian agent records indicate a relatively steady population increase since the latter half of the nineteenth century in spite of intermittent epidemics.

The descriptive name Umóⁿhoⁿ refers to going "against the current" or "upstream," and has been recorded for more than 450 years. The name reflects the oral histories of migrations and divisions from other kindred *Dhegiha* groups (Ponca, Osage, Quapaw, Kaw). Over time the Omaha parted company and moved up the Mississippi River drainage. These historic relations are seen in how the Omaha language is related, with increasing distance, to the *Ponca, Osage, Kansa,* and *Quapaw* languages, all within the larger *Siouan* language family. Nineteenth-century linguists described Omaha and Ponca as dialects of the same language.

Omaha oral traditions acknowledge a migration to the Great Plains from the east. Archaeological evidence generally points to the Ohio River Valley region as a probable point of origin or solidification.[7] This region with its distinctive cultural patterns is identified by archaeologists as the *Mississippian culture complex*. There is an ongoing debate among scholars as to whether the Omaha evolved from, or replaced, the *Oneota culture complex* as they moved toward the margins of the Great Plains. Colonial European documents note that the Omaha were in southwest Minnesota and northwest Iowa by the 1670s. Omaha oral history tells of a period of time in which they controlled the *pipestone* quarries in southwestern Minnesota before being displaced by other groups. The Omaha arrived at the Missouri River by 1714. For a time they dominated the Missouri River fur trade and had relations with French, Spanish, British, and later American traders.

In the first half of the nineteenth century, increasing American frontier settlement pressured the Omaha and other tribes to sign a treaty ceding lands east of the Missouri River. Introduced diseases and encroaching hostile groups from the north drove the Omaha to the mouth of the Platte River in the 1840s. An 1854 treaty established the current Nebraska reservation while relinquishing all other Nebraska lands. Northern portions of the reservation were sold to the Winnebago in 1865 and 1874.

The Omaha were immediately subjected to American colonial pressures of *assimilation* on the reservation, which sought to intervene in all aspects of their culture and society. The Omaha were the first U.S. tribe to participate in land allotment. They have experienced land loss, boarding schools, and Christianization.

The Omaha occupied sites in Minnesota and South Dakota prior to moving into the Nebraska region. Their most prominent Nebraska village was Ttónwonttonga, Big Village, on Omaha Creek in Dakota County. Occupied from 1775 to 1845, it was deserted several times due to disease and enemy attacks. The Omaha returned to the area on the newly formed reservation in 1855 and divided into three villages.

The villages reflected important sociopolitical divisions emerging in the group. The northern village, Winjáge, was situated near the Presbyterian Mission and consisted of milled-wood homes. Parents sent their children to school and encouraged the speaking of English. Hence it was dubbed the "Make-Believe White Men" village. A larger centralized village, Bikkúde, consisted of earth lodges and tipis. Its inhabitants maintained many pre-reservation cultural practices (society dances, buffalo hunting, clothing styles), continued to speak the Omaha language, and were often referred to by the Indian agents as "primitive." Residents of Zhontháthe (Wood Eaters) south of Bikkúde acquired their name from the practice of cutting timber from the Missouri River bluffs and selling it to the steamboat crews who stopped at nearby Decatur.

Oral histories of pre-reservation life recount that the Omaha learned about the earth lodge from the Arikara or Pawnee. While in the eastern woodlands the Omaha had used bark-covered houses. Earth lodges up to forty feet in diameter were built for village use and often arranged in relation to matrilocal residence patterns. The buffalo hide tipi was employed during bison hunts and erected in association with patrilineal clan patterns.

By the late nineteenth century, earth lodges had given way to mill-cut lumber houses built on the floor plan of area white settlers. Tipi covers were sewn from cotton canvas material and then faded from general use. By the end of the twentieth century, tipis were used only by the Native American Church for all-night prayer services and by a few community members at the annual August powwow. Most Omaha at Macy reside in housing projects built through federal programs and managed by the tribe. Other tribal members rent or own houses, apartments, or mobile homes in the surrounding countryside and non-Indian towns. A general shortage of quality affordable housing on the reservation was a chronic issue during the latter half of the twentieth century.

Pre-reservation Omaha practiced an annual cycle of spring planting, summer hunting, fall harvesting, and winter hunting. Women owned and worked the garden plots containing maize, beans, and squash. They also exploited a wide range of native plants for food and medicines. The tribe participated in annual summer and winter buffalo hunts into western Nebraska and Kansas. While the buffalo held great ceremonial and economic significance, the people also depended upon deer, antelope, bear, smaller mammals, birds, fish, and crustaceans. The Omaha were active in the fur trade until its collapse at the end of the nineteenth century. They successfully transitioned to American-style farming and produced annual surpluses using imported seeds and agricultural techniques.

As a result of the loss of land ownership following allotment, many Omaha innovated and began leasing their dwindling land base. Today the post-reorganization tribal government and the local public school district provide the majority of the jobs in an otherwise economically depressed rural agricultural area.

Ceremonial and utilitarian arts that were practiced prior to the early 1900s but that have since disappeared include the manufacturing of woven rush mats, painted rawhide containers, wooden burl bowls, buffalo horn spoons, canvas or hide tipi covers, bows, arrows, heddle-woven beadwork, finger-woven sashes, and bags.

Today, the majority of the Omaha tribe participates in ceremonial activities by attending handgames, war dances, gourd dances, Native American Church meetings, funerals, sweat lodge ceremonies, and the recently acquired sun dance. Most participants rely on a small number of community members to fabricate the dance regalia, ceremonial objects, and traditional giveaway objects needed for these activities. While many community members can produce common beadwork items (belts, hair barrettes, moccasins), few individuals create the more technically challenging beadwork pieces (appliqué breechcloths and dance blankets, net-beaded feather fans and gourd rattle handles, diagonal hair pendants). Few individuals have maintained the arts in other traditional media (feather, wood, ribbon, cloth, stone, rawhide, leather, bone, and quill). While maintaining several distinct features and motifs in their *material culture*, the Omaha also borrow and innovate from surrounding cultures.

The Omaha provided quantities of fur-bearing animal hides, bison robes, and related products, along with agricultural produce (primarily corn) and horses to the fur trade of the late eighteenth and early nineteenth century. As bison declined, agricultural production of corn, wheat, and potatoes increased, and they were routinely traded to whites and neighboring tribes. The Omaha were noted for maintaining quality blooded horses through the early 1900s.

Over time the tribe lost lands and experienced a shift to a wage labor economy. Today the tribal government and its members produce only small quantities of agricultural products for market. A few individuals maintain private gardens from which small amounts of dried corn and hominy are produced for sale, trade, or gift giving in an informal market. Dance regalia and other ceremonial paraphernalia are also produced in limited quantities for sale, trade, or as gifts.

Prior to the 1850s the Omaha divided much of the labor along gender and age lines. Females were responsible for all child- and home care, including collecting firewood, hauling potable water, moving and maintaining the tipi, and building and maintaining earth lodges. They developed and maintained the gardens as well as gathering other plant materials for home use. They shared these duties with their female kin and offspring. The result was that the tipi, earth lodge, and products of the garden were the property of the woman. The husband and other male kin would assist in some of the heavier duties related to earth lodge construction and gardening. Participation in the fur trade placed extra burdens upon the females to prepare furs and hides for market.

Males traditionally hunted, trapped, fished, and provided defensive protection for the community. Political organization and ceremonial duties were the responsibility of the men, although the completion of such duties often relied upon the labor and cooperation of the wife and female kin. Young boys herded the horses and hunted small game. Young girls provided childcare to younger siblings while assisting their female kin in other duties. The assimilation pressures of the reservation have removed many of the hunting and defensive warfare duties from the men. Men still fill ceremonial and political roles. Female roles related to home and childcare have not changed.

Since World War II women have expanded into the wage labor economy by taking jobs in all areas of the community. Some women have entered the political arena and have served on the tribal council or as government program directors. Beyond gender and age, some ceremonial duties remain fixed according to clan membership.

Garden plots and earth lodge sites were generally the property of the wife, her sister(s), and daughter(s). The tribe collectively laid claim to the lands upon which they routinely hunted. The communally held reservation lands were allotted to individuals beginning in 1871 and continuing through the early 1900s. "Surplus" communal lands were sold to white settlers and land speculators. Lacking funds to develop their newly acquired farmsteads, many Omaha resorted to leasing their lands to neighboring whites.

Much of the land is in federal trust status, so it cannot be used as collateral for development loans. The bulk of Omaha lands have been sold or lost to outsiders. The economic options available for the remaining lands have often been limited. Without estate planning, many allotments pass into undivided ownership among an increasing number of patrilineal and/or matrilineal heirs. The result is that land remains leased to local white farmers, the original allot-

ment house stands empty, and the heirs reside in tribally managed housing in Macy. The tribal government is currently developing land management programs to protect natural resources such as game, water, and soil.

There are ten major clans, of which many are further divided into smaller discrete subclans. Collectively the clans are visualized as a circular encampment called the Húthuga, symbolizing the universe. The clans are equally divided along an east-west axis into a *moiety* system often described as the northern, male, or sky clans and complemented by the southern, female, or earth clans. The clan governs its own duties, rights, taboos, and personal names. Membership is ideally patrilineal but increasingly includes members tracing their lineage through the mother's side due to children arriving from non-Omaha fathers. The role of the clan has atrophied in some families but remains a symbol of identity throughout the community. Today most contemporary Omaha summarily refer to the existence of only seven clans, usually listing clans associated with the pre-reservations Council of Seven.

Kinship follows a *bifurcate merging* pattern. Cross cousins are referred to as "Aunt" and "Uncle." As generational distance increases, these terms are often modified to become "Little Aunt" and "Little Uncle." Parallel cousins in the first generation are referred to as "Brother" and "Sister." The traditional Omaha kinship system is used as a model of one of the major classification systems in anthropology relating to cousin terms. The imposition of the Euro-American descent model has since created a mixture of surname options and kinship patterns, including the acceptance of the term "Cousin." Public and private use of correct kin terms, although increasingly rendered in the English language, remains a cultural value. Kin terms are used to account for blood, marriage, fictive (including Pan-Indian and non-Native), ceremonial, and potential relationships. Individual kin terms are linguistically marked by the gender of the speaker.

Clan exogamy is the preferred practice, and *moiety exogamy* is held as the cultural ideal. Potential marriage partners are identified through the use of kin terms that reflect the possibility of future claims. Traditionally the practice of both *sororate* and *levirate* marriage rules helped to hold the family together, especially for supporting children in the event of the death of a parent. In the early reservation era friends served as courtship go-betweens. Since chaperones routinely escorted all girls when outdoors, young men had to wait surreptitiously at the water spring or other location for an opportune moment to talk to a girl. Love songs played on a flute from afar were one method of indicating an interest in a girl.

Marriage was often by elopement in order for the girl to escape the claims of all her potential marriage partners. After escaping to the home of one of the boy's relatives, the young couple would return a few days later to the girl's parents' home. The boy's relatives presented gifts to the girl's relatives. If they were accepted, it signaled the recognition of the marriage.

Post-marital residence depends upon the resources available from the families of the bride and groom and may shift between *matrilocal* and *patrilocal* before becoming *neolocal*. *Polygamy* existed into the early twentieth century, although it was not the rule. A man rarely

had more than two wives, and these were generally sisters or aunt and niece. The practice was more often found among the prominent men who had political and ritual duties requiring extra labor and resources.

Divorce was not uncommon. An abusive husband could be turned out, the children remaining with the mother, and the father's male kin expected to continue to support the family. An immoral wife could be turned out and punished by her husband. Generally the Omaha did not favor the changing of the marriage relation due to whim. Today courtship behaviors more closely follow mainstream white society, and serial monogamy is the general practice. Long-term, stable marriages remain the honored ideal.

From the earliest reservation days most families lived in *extended collateral households* to varying degrees, consisting of a husband, wife, children, one or more grandparents, and occasionally the married or unmarried sibling(s) of the parents or children and their family. The pattern continues through the twentieth century, although single-parent and female-headed households are not uncommon. The composition of the household is flexible as the needs of other kin change. Some households include one or more unrelated persons living with, and assisting, the family. Overall composition remains linked to economic factors, availability of housing, and personal preferences.

The father is recognized as having the highest authority, but the mother exercises equal authority regarding the welfare of the children. The grandparent(s) are often the primary caregivers while the parents and other adults are working or absent.

Inheritance of clan name, clan rights, land,

and other tangible objects usually follows a patrilineal pattern. However, ritual knowledge and rights may also pass from the wife's kin to her husband or children depending upon the receiver having shown a marked interest in such knowledge. Most of a person's personal property is distributed to kin and non-kin mourners at the funeral. Without estate planning, most land passes into undivided ownership among increasing numbers of patrilineal and/or matrilineal heirs, sometimes including adopted kin and step-children.

The first line of socialization for all children is the mother, who may be supported by other adults in the extended family. Physical punishment is not the first response to bad behavior. Good manners, including respect for self and others, are the ideal. Children are viewed as individuals and are understood to develop at their individual pace. The Turning of the Child and other pre-reservation rites of passage have given way to preschool, kindergarten, and high school graduation ceremonies.

Those children who show an interest in the dance arena or any of the various religious ceremonies are introduced individually into those respective venues. Long-term relationships are often established with adults who serve as mentors and sponsors. Teasing as a socialization tool is widespread and is applied to both children and adults, especially between particular kin.

The community remains loosely organized around the clan and moiety system with membership being ideally patrilineal. The clans are *symbiotic* in that the performance of most social or religious rites requires the assistance of other clans. *Social stratification* is moderately flexible and quite complex. It is based upon a family's historic and contemporary practice of religious ceremonies, an individual's ownership of ceremonial materials, relationship to traditional leaders and/or women bearing the Mark of Honor, clan membership, blood quantum, and attainment of educational or economic standing. Until World War II several secret societies existed in which membership was attained by virtue of a dream, vision, or purchase. Social groups and clubs focused on the maintenance of Omaha cultural practices continue to emerge and evolve both on- and off-reservation.

Through the late nineteenth century the Omaha were governed by the Council of Seven, whose representatives came from seven specific subclans. The council's authority originated from, and was sanctioned by, the existence and use of two Sacred Pipes that represented the moiety system. Keepers of the Sacred Pipes, Sacred Tent of War, Sacred Buffalo Hide, and Sacred Pole attended council meetings but held no voting authority. There was no tribal assembly or tribal council, per se.

Duties of the Council of Seven included maintaining internal peace and order, securing allies, setting the date of the annual buffalo hunt, and confirming the man who was to act as leader for that hunt. Soldiers were appointed by the council to carry out their commands and to mete out punishment for transgressions of tribal law. Aggressive warfare was sanctioned and controlled by the Sacred Packs of War. Clans did not have a chief or council, nor could a clan act by itself in a political sense. United States government officials appointed pliant men as "paper chiefs" whose presence and influence disrupted the traditional order.

The effects of generations of poverty, alcoholism, and conflicting policies implemented by non-Omaha agencies have wreaked havoc on the Omaha social control system. In pre-reservation days, the authority of the chiefs and social order was safeguarded by various punishments.

In modern times as in the past, most offenses are directed toward an individual and tend to be dealt with by the families involved, although taking the law into one's own hands is publicly frowned upon. Perpetrators of physical assault can expect themselves or their relatives to be attacked by the victim's family. The husband or near relatives often will administer punishment to a man committing adultery. A wife might assault a woman who shows undue attention toward her husband.

Mainstream U.S. and tribal law codes and institutions are in place, but questions about jurisdiction and enforcement create conflict. Within the family unit, an adult talking to or admonishing a child is the primary form of social control. Corporal punishment is generally frowned upon. Teasing is a common control tactic. Ostracism is occasionally used. The belief in a supernatural penalty for inappropriate actions, and attempts to direct supernatural punishment toward someone, are fragmentary. Tribal government leaders, Native American Church leaders, and respected Elders are occasionally called upon to arbitrate conflicts.

While the Omaha have maintained a legacy of "peace" with the federal government, armed conflicts with other tribes were not uncommon prior to the 1900s. In order to maintain control of the fur and gun trade of the Middle Missouri, the Omaha battled on one occasion with the Spanish.

Causes for battles with surrounding tribes included raids by encroaching groups, retaliation, and the seeking of war trophies and battlefield prestige. Adversaries included various bands of Dakota and Lakota Sioux, Arikara, Cheyenne, Pawnee, Otoe, and the Omaha's nearest kin, the Ponca. Alliances and peace were established and breached through time. The performance of the Wawa^n or Calumet Ceremony was one method of establishing peace. Peace with the Arikara probably facilitated the transfer of local strains of maize and earth lodge technology to the Omaha. Peace with the Pawnee permitted joint use of the prime buffalo hunting grounds of the central Great Plains.

Omaha citizens have served in the American military from earliest times. Over 260 men reportedly enlisted in the Union Army by 1865.[8] Many served in World War I, World War II, and more recent conflicts in Vietnam, Korea, and the Middle East. Struggles with outside groups in the twentieth century included bloodless but fiercely fought legal battles to retain or reclaim sovereign Omaha rights and resources. The unarmed occupation of the Blackbird Bend area of Iowa, followed by lengthy court battles, resulted in the return of some lands reserved under the 1854 treaty. Occasional legal actions against the neighboring Winnebago seem to reflect competition for limited resources rather than any underlying animosity.

Prior to the influences of Christianization and Americanization, the Omaha believed in a continuous and invisible life force called Wak-kó^{n}da (UNL usage, as in part 2 of this book; spelled Wakó^{n}da in Macy Standard Orthography, as in part 1). This force manifested itself in the duality of motion and the action of mind and body as well as in the permanency of structure and form as seen in the physical environment. This duality was further developed in the conceptualization of the universe as containing male and female parts whose union perpetuated order in all living things, including people's lives. Religious rites and social organizations such as the Húthuga moiety system and the presence of two principal chiefs symbolized this concept. Young males would maintain a solitary fast for four days on a hilltop, praying to Wakkónda for help throughout life. Since the early 1900s, traditional beliefs have melded with multiple denominations of mainstream American Christianity, the Bahá'í religion, and the *syncretic* peyote religion as manifested in the Native American Church. The result is a complex, and sometimes conflicting, worldview. The concept of Wakkónda has acquired many of the anthropomorphic characteristics associated with the Christian God, including becoming the father of Jesus Christ.

Prior to the 1900s every clan and subclan had a particular family to which belonged the hereditary right to furnish a male keeper of the sacred objects of the clan together with its rituals and rites. The keeper alone possessed the authority to perform the ceremony. His son would follow him in this duty. Assimilation, Christianization, and the deleterious effects of alcohol have contributed to the decline and disappearance of nearly all pre-reservation practices.

The majority of Omaha maintain a pluralistic religious practice through participation in Native American Church, traditional Omaha, and mainstream Christian ceremonies. Leaders of the Native American Church acquire their authority by demonstrating a belief in the church and its worldview, sponsoring prayer meetings, and receiving the ceremonial instruments with the blessing of church leaders through petition or inheritance. The use of personal medicine bundles, pipes, sweat lodge ceremonies, and the newly acquired sun dance ceremony follow a similar pattern.

All important changes in life are marked, to varying degrees, with either a family or public ceremony. All ceremonies involve the offering of prayers to Wakkónda. All include the sharing of food provided by the ceremony's sponsor and the redistribution of material goods through gift giving. Family or public feasting marks such life events as birth and birthdays, recovery from illness, graduation or social promotion of any kind, marriage and anniversary, homecoming, death, and memorials. Tribal and national holidays are also observed.

Joyous occasions may also be marked by the addition of a war dance, handgame, gourd dance, or Native American Church prayer service. One child may be singled out of a family to be the focus of a total of four yearly birthday dances or church meetings. Memorial meetings or feasts often follow this four-year pattern. Since the mid-twentieth century, prayer service leaders in the Native American Church have primarily filled the role of Man-in-Charge at most ceremonial and social functions.

In the twentieth century, artistic production and performance remain culturally centered on activities around the big drum of the dance arena and the small drum of the Native American Church prayer service. The ability to render old songs accurately and create new songs is an honored skill that requires a lifetime commitment. Unlike with other tribes, Omaha singing and drumming are a male role. A spouse or other female relative may sit behind the singers. They will harmonize the chorus of the songs and are routinely referred to as the "canaries." A few males play the cedar flute.

Types of dancing are identified by the style of movement and distinctive regalia, including male traditional war dance or Hethúshka, fancy dance, straight dance, grass dance, female traditional buckskin, traditional cloth, fancy shawl, and jingle dress. The Kiowa gifted the gourd dance to the Omaha in the late 1960s. Literary production, mostly in the form of poetry or ethnohistorical sketches, is limited. A few individuals play Western musical instruments beyond the public school music program for their own enjoyment. A handful of community members work in oil, water colors, charcoal, and pen and ink media for local consumption.

Prior to allotment, several secret societies had knowledge of medicine, roots, plants, and curative practices. Original knowledge was gained through visions or dreams and tended to be specialized within each society. For example, the Ttéitha'ethe, "those whom the buffalo have shown compassion," had knowledge for the curing of wounds. The Omaha utilized a vast pharmacopoeia derived from plants, animals, and minerals. Other techniques included the use of prayer, song, massage, sucking, and hacking (controlled bloodletting).

By the late twentieth century all traditional knowledge and practice of medicine had nearly disappeared. Western medicine is used for most daily or chronic medical needs, and several Omaha have entered the health care field. Some community members rely on Native American Church prayer services and the ritual ingestion

of peyote (*Lophophora williamsii*) to treat a wide range of illness. Sweat lodge and other prayer ceremonies are sometimes used to treat physical and mental illness.

Through the early 1900s the Milky Way was believed to be the path made by the spirits of people as they passed to the realm of the dead. The family or the society in which the deceased was a member prepared the body for burial. Burial was usually within a day of death. The deceased was placed in a shallow hilltop grave in a seated position facing east. Poles were arranged over the opening upon which earth was heaped into a mound. Personal belongings were left at the grave. Some mourners cut their hair or made blood offerings by slashing the forearms. A fire was kept burning at the grave for four days to cheer the deceased on the journey. Food was left at the grave as a token of remembrance. The spirit of a murderer never reached the afterworld but was forced to wander the earth.

By the end of the twentieth century the Omaha funeral had undergone profound changes. The embalmed body lies in state, usually in the home of kin, for four nights. It is buried after a public funeral on the fifth day. Mourners visit the family, partake of regular meals and prayers for the deceased, and keep all night vigils. A wake service or Native American Church funeral service marks the fourth night. A key component of the final all night vigil is the opportunity for family members to speak to the deceased for the last time. This is consonant with the older belief that under certain conditions the realm of the dead is accessible to the living, and the dead can lend their assistance in the avocations with which they have been familiar. As in the past, the environment of the afterlife is believed to be similar to the physical world, although free of want and illness. It appears that the belief in supernatural punishment and reward after death is the result of Christianization.

The modern funeral involves a communal feast, distribution of gifts to mourners, and a graveside blessing. Males assist in both digging and filling the grave. Interment is in a modern casket inserted into a rough board box. Stone markers are used. There is a central hilltop tribal cemetery at Macy and several smaller cemeteries are near old allotment homes. Dancing, singing, and other social events are normally canceled while a body is above ground. Stories of ghostly visitors remain common, especially in old village sites, at abandoned or old allotment homes, and near certain geographical sites. Of all the ceremonies performed in the twentieth century, it can be said that the Omaha funeral is the single activity in which nearly all Omaha, whether traditionalist or assimilated, will participate. It embodies the fundamentals of Omaha worldview, including the values of kinship, food sharing, self-sacrifice, reciprocity, and the interrelation of the physical body and spiritual soul.

In the summer and fall of 1930 anthropologist Margaret Mead and her husband, Reo Fortune, performed fieldwork on the Omaha Reservation. Fortune was interested in the esoteric knowledge and its organization in the community. His findings became part of *Omaha Secret Societies* (1932), a monograph in the Columbia University Contributions to Anthropology series. Mead reported that Fortune used interpreters to interview the elderly informants, which suggests that the elderly keepers of knowledge preferred to use the Omaha language.

Mead, on the other hand, worked secretly, observing and talking to women and children for her own study on the condition of Indian women, later published in *The Changing Culture of an Indian Tribe*. She remarked, "The conditions of work and the lack of the [Omaha] language precluded research on little children."[9] This suggests that children were still being born in the late 1920s as Omaha-only speakers. This barrier to research was balanced by her belief that the existence of three generations of English-speaking people would produce sufficient data. Mead surmised that it was not justifiable to take the time to learn the language for the purpose of fieldwork in a disintegrated culture.

Mead's description of Macy and its environs came a generation after the Omaha received fee patents to their trust lands, allowing land to be sold. Tribal economy had already eroded with the increasing loss of land to white setters and speculators. The list of the commercial establishments available at the time included two stores, "two restaurants, a post office, a shoe and harness repair shop, two filling stations, a garage and car wrecking establishment, a blacksmith, a Pentecostal church, a deserted white Presbyterian church, a pretentious school building . . . , the agency buildings, . . . and the mission."[10] Mead describes the 1930 Omaha culture as "deleted and attenuated, . . . existing in a state of just attained and slender equilibrium."[11] Some of the attenuated (shortened) aspects of Omaha culture that remained included: "notably the accumulation of counts so that one's daughter might be tattooed, burial and mourning ceremonials including the 'give away' of all the personal possessions of the deceased, the watch at the grave, the contribution to the mourners, and the mourner's subsequent distribution of gifts to 'end mourning.' The kinship system was kept, in terminology-exogamic rules and gentile taboos."[12] Completely abandoned customs included use of the menstrual hut and menstrual taboos, early childhood rituals (e.g., Turning of the Child, Dedication of the Boys to Thunders), fasting for religious experience, and both military and civil chieftainship.

Mead recognized that the Omaha made a significant adjustment to white culture with the adoption of the syncretic peyote religion, which arrived in 1906. She noted that other adjustments had been made "without sacrificing their tribal individuality, without giving up their language, [but notably] with the surrender of half of their institutions, their political autonomy, and their existence as a self-governing community, and by absorbing a fair number of traits of white material culture. But they had made for themselves a sort of existence, although it was only the shadow of the rich complexity of their former lives."[13]

Although she acknowledged this existence as still comprising a coherent standard, Mead surmised that if the economic base had been left intact, further changes would have been kept at bay for a generation or more. In other words, the loss of a land base resulted in the loss of a viable economy and hence was a catalyst for dramatic changes in both cultural beliefs and social practices.

An attempt to reverse land loss came with the passage of the Indian Reorganization Act of 1934. While permitting tribes to reorganize their traditional governments under a more Western model, it halted land allotments and returned unallotted surplus lands to tribal ownership. The Omaha ratified a constitution and bylaws by a vote of 311 to 27 in an early 1936 election. Later that year a corporate charter was ratified by a vote of 221 to 14. With these actions the Omaha shifted to a popularly elected seven-member Tribal Council holding three-year terms. Off-reservation tribal members were not allowed to vote or hold office. Council members were immediately faced with a growing population and a lack of revenues. Tribal lands were cleared east of Macy, and the timber was sold to finance government operations. The cleared lands became part of a farming operation to supply additional funds.[14]

Data from a 1946 survey compiled by Bureau of Indian Affairs (BIA) personnel for inclusion in an unidentified congressional report noted that of 175 families, 134 had an income under $250 per annum, 20 under $500 per annum, 9 under $1,000 per annum, and only 12 above $1,250 per annum.[15] In the years following World War II the Omaha had lost most of their western lands and were regrouping along the Highway 75 corridor on the eastern Missouri River bluffs, the location of the early reservation villages. Of the 1,127 persons living on the reservation in 1956, nearly 75 percent were half-blood Omaha or more. Of the 1,087 enrolled members living off-reservation, over 50 percent congregated in Lincoln, Omaha, and Sioux City. Overall, the Omaha remained impoverished.

In A. R. Longwell's thesis on the status of Omaha lands in the mid-1950s, he reported high unemployment, the lack of demand for Indian labor for farm work, and the lack of industry on the reservation. The depressed economic situation mirrored his assessment of the education environment, including poorly maintained facilities, educators untrained to meet the particular cultural and social needs of the Omaha children, and a generalized lack of interest in the community toward acquiring an adequate education, which resulted in a high truancy rate.

Many policies of the Indian New Deal were reversed following WWII. In retrospect, policies such as the Indian Reorganization Act helped to further the assimilation of communal tribal nations into the Western mainstream model. Termination of federal responsibilities for Indian affairs began in the 1950s. While the Omaha avoided termination of their tribal status, they were alarmed when the BIA discussed transferring many Omaha services to county and state agencies as cost-cutting measures. The Tribal Council chairman surmised that the tribe would experience the same effect as termination.[16] The Omaha were especially anxious when their close kin, the Northern Ponca, were terminated in 1962.

Thus the Omaha continued to struggle with many fundamental survival issues. They had a growing population; a diminishing viable land base, as properties acquired heirs in an exponentially expanding manner; insufficient housing; and insecure revenues for the operation of their government. Nearly one-half of the enrolled population was disenfranchised due to their off-reservation residence. In 1958 an urban journalist characterized the Omaha as being "among the most culturally disintegrated and socially ill in the country. . . . The eight hundred residents were a divided people, barely able to recall the last time they all did something

together."[17] While this was surely an exaggerated assessment, it was probably widely held by non-Indians. Tribal Council Chairman Alfred "Buddy" Gilpin summed up the situation when he characterized the BIA as having taken care of the Omaha in a way that made the Omaha forget how to care for themselves. Perhaps he had caught a glimpse of the future when he told a *World Herald* reporter, "Today, [the Omaha] are just waking up and beginning to hate this helplessness."[18]

For the Omaha, the current cultural renaissance has been ongoing since at least the late 1960s and early 1970s. The stimuli for the renaissance are a combination of many factors. These include increased expressions of Native sovereignty brought about by the economic and political reforms demanded by grassroots and national groups such as the American Indian Movement (AIM). Members of the Omaha tribe participated in the AIM occupation of Wounded Knee, South Dakota, the occupation of Alcatraz Island, and several protest demonstrations in Nebraska. Federal policies began shifting to encourage self-determination without termination. The 1975 Self-Determination and Education Assistance Act gave the tribal government the opportunity to contract for Bureau of Indian Affairs–controlled programs and garner overhead costs that they could apply to other tribal programs.

Significant monetary awards realized through Indian Claims Commission settlements funded early housing construction and infrastructure improvements at Macy. This was followed by Housing and Urban Development programs aimed at reducing the critical housing shortage across the reservation. The 1978 Indian Child Welfare Act returned a measure of control over the welfare of Omaha children to the Omaha government.

Changes in the political climate, as well as the initiation of casino gaming and other economic ventures, have attracted the return of many expatriate Omaha to the reservation. In 1994 the Omaha Tribe reported an enrolled population of more than seven thousand. Well over one-half of the enrolled members of the tribe live off-reservation in neighboring urban areas. The tribal government is struggling to create jobs and provide housing for its growing population.

Northeast Nebraska is primarily an agricultural district. Remaining Omaha lands consist mainly of the heavily timbered and non-arable Missouri River bluffs, with limited economic development potential. In past years the Omaha Tribe has run a tribal farm and dairy operation on the Nebraska side of the river. A small but lucrative casino was established on the Iowa side of the river in the 1990s. Competition from surrounding casino operations, both Indian and non-Indian, has since reduced profitability. The tribe continues to expand its gaming facilities on both sides of the river. Other economic development ideas that have been considered or attempted since the 1970s have included an ethanol plant, classic car business, cigarette manufacturing plant, farm equipment manufacturing plant, sportsman camping area, and convenience store/gasoline station.

Evidence of an Omaha reassertion of political sovereignty includes the partially successful litigation for reclaiming reservation lands at Blackbird Bend. There are continuing negotiations to remedy jurisdictional problems in law enforcement as well as efforts to control other federal programs operating on the reservation.

On the cultural front, in 1989 the Omaha successfully retrieved two of their paramount sacred objects, the Sacred Pole and the White Buffalo Hide, from eastern museums. The tribe stated a desire to provide a cultural heritage center facility to house these and other artifacts and archives for tribal members' use.

As the twenty-first century opens a new millennium, the Omaha find themselves continuing to struggle with uninterrupted assimilation pressures. They remain active participants in national discourse related to high profile Native issues of tribal sovereignty, human remains and grave goods repatriation, and economic development through casino gaming. The Omaha people continue to battle upstream against the current of mainstream pressures.

KEY CONCEPTS

Allotment: the process of dividing something (land, money, etc.) into individual shares or portions.

Appropriate authority: people whose knowledge or skills were obtained through proper or acceptable channels, and who are recognized by the community-at-large as being qualified to impart that knowledge or exercise that skill in a culturally correct manner.

Assimilation: the process in which one group takes on the cultural and other traits of a larger group.

Bifurcate merging kinship: a system in which Ego's two sides (mother's and father's) merge the term "father" to include all of Ego's father's brothers, and the term "mother" to include all of Ego's mother's sisters.

Clan exogamy: to marry outside one's own clan or lineage.

Dhegiha: "belonging to the people of this land" or "those dwelling here." Dorsey (1890) reports applying this term to the group of tribes in the Siouan language family (Omaha, Ponca, Osage, Kansa, and Quapaw). It is the name of a particular language in that family tree. Contemporary Umóⁿhoⁿ people do not use the term when referring to themselves.

Epidemic: an outbreak of a disease that spreads more quickly and more extensively among a group of people than would normally be expected.

Extended collateral households: include members of multiple generations (extending from grandparents through grandchildren) and siblings with spouses.

Gendered behavior: the social roles that are based upon one's gender. For example, in today's Umóⁿhoⁿ society a woman's duties include child rearing and food preparation. A man's roles include public speaking, decision making regarding religious ceremonies, and protection of the tribe and family from external dangers.

Gendered knowledge: knowledge and/ or skills that are recognized by the community to belong to males: nú ūshkoⁿ (men's customs), or females: waʾú ūshkoⁿ (women's customs), as part of their regular social, political, or religious roles.

Kansa: Kóⁿze, meaning undetermined. Also named as the Kaw.

Levirate: the practice of a man marrying his deceased wife's sister.

Macy Standard Orthography (MSO): the writing system used at the Umóⁿhoⁿ Language and Culture Center at Umóⁿhoⁿ Nation Public School, modified from the Fletcher and La Flesche system.

Material culture: the objects created by humans. Studying the material culture of a people can give insights into the life ways and value systems shared by the group.

Matrilocal: residence, especially after marriage, when the bride and groom live with the wife's relatives.

Mississippian culture complex: an archaeological term applied to multiple sites centered on the Mississippi drainage and the lower part of the eastern woodland culture area. The Mississippian period dates from around 800–900 AD through 1500–1600 AD. There are regional variations. Intensive agriculture, vast trade networks, and monumental earthen mounds are diagnostic characteristics. Cahokia in the area of East St. Louis, Illinois, is the largest city complex of the Mississippian culture.

Moiety: a society that is divided into two halves that may serve complementary relations in political, religious, and social functions.

Moiety exogamy: to marry outside one's moiety.

Neolocal: residence, especially after marriage, where the bride and groom establish an independent home.

Omaha: Umóⁿhoⁿ, "against the wind or current," is also sometimes interpreted as "the upstream people." Historic and contemporary variations of the spelling of Umóⁿhoⁿ include Máha and Umáha. A person may respond to the question "What tribe are you?" by saying, Umóⁿhoⁿ bthíⁿ, "I am Omaha."

Oneota culture complex: an Algonquin term used by archaeologists to describe groups of village horticulturists in the Midwest region, including the Blood Run site in Iowa. Radiocarbon dates for Oneota villages range between about 1000 and 1650 AD.

Osage: Wazházhe, meaning undetermined.

Patrilocal: residence, especially after marriage, when the bride and groom live with the groom's relatives.

Pipestone: a reddish or pinkish stone resembling clay in consistency that some Native North Americans harden and use for decorative objects and long, often ornate pipes. The pipestone quarries in southwest Minnesota continue to yield stone for Native use. Umóⁿhoⁿ people consider the stone to be sacred and give great respect to the tribal pipes crafted from this stone.

Polygamy: marriages involving plural spouses of either sex.

Ponca: Ppóⁿkka, meaning undetermined.

Post-marital residence: where the bride and groom live after marriage.

Proprietary knowledge: the concept that knowledge, skills, and duties may belong to an individual, family, or clan and not to the tribe or community. The exercising of the skills and duties, or the transmittal of the knowledge, is a right of the owner of that knowledge. For example, in Umóⁿhoⁿ society each clan owns the personal names associated with that clan. They regulate who receives the names. People cannot claim the right or use of a clan name for clans from which they are not descended.

Quapaw: Ugáx̣pa, "downstream people."

Reservation: an area of land set aside for a particular purpose, especially in North America for the use of a Native North American people. The Umóⁿhoⁿ acquired their reservation by treaty in 1854.

Siouan: the term as used in this textbook applies to the language family that includes the Dhegiha tribes; the other Missouri Valley Siouan tribes including the Winnebago, Otoe, Iowa, Missouria, Lakota, Dakota, and Nakoda; and other related tribes like the Mandan, Hidatsa, Crow, Biloxi, Ofo, and Tutelo.

Social stratification: a ranked society in which some persons have greater access to resources, power, and authority.

Sororate: the practice of a woman marrying her deceased husband's brother.

Subsistence practices: how a group of people makes their living; how they secure food, clothing, and shelter.

Symbiotic: a close association of animals or plants of different species that is often, but not always, of mutual benefit; used here to describe the close association of clans.

Syncretic: the combination of different systems of philosophical or religious belief or practice.

Treaty: a formal contract or agreement negotiated between countries or other political entities. The Umóⁿhoⁿ, as a sovereign independent nation, signed several treaties with the United States government.

NOTES

1. Omaha Tribe of Nebraska, "Omaha Language Preservation Project" (Macy: Omaha Tribe of Nebraska, 1994).

2. Nebraska Department of Education, *Challenge for a New Era: Nebraska K-12 Foreign Language Frameworks* (Lincoln: Nebraska Department of Education, 1996).

3. James Edwin, *Account of an Expedition from Pittsburgh to the Rocky Mountains . . .*, ed. Reuben Gold Thwaites (Cleveland: Arthur H. Clark Company, 1905), and Reuben Gold Thwaites, ed., *Travels in the Interior of North America* (Cleveland: Arthur H. Clark Company, 1906).

4. See selected publications from James Owen Dorsey in the bibliography.

5. See selected publications from Alice Cunningham Fletcher and Francis La Flesche in the bibliography.

6. Mark Awakuni-Swetland, "The Omaha," in *Encyclopedia of World Cultures Supplement*, ed. Carol R. Ember, Melvin Ember, and Ian Skoggard (New York: Macmillan Reference USA, 2001), 257–63.

7. John M. O'Shea and John Ludwickson, *Archaeology and Ethnohistory of the Omaha: The Big Village Site* (Lincoln: University of Nebraska Press in cooperation with the American Indian Studies Research Institute, Indiana University, 1992).

8. U.S. Department of the Interior, Office of Indian Affairs, *Annual Report of the Commissioner of Indian Affairs, for the Year 1865* (Washington DC: Government Printing Office, 1865), 576.

9. Margaret Mead, *The Changing Culture of an Indian Tribe* (1932; repr., New York: Capricorn Books, 1966), xiii.

10. Mead, *The Changing Culture of an Indian Tribe*, 32.

11. Mead, *The Changing Culture of an Indian Tribe*, 30.

12. Mead, *The Changing Culture of an Indian Tribe*, 28.

13. Mead, *The Changing Culture of an Indian Tribe*, 29.

14. Mark Awakuni-Swetland, *Dance Lodges of the Omaha People: Building from Memory* (New York: Routledge, 2001), 54–56.

15. A. R. Longwell, "Lands of the Omaha Indians," MA thesis, University of Nebraska-Lincoln, 1961, 23.

16. Awakuni-Swetland, *Dance Lodges*, 65–66.

17. Joy Miller, "Omahas Take Control of Tribe Rehabilitation," *World Herald* (Omaha NE), September 2, 1958, 2.

18. "'Chief' Fears End of Tribe," *World Herald* (Omaha NE), April 27, 1958, B11.

BIBLIOGRAPHY

Awakuni-Swetland, Mark. *Dance Lodges of the Omaha People: Building from Memory*. New York: Routledge, 2001; repr., Lincoln: University of Nebraska Press, 2008.

———. "The Omaha." In *Encyclopedia of World Cultures Supplement*, edited by Carol R. Ember, Melvin Ember, and Ian Skoggard, 257–263. New York: Macmillan Reference USA, 2001.

Barnes, R. H. *Two Crows Denies It: A History of Controversy in Omaha Sociology*. Lincoln: University of Nebraska Press, 1984; repr., Lincoln: University of Nebraska Press, 2005.

Bennett, Paula Porter. "Wisdom Great and Small: Omaha Indian Grandmothers Interpret Their Lives." PhD diss., University of Nebraska-Lincoln, 1996.

Boughter, Judith A. *Betraying the Omaha Nation, 1790–1916*. Norman: University of Oklahoma Press, 1998.

"'Chief' Fears End of Tribe." *World-Herald* (Omaha NE), April 27, 1958.

Common Omaha Recipes (bilingual recipes with audio files). UNL Omaha class website, http://omahalanguage.unl.edu. Macy, 2002.

Cook, Thurman. *Umonhon iye te ede'nonya?: How do you say in Omaha?* Unpublished dictionary and lessons. Macy, 1997.

Dorsey, James Owen. *The Ȼegiha Language*. Contributions to North American Ethnology vol. 6. Washington DC: Government Printing Office, 1890. https://archive.org/details/ldpd_8627114_000.

———. *Omaha and Ponka Letters*. Bureau of American Ethnology Bulletin 11. Washington DC: Government Printing Office, 1891. https://archive.org/details/omahaandponkale-00dorsgoog.

———. "Omaha Dwellings, Furniture, and Implements." In *Bureau of American Ethnology 13th Annual Report*, edited by J. W. Powell, 263–88. Washington DC: Government Printing Office, 1896.

———. *Omaha Sociology*. In *Bureau of American Ethnology 3rd Annual Report*, edited by J. W. Powell, 205–307. Washington DC: Government Printing Office, 1884.

Edwin, James. *Account of an Expedition from Pittsburgh to the Rocky Mountains, performed in the Years 1819, 1820 . . . under the Command of Maj. S. H. Long*. Early Western Travels series, vols. 14–17, edited by Reuben Gold Thwaites. Cleveland: Arthur H. Clark Company, 1905.

Fletcher, Alice Cunningham. *Historical Sketch of the Omaha Tribe of Indians in Nebraska*. Washington: Judd & Detweiler, 1885.

———. "Observations on the Laws and Privileges of the Gens in Indian Society." *Proceedings of the American Association for the Advancement of Science* 32 (1885): 395–96.

———. "Tribal Life among the Omahas." *Century Magazine* 51 (January 1896): 450–61.

Fletcher, Alice Cunningham, and Francis La Flesche. *The Omaha Tribe.* Bureau of American Ethnology 27th Annual Report, 1905–6. 2 vols. Washington DC: Government Printing Office, 1911; repr., Lincoln: University of Nebraska Press, 1992.

Fortune, Reo F. *Omaha Secret Societies.* New York: Columbia University Press, 1932.

Gilmore, Melvin R. *Uses of Plants by the Indians of the Missouri River Region.* MA thesis, University of Nebraska–Lincoln, 1914; repr. Lincoln: Bison Books, University of Nebraska Press, 1991.

Kinbacher, Kurt. "Immigration, the American West, and the Twentieth Century: German from Russia, Omaha Indian, and Vietnamese-Urban Villages in Lincoln, Nebraska." PhD diss., University of Nebraska–Lincoln, 2006.

Koontz, John E. "Preliminary Sketch of the Omaha-Ponka Language." Draft dissertation manuscript, University of Colorado–Boulder, 1984; rev., 1988.

La Flesche, Francis. *The Middle Five: Indian Schoolboys of the Omaha Tribe.* 1900; repr., Lincoln: University of Nebraska Press, 1978.

Larson, Rory M. "Acculturation Terms in Omaha." MA thesis, University of Nebraska–Lincoln, 2005.

Longwell, A. R. "Lands of the Omaha Indians." MA thesis, University of Nebraska–Lincoln, 1961.

Marshall, Carol. *Umonhon iye wagatha' baçe = Omaha language workbook of Elizabeth Stabler.* Mimeograph copy. 197?.

Mead, Margaret. *The Changing Culture of an Indian Tribe.* 1932; repr., New York: Capricorn Books, 1966.

Miller, Joy. "Omahas Take Control of Tribe Rehabilitation." *World-Herald* (Omaha NE), September 2, 1958.

Nebraska Department of Education. *Challenge for a New Era: Nebraska K-12 Foreign Language Frameworks.* Lincoln: Nebraska Department of Education, 1996.

Nelson, Elaine. "Eunice Woodhull Stabler, Omaha Indian Writer, 1885–1963." MA thesis, University of Nebraska–Lincoln, 2004.

Omaha Tribe of Nebraska. "Omaha Language Preservation Project." Grant proposal to Administration for Native Americans, program announcement #93.612–943. Macy: Omaha Tribe of Nebraska, 1994.

O'Shea, John M., and John Ludwickson. *Archaeology and Ethnohistory of the Omaha: The Big Village Site.* Lincoln: University of Nebraska Press in cooperation with the American Indian Studies Research Institute, Indiana University, 1992.

Ridington, Robin, and Dennis Hastings (Ín'aska). *Blessing for a Long Time: The Sacred Pole of the Omaha Tribe.* Lincoln: University of Nebraska Press, 1997.

Saunsoci, Alice, and Ardis Eschenberg. *500+ Verbs in Umonhon (Omaha): Doing Things in the Umonhon Way.* Lexington: CreateSpace Independent Publishing Platform, 2016.

Scherer, Mark R. *Imperfect Victories: The Legal Tenacity of the Omaha Tribe, 1945–1995.* Lincoln: University of Nebraska Press, 1999.

Stabler, Elizabeth, and Mark J. Swetland. *Umonhon iye of Elizabeth Stabler: A Vocabulary of the Omaha Language.* Winnebago: Nebraska Indian Press, 1977.

———. *Umonhon iye of Elizabeth Stabler: A Vocabulary of the Omaha Language with an Omaha to English Lexicon.* Macy: John Mangan Printing, 1991.

Stabler, Hollis D. *No One Ever Asked Me: The World War II Memoirs of an Omaha Indian Soldier.* Edited by Victoria Smith. Lincoln: University of Nebraska Press, 2005.

Summers, Wynne L. *Women Elders' Life Stories of the Omaha Tribe: Macy, Nebraska, 2004–2005.* Lincoln: University of Nebraska Press, 2009.

Swetland, Mark J. "'Make-Believe White-Men' and the Omaha Land Allotments of 1871–1900." *Great Plains Research* 4 (1994): 201–36.

Tate, Michael L. *The Upstream People: An Annotated Research Bibliography of the Omaha Tribe.* Metuchen: Scarecrow Press, 1991.

Thwaites, Reuben Gold, ed. *Travels in the Interior of North America.* In Early Western Travels series, vols. 22–24. Cleveland: Arthur H. Clark Company, 1906.

Tibbles, Thomas H. *Buckskin and Blanket Days.* Lincoln: University of Nebraska Press, 1957.

UNL Omaha Language Class. Common Omaha Cooking (bilingual recipes with audio files). Omaha Language Curriculum Development Project. Lincoln: UNL, 2002. http://omaha language.unl.edu/recipes/index.html.

UNL Omaha Language Class, Alberta Grant Canby, Emmaline Walker Sanchez, Rory Larson, and Mark Awakuni-Swetland. "Iⁿdénoⁿba Núzhiⁿga Noⁿbéda: Two Faces and the Twin Brothers." Omaha Language Curriculum Development Project. Lincoln: UNL, 2006. http://omahalanguage.unl.edu/two-faces /oml.0002.html.

———. *Umóⁿhoⁿ Tí Ukéthiⁿ tʰe: The Common Omaha House.* Lincoln: UNL Anthropology / Ethnic Studies / Native American Studies, 2007.

U.S. Department of the Interior, Office of Indian Affairs. *Annual Report of the Commissioner of Indian Affairs, for the Year 1865.* Washington DC: Government Printing Office, 1865.

Welsch, Roger. *Omaha Tribal Myths and Trickster Tales.* Chicago: Swallow Press, 1981.

Wishart, David J. *An Unspeakable Sadness: The Dispossession of the Nebraska Indians.* Lincoln: University of Nebraska Press, 1994.

Part 1

Lessons from the Umón̓hoⁿ Language and Culture Center, Umón̓hoⁿ Nation Public School, Macy, Nebraska

Different Sounds

Some Umóⁿhoⁿ letters don't sound like anything in English.

> **K** as in **ké** ("turtle") sounds like a cross between English K and G.
>
> **P** as in **péxe** ("gourd") sounds like a cross between English P and B.
>
> **T** as in **té** ("buffalo") sounds like a cross between English T and D.

When you say Umóⁿhoⁿ K, P or T, try it like this: Hold your hand in front of your lips and make the English sound K, P, or T. What you did should make a puff of air hit your hand—which is the same as Umóⁿhoⁿ Kᴴ, Pᴴ and Tᴴ. Now try doing the same thing without that puff of air. This is the Umóⁿhoⁿ K, P and T.

> **P'** as in **wanóⁿp'iⁿ** ("necklace") sounds like a cross between English P and B with a jump in the throat.
>
> **T'** as in **t'é** ("dead") sounds like a cross between English T and D with a jump in the throat.
>
> **X** as in **xúde** ("gray") sounds like English K without the K sound—or like a soft version of the throaty sound in some German words. Try making a K sound but holding it and making a soft hiss with the back top of your tongue.

Soundalikes

Some Umóⁿhoⁿ letters have the same sound, or nearly the same sound, as they do in English.

B CH D G H J M N S SH W Y Z

Special Soundalikes

> **TH** as in **Óⁿtha Thétha** ("throw it") sounds like **TH** in **this**, not like **TH** in **thin**.
>
> **ZH** as in **zhiⁿgá** ("small") sounds like S in **vision** or GE in **garage**.
>
> **Kʰ** as in **kʰagého** ("friend") sounds like English K.
>
> **Pʰ** as in **pʰí** ("I went there") sounds like English P.
>
> **Tʰ** as in **tʰe** ("the") sounds like English T.

Vowel Soundalikes

> **A** as in **father**, **E** as in **Las Vegas**, **I** as in **pizza**, **O** as in **aho**, **U** as in **flu**
>
> **Iⁿ** as in **mean** / **dream** / **sing** / **finger**
>
> **Oⁿ** as in **mom** / **song** / **laundry** / **longer**

See the "Writing System Extension" in chapter 8 for more in-depth coverage of spelling issues.

1.2 ARTICLES

Example sentences: Marcella Woodhull Cayou; source posters: Vida Woodhull Stabler.

"the (living)"

akʰa: One subject

Núzhiⁿga-akʰa wachígaxe thipʰí: The boy knows how to dance.

ama: More than one subject

Shémizhiⁿga-ama kigthíbuta wachígaxa: The young women round-danced.

thiⁿkʰe: One minor subject or living being who is acted on

Pasóⁿ-thiⁿkʰe áta: The bald eagle is the highest / best.

thoⁿkʰa: More than one minor subjects or living beings who are acted on

Pasóⁿ-thoⁿkʰa awátoⁿbe: I saw the bald eagles.

ma: More than one minor subjects or living beings who are acted on

Shóⁿge wáthiⁿ-ma awátoⁿbe: I saw the horses he has.

"the (non-living)"

thoⁿ: round / self-contained / symmetrical

Mízhiⁿga-akʰa sézi-thoⁿ gthízhabe: The girl peeled her orange.

kʰe: long / flat / horizontal / deceased

Zhoⁿmóⁿthiⁿ-kʰe ugthíⁿ áhigi: The limo seats many people.

tʰe: tall / vertical / group / idea

Tizhébe-tʰe ánoⁿsa: The door is locked.

ge: scattered / many groups / all over / different ones

Híⁿska-ge ubúde uxpátha, zhoⁿbtháska-kʰe-di: The beads fell in pieces, all over the floor.

There are two other, older Umóⁿhoⁿ articles, which today are typically heard only in old songs, stories, prayers and names: **thiⁿ** "the (moving)" and **tʰoⁿ** "the (standing)." One exception still in common use is the article **thiⁿ** with **masóⁿ** ("snowflake"), as in **Masóⁿ-thiⁿ ashkáde abthíⁿ**, "I have snowflakes and am playing with them."

1.3 ELDERS' VERB PATTERNS

The "a" verb pattern: Donna Morris Parker; "bth" verb pattern: Donna Morris Parker and Marcella Woodhull Cayou; "nóⁿxeskazhi" verb pattern: Marcella Woodhull Cayou and Donna Morris Parker; "gáxe" verb pattern: Donna Morris Parker; elicitation/transcription and lesson introduction: Vida Woodhull Stabler. "As my elicitation and documentation skills became better, I would ask the Elders to conjugate verbs as they came up when planning lessons. The environment was sitting in our Title VI office drinking coffee. I would sit at my computer across from the Elder(s). I would ask the Elders to use the verb in a sentence. The following is what they shared. This is a sample of their work." — Vida Woodhull Stabler

"a" Verb Pattern

NOⁿ'Óⁿ: HEAR

—: s/he/they

a-: I

tha-: you

oⁿ-: we

Anóⁿ'oⁿ: I hear it.

Iⁿgthóⁿga-thiⁿkʰe anóⁿ'oⁿ: I heard the cat.

Thanóⁿ'oⁿ: You hear it.

Kipáda-thiⁿkʰe thanóⁿ'oⁿ-a?: Did you hear the hatchling / duckling / chick?

Noⁿ'óⁿ: S/he / they hear it.

Ewázhiⁿnoⁿge-kʰe noⁿ'óⁿ: She can hear the train.

Shé-akʰa wazhíⁿga-thiⁿkʰe noⁿ'óⁿ: That one heard the bird.

Oⁿnóⁿ'oⁿ: We hear it.

Iyébaha-thiⁿkʰe oⁿnóⁿ'oⁿ-bazhi: We can't hear the camp crier.

We have used the shortcut s/he to indicate that the subject may be either male or female. Umóⁿhoⁿ grammar does not distinguish between "he" and "she," and English grammar has no way to refer to a single third person sentient subject without doing so. Thus, **noⁿ'óⁿ** can mean "she hears it," or "he hears it," or "it hears it," without distinction of gender.

More Advanced Conjugations

Winóⁿ'oⁿ: I hear you.

Winóⁿ'oⁿ-mazhi: I don't hear you.

Oⁿtháⁿnoⁿ'oⁿ: You hear me.

Vida, oⁿtháⁿnoⁿ'oⁿ-a?: Vida, do you hear me?

Watháⁿnoⁿ'oⁿ: You hear them / us.

Gahíye-ama ugthíⁿ ázhi kigthíazhi edái-tʰe watháⁿnoⁿ'oⁿ-a?: The Tribal Council candidates were talking about changing seats, did you hear what was said? ("The Tribal Council were talking about changing their different people seated there, did you hear what they said?")

Oⁿnóⁿ'oⁿ: S/he / they hear me.

Shé-ama oⁿnóⁿ'oⁿ: They all heard me.

Wóⁿgithe oⁿnóⁿ'oⁿi-a/ga: All of you listen to me. ("hear me")

Áthinoⁿ'óⁿ: S/he / they listen to you.

Shémizhiⁿga áthinoⁿ'oⁿ-a?: Did your daughter listen to you? ("Did the young woman listen to you?")

Áthaginoⁿ'oⁿ: You listen to your own.

Thihóⁿ íye-tʰe áthaginoⁿ'oⁿ-a?: Did you listen to your mother talk?

"bth" Verb Pattern

THAXTÁ: BITE; THASHPÉ: BITE A PIECE OFF; THIXÓⁿ: BREAK; THIDÚZHE: BUST; THIWÍⁿ: BUY

—: s/he/they

bth-: I

n-: you

oⁿth-: we

Btháxta: I bite it.

Náxta: You bite it.

Thaxtá: S/he / they bite it.

Oⁿtháxta: We bite it.

Wamóⁿska shúga-thoⁿ btháxta: I bit the cowboy bread.

Shé-thoⁿ náxta: You bit that one.

Zhoⁿní-thoⁿ thaxtá: She bit the candy.

Wóⁿgithe tanúka oⁿtháxta: We all bit the meat.

Btháshpe: I bite a piece off.

  Náshpe: You bite a piece off.

  Thashpá: S/he / they bite a piece off.

  Oⁿtháshpa: We bite a piece off.

Shé-thoⁿ btháshpe: I took a bite off the apple.

Tanúka-thoⁿ hébe náshpe-a?: Did you bite a piece off the meat?

Shé-thoⁿ hébe thashpá: She bit a piece off the apple.

Wóⁿgithe zhoⁿní zízige oⁿtháshpa: We all bit pieces off the taffy.

Bthíxoⁿ: I break it.

  Níxoⁿ: You break it.

  Thixóⁿ: S/he / they break it.

  Oⁿthíxoⁿ: We break it.

Miídoⁿbe wiwíta-thoⁿ bthíxoⁿ: I broke my clock.

Wébaxu-kʰe níxoⁿ-a?: Did you break your pencil?

Mízhiⁿga-akʰa zhóⁿzhiⁿga-kʰe thixóⁿ: The girl broke the stick.

Móⁿze waóⁿ oⁿthíxoⁿ: We broke the radio.

Bthíduzhe: I bust it.

  Níduzhe: You bust it.

Thidúzha: S/he / they bust it.

  Oⁿthíduzha: We bust it.

Wazhíde-thoⁿ bthíduzhe: I busted the tomato.

Hazízige ní uzhí níduzhe-a?: Did you bust the water balloon?

Wa'ú-akʰa wéta áhigi uthíxpatha wóⁿgithe gadúzha: The woman dropped a lot of eggs and broke them all. (**gadúzha** instead of **thidúzha** because of the force of the break, **ga** verb pattern)

Kóⁿde oⁿbáhi, káshi-áchoⁿ gthíⁿ, wóⁿgithe dúzheoⁿtha: We picked a lot of plums, they sat too long so we spoiled them all. (**dúzhethe**, "cause to bust open," **a** verb pattern)

Bthíwiⁿ: I buy it.

  Níwiⁿ: You buy it.

  Thiwíⁿ: S/he / they buy it.

  Oⁿthíwiⁿ: We buy it.

Niⁿdágthe bthíwiⁿ: I bought diapers.

Kinóⁿnoⁿge wíⁿ níwiⁿ-a?: Did you buy a car?

Hiⁿbé téga thiwíⁿ: She bought new shoes.

Háthe oⁿthíwiⁿ: We bought clothes.

More Advanced Conjugations

Oⁿtháxta: S/he / they bite me.

Shíⁿnudoⁿ xthítu-akʰa oⁿtháxta: The mean dog bit me.

Agthíxoⁿ: I break my own.

Miídoⁿbe axíbe agthíxoⁿ: I broke my watch.

Gthíxoⁿ: S/he / they break their own.

Mízhiⁿga-akʰa móⁿzestugthoⁿ gthíxoⁿ: The girl broke her glasses.

Kigthíwiⁿ: S/he / they buy it for themselves.

Wa'ú-akʰa hiⁿbé téga kigthíwiⁿ: The woman bought herself new shoes.

Oⁿkígthiwiⁿ: We buy it for ourselves.

Wóⁿgithe háthe téga oⁿkígthiwiⁿ-taoⁿgatʰoⁿ: We're all going to buy ourselves new clothes.

Stative Verb Pattern

NÓⁿXESKAZHI: DIZZY;
GASKÍ-ÁCHOⁿ: BREATHLESS

—: s/he/they

oⁿ-: I am

thi-: you are

wa-: we are

Nóⁿxeoⁿska-mazhi: I'm dizzy.

Nóⁿxethiskazhi: You're dizzy.

Nóⁿxeska-bazhi: S/he / they are dizzy.

Wóⁿgithe nóⁿxewaska-bazhi: We're all dizzy.

Nóⁿxeska-bazhi íkipahoⁿzhi aíatha: She got dizzy and fainted. ("Dizzy, she went not knowing herself.")

Oⁿáski-áchoⁿ: I'm really out of breath.

Thiáski-áchoⁿ: You're really out of breath.

Mízhiⁿga-akʰa gaskí-áchoⁿ: The girl's really out of breath.

Wáski-áchoⁿ: We're really out of breath.

Núzhiⁿga-akʰa tabé shkádai-ki noⁿhéga-bazhi gaskí-áchoⁿ: When the boy was playing ball, he got out of breath from running fast.

Wóⁿgithe oⁿmóⁿthiⁿ waSékoⁿ oⁿgúiⁿhai-ki wáski-áchoⁿ: When we joined in the fast walk we all got out of breath.

Irregular Verb Pattern

GÁXE: MAKE / DO

Páxe: I make it.

Washíⁿzhegthoⁿ páxe: I made frybread.

Wi ebthégoⁿ-tʰegoⁿ páxe: I'll make it the way I want. ("I'll make it according to my own thoughts.")

Shkáxe: You make it.

Watʰé iⁿthéshkaxe-aʔ: Did you make me a dress? (**iⁿthé-**, "you for me")

Gáxa: S/he / they make it.

Wa'ú-akʰa washíⁿzhegthoⁿ gáxe góⁿtha: The woman wants to make frybread. (**gáxe** not **gáxa** because before another verb)

Oⁿgáxa: We make it.

Wóⁿgithe taní oⁿgáxe-taoⁿgatʰoⁿ: We're all going to make soup. (**oⁿgáxe** not **oⁿgáxa** because before -**ta** future ending)

Páze-ki óⁿguhoⁿi-ki taní oⁿgáxe-taoⁿgatʰoⁿ: This evening when we're cooking we're going to make soup.

More Advanced Conjugations

Wípaxe: I made it for you.

Watʰé-thoⁿ wípaxe: I made the dress for you.

É gáxa: S/he / they're the one who made it.

Shé-akʰa wa'ú-akʰa háwatʰe é gáxa: The woman's the one who made the buckskin dress.

Thígaxa: S/he / they make it for you.

Rick-akʰa sáhiⁿ é thígaxa: Rick's the one who made you your basket.

Mrs. Rogers-ama waxtá úzhoⁿ é thígaxa: Mrs. Rogers is the one who made you a flowerbed.

agípaxe: I made mine. / I made it for my relative.

Ikʰáge wiwíta sáhiⁿ-tʰe agípaxe: I made a basket for my friend.

2.1 GUIDE TO USING QUICK SHEETS: WAGTHÁBAZE ÚMAKʰA

The Situation Quick Sheets section provides the learner with Umóⁿhoⁿ language handouts of common phrases within a variety of learning situations. It is activity based. Quick sheets are short enough, one or two pages, to allow for easy copying without being overwhelming. They are user friendly and encourage use of Umóⁿhoⁿ by providing a written tool to read and practice speaking the Umóⁿhoⁿ language before or during the appropriate activity. Situation Quick Sheets allow you to engage in language with learners and speakers of varying abilities. They can be used to promote a cultural environment within situations.

2.2 ANIMAL CHARACTERISTICS: WANÍTA ÚSHKOⁿ

Translation: Marcella Woodhull Cayou and Donna Morris Parker; elicitation/transcription/lesson plan: Vida Woodhull Stabler.

This material may be used for an extended breakdown activity. Have students break down the following phrases, underlining the verb forms.

> Iⁿdádoⁿ thatʰé-noⁿ-a?: What do they eat?
>
> Iⁿdádoⁿ nátʰe-taniⁿkshe-a?: What are you going to eat?

Tibáxiatha-akʰa tí-tʰe éthoⁿska noⁿzhíⁿ: The elephant stands as big / tall as the house.

Tibáxiatha-akʰa tí éthoⁿska égoⁿ: The elephant is about as big as a house.

Káxe-akʰa wahába wagthíshka edábe wathatʰe-noⁿ: The crow eats corn, bugs and worms.

Wés'a-akʰa iⁿchóⁿga wathatʰe-noⁿ: The snake eats mice.

Pasóⁿ-akʰa wés'a, iⁿchóⁿga, huhú edábe wathatʰe-noⁿ: The bald eagle eats snakes, fish and mice.

Pasóⁿ-akʰá wés'a, huhú wathatʰai-tʰe, waníta thatʰe éthoⁿska, wagthíshka zhiⁿga wathatʰa: The bald eagle ate little bugs and worms as well as snakes and fish and four-legged animals of that same size.

Míka-akʰa wathátʰe pahóⁿga thizhá-noⁿ: The raccoon washes its food first.

Míka-akʰa wathátʰe etái-tʰe thizhá thatʰé-noⁿ: The raccoon eats washing its food.

Míka-akʰa wathátʰe etái-tʰe iⁿchóⁿga, moⁿshtíⁿge-shti wathátʰe-noⁿ: The raccoon's food is those little ones that can't help themselves (mice and rabbits).

Móⁿga-akʰa bthóⁿ-tʰe píazhi-áchoⁿ: The skunk smells bad.

Moⁿchʰú-akʰa huhú thatʰe xtátha:
The brown bear likes to eat fish.

Moⁿchʰú-akʰa hugási íbahoⁿ. Huhú
wathatʰe-noⁿ: The brown bear knows
how to fish. He eats fish.

Iⁿchóⁿga-akʰa wathátʰe uthíxide-noⁿ:
The mouse looks for food.

Iⁿchóⁿga-akʰa wamóⁿthoⁿ-shtóⁿ: The
mouse is always stealing.

Iⁿchóⁿga-akʰa wathátʰe uthéwiⁿtha góⁿki
ánoⁿ'u: The mouse gathered the food
and stashed it underground.

Iⁿchóⁿga-akʰa wathátʰe móⁿthoⁿ shi
ánoⁿ'u: The mouse stole food and
stashed it underground.

Táxti-akʰa wadóⁿbe noⁿzhíⁿ: The deer is
standing looking at us.

Táxti-ama móⁿzemoⁿ noⁿhégazhi gíoⁿhe
moⁿthíⁿ: The deer are dodging (fleeing
fast from) bullets.

Táxti-akʰa iⁿdádoⁿ ubésni-egoⁿ
xthabé-kʰe-di óⁿhe íkinoⁿxtha: The
deer sensed something, so he ran
through the trees to hide.

Páhiⁿ waníta-ama xthítu-biama: The
porcupine animal is mean, they say.

Páhiⁿ-akʰa xthítu: The porcupine is mean.

Síⁿga-akʰa táge uthéwiⁿthe-noⁿ-biama:
The squirrel gathers nuts, they say.

Kétoⁿga-akʰa ní shkúbe-kʰe-di
gthíⁿ-noⁿ-biama: The snapping turtle
lives in deep water, they say.

Kétoⁿga ní móⁿtʰe gthíⁿ: Snapping turtles
live in the water.

Wagthíshka-akʰa waxtá thatʰe xtátha:
The bug likes to eat flowers.

Waníta nóⁿka t'úsa wa'íⁿ skíge
'íⁿ-noⁿ-biama / Nóⁿxahi t'úsa-ama
wa'íⁿ skíge 'íⁿ-noⁿ-biama: Camels carry
heavy loads on their back, they say.

Nóⁿxahi t'úsa-akʰa wé'iⁿ: The camel
carried for somebody.

Té-ama wabáhi moⁿthíⁿ: The buffalo are
grazing.

Shóⁿtoⁿga-akʰa hóⁿ-noⁿ-di hú gthíⁿ-noⁿ-
biama: The wolf howls at night, they say.

Pánuhu ába'e gíudoⁿ. Iⁿchóⁿga uthíxide-
noⁿ-biama: The hoot owl likes to hunt. It
looks for mice, they say.

Pánuhu ába'e gíudoⁿ: Hoot owls like to hunt.

Iⁿgthóⁿ sí snéde-akʰa tanúka thatʰá /
Waníta móⁿtʰanoⁿha-akʰa tanúka
thatʰá: The mountain lion / cougar /
wildcat ate meat.

Zhábe-akʰa ní-kʰe-di gthíⁿ xthabé
thabthízhe théthe-noⁿ: The beaver
lives along the stream and fells trees
by gnawing on them.

2.3 ANIMAL DRAWING: WANÍTA GTHÍXU-A/GA

Translation: Marcella Woodhull Cayou and
Rufus White; elicitation/transcription/lesson
plan: Vida Woodhull Stabler.

Lesson: Animal Names and Characteristics

OBJECTIVE

Practice talking about characteristics and
actions as related here to animals, speaking in
complete sentences.

MATERIALS

Timber animals, Stabler-Swetland dictionary

Introduction

What animals live in the timbers? What do you know about them? Is there an animal you especially like? Why?

waníta animal

Thixú-a/ga. Draw it.

thithíta your

wiwíta my

izházhe name

iⁿdádoⁿ what

águdi where

gáxe do

udóⁿbe appearance

Example Q&A

wémoⁿxe question

edégithoⁿ answer

Waníta thithíta izházhe-tʰe iⁿdádoⁿ-a?
  What is your animal's name?

Waníta wiwíta izházhe-tʰe _____.
  My animal's name is _____.

**Waníta thithíta-thiⁿkʰe iⁿdádoⁿ
  thatʰé-noⁿ-a?** What does your
  animal eat?

_____ **thatʰé-noⁿ.** It eats _____.

**Waníta thithíta-thiⁿkʰe udóⁿbe
  iⁿdádoⁿ-a?** What does your animal
  look like?

Udóⁿbe-tʰe _____. It looks _____.

**Waníta thithíta-thiⁿkʰe iⁿdádoⁿ
  gáxe-noⁿ-a?** What does your animal
  do well?

_____ **thipʰí.** It's good at _____.

Activities

Waníta thithíta thixú-a: Draw your
  animal. (female speaker)

Waníta thithíta thixú-ga hó: Draw your
  animal. (male speaker)

LEARN

Students are given the preceding **wémoⁿxe** (questions) either as a worksheet or on the board, and Elders or Wagóⁿze say the first sentence. Students decipher the sentence word by word to get the meaning, with the help of Elders and Wagóⁿze-ama. When the question is understood, students are to reply.

DISCUSSION

After learning the vocabulary students may use the Umóⁿhoⁿ Q&A to practice speaking full sentences and answering questions.

Cultural Note

At one time our prairie and timbered land were abundant in size. Big machinery and land lease of tribal lands has made it possible for areas to be cleared for more farmable land. Animals are being forced to live on smaller areas of land. The animals living in our timbers need the protection of leadership to ensure their survival.

There are clans of the Umóⁿhoⁿ represented by animals such as the deer, elk, and buffalo. Deer remain and thrive in the timbered areas. Elk have migrated to colder mountainous areas. The tribe now has small herd of buffalo that are nurtured with great care. Tribal lands still include several types of landscapes:

híde-ata: down bottom

Óⁿpʰoⁿ Toⁿga: Big Elk [Park]

uchʰízhe: brush

snóⁿsnoⁿ: bottomlands / flat prairie

uxthábe: timberlands

xthabé-ata: into the timbers

xáde-ata: into the grass / prairie

móⁿtʰanoⁿdi: out in the wild

xeútʰoⁿnadi: floodplain (literally "between bluffs")

bahóⁿhoⁿ: rolling hilly prairie

snóⁿsnoⁿ thiⁿge: no flatlands, very hilly with ravines

tóⁿde-ata: uphill / upland / away from the bottomlands

xé: bluff / mountain

xéki / xékigtha: foot of a bluff

skída: saddle / notch between bluffs

áthiⁿ: ridge

patháge: dead-end bluff

pahé: hill

ápathage: headland ("hill's hat")

pahé zúbe: hilltop

baxú: sharp rocky peak

bazú: round peak

2.4 ANIMAL NAMES: WANÍTA IZHÁZHE ETÁI-GE

Translation: Marcella Woodhull Cayou, Donna Morris Parker, and others; elicitation/transcription: Vida Woodhull Stabler; orthography check: Bryan James Gordon.

Words for Animals

waníta: animal / four-legged ones

móⁿtʰanoⁿha: wild

washtáge: tame

wanágthe: domesticated / livestock

wazhíⁿga: bird / winged ones

wagthíshka: bug / reptile / crawling ones

Animal Names

Alligator: **Wagthíshka sihí dúba, wagthíshka hí dúba**

Bear: **Moⁿchú** ("brown bear"), **Wasábe** ("black bear")

Beaver: **Zhábe**

Bee: **Kigthóⁿxe**

Bird (also chicken): **Wazhíⁿga**

Buffalo: **Té**

Bull: **Téska núga**

Bug: **Wagthíshka, wagthishka zhiⁿga** ("little bug")

Bunny: **Moⁿshtíⁿga zhiⁿga**

Butterfly: **Watʰíninika** (sometimes **Wachíninika**)

Calf: **Téska Zhiⁿga**

Cat: **Iⁿgthóⁿga**

Chipmunk: **Tashníⁿga**

Crane: **Pétoⁿ sóⁿ** ("white crane"), **pétoⁿ xude** ("grey crane"), **pétoⁿ sóⁿ Áhiⁿtaxe sabe** ("white crane with black wing tips")

Cow: **Téska, téska míⁿga**

Cricket: **Síⁿgthe**

Deer: **Táxti**

Dog: **Shíⁿudoⁿ** (sometimes **shíⁿnudoⁿ**)

Donkey: **Nitá toⁿga**

Dove: **Thíta**

Eagle: **Pasóⁿ** ("bald eagle"), **xithá** ("golden eagle")

Ewe: **Haxúde míⁿga**

Firefly: **Wanáxoⁿxoⁿ**

Fish: **Huhú**

Foal: **Shóⁿzhiⁿga**

Giraffe: **Pasiáta watháᵗʰe** ("eats at the treetop")

Goat: **Héskiba, hésakʰiba**

Gopher: **Moⁿthíⁿga**

Groundhog / prairie dog: **Kinóⁿxa** ("buries itself using its feet"), **Moⁿthíⁿxude**

kinóⁿxe gitóⁿba-bazhi. "Groundhog didn't see his shadow."

Hatchling: **Kipáda**

Hen: **Wazhíⁿga míⁿga**

Hippopotamus: **Niádi Wakóⁿda**

Horse: **Shóⁿge**

Kitten: **Iⁿgthóⁿga zhiⁿga**

Lady Bug: **Wagthíshka**

Lamb: **Haxúde zhiⁿga**

Leopard: **Iⁿgthóⁿga gthezáza**

Lightning Bug: **Wanáxoⁿxoⁿ**

Lion: **Waníta wáxa**

Mare: **Shóⁿge míⁿga**

Mouse: **Iⁿchóⁿga**

Ostrich: **Wazhíⁿga toⁿga óⁿsagi** ("big fast-running bird")

Wazhíⁿga zhíbe snéde

Ostrich Chick: **Wazhíⁿga toⁿga óⁿsagi kipáda**

Panther: **Iⁿgthóⁿ si snéde**

Peacock: **Wazhíⁿga íⁿbe gabthá** ("bird spreading tailfeathers")

Penguin: **Míxa níkashiⁿga égoⁿ**

Pig: **Kúkusi**

Piglet: **Kúkusi zhiⁿga**

Porcupine: **Pahíⁿ**

Puppy: **Shíⁿudoⁿ zhiⁿga, shíⁿnudoⁿ zhiⁿga**

Prairie Dog: **Moⁿthíⁿxude**

Rabbit: **Moⁿshtíⁿga**

Raccoon: **Miká**

Rooster: **Wazhíⁿga núga**

Skunk: **Móⁿga**

Seal: **Huhú shnaha**

Sheep: **Haxúde**

Snail: **Nihá**

Snake: **Wés'a**

Snapping Turtle: **Ké toⁿga**

Sow: **Kúkusi miⁿga**

Spider: **Ukʰígthiski, ukígthiske**

Squirrel: **Síⁿga**

Tiger: **In̄gthón̄ si snéde, in̄gthón̄ hí-thon̄ gthezáza** ("cat with striped fur")

Tortoise: **Ké ton̄ga**

Whale: **Huhú ton̄ga**

Wolf: **Shón̄ton̄ga**

Zebra: **Shón̄ge gthéze**

Cultural Note

The richness of Umón̄hon̄ language knowledge led to the development of new words as our surrounding world evolved. I am not sure what process took place long ago, but I did witness new words development within our school environment. The Elders working/consulting would be sitting around a table at school drinking coffee. They always spoke to one another fluently in the Umón̄hon̄ language.

A lesson would require a translation because no word was known to them. After discussion, there was a kind of consensus that took place among them. This happened with words like "ostrich," "peacock," and "seal." Aunt Marcella would be the voice of the newly developed word and speak it to me. I would document the word.

As time went on there were fewer and fewer women in the group, and reliance fell to two fluent Elder women and eventually one. No doubt, in past times, there were many others in our community of Umón̄hon̄ speakers who developed new words. New word development is a trait of fluency in a community where change is present. I first heard the term for computer from Elder Thurman Cook. He spoke the words **wathígthon̄ wasékon̄** ("fast mind") to me in 1995. This was his way to describe a computer.
—Vida Woodhull Stabler

2.5 BIRTHDAY CELEBRATION PHRASES

Translation: Donna Morris Parker; elicitation/transcription: Vida Woodhull Stabler.

Ón̄bathe Wagón̄ze ón̄ba ída etá-tʰe: Today is Teacher's birthday.

Ón̄ba ída thithíta-tʰe-a?: Is your birthday today?

Umón̄thin̄kʰa ánon̄ nín̄-a?: How old are you?

Ón̄bathe ón̄ba ída etá-tʰe-a?: Is it his birthday today?

Umón̄thin̄kʰa ánon̄?: How old is s/he?

On̄shkáde-taon̄gatʰon̄: We will play today.

Wéuzhawa-taon̄gatʰon̄: We will enjoy ourselves.

Úzhawa-áchon̄: That was a lot of fun.

Ín̄uzhawa: I'm having fun.

Musical Chairs with Umón̄hon̄ Music

Ágthin̄ uthízon̄ itʰéthai-a/ga: Put the chairs in the middle.

Món̄ze waón̄ wi áakʰihide-tamin̄kʰe: I'm going to watch out for the stereo.

Món̄ze waón̄ bthínon̄ge-tamin̄kʰe: I'm going to turn on the stereo.

Uthíshon̄ mon̄thín̄i-a/ga: Walk in a circle.

Món̄ze waón̄ bthínazhi-ki hin̄thékithe gthín̄i-a/ga: Sit fast when I turn off the stereo.

Balloon Game

Hazízige tabé-thoⁿ thizái-a/ga:
Get the balloon.

Thizíi-a/ga: Stretch it.

Hazízige tabé-thoⁿ ubíxoⁿi-a/ga:
Blow the balloon up. ("Blow in it.")

Tabé-thoⁿ hazízige koⁿt^hóⁿi-a/ga:
Tie the balloon in a knot.

Tizhébe-tathishoⁿ noⁿhéga-bazhii-a/ga:
Run to the door.

Wíugoⁿba toⁿga-tathishoⁿ noⁿhéga-bazhii-a/ga: Run to the big windows.

Thishtóⁿ théthai-a/ga: Let it go.

Thenóⁿ égoⁿ gáxai-a/ga: Do it again.
("Do that way another time.")

Hazízige ágthiⁿi-a/ga: Sit on the balloon.

Bibtházai-a/ga: Pop it.

Take Care of the Cake

The cake represents the butchering — or taking care — of the buffalo, which is the responsibility of the Iⁿkésabe (Black Shoulder of the Buffalo) Clan. Iⁿkésabe men are often asked to mark the cake and then a female Iⁿkésabe is asked to cut the cake and give to those present. The ceremony represents the butchering of the buffalo after a successful hunt. Each camp would then have their share of food to feed their families.

Wamúska skíthe oⁿthát^he-taoⁿgat^hoⁿ: We will eat cake.

Sheúzhegthoⁿ oⁿthát^he-taoⁿgat^hoⁿ: We will eat pizza / pie.

Wabthát^he-tamiⁿk^he: I will eat.

2.6 CLASSROOM PHRASES FOR ACTION VERBS

Translation: Marcella Woodhull Cayou and Donna Morris Parker; elicitation/transcription: Vida Woodhull Stabler; consolidated from "Classroom Conversation Phrases" and "Classroom Conversation Table," "Teacher Classroom Phrases," "Useful Classroom Phrases," "General Teacher Phrases for the Classroom," "Basic Umóⁿhoⁿ Classroom Phrases," "Basic Umóⁿhoⁿ Classroom Praise Phrases," "Roll Call," "Elder Lesson Plan," "Roll Call Winter," and "TPR Complete Phrases"; orthography check and consolidation: Bryan James Gordon.

Teaching Note

In order to learn the Umóⁿhoⁿ language, our ears must "be tickled" time and time again for us to develop our listening ear. We must hear our language spoken frequently. It is helpful to hear common phrases repeatedly as well as having new phrases introduced. The classroom phrases require modeling for the appropriate physical response. When the lesson is introduced, first call upon another teacher or student to model the desired action.

Wagáxe Gáxe: Making Gestures

Noⁿbé-t^he thitútushi-a/ga: Snap your fingers (more than once).

Noⁿbéshka thibúta/ga: Make a fist.

Noⁿbé-tʰe gachʰáki-a/ga: Clap your hands (once).

Noⁿbé-tʰe gachʰáchʰaki-a/ga: Clap your hands (more than once).

Íxazhiⁿga/ga: Smile.

Íxa thahégazhi-a/ga: Laugh out loud.

Iⁿshtá thip'íⁿza/ga: Close your eyes.

Iⁿshtá thibthá/ga: Open your eyes.

Iⁿshtá thip'íⁿp'iⁿza/ga: Blink your eyes.

Iⁿshtáxoⁿxoⁿ/ga: Squint.

Sí thátʰa ábazu-a/ga: Point to your left foot.

Noⁿbé wéthitʰoⁿ ábazu-a/ga: Point to your right hand.

Iⁿdádoⁿ-shte pézhitu ábazu-a/ga: Point to something green.

Áshi-ta Thé: Going Outside

Tizhébe áshi-ta-ta moⁿthíⁿi-a/ga: Go to the outside door.

Thishíbai-a/ga: Open it.

Áshi-ta moⁿthíⁿi-a/ga: Go outside.

Óⁿba eyóⁿ-tʰe dóⁿbe thé-wathe: Let's go see how the weather is.

Tóⁿde-thoⁿ átʰoⁿi-a/ga: Stand on the ground / dirt.

Haská-thoⁿ-ta noⁿzhíⁿi-a/ga: Stand by the flag.

Uhéatʰoⁿ-thoⁿ-ta noⁿzhíⁿi-a/ga: Stand by the steps.

Uhéatʰoⁿ-thoⁿ átʰoⁿi-a/ga: Stand on the steps.

Kinóⁿnoⁿge-ma wawégaxai-a/ga: Wave to the cars.

Tizhébe-tʰe wéthishiba/ga: Open the doors for them.

Gahíye Tí-ata moⁿthíⁿi-a/ga: Go to Council.

Wachʰígaxe Tí-ata moⁿthíⁿi-a/ga: Go to Alfred Gilpin Building.

Wathíze Tí-ata moⁿthíⁿi-a/ga: Go to Social Services.

Wéthihoⁿ Thihóⁿ Tí-ata moⁿthíⁿi-a/ga: Go to Four Hills of Life.

Úthiwiⁿ Tí-ata moⁿthíⁿi-a/ga: Go to C-Store.

Úshkade-ta moⁿthíⁿi-a/ga shkádai-a/ga: Go to the park and play.

Zhoⁿ'ábe dúba uthíxidai-a/ga: Look for four leaves.

Zhoⁿ'ábe dúba bahíi-a/ga: Pick up four leaves.

Xátha thé-wathe: Let's go back.

Xátha moⁿgthíⁿi-a/ga: Go back.

Úshkoⁿ Ázhi-thoⁿthoⁿ: Different Situations

Waskíthe ánoⁿxtha/ga: Hide the fruit.

Wézhezhi-tʰe-di uzhí-a/ga: Put it in the skillet.

Wamúske-tʰe wézhezhi-tʰe-di uzhí-a/ga: Put the bread in the skillet.

Wéta zhézhi-a/ga: Fry the egg.

Nióⁿba noⁿbá thixúi-a/ga: Draw two moons.

Miká'e noⁿbá thixúi-a/ga: Draw two stars.

Wagthíshka thixúi-a/ga: Draw a bug.

Wagthíshka-thi^{n}k^{h}e zí ugái-a/ga: Color the bug yellow.

Wazhí^{n}ga thixúi-a/ga: Draw a bird.

Wazhí^{n}ga-thi^{n}k^{h}e tú ugái-a/ga: Color the bird blue.

Waxchá thixúi-a/ga: Draw a flower.

Waxchá-tho^n zhíde ugái-a/ga: Color the flower red.

Wagthíshka-thi^{n}k^{h}e thisái-a/ga: Cut out the bug.

Wazhí^{n}ga-thi^{n}k^{h}e thisái-a/ga: Cut out the bird.

Waxchá-tho^n thisái-a/ga: Cut out the flower.

Í^{n}bahai-a/ga: Show them to me.

Thisó^{n}thai-a/ga: Turn them over.

Izházhe gipáxui-a/ga: Write your name.

Wahó^n-k^{h}e thisái-a/ga: Cut the yarn.

Weáthaskabe-k^{h}e 'ó^{n}i-a/ga: Use the tape.

Xthabé-t^{h}e-di ubát^{h}i ithó^{n}thai-a/ga: Hang them in the tree.

2.7 CLASSROOM PHRASES FOR ASKING AND TALKING: WÉMO^{N}XE T^{H}E, ÍYE UTHÁ

Translation: Marcella Woodhull Cayou and Donna Morris Parker; elicitation/transcription: Vida Woodhull Stabler; consolidated from "Classroom Conversation Phrases," "Classroom Conversation Table," "Teacher Classroom Phrases," "Useful Classroom Phrases," "General Teacher Phrases for the Classroom," "Basic Umó^{n}ho^n Classroom Phrases," "Basic Umó^{n}ho^n Classroom Praise Phrases," "Roll Call" "Elder Lesson Plan," and "Roll Call Winter"; orthography check and consolidation: Bryan James Gordon.

Wémo^{n}xe T^{h}e: Asking

Ko^{n}há ímo^{n}xa/ga: Ask Grandma. (spoken to female)

 Ko^{n}há ímo^{n}xai-a/ga (spoken to more than one)

Ko^{n}hó ímo^{n}xa/ga: Ask Grandma. (spoken to male)

 Ko^{n}hó ímo^{n}xai-a/ga (spoken to more than one)

Thikó^n-thi^{n}k^{h}e ímo^{n}xa/ga: Ask your Grandma. (spoken to either gender)

 Thikó^n-thi^{n}k^{h}e ímo^{n}xai-a/ga (spoken to more than one)

Tigo^{n}há ímo^{n}xa/ga: Ask Grandpa. (spoken to female)

 Tigo^{n}há ímo^{n}xai-a/ga (spoken to more than one)

Tigo^{n}hó ímo^{n}xa/ga: Ask Grandpa. (spoken to male)

 Tigo^{n}hó ímo^{n}xai-a/ga (spoken to more than one)

Thitígo^n-thi^{n}k^{h}e ímo^{n}xa/ga: Ask your Grandpa. (spoken to either gender)

Thitígo^n-thi^{n}k^{h}e ímo^{n}xai-a/ga (spoken to more than one)

Wi o^{n}thó^{n}mo^{n}xa/ga: Ask me.

 Wi o^{n}thó^{n}mo^{n}xai-a/ga (spoken to more than one)

Wémo^{n}xa/ga: Ask them.

 Wémo^{n}xai-a/ga (spoken to more than one)

Edíye thékʰitha/ga: Answer her/him.

Edíye thékʰithai-a/ga (spoken to more than one)

Íye: Talking

Égoⁿ: Yes, I agree / It is so / Mhm.

Égoⁿ hó (male voice)

Égithoⁿ/ga: Say it (to somebody).

Égithoⁿi-a/ga (spoken to more than one)

Shi égithoⁿ/ga: Say it again.

Égipʰe / Égishe / Égithoⁿ: I / you / s/he said it (to somebody).

Eóⁿgithoⁿ / Égisha / Égithoⁿ: We / you / they said it (to somebody).

Wi égipʰe: I'm the one who said it.

Oⁿgu eóⁿgithoⁿ: We're the ones who said it.

Á/ga: Say it (out loud).

Ái-a/ga (spoken to more than one)

Edéshe-a?: What did you say? / Did you say something?

Edéshai-a? (spoken to more than one)

Edéha-mazhi / Edéshazhi / Edá-bazhi: I / you / s/he didn't say anything.

Edóⁿthoⁿ-bazhi / Edésha-bazhi / Edá-bazhi: We / you / they didn't say anything.

Ehé / Eshé / Á: I / you / s/he said it (out loud).

Oⁿthóⁿ / Eshá / Á: We / you / they said it (out loud).

Íye thahégazhi-a/ga: Talk louder.

Íye thahéga-bazhíi-a/ga (spoken to more than one)

Umóⁿhoⁿ úwakia/ga: Talk Umóⁿhoⁿ to them.

Umóⁿhoⁿ úwakiai-a/ga (spoken to more than one)

Umóⁿhoⁿ íye xtáathe: I like to talk Umóⁿhoⁿ.

Umóⁿhoⁿ íye xtáoⁿtha: We like to talk Umóⁿhoⁿ.

Cultural Note

Speaking within a classroom environment is very different than when you speak at a gathering of Umóⁿhoⁿ people. It is good to observe the protocol of public speaking and to learn how to give thanks. Considerations include: before asking the Person in Charge for permission to speak, wait to see if an Elder relative speaks first, as that person may cover what you wish to say. If you are a younger woman, talk to a male head of household or other male relative, and ask that he speak in behalf of your family. Above all, be patient and don't interrupt. This behavior is modeled repeatedly at cultural events or doings—watch and learn.

2.8 CLASSROOM PHRASES FOR BEGINNING OF CLASS

Translation: Marcella Woodhull Cayou and Donna Morris Parker; elicitation/transcription: Vida Woodhull Stabler; consolidated from "Classroom Conversation Phrases," "Classroom Conversation Table," "Teacher Classroom Phrases,"

"Useful Classroom Phrases," "General Teacher Phrases for the Classroom," "Basic Umó^{n}ho^n Classroom Phrases," "Basic Umó^{n}ho^n Classroom Praise Phrases," "Roll Call," "Elder Lesson Plan," "Roll Call Winter," and "TPR Complete Phrases"; orthography check and consolidation: Bryan James Gordon.

Cultural Note

Be sure to make our children (students) feel welcome when they walk into their classroom. Greet them in Umó^{n}ho^n by saying, "**That^{h}i-t^{h}e údo^n**" ("it's good you are here"). You can also greet the entire class by saying, "**Wó^{n}githe, that^{h}i-t^{h}e údo^n**."

Mó^{n}t^{h}e At^{h}í-ki: When They Come Inside

Eyó^n ní^n-a?: How are you?

Eyó^n ní^n-hó?: How are you? (male)

Agudí-shte gthí^n-a/ga: Sit somewhere.

Agudí-shte gthí^{n}i-a/ga (spoken to more than one)

Ágigthi^n-a/ga: Sit in your own seat.

Ágigthi^{n}i-a/ga (spoken to more than one)

Shéhi-ta gthí^n-a/ga: Sit over there.

Shéhi-ta gthí^{n}i-a/ga (spoken to more than one)

Zhuó^{n}gthe gthí^n-a/ga: Sit by me.

Zhuó^{n}gthe gthí^{n}i-a/ga (spoken to more than one)

Gthí^n-azhi-a/ga: Don't sit.

Gthí^n-bazhíi-a/ga (spoken to more than one)

Ágthi^n sabe to^{n}ga-tho^n ágthi^n-a/ga: Sit in the big black chair.

Gá-t^{h}e-di gthí^n-a/ga: Sit right here.

Eshó^n gthí^n-a/ga: Sit closer.

Eshó^n gthí^{n}i-a/ga (spoken to more than one)

Áwa-t^{h}e-égo^n eáto^n ní^n?: What happened to you? / What's the matter with you?

Hithái-t^{h}e-di i^{n}dádo^n shkáxe?: What did you do Saturday?

Zhápa-tho^n shíshige úzhi-t^{h}e-di ó^{n}tha/ga: Throw your gum in the trash.

Zhápa-tho^n shíshige úzhi-t^{h}e-di ó^{n}thai-a/ga (spoken to more than one)

Ó^{n}ba-t^{h}e: Daily Routine

Ó^{n}ba wéno^{n}ba: It's Tuesday.

Ó^{n}bathe ó^{n}ba wéno^{n}ba: Today is Tuesday.

Mí-k^{h}e Peníshka Mí Etái-k^{h}e: The month is March.

Ó^{n}ba-t^{h}e agthí^n sáto^n: It's the fifteenth.

Ebé ní^n-a?: Who are you?

Ebé ní^n-hó? (male voice)

Izházhe i^{n}dádo^n aní^n-a?: What name do you have?

Izházhe thithíta-t^{h}e i^{n}dádo^n?: What is your name?

Ebé bthí^n-t^{h}e uwíbtha-tami^{n}k^{h}e: I'm going to tell you who I am.

Izházhe wiwíta-t^{h}e _____: My name is _____.

_____ **izházhe abthíⁿ:** I have the name
_____ .

Óⁿba-tʰe eyóⁿ-a?: How is the weather?

Ebé Tʰí: Roll Call

Atʰí-a?: Is s/he / they here?

Thatʰí-a?: Are you here?

Thatʰí-tʰe údoⁿ: Welcome / It's good that you came here.

Shi thatʰí-a?: You came again? (a greeting)

Thagthí-tʰe údoⁿ: Welcome back.

Shi thagthí-a?: You came back? (a greeting)

Atʰí-thoⁿzha wasnída: S/he's here but late.

Shi atʰí: I'm here again.

Atʰí: I'm here.

   Atʰí hó (male voice)

Atʰí: S/he / they are here.

Atʰí-bazhi: S/he / they aren't here.

_____ **-akʰa é-shti atʰí:** _____ is here too.

Shi atʰí-bazhi: S/he / they didn't come again.

Atʰóⁿ-ki atʰí-taakʰa?: When are s/he / they going to get here?

Atʰóⁿdi thatʰí? When did you get here?

Wathísnide thatʰí: You're late.

Eátoⁿ wathísnide-a? Why are you late?

Atʰí-bazhi: S/he / they didn't come.

Awagí wathísnide-a?: Where did you come from so late?

Wasnídazhi-a/ga: Don't be late.

   Wasnída-bazhíi-a/ga (spoken to more than one)

Wasníde-taakʰa: S/he'll be late.

Wasníde-taama: They'll be late.

Wagóⁿze-ama wasníde atʰí-bazhi-noⁿ: Teachers don't come late.

Wóⁿgithe wawásnide atʰí: We all came late.

Wa'ú-akʰa miídoⁿbe noⁿshnóⁿ-shóⁿshoⁿ: The woman always misses the time.

Nu-akʰa wasníde-shóⁿshoⁿ: The man is always late.

Cultural Note

It is good to acknowledge the presence of people as they arrive to a doings. Often you will hear the Master of Ceremony or Man in Charge welcoming the relative as they arrive. Arriving late or leaving an event early is noticed by those in attendance. Often, if people arrive late and wish to address the crowd, they may first ask to be excused for their tardiness before they give their heartfelt appreciation for the event taking place. Likewise, if a person leaves an event before the Man in Charge excuses the people, as the individual departs, they often explain to the Man in Charge or Master of Ceremony their reason for leaving early. The departing individual may choose to leave a monetary gift for the honoree "on the table."

2.9 CLASSROOM PHRASES FOR ENDING/LEAVING: AÍATHAI-KI UTHÁ

Translation: Marcella Woodhull Cayou and Donna Morris Parker; elicitation/transcription: Vida Woodhull Stabler; consolidated from "Classroom Conversation Phrases," "Classroom Conversation Table," "Teacher Classroom Phrases," "Useful Classroom Phrases," "General Teacher Phrases for the Classroom," "Basic Umóⁿhoⁿ Classroom Phrases," "Basic Umóⁿhoⁿ Classroom Praise Phrases," "Roll Call," "Elder Lesson Plan," "Roll Call Winter," and "TPR Complete Phrases"; orthography check and consolidation: Bryan James Gordon.

Ní Kigthíze: Getting Water

Nitháto ⁿ-ta moⁿthíⁿ-a/ga: Go to the fountain.

Thinóⁿga/ga: Turn it on.

Ní niúthato ⁿ-tʰe ugípi uzhí-a/ga: Fill the cup with water.

Thinázhi-a/ga: Turn it off.

Xátha moⁿgthíⁿ-a/ga: Go back.

Thatóⁿ/ga: Drink it.

Aíathai-ki: When They Leave

Óⁿbathe áhigi bthípʰi: Today I learned a lot.

Óⁿbathe áhigi oⁿthípʰi: Today we learned a lot.

Óⁿbathe wabthítoⁿ-achoⁿ: Today I really worked hard.

Óⁿbathe oⁿwóⁿthitoⁿ-achoⁿ: Today we really worked hard.

Shénoⁿ: That's all.

Shénoⁿ gáxa: They finished it.

Shíshige-tʰe bahí-a/ga: Pick up the trash.

Shíshige-tʰe bahíi-a/ga (spoken to more than one)

(Xátha) Itʰétha/ga: Put it away (upright / group) / Put them (group of items) away.

(Xátha) Itʰéthai-a/ga (spoken to more than one)

Thipʰi itʰétha/ga: Put it away right.

Thipʰi itʰéthai-a/ga (spoken to more than one)

(Xátha) Ihétha/ga: Put it away (flat).

(Xátha) Ihéthai-a/ga (spoken to more than one)

(Xátha) Ithóⁿtha/ga: Put it away (contained / round / bundled).

(Xátha) Ithóⁿthai-a/ga (spoken to more than one)

Hide itʰétha/ga: Put it down.

Moⁿshtíⁿge wáthatʰe gahá ithóⁿtha/ga: Put the rabbit on the table.

Wébaxu ágthiⁿ kigthá-ta ihétha/ga: Put the pencil under the chair.

Niúthatoⁿ wáthatʰe kigthá-ta itʰétha/ga: Put the cup under the table.

Taní úzhi ágthiⁿ kigthá-ta ithóⁿtha/ga: Put the bowl under the chair.

Waskíthe wáthatʰe gahá itʰétha/ga: Put the fruit on the table.

Waskíthe wíⁿ niúthatoⁿ-tʰe-di ugthóⁿ/ga: Put one fruit in the cup.

Waskíthe wíⁿ taní úzhi ugthóⁿ/ga: Put one fruit in the bowl.

Watháge-thoⁿ thagái-a/ga: Put on your hats.

Unónzhin-thon unónzhini-a/ga: Put on your jackets.

Hinbékon-tʰe íkonтʰoni-a/ga: Tie your shoes.

Ukiáwatʰonтʰon nonzhíni-a/ga: Line up.

Tizhébe-tʰe thishíba/ga: Open the door.

Tizhébe-tʰe ánonsa/ga: Close the door.

Thishíbazhi-a/ga: Don't open it.

　Thishíba-bazhíi-a/ga (spoken to more than one)

Tizhébe áshi-ta éta monthíni-a/ga: Go to the outside doors.

Áshi-ta monthíni-a/ga: Go outside.

Nonhéba/ga: Wait / Hold on / Just a minute.

　Nonhébai-a/ga (spoken to more than one)

Weápa/ga: Wait for them.

　Weápai-a/ga (spoken to more than one)

Ithápa/ga: Wait for her/him.

　Ithápai-a/ga (spoken to more than one)

Onthápa/ga / Onthónapa/ga: Wait for me.

　Onthónapai-a/ga (spoken to more than one)

Ínpa/ga: Wait for me (I'm stopping for just a second).

　Ínpai-a/ga (spoken to more than one)

Íncʰon shi ongáthe-taitʰé: Now we'll go on.

Monthíni-a/ga: You can go / leave.

Ónbathe onwónsnide: Today I ran late.

　Ónbathe wawásnida: Today we ran late.

2.10 CLASSROOM PHRASES FOR PLACES AND MOVEMENT

Translation: Marcella Woodhull Cayou and Donna Morris Parker; elicitation/transcription: Vida Woodhull; consolidated from "Classroom Conversation Phrases," "Classroom Conversation Table," "Teacher Classroom Phrases," "Useful Classroom Phrases," "General Teacher Phrases for the Classroom," "Basic Umónhon Classroom Phrases," "Basic Umónhon Classroom Praise Phrases," "Roll Call," "Elder Lesson Plan," "Roll Call Winter," and "TPR Complete Phrases"; orthography check and consolidation Bryan James Gordon.

Cultural Note

Movement in the classroom gives opportunity to teach movement of Umónhon people in a traditional sense. When dancing, we follow the path of the sun. We enter east and move left around the drum. During times of prayer, when cedar or water is used, we stand east where the sun rises. There is also purposeful thought given to movement protocol to learn and follow when participating in other Umónhon ceremonies.

Shkón-tʰe Shkáde-tʰeshti: Movement and Play

　Gthín-a/ga: Sit down.

　　Gthíni-a/ga (spoken to more than one)

　Nonzhín-a/ga: Stand up.

　　Nonzhíni-a/ga (spoken to more than one)

　Eshón gí-a/ga: Come closer.

Eshó^n gíi-a/ga (spoken to more than
one)

Kigthíso^{n}tha/ga: Turn around.

Kigthíso^{n}thai-a/ga (spoken to more
than one)

Wéthit^{h}o^n-tathisho^n kigthíso^{n}tha/ga:
Turn toward the right.

Wéthit^{h}o^n-tathisho^n kigthíso^{n}thai-a/ga
(spoken to more than one)

Tháta-tathisho^n kigthíso^{n}tha/ga: Turn
toward the left.

Tháta-tathisho^n kigthíso^{n}thai-a/ga
(spoken to more than one)

Wéthit^{h}o^n mo^{n}thí-a/ga: Walk right.

Wéthit^{h}o^n mo^{n}thí^{n}i-a/ga (spoken to
more than one)

Tháta mo^{n}thí^n-a/ga: Walk left.

Tháta mo^{n}thí^{n}i-a/ga (spoken to more
than one)

Uthísho^n mo^{n}thí^n-a/ga: Walk around the
circle.

Uthísho^n mo^{n}thí^{n}i-a/ga (spoken to more
than one)

Tó^{n}thi^n-a/ga: Run.

Tó^{n}thi^{n}i-a/ga (spoken to more than one)

No^{n}hégazhi-a/ga: Run fast.

No^{n}héga-bazhíi-a/ga (spoken to more
than one)

Waséko^n mo^{n}thí^n-a/ga: Walk fast.

Waséko^n mo^{n}thí^{n}i-a/ga (spoken to
more than one)

Ó^{n}the-xchi mo^{n}thí^n-a/ga: Walk slowly /
carefully.

Ó^{n}the-xchi mo^{n}thí^{n}i-a/ga (spoken to
more than one)

Gthí^{n}azhi-a/ga: Don't sit.

Gthí^n-bazhíi-a/ga (spoken to more than
one)

Gí-a/ga: Come here / this way / back.

Gíi-a/ga (spoken to more than one)

No^{n}shtó^n/ga: Stop.

No^{n}shtó^{n}i-a/ga (spoken to more than
one)

Wach^{h}ígaxa/ga: Dance.

Wach^{h}ígaxai-a/ga (spoken to more than
one)

U'ó^{n}si-tho^{n}tho^n/ga: Jump up and down.

U'ó^{n}si-tho^{n}tho^{n}i-a/ga (spoken to more
than one)

Íxazhi^{n}ga/ga: Smile.

Íxazhi^{n}gai-a/ga (spoken to more than
one)

Thí-paho^{n}ga gí-a/ga: You come first.

Thípaho^{n}ga mo^{n}thí^n-a/ga: You go first.

Thi mo^{n}thí^n-a/ga: You go.

Thi mo^{n}thí^{n}i-a/ga (spoken to more than
one)

Zho^{n}btháska-ta mo^{n}thí^n-a/ga: Go to the
board.

Zho^{n}btháska-ta mo^{n}thí^{n}i-a/ga (spoken
to more than one)

Thi aní^n: Your turn / You have it.

Wi abthí^n: My turn / I have it.

Xátha gí-a/ga: Come back.

Xátha gíi-a/ga (spoken to more than
one)

Ágthiⁿ íkikawiⁿthai-a/ga: Switch seats with each other.

Ebé thé-tathiⁿkʰe?: Who will go?

Móⁿze íutha-ta moⁿthíⁿ-a/ga: Go to the phone.

Shé-tʰe wóⁿgithe athíⁿ gí-a/ga: Bring all of that.

Tabé-thoⁿ uhá thétha/ga: Pass the ball.

Tabé-thoⁿ thátʰa-tathishoⁿ uhá thétha/ga: Pass the ball left.

Éta Noⁿzhíⁿ-a/ga: Stand by There

Théthudi noⁿzhíⁿ-a/ga: Stand over here.

    Théthudi noⁿzhíⁿi-a/ga (spoken to more than one)

Tizhébe-tʰe-ta eshóⁿ noⁿzhíⁿ-a/ga: Stand close to the door.

    Tizhébe-tʰe-ta eshóⁿ noⁿzhíⁿi-a/ga (spoken to more than one)

Tizhébe-thoⁿ-ta noⁿzhíⁿ-a/ga: Stand by the door.

    Tizhébe-thoⁿ-ta noⁿzhíⁿi-a/ga (spoken to more than one)

Kúge-thoⁿ-ta noⁿzhíⁿ-a/ga: Stand by the drum.

    Kúge-thoⁿ-ta noⁿzhíⁿi-a/ga (spoken to more than one)

Mázi xthabé-ta noⁿzhíⁿ-a/ga: Stand by the cedar tree.

    Mázi xthabé-ta noⁿzhíⁿi-a/ga (spoken to more than one)

Shíshige úzhi-tʰe-ta noⁿzhíⁿ-a/ga: Stand by the trash can.

Shíshige úzhi-tʰe-ta noⁿzhíⁿi-a/ga (spoken to more than one)

U'óⁿhe-kʰe-ta noⁿzhíⁿ-a/ga: Stand by the baby board.

    U'óⁿhe-kʰe-ta noⁿzhíⁿi-a/ga (spoken to more than one)

Táxtiha-thoⁿ-ta noⁿzhíⁿ-a/ga: Stand by the deer hide.

    Táxtiha-thoⁿ-ta noⁿzhíⁿi-a/ga (spoken to more than one)

Wáiⁿ-thoⁿ-ta noⁿzhíⁿ-a/ga: Stand by the blanket.

    Wáiⁿ-thoⁿ-ta noⁿzhíⁿi-a/ga (spoken to more than one)

Móⁿze íutha-ta noⁿzhíⁿ-a/ga: Stand by the phone.

    Móⁿze íutha-ta noⁿzhíⁿi-a/ga (spoken to more than one)

Unéthe-tʰe-ta noⁿzhíⁿ-a/ga: Stand by the stove.

    Unéthe-tʰe-ta noⁿzhíⁿi-a/ga (spoken to more than one)

Kinóⁿnoⁿge sabe-kʰe-ta noⁿzhíⁿ-a/ga: Stand by the black car.

    Kinóⁿnoⁿge sabe-kʰe-ta noⁿzhíⁿi-a/ga (spoken to more than one)

Tóⁿde-thoⁿ-ta noⁿzhíⁿ-a/ga: Stand on the ground / dirt.

    Tóⁿde-thoⁿ-ta noⁿzhíⁿi-a/ga (spoken to more than one)

Haská-thoⁿ-ta noⁿzhíⁿ-a/ga: Stand by the flag.

    Haská-thoⁿ-ta noⁿzhíⁿi-a/ga (spoken to more than one)

Uhéat^{h}o^n-tho^n-ta no^{n}zhí^n-a/ga: Stand on the steps.

   Uhéat^{h}o^n-tho^n-ta no^{n}zhí^{n}i-a/ga (spoken to more than one)

Nó^{n}ze-k^{h}e-ta no^{n}zhí^n-a/ga: Stand by the fence.

   Nó^{n}ze-k^{h}e-ta no^{n}zhí^{n}i-a/ga (spoken to more than one)

Agudí: Where

gá-t^{h}e-di: right here / there

shéhi-ta: over there

théthudi: around here / this area

agudí-shte: wherever / somewhere

uthúshi: in front

uthízo^n / ído^{n}be: in the middle

Uthísho^n mo^{n}thí^n-a/ga: Walk around the circle.

   Uthísho^n mo^{n}thí^{n}i-a/ga (spoken to more than one)

Tó^{n}thi^n-a/ga: Run.

   Tó^{n}thi^{n}i-a/ga (spoken to more than one)

Waséko^n mo^{n}thí^n-a/ga: Walk fast.

   Waséko^n mo^{n}thí^{n}i-a/ga (spoken to more than one)

Gá-t^{h}e-di gthí^n-a/ga: Sit here (where I'm pointing).

   Gá-t^{h}e-di gthí^{n}i-a/ga (spoken to more than one)

Gá-t^{h}e-di no^{n}zhí^n-a/ga: Stand here (where I'm pointing).

Gá-t^{h}e-di no^{n}zhí^{n}i-a/ga (spoken to more than one)

Shéhi-ta gthí^n-a/ga: Stand over there.

   Shéhi-ta gthí^{n}i-a/ga (spoken to more than one)

Zhuó^{n}gthe / Zhó^{n}gthe gthí^n-a/ga: Sit by me.

   Zhuó^{n}gthe / Zhó^{n}gthe gthí^{n}i-a/ga (spoken to more than one)

Uthízo^n agthí^n-tami^{n}k^{h}e: I'm going to sit in the middle / between you.

Uthúshi no^{n}zhí^n-a/ga: Stand in front.

   Uthúshi no^{n}zhí^{n}i-a/ga (spoken to more than one)

Agudíshte Thé-k^{h}e: Going Somewhere

Agímo^{n}thi^n-a/ga: Go get it.

   Agímo^{n}thi^{n}i-a/ga (spoken to more than one)

Xátha gí-a/ga: Come back.

   Xátha gíi-a/ga (spoken to more than one)

Pá-t^{h}e ázhi bthé: I'm going to go blow my nose.

Pá-t^{h}e tházhi né-te: You should go blow your nose.

Áwa-k^{h}e-ta né-a?: Where are you going?

Tizhí^{n}ga-ta bthé kó^{n}btha: I want to go to the bathroom.

Áwa-ta / Áwa-tho^n-ta shí-a?: Where did you go?

Tizhí^{n}ga-ta p^{h}í: I went to the bathroom.

Áwa-ta-t^{h}o^n shkí-a?: Where are you coming from?

Hidé-ata-tʰoⁿ pí: I'm coming from down bottom / Decatur.

2.11 CLASSROOM PHRASES FOR PRAISE AND CARING: ÓⁿXTIWATHE, WATHÁNOⁿBE, WÁKʰIHIDE UTHÁ

Translation: Marcella Woodhull Cayou and Donna Morris Parker; elicitation/transcription: Vida Woodhull Stabler; consolidated from "Classroom Conversation Phrases," "Classroom Conversation Table," "Teacher Classroom Phrases," "Useful Classroom Phrases," "General Teacher Phrases for the Classroom," "Basic Umóⁿhoⁿ Classroom Phrases," "Basic Umóⁿhoⁿ Classroom Praise Phrases," "Roll Call," "Elder Lesson Plan," "Roll Call Winter," and "TPR Complete Phrases"; orthography check and consolidation: Bryan James Gordon.

Cultural Note

The Umóⁿhoⁿ people come from a history and culture where we think as a tribe and for one another. The beliefs that "We Are One" and that "We Are All Related" are evident in our Huthuga clan system. Our culture has countless examples of the care we have for one another as a people.

Today we teach our language and culture within a classroom environment. We aim to teach in a natural setting, through situations that mimic community and home life. This nurturing environment promotes the growth of our language and culture and supports the family teachings. Unfortunately, the Boarding School experiences and sometimes other educational institutions have left a negative effect that must be overcome. Praise and encouragement is directed toward the group of students within the classroom, though it is good to praise individually and when culturally appropriate. We nurture our children as they go along, through one stage of life to the next. With a nurturing voice, we learn the value, to "talk right" to one another. Teasing is also a part of our culture, but we must teach people to not go "too far or get too carried away" with it. Praise and care are shown through our actions. The respect and consideration shown toward one another is one of our most important values.

Óⁿxtiwathe, Wathánoⁿbe, Wákʰihide: Praise, Caring

Údoⁿ: It's good. / Okay.

Wehéd': Excellent. / Awesome.

Úd'shkaxe: You did good.

    Úd'shkaxa (spoken to more than one)

Wasísige: S/he's energetic / lively / a go-getter.

Wathísisige: You're energetic / lively / a go-getter.

Áwikʰihide: I'm looking out for you / watching you.

    Áwikʰihida (spoken to more than one)

Witóⁿbe atʰí: I came to see you.

Oⁿthídoⁿbe oⁿgátʰi: We came to see you.

Washkóⁿ/ga: Try hard. / Do your best.

    Washkóⁿi-a/ga (spoken to more than one)

Ígaskoⁿtha/ga: Try it.

Ígaskoⁿthai-a/ga (spoken to more than one)

Íkigthaskoⁿtha/ga: Practice speaking / rehearse.

Íkigthaskoⁿthai-a/ga (spoken to more than one)

Wíⁿ ígaskoⁿtha/ga: Try one.

Wíⁿ ígaskoⁿthai-a/ga (spoken to more than one)

Égoⁿ oⁿgáxe oⁿthíshtoⁿ. Íshpahoⁿ / Íthashpahoⁿ: We've done like this before. You know it.

Iⁿwíⁿkoⁿ/ga: Help me.

Uíkoⁿ/ga: Help him/her.

Uíkoⁿi-a/ga (spoken to more than one)

Úwakoⁿ/ga. / Úwagikoⁿ/ga: Help them.

Úwakoⁿi-a/ga. / Úwagikoⁿi-a/ga (spoken to more than one)

Íthae-tʰe údoⁿ: You sound good / speak well.

Hú-tʰe údoⁿ: Your voice sounds good.

Nóⁿde údoⁿ níⁿ: You are good-hearted.

Úshk'udoⁿ níⁿ: You have good ways.

Wathígthoⁿ-tʰe údoⁿ: Your mind is good / Good thinking.

Thipʰi shkáxe: You did a good job.

Umóⁿhoⁿ íye thipʰi-achoⁿ: They really know Umóⁿhoⁿ Íye.

Wanípʰi-achoⁿ: You're really good at it. / You really learned well.

Íkizhuwathe: It's something to be proud of.

Umóⁿhoⁿ-ama íkizhu: It made the Umóⁿhoⁿ people proud.

Wáspe-tʰe Wákʰihide tʰe:
Good Behavior and Paying Attention

Wáspa/ga: Behave.

Bahé théthazhi-a/ga: Don't push him/her.

Kipáhe thétha-bazhíi-a/ga: Don't push each other.

Ánoⁿ'oⁿ/ga: Listen.

Ánoⁿ'oⁿi-a/ga (spoken to more than one)

Óⁿnoⁿ'oⁿ/ga: Listen to me.

Óⁿnoⁿ'oⁿi-a/ga (spoken to more than one)

Thikóⁿ / Koⁿhá / Koⁿhó íye-tʰe ánoⁿ'oⁿ/ga: Listen to Grandma talk.

Thikóⁿ / Koⁿhá / Koⁿhó íye-tʰe ánoⁿ'oⁿi-a/ga (spoken to more than one)

Thitígoⁿ / Tigoⁿhá / Tigoⁿhó íye-tʰe ánoⁿ'oⁿ/ga: Listen to Grandpa talk.

Thitígoⁿ / Tigoⁿhá / Tigoⁿhó íye-tʰe ánoⁿ'oⁿi-a/ga (spoken to more than one)

Thipʰi wanóⁿ'oⁿ/ga / Wákʰihida/ga: Pay attention.

Thipʰi wanóⁿ'oⁿi-a/ga / Wákʰihidai-a/ga (spoken to more than one)

Thiwágazu-a/ga: Look hard / Recognize / Examine.

Thiwágazui-a/ga (spoken to more than one)

Dóⁿbe thá/ga: Go look.

Dóⁿbe thái-a/ga (spoken to more than one)

Óⁿkʰihida/ga: Watch (out for) me.

Óⁿkʰihidai-a/ga (spoken to more than one)

Oⁿdóⁿba/ga: Look at me.

Oⁿdóⁿbai-a/ga (spoken to more than one)

Wadóⁿba/ga: Look at them.

Wadóⁿbai-a/ga (spoken to more than one)

Witóⁿbe: I'm watching you.

Oⁿthídoⁿba: We're watching you.

2.12 CLASSROOM PHRASES FOR TEACHING: WÉGOⁿZE-DOⁿ UTHÁ

Translation: Marcella Woodhull Cayou and Donna Morris Parker; elicitation/transcription: Vida Woodhull Stabler; consolidated from "Classroom Conversation Phrases," "Classroom Conversation Table," "Teacher Classroom Phrases," "Useful Classroom Phrases," "General Teacher Phrases for the Classroom," "Basic Umóⁿhoⁿ Classroom Phrases," "Basic Umóⁿhoⁿ Classroom Praise Phrases," "Roll Call," "Elder Lesson Plan," and "Roll Call Winter"; orthography check and consolidation: Bryan James Gordon.

Izházhe Wa'í: Giving Names

Iⁿdádoⁿ-a?: What is this?

Háshi-tʰe iⁿdádoⁿ oⁿthádai-a?: What did we call it last time?

Iⁿdádoⁿ-tʰe uáwagitha/ga: Tell us what it is.

Iⁿdádoⁿ-tʰe uáwagithai-a/ga (spoken to more than one)

Gátʰe Umóⁿhoⁿ íye-tʰe awatʰégoⁿ?: What is this (pointing or holding it) called in Umóⁿhoⁿ Íye?

Thétʰe Umóⁿhoⁿ íye-tʰe awatʰégoⁿ?: What is this here (close to me) called in Umóⁿhoⁿ Íye?

Shétʰe Umóⁿhoⁿ íye-tʰe awatʰégoⁿ?: What is that over there called in Umóⁿhoⁿ Íye?

Ebé etá?: Whose is it?

Wiwíta: It's mine.

Wiwíta-mazhi: It's not mine.

Thithíta: It's yours.

Thithítazhi: It's not yours.

Oⁿgúta: It's ours.

Oⁿgúta-bazhi: It's not ours.

Etá: It's hers/his/theirs.

Etá-bazhi: It's not hers/his/theirs.

_____ oⁿtháde-noⁿ: We call it _____.

_____ thadé-noⁿ: It's called _____.

Wégoⁿze-doⁿ: While Teaching Them

Ebé íbahoⁿ?: Who knows it?

Íbahoⁿ: S/he / they know.

Bthípʰi kóⁿbtha: I want to learn.

Thipʰí: S/he / they know how / are learning.

Thígoⁿze-taakʰa: S/he'll teach you.

Wípoⁿze-tamiⁿkʰe: I'll teach you.

Gióⁿza/ga: Teach her/him.

Gióⁿzai-a/ga (spoken to more than one)

Wégoⁿza/ga: Teach them.

Wégoⁿzai-a/ga (spoken to more than one)

Íⁿgoⁿza/ga: Teach me.

Íⁿgoⁿzai-a/ga (spoken to more than one)

Gíbaha/ga: Show her/him.

Gíbahai-a/ga (spoken to more than one)

Íⁿbaha/ga: Show me.

Íⁿbahai-a/ga (spoken to more than one)

Iⁿdádoⁿ shkáxe-tʰe íⁿbaha/ga: Show me what you did.

Iⁿdádoⁿ shkáxai-tʰe íⁿbahai-a/ga (spoken to more than one)

Agísitha-mazhi: I forgot it.

Ithápahoⁿ-mazhi: I don't know.

Tápuska Móⁿtʰe Wágazhi-ge: Classroom Action Commands

Thinákoⁿga: Turn (lights) on.

Thinázhi-a/ga: Turn (lights) off.

Thinóⁿga/ga: Turn (machine) on.

Ánoⁿsa/ga: Turn (machine) off / Lock it / Close it.

Thishíba/ga: Open it.

Wagthábaze ágaxada/ga: Close / Cover your book.

Áthaskabetha/ga: Glue this onto that.

Pá-tʰe gazhíⁿ-a/ga: Blow your nose.

Pá-tʰe áazhi bthé: I'm going to go blow my nose.

Pá-tʰe tháazhi né-te: You should go blow your nose.

Zhoⁿbtháska-kʰe thisíhi-a/ga: Clear the board.

Zhoⁿbtháska-kʰe thisíhii-a/ga (spoken to more than one)

Zhoⁿbtháska-kʰe gthísihi-a/ga: Clear your board.

Zhoⁿbtháska-tʰe gthísihi-a/ga: Clear your boards.

Baxú-a/ga: Write it.

Shékʰe paháshi thisíhi-a/ga: Erase that part on top.

Izházhe thithíta-tʰe ábaxu-a/ga / ágipaxu-a/ga: Write your name on it.

Wáxe íye-kʰedi baxú-a/ga: Write it in English.

Wébaxuni aníⁿ-a?: Do you have a pen?

Ebé baxú-tathiⁿkʰe?: Who is going to write it?

Wébaxun kóⁿbtha: I want a pencil.

Wiúga-kʰe bíze: The marker is dry.

Pi'óⁿ/ga: Fix it.

Wébaxu oⁿ'í-a/ga: Give me a pencil.

Thenóⁿ wíⁿ oⁿ'í-a/ga: Give me another.

Óⁿgazhiazhi-a/ga: Don't tell me what to do.

Áwigazhi: I told you (to do something).

Wáagazhi: I told them (to do something).

Ágazhi-a/ga: Tell her/him (to do it).

Wágazhi-a/ga: Tell them (to do it).

2.13 CLOTHING AND WEATHER: HÁTHE-TʰE ÓⁿBA-AKʰA-SHTI

From "Fall Phrases" by Marcella Woodhull Cayou, Donna Morris Parker, and Susan Freemont; "Seasonal Weather Terms" by Marcella Woodhull Cayou and Donna Morris Parker; "Morning Routine Commands" by Marcella Woodhull Cayou and Donna Morris Parker; "Clothing Items"; "New and Old Game"; "Shíⁿgazhiⁿga Everyday Phrases"; "Stuffed Bear Phrases"; elicitation/transcription: Vida Woodhull Stabler.

Íye Atʰóⁿ-shte É-noⁿ: Words for Whenever (General Clothing and Weather Terminology)

háthe / wáthaha: clothes

Óⁿba-tʰe eyóⁿ-a? / Óⁿba-akʰa eyóⁿ-a?: How's the weather?

waxíⁿha: material / cloth / fabric

Tadésagi: It's windy.

wáthaha áthaha / wáthaha tóⁿ / háthe 'óⁿ / thahá: get dressed

Tadésagi-áchoⁿ: It's very windy.

Háthe 'óⁿ/ga. / Wáthaha tóⁿ/ga: Get dressed.

Mí-akʰa unágoⁿba: The sun is shining.

Wáthaha údoⁿ ágthaha/ga: Put on your best clothing.

Móⁿxe-kʰe kétha. / Móⁿxe-kʰe usíhi: The sky is clear.

'óⁿ: wear / put on (general)

Kétha-áchoⁿ: It's very clear.

'óⁿkʰithe: get somebody dressed

Kétha í: It's getting clearer.

Zhiⁿgá-thiⁿkʰe unóⁿzhiⁿ 'óⁿkʰitha/ga: Put baby's shirt on for her.

Gakíza: The clouds parted.

Níⁿde ágthoⁿ ázhi 'óⁿkʰitha/ga: Change her/his diaper.

Móⁿxe-kʰe gasíhi-tʰe údoⁿ: It's good that the wind is clearing the sky.

unóⁿzhiⁿ: wear / put on (on torso)

Mí-akʰa tʰigthágtha: The sun is coming and going.

utóⁿ: wear / put on (on lower body)

Mí-akʰa gaéthoⁿbe ihé-thoⁿthoⁿ gthíⁿ: The sun keeps appearing suddenly over and over.

thagé: wear / put on (on head)

Móⁿxe-kʰe ámoⁿxpi: The sky is cloudy.

'íⁿ: wear / put on (wrapped around body)

Ámoⁿxpi. / Moⁿxpí: It's cloudy.

ágashke: fasten / button / velcro / pin on

Mí-thoⁿ wathíshnazhi: The sun is out of sight.

Niⁿdúthishiⁿ-thoⁿ ágigthashka/ga: Buckle / snap your pants.

Shtáge. / Sníshtage: It's lukewarm.

Watʰé-thoⁿ ágigthashka: Pin your dress.

Tʰíⁿ: It's dewy / moist / damp.

égashke: fasten / button / velcro / pin on for somebody

zhídoⁿ: dew

Unóⁿzhiⁿ móⁿge égashka/ga: Button his shirt.

tushníge: rainbow

háthukathi^n: naked

kigthíhathukathi^n: get undressed

*I^{n}dádo^n-shte Ázhi-tho^{n}tho^n 'ó^n-no^n:
Other Things That Are Worn (Accessories)*

wéki'o^n: jewelry

áxibe: bracelet

no^{n}béuthixtho^n: ring

Áxibe xtáathe-tho^n agímo^n: I'm wearing my favorite bracelet.

No^{n}béuthixtho^n mó^n: I'm wearing a ring.

miído^{n}be / áxibe miído^{n}be: watch

No^{n}béuthixtho^n upásno^n: I put on a ring.

Áxibe miído^{n}be mó^n: I'm wearing a watch.

No^{n}béuthixtho^n uágipasno^n: I put on my ring.

úwi^n: earrings

No^{n}béuthixtho^n i^{n}wí^{n}basno^n: S/he put a ring on me.

wanó^{n}p'i^n: necklace

mó^{n}zi^{n}shtugtho^n / mó^{n}zestugtho^n: glasses ("metal eye sockets")

hí^{n}ska: beadwork

Mó^{n}zi^{n}shtugtho^n mó^n: I'm wearing glasses.

Égithe mó^{n}zestugtho^n gthíxo^{n}zhi-a/ga: Watch out so you don't break your glasses.

Mó^{n}zi^{n}shtugtho^n gthísihi bik^{h}á/ga: Wipe your glasses clean.

Háthe-t^{h}e éthigito^n: Your clothes look good on you.

Nú-ak^{h}a sébe-xchi mo^{n}thí^n: The man's going around dressed neatly. ("sébe" refers to dark color)

2.14 COFFEE PHRASES: MO^{n}KÓ^{n}SABE UTHÁ

Translation: Marcella Woodhull Cayou and Donna Morris Parker; transcription: Vida Woodhull Stabler.

Vocabulary

mo^{n}kó^{n}sabe ígaxe: coffee pot

niútható^n: coffee cup

tehé zhi^{n}ga: small spoon

téska mo^{n}zéni: milk

zho^{n}ní: sugar

Phrases

Mo^{n}kó^{n}sabe btháto^n: I'm drinking coffee.

Mo^{n}kó^{n}sabe náto^n-a?: Are you drinking coffee?

Mo^{n}kó^{n}sabe tható^n/ga: Drink the coffee.

Mo^{n}kó^{n}sabe o^{n}tháto^n: We're drinking coffee.

Mo^{n}kó^{n}sabe-t^{h}e níde: The coffee is ready.

Mo^{n}kó^{n}sabe-t^{h}e shó^n: The coffee is done.

Mo^{n}kó^{n}sabe-t^{h}e ábixo^n thishtó^n: The coffee is finished boiling.

Mo^{n}kó^{n}sabe-t^{h}e pá-ácho^n: The coffee is very bitter.

Moⁿkóⁿsabe-tʰé múpa-áchoⁿ:
The coffee is very bitter (oversteeped).

Moⁿkóⁿsabe-tʰe washkóⁿtoⁿga:
The coffee is strong.

Moⁿkóⁿsabe-tʰe skíthe: The coffee
is sweet.

Moⁿkóⁿsabe-tʰe washkóⁿ thiⁿgé:
The coffee is weak.

Moⁿkóⁿsabe páxe: I made coffee.

Moⁿkóⁿsabe shkáxe-a?: Will you
make coffee?

Moⁿkóⁿsabe-tʰe oⁿthóⁿbthoⁿ: I've had
enough coffee.

**Moⁿkóⁿsabe Thitígoⁿ / Tigoⁿhá / Tigóⁿho
'í-a/ga:** Give Grandpa coffee.

**Moⁿkóⁿsabe Thikóⁿ / Koⁿhá / Koⁿhó 'í-a/
ga:** Give Grandma coffee.

Zhoⁿní-shti wagthábaze úzhi 'í-a/ga:
Give her a sugar packet too.

Wagóⁿze dúba 'í-a/ga: Give Teacher
some.

Wi háshi-shti wíⁿ oⁿ'í-a/ga: Give one to
me last, too.

Moⁿkóⁿsabe nátoⁿ-noⁿ-a?: Do you drink
coffee?

Shi níshtoⁿ-ki Wagóⁿze 'í-a/ga: Give
Teacher some when you're done.

Wóⁿgithe úwazhi-a/ga: Serve everybody.

**Niúthatoⁿ-tʰe wíⁿ-thoⁿthoⁿ sheáma
wa'í-a/ga:** Give a cup to each person.

Moⁿkóⁿsabe sabázhi náxthude-tai: You
might choke on your coffee. ("You might
get coffee nerves.")

Cultural Note

Coffee (**moⁿkóⁿsabe**, "black medicine") has
become an integral part of Umóⁿhoⁿ daily life.
Many a good visit has taken place where coffee
is the preferred hot drink. Before coffee came
along, we drank **tabéhi** ("ball plant," named for
its snowball-like flowers), our wild tea, harvested from our land. The general term for different
kinds of tea is **xáde moⁿkoⁿ** ("grass medicine").

Today most homes have a speckled enamelware coffee pot sitting on top of a kitchen cupboard or still in use sitting on top of the stove.
One can only imagine that very first shared cup
of coffee between an Umóⁿhoⁿ man and French
trader coming up the Missouri. You can take the
thought one step further and imagine what was
bartered. Perhaps it was an animal pelt traded
for a sack of coffee.

2.15 COFFEE SCRIPT: MOⁿKÓⁿSABE UTHÁ UKÍKʰIA

Five-minute immersion lesson. Elders and conversation participants: Clifford Wolfe Jr., Francine Cayou, Susan Freemont, Pat Phillips, Vida
Woodhull Stabler, Rufus White, and Octa Mitchell Keen. Recorded October 12, 2011.

SETTING: All the relatives sitting are sitting
around the table. It's break time and they are
ready for their coffee break.

CW: **Moⁿkóⁿsabe níde:** The coffee is done.

FC: **Moⁿkóⁿsabe ebé gáxe-a?:** Who made
coffee?

SF: **Pat moⁿkóⁿsabe-tʰe gáxa:** Pat made the coffee.

PP: **Wi páxe:** I made it.

VS: **Moⁿkóⁿsabe-tʰe údoⁿ-áchoⁿ:** The coffee is excellent.

FC: **Moⁿkóⁿsabe thiⁿgé. Xthú'a:** The coffee is gone. ("No coffee. It's empty.")

SF: **Tushpahá moⁿkóⁿsabe wíⁿ agímoⁿthiⁿ-a. Thiwíⁿ moⁿthíⁿ-a:** Granddaughter, go get a coffee. Go buy it.

VS: **Móⁿzeska oⁿthíⁿge:** I don't have money.

RW: **Wagáxe ná-ga:** Borrow some. ("Ask for a loan.")

OK: **Gá, móⁿzeska wi'í. Thiwíⁿ moⁿthíⁿ-a:** Here, I'll give you money. Go buy some.

VS: **Wíbthahoⁿ:** Thank you.

For Umóⁿhoⁿ Íye immersion maintenance, use as needed the phrases **Shi égithoⁿ/ga** ("Say it again"); **Edéshe?** ("What did you say?"); and **Winóⁿ'oⁿ-mazhi** ("I didn't hear you").

2.16 COLORS: ÚGAXE ÁZHI-THOⁿTHOⁿ

Translation: Marcella Woodhull Cayou; elicitation/transcription: Vida Woodhull Stabler.

zhíde: red

shé zhíde: red apple

Shé zhíde-thoⁿ abthíⁿ: I have the red apple.

Tom-akʰa shé zhíde athíⁿ: Tom has a red apple.

zhí-egoⁿ: pink

Watʰé-móⁿtʰe zhí-egoⁿ abthíⁿ: I have a pink underskirt.

sézi-egoⁿ: orange

ágthiⁿ sézi-egoⁿ: orange chair

Ágthiⁿ sézi-egoⁿ abthíⁿ: I have an orange chair.

zí: yellow

waxtá thigúzhe zí / téthawa zí: yellow banana

Waxtá thigúzhe zí bthátʰe: I ate a yellow banana.

pézhitu: green

iⁿdé íbikʰa pézhitu: green face towel

Iⁿdé íbikʰa pézhitu abthíⁿ: I have a green face towel.

tú: blue

kinóⁿnoⁿge tú: blue car

Jane-akʰa kinóⁿnoⁿge tú dóⁿba: Jane saw a blue car.

házi-egoⁿ: purple

móⁿzeska úzhi házi-egoⁿ: purple purse

Mary-akʰa watʰé házi-egoⁿ óⁿ: Mary is wearing a purple dress.

zíshabe: brown

hiⁿbé zíshabe: brown shoes

Hiⁿbe zíshabe noⁿbá abthíⁿ: I have two brown shoes.

sábe: black

shóⁿge sábe: black horse

Shóⁿge sábe wíⁿ áagthiⁿ: I rode a black horse.

Tom-akʰa kinóⁿnoⁿge sábe ugthíⁿ: Tom is riding in a black car.

ská: white

unóⁿzhiⁿ ská: white shirt

Unóⁿzhiⁿ ská abthíⁿ: I have a white shirt.

Jim-akʰa unóⁿzhiⁿ ská óⁿ: Jim is wearing a white shirt.

sóⁿ: light / lighter / pale / bright

shábe: dark / darker / deep

2.17 DAYS OF THE WEEK

Sunday: **Óⁿba Xubé** ("Holy / Sacred Day")

Monday: **Óⁿba Xubé Thishtoⁿ** ("Holy Day Finished")

Tuesday: **Óⁿba Wénoⁿba** ("Second Day")

Wednesday: **Óⁿba Wéthabthiⁿ** ("Third Day")

Thursday: **Óⁿba Wéduba** ("Fourth Day")

Friday: **Óⁿba Wésatoⁿ** ("Fifth Day")

Saturday: **Hithái** ("Bath Day")

Sunday is also referred to as **Óⁿba Waxúbe.**

Sundays are commonly used to count weeks. "In one week" may be expressed as **Óⁿba Xubé wiⁿóⁿxchi-ki**; "five weeks ago" as **Óⁿba Xubé sátoⁿ athá**; "two weeks' time" as **Óⁿba Xubé noⁿba-tʰe shetʰoⁿ.**

In the name for Wednesday either of the first two syllables may be stressed: **Óⁿba Wéthabthiⁿ** or **Óⁿba Wethábthiⁿ.**

Further information on the name for Saturday, **Hithái**, may be found in the "What Are You Going to Do This Summer?" activity (section 7.21).

2.18 DOINGS PHRASES: ÚZHAWA ÍYE

Wóⁿgithe thatʰí-　tʰe　údoⁿ.
everybody　you come　that　good
It's good that all of you came.

Wóⁿgithe oⁿgátʰi-　tʰe　údoⁿ.
everybody　we come　that　good
It's good that we all came.

Shetáthishoⁿ wa'í-　bazhi.
toward there　give out　not
That side didn't get any (food) yet.

Shetáthishoⁿ wa'í-　bazhi.
toward there　give out　not
That side didn't get any (food) yet.

Shetʰóⁿnoⁿ wáthatʰe- kʰe shetáthishoⁿ shígtha- bazhi.
still　　　table　the toward there　dip　　not
The servers didn't serve on that side yet.

Shígthe is a special verb used today mostly just for the dipping of soup with a ladle at ceremony. Dorsey said that in the late 1800s the word was used for soup that had more water than meat and had the water floating on the surface, and it could also be used for skimming grease off the top.

you dipped: **shíthagthe**; I dipped: **shiágthe**;
we dipped: **shióⁿgtha**; s/he/they dipped:
shígtha

Wathátʰe uthízhi-   mashe   wathátʰai-ga.
food   filled for you you who eat
Those of you given food, go ahead and eat.

Úhoⁿ,   shígthe- ama wathátʰe uthízhi
cook   dip   the food   filled for you

thishtóⁿ-   ama   wathátʰai-ga.
already   the   eat
The cooks and servers who already have food
can go ahead and eat.

Kúge-   thoⁿ   kugé-   achoⁿ.
drum   the   drum   sound very
The drum is loud.

Kugé refers to "hollow" sounds. The sound
of beating on a drum is just one of these.
It is used in verbs like **gakúge** "beat
drum," which is sometimes said **gakú**, and
thikúge "make a hollow sound pulling a
wagon or sled." It does not mean "loud"
by itself. The idea of "loud" comes in
combination with the ending -**achoⁿ**.
Umóⁿhoⁿ Íye has different words for
"loud" depending on the source of the
sound. Loud speech is **thahégazhi** or **íye
sagí**, loud yelling **thadíⁿdiⁿ**, loud singing
thatóⁿga, a loud gunshot **múhegazhi** or
múzhawa, a loud popping sound **gatúshi**,
and many more.

Xúka-ma   épahoⁿga   íwathishi-a/ga.
sing the   them first   feed them
Serve the singers first.

Hóⁿdi   úhoⁿ- ama wathátʰe-kʰe áshita uhóⁿ.
night at cook the   food   outside cook it
Last night the cooks cooked the food outside.

Wamóⁿske skíthe- thoⁿ gthíxukʰitha-a/ga.
bread   sweet   the   let her/him cut
her/his own
The clan that cuts the cake, let her go ahead
and cut it.

This sentence is special. There are many
ordinary verbs for "cut," including **páde,
sú, máse, máxoⁿ, máshpe, mázha,
mámu, gasé, gashpé, gashná, gazhá,
thisé**, and many more. But here a different
verb is used, **thixú**, which is used for
"drawing" and "marking." Ceremonially
the clan member is "marking" the cake.
The powerhouse **thixú** becomes **gthíxu**
to signify that the clan member has
ceremonial ownership. And because we are
letting the clan member cut it instead of
making her do it, the special ending -**kʰithe**
is used.

**Iⁿkésabe- thiⁿ kʰe wamóⁿske skíthe gthíxukʰitha-
a/ga.**
Iⁿkésabe   the   bread   sweet let her/him cut
her/his own

Let the Iⁿkésabe mark her cake.

Wa'ú- akʰa wamóⁿske skíthe máxoⁿxoⁿ.

woman the bread sweet cut in pieces

The woman cut the cake (into many pieces).

Ukʰéthiⁿxchi góⁿ gáxa.

really ordinary like made it

Nothing fancy, she made it simple.

Tha'étʰewathe íya.

humble speak

Talking humble / pitiful. (Donna Morris Parker and Marcella Woodhull Cayou)

Íye waxú'exchi íya.

word really humble speak

She spoke very humble. (Marcella Woodhull Cayou and Donna Morris Parker)

Xu'é is a sound word referring to the soft, steady sound of the speaker's voice rather than the idea of "humble" expressed by **tha'étʰewathe** in the previous sentence. Other things that are said to **xu'é** include the waves in a stream or the flow of the stream, sand in an hourglass, paper being torn, sucking noises made by **wazétheama**, grass being crawled on, grain pouring out of a bag, buzzing of flying birds, scraping wood, tearing fabric, and whirling something around on a string. It is related to **su'é**, the loud sound of pouring rain and of dragging long ropes on the ground. **Xu'é** is softer than **su'é**, as can be seen by comparing the examples.

Gíku pʰí.

feast I went

I went to a feast / dinner.

Awáchʰigaxe pʰí.

I dance I went

I went to powwow.

Wachʰígaxe athíⁿ-ma

dance the ones having

wachígaxe-ma wáapanoⁿ pʰí.

the dancers I look on I went

They were having a powwow, I went to look on.

2.19 DOINGS CULTURAL NOTE

Umóⁿhoⁿ people attend a variety of community gatherings, which they refer to as "doings." The events include times of celebration as well as more somber events, such as a memorial dinner or funeral. Among the types of gatherings are handgames, feasts, Memorial remembrances, War Dance, Gourd Dance, Umóⁿhoⁿ naming ceremony; and Native American Church fundraisers. There are behaviors practiced by Umóⁿhoⁿ people that are very specific to our culture.

Umóⁿhoⁿ people always bring their own "tied dish bundle." They often carry their dish bundle in a basket. Items that are a must include plates, bowls, cups, spoon, salt, and soup bucket.

Umóⁿhoⁿ people carry a chair and pillow. Singers will carry their chair and drum stick.

Food is placed on the ground or floor in the center of the gathered people sitting in a circle.

The Man in Charge will call for help to serve the food.

The protocol for how food is served will be directed by the People in Charge (male and female).

It is polite to watch over the plate of a person serving.

At a dance the singers are always served first.

Respect is shown by maintaining silence (no side conversations or talking) when eating or when a person is addressing the gathered people.

It is expected that children will sit quietly if brought to doings. If they have a lively spirit it may be best to leave them home with family.

Prayer is offered over the food by the Man in Charge.

He will also make prayers for the honoree(s) and family as needed.

2.20 DOOR-ANSWERING PHRASES FOR SEE YOU LATER, GREETINGS

Translation: Marcella Woodhull Cayou and Donna Morris Parker; elicitation/transcription: Vida Woodhull Stabler.

Áwa-kʰe-ta né-a?
Where are you going?

Agthé.
I'm going home.

Kʰe bthé.
Okay, I'm going.

Thagthé-a?
You going home?

Né-a?
Are you going?

Gasóⁿthiⁿ witóⁿbe-tamiⁿkʰe, shí.
Tomorrow I will see you,   again.

Shi   witóⁿbe-tamiⁿkʰe, gasóⁿthiⁿ.
Again I will see you,   tomorrow.

Gasóⁿthiⁿ agthí-tamiⁿkʰe.
Tomorrow I'll be back.

Góⁿchʰe agthí-tamiⁿkʰe.
Later   I will return.

Hóⁿ-ki witóⁿbe-tamiⁿkʰe.
Tonight I'll see you.

Páze-ki   witóⁿbe-tamiⁿkʰe.
This evening I'll see you.

Óⁿba Xube Thishtóⁿ witóⁿbe-tamiⁿkʰe.
Day   Sacred Finishes   I'll see you.
     ("I'll see you Monday.")

Páze hí-ki witóⁿbe-tamiⁿkʰe.

Evening when it arrives I'll see you.

("I'll see you toward evening.")

Wóⁿgithe thatʰí-tʰe údoⁿ.

everybody that you're here is good.

("Welcome everybody.")

Káshi-xti witóⁿba-mazhi.

really long time I have not seen you.

("Long time no see.")

Atʰóⁿ-ki thagthí-taniⁿkshe?

when will you be back?

("When will you come back?")

2.21 FIVE SENSES: WÍUBESNI SÁTOⁿ

Translation: Susan Freemont; prior translation: Marcella Woodhull Cayou and Donna Morris Parker; elicitation/transcription: Vida Woodhull Stabler.

Dóⁿba/ga: Look at it.

wadóⁿbe-tʰe: seeing

udóⁿbe-tʰe: looks / appearance

Uthíbthoⁿ/ga: Smell it.

uthíbthoⁿ-tʰe: smelling

bthóⁿ-tʰe: smell / odor

Thastúba/ga: Taste it (put it in your mouth).

Ígaskoⁿtha/ga: Taste / try it.

Noⁿ'óⁿ/ga: Listen to it.

wanóⁿ'oⁿ-tʰe: listening / hearing

noⁿxíde-tʰe: ear / sense of hearing

Ábitʰa/ga: Touch it.

wathítʰoⁿ-tʰe: feeling around

2.22 BAKING A CAKE: WAMÓⁿSKE SKÍTHE OⁿGÚHOⁿI-TʰE

Translation: Donna Morris Parker and Susan Freemont; elicitation/transcription: Vida Woodhull Stabler; additional phrases: Donna Morris Parker.

Cultural Note

The cake symbolizes the buffalo meat provided and dispensed to the Umóⁿhoⁿ people by the Iⁿkésabe clan. Therefore, when there is cake at a community doings, it is protocol to ask an Iⁿkésabe clan member to deal with the cake. It is their right or duty. An Iⁿkesabe man may mark the cake first, representing his duty in the hunt and killing of the buffalo.

More frequently, an Iⁿkésabe woman is asked to take care of the cake in her way. She may first ask younger relatives to show the sheet cake around to the people before it is cut. When the cake has made a complete circle around to the people, she cuts the cake. She may decide to pass the cake around herself or she may ask relatives to help her pass the cake out to people. Once the cake is dispensed to all present, she may take the prerogative to stand and give her thanks to the family for the honor of taking care of the ceremonial cake.

Wágazhi-ge: Commands

Oⁿgúhoⁿ oⁿthátʰe-taoⁿgatʰoⁿ: We will bake and eat it.

Óⁿbathe noⁿbé-tʰe kigthízhai-a/ga: All of you wash your hands.

Uxpé toⁿga-tʰe thizá/ga: Get the big bowl.

Kúge-tʰe thishíba/ga: Open the box.

Wamúske ígahi-tʰe uzhí-a/ga: Pour the mix in.

Kúge shíshige úzhi-tʰedi óⁿtha/ga: Throw the box in the trash can.

Wéta thizá/ga: Get the eggs.

Ní thizá/ga: Get the water.

Wégthi-tʰe thizá/ga: Get the oil.

Tehé toⁿga wíⁿ thizá/ga: Get a big spoon.

Uthúgahi-a/ga: Mix it.

Wíuhoⁿ wégthi íbikʰa thizá/ga: Get a cake pan and smear grease on it.

Wamúska xúde thizá/ga: Get flour.

Wáku thizá/ga: Get a fork.

Wasékoⁿ uthúgahi-a/ga: Mix it fast.

Tehé toⁿga wíⁿ thizá/ga: Get a big spoon.

Uzhí thishtóⁿ/ga: Put it all in.

Wégoⁿze niúthatoⁿ thizá/ga. Shétʰe athíⁿ-gi-a/ga: Get the measuring cup. Bring that to me.

Wégazu thizá/ga: Spread out straight (to the four corners).

Tehé gasíhi-a/ga: Scrape the spoon.

Shkóⁿzhi gthíⁿ-a/ga: Sit and don't move. (spoken to kids helping out)

Wéthihide edábe: The utensils too. (put them in the sink)

Óⁿma-kʰe thizá/ga: Get the other one too.

Uzhí thishtóⁿ: It's already in there. (said of utensils in sink or cake in oven)

Wamúska xúde itʰétha/ga: Put the flour away.

Wéta itʰétha/ga: Put the eggs away.

Wamúska skíthe níde-a?: Is the cake done?

Óⁿhoⁿ, wamúska skíthe níde: Yes, the cake is done.

Wamúska skíthe gashíbe thizá/ga: Take the cake out.

Sní ithóⁿtha/ga: Set it out to cool.

Ní ámusni thétha/ga: Pour water over them to cool them off (hot dishes).

Ní uzhí itʰétha/ga: Add water, leave it.

Wáthatʰe thishúpa/ga thisíhi-a/ga: Gather up / Clean up / Clear off the table.

Shíshige úzhi-tʰedi uzhí-a/ga: Throw it in the trash can.

Wégthi óⁿma-tʰe itʰétha/ga: Put the other lard away.

Wamúska skíthe-tʰe uspé aíatha: The cake fell.

ugáspe: indented (as if by a finger dipped in)

Wémoⁿxe Edégithoⁿ-ge-shti:
Questions and Answers

Sam, noⁿbé-tʰe nízha?: Sam, did you wash your hands?

Noⁿbé-tʰe akígthizha: I washed my hands.

Uxpé-tʰe níze-a?: Did you get the bowl?

Uxpé-tʰe bthíze: I got the bowl.

Wagthábaze níshibe-a?: Did you open the box?

Wagthábaze shuga bthíshibe bthíshto^n: I'm done opening the cardboard box.

Wamó^{n}ske xúde ígahi-t^{h}e uxpé-t^{h}edi utházhi-a?: Did you pour the mix in the bowl?

Wamó^{n}ske xúde ígahi-t^{h}e uázhi: I poured the mix in.

2.23 PRAYING OVER FOOD: O^{n}WÓ^{n}HO^n'A

Translation: Donna Morris Parker; transcription: Vida Woodhull Stabler.

Cultural Note

Our Umó^{n}ho^n ways teach us that "prayer comes first."

Dadího / Dadihá Wakó^{n}da,

Father (male / female speaker) Wakó^{n}da

wathát^{h}e   o^{n}thát^{h}e-tao^{n}gat^{h}o^n

food   we will eat

údo^n wégaxa/ga.

good make it for us (female / male speaker)

Wíbthaho^n.

I thank you.

Dadihá Wakó^{n}da, wathát^{h}e o^{n}thát^{h}e-tao^{n}gat^{h}o^n údo^n wégaxa.

Father God, I thank you for the food we will eat, make it good for us. (female speaker)

Dadího Wakó^{n}da, wathát^{h}e o^{n}thát^{h}e-tao^{n}gat^{h}o^n údo^n wégaxa/ga.

Father God, I thank you for the food we will eat, make it good for us. (male speaker)

Other Versions

Dadího / Dadihá Wakó^{n}da, wathát^{h}e o^{n}thát^{h}ai-t^{h}e wíbthaho^n.

Father God, I thank you for the food we ate.

Wakó^{n}da wathát^{h}e o^{n}gó^{n}tha-tait^{h}é údo^n wégaxa/ga.

Wakó^{n}da please make the food good for us that we will want to eat.

Mithúmo^{n}shi thé théthudi údo^n wégaxa/ga.

Make this noonday (meal) here good for us.

2.24 SITTING AROUND THE TABLE: WÁTHAT^{h}E UTHÍSHO^n O^{n}GTHÍ^n

Translation: Marcella Woodhull Cayou; transcription: Vida Woodhull Stabler; orthography check: Bryan James Gordon.

Cultural Note

These phrases were elicited with a family sitting around a dinner table in mind. If you are at a feast or doings, you will hear the phrase "**Wathát^{h}ai-ga**" spoken by the Man in Charge giving all permission to eat. Everyone must wait until this phrase is spoken. It is also good Umó^{n}ho^n etiquette always to take what you are served. Don't turn the food away when offered it. Once the food makes its way around to all, the remaining food will be served until gone. Soup will be served around to all. Soup buckets may be filled once it has made its way around to all.

Phrases

Iⁿdádoⁿ oⁿtháthe-taóⁿgathoⁿ?: What are we going to eat?.

Watháthe ázhi-thoⁿthoⁿ oⁿthóⁿnoⁿpehi: The different foods make me hungry.

Watháthe gí-a/ga: Come eat.

Hiⁿthékitha/ga, noⁿpeóⁿhi (noⁿpóⁿhi): Hurry up, I'm hungry.

Niskíthe-the úha thétha/ga: Pass the salt around.

Nú-the úha gítha/ga: Pass the potatoes back this way.

Moⁿkóⁿsabe-the dúba oⁿ'í-a/ga: Give me some of the coffee.

Watháthai-a (f.) / Watháthai-ga hó (m.): Eat! (said to two or more people)

Shi dúba shkóⁿna?: Want some more?

Males may also say, **"Shi dúba shkóⁿna-ho?"**

When speaking to two or more people, one may say, **"Shi dúba shkóⁿnai-a?"**

Wiⁿdénoⁿ uzhí-a/ga: Pour / fill / load it halfway

When speaking to two or more people, say, **"Wiⁿdénoⁿ uzhíi-a/ga."** (female / male speaker)

Wiⁿdéthoⁿ oⁿ'í-a/ga: Give me half (cut lengthwise)

"Wiⁿdéthoⁿ" usually refers to half the length, height, distance, or time or to half of something linear. This is why the speaker translated this as "cut lengthwise." **"Wiⁿdéthoⁿska"** and **"wiⁿdénoⁿ"** usually refer to half of a mass or abstract quantity—something nonlinear.

Wiⁿdéthoⁿska oⁿ'í-a/ga: Give me half (round or square object).

Shethóⁿnoⁿ wanáthe-a?: Are you still eating?

Shénoⁿ / Shóⁿ: I'm done / I've had enough / I have enough / That's all.

Shénoⁿ bthégoⁿ: I think I'm done.

Weóⁿnoⁿde: I'm full.

Weóⁿnoⁿde, wíbthahoⁿ: I'm full, thank you.

Weóⁿnoⁿde-xti-móⁿ: I'm really full.

Weóⁿnoⁿde ebthégoⁿ: I think I'm full.

Weóⁿnoⁿdextimoⁿ, wíbthahoⁿ: I'm really full, thank you.

Égoⁿ bthégoⁿ: I think so / I'm not sure.

Watháthe-the údoⁿ: The food is / was good.

Oⁿthásniⁿ: We swallowed it down / gobbled it up.

Watháthe-thoⁿ thishúpa/ga: Pack away the food.

Watháthe-thoⁿ thisíhi-a/ga: Clear the food.

Uxpé-the thizhái-a/ga: Wash the dishes.

úthashte: food that has been prayed over, taken home from a doings or feast

Wéta noⁿba ushté: There are two eggs left.

Énoⁿ: That's all.

Usní-atathishoⁿ
toward the cold weather

Itʰáxe-tathishoⁿ
toward the headwaters

Mí
ithé-thoⁿtathishoⁿ
toward where the sun leaves

Mí
uéthoⁿba-tathishoⁿ
toward where the sun appears

Óⁿba í-tathishoⁿ
toward the coming daylight

Moⁿshté-atathishoⁿ
toward the warm weather

Hidé-atathishoⁿ
down bottom / downriver

Shóⁿ: Enough. (Said when you've had enough. I've had the right amount.)

shóⁿ gáxe: to quit

Shóⁿ gáxa: S/he / they quit.

baniúski (also **banúski, núski, niúski**): to hiccup/burp

you hiccup/burp: **shpániuski / niúthaski;** I hiccup/burp: **pániuski / niuáski;** we hiccup/burp: **oⁿbániuski / niuóⁿski**

uthúbidoⁿ: dip / dunk / press something (like a cookie or frybread) in something else

2.25 FOUR WINDS/DIRECTIONS: TADÉ DÚBA

Translation: Marcella Woodhull Cayou and Donna Morris Parker; elicitation/transcription: Vida Woodhull Stabler.

Cultural Note

In addition to the four directions known by many, Umóⁿhoⁿ people know of two additional directions or connections to the spiritual realm. The first is a person's connection to the heavens, **Móⁿxe-atathishoⁿ**. The second is a person's connection to the earth, **Tóⁿde-atathishoⁿ**.

2.26 FOUR SEASONS

Translation: Elders; elicitation/transcription: Vida Woodhull Stabler.

> **Mépahoⁿga:** spring
> **Nugé Moⁿshté:** summer
> **Toⁿgáxthoⁿ:** fall
> **Mágashude:** winter

2.27 HANDGAME GREETINGS: Íⁿ'UTʰIⁿ THATⁿÍ

Translation: Marcella Woodhull Cayou; elicitation/transcription: Vida Woodhull Stabler; orthography check: Bryan James Gordon.

Cultural Note

The Man in Charge or the Master of Ceremony (emcee or MC) will welcome the participants. He will do this by saying the following:

> **Wóⁿgithe thatʰí-tʰe   údoⁿ, wíbthahoⁿ.**
> everybody you come that good thank you

> **Úgthiⁿ- kʰe áhigi edí.**
> seat   the lots there are

> **Thatʰí- ama gthíⁿi-ga.**
> you come the sit down
>   It's good that you all came. Thank you.
>   There are a lot of places to sit.
>   If you're just arriving, take a seat.

The Master of Ceremony, "Iyébaha / Éabaha" or Man in Charge, "Nudoⁿhoⁿga," will tell the purpose of the handgame and explain the "wager" if there

is any prior to the start of the game. The Man in Charge will sit next to the MC at the main table, so that he can relay information throughout the evening. The Man in Charge and Companion Wife both sit at the table to share the responsibility of "moving sticks" or keeping score for their side. The woman also oversees the cooking and serving of food. There is much more responsibility for all those involved in Umóⁿhoⁿ handgame. This summary tells of only a few important duties of those In Charge.

> **Oⁿdóⁿbai-a/ga. Uwíhi-tamiⁿkʰe.**
> watch me   I will beat you

Menfolk will purposely show the stone to their opponent (feather carrier of the other side).

> **Káshi ánoⁿxtha-a/ga:** Don't let them get you right away. ("Hide it a long time.")
> **Káshi thithíze thi'á:** They can't get you for a long time.
> **Wáoⁿ thashtóⁿi-a/ga:** Stop the singing.
> **Íⁿ'e uthíxpatha-bazhi-a/ga:** Don't drop the stone.

2.28 HANDGAME SETUP AND INSTRUMENTS

Translation: Marcella Woodhull Cayou, Oliver Cayou Sr., and Donna Morris Parker; elicitation/transcription: Vida Woodhull Stabler.

Setup Instructions

> **Gáthoⁿ thibthá-a/ga:** Spread that (cloth) out.

Zhóⁿzhiⁿga dúba-thoⁿthoⁿ itʰétha/ga: Put down four sticks at a time.

Íⁿ'e-tʰe noⁿbá-thoⁿthoⁿ itʰétha/ga: Put down two stones each.

Móⁿshoⁿ-tʰe édi itʰétha/ga: Put the feathers there.

Íⁿ'utʰiⁿ shkáde théwathe: Let's go play handgame.

Íⁿ'utʰiⁿ wábanoⁿ théwathe: Let's go look on at handgame.

Kʰé íⁿchʰoⁿ íⁿ'utʰiⁿ 'óⁿwathe: Come on now, let's put on a handgame.

Kʰé íⁿchʰoⁿ íⁿ'utʰiⁿ shkádewathe: Come on now, let's play handgame.

Móⁿzeska uthéwiⁿtha: To raise money.

Zhiⁿgá-ama móⁿzeska uthéwiⁿ-wákʰitha: They raised money for the children.

Shémizhiⁿga-ama ihóⁿ-thiⁿkʰe xtágitha tha'égitha úzhawa wathígthoⁿ sítha: The young women remember how their mothers loved them, took pity on them and had fun with them.

Reminiscence from Marcella Woodhull Cayou

My grandpa was a gambler and liked to play cards. Grandma liked handgames. People in the countryside with large living rooms often held handgames. Grandma would go there to play. Bonehead George Mitchell had a large place to play. We would have them on holidays. People would cook chickens potluck, not buy $200 dollars worth of meat like today. Whole chickens cost maybe 29–39 cents apiece. Somebody would get five chickens and that would be enough for a handgame. People helped make those things in those days; it seemed easy. Today people only seem to help their own. Oliver and I always liked handgames. We would go way down south of Macy to play.

2.29 HANDGAME ENCOURAGEMENTS AND GAMEPLAY

Translation: Marcella Woodhull Cayou, Oliver Cayou Sr., and Donna Morris Parker; elicitation/transcription: Vida Woodhull Stabler; additions: Donna Morris Parker and Rufus White; orthography check: Bryan James Gordon.

Gathíⁿgai-a/ga: Go all the way. (**Gathíⁿge** means "get rid of it by hitting it"; here it refers to getting rid of the sticks on the opposing team's side.)

Wiⁿóⁿxchi uáwatʰiⁿ: S/he/ they hit us in one / on the first time.

Wiⁿóⁿxchi utʰíⁿ-a?: Did they hit one?

Ánoⁿxthai-a/ga. Gathíⁿgai-a/ga: Hide it. Go all the way.

Shi óⁿguhi: We won again.

Uthúshi thá-bazhii-a/ga: Don't go in between the players.

(**Uthúshi** means "in front." Here it refers to walking between the feather and stone carriers and the players—which would mean walking in front of them, although the English translation uses the word between to describe this same position.)

Íⁿ'utʰiⁿ shkáda, íhe thá-bazhii-a/ga: Don't go in front of players.

(Here is the verb **íhe thá-bazhii-a**, "don't pass by," to discourage people from the same kind of motion as in the previous example.)

Íⁿ'utʰiⁿ oⁿ'óⁿ-ta: We're going to put on a handgame.

Tháta-tathishoⁿ utʰíⁿ-a/ga: Hit her/him on the left side.

Wéthitʰoⁿ-tathishoⁿ utʰíⁿ-a/ga: Hit her/him on the right side.

Ágthoⁿ gahá/Ákigthaha utʰíⁿ-a/ga: Hit her/him on the outside.

Uthízoⁿ utʰíⁿ-a/ga: Hit her/him down the middle.

("Down the middle" can be **ídoⁿbe** as well as **uthízoⁿ**; "outside" can be **ákigthaha** as well as **áshita**. **Ákigthaha** literally means "one on top of the other" and can refer to the hand held over the feather below.)

Wáthiza-bazhi: He didn't get them.

Wáthiza/ga: Get them.

Wathíza: They got us.

Íⁿ'utʰiⁿ oⁿshkáde-ta: We will play handgame.

Wiⁿóⁿxchi ushté: One (stick) left.

Íⁿ'utʰiⁿ wáapanoⁿ pʰí: I went to watch handgame.

Íⁿe uthíxpathazhi-a/ga: Don't drop the stone.

Áwatʰegoⁿ páxe bthí'a: I can't do it no matter what.

Iⁿwíⁿkoⁿ/ga: I need help.

Uíkoⁿ/ga: Help her/him.

Péxe-thoⁿ thisáthu / gasáthu: S/he shakes the gourd.

Zhóⁿzhiⁿga-tʰe shkóⁿzhixtioⁿ: The sticks haven't moved at all.

Shetʰóⁿnoⁿ shóⁿ-bazhi: S/he's not ready.

Shetʰóⁿnoⁿ ánoⁿxtha-bazhi: S/he hasn't hidden it yet.

Itʰétha/ga: Put it away.

Noⁿbé-tʰe thibthá/ga: Open your hands.

Donna Morris Parker's Additions

Thípahoⁿga ánoⁿxtha/ga: You hide first.

Wathíza-bazhi. Pʰi ánoⁿxtha/ga: They didn't get us. Hide it again.

Wáthiza/ga: Get them.

Wóⁿdoⁿ wáthiza/ga: Get them both.

Thípʰi shkáda/ga: Play right.

Íⁿe-thoⁿ ánoⁿxtha/ga: Hide the stone.

Gthíⁿ-wákʰitha/ga: Make them sit down.

Gthíⁿkʰitha/ga: Make her/him sit down.

Wániza?: Did you get them?

Níze-a?: Did you get her/him?

Thípahoⁿga moⁿthíⁿ-a/ga: You go first.

Thi-táthishoⁿ: Your side (hides first).

Shé-tathishoⁿ ánoⁿxtha: That side hides.

Thégithishoⁿ ánoⁿxthe-taama: This side will hide.

Óⁿganoⁿxthe-taoⁿgatʰoⁿ: Our side will hide.

Úhi-ma íⁿe-thoⁿ xátha wé'i-a/ga: Give the stone back to the winners.

Wa'ú-akʰa úhi: The women won.

Úhi-ama gíthe wachígaxa: The winners round-dance happily.

Íⁿbaha/ga: Show me.

Rufus White's Additions

Noⁿbé iⁿwíⁿtʰiⁿ-a/ga: Clap for me. (Pronounced with a short **iⁿ** sound where the two words meet: **noⁿbiⁿwíⁿtʰiⁿga**.)

Oⁿwóⁿtʰiⁿ-a/ga: Hit me.

2.30 HANDGAME GAMEPLAY PHRASES: ÍⁿUTʰIⁿ SHKÁDE-KʰE UTHÁ

Translation: Donna Morris Parker; elicitation/transcription: Vida Woodhull Stabler; orthography check: Bryan James Gordon; additions: Rufus White.

Cultural Note

We started playing "Handgame Friday" to teach the Umóⁿhoⁿ language students how to play Umóⁿhoⁿ handgame. We tell them we can play as long as there is no one "lying in state." We put the game away if the community is mourning the passing of a relative. Otherwise it is regularly played and enjoyed by our students.

Thípahoⁿga ánoⁿxtha/ga: You hide first.

Wathíza-bazhi. Pʰi ánoⁿxtha/ga: They didn't get us. Hide it again.

Wáthiza/ga: Get them.

Wóⁿdoⁿ wáthiza/ga: Get them both.

Thípʰi shkáda/ga: Play right.

Íⁿe-thoⁿ ánoⁿxtha/ga: Hide the stone.

Gthíⁿ-wákʰitha/ga: Make them sit down.

Gthíⁿkʰitha/ga: Make her/him sit down.

Wániza?: Did you get them?

Níze-a?: Did you get her/him?

Thípahoⁿga moⁿthíⁿ-a/ga: You go first.

Thi-táthishoⁿ: Your side (hides first).

Shé-tathishoⁿ ánoⁿxtha: That side hides.

Thégithishoⁿ ánoⁿxthe-taama: This side will hide.

Óⁿganoⁿxthe-taoⁿgatʰoⁿ: Our side will hide.

Úhi-ma íⁿe-thoⁿ xátha wé'i-a/ga: Give the stone back to the winners.

Wa'ú-akʰa úhi: The women won.

Úhi-ama gíthe wachígaxa: The winners round-dance happily.

Íⁿbaha/ga: Show me.

2.31 HANDGAME Q&A

Translation: Marcella Woodhull Cayou, Oliver Cayou Sr., and Donna Morris Parker; elicitation/transcription: Vida Woodhull Stabler.

Handgame Questions

Ebé nudóⁿhoⁿga?: Who are the sponsors?

UNPS Tápuska Shíⁿgazhiⁿga-ama Tíuzhi-amaé.

Zhiⁿgá-ama é nudóⁿhoⁿga gthíⁿ.

Ebé nudóⁿhoⁿga gthíⁿi-a?: Who's in charge?

(Although **nudóⁿhoⁿga** can refer either to the sponsoring family or to the People in Charge, here we can tell it's the People in Charge because of the describing verb **gthíⁿ**, "sit.")

Ebé íⁿ'utʰiⁿ-tʰe nóⁿgethe-a?: Who's in charge?

Íⁿ'utʰiⁿ-tʰe ebé nóⁿgethe-a?: Who's in charge?

Mr. & Mrs. Oliver Cayou Sr. nóⁿgetha.

Mr. & Mrs. Bill Canby é nóⁿgethe-taama.

Ebé Iyébaha?: Who is the Master of Ceremonies / Camp Crier?

Chris Fremont Iyébaha.

Mitchell Parker Iyébaha.

Ebé móⁿshoⁿ athíⁿ-a?: Who carried the feather?

Móⁿshoⁿ-kʰe ebé athíⁿ-a?: Who carried the feather?

Ázhi-thoⁿthoⁿ móⁿshoⁿ-kʰe athíⁿ: Different people carried it.

Wagóⁿze-akʰa móⁿshóⁿ athíⁿ: Teacher carried it.

Ebé íⁿ'eákʰihide?: Who watched the stones?

Wagóⁿze-akʰa íⁿ'e ákʰihida: Teacher watched them.

Ebé íⁿ'e athíⁿ?: Who carried the stones?

Wagóⁿze-akʰa íⁿ'e athíⁿ: Teacher carried them.

zhóⁿ athíⁿ: the ones who have the sticks

Ebé úhi?: Who won?

Mí u'éthoⁿba-tathisoⁿ-ama úhi: East won.

Óⁿmoⁿ-tathisoⁿ-ama úhi: The other side won.

Mí íthe-tathisoⁿ úhi: West side they won.

Mí íthe-thoⁿtathisoⁿ úhi-bazhi: The west side lost all games.

Móⁿge wáxa: They skunked them.

Mí u'éthoⁿba-tathisoⁿ gthíⁿ-ama úhi: Those sitting to the east won. (Senior citizens sit on the east side.)

Senior citizens gthíⁿ-noⁿ: Senior citizens always sit there.

Ebé Xúka Nudóⁿhoⁿga?: Who is the head singer?

Ebé Xúka-thoⁿ Nudóⁿhoⁿga / Ebé Wáoⁿ Nudóⁿhoⁿga: Who is the head singer?

Mitch Sheridan Xúka Nudóⁿhoⁿga.

Xúka Nudóⁿhoⁿga Rufus White.

Erwin Morris Xúka Nudóⁿhoⁿga.

Hóⁿadi, niáshiⁿga-ama móⁿzeska gthéboⁿhiⁿwiⁿ thábthiⁿ-ki édi gthéboⁿ dúba-ki édi thábthiⁿ thi'í: Last night, the people gave you three hundred and forty-three (343) dollars.

Íⁿ'utʰiⁿ ebé gáxe?: Who made the handgame?

2.32 HANDGAME WORKSHEET 1

Translation: Marcella Woodhull Cayou and Oliver Cayou Sr.; elicitation/transcription: Vida Woodhull Stabler; orthography check: Bryan James Gordon.

Directions

Translate the Umóⁿhoⁿ questions into **Wáxe Íye** and then fill in the blanks in the Umóⁿhoⁿ answers.

Handgame Questions

Ebé nudóⁿhoⁿga? _____

UNPS **Tápuska Shíⁿgazhiⁿga-ama Tiúzhi-ama é.**

Ebé íⁿut^{h}iⁿ-t^{h}e nóⁿgethai-a?

_____

nóⁿgetha. _____

Ebé Íyebaha? _____

_____ **Íyebaha.**

Ebé móⁿshoⁿ athíⁿ-a? _____

Ázhi-thoⁿtho móⁿshoⁿ-k^{h}e athíⁿ.

Ebé Xúka Nudóⁿhoⁿga?

_____

_____ **Xúka Nudóⁿhoⁿga.**

Xúka Nudóⁿhoⁿga _____.

Ebé úhi? _____

Mí u'éthoⁿba-tathishoⁿ-ama úhi.

2.33 HANDGAME WORKSHEET 2

Translation: Donna Morris Parker; elicitation/transcription: Vida Woodhull Stabler.

Translation

Directions: Break down the Umóⁿhoⁿ phrases below. Put the English meaning below each Umóⁿhoⁿ word. Write the complete English sentence translation to the right in the space provided. [The worksheet's top four lines are for name, date, and sample word-by-word and complete sentence translations; notes in English farther down are hints.]

Izházhe Wiwíta-t^{h}e _____

  Óⁿbathe _____

Umóⁿhoⁿ Íye "Complete Sentence" English Translation

Íⁿ'ut^{h}iⁿ   shkáde thé- wathe: Let's go play handgame.

handgame play   go   let's

Ebé Nudóⁿhoⁿga gthíⁿ-a? _____

_____

or Íⁿ'ut^{h}iⁿ ebé nóⁿgethe-a? _____

Ebé Íyebaha? _____

_____

Móⁿshoⁿ-k^{h}e ebé athíⁿ-a? _____

Ebé úhi-a? _____

_____

Ebé Xúka-thoⁿ Nudóⁿhoⁿga? _____

or Ebé Wáoⁿ Nudóⁿhoⁿga? _____

Gathíⁿgai-a/ga: Get rid of the sticks by hitting / Beat them.

Ánoⁿxthai-a/ga! Gathíⁿgai-a/ga!

_____

Wiⁿóⁿxchi uáwat^{h}iⁿ: They caught/hit us on the first time.

Wiⁿóⁿxchi ut^{h}iⁿ-a/ga: _____

_____

Shi óⁿguhi: _____

_____

Óⁿma-tathishoⁿ-ama úhi: _____

_____

Q&A

Directions: Follow along as Wagóⁿze-akʰa reads the following question and answer script. Take turns reading both the question and response. Break down the sentences after you've had time to listen and practice.

> Q: **Ebé Nudóⁿhoⁿga?**
> R: **Zhiⁿgá-ama é Nudóⁿhoⁿga gthíⁿ.**
>
> Q: **Íⁿ'utʰiⁿ-tʰe ebé nóⁿgethe-a?**
> R: **Mr. & Mrs. Cayou é Nóⁿgethe-taama.**
>
> Q: **Ebé Íyebaha?**
> R: **Mitchell Parker-akʰa Íyebaha-akʰa.**
>
> Q: **Ebé móⁿshoⁿ athíⁿ?**
> R: **Wagóⁿze-akʰa móⁿshoⁿ athíⁿ.**
>
> Q: **Ebé íⁿ'e athíⁿ?**
> R: **Wagóⁿze óⁿma-akʰa íⁿ'e athíⁿ.**
>
> Q: **Ebé Xúka Nudóⁿhoⁿga?**
> R: **Erwin Morris-akʰa Xúka Nudóⁿhoⁿga-akʰa.**
>
> Q: **Ebé úhi?**
> R: **Mí Ithé-thoⁿtathishoⁿ-ama úhi.**

2.34 HANDGAME FLYER

Cultural Note

The community of Macy has a long history of producing "flyers" for inviting the whole community to an event. They are hung at the Tribal Building, post office, and C-Store in Macy and also in neighboring Walthill. The flyers give details such as the names of the people and their roles and duties during the event and where and when the event will take place. There are times when the event requires the ceremonial carrying of tobacco to a family's home to request their help in taking care of a particular event.

Handgame & Gourd Dance

Saturday, April 20, 2002
4:00 p.m. (Gilpin Building)

Honoring Oliver Cayou, Sr.
Sponsored by His Children

Head Singer: Mitch Sheridan
Head Man Dancer: Chris Fremont
Head Lady Dancer: Pat Thundercloud
Master of Ceremony: Doran Morris
In Charge: Mr. & Mrs. Jeff Gilpin
Host Dancers: Tia Piah Society

Everyone is Invited
Special Invitation To: Macy Senior Citizens
Native American Church
Veterans of Foreign Wars

Íⁿ'utʰiⁿ, Péxe Wachígaxe-shti oⁿgáthiⁿ-taoⁿgathoⁿ

Hithái-ki, Óⁿba 20, Mí Eátoⁿ Thiⁿge-kʰe, 2002, Miídoⁿbe 4
Umóⁿhoⁿ Wachigaxe Tí Toⁿga kʰe di

Oliver Cayou, Sr., óⁿxtithe-tegoⁿ
Inísi-ama Nudóⁿhonga gthíⁿ-taama.

Mitch Sheridan Xúka Nudóⁿhoⁿga
Chris Fremont Nú Nudóⁿhoⁿga Wachígaxe
Pat Thundercloud Wa'ú Nudóⁿhoⁿga Wachígaxe
Doran Morris Iyépahoⁿ
Mr. & Mrs. Jeff Gilpin Nóⁿgethe-taama
Tia Piah Gikubanoⁿ-ma Wachígaxe Íⁿku

Wóⁿgithe iⁿthíku hó.
Thanóⁿ-mashe,
Native American Church-mashe,
Veterans of Foreign Wars-mashe-shti
thi-é-xchi iⁿthíku.

2.35 HANDWASHING: NOⁿBÉ KIGTHÍZHA-TʰE

Translation: Donna Morris Parker; transcription/elicitation: Vida Woodhull Stabler.

This material is to be used with daily routine sequence cards and integrated into daily routine in the Umóⁿhoⁿ Íye classroom. The objective is for students to be able to perform the steps as directed. The commands are given in plural form.

> **Ní-tʰe thinóⁿgai-a/ga:** Turn on the water.
>
> **Wéthitega dúba 'óⁿi-a/ga:** Use some soap.
>
> **Noⁿbé-tʰe thizhái-a/ga:** Wash your hands.
>
> **Noⁿbé-ge bigúdai-a/ga:** Scrub your hands. ("Rub the hands all over each other.")
>
> **Noⁿbé-tʰé gipíkai-a/ga:** Wipe your hands dry.
>
> **Noⁿbé íbikʰa shíshige-tʰe-di óⁿthai-a/ga:** Throw the hand towel in the trash.

2.36 HOUSEHOLD OBJECTS: IⁿDÁDOⁿ-SHTE TÍ-ADI-GE

Translation: Marcella Woodhull Cayou; elicitation/transcription: Vida Woodhull Stabler; additional phrases from "TPR Complete Phrases."

Tí Zhiⁿga: Bathroom

> **noⁿbé íbikʰa:** hand towels
>
> **iⁿdé íbikʰa:** face towel
>
> **ígadi / unézheti wagthábaze:** toilet paper
>
> **niúkigthaziⁿ:** mirror
>
> **unézheti wéthisihi:** toilet brush

> **Hí-kʰe thizhá/ga, Hí-kʰe kigthízha/ga:** Brush your teeth.
>
> **Noⁿbé-tʰe thizhá/ga, Noⁿbé-tʰe kigthízha/ga:** Wash your hands.
>
> **Sí-tʰe thizhá/ga, Sí-tʰe kigthízha/ga:** Wash your feet.
>
> **Noⁿshkí-tʰe thizhá/ga, Noⁿshkí-tʰe kigthízha/ga:** Wash your head.
>
> **Pá-tʰe thizhá/ga, Pá-tʰe kigthízha/ga:** Wash your nose.
>
> **Í-tʰe thizhá/ga, Í-tʰe kigthízha/ga:** Wash your mouth.
>
> **Iⁿshtá-thoⁿ thizhá/ga, Iⁿshtá-thoⁿ kigthízha/ga:** Wash your eyes.
>
> **Noⁿxíde-tʰe thizhá/ga, Noⁿxíde-tʰe kigthízha/ga:** Wash your ears.
>
> **Iⁿdé-thoⁿ thizhá/ga, Iⁿdé-thoⁿ kigthízha/ga:** Wash your face.
>
> **Astúhi-thoⁿ thizhá/ga, Astúhi-thoⁿ kigthízha/ga:** Wash your elbows.

Uzhóⁿ Tí: Bedroom

> **miká'e wáiⁿ pʰúga:** star quilt
>
> **iⁿbehi:** (feather) pillow
>
> **Thizú'e zhóⁿ/ga:** Lie down stretched out.
>
> **Zhóⁿ gáxa/ga:** Pretend to sleep.
>
> **Íkitha/ga:** Wake up.
>
> **Kigtházi-a/ga:** Stretch.

Uthátʰe Tí: Dining Room

> **wáthatʰe:** table
>
> **ágthiⁿ:** chair

Tiút^{h}o^{n}na: Hallway

tibábexi^n: broom

tibábexi^n-no^n: sweeper

tí wéthisihi: vacuum cleaner

Tí Ó^{n}ma-t^{h}e: Other Rooms

shíshige úzhi: garbage can

wéthishibe uthó^n: keyring

i^{n}gthó^{n}ga shíshige: cat litter

wathígtho^n waséko^n: computer

mó^{n}ze waó^n: radio / CD player

waó^n wathíze: CD / record

háthe wéthizha: washing machine

wabásada: ironing board

wéthitega úzhi: soapbox

úzhizhi: box for different things

paháshi-ta: upstairs

Táp'ska-t^{h}e-di: At School

zho^{n}mó^{n}thi^n wanó^{n}mo^{n}shi: elevator

íutha ithó^{n}thai-tho^n: the bulletin board

zho^{n}btháska ska: whiteboard

wébaxu: pencil

wébaxuni: pen

wagthábaze / wabthágaze / waxí^{n}ha: paper

weáthaskabe: tape

Tí Ágipaxui-a/ga: Write on Your House

ACTIVITY

- OBJECTIVES: Create useful phrases centered around home life, reinforce "I" form of future tense **tami^{n}k^{h}e** and **bth** verb pattern, and introduce new verb **áthade** ("read").
- MATERIALS: Paper, markers, pencils, household objects

Students or households may create sentences about activities in their house using available vocabulary and eliciting sentences from Elders, drawing scenes and labeling them with the sentences to display at home. Some sentences we created in class:

Úgaxe shkó^{n}shko^n téga bthíwi^n: I bought a new TV ("moving picture").

Waxtáhi-t^{h}e újo^n: The plant is pretty.

Wagthábaze ábthade-tami^{n}k^{h}e: I am going to read a book.

Úgaxe shkó^{n}shko^n ápano^n-tami^{n}k^{h}e: I am going to watch TV.

Úgaxe shkó^{n}shko^n-k^{h}e íutha-no^n: The TV tells the news.

Thigthíze wíuho^n-t^{h}e-di úaho^n-tami^{n}k^{h}e: I am going to cook in the microwave.

Ó^{n}aze-tho^n thimó^{n}shi-a/ga: Raise the shade.

Ó^{n}aze-tho^n thihída/ga: Lower the blind.

2.37 INVITING AND VISITING: WÉKU TIÚPE ÉTHOⁿBA

Translation: Marcella Woodhull Cayou; elicitation/transcription: Vida Woodhull Stabler.

Wóⁿgithe wíku: I invite all of you.

Mí-thoⁿ umóⁿshi watháthe wíku (Míthumoⁿshi watháthe wíku): I invite you for the noon meal.

Watháthe zhuóⁿgthe íi-a/ga (zhóⁿgthe): Come eat with me.

Watháthe-the íia-ga: Come eat.

Shi xátha gíi-a/ga: Come back again.

Shi tiúpe athí-tamiⁿkhe: I will visit again.

Shi tióⁿwoⁿpa/ga: Visit me again.

Tiúpe shuphí-tamiⁿkhe: I will come by to visit you.

2.38 IN THE KITCHEN: ÚHOⁿ TÍ-ADI

Translation: Marcella Woodhull Cayou and Donna Morris Parker; elicitation/transcription: Vida Woodhull Stabler.

Íye Úmakha-ge: Basic Vocabulary

úhoⁿ tí: kitchen ("cooking house")

wágthe: counter ("stand things up on")

tehé úzhi: drawer ("put spoons in")

wáthathe: table ("eat on")

ágthiⁿ: chair ("sit on")

miídoⁿbe: clock ("see sun with")

shíshige úzhi: garbage can ("put garbage in")

wíugoⁿba: window ("illuminate with")

wíugoⁿba ithágaxade: curtain ("cover window with")

úzhi kúge: shelf ("box to put in")

uxpé úgthe: cupboard ("stand dishes up in")

uxpé úzhi: dish rack / cupboard / cabinet ("put dishes in")

úhoⁿ wagthábaze áthade: read a cookbook

nóⁿxe wamúske skíthe úzhi: cookie jar ("glass to put sweet bread in")

wéganazhi: fire extinguisher ("tool to blow out fire with")

Uxpé, Úzhi-shti Ázhi-thoⁿthoⁿ: Dishes and Containers

uxpé: plate

taní uxpé / taní úzhi uxpébuta: bowl ("soup dish / put soup in / round dish")

uxpé basása: divided plate ("cut-up dish")

niúthatoⁿ: cup ("drink water in")

moⁿkóⁿsabe niúthatoⁿ: coffee cup

nóⁿxe: glass

tehé: spoon ("buffalo horn")

wáku: fork ("piercer / awl")

móⁿhi: knife

noⁿbé íbikha: napkin ("wipe hand with")

móⁿze ubéthoⁿ / móⁿze bethóⁿtoⁿ: tin foil ("wrap in metal / wrap and wrap metal")

móⁿze úzhi: can ("put in metal")

úthashte úzhi: ziploc / tupperware ("put leftovers in")

wamúska xúde úzhi: flour canister ("put grey wheat in")

zhoⁿní úzhi: sugar canister ("put tree sap in")

moⁿkóⁿsabe úzhi: coffee can ("put black medicine in")

wawégahi úzhi / wawíugahi úzhi: baking powder / frosting can ("put what is mixed in")

wégthi úzhi: grease can ("put grease in")

péxeha toⁿga: gallon container ("big gourd rattle")

wégoⁿze: gallon ("measurement / amount")

Úhoⁿ Wéthihide Ázhi-thoⁿthoⁿ: Cooking Utensils and Appliances

wébasoⁿtha: spatula ("turn by pushing with")

tehé toⁿga: serving spoon ("big buffalo horn")

wébashnade: tongs ("pluck bare with")

wamúska íbibthaska: rolling pin ("pull bread flat with")

móⁿze wéthishibe: can opener ("open metal with")

uxpé úzhi: dish rack / cupboard / cabinet ("put dishes in")

ukígthizha: sink ("wash oneself in")

uxpé ukígthizha / úhoⁿ tí ukígthizha: kitchen sink

umútoⁿthiⁿ: turn (water) on in (sink) ("make it flow and run in")

ní-tʰe thixtóⁿ: faucet ("pours the water")

uxpé íbikʰa: dishtowel ("wipe dishes with")

uxpé íthizha wéthihide: dishwasher ("tool to wash dishes with")

wíuhoⁿ: pot / pan ("cook with")

weáthitabe: pot holder

íkóⁿthe: handle ("hold steady with")

néxe: skillet / kettle ("bladder")

néxe shuga wézhegthoⁿ: cast-iron skillet ("thick bladder to roast / fry with")

wézhezhi: skillet / frying pan ("tool to fry / roast with")

thigthíze wíuhoⁿ: electric skillet / microwave "(forked lightning to cook with")

uxpé ugáu'ude: strainer ("dish with holes beat in it")

wanáxude ígaxe: toaster ("make burnt-gray with")

móⁿze unéthe: stove ("metal fireplace")

uzhégthoⁿ: oven ("roast / fry in")

uzhéoⁿhe: stove / oven ("roast in")

péde / pédinaxthiⁿ: match ("fire / use to light fire")

thigthíze uzhégthoⁿ: microwave ("forked lightning to roast / fry in")

núxe úzhi: icebox / refrigerator ("put ice in")

Uxpé-tʰe móⁿze gasása-tʰe uzhí-a itʰétha, gabíze-taakʰa: Put the dishes in the metal rack ("divided up metal") and they will dry.

Ukígthizha úhoⁿ tí, uxpé uthízha-tʰe, uxpé uzhí-a, ní-tʰe umútoⁿthiⁿ-a: The kitchen sink, to wash dishes, put the dishes in and turn the water on.

Wéta-tʰe núxe úzhi-tʰedi itʰétha/ga: Put the eggs in the fridge.

2.39 MONEY: MÓⁿZESKA

Translation: Marcella Woodhull Cayou; elicitation/transcription: Vida Woodhull Stabler.

Bills

wíⁿbthuga: one dollar

móⁿzeska sátoⁿ: five dollars

móⁿzeska gthéboⁿ: ten dollars

móⁿzeska gthéboⁿ noⁿbá: twenty dollars

móⁿzeska gthéboⁿ sátoⁿ: fifty dollars

móⁿzeska gthéboⁿhiwiⁿ: one hundred dollars

kúge wíⁿ: one thousand dollars

Coins

wéthawa zhíde: penny ("red counter")

wéthawa: nickel ("counter")

shugá zhiⁿga: dime ("little thick one")

mikáha íthawa: quarter ("used to count coonskins")

moⁿsóⁿthiha: half dollar

móⁿzeska wíⁿbthuga: silver dollar

Phrases

Ánoⁿ íthawa? / Ánoⁿ íthawai-a?: How much does it cost?

íthawa áhigi: something that costs a lot

móⁿzeska áhigi-áchoⁿ: an awful lot of money / too expensive

Ánoⁿ-a?: How much?

íkikawiⁿthe: change

Móⁿzeska ánoⁿ oⁿthá'i-a?: How much money do you give me?

Wíⁿbthuga oⁿwóⁿ'i-a/ga: Can I borrow a dollar? ("Lend me a dollar.")

Oⁿthá'i-te: Please give it to me.

2.40 MONTHS OF THE UMÓⁿHOⁿ CALENDAR YEAR: MÍ-Kᴴᴇ

Translation: Marcella Woodhull Cayou and Donna Morris Parker; published source: Fletcher and La Flesche, *The Omaha Tribe*.

There are several points to make regarding the months of the Umóⁿhoⁿ year. First, the new year is heralded in with the First Thunder in traditional Umóⁿhoⁿ belief. This usually happens from March to April. However, for the purpose of this book, we start with January, in line with how the months are started in *The Omaha Tribe* by Alice C. Fletcher and Francis La Flesche. Discussions with fluent Elders Marcella Cayou and Donna Morris Parker generated alternative ways to say in Umóⁿhoⁿ the English meaning. Some of these changes were as minor as the inclusion of one word here or there. Following are the months used at Umóⁿhoⁿ Nation Public School.

January: **Hóⁿga Umúbthii-kʰe** ("When the snow drifts into the tents of the Hóⁿga")

February: **Míxa toⁿga mí agthíi-kʰe** ("When the geese come home")

March: **Pénishka mí etái-kʰe** ("The little frog moon")

April: **Mí eátoⁿ thiⁿgé-kʰe** ("The moon in which nothing happens")

May: **Mí wá'ai-k^{h}e** ("The moon in which they plant")

June: **Tenúga míga unái-k^{h}e** ("The moon when the buffalo bull looks for buffalo cows")

July: **Té hút^{h}o^{n}i-k^{h}e** ("The moon when the buffalo bellows")

August: **Ó^{n}p^{h}o^n hút^{h}o^{n}i-k^{h}e** ("The moon when the elk bellows")

September: **Táxti mo^{n}nó^n'ai-k^{h}e** ("The moon when the deer paw the earth")

October: **Táxti kigthíxai-k^{h}e/Táxti kigthígtho^{n}i-k^{h}e** ("The moon when the deer rut")

November: **Táxti hé baxó^{n}i-k^{h}e** ("The moon when the deer shed antlers")

December: **Wasábe zhi^{n}ga ídai-k^{h}e** ("The moon when the little black bear is born")

The names for the months corresponding to May and September both have the same verb root, **'é** referring to "scattering." The stem, or powerhouse, in the name given for May is **á'e** "scatter on something," referring to the sowing of seeds; in the name for September it is **mo^{n}nó^n'e** "scatter earth using one's feet," referring to pawing. The vowel becomes **a** because it is followed by the verb ending **-i**.

2.41 NUMBERS: WATHÁWA

wí^n / wi^{n}o^n-xchi: one / just one

no^{n}ba: two

thábthi^n: three

dúba: four

sáto^n: five

shápe: six

pétho^{n}ba: seven

pethábthi^n: eight

shó^{n}ka: nine

gthébo^n: ten

agthí^n wí^n: eleven

shápe no^{n}bá: twelve ("two sixes")

agthí^n thábthi^n: thirteen

agthí^n dúba: fourteen

agthí^n sáto^n: fifteen

agthí^n shápe: sixteen

agthí^n pétho^{n}ba: seventeen

agthí^n pethábthi^n: eighteen

agthí^n shó^{n}ka: nineteen

gthébo^n no^{n}ba: twenty ("two tens")

gthébo^n no^{n}bá k^{h}i édi wi^{n}ó^n-xchi: twenty-one

gthébo^n no^{n}ba k^{h}i édi no^{n}bá: twenty-two

gthébo^n tháthi^n: thirty

gthébo^n dúba: forty

gthébo^{n}hiwi^n: one hundred

gthébo^{n}hiwi^n k^{h}i édi wi^{n}ó^n-xchi: one hundred and one

gthébo^{n}hiwi^n k^{h}i édi gthébo^n: one hundred and ten

gthébo^{n}hiwi^n k^{h}i édi agthí^n shó^{n}ka: one hundred and nineteen

gthébo^{n}hiwi^n no^{n}ba: two hundred

gthébo^{n}hiwi^n thábthi^n: three hundred

gthéboⁿhiwiⁿ dúba kʰi édi gthéboⁿ sátoⁿ
kʰi édi péthoⁿba: four hundred fifty-
seven

kúge / kúge wíⁿ: one thousand

kúge wíⁿ kʰi édi gthéboⁿhiwiⁿ shóⁿka
kʰi édi gthéboⁿ shóⁿka kʰi édi shóⁿka:
nineteen ninety-nine

2.42 OPPOSITES

Translation: Donna Morris Parker, Marcella Woodhull Cayou, and Susan Freemont; elicitation/transcription: Vida Woodhull Stabler.

gíthe: happy

gítha-bazhi: sad

usíhi: clean

shnábe: dirty

zhóⁿ: sleep / lie down

íkithe: wake up

pá-ta / itʰóⁿthiⁿ-ata: in front

náze / náza-ta: in back

ágaha: on top / outside

kigthá-ta: at the bottom

áshi-ta: outside

móⁿtʰa-ta: inside / underneath

bóⁿ thahégazhi: yell

xthíazhi: be quiet

za'é: noise

núka: wet

bíze: dry

shtíde: warm

ásni: cool

nákʰade: hot

usní: cold

toⁿga: big

zhiⁿga: little

wéthitʰoⁿ: right

thátʰa: left

moⁿshíadi: tall

chéshka: short

móⁿshi: high up

hide: low down

noⁿzhíⁿ: stand

gthíⁿ: sit

téga: new

itʰóⁿthiⁿadi: old (The word for "old," itʰóⁿthiⁿadi, breaks down to "in front," because the Umóⁿhoⁿ cultural metaphor of the past is in front, where we can see it, not behind us as in English.)

wasékoⁿ: fast

wasníde: slow

úmakʰa: cheap

hégazhi: expensive / a lot

téxi: difficult

úmakʰa: easy

júba-xchi: a little bit

áhigi-áchoⁿ: a lot

xthá: skinny

shíⁿ: fat

Mépahoⁿga: spring

Toⁿgáxthoⁿ: fall

Moⁿshté / Nugé: summer

Usní / Mágashude: winter

2.43 OUTSIDE AND PLAY: ÁSHI SHKÁDE THÉ-WATHE

Translation: Marcella Woodhull Cayou, Susan Freemont, and Donna Morris Parker; elicitation/transcription: Vida Woodhull Stabler.

Today is a bright, warm day. We want to take the young girls outside to play. We played kick ball. We played running games also. We were really having a good time but the bugs started to bite us. They were biting us so much we had to go back inside the school. We went inside to dance. I taught the girls to put shawls on each other. They shook hands with each other too.

Tabé-tho^n no^{n}t^{h}á/ga: Kick the ball.

Tabé-tho^n thanó^{n}t^{h}e-a?: Did you kick the ball?

Tabé-tho^n anó^{n}t^{h}e: I kicked the ball.

Házhi^{n}ga u'ó^{n}si-tho^{n}tho^n/ga: Jump rope.

Házhi^{n}ga-k^{h}e uthá'o^{n}sisi-a?: Did you jump rope?

Házhi^{n}ga uá'o^{n}sisi: I jumped rope.

No^{n}hégazhi mo^{n}thí^n-a/ga: Run fast!

Thanó^{n}hegazhi-a?: Did you run fast?

Anó^{n}hega-mazhi (Anó^{n}hegamash): I ran fast.

2.44 RELATIONSHIP TERMS: ÉAWATHE

Translation: Marcella Woodhull Cayou, Donna Morris Parker, Rufus White, and Clifford Wolfe Jr.; elicitation/transcription: Vida Woodhull Stabler.

FEMALE SPEAKING TO	MALE SPEAKING TO	SPEAKING ABOUT MY	ENGLISH TRANSLATION
Dadihá	Dadího	I^{n}dádi-ak^{h}a	father
No^{n}há	No^{n}hó	Í^{n}no^{n}ha-ak^{h}a	mother
Mámato^{n}ga /		Í^{n}no^{n}ha to^{n}ga-ak^{h}a	mother's big sister
Mámazhi^{n}ga		Í^{n}no^{n}ha zhi^{n}ga-ak^{h}a	mother's little sister
Tigo^{n}há	Tigó^{n}ho	Witígo^n-ak^{h}a	grandfather
Ko^{n}há	Ko^{n}hó	Wikó^n-ak^{h}a	grandmother
Tinuhá		Witínu-ak^{h}a	female's big brother
	Zhi^{n}thého	Wizhí^{n}the-ak^{h}a	male's big brother
Zho^{n}thehá		Wizhó^{n}the-ak^{h}a	female's big sister
	To^{n}gého	Witó^{n}ge-ak^{h}a	male's sister
Wihé / Wihézhi^{n}ga		Wihé-ak^{h}a / Witó^{n}ge-ak^{h}a	female's little sister
K^{h}agézhi^{n}ga		Wik^{h}ágezhi^{n}ga-ak^{h}a	female's little brother
	K^{h}agéso^{n}gaho	Wik^{h}ágeso^{n}ga-ak^{h}a	male's little brother

FEMALE SPEAKING TO	MALE SPEAKING TO	SPEAKING ABOUT MY	ENGLISH TRANSLATION
Kʰagé	Kʰagého	Wikʰáge-akʰa	friend
Thanóⁿ		Wiégthoⁿge-akʰa	husband
	Wigáxthoⁿ / Thanóⁿho	Wigáxthoⁿ-akʰa	wife
Shikoⁿhá		Wishíkoⁿ-akʰa	female's sister-in-law
	Hoⁿgáho	Wihóⁿga-akʰa	male's sister-in-law
Wishí'e		Wishí'e-akʰa	female's brother-in-law
	Tahóⁿho	Witáhoⁿ-akʰa	male's brother-in-law
Negihá	Negího	Winégi-akʰa	uncle
Timihá	Timího	Witími-akʰa	aunt
Wihé	Nisího	Wizhóⁿge-akʰa / Winísi-akʰa	daughter / female's sister's daughter / male's brother's daughter
Kʰagé	Nisího	Wizhíⁿge-akʰa / Winísi-akʰa	son / female's sister's son / male's brother's son
Tushpahá / Wihé	Tushpáho	Witúshpa-akʰa	granddaughter
Tushpahá / Kʰagé	Tushpáho	Witúshpa-akʰa	grandson
Wihé		Witúzhoⁿge-akʰa	female's niece (brother's daughter)
	Tizhóⁿho	Witízhoⁿ-akʰa	male's niece (sister's daughter)
Tushkahá		Witúshka-akʰa	female's nephew (brother's son)
	Toⁿshkáho	Witóⁿshka-akʰa	male's nephew (sister's son)
	Toⁿdého	Witóⁿde-akʰa	son-in-law
Míwathixe / Tinihá		Míwathixe-akʰa / Witíni-akʰa	daughter-in-law

Conjugation of éthe: related

SPEAKING ABOUT	ENGLISH TRANSLATION	SPEAKING TO
éthe	her/his relative	
étha	their relative	
éthathe	your relative	
éthatha	you-all's relative	
éathe	my relative	éwithe
éonᵗha	our relative	éonᵗhithe
éwathe	her/his relatives	
éwatha	their relatives	
éwathathe	your relatives	
éwathatha	you-all's relatives	
éawathe	my relatives	éwitha
éonwonᵗha	our relatives	éonᵗhitha

Cultural Note

I was told that **Wihé** could be used by an older female when she addresses a younger female. I would think this might happen when the relationship is not known. Therefore, respect is still shown by using **Wihé** to address the female relative. — Vida Woodhull Stabler

Reminiscence from Marcella Woodhull Cayou

My childhood friends included Mary Louise Grant, my step-father's sister. She lived down bottom. She'd come home with me and stay with us. Others came over to stay, too. They would help around the house and stay with us. It was common to have extended family members staying with us.

I met my future husband when he was in the service. He was seven years older than me. His girlfriend introduced me to him. She still doesn't like me today. Living out in the countryside was better than how we are gathered together today. You could have animals. We had a dog named Jiggs. He would come meet us as we rode the wagon home down bottom. He would bark at us all the way home. It did not bother the horses. Grandma would always feed him when we got home. Maybe that is why he would never stray far from home. We were married in 1952. We had four girls and three boys.

My grandmother on my mother's side lived a long time, as did her mother. Now that Oliver is gone I miss them, too. Orville is the first born son. He was born 1953, when I was seventeen years old. We were living in Omaha at the time. Grandma Margaret and Grandma Jeanette and others would come and check on us. They would put Orville on the baby board and help take care of him. Other relatives living nearby would also check on us and the baby. He was small, but then many of our family on one side were small. On the other side many were taller and larger.

Oliver worked at United States Cold Storage in South Omaha. Orville was eight or ten years old. Then we had Janice, Junior, and Vanessa. Oliver said he did not want to raise his children in the city. He said let's just go home and he would find something there. So we returned to Macy. Orville had already started school in Omaha.

**2.45 RESTROOM PHRASES:
TÍ ZHIⁿGA UTHÁ**

Translation: Donna Morris Parker; transcription/elicitation: Vida Woodhull Stabler.

Tí zhiⁿga-ta bthé kóⁿbtha: I want to go to the bathroom.

Tí zhiⁿga-tʰe águdi-a?: Where is the bathroom?

Tí zhiⁿga-tʰe-di wíⁿ edí. Tizhébe-tʰe uthídoⁿ: There's somebody in the bathroom. The door is locked.

Tí zhiⁿga-tʰe usíhi, thizhá: The bathroom is clean, they washed it.

Tí zhiⁿga-tʰe ígadi thiⁿgé: The bathroom is out of toilet paper.

Tí zhiⁿga-ta pʰí ígadi-tʰe édi dúba itʰétha: I went to the bathroom, they put some toilet paper in there.

Ígadi dúba uzhí pʰi-tʰe, tí zhiⁿga-tʰe-di: I must have gone to put some toilet paper in the bathroom.

Tí zhiⁿga-tʰe-di zhoⁿbtháska-kʰe úsihi: The bathroom floor is clean.

Tí zhiⁿga-tʰe-di zhoⁿbtháska-kʰe shnábe: The bathroom floor is dirty.

Tí zhiⁿga-tʰe-di zhoⁿbtháska-kʰe núka: The bathroom floor is wet.

Noⁿbé-tʰe thizhá/ga: Wash your hands.

Noⁿbé-tʰe thizhái-a/ga: All of you wash your hands.

Tí zhiⁿga-ta shí níshtoⁿ-ki noⁿbé-tʰe thizhá/ga: When you're done going to the bathroom wash your hands.

Noⁿbé-tʰe thizhádoⁿ bibíza/ga: Dry your hands (while spreading your fingers wide—**thizhádoⁿ**, "to get between the fingers").

Cultural Note

Tí zhiⁿga ("house little") refers to a time when outhouses were in common use. Umóⁿhoⁿ has words to describe detail regarding restroom phrases.

**2.46 TELEPHONE PHRASES:
MÓⁿZE ÍUTHA UTHÁ**

Translation: Donna Morris Parker; additional translations: Susan Freemont; elicitation/transcription: Vida Woodhull Stabler.

ULCC at Umóⁿhoⁿ Nation Public School

Begin with one of these phrases:

Óⁿba-tʰe údoⁿ: The day is good.

Édi níⁿ-a?: Are you there?

Eyóⁿ níⁿ-a?: How are you?

Wí-e-bthiⁿ: It's me.

Ms. Woodhull bthíⁿ: It's me, Ms. Woodhull.

Respond with one of these phrases:

Édi bthíⁿ: I'm here.

Ebé uthákʰiye shkóⁿna?: Who do you want to talk to?

Iⁿdádoⁿ shkóⁿna?: What do you want?

Ebé shkóⁿna?: Who do you want?

Ebé nín, indádon shkónna?: Who are you, and what do you want?

Eáton-a?: What's the matter?

Continue:

Uwíkhiye kónbtha: I want to talk to you.

Ms. Woodhull uákhiye kónbtha: I want to talk to Ms. Woodhull.

Nú-akha uthíkhiye góntha: He wants to talk to you.

Edí-bazhi: S/he's not here.

Nonhéba/ga, tí ónma-khe-ta: Wait, s/he's in the other room.

Nonhéba/ga, apíbthe-taminkhe: Wait, I'll go get her/him.

Théthudi-bazhi: S/he's not around here.

Agthí-bazhi: S/he hasn't come back yet.

Shethónna athí-bazhi: S/he isn't here yet.

Mónze íutha gónche gíbon/ga: Call for her/him later.

Shethónna zhón: S/he's still asleep.

2.47 TIME (TELLING TIME FROM THE CLOCK): MIÍDONBE ÁNON-A?

Sources: ULCC materials "Telling Time," "Morning Commands," and "Prom Script" (Creighton Saunsoci and Austin Kaaihue); material from teacherspayteachers.com; and "Roll the Time" by "Miss Giraffe."

Íye-ge: Phrases

You won't need all of these phrases for your game, but they are provided so you can learn them.

- **Miídonbe-thon donbá/ga:** Look at the clock.

- **miídonbe ánon-ki:** at what time (used in a sentence about something that hasn't happened yet)

- **miídonbe ánon-thedi:** at what time (used in a sentence about something that has already happened)

- **Miídonbe ánon-thedi íthakithe?:** What time did you get up this morning?

- **Miídonbe ánon-a?:** What time is it?

- **miídonbe _____ ákhusonde:** past _____ o'clock

- **miídonbe _____ -ki edi windéthon:** half past _____

- **miídonbe _____ -ki edi mikáhithawa:** quarter past _____

- How to say complicated times like "8:38": **miídonbe _____ -ki edi _____**

- (8:38 = **miídonbe pethábthin-ki edi gthébon thábthin-ki edi pethábthin**)

Sudden-Elimination Tournament

Sit in groups of three. One student rolls while two try to survive elimination. Half the groups sit to the south, half of them to the north. North plays against south in the final round. Students left over with no group of three automatically advance.

Roller rolls two dice and announces the outcome. (E.g., **"Shóⁿka aóⁿbtha."**)

Roller rolls two dice again and announces the outcome. (E.g., **"Péthoⁿba aóⁿbtha."**)

The player who says the time in Umóⁿhoⁿ Íye first advances.

Roller decides which answers were correct and which one was first. In the event of a tie, roller may roll again.

Each group member takes turn rolling so that everybody has two chances to avoid elimination. After everybody has rolled once in all groups, students who have not said the time first are eliminated and new groups are formed for the next round.

Form new groups on the same side of the room. If you have to make a group out of both north and south (like in the final round), they sit on the north and south sides of a table in the middle.

Students who are eliminated may choose another student on the same side (north or south) and help them by whispering hard numbers to them. Each player can have only one helper at a time.

When there are only three students left, all three take turns rolling as usual. If one of them wins twice, that person wins the tournament. If all three win once, then an overtime round must be played.

If all students from one side are eliminated before the final round, the other side wins, but students may continue playing to find a final individual winner too. (This won't happen if the groups are formed evenly like in the examples that follow.)

Example Games

10 students in class:

Round 1 has 2 groups on south side and 1 on north with 1 student left over. South eliminates 2 and north eliminates 1.

In round 2 form 1 group on south side with 1 left over. North forms 1 group. Each eliminates 1.

In round 3 form 1 group on south side with 2 students waiting on north. South eliminates 1.

Round 4 has 1 group in the middle with 2 south students and 1 north. The other north student waits. 1 is eliminated.

16 students in class:

Round 1 has 3 groups on south side and 2 on north with 1 student left over on north. South eliminates 3 and north eliminates 2 in round 1.

In round 2 form 2 groups on south side and 1 group on north with 2 students left over. South eliminates 2 and north eliminates 1 in round 2.

In round 3 form 1 group on south side with 1 student left over, and 1 group on north with 1 student left over. Both sides eliminate 1 student.

In round 4 form 1 group on each side and eliminate 1 on each.

In round 5 form 1 group in the middle with 2 students from south and 1 from north. 1 north student is left over.

Round 6 is the final round unless overtime is needed.

13 students in class:

Round 1 has 2 groups on each side with 1 student left over on south. 2 are eliminated from each side.

Round 2 has 1 group on each side, with 2 left over on south and 1 left over on north. 1 is eliminated from each side.

Round 3 has 1 group on each side, with 1 left over on south. 1 is eliminated from each side.

Round 4 has 1 group on south, and 2 students waiting on north. South eliminates 1.

Round 5 has 1 group in the middle with 2 south students and 1 north. The other north student waits. 1 is eliminated.

2.48 TIME (YESTERDAY, TODAY, TOMORROW): SIDÁDI Ó^{n}BATHE GASÓ^{n}THI^n

Mystery Sentence

Sidádi	Wakó^{n}da	watháho^n	p^{h}í.
yesterday	Wakó^{n}da	pray / give thanks	I went

Yesterday I went (to make prayers / give thanks to God).

Vocabulary

What kinds of words do we need to express when we do or have done things? Today we'll learn a few.

sidádi: yesterday

ó^{n}bathe: today

gasó^{n}thi^n: tomorrow

The word for asking "when" is **at^{h}ó^n**. It is used with the ending **-ki** "when / if," **-kizhi** "if," or **-shte** "whenever / if ever maybe," when we ask when something will happen that has not yet happened. When we ask when something happened in the past, we use this word with the ending **-di** "at / on / in."

2.49 TIME OF DAY

Translation: Marcella Woodhull Cayou and Donna Morris Parker; compiled by Bryan James Gordon from "Door Phrases," "Clue Gameplay," and Dorsey and Elizabeth Stabler.

hé^{n}go^{n}ch^{h}a-xchi: early morning

ó^{n}ba aí / ó^{n}ba zhíde: dawn ("day is coming")

hé^{n}go^{n}ch^{h}e, also **ho^{n}égo^{n}ch^{h}e, hé^{n}gach^{h}e:** morning ("when it is a little dark")

míthumo^{n}shi híazhi: mid-morning ("not yet noon")

míthumo^{n}shi zhi^{n}ga: just before noon

míthumo^{n}shi-xti: exact noon / high noon / 12:00

míthumo^{n}shi, also **mítho^{n}mo^{n}shi, mítho^n umó^{n}shi:** afternoon ("the sun is high")

míthumo^{n}shi ák'so^{n}de / míthumo^{n}shi thishtó^n / míthumo^{n}shi átasho^n: past noon

páze: evening / twilight

hó^n: night / darkness

hó^n wi^{n}dét^{h}o^n / hó^{n}skaska: midnight

Noon / afternoon is often expressed as **mí-tho^n mó^{n}shi** "the sun is high" or **mí-tho^n umó^{n}shi** "the sun is high." These ways of saying it have the same meaning as **míthumo^{n}shi.** (**Míthumo^{n}shi** in fact is a shortened way of saying **mí-tho^n umó^{n}shi.**)

These words originally referred to a point in the sun's journey and the presence or absence of light. Today they have come to take on modern meanings referring to the times *after* those points. "Morning" is the time *after* it is a little dark. "Afternoon" is the time *after* the sun is high. "Evening" is the time during and *after* twilight (except from May to July when our modern "evening" begins well before sunset).

Umó^{n}ho^n Íye uses the ending **-di** to refer to the most recently passed time. So **hé^{n}go^{n}ch^{h}a-di** means "this morning" after the morning has passed, and **páze-adi** means "yesterday evening" or even "last night before bedtime." The past afternoon is **míthumo^{n}shi-adi.** "Last night" is **hó^n-di.**

Use the ending **-ki** if the time has not yet come. So "tomorrow morning" is **hé^{n}go^{n}ch^{h}e-ki,** the following afternoon is **míthumo^{n}shi-ki,** "this evening" before it arrives is **páze-ki,** and "tonight" before it arrives is **hó^n-ki.**

Cultural Note

There is a time to do things, for actions to take place. Umó^{n}ho^n people believe in rising early and getting busy with the day to come. First, greet the day with prayer. With a clear mind, the rest of day can take shape. Throughout the day, whatever you're doing, do the best you can. Cook early enough so you can feed your family before dark. If attending a doings, don't leave your food unattended outside, and take it home with you, if possible before dark. Don't remain outside in the dark to play. Always return home before dark. There are many Umó^{n}ho^n beliefs regarding night. Ask your family members to teach them to you.

2.50 UMÓ^{N}HO^N LANGUAGE PLEDGE: WÓ^{N}GITHE O^{N}THÍP^{H}I

Translation: Marcella Woodhull Cayou and Donna Morris Parker; elicitation/transcription: Vida Woodhull Stabler.

Wó^{n}githe o^{n}thíp^{h}i.

We all learn it.

Wó^{n}githe eó^{n}githo^n.

We all speak it.

Wó^{n}githe i^{n}wí^{n}go^{n}za.

We all teach it.

Wó^{n}githe o^{n}thó^{n}baho^n.

We all know it.

Wó^{n}githe o^{n}níta o^{n}mó^{n}thi^n.

We all live it.

Ó^{n}ba itháugthe o^{n}gát^{h}i.

Every day we're here.

Cultural Note

Vida Woodhull Stabler.

This pledge to speak the Umóⁿhoⁿ language came about because we want our children and our people to commit to speaking what they learn both at home and here at school. We need to break through the fear we have of making mistakes, mispronouncing words, and the struggle we feel when speaking our language. Our Elders learned how to speak in a natural way in their homes, from their mothers first. They learned and grew in language over the course of the stages of life. They had the support of family and community rich in our language. It was spoken by all. Today it is difficult to find a place to hear fluent Umóⁿhoⁿ language. Given this challenge, we must continue in our daily lives to try our best to speak and to contribute to the life of our language. Be brave—**Umóⁿhoⁿ iye shoⁿshoⁿ. Washkóⁿ-a**!

2.51 WELLNESS ACTIONS AND THE FOUR HILLS OF LIFE WELLNESS CENTER: NIYÉ THIⁿGÉ TÍ-ADI WÁGAZHI, PAHÉ DÚBA NÍTA MOⁿTHÍⁿ

Translation: Marcella Woodhull Cayou and Donna Morris Parker; additions from "TPR Complete Phrases"; elicitation/transcription: Vida Woodhull Stabler.

Cultural Preface

From Pauline Tyndall, "Addressing the Healers," 1984; permission for use granted by Dennis Tyndall on June 8, 2016.

The Umoⁿhoⁿ people believe in the oneness of life, the interconnectedness of all of life, and respect for every living thing. Traditionally the people went to one person, a medicine man, for healing. Many people continue this practice today. The medicine man never treats only one aspect of the person's condition. He treats the whole person and has a deep understanding of the interconnectedness of the mind, body, and spirit. For this reason it is difficult for many of our population to comprehend the dominant culture's practice of going to a particular person for one type of problem and another for something else. The overspecialization that has resulted in fragmented knowledge and services to the people has not yet occurred here. It should be avoided if we are to provide services in a way that is congruent with the values and ways of the people. Within this program, services must be provided holistically in order that the client may feel trust and confidence in the provider as well as for the provider to have more complete understanding of the individual.

Shtídekithe: Warmup

ÁBITʰAI-A/GA SHI THIHÓⁿI-A/GA

Noⁿshkí-thoⁿ ábitʰai-a/ga: Touch your head.

Pá-tʰe ábitʰai-a/ga: Touch your nose.

Í-tʰe ábitʰai-a/ga: Touch your mouth.

Iⁿshtá-thoⁿ ábitʰai-a/ga: Touch your eye.

Noⁿxíde-tʰe ábitʰai-a/ga: Touch your ears.

Iⁿdé-thoⁿ ábitʰai-a/ga: Touch your face.

Noⁿzhíha-thoⁿ ábitʰai-a/ga: Touch your hair.

Iⁿkʰéde-thoⁿ ábitʰai-a/ga: Touch your shoulders.

Sí-tʰe ábitʰai-a/ga: Touch your feet.

Noⁿbé-tʰe ábitʰai-a/ga: Touch your hand.

Á-kʰe ábitʰai-a/ga: Touch your arm.

Zhíbe-kʰe ábitʰai-a/ga: Touch your leg.

Páhi-kʰe ábitʰai-a/ga: Touch your neck.

Núde-kʰe ábitʰai-a/ga: Touch your throat.

Astúhi-thoⁿ ábitʰai-a/ga: Touch your elbow.

Shinóⁿde-thoⁿ ábitʰai-a/ga: Touch your knee.

Noⁿbéhi ábitʰai-a/ga: Touch your fingers.

Sipá-tʰe ábitʰai-a/ga: Touch your toes.

Sikóⁿ ábitʰai-a/ga: Touch your ankles.

Thi'é-kʰe ábitʰai-a/ga: Touch your side.

Níxa-thoⁿ ábitʰai-a/ga: Touch your stomach.

Móⁿge-thoⁿ ábitʰai-a/ga: Touch your chest.

Tashtáde ábitʰai-a/ga: Touch your waist.

Síⁿdehi ábitʰai-a/ga: Touch the back of your hips.

Nóⁿkʰa ábitʰai-a/ga: Touch your back.

Á-kʰe thihóⁿi-a/ga: Lift your arms.

Iⁿkʰéde-thoⁿ thihóⁿi-a/ga: Lift your shoulders.

Zhíbe-kʰe thihóⁿi-a/ga: Lift your legs.

Sí thátʰa ábazui-a/ga: Point to your left foot.

Noⁿbé wéthitʰoⁿ ábazui-a/ga: Point to your right hand.

Iⁿdádoⁿ-shte pézhitu ábazui-a/ga: Point to something green.

Cultural Note

The wellness center in Macy is named the Four Hills of Life Wellness Center. It is aptly named to acknowledge the stages of life of an Umóⁿhoⁿ. From the early days after birth, when a child receives an Umóⁿnoⁿ name, prayers are made. One can hear the prayerful words to Wakóⁿda, spoken from a Grandfather or Grandmother as they mention the Four Hills of Life, so the infant child will have a long life to that fourth hill.

u'óⁿhe: baby on board

shíⁿgazhiⁿga: toddler / daycare age / young child

mízhiⁿga: girl

núzhiⁿga: boy

shémizhiⁿga: young woman

shénuzhiⁿga: young man

wa'ú: woman

nú: man

wa'úzhiⁿga: Elder woman

iⁿsh'áge: Elder man

nóⁿ / nóⁿ-xti: Elder / mature / aged

nóⁿ-ama / nóⁿ-xti-ama: the Old People

thanóⁿ-xti thagthíⁿ-mashe: those of you who are Elders (used in addressing a group)

Niyé Thiⁿgé Tí-ata Thé-Wathe:
Let's Go to Wellness

Wéthihide háhade-thoⁿ thizá/ga: Get the light weight.

Dúboⁿ thimóⁿshi-a/ga: Lift it four times.

Wéthihide skíge-thoⁿ thizá/ga: Get the heavy weight.

Bamóⁿshi-a/ga: Push it up. / Lift it by pushing.

Wéthihide skíge-égoⁿ thizá/ga: Get the kind of heavy weight.

Wéthihoⁿ ánoⁿ-a? : How much does it weigh?

Wéthihide háhade-égoⁿ thizá/ga: Get the kind of light weight.

Thihída/ga: Lower it.

wéthihide / wéthihoⁿ / móⁿzeskige: weights

Thanóⁿzhiⁿi-a/ga, íkikawiⁿthai-a/ga: Stand and switch places.

Hide ithóⁿtha/ga: Put it down.

Thipʰi xátha itʰétha/ga: Put it back right.

Shéhi-tʰe ithóⁿtha/ga: Put it over there.

Tabé úgasnoⁿ-thoⁿ-ta moⁿthíⁿ-a/ga: Go to the basketball hoop.

Gá-tʰe-di ihétha/ga: Put it down flat right here.

Édi itʰétha/ga, ídoⁿbe: Put it there, in the middle.

Uhéatʰoⁿ-ta moⁿthíⁿ-a/ga: Go to the stairs / ladder.

Nóⁿze-kʰe-ta moⁿthíⁿ-a/ga: Go to the fence.

Nóⁿze-thoⁿ-ta oⁿnóⁿzhiⁿ: We're standing at the fence.

Nóⁿze-kʰe ábitʰa/ga: Touch the fence.

Nóⁿze-kʰe ápitʰa: I'm touching the fence.

Ágapʰuga-kʰe Átʰoⁿ Kígtházi: Stretching on the Mat

Ágapʰuga-ta moⁿthíⁿ-a/ga: Go to the mat.

Zhíbe wéthitʰoⁿ-kʰe thipúxa/ga: Fold in your right leg.

Noⁿbéhi-tʰe sipá-tʰe ábitʰa/ga: Touch your fingers to your toes.

Zhíbe óⁿma thipúxa/ga: Fold in your other leg.

Thizúe zhóⁿ/ga, kipáhoⁿ/ga: Lie down stretched out and sit up again.

Shi óⁿma-tathishoⁿ: Again with the other side.

Moⁿgthíⁿ gthíⁿ-a/ga: Sit back up.

Kipímoⁿshi-a/ga: Do a push-up.

U'óⁿsi-thoⁿthoⁿ/ga: Do jumping jacks.

Á thisáda thipúxa-thoⁿthoⁿ/ga: Straighten and fold in your arm repeatedly.

Íye Ázhi-thoⁿthoⁿ: Various Other Phrases

Kinóⁿsada/ga: Go walk / jog.

Sigthé-kʰe wíuha/ga: Follow them.

Úhe-kʰe áha/ga: Follow the path.

Sigthé-kʰe uíha/ga: Follow her/him.

Égithe sí íthikʰashe-te: Watch out, you might catch your foot.

Égithe thakínoⁿsa-te: Watch out, you might trip.

Sagígi-a/ga: Harder / Faster.

Ákikʰihida/ga: Watch out for yourself.

Wagtháwasisiga/ga: Encourage your relatives / friends to be active.

Wák^{h}ihida/ga: Watch out / Pay attention.

Wathísisige moⁿthíⁿ-a/ga: Stay active.

Wasísiga/ga: Be active / energetic.

Kigthíwashkoⁿtoⁿga/ga: Get stronger.

Kióⁿza/ga: Rest.

Shóⁿ bthégoⁿ. Thé-wathe: I think that's it, let's go.

Shinóⁿde-thoⁿ bizhú-a/ga: Rub your knee.

Sí-t^{h}e thi'ú-a/ga: Scratch your foot.

Verb Vocabulary by Pattern

BTH PATTERN

thizé: take

thihóⁿ: lift

thimóⁿshi: lift

thihíde: lower

thipúxa: fold in

moⁿthíⁿ: walk

thisáda: straighten out

A PATTERN

it^{h}éthe, ithóⁿthe, ihéthe: put

gthíⁿ: sit

noⁿzhíⁿ: stand

kipáhoⁿ: get up / sit up

kigtházi: stretch

kipímoⁿshi: do a push-up

u'óⁿsi: jump

kinóⁿsa: trip

kinóⁿsada: go for a walk / jog

gtháwasisige: encourage to be active

kigthíwashkoⁿtoⁿga: get stronger

kióⁿze: rest

ák^{h}ihide: watch

ákik^{h}ihide: watch self

SHP PATTERN

ábit^{h}a: touch

bamóⁿshi: push upward

bimóⁿshi: pull upward

Games: Úshkade

3.1 GAMES HOW-TO

Cultural Note

"My grandpa was a gambler and liked to play cards." — Marcella Woodhull Cayou

Umóⁿhoⁿ people have been playing games throughout their history. There were games of chance and also games that required physical endurance and strength. The earliest card game played is the traditional card game **Tóⁿkawe**. Umóⁿhoⁿ games like **Tóⁿkawe**e and Umóⁿhoⁿ **Íⁿ'utʰiⁿ** ("handgame") are a part of our history and continue being played today. Later on, 500 Rummy and Pitch became common card games. It was common for the sponsors of a card game to get a little side money out of the pot called the "house pot." The sponsors then provided a meal for the card players as it was common for the playing to go into the late hours. The love of playing games continues today. The games in this textbook are modern common board games and card games. The translations for all the games were elicited while playing the game or discussing it immediately after play. We always had a good time, just like in days past.

3.2 CARD GAME PLAY PHRASES: WATHÍBABA ÍSHKADE UTHÁ

Translation: Marcella Woodhull Cayou, Donna Morris Parker; elicitation/transcription: Vida Woodhull Stabler; orthography check and compilation: Bryan James Gordon.

Shkáde-wathe: Let's play.

Gasá/ga: Cut it.

Wíⁿ thisóⁿtha/ga: Turn one over.

Wiⁿdétʰoⁿ gasá/ga: Cut it in half.

Wathíbaba-tʰe basnída/ga: Shuffle the cards.

Wathíbaba-tʰe basnída: S/he shuffled the cards.

Ebé pahóⁿga moⁿthíⁿ-a? : Who goes first?

Thí-pahoⁿga moⁿthíⁿ-a/ga: You go first.

Ebé thé? : Whose turn is it? / Who goes?

Thi moⁿthíⁿ-a/ga: Go / It's your turn.

Íⁿchʰoⁿ wí-e-bthiⁿ: Now it's my turn.

Thí-e-niⁿ: It's your turn.

Dúakʰa thátʰa gthíⁿ-akʰa é-pahoⁿga: The one to the left of this one (the dealer) goes first.

Wíⁿ-thoⁿthoⁿ moⁿthíⁿi-a/ga: Take turns. ("Go one by one.")

íⁿe ska / íⁿepa: diamonds

núzhiⁿga: jack ("boy")

wétʰiⁿ: clubs

wa'ú: queen ("woman")

móⁿzepe: spades ("hatchet")

iⁿsh'áge: king ("Elder male")

nóⁿde: hearts

ugátigthoⁿ: ace

niáshiⁿga wawéxaxa: joker ("person who makes fun of others")

tí ugípi: full house

Wathíbaba oⁿʼí-a/ga: Give me a card / Give me cards.

Wiⁿóⁿxchi kóⁿbtha: I want one.

Thi athíⁿ-a/ga: You keep it / Hold it.

Iⁿdádoⁿ aníⁿ-a?: What do you have?

Uwíʼi: I loan/loaned it to you.

Úthahi-ki íⁿʼi-a/ga: When you win, give it back.

Akíʼi: I give/gave it to myself.

Uéhe: I'm in / I go in.

Oⁿgu óⁿguhi: We won!

Uéha-mazhi: I fold / I'm out.

Uhí uthíshi-noⁿ: S/he can't be beat.

wékʰitʰe-tʰe: cheating

Wékʰitʰa: S/he is cheating. (teasing phrase)

Égoⁿxti-azhi égoⁿi-tʰe: S/he's getting carried away. (slang for "going too far"—literally "S/he seems to be kind of not exactly right.")

Wathíbaba moⁿshíadi athíⁿ-thiⁿkʰe uhí-tathiⁿkʰe: Whoever has the high card will win.

Wathíbaba-tʰe waxchá-thoⁿ-ta íbiski noⁿzhíⁿ: The cards are next to the flowers.

Wóⁿgithe uwíhii: I beat all of you.

Uwíhii-áchoⁿ wóⁿgithe / Wóⁿgithe uwíhii-áchoⁿ: I really beat all of you.

Wathíbaba óⁿska waʼú-akʰa uáwahi-áchoⁿ: Well! The woman really beat us at cards.

Uáhi: I won.

Uhí téxi-áchoⁿ: It was a hard one to win.

Wathíbaba-tʰe kúge zhiⁿga-tʰedi xátha uzhí-a/ga: Put the cards back in the box.

3.3 BOARDGAME PLAY PHRASES: ZHOⁿBTHÁSKA ÁSHKADE UTHÁ

Translation: Marcella Woodhull Cayou and Donna Morris Parker; elicitation/transcription: Vida Woodhull Stabler.

Shkáde-wathe: Let's play.

Kúge thibthá/ga: Open the box. (**thibthá,** "spread open like a book or folded blanket," spreading open the board)

Thí-pahoⁿga moⁿthíⁿ-a/ga: You go first.

Thi moⁿthíⁿ-a/ga: You go / Your turn.

Wi-étoⁿthiⁿ / Wí- toⁿthiⁿ / Wí-pahoⁿga bthíⁿ: I'm first.

Wi bthé-tamiⁿkʰe: I'll go / It'll be my turn.

Íⁿchʰoⁿ wi bthé-a?: Now do I go?

Thomas-akʰa é-pahoⁿga-taakʰa / Thomas-akʰé-pahoⁿga-taakʰa: Thomas goes first.

Íⁿchʰoⁿ wí-e-bthiⁿ: Now I go / Now it's me.

Wí-e-bthiⁿ-a? / Wi wí-e-bthíⁿ-a?: Is it my turn?

Shi bthé-tamiⁿkʰe: I will go again.

Noⁿhéba/ga: Wait.

Né níʼa: You can't move.

Bthé bthíʼa: I can't move.

Xátha moⁿgthíⁿ-a/ga: Go back.

Dúba nístu moⁿthíⁿ-a/ga: Move back four.

Íkikawiⁿthai-a/ga: Trade places / Exchange (bingo cards, etc.).

Pahóⁿga moⁿthíⁿ-a/ga / Pahóⁿga-tathishoⁿ moⁿthíⁿ-a/ga / Sí thizá/ga: Move forward.

Nístu moⁿthíⁿ-a/ga / Xátha moⁿthíⁿ-a/ga: Move backward.

Shi xátha gí-a/ga: Come back again.

Íⁿthisnu-a/ga: Move that for me. (**thisnú,** "pull / draw / drag / lead")

Weáhide gastákʰi thétha: S/he knocked it far.

Kóⁿsi-tʰe oⁿ'í-a/ga: Give me the dice.

Kóⁿsi-tʰe óⁿtha thétha/ga: Throw the dice.

Kóⁿsi-tʰe ganóⁿge thétha/ga: Roll the dice.

Kóⁿsi wíⁿ óⁿtha thétha/ga: Throw one die.

Kóⁿsi wóⁿdoⁿ óⁿtha thétha/ga: Throw both dice.

Kóⁿsi thátʰa wíⁿ 'í-a/ga: Give one die to the left.

Águdi níⁿ-a?: Where are you?

Áwa-kʰe-ta né-a? /Áwaxta né-a?: Where are you going?

wékʰitʰe-tʰe: cheating

Wawékʰitʰazhi-a/ga: Don't cheat.

Égoⁿxti-azhi égoⁿi-tʰe: S/he's carried away. (slang for "going too far"—literally, "S/he seems kind of not quite right")

Téxi uhá: Too bad. (used when teasing during gameplay; literally, "difficulty going around")

Ebé thé?: Who goes? / Whose turn is it?

Thi athíⁿ-a/ga: You keep it / Hold it.

Awíⁿoⁿwa-thiⁿkʰe níⁿ?: Which one are you?

Thí-e-niⁿ, zí: That's you, the yellow one.

Áashnoⁿ: I missed.

Gashnóⁿ: S/he missed.

Tháshnoⁿ: You missed.

Éakʰa óⁿthiⁿ-noⁿ uhí-bathiⁿ: S/he almost won.

Úthahi-ki íⁿ'i-a/ga: If you win give it back to me.

Uwí'i: I loaned it to you.

Akí'i: I gave it to myself.

Wathátʰe-thoⁿ-ta íi-a/ga / gíi-a/ga: Come to the table.

Éthihi-áchoⁿ: You're very lucky.

Éhi-áchoⁿ: S/he is very lucky.

Éhi-bazhi: S/he is unlucky.

Shóⁿ páxe: I'm done.

Wazhíⁿshta-bazhii-a/ga: Don't be pouting around. (spoken to more than one person)

Wazhíⁿpi-bazhi: S/he's not mad.

Thípʰi shkádai-a/ga: Play right. (spoken to more than one person)

3.4 BALLGAME PLAY PHRASES: TABÉ ÍSHKADE UTHÁ

Translation: Marcella Woodhull Cayou; elicitation/transcription: Vida Woodhull Stabler.

Óⁿtha: Throw

Óⁿtha thétha/ga: Throw it.

Tabé-thoⁿ wáthatʰe-kʰe-tathishoⁿ óⁿtha thétha/ga: Throw the ball at the table.

Tabé-thoⁿ úgaxe shkóⁿshkoⁿ-ta óⁿtha thétha/ga: Throw the ball at the TV.

Nóⁿze-kʰe-ta óⁿtha thétha/ga: Throw the ball at the fence.

Ubázu-thoⁿ-ta óⁿtha thétha/ga: Throw it at the corner.

Tizhébe-tʰe-ta óⁿtha thétha/ga: Throw it at the door.

Mázi xthabé-tʰe-ta óⁿtha thétha/ga: Throw it at the cedar tree.

Uthóⁿ: Catch

Tabé-thoⁿ uthóⁿ/ga: Catch the ball.

Noⁿtʰé: Kick

Tabé-thoⁿ noⁿtʰá/ga: Kick the ball.

Tabé-thoⁿ ubázu-thoⁿ-ta noⁿtʰé thétha/ga: Kick the ball to the corner.

Tabé-thoⁿ wáthatʰe-kʰe-ta noⁿtʰé thétha/ga: Kick the ball to the table.

Tizhébe-ta noⁿtʰé thétha/ga: Kick it to the door.

Ágthiⁿ sabe-thoⁿ-ta noⁿtʰé thétha/ga: Kick it to the black chair.

Shíshige úzhi-tʰe-ta noⁿtʰé thétha/ga: Kick it to the trash.

Shíshige úzhi-tathishoⁿ noⁿtʰé thétha/ga: Kick it toward the trash.

Ganóⁿge: Roll

Tabé-thoⁿ ganóⁿge thétha/ga: Roll the ball.

Gasnú: Slide

Tabé-thoⁿ gasnú-a/ga: Slide the ball.

Tabé-thoⁿ gasnú thétha/ga: Slide the ball away somewhere / Give the ball a good slide.

Tabé-thoⁿ shíshige úzhi-ta gasnú thétha/ga: Slide the ball to the trash.

Ágthiⁿ sabe-thoⁿ-tathishoⁿ gasnú thétha/ga: Slide it toward the black chair.

Ubázu-tathishoⁿ gasnú thétha/ga: Slide it toward the corner.

Ugásnoⁿ: Make a Basket

Tabé-thoⁿ shíshige úzhi-tʰe-di ugásnoⁿ/ga: Throw the ball in the trash can.

Ugásnoⁿ means "force to pass through," and shares the same root **snoⁿ** as other verbs like **basnóⁿ**, "put a spit through food to roast it"; **uthísnoⁿ**, "put thread through a needle / put a horse to a wagon / lace a shoe"; and **uíbasnoⁿ**, "put a ring on somebody." Two other roots with the same sound **snoⁿ** are used in other verbs having to do with shelling beans and ripping things.

3.5 GO FISH PHRASES: HUGÁSI MOⁿTHIⁿ-A/GA UTHÁ

Translation: Marcella Woodhull Cayou; elicitation/transcription: Vida Woodhull Stabler.

Hugási Moⁿthíⁿ-a/ga uses a regular deck of cards. The rules are simple. Just match the cards by taking turns and asking another player for the one needed. Gameplay phrases follow:

Wathíbaba sátoⁿ-thoⁿthoⁿ wa'í-a/ga: Deal out five to each player.

Wíⁿ-thoⁿthoⁿ wathíbaba ímoⁿxe-taakʰa, izházhe wánade: They take turns asking about cards, you call out their name.

Ékʰigoⁿ wíⁿ aníⁿ-ki híde itʰétha/ga: If you get a match lay it down.

Aníⁿ-azhi-ki hú ugási moⁿthíⁿ-a/ga: If you don't have one go fishing.

Wathíbaba aníⁿ-ki shi moⁿthíⁿ-a/ga: If you get the card go again.

Wathíbaba thithíⁿge-tʰedi úthahi-taniⁿkshe: When you are out of cards you will win.

Ékʰigoⁿ áhigi aníⁿ-ki úthahi-taniⁿkshe: You'll win if you have a lot of matches.

Wa'ú aníⁿ-a?: Do you have a queen?

Wa'ú abthíⁿ: I have a queen.

Núzhiⁿga aníⁿ-a?: Do you have a jack?

Núzhiⁿga abthíⁿ-mazhi / Núzhiⁿga oⁿthíⁿge: I don't have any jacks.

Iⁿsh'áge aníⁿ-a?: Do you have a king?

Iⁿsh'áge abthíⁿ: I have a king.

Ukátigthoⁿ aníⁿ-a?: Do you have an ace?

Ukátigthoⁿ abthíⁿ-mazhi: I don't have an ace.

Sátoⁿ oⁿ'í-a/ga: Give me a five.

Sátoⁿ wi'í: I give you a five.

3.6 AN UMÓⁿHOⁿ CARD GAME: TÓⁿKAWE

Translation: Marcella Woodhull Cayou and Donna Morris Parker; elicitation/transcription: Vida Woodhull Stabler; orthography check: Bryan James Gordon.

Umóⁿhoⁿ Niáshiⁿga-ama and the History of Tóⁿkawe

Story: Marcella Woodhull Cayou; elicitation: Vida Woodhull Stabler.

Umóⁿhoⁿ people have a history of participation in a variety of games. One game is the card game known as **Tóⁿkawe**. Tóⁿkawe was originally a women's card game that was played in people's homes. In past times knickknacks (gíshi) were used as ante if there was no money. Today change is often used for the pot.

The Elders say they saw the game played by the women in their families. Mothers, aunts, and grandmothers have enjoyed playing Tóⁿkawe for many years.

Mrs. Marcella Cayou describes the game being played in her home for as long as she can recall. Mrs. Cayou remembers how Tóⁿkawe was played during the summer months. "If you lived in the country, the womenfolk would go from house to house to play Tóⁿkawe. Most Umóⁿhoⁿ people lived in the country back in those days. Our people lived out south, west, north, and east. We would play early in the evening and go home before dark."

Today, Umóⁿhoⁿ Íye students learn Tóⁿkawe from Elders in the language classroom. Many tribal members continue to play Tóⁿkawe at the Macy Senior Center, Umóⁿhoⁿ Nation Public School, and in homes around and in the community of Macy.

Kigthítoⁿ: Getting Ready

wabáxte: bundle (of things for betting)

kʰíde: shoot (cards)

Águdi kʰídai-a?: Where are they shooting cards?

Oⁿkʰída: We're shooting cards.

Kʰída/ga: Shoot.

Pahóⁿga-di: Before the Hand

wéshi: ante / pot

Móⁿzeska uthéwiⁿ itʰétha/ga: Gather and pile up the money / Ante up.

Móⁿzeska uázhi / Móⁿzeska uázhi bthíshtoⁿ: I already put in my money.

Shkáde-doⁿ: During the Hand

Iⁿdádoⁿ-shte údoⁿ oⁿʼí-a/ga: Give me something good.

Iⁿshʼáge é-noⁿ-xchi kóⁿbtha: I only need the king.

É-azhi: That's not the one I want. ("It's not it.")

Ugína/ga: Your hunt. ("Search for yours.")

Thábthiⁿ ékʰigoⁿ híde itʰéthai-a/ga: Put threes of a kind down.

giná: call / ask for one's own

Agína, oⁿʼí-a/ga: I'm calling for my card, give it to me!

Giná: S/he called for her/his card.

Giná gthíⁿ: S/he's calling for her/his card.

Waʼú-akʰa giná gthíⁿ: The queen is (sitting there) calling.

Bthíze: I'll take it.

gashnúde: give (card) up

gashnúdekʰithe: get (somebody) to give (card) up

Wathíbaba kóⁿbtha athíⁿ. Gashnúde-ákʰithe: She had the card I wanted. I made her give it up.

Wathíbaba kóⁿbtha-kʰe waʼú-akʰa athíⁿ. Wathíbaba kóⁿbtha gashnúda: The woman had the card I wanted. She gave up the card I wanted.

Shugthé: It's going back around toward you.

Shápe shugthé: Six is going back around toward you.

Shugí: It's coming back around toward you.

Iⁿshʼáge shuthé: The king is going your way.

Wathíbaba uhá thé-tʰe: The card must be going around.

Shi oⁿgátha / Shoⁿgátha: We're going around (more than one card).

Wiⁿóⁿ-xchi kóⁿbtha (Móⁿga abthíⁿ) : I want one. (I have a skunk hand.)

Móⁿga wípaxe: I skunked you.

Nízazhi-tʰedi-ki ("nízashtidik") bthíze-tamiⁿkʰe: When you don't get it, I will.

Nízazhi shi wi bthíze-tamiⁿkʰe: You're not going to get it and I will.

Óⁿthanoⁿse: You cut me off.

Wathíbaba uétha-achoⁿ: I didn't get nothing. ("The cards were too scattered.")

Wí-shti bthíza-mazhi: I didn't get one either.

Wiⁿóⁿ-xchi uíⁿshte: I only have one left.

Háshi-doⁿ: After the Hand

Wathíbaba oⁿthóⁿt'e: The card killed me. (Somebody else got it; literally, "I am dead by the card")

Páshethoⁿ: I've laid down (to win). ("I've pushed out to finish.")

Bashéthoⁿ: S/he laid down (to win).

3.7 REAL ESTATE BOARDGAME PHRASES

Translation: Marcella Woodhull Cayou and Donna Morris Parker; elicitation/transcription: Vida Woodhull Stabler.

Directions: Use a real estate boardgame set to play. Names were elicited and changed on the board to reflect the places in the Macy community. The students and Elders chose the names for the new gameboard.

Zhoⁿbtháska Uthíshoⁿ Moⁿthíⁿ-tʰe: Moving around the Board

_____-ta bthé-tamiⁿkʰe: I'll go to _____.

Thigthíze tí-ta bthé: I'm going to the Electric House.

Zhoⁿbtháska-kʰe-ta moⁿthíⁿ-a/ga: Go to Boardwalk.

Thigthíze móⁿtʰe agípashethoⁿ bthé: I'm going to pay my electric bill. ("I'm going to put down to settle mine inside the electric house.")

Uágashoⁿ bthé: I'm going traveling.

Moⁿzhóⁿ Basása-ge Thiwíⁿ-tʰe: Buying Pieces of Land

Níwiⁿ shkóⁿna-a? : You want to buy it?

Ánoⁿ íthawai-a? : How much does it cost? ("How much is counted with it?")

Ánoⁿ-a?: How much?

Íthawa moⁿshíadi: It's too expensive. ("high price")

Móⁿzeska áhigi-áchoⁿ íthawa: It costs too much money. ("A lot of money is counted with it.")

Móⁿzeska íthawa uthíshi: It costs millions. ("The amount of money counted with it is impossible.")

Moⁿzhóⁿ bthíwiⁿ kóⁿbtha: I want to buy the land.

Bthíwiⁿ-tamiⁿkʰe: I will buy it.

É-shti bthíwiⁿ kóⁿbtha: I want to buy that one too.

Ewázhiⁿnoⁿge (ewáshnoⁿge) bthíwiⁿ kóⁿbtha: I want to buy the railroad.

Ebé athíⁿ-a?: Who has it?

Ebé-shtewoⁿ athíⁿ-azhi: Nobody has it.

Ebé etá?: Whose is it?

Wiwíta: It's mine.

Wagóⁿze-akʰa etá (Wagóⁿze-akʰéta): It's Teacher's.

Uzhóⁿiti bthíwiⁿ kóⁿbtha: I want to buy a hotel.

Tí óⁿma-tʰe Thitígoⁿ-thiⁿkʰe / Tigoⁿhá / Tigóⁿho 'í-a/ga: Give the other house to Grandpa.

Ugthíⁿ, Wathíbaba-shti Ázhi-thoⁿthoⁿ: Different Places and Cards

Kʰagehá / Kʰagého, wathíbaba wíⁿ oⁿʼí-a/ga: Friend, give me a card.

waxpáthiⁿ wagáxe: poor tax

uʼóⁿthiⁿge unóⁿshtoⁿ: free parking

wéshi itʰétha: jackpot ("They put their antes / winnings / prizes / rewards.")

Umóⁿhoⁿ Úhe-kʰe-ta moⁿthíⁿ-a/ga: Go to Omaha Road.

Wawéshi Úhe-kʰe-ta moⁿthíⁿ-a/ga: Go to Paycheck Road.

Híde-ata: Down Bottom

Umóⁿhoⁿ Tí: Umóⁿhoⁿ Lodges

Mí Éthoⁿbe: Sunrise

Nóⁿ-ama: Old Ones

Umóⁿhoⁿ Wáʼai: Tribal Farm

Búta: Circle

Nóⁿde Móⁿze: Iron Heart

Móⁿga Úhe: Skunk Hollow

Unáhe Tí: Firehouse

Moⁿgthíxta: Blackbird Hill

Úthiwiⁿ Tí: C-Store

Wakóⁿda Wathahoⁿ Niáshiⁿga Iⁿshʼáge: Old Mission

Wazéthe Tí: Carl T. Curtis Health Center

Óⁿpʰoⁿ Toⁿga Moⁿzhóⁿ: Big Elk Park

Úthixide Thétha Moⁿzhóⁿ: Lookout Point

Íⁿʼe Uʼúde / Iⁿʼe Moⁿshóⁿde: Hole-in-the-Rock

Ní Wathítʰoⁿ: Water Works

Tibúta Íye: Jail Phrases

tibúta kinóⁿshibe: Get out of jail (getting oneself out; i.e., "breaking out free")

Tibúta uágthiⁿ-tamikʰe: I'm going to sit in jail.

Tibúta-ta bthé: I'm going to jail.

Tibúta-tʰe-di-tʰoⁿ akínoⁿshibe: I broke out of jail.

Gashíbe agthí: I came back out.

Tiúpe né-a?: Are you going to visit?

Tiúpe pʰí: I went to visit.

Wagáxe Íye: Rent Phrases

Wagáxe íⁿthaniⁿ: You owe me. ("You have a bill from me.")

Wagáxe wéthaniⁿ: You owe them. ("You have a bill from them.")

Gthéboⁿ oⁿʼí-a/ga: Give me ten.

Gthéboⁿ bashéthoⁿ/ga: Pay ten / Settle for ten.

Wagáxe bashéthoⁿ / gipáshethoⁿ: S/he paid their bill.

Wagáxe páshethoⁿ / agípashethoⁿ: I paid my bill.

Bashéthoⁿ/ga: Pay it.

Íye Óⁿma Ázhi-thoⁿthoⁿ-ge: Other Phrases

Nóⁿde údoⁿ bthíⁿ. Móⁿzeska gthéboⁿ wiʼí-tamikʰe: I am good-hearted. I'll give you ten dollars.

Wanítʰe-áchoⁿ: S/he's very stingy.

Óⁿxoⁿ bthé: I'm going broke / running out of money / going along without money.

Niyé thiáxe-taakʰa. Thithíxoⁿ-taakʰa: S/he'll hurt you. S/he'll break you.

Údoⁿ níwiⁿ-tʰe: That was a good buy. ("It must be that you bought well.")

Iⁿdádoⁿ níwiⁿ-tʰe Wagóⁿze-thiⁿkʰe 'íi-a/ga: What you bought, give to Teacher.

Waxpáthiⁿ-ma wa'í-a/ga: Give to the poor.

Thenóⁿ wíⁿ ushté: Only one left.

Ewázhiⁿnoⁿge thenóⁿ wíⁿ ushté / Thenóⁿ wíⁿ ushté, ewázhiⁿnoⁿge: Only one railroad left.

Wéthawa-tʰe eyóⁿ-a?: How is the money? ("Is it accounted for?")

3.8 GRANDMA SAYS: THIKÓᴺ ÁTHIGAZHI

Translation: Marcella Woodhull Cayou; elicitation/transcription: Vida Woodhull Stabler.

Directions

Wagóⁿze will call one student to the center circle and give the command to one first. This game requires little practice if students are already familiar with basic action verb commands. Be sure and "tickle" the ear of your students by speaking the Umóⁿhoⁿ phrases to them repeatedly. The verb action vocabulary should be modeled, and the teacher should check for understanding before progressing with the game. Once an oral check is done, the game can progress to two to four teams, depending on class size. The first in line from each team will step forward, separating from the rest of the team. Each of the leaders will stand ready to perform the action verb spoken by the teacher. Also, be aware that the verb will change from singular to plural forms once game is in play. Trick: This game can be enhanced by adding **noⁿshtóⁿ** after action verbs. Choose the relationship term appropriate for the person giving the command:

Relationship Term		Article	'to do this'		'tells you'
Thikóⁿ	'Your Grandmother'		gthíⁿ	'sit'	
Thitígoⁿ	'Your Grandfather'		noⁿzhíⁿ	'stand'	
Thitími	'Your Aunt'		u'óⁿsi	'jump'	
Thinégi	'Your Uncle'		kigthísoⁿtha	'turn around'	
Thihóⁿ	'Your Mother'	-akʰa	noⁿshtóⁿ	'stop'	áthigazhi.
Thiádi	'Your Father'		noⁿshkí-tʰe ábitʰa	'touch your head'	
Thizhíⁿthe	'Your [female's] Older Brother'		noⁿbéhi-tʰe ábitʰa	'touch your fingers'	
Thitínu	'Your [male's] Older Brother'		zhíbe-kʰe ábitʰa	'touch your leg'	
Thizhóⁿthe	'Your [female's] Older Sister'		zhíbe-tʰe ábitʰa	'touch both legs'	
Thisóⁿga	'Your [male's] Sister'		sí-tʰe ábitʰa	'touch your feet'	
Thitóⁿge	'Your [female's] Little Sister'		noⁿxíde-tʰe ábitʰa	'touch your ears'	
Thisóⁿtha	'Your [female's] Little Brother'		tóⁿthiⁿ	'run'	
Thikʰágesoⁿga	'Your [male's] Little Brother'		moⁿthíⁿ	'walk'	

3.9 NATURAL BODY ACTION/ TOTAL PHYSICAL RESPONSE

Translation: Marcella Woodhull Cayou, Rufus White, and Donna Morris Parker; elicitation/transcription: Vida Woodhull Stabler.

How to Play

Students should already be familiar with basic action verb commands in order to play Natural Body Action/Total Physical Response. Separate students into teams of two. Give one command to the pair. The first to perform appropriate action remains in game play. The other moves to the back of their line. Go through the different body action phrases to continue game play.

> **Iⁿshtá thip'íⁿzai-a/ga:** Close your eyes.
>
> **Iⁿshtá thibthái-a/ga:** Open your eyes.
>
> **Iⁿshtá thip'íⁿp'iⁿzai-a/ga:** Blink your eyes.
>
> **Iⁿshtáxoⁿxoⁿi-a/ga:** Squint.
>
> **Iⁿshtá-thoⁿ bigúdai-a/ga:** Rub your eye.
>
> **Shinóⁿde-thoⁿ bizhúi-a/ga:** Rub your knee.
>
> **Sí-tʰe thi'úi-a/ga:** Scratch your foot.
>
> **Noⁿbé-tʰe thitútushii-a/ga:** Snap your fingers.
>
> **Noⁿbé-tʰe thitúshii-a/ga:** Snap your fingers once.
>
> **Noⁿbé-tʰe gachʰáchʰakii-a/ga:** Clap your hands.
>
> **Noⁿbé-tʰe gachʰákii-a/ga:** Clap your hands once.
>
> **Kigtházii-a/ga:** Stretch.

> **Á-kʰe thihóⁿi-a/ga / Á-kʰe thimóⁿshii-a/ ga:** Raise / Lift your arms.
>
> **Á-kʰe thihídai-a/ga / Á-kʰe híde théthai-a/ ga:** Lower your arms.
>
> **Sikóⁿ-tʰe kigthízhai-a/ga:** Wash your ankles.
>
> **Pá-tʰe gazhíⁿ-a/ga:** Blow your nose.

3.10 I'M SORRY: UTHÚAMA

Translation: Marcella Woodhull Cayou; elicitation/transcription: Vida Woodhull Stabler.

Activity

All students will take turns rolling the dice to determine who goes first. Play will continue clockwise following Sorry game-playing rules. An Elder will act as the person in charge with the responsibility of asking basic questions (see phrases following). Each student learns one phrase from the list and is responsible for using the phrase repeatedly when appropriate. This format allows each student to become familiar with one phrase, with new phrases added as the game progresses.

Materials

Gameboard and pieces, translated Umóⁿhoⁿ cards

Phrases

> **Wíuga awíⁿoⁿwa shkóⁿna?:** What color do you want?

Wathíbaba-tʰe basnída/ga: Shuffle the cards.

Uthúama: Sorry.

Gasnú-a/ga: Slide.

Uwítʰiⁿ, uthúama: I hit you, I'm sorry.

Uwítʰiⁿ, pahóⁿga-ta moⁿgthíⁿ-a/ga: I hit you, go back to start.

Étoⁿthiⁿ-atathishoⁿ moⁿthíⁿ-a/ga: Move forward.

Nístu moⁿthíⁿ-a/ga: Move backward.

Xátha moⁿgthíⁿ-a/ga: Go back (where you came from).

Wiⁿóⁿxchi kóⁿbtha: I want one.

Kʰé bthé: Okay, I'm going.

Ukʰí wiwíta agthé-tamiⁿkʰe: I'm going home.

Goⁿ-égoⁿ-xchi akʰí: I'm sort of getting home.

Eshóⁿ-xchi akʰí: I'm nearly home.

Káshi íthathape: You waited a long time.

Thi thakʰí: You're home.

Éakʰa eshóⁿ-xchi akʰí: S/he's nearly home.

Agthí: I'm home.

Agthé thi'á: S/he can't get home.

3.11 POKENO PHRASES: POKENO UTHÁ

Translation: Marcella Woodhull Cayou and Donna Morris Parker; elicitation/transcription: Vida Woodhull Stabler.

Pokeno áthade: Pokeno caller

thútʰoⁿ: straight-line bingo

noⁿbá / ákigthaha: double-line bingo ("two / one on top of another")

íⁿe ska toⁿga: big diamond

ágaxade: blackout ("cover whole card")

wathíbaba: cards

u'óⁿthiⁿge: free space

gthéboⁿ nóⁿde: ten of hearts (See section 3.2, Card Game Play Phrases, to construct other combinations.)

shóⁿka íⁿepa: nine of diamonds

Híⁿska dúba thizá/ga: Take some beads.

Wíⁿ thizá/ga: Take one.

Wathíbaba-tʰe thátʰa uhá thétha/ga: Pass the cards to the left.

Ebé nóⁿ-a?: Who's the oldest?

Shéakʰa é-noⁿ nóⁿ (Shéakʰénoⁿ nóⁿ): That one's the oldest.

Thi thanóⁿ: You're the oldest.

Awíⁿoⁿwa-thoⁿkʰáshe thanóⁿi-a?: Which of you all is the oldest?

Wi anóⁿ-xti: I am truly old.

Thi thanóⁿ-a?: Are you the oldest?

Égoⁿ / Óⁿkazhi / Óⁿka-mazhi: Yes / No / No, I'm not.

Ebé zhiⁿgá?: Who's the youngest?

Éakʰa é-noⁿ zhiⁿgá (Éakʰenoⁿ zhiⁿgá): That one is the youngest.

Wí-noⁿ oⁿzhíⁿga: I'm the youngest.

Wóⁿgithe wazhíⁿga: We're all small / young.

3.12 YOU'RE IN TROUBLE PHRASES: PÍAZHI SHKÁXE UTHÁ

Translation: Donna Morris Parker; elicitation/transcription: Vida Woodhull Stabler.

Follow the directions to the boardgame while using the phrases below.

Wíuga awíⁿoⁿwa shkóⁿna?: Which color do you want?

_____**kóⁿbtha:** I want_____.

Thithíta gá-tʰe-di ugthóⁿ/ga: Put yours here.

Tabé uthízoⁿ-di gthíⁿ bispóⁿ: Press the center ball.

Shápe bthé-tamiⁿkʰe: I'll go six.

Nístu moⁿgthíⁿ-a/ga: Go back.

Eshóⁿ-xchi akʰí: I'm nearly home.

Noⁿbá-xchi kóⁿbtha: I just want two.

Shápe níze shi moⁿthíⁿ-a/ga: You took six, go again.

Ashkóⁿ bthí'a: I can't move.

Thashkóⁿ ní'a: You can't move.

3.13 IT WILL FALL PHRASES: UXPÁTHE-TAAKʰA UTHÁ

Follow the directions to the game with blocks while using the phrases that follow.

Zhóⁿzhiⁿga wíⁿ thizá/ga: Take one little block.

Óⁿma-tathishoⁿ moⁿthíⁿ-a/ga: Go to the other side.

Shéakʰa athé-taakʰa: That one is going.

Ákʰihida/ga: Watch it.

Uxpáthe taakʰa: It will fall.

3.14 TWIST AND BEND YOUR BODY: ZHÚ THIBÉNI

Translation: Marcella Woodhull Cayou; elicitation/transcription: Vida Woodhull Stabler.

Zhú Thibéni introduces a new verb **átʰoⁿ** "stand/step on" as well as reinforcing colors, left/right, and foot/hand. Prior to introducing **Zhú Thibéni** add **noⁿbé-tʰe thihóⁿi-a/ga** "raise your hands" and **sí-tʰe thihóⁿi-a/ga** "raise your feet" to ACTION VERB routine.

Review colors by spinning the color wheel and asking students what color they see. Next, command each student to spin the wheel.

Thikúwiⁿxa/ga: Spin it.

Átʰoⁿ/ga: Step on it.

Thihóⁿ/ga: Raise / lift it.

tú: blue

zí: yellow

pézhitu: green

zhíde: red

thátʰa: left

wéthitʰoⁿ: right

sí: foot

noⁿbé: hand

Sí wéthitʰoⁿ-tʰe pézhitu átʰoⁿ/ga: Right foot step on green.

If students are reluctant, or if **Zhú Thibéni** has already been played a number of times, a variation may be introduced. Each student finds three to five objects (depending on the number of students) to place in the center for game play. The Elder or Wagóⁿze tells students to place one or more objects on a color space; for example, to "put the bowl on red." Students respond appropriately as they show understanding. After a few turns, students practice making similar commands to each other based on previously acquired vocabulary.

Ithábashna-kʰe pézhitu ihétha/ga: Put the scissors on green.

Moⁿhí-kʰe pézhitu ugthóⁿ/ga: Put the knife in the green.

Moⁿhí-kʰe uxpé-tʰe ugthóⁿ/ga: Put the knife in the bowl.

Wagóⁿze 'í-a/ga: Give it to Teacher.

Niskíthe-tʰe éthiⁿkʰe a'í-tamiⁿkʰe: I'll give the salt to him/her.

Gthíza/ga: Take it back.

Xátha itʰétha/ga: Put it back.

Wébaxu-kʰe zí-tʰe gahá itʰétha/ga: Put the pencil on the yellow.

3.15 BLACKJACK PHRASES: GTHÉBOⁿ NOⁿBÁ KʰI ÉDI WIⁿÓⁿXCHI UTHÁ

Translation: Marcella Woodhull Cayou; elicitation/transcription: Vida Woodhull Stabler.

Use a regular deck of cards. Take out the jokers.

Oⁿwóⁿtʰiⁿ-a/ga: Hit me.

Shéna: Stop / That's enough.

Áhigi-áchoⁿ: Too much.

Eshóⁿ-xchi shí: You're almost there.

Eshóⁿ-xchi pʰí: I'm almost there.

Eshóⁿ-xchi ahí: S/he's almost there.

Uthóⁿ: S/he held.

wékʰitʰe-tʰe: cheating

Oⁿthóⁿkʰitʰe gthíⁿ: S/he's cheating me.

Wawékʰitʰe gíudoⁿ: S/he likes to cheat.

Weákʰitʰe agthíⁿ: I'm cheating.

Híde itʰétha/ga: Put them down.

Wéthawa zhíde oⁿthóⁿkikoⁿ: We're playing each other with pennies. (phrase for "penny-ante")

Wawéthakʰitʰe thagthíⁿ: You're cheating.

Wathíbaba-tʰe gamóⁿtha/ga: Lay down your cards.

Wathíbaba-tʰe thisóⁿtha/ga: Turn over your cards.

Wathíbaba-tʰe gasóⁿtha itʰétha/ga: Slap your cards down.

Wathíbaba-tʰe nísoⁿtha?: Did you turn your cards over?

Wathíbaba-tʰe oⁿthóⁿnoⁿsa: S/he got the card I needed. ("cut me off")

Wathíbaba kóⁿbtha aníⁿ éiⁿtʰe gítha/ga: If you happen to have the card I want, pass it.

Wathíbaba shkóⁿna-tʰe thi shukʰí: The card you wanted came home to you.

wawéxaxa: joker

Wi pásnide, wi uáhi: I won, I'll shuffle.

3.16 DARTS PHRASES: MÓⁿDEHI ÓⁿTHA THÉTHA/GA UTHÁ

Translation: Donna Morris Parker; elicitation/ transcription: Vida Woodhull Stabler.

> **Aóⁿbtha théathe:** I threw it.
>
> **Thaóⁿna théthathe:** You threw it.
>
> **Óⁿtha thétha:** S/he / they threw it.
>
> **Oⁿóⁿtha théoⁿtha:** We threw them.
>
> **móⁿda / móⁿde / móⁿdehi:** dart
>
> **Eshóⁿ agthí / Eshóⁿ agí:** I'm getting close to home.
>
> **Eshóⁿ thakʰí / Eshóⁿ thagthé:** You're getting close to home.
>
> **Eshóⁿ agthá / Eshóⁿ akʰí:** S/he's getting close to home.
>
> **Thipʰi óⁿtha thétha/ga:** Throw it the right way.
>
> **Gamóⁿshi óⁿtha thétha/ga:** Throw it high.
>
> **Gahíde óⁿtha thétha/ga:** Throw it low.
>
> **Ídoⁿbe óⁿtha thétha/ga:** Throw it center.
>
> **Gashíbe óⁿtha thétha/ga:** Throw it outside.

3.17 BADMINTON/RACQUETBALL: WAZHÍⁿGA ZHIⁿGA UTʰÍⁿ-A/GA

Translation: Donna Morris Parker; elicitation/ transcription: Vida Woodhull Stabler.

Game Play Directions

This game is great for practicing knowledge of counting in Umóⁿhoⁿ. A point is added each time the birdie is struck by the racket. Tell the students to try to keep the birdie in action to the count of 5, 10, 15, and 20. All the while they should count in Umóⁿhoⁿ.

Vocabulary and Phrases

> **wétʰiⁿ:** racket
>
> **wétʰiⁿ zázade:** racket ("hitting-tool that splays outward like a fan")
>
> **Wétʰiⁿ zázade thizá/ga:** Take the racket.
>
> **Wazhíⁿga zhiⁿga-kʰe wóⁿdoⁿ utʰíⁿ shkádai-a?:** Are both of them playing hitting the birdie?
>
> **Áshi-ta oⁿgáthe wóⁿgithe:** We all go outside.
>
> **Wétʰiⁿ zázade thizá/ga:** Take the racket.
>
> **Thútʰoⁿ utʰíⁿ-a/ga:** Hit it straight.
>
> **Gamóⁿshi thétha/ga:** Hit it high.
>
> **Wazhíⁿga zhiⁿga óⁿtha/ga:** Throw the birdie.
>
> **Wasékoⁿ óⁿtha thétha/ga:** Throw it fast.
>
> **Gadíⁿdiⁿ óⁿtha thétha/ga:** Throw it hard.
>
> **Thipʰi óⁿtha thétha/ga:** Throw it the right way.
>
> **Gamóⁿshi óⁿtha thétha/ga:** Throw it high.
>
> **Gahíde óⁿtha thétha/ga:** Throw it low.
>
> **Ídoⁿbe óⁿtha thétha/ga:** Throw it center.
>
> **Gashíbe óⁿtha thétha/ga:** Throw it outside.

3.18 JUMP ROPE AND TUG-OF-WAR PHRASES: HÁZHIⁿGA U'ÓⁿSISI, HÁZHIⁿGA THIDÓⁿ UTHÁ

Translation: Donna Morris Parker and Octa Keen; elicitation/transcription: Vida Woodhull Stabler.

"Moⁿchʰú Moⁿchʰú U'óⁿsisi": Teddy Bear Song

Students jump rope while singing the song. They perform the actions as the words come up in the rhyme. For example, when they say **úhe átʰoⁿ/ga**, they may lift their legs and pretend to climb the steps.

Moⁿchʰú Moⁿchʰú thawá shóⁿshoⁿ/ga: Teddy Bear Teddy Bear count and keep counting.

Moⁿchʰú Moⁿchʰú kigthísoⁿtha/ga: Teddy Bear Teddy Bear turn around.

Moⁿchʰú Moⁿchʰú tóⁿde ábitʰa/ga: Teddy Bear Teddy Bear touch the ground.

Moⁿchʰú Moⁿchʰú móⁿxe ábitʰa/ga: Teddy Bear Teddy Bear touch the sky.

Moⁿchʰú Moⁿchʰú zhóⁿzhiⁿga bahí-a/ga: Teddy Bear Teddy Bear pick up sticks.

Moⁿchʰú Moⁿchʰú shi thawá/ga: Teddy Bear Teddy Bear count again.

Moⁿchʰú Moⁿchʰú Wakóⁿ-wathahoⁿ/ga: Teddy Bear Teddy Bear say your prayer.

Moⁿchʰú Moⁿchʰú táp'ska moⁿthíⁿ-a/ga: Teddy Bear Teddy Bear go to school.

Moⁿchʰú Moⁿchʰú úhe átʰoⁿ/ga: Teddy Bear Teddy Bear climb the step.

Gameplay Phrases

Házhiⁿga shkáde-wathe: Let's play rope.

Házhiⁿga u'óⁿsisi oⁿshkáda: We play jump rope.

Házhiⁿga thipʰi ganóⁿgai-a/ga: Turn the rope the right way.

Tabé ganóⁿge oⁿwóⁿoⁿsisi: We're jumping skipball.

Házhiⁿga-kʰe thidóⁿ ákikʰitha-taama: They're going to play tug-of-war against each other. ("pull the rope")

Házhiⁿga u'óⁿsi-thoⁿthoⁿ/ga: Jump rope.

Házhiⁿga-kʰe uthá'oⁿsisi-a?: Did you jump rope?

Házhiⁿga uá'oⁿsisi: I jumped rope.

Thipʰi shkádai-a/ga: Play right.

Házhiⁿga uá'oⁿsisi kóⁿbtha: I want to jump rope.

Házhiⁿga-kʰe ánoⁿge kóⁿbtha: I want to hold / swing the rope.

Thi házhiⁿga-kʰe ganóⁿga/ga: You hold / swing the rope.

Oⁿdóⁿba/ga. Thégoⁿ gáxa/ga: Watch me. Do it like this.

Shéhi-ta noⁿzhíⁿ-a/ga: Stand over there.

Uthúakiwatʰoⁿtʰoⁿ noⁿzhíⁿ-a/ga: Stand in line.

Wabáhe théthazhi-a/ga: Don't push.

Kipáhe thétha-bazhii-a/ga: Don't push each other.

Shéakʰa házhiⁿga-kʰe ganóⁿge-ta: That one will hold the rope.

Óⁿthe ganóⁿgai-a/ga: Swing it slower.

Wasékoⁿ ganóⁿgai-a/ga: Swing it faster.

Watháwa/ga: Count.

Ebé éduwatʰoⁿ u'óⁿsisi-tathiⁿkʰe?: Who will jump next?

Shi pʰí uá'oⁿsisi kóⁿbtha: I want to jump again.

Noⁿhébai-a/ga: Wait.

Oⁿthóⁿapa/ga: Wait for me.

Wí-pahoⁿga oⁿdóⁿbai-a/ga: Watch me first.

Thakígthishtoⁿ-a?: Are you ready?

Akígthishtoⁿ: I'm ready.

Akígthishtoⁿ-mazhi: I'm not ready.

Wí-pahoⁿga uá'oⁿsisi-thoⁿthoⁿ-tamiⁿkʰe: I'll jump first.

U'óⁿsisi tʰigthá/ga: Jump in. ("Start jumping.")

Washkóⁿ/ga: Try hard.

Uthákihi: You can do it.

Íye agísitha-mazhi: I forgot the word.

Thi égithoⁿ/ga: You say it.

Iⁿwíⁿkóⁿ/ga: Help me.

Uíkoⁿ/ga: Help her/him.

Shéma úwagikoⁿ/ga: Help them.

Summer: Nugé Mon shté

4.1 "TAPS" SONG AND MEMORIAL DAY

Translation: Susan Freemont; elicitation/transcription: Vida Woodhull Stabler; requested by UNPS Music Director John Mangan; spellcheck: Bryan James Gordon.

In May 2007 Music Director John Mangan, "Hexága-zhin ga," came into the ULCC with a request for the translation of "Taps," an end-of-the day bugle call for military servicemen and women. Grandmother Susan Freemont agreed to meet his request. I was to elicit and document the process so that the translation work could be used by the school. The following is a little background on "Taps" within our school and our community.

John Mangan has been blowing "Taps" on the hill (Macy Cemetery) for over forty years. As the band teacher, he has also been teaching Umón hon children to carry on the tradition of blowing "Taps." The following story is what took place on Monday, May 30, 2016, during the annual Memorial Day ceremony at the Macy Cemetery.

As is tradition, as soon as the reading aloud of servicemen and servicewomen's names was completed, Elder Eugene Pappan sang an Umón hon song to honor the Warriors. Following protocol, the Veterans performed the anticipated rifle salute.

It was now the time for the students. They had stood through the Veteran Roll Call and now positioned themselves to play their bugles.

The three UNPS students stood north, overlooking the soldier burial grounds. Under the direction of John Mangan, they began to render "Taps." Leader Kyleigh Merrick, with the assistance of Quinc Dick and Quentin Dick, warmed the hearts of so many on that day.

In closing, there are many traditions practiced by Umón hon people on Memorial Day and at many other times throughout the year to commemorate and remember loved ones.

Memorial Day is a time for families to gather and to share a meal as they remember all the relatives who have passed on. Another tradition is the giving of memorial bowls to relatives and friends of the deceased family members. The preceding story tells of the special way Umón hon people remember loved ones. It is good to attend the ceremonies and to see all that takes place during these times.

Ón ba thishtón.

Day is done.

Mí-ak^h a aíatha.

The sun has gone.

Pahé-thon tát^h on,

From the hill,

Niúthishon -tát^h on.

From the lake.

I^{n}dádo^n-t^{h}e údo^n no^{n}zhí^n.

Something stands good.

Úmak^{h}a ígashno^n.

Rest easy.

Wakó^n-ak^{h}a eshó^n.

Wakó^{n}da / Sacredness is near.

The line "from the sky" was mistakenly omitted from elicitation on that day.

4.2 NAMES OF MONTHS

Transcription: Vida Woodhull Stabler.

June: **Tenúga míga unái-k^{h}e**

The moon when the buffalo bull looks for buffalo cows.

July: **Té hút^{h}o^{n}i-k^{h}e**

The moon when the buffalo bellows.

August: **Ó^{n}p^{h}o^n hút^{h}o^{n}i-k^{h}e**

The moon when the elk bellows.

These names for months come directly from *The Omaha Tribe*, volumes 1 and 2, by Alice Fletcher and Francis La Flesche. There has been discussion concerning alternative or different ways to say a few of the names. The phrases are written as they appear in *The Omaha Tribe* with a few spelling updates to adapt them to the present orthography. When discussing existing names for months, one Elder said, "I stand to be corrected. Those were the Old People back then."

4.3 MILKWEED AND BERRIES: WAXTHÁ WAXTÁ SKÍTHE ÉTHO^{n}BA

Translation: Pat Phillips; elicitation/transcription: Vida Woodhull Stabler.

Vocabulary

waxthá: milkweed

> **Waxthá** extends to introduced vegetables like "cabbage" and "broccoli." To distinguish, we say **waxthá mo^{n}táno^{n}ha**, "wild **waxthá**," because it doesn't come from the grocery store.

táshi/táshe: swellings/buds

waxthá táshe: milkweed buds. If purple, do not pick. They're on the overripe side then.

Cultural Note

Many of the fields where milkweed once grew in abundance are now sprayed with chemicals to prevent growth of plants considered by some to be weeds. It is difficult to find harvest sites free of chemical spraying where **waxthá** can be picked. Still, dedicated foragers know where to locate clean **waxthá**. With watchful eyes they watch the growing plant. They know the fields and the best time to pick **táshi**.

The traditional soup known as **Waxthá taní** is a delicacy much loved by Umó^{n}ho^n people. Once it is washed properly, táshi is added to the soup pot along with a few leaves, potatoes, dumplings, and a preferred meat of bacon/salt pork or hamburger. Recipes vary depending on how the family prefers to cook their **Wax thá taní.**

Other Fruits from Our Lands: Berries

agthóⁿgamoⁿge: raspberry / blackberry

bashté: strawberry

batúshi: elderberry

gubéhi: hackberry

kóⁿde: plum

noⁿshámoⁿ: loganberry

pézi: gooseberry

zhóⁿxude: juneberry

zhóⁿzi: mulberry

Cultural Note

The first berries to harvest in the summer are gooseberries, **pézi.** You can tell by the size (fingernail size) and color when they are ready. **Pézi** are harvested when green and firm, usually in early to mid-June. Mulberries, **zhóⁿzi**, are also ready in June. The strawberries, raspberries, and blackberries will be ready to pick in July. Plums, **kóⁿde**, come in August right around our harvest celebration.

Reminiscence from Marcella Woodhull Cayou

We stayed with my grandfather Scott, south of Macy near Decatur. My grandparents had a home there. Grandpa Ed Mitchell lived nearby and had a log cabin single room. We used woodstove heat. There was well water with a pump to fill a nearby tank for use. My grandmother would home-can vegetables in the summertime. There were not too many kids. Grandpa made a large garden. He dug a cellar for the potatoes. We had tomatoes and string beans. He did not have a steady job, but worked for a neighbor as a farmer's helper, fixing fence, and feeding hogs and cows.

We hauled water from the well using big cans. Dad plowed his own garden with his horses. We had one old horse and one lazy young horse. The old horse would get after the lazy one.

Grandpa Ed Mitchell traveled to town daily to buy tobacco and meat. He liked beef ribs and soup. We did all of our cooking on a wood stove which was better than modern stoves.

The house was close to the timber. We would go down bottom with Grandma to collect raspberries, gooseberries for canning and to store in the cellar for winter pies. We could fill our buckets up right away. After supper we would clean them. Sometimes she would not cook them completely, just enough to put in jars. Then cook over when opening the jar. Gooseberries were for pies. Raspberries were for pies and desserts after supper.

4.4 NATURE WALK LESSON PLAN

Translation: Donna Morris Parker; elicitation/transcription: Vida Woodhull Stabler; additions: Bryan James Gordon.

Lesson: Appreciation of Nature
("Liking" Wakóⁿda's Creations)

Wakóⁿda wegáxa: Wakóⁿda's creations
("Wakóⁿda makes/made it for us")

Objectives

- Reinforce **xtáathe**, "I like."
- Learn of Wakóⁿda's gifts to us in nature.
- Students will identify "senses" and practice using their senses while hiking with their classmates and teachers.
- MATERIALS: clipboard, pencil, blanket

Introduction

Grandpa discussed how nature is a gift from Wakóⁿda for us to appreciate. When we walk outside we have all these wondrous things that sometimes we take for granted, forgetting that these are gifts. Today, we'll walk and appreciate these.

Specific Assignment

Áshi-ta thé-wathe: Let's walk outside. While we're walking, students need to write down at least two phrases in English about what they see in nature that they like, and say one phrase in Umóⁿhoⁿ Íye about what they like.

Rules

We will all walk in a group and be quiet: **Wáxthi-bazhi-taoⁿgatʰoⁿ.**

We will be listening to the sounds, observing the sights and feeling the sensations (wind, sun, etc.): **Wóⁿganoⁿ'oⁿ-taoⁿgatʰoⁿ.**

Students will listen to stories from an Elder walking with them.

Students will discuss the matter at hand (nature): **Ukíkʰiye-taama.**

Activity

Students and Elders walk together, first listening and then discussing. At the end of the road, the group gathers to give some of their English examples as well as the Umóⁿhoⁿ phrases they have created. If possible, it is good to stop and discuss this while sitting on a blanket. Upon returning to the classroom, the Elders and students can work to translate their English sentences into Umóⁿhoⁿ Íye.

Examples

Xthabé xtáathe: I like trees.

Mí xtáathe: I like the sun.

Má'a toⁿga xtáatha-mazhi. Hiⁿxpékʰe gahítha ithát'abthe: I don't like cottonwood trees. I don't like the drifting cottonwood seed fluff.

Thióⁿba, má'a toⁿga uhúthe kʰútha: Lightning—cottonwood is quick to attract it.

Zhoⁿ'ábe xtáathe: I like leaves.

Moⁿzhóⁿ xtáathe: I like the earth.

Tadé xtáathe: I like the wind.

Wahába xtáathe: I like corn.

Wazhí^{n}ga hút^{h}o^n awáno^n'o^n xtáathe: I like to hear the birds singing.

Cultural Note

This lesson provides a good time to discuss behaviors valued by Umó^{n}ho^n people. Our Umó^{n}ho^n Ushkó^n-t^{h}e teaches us to be observant and to watch what is going on around us. Silence and the ability to listen are also admirable characteristics in Umó^{n}ho^n culture. You will hear many stories of the importance of teaching children to sit and listen to people when they speak. When a child has the ability to sit quietly at a doings, that child is viewed as having "good teachings."

4.5 UMÓ^{N}HO^N LANGUAGE AND CULTURE CENTER MISSION STATEMENT

Translation: Marcella Woodhull Cayou; elicitation/transcription: Vida Woodhull Stabler.

Umó^{n}ho^n **niáshi^{n}ga-** **ma** **táp'ska**
Umó^{n}ho^n people the school
o^{n}gúta- **tait^{h}é-** **t^{h}edi,**
ours will be in the

wathít^{h}o^n **údo^n** **i^{n}thí^{n}wi^{n}gasko^{n}tha-**
work good we try for their sake
tao^{n}gat^{h}o^n.
we will

Wó^{n}githe **o^{n}gúta-** **ma** **wawégo^{n}ze**
all ours the teach them things
taama.
they will

Our teachers will work with our Umó^{n}ho^n people in a good way.

(literal word-for-word: "In what will be us Umó^{n}ho^n people's own school, we will try to do good work for them, and they will teach all of our people.")

Zhi^{n}gá- **ama** **i^{n}dádo^n-shte** **údo^n**
child the thing good
kikáxe **i^{n}wí^{n}go^{n}tha,**
make for selves we want for them

shi **niáshi^{n}ga** **áshi-** **amáshti** **ethégo^n**
and person different the also think of
i^{n}wí^{n}go^{n}tha- **tao^{n}gat^{h}o^n.**
we want for them we will
We will teach our children how to provide for themselves, but also to think of others.

Táp'ska **o^{n}gúta-** **tait^{h}é** **údo^n**
school ours will be good
no^{n}zhí^n **o^{n}gíkó^{n}tha.**
stand we want ours
We want our school to be a safe and good place to be.

Zhi^{n}gá- **ama** **Umó^{n}ho^n** **Íye,** **Umó^{n}ho^n**
child the Umó^{n}ho^n Language Umó^{n}ho^n
Úshko^n- **k^{h}e** **thipi** **gáxe** **i^{n}wí^{n}go^{n}tha,**
Ways the well do we want for them

thiézhuba **i^{n}wí^{n}go^{n}tha.**
respect it we want for them
We will teach our children about Respect for their Umó^{n}ho^n culture.

Our teachers will work with our Umó^{n}ho^n people in a good way.

We will teach our children how to provide for themselves, but also to think of others.
We want our school to be a safe and good place to be.
We will teach our children about *Respect* for their Umóⁿhoⁿ culture.

Cultural Note

Vida Woodhull Stabler.

The Language and Culture Center mission statement came from a Title VII Parent Committee meeting in the spring of 2005. At that meeting I asked the five parents assembled what they think our school should teach our children. The preceding sentences identifying our mission were their responses. Later, in February, I sat with Aunt Marcella and documented the phrases she had translated.

4.6 HIGH SCHOOL UMÓⁿHOⁿ ÍYE I, 2, AND 3 SCOPE AND SEQUENCE

Wagthábaze páxe: Vida Woodhull Stabler, Peníshka Mí Etái-kʰe, Óⁿba Wénoⁿba, Agthí-Pethábthiⁿ; contributors: Donna Morris Park-er, Marcella Woodhull Cayou, Vida Woodhull Stabler, Pat Phillips, and Rufus White.

This chart shows how Umóⁿhoⁿ Íye is taught following the timeline of seasons of the year. Some concepts are introduced during the appropriate month. Other concepts, such as grammar, begin in the late summer with our fall semester and are built upon throughout the year through a variety of activities and lessons. All begin with an oral assessment, and as skills are learned they are assessed via written and portfolio assignments.

Our academic calendar runs a little ahead of the actual seasons, so that we introduce **Toⁿgáxthoⁿ** (fall) themes beginning in August, **Mágashude** (winter) themes beginning in November, **Mépahoⁿga** (spring) themes beginning in February, and **Nugé Moⁿshté** (summer) themes during our short time in May. The scope and sequence in this book follow the school academic calendar. On the other hand, we have divided our other seasonal offerings in the rest of this textbook based on the actual seasons, keeping in mind that the school is not the only place where the book can be of use for Umóⁿhoⁿ people.

ELDER GUIDANCE **SPIRITUALITY** ELDER DIRECTION

	TOⁿGÁXTHOⁿ (FALL) August / September / October	MÁGASHUDE (WINTER) November / December / January	MÉPAHOⁿGA (SPRING) February / March / April	NUGÉ MOⁿSHTÉ (SUMMER) May only
ÓⁿBA-T^{H}E 'Weather'	Óⁿba-t^{h}e eyóⁿ-a? 'How is the day?' ásni 'cool' két^{h}a 'bright' ámoⁿxpi 'cloudy' moⁿshté 'warm' nák^{h}ade 'hot' noⁿzhíⁿ 'rain' Teacher Q&A Student-to-Student Q&A Outside Weather Person	Óⁿba-t^{h}e eyóⁿ-a? 'How is the day?' usní 'cold' núxe 'ice' mát^{h}e 'snow' mát^{h}ithoⁿt^{h}oⁿ 'drifts' mágashude 'blizzard' First Snow, Hígoⁿ How the Umóⁿhoⁿ People Got Corn	Weather Person Q&A First Thunder noⁿzhíⁿ 'rain' moⁿshté 'warm' Give Thanks, Mépahoⁿga, The Awakening Hints of Spring: trees, geese, grass, bird sounds Creation Story	nák^{h}ade 'hot' up'úthoⁿ / t^{h}íⁿ 'humid' noⁿzhíⁿ 'rain' Growing Season Review Year ** Weather Slideshows
HÁTHE 'Clothing'	Noun – Color combination hiⁿbé 'shoes' níⁿdushiⁿ 'pants' unóⁿzhiⁿ 'blouse / shirt' listening-skills activities Háthe Thixú-a/ga 'draw clothing' Wágazhi 'command activities / TPR' Hidden Pictures activities	unóⁿzhiⁿtoⁿga 'coat' hiⁿbé snéde 'boots' paút^{h}ishiⁿ 'scarf' wat^{h}áge 'hat' listening-skills activities Wágazhi 'command activities / TPR / go to ____' Q&A understand	Q&A converse noⁿzhíⁿunoⁿzhíⁿ 'raincoat' wat^{h}áge 'cap' listening-skills activities Wágazhi 'command / TPR'	Review Year Q&A shorts, light shirt, sandals
ÁWAT^{H}EGOⁿ ÍYE-NOⁿ 'Grammar'	Writing System Introduce vowel sounds 'a e i o u' Nasal sounds / super-n's 'iⁿ oⁿ' Special sounds Letter x Whiteboard spelling Games: Sound Games			

ELDER GUIDANCE **SPIRITUALITY** ELDER DIRECTION

	TOⁿGÁXTHOⁿ (FALL) August / September / October	MÁGASHUDE (WINTER) November / December / January	MÉPAHOⁿGA (SPRING) February / March / April	NUGÉ MOⁿSHTÉ (SUMMER) May only
TÓⁿWOⁿGTHOⁿ ÚSHKOⁿ 'Tribal Life'	Hethúshka, Hédewach^{h}i, Harvest Celebration, Nióⁿba Full Moon Íⁿ'ut^{h}iⁿ Iⁿdéugt^{h}oⁿ 'handgame masquerade' Walk & Runs Gahíye – Tribal Council Stated Meeting Veterans Day Honor Haská-thoⁿ égoⁿ-xti ébthiezhuba 'Pledge of Allegiance' Gahíye – Tribal Council Election	wáthisnu 'óⁿ 'sledding' núzoⁿ 'óⁿ 'ice skating' má badíⁿ 'shovelling snow' Íⁿ'ut^{h}iⁿ 'handgame'; past / present, Groups (Big Crazies, Sí Sabe, Group Nine / Henry Dick) Wathát^{h}e 'food' Gahíye – Tribal Council Stated Meeting Umóⁿhoⁿ Language Pledge Four Hills of Life American Indian Heritage Month Umóⁿhoⁿ Quotes Family Trees, P. Brille	Teníxa Ugthézhe Uná 'mushroom hunting' Wá'e 'planting gardens' Sports, Softball, Bikeriding, Íⁿ'ut^{h}iⁿ Gahíye – Tribal Council Stated Meeting Umóⁿhoⁿ Íye Mother's Day	Memorial Day Church Activities Travel Tribal Events Tipi Meetings Gahíye – Tribal Council Stated Meeting Timóⁿgthe 'raise the tipi'
WATHÁT^{H}E, ÚHOⁿ 'Food & Cooking'	Thískie oⁿwóⁿthat^{h}e-noⁿ 'We eat together' Food Vocabulary Plastic Foods with verbs School Daily Menu Food Q&A Birthday Cakes Breakfasts, Fruit Salad, Ice Cream, Breakfast Cereal, Breakfast Burritos Importance of Salt	Birthday Cakes Fruit Donuts & Milk Breakfast: Crazy Eggs / Pancakes Variety of Foods Caramel Apples Winter Fruit & Vegetables Traditional Food: Washóⁿge Importance of Salt	Birthday Cakes ** Teníxa Ugthézhe uná, uhóⁿ, that^{h}é 'hunt, cook and eat mushrooms' *** Field Trip to Úthiwiⁿti 'grocery store' ** Indian Tacos / Cowboy Bread Easter Eggs, color, hunt Egg-Salad Sandwiches ** Hard-Boiled Egg with salt Importance of Salt	Preparing the Earth Heirloom Seeds Wá'e 'planting' Moⁿshté-ama 'summer weather' Nature effects on garden Tour to identify berries

ELDER GUIDANCE **SPIRITUALITY** ELDER DIRECTION			
ToⁿGÁXTHOⁿ (FALL) August / September / October	MÁGASHUDE (WINTER) November / December / January	MÉPAHOⁿGA (SPRING) February / March / April	NUGÉ MOⁿSHTÉ (SUMMER) May only
WÉTHIHIDE 'Technology' How to make super-n's and super-h's Body-part slideshow Emotions slideshow Community calendar	Documentation Digital photography Community calendar	Tripod Basic self-introduction slideshow Íⁿ'utʰiⁿ wagáxe 'recording handgame' Community calendar *** Iⁿdé Wagáxe Shkóⁿshkoⁿ Making movies	Year Portfolio Reflection Slideshow ** Community calendar *** Iⁿdé Wagáxe Shkóⁿshkoⁿ
ÍⁿNOⁿHA TÓⁿDE 'Nature' táxti 'deer' zizíka 'turkey' móⁿga 'skunk' síⁿga 'squirrel' xithá pasóⁿ 'eagle' gthedóⁿ 'hawk' nihóⁿga 'spring' – sacred Environmental Changes Days Shorter Harvest of Corn Beans Squash Wahába Hiⁿbthiⁿ Watʰóⁿ Tʰóⁿ Wahába Ukʰéthiⁿ 'Indian Corn' White Corn, Washóⁿge Moⁿzhóⁿxe 'onions' / lay down Pézhexuta 'sage' Tabéhi 'wild tea' Offer Prayer Sumac Color Change Browning of Land	Winter Hikes: ÓⁿpʰoⁿToⁿga 'Big Elk', uxthábe 'timbers', Old Mission River Freeze Discuss Types of Animals Traditional Foods Dried Meat	Clay / mud Mépahoⁿga Animal babies Preparation: Washóⁿge, walnuts days longer healing plants tabéhi 'Indian tea' teníxa ugthézhe 'morel mushrooms' nubthóⁿ 'Indian perfume (medicine)' Waxchá Uzhí Planting Flower Seeds Sounds of Nature Sigthé Íbahoⁿ 'Animal Track Identification'	pézi 'gooseberry' agthóⁿkamoⁿge 'raspberry' kóⁿde 'plum' bashté 'strawberry' waxthá táshe 'milkweed buds' Offer Prayer

ELDER GUIDANCE **SPIRITUALITY** ELDER DIRECTION			
ToⁿGÁXTHOⁿ (FALL) August / September / October	MÁGASHUDE (WINTER) November / December / January	MÉPAHOⁿGA (SPRING) February / March / April	NUGÉ MOⁿSHTÉ (SUMMER) May only
TÓⁿWOⁿGTHOⁿ-DI 'In the Community' Umóⁿhoⁿ Places Game	Winter / Christmas Songs	Dr. Seuss 'The Foot Book' Nursing-Home Visits Jumprope for Heart Girl-Scout Cookies	

4.7 FIRST DAYS OF SCHOOL AND BASIC SELF-INTRODUCTIONS

Translation: Marcella Woodhull Cayou.

Cultural Note

The first days of school are always filled with the school's rules and expectations that are determined by the UNPS curriculum. As regards Umó^{n}ho^n Culture, we also address what we hope to teach from an Umó^{n}ho^n perspective. In the teaching of our children we ask them how they see "Respect" shown between our people within our communities. They are always "spot on" when describing a situation. The teaching of Umó^{n}ho^n Language and Culture also has behavior expectations. The Elders taught us that the most important teachings are to "help one another," "pity one another," and "be careful what you say."

First Lesson on Culture and Respect, Umó^{n}ho^n Ushkó^n-t^{h}e: The Umó^{n}ho^n Way

OBJECTIVES

- To instill an atmosphere of respect in the classroom
- To introduce the Elders and help students to relate to them
- To develop familiarity with the vowel sounds of Umó^{n}ho^n Íye
- To serve as the first building block of an all-year self-introduction curriculum

MATERIALS

Vowel sounds/symbols written on large cards for display on the wall (with a similar sound in an English word, and an example Umó^{n}ho^n word): use lesson 1.1, the Writing System Quick Sheet: **Umó^{n}ho^n Íye-t^{h}e Áwat^{h}ego^n Baxú-No^n**; walkie-talkies (or updated technology); word sheet in random order to read into the walkie-talkies in the exercise below; binders, pens

Activities

First, introduce the Elders and allow them to speak about themselves and respect. (Ask Elders to share a story of when they saw respect shown. What does "respect" mean to them?)

Provide listening, reading and writing activities in a game-playing format (dice games, hangman, You're-the-Teacher, etc.).

Review

What do the following mean?

- **Ko^{n}há**
- **Ko^{n}hó**
- **Negíha**
- **Negího**
- **Wagó^{n}ze**

How do you say the following?

- Hello: **Ahó / Eyó^n ní^n-a?**
- Grandmother!: **Ko^{n}hó / Ko^{n}há!**
- My name is_____: **Izházhe wiwíta-t^{h}e_____.**

New Vocabulary

Wíbthahoⁿ: I thank you.

Óⁿhoⁿ/Áoⁿ/Égoⁿ: Yes.

Óⁿkazhi: No.

Tigóⁿho/Tigoⁿhá: Grandpa (used when speaking to)

Student Reflection: The Umóⁿhoⁿ Way

- How do we call people in Umóⁿhoⁿ Íye to show that we respect them?
- What do our Elders have to say about showing respect?

Sounds of Umóⁿhoⁿ

Using your vowel cards and the Writing System Quick Sheet: **Umóⁿhoⁿ Íye-tʰe Áwatʰegoⁿ Baxú-Noⁿ** quick reference in lesson 1.1, rehearse the sound-symbol correspondences of the Umóⁿhoⁿ vowels. Additional teachings for the nasal vowels:

oⁿ as in **óⁿhoⁿ:** yes

You can practice making this sound by starting to say "on," and drawing out the vowel for a long time. Oⁿ is the vowel sound you hear before you say the consonant n.

iⁿ as in **wíⁿ:** one

This sound can be practiced by saying "mean" and drawing out the vowel the same way you did for "on."

Exercises

Practice saying each sound individually. (Oral practice)

Model the sound three times for students and have each student say the sound.

Repeat this with all the vowel sounds.

Practice saying all the sounds in a row.

Say the following in a row and have students repeat it: a e i o u oⁿ iⁿ.

You can vary this (e.g., do it once slowly, once fast).

Play a Sound Game using the Umóⁿhoⁿ Sound Guide board and pointer.

Divide the students into two groups, the Earth and Sky. They should stand in two lines. Wagóⁿze points to a vowel on the sound guide board. The student to pronounce it correctly wins one point for that side. This should be played until oral observation shows the students understand Umóⁿhoⁿ vowel sounds.

WALKIE-TALKIE EXERCISE

Divide the students into two groups. Give each group its list of sets ordered for reading into the walkie-talkie. The students separate. The first (odd) group will read the words in their set in Umóⁿhoⁿ only. The group hearing the word will try to figure out which word it is and tell the English meaning. If they guess right, the group gets 1 point. If they guess wrong, the group reading the word gets 1 point. Elders can help the students practice pronouncing before they talk into the mic. The sets are to be done in order (1, 2, 3, 4 . . .).

set 1	set 2
tá: dried meat	**há:** skin
té: buffalo	**hé:** lice
tí: house	**hí:** tooth
tú: blue	**hú:** voice

set 3	set 4
wí: I	**tí:** house
wí^n: one	**tí^n:** dewy/humid

set 5	set 6
ahó: hello	**ha:** lips
hó^n: night	**ihó^n:** mother

set 7	set 8
eáto^n: why	**gaxá:** branch
É áta: It is important.	**gaxó^n:** break by striking

set 9	set 10
shó^n: quit/ready	**dúba:** four
shú: prairie chicken	**dó^{n}ba:** look at it

SELF-INTRODUCTION

Target vocabulary (**wémo^{n}xe**, "question"; **edíye**, "answer"):

wémo^{n}xe-k^{h}e: Ebé ní^n-a?/Ebé ní^n-hó?: Who are you?

edíye-k^{h}e: Ebé bthí^n-t^{h}e uwíbtha-tami^{n}k^{h}e. Izházhe wiwíta-t^{h}e _____ : I'll tell you who I am. My name is _____ .

METHOD AND ORDER

Have the teacher work with an assistant, Elder, or other teacher to model this exchange—in both directions. *Wait until another day before advancing.*

On the day that you plan to have students participate for the first time (day 1), simplify by dropping **Ebé bthí^n-t^{h}e uwíbtha-tami^{n}k^{h}e** (unless you know that students know this phrase from previous exposure).

Day 1: Model again with assistant, Elder, or teacher, then use the **wémo^{n}xe** ("question") to prompt a couple of students you believe will be able to answer.

Day 2: Prompt the same students as yesterday, then go round-robin, prompting each student.

Day 3: Add **Ebé bthi^n-t^{h}e uwíbtha-tami^{n}k^{h}e** if you have not used it so far. Offer a teaching for why this is added.

Day 4: Model with assistant/Elder/teacher by going through the exchange and then one of you tells the other, **Ímo^{n}xa/ga**—asking the helper to ask the first student. That person asks the first student and then says, **Ímoⁿxa/ga**, asking that student to ask the next student. It may take a few days for students to master this routine.

After students have mastered asking each other, begin to reinforce by building the vocabulary into other activities, and move on to the next self-introduction units—lesson 4.8 Self-Introduction Basic Curriculum and its concluding Question and Answer segment, following here, and lesson 6.3 Self-Introductions: Additional Phrases and Tisha Webster's Example " in the Winter: Mágashude chapter.

4.8 SELF-INTRODUCTION BASIC CURRICULUM: EBÉ BTHÍ^N-T^{H}E UWÍBTHA-TAMI^{N}K^{H}E

Translation: Marcella Woodhull Cayou; elicitation/transcription: Vida Woodhull Stabler.

Quick Reference: Vocabulary Goals for Basic Self-Introduction

As students progress, add more material until they achieve mastery.

Ebé bthíⁿ-tʰe uwíbtha-tamiⁿkʰe: I'll tell you who I am.

Izházhe wiwíta-tʰe _____ : My name is
_____ .

or **Umóⁿhoⁿ izházhe wiwíta-tʰe**
_____ **shi.**

Wáxe izházhe wiwíta-tʰe _____ : My Umóⁿhoⁿ name is _____ and my English name is _____ .

Iⁿdádi izházhe etá-tʰe _____ : My father's name is _____ .

Íⁿnoⁿha izházhe etá-tʰe _____ : My mother's name is _____ .

Witígoⁿ izházhe etá-tʰe _____ : My grandfather's name is _____ .

Wikóⁿ izházhe etá-tʰe _____ : My grandmother's name is _____ .

_____ **-kʰe íⁿthiⁿge:** My _____ is passed.

_____ **bthíⁿ:** I am [clan].

or _____ **núzhiⁿga / mízhiⁿga / shénuzhiⁿga / shémizhiⁿga / wa'ú / nú bthíⁿ:**

I am a _____ [clan] boy / girl / young man / young woman / man / woman.

_____ **ithátʰa-mazhi-noⁿmóⁿ:** I don't touch _____ .

_____ **oⁿthóⁿtʰa-bazhi-noⁿ:** We don't touch _____ .

Umóⁿhoⁿ bthíⁿ: I am Umóⁿhoⁿ.

or **Umóⁿhoⁿ núzhiⁿga / mízhiⁿga / shénuzhiⁿga / shémizhiⁿga / wa'ú / nú bthíⁿ:** I am a Umóⁿhoⁿ boy / girl / young man / young woman / man / woman.

Cultural Note

The preceding self-introduction is not the only way to introduce oneself. Here are a few considerations you make during an introduction: If you are introducing yourself to an Elder person, you would mention a grandparent or even an earlier generation that the Elder may be more likely to have known. Also, if only one of your parents is Umóⁿhoⁿ you would mention your family name and father's or mother's clan. This is important because this is how relationships are established. There are different ways to self-introduce if in a public gathering addressing a group of Umóⁿhoⁿ people or relatives. If this is the case, acknowledge the Elders in the group first before speaking.

Question & Answer: Phrases for Prompts, Games, and Round-Robin

Ebé níⁿ-a?/Ebé níⁿ-hó? : Who are you?

Ebé bthíⁿ-tʰe uwíbtha-tamiⁿkʰe: I'll tell you who I am.

Izházhe thithíta-tʰe iⁿdádoⁿ-a? : What is your name?

Izházhe wiwíta-tʰe _____: My name is _____.

Iⁿdádoⁿ izházhe níⁿ-a? : What is your name?

_____ izházhe bthíⁿ: I am _____ by name.

Izházhe iⁿdádoⁿ aníⁿ-a?: What name do you have?

_____ izházhe abthíⁿ: I have the name _____.

Izházhe iⁿdádoⁿ thíthadai-a?: What name did they call you?

_____ izházhe íⁿthada: They called me by the name _____.

Izházhe iⁿdádoⁿ thi'í?: What name did they give you?

_____ izházhe oⁿ'í: They gave me the name _____.

Ebé izházhe-tʰe thigí'i?: Who gave you your name?

Witígoⁿ _____-akʰa izházhe-tʰe oⁿgí'i: My grandfather _____ gave me my name.

Thiádi ebé-a?: Who is your father?

Iⁿdádi izházhe etá-tʰe _____: My father's name is _____.

Thihóⁿ ebé-a?: Who is your mother?

Íⁿnoⁿha izházhe etá-tʰe _____: My mother's name is _____.

Thitígoⁿ ebé-a?: Who is your grandfather?

Witígoⁿ izházhe etá-tʰe _____: My grandfather's name is _____.

Thikóⁿ ebé-a?: Who is your grandmother?

Wikóⁿ izházhe etá-tʰe _____: My grandmother's name is _____.

Tóⁿwoⁿgthoⁿ thithíta iⁿdádoⁿ-a?: What is your clan?

or **Tóⁿwoⁿgthoⁿ iⁿdádoⁿ níⁿ-a?:** What clan are you?

or **Tóⁿwoⁿgthoⁿ thithíta ebé-a?:** Who is your clan?

_____ bthíⁿ: I am [clan].

Tóⁿwoⁿgthoⁿ thithíta-mashe iⁿdádoⁿ íthatʰa-bazhi-noⁿ-a?: What doesn't your clan touch?

_____ oⁿthóⁿtʰa-bazhi-noⁿ: We don't touch _____.

4.9 CLOTHING AND WEATHER: HÁTHE, MOⁿSHTÉ

Translation: Marcella Woodhull Cayou, Donna Morris Parker, and Susan Freemont; from: "Fall Phrases," "Seasonal Weather Terms," "Morning Routine Commands," "Clothing Items," "New & Old Game," "Shíⁿgazhiⁿga Everyday Phrases," and "Stuffed Bear Phrases"; transcription/elicitation: Vida Woodhull Stabler.

Moⁿshté-doⁿshte: Whenever It's Warm Weather

unóⁿzhiⁿ: shirt

Unóⁿzhiⁿ móⁿ / Unóⁿzhiⁿ uánoⁿzhiⁿ: I'm wearing a shirt.

Unóⁿzhiⁿ itóⁿthiⁿadi uáginoⁿzhiⁿ: I'm wearing my oldest shirt.

watʰé: dress /skirt

watʰé snéde: long Umóⁿhoⁿ dress

níⁿdeuthishiⁿ / niⁿdúthishiⁿ / níⁿdushiⁿ: pants

Níⁿdushiⁿ sabe uátʰoⁿ: I'm wearing black pants.

niⁿdúthishiⁿ móⁿtʰe / níⁿdushiⁿ móⁿtʰe: underwear

níⁿde ágthoⁿ: diaper

unóⁿzhiⁿ móⁿtʰe: undershirt

hiⁿbé: shoes

Hiⁿbé tega uthátʰoⁿ-a?: Are you wearing new shoes?

Hiⁿbé watháwa ánoⁿ uthátʰoⁿ?: What size shoes do you wear?

hiⁿbékoⁿ: shoelaces

Hiⁿbékoⁿ koⁿtʰóⁿ/ga: Tie your shoes.

hiⁿbé ukʰéthiⁿ / hiⁿbéukʰethiⁿ / hiⁿbé: moccasins

hiⁿbéagahadi / hiⁿbéakigthaha: rubber boots / overboots

Hiⁿbé-tʰe páhiⁿ ithápatʰe: I stitched quillwork onto my moccasins.

hiⁿbégawiⁿxe / hiⁿbékuwiⁿxe / hiⁿbéugaxe / hiⁿbébuxe: socks

móⁿge ithágashke: button (chest)

ípithage: belt

ithágashke: buckle / pin

noⁿzhíⁿunoⁿzhiⁿ: raincoat

weágashke: safety pin

hóⁿdoⁿ háthe / hóⁿdoⁿ wáthaha: pajamas

Mépahoⁿga: Spring/First Thunder

Mépahoⁿga atʰí: Spring is here/First Thunder has come.

Iⁿgthóⁿhutʰoⁿ: Thunder roars.

Witígoⁿ-ama agthí: Those Grandfathers are back.

Thióⁿba: Lightning flashes.

Thigthíze: Lightning forks.

Mémathe: spring snow

Noⁿzhíⁿ: It's raining.

Noⁿzhíⁿubixoⁿ / Niúbixoⁿ: It's misting.

Óⁿthe-xchi ubíxoⁿ noⁿzhíⁿ: It's sprinkling slow.

Tadóⁿhe: whirlwind / dust devil

Moⁿgáshude: dust storm / dust devil

Tadésagi toⁿga / tadóⁿhe toⁿga: tornado

Mási uxpáthe: It's hailing.

Óⁿbathe mási: There was hail today.

Shúdemoⁿhoⁿ: It's foggy.

Mási-tʰe gá-thoⁿska-thoⁿthoⁿ, mikáhithawa é-thoⁿska-xti égoⁿ: The hail was this big, the same size as a quarter.

Su'é noⁿzhíⁿ / Su'é-áchoⁿ: It's pouring down rain. (sound word)

Moⁿshté-ama gí: The warm days are coming.

Óⁿba-tʰe hébe shóⁿ égoⁿ: The weather has eased up a little (kind of partly stopped).

Up'úthoⁿ: It's sticky / steamy / humid.

Óⁿnakʰade-áchoⁿ-egoⁿ iⁿshtá bthíp'iⁿze: The sun is shining on me so hot I have to close my eyes.

Nákʰade-áchoⁿ (Nákʰadach.): It's very hot.

Cultural Note

As longtime residents of the Great Plains, the Umóⁿhoⁿ people are intimately aware of the weather. In the pre-reservation days our very survival depended upon watching the weather signs and being prepared to find safety in times of extremes of temperature, wind, and storms. Today we continue to be respectful of the power of the Thunder Beings, storms, and other weather-related conditions. We are concerned for the safety of our family members as they make their way to and from school and work when there are threatening weather conditions. It is common to greet another person in passing by talking about the weather within the Umóⁿhoⁿ community. Talking about the weather provides an excellent opportunity to use our Umóⁿhoⁿ language on a daily basis. In every class meeting the Elders and students are encouraged to ask each other about what sort of day it is. The responses can vary from simple to complex. Practice the following pattern by filling in the blank with an appropriate word that describes the day:

> Q: **Óⁿba-tʰe eyóⁿ-a?**
> R: **Óⁿba-tʰe** _____ .

4.10 UMÓ^NHO^N FLAG SONG

Translation: Rufus White and Marcella Woodhull Cayou.

Shé-thoⁿ moⁿzhóⁿ shí-thoⁿ-ta
that   land   you went to the
The land over there where you were

Haská   thé-thoⁿ   watháʼi.
flag   this   you gave it to us
This flag was given to us by you.

Kʰagé   thí-e-niⁿ-goⁿ   aníta.
brother   it's because of you   I live.
Brother, because of you I'm alive.

History of the Umóⁿhoⁿ (United States) Flag Song Use within Our Umóⁿhoⁿ Community

Umóⁿhoⁿ people respect the flag of our country. The Umóⁿhoⁿ Flag Song is sung regularly during many occasions. It is sung during our annual Hédewachi harvest celebration when Veteran Flags are flown in the center of the dance arena.

During this time, the Umóⁿhoⁿ Flag Song is sung twice daily over the four days. The committee opens each of the four days by flying a different Veteran's Flag. Family will answer that call and request for their family member's flag to be flown. The Umóⁿhoⁿ Flag Song is sung both when the flag is raised and when it is retired.

At Umóⁿhoⁿ Nation Public School, respected traditional singer Elder Rufus White sings the Umóⁿhoⁿ Flag Song to young relatives attending school. He wants them to understand the meaning and to "know their Flag Song so they can sing it for returning Soldiers and when they are called upon to sing."

4.11 HÚTHUGA: WAYNE TYNDALL-AKᴴA HÚTHUGA UTHÁI-TᴴE

From "Traditional Umóⁿhoⁿ Foods" pamphlet by Wayne Tyndall, Shah Roohi, Linda Bird, Judy Held, Diane Dodendorf, and Marjorie Coffey, published by the Carl T. Curtis Health Education Center with support from the Health Promotion and Education Programs at the Nebraska Department of Health.

The Umóⁿhoⁿ Húthuga (Great Tribal Circle) consists of ten major clans: five clans to the south are designated mother earth people, while the five clans to the north comprise father sky people. See figure 01, The Clans, Húthuga, at the front of the book. Each clan had its own rites, responsibilities, and a place in the Great Tribal Circle. Some clans served as soldiers, warriors, or chiefs; and some were responsible as keepers and priests for ceremonial rites of the Umóⁿhoⁿ

Nation. In addition to clan duties and responsibilities, many Umóⁿhoⁿ belonged to social and secret societies that served the people in other good ways. The Buffalo Society, for example, were practitioners for the sick and mentally ill. Women of the Blessed Night Society took care of social problems within the tribal circle.

All clans were designated by an emblem, such as deer, buffalo, or elk or were named after the cosmic forces, such as rain, wind, or thunder. Each clan had certain foods that were forbidden, such as fowl, deer, elk, turtle, or oysters; these restrictions included no touching of elk or deer skin, ashes, red corn, insects or reptiles.

Farming and the hunt for buffalo and other smaller game played an important role in Umóⁿhoⁿ life. On the earth side the Elk Clan was in possession of the Sacred War Tent and responsible for the protection of the people. The Thundergod was protector of all warriors from infancy throughout life.

The Hóⁿga Clan on the earth side were keepers of the Sacred Pole, which represented the autonomy of the Umóⁿhoⁿ Nation, and of the Sacred White Buffalo Robe that was used ceremonially during the buffalo hunt and the gathering of maize during harvest. The Buffalo Clan were keepers of the two sacred pipes representing the two grand divisions of the tribal circle. This clan also led the two annual buffalo hunts. The Wind Clan was in charge of recreation, while the Earth-Lodge Makers had charge of the four sacred stones. Seven clans possessed hereditary chiefs who made up the chieftain circle and led the people within the tribal circle. The Thunder Clan had charge of the ceremonies for Umóⁿhoⁿ children's entrance into the world and supplemental rites before they became adults. The Deer Clan had rites pertaining to the stars and universe and the afterlife.

The Umóⁿhoⁿ kept active in their daily lives and ate foods that did not contain too much fat, sugar, and certainly no alcohol, and thereby lived to be more than one hundred years old. They did not abuse the sacred tobacco.

4.12 HARVEST CELEBRATION: HÉDEWACHᴴI/HETHÚSHKA

Translation: Rufus White; lesson: Vida Woodhull Stabler: transcription: Bryan James Gordon.

Objectives

- Learn about the annual ceremonial Hédewachʰi Harvest Celebration.
- History: Carnival Story, Princess Story, One Center Drum, no Grand Entry, Arena Director walks in and out, use of East Door for entry.

Cultural Note

The full moon in August determines the time when the annual dance will take place. It makes good sense as it allows natural light later into the evening. In past days there was always plenty to eat at that time too. Prior to the start of the four-day ceremony, during sunrise early on a Wednesday morning, the ceremonial dance grounds are blessed by a respected Elder. All those who will be involved over the days to come are there to witness the ceremony. Afterward a meal is provided by a family. Our ceremonial dance begins at noon on a Thursday and continues until all ceremony is done on Sunday evening.

In the year 2016 the annual Hédewachʰi ceremony was counted as the two hundred and twelfth celebration. However, history tells us the act of counting or documentation begun just over two hundred years ago was not the actual start year of our dance. Oral history reflects that our dancing to give thanks, whether in celebration of a good harvest or to acknowledge war deeds through a Hethúshka dance, was practiced for many years prior to any written date. The Umóⁿhoⁿ Tribe is credited as being the "originators" of the Hethúshka dance.

Introduction

Úzhawa wiⁿóⁿwa-kʰ etáthishoⁿ oⁿgátha?
doings which towards the we go
What special annual event is about to happen?

Úzhawa- tʰe óⁿba atʰóⁿ-ki wachígaxe
doings the day when dance
tʰithá- tʰe eyóⁿ ígthigthoⁿ-noⁿ?
start the how they decide theirs
How is the date for this annual event determined?

Moⁿzhóⁿ waxúbe- thoⁿ átʰoⁿ góⁿtha-
grounds sacred the stand on want
ki, iⁿdádoⁿ pahóⁿga gáxe-noⁿ etʰégoⁿ?
when what first they do have to
What takes place first before people can enter ceremonial grounds?

- MATERIALS: Video *To Sing for Someone* (1982 but labeled as 1992); video *Dancing to Give Thanks*; Gerine Woodhull Davidson Story

Activities

Watch video. Follow-up questions:

Q: **Wachígaxe- ama úwachigaxe- thoⁿta**
dancers   the   arena   to the
wiⁿóⁿwatatʰoⁿ   oⁿ upé-noⁿ?
from which side   they enter
From what direction do the dancers enter the arena?

A: **Mí éthoⁿba- tatʰoⁿ upé-noⁿ.**
sun appear   from   they enter
They enter from the east.

Q: **Kúge-   akʰa iⁿdádoⁿ éwakʰa?**
drum   the   what   refers to
What does the drum represent?

A: **Nóⁿde-   thoⁿ gakúku- tʰe éwakʰa.**
heart   the   beating   the refers to
It refers to the heartbeat.

Q: **Káxe- kʰe móⁿshoⁿ iⁿdádoⁿ**
bustle the feather   what kind
ígaxe-noⁿ?
they make it with
What kind of feathers is a traditional Umóⁿhoⁿ bustle made of?

A: **Káxe móⁿshoⁿ   ígaxe-noⁿ.**
crow feather   they make it with
They make it out of crow feathers.

Q: **Hethúshka- tʰe umóⁿthiⁿkʰa ánoⁿxti-**
Hethúshka the year   just how many
tatʰoⁿ   íthawa-noⁿ?
since   they count it
How many years have they been counting the Hethúshka?

A: **Umóⁿthiⁿkʰa kúge   noⁿba- ki**
year   thousand two   when
édi   agthíⁿ shápe-   kʰedi
then teen   six   in the

Hethúshka gthébóⁿhiⁿwiⁿ noⁿba- ki   édi
Hethúshka hundred   two   when then
shápe   noⁿba   íthawa-taitʰé.
sixes   two   they will count it
In the year 2016, the two hundred twelfth Hethúshka will be counted.

On Powwow Grounds: Úwachʰigaxe-thoⁿdi

Ebé wawéhoⁿ'e?: Who made the prayer?
Ebé wanóⁿshe?: Who's the whipman?
Ebé síⁿde?: Who are the taildancers?

Cultural Note

In the past, a "Camp Crier" would herald the coming day to the people at their campsites. It was his duty to encourage the people to make ready for the day to come. He would walk through the campsites, cane in hand, and talk about what would take place. "Hurry up, clean up your campsites and get ready. The visitors will be here to look on."

Ebé iyébaha?/Ebé éabaha?/Ebé wajépa?/ Ebé íyek^{h}ithe?: Who's Camp Crier?

Ebé xúkaho^{n}ga?: Who's Head Singer?

Áwa-tho^n-ta thatí?: Where's your camp?

Ebé íwathishi?: Who's feeding the people?

4.13 HARVEST CELEBRATION PHRASES: HÉDEWACH^{H}I/HETHÚSHKA UTHÁ

Translation: Marcella Woodhull Cayou and Donna Morris Parker; elicitation/transcription: Vida Woodhull Stabler.

Iyébaha/Éabaha to Campsites

Wó^{n}githe hi^{n}thékithai-ga!: Everybody hurry!

Wáxe-ama áthibano^n at^{h}í-taama: The White people will come to watch.

Íkithai-ga, híkithai-ga: All of you wake up and clean (yourselves) up.

Tiút^{h}o^{n}no^n thisíhii-ga: Clean up your area.

Iyébaha/Éabaha to Dancers

Hethúshka hi^{n}thék^{h}ithai-ga-hó!: Hethúshka hurry!

Wáxe-ama áthibano^n at^{h}í-taama: The White people will come to watch.

Iyébaha/Éabaha to Onlookers

Thísho^{n}i-ki no^{n}bé gachák^{h}ii-ga: If satisfied with performance, clap your hands.

Wó^{n}githe gíthe-wathe: Let's all be happy.

Wó^{n}githe wachígaxe wábano^n gíthe-wathe: All of you watching, enjoy the dancing.

4.14 UMÓ^{N}HO^N REGALIA, MEN'S AND WOMEN'S: NÚ WÁTHAHA, WA'Ú WÁTHAHA

Drawn from materials by Úthixide (Mark Awakuni-Swetland) based on work with Umó^{n}ho^n male Elders; additions for women's regalia from Donna Morris Parker, Marcella Woodhull Cayou, and Octa Mitchell Keen.

Nú Wáthaha: Men's

hi^{n}bé / hi^{n}béuk^{h}ethi^n: moccasins

mó^{n}ze gatámo^n / mó^{n}ze gamó^{n}the: bells

Umó^{n}ho^n hi^{n}bé: Umó^{n}ho^n moccasins

mó^{n}sho^n: feather

wágtho^n: pin / brooch / medallion / slide

xithá mó^{n}sho^n: eagle feather

hítho^{n}wi^n: garters

wanó^{n}p'i^n: choker

ípithage: belt / sash

úwi^{n}gazode: sidestitch choker

hí^{n}ska: beadwork

nubthó^n: perfume (traditional plant)

páhi^{n}bat^{h}e: quillwork

unóⁿzhiⁿ: shirt

paúthishiⁿ: neck scarf

wáyiⁿ: blanket / shawl / robe

táxtiha: deer hide / buckskin

wáyiⁿshnaha: broadcloth / apron

tezhíⁿhiⁿde: finger weave

wabát^{h}e: suitcase

weágashke: safety pin

wábat^{h}e: ribbonwork / appliqué

káxe: bustle

waxíⁿha: fabric / cloth / calico

zheátigthoⁿ: breechcloth

waxíⁿha nágoⁿba: ribbon

móⁿshoⁿpagthoⁿ: eagle tail-feather war bonnet

utóⁿ: leggings

utóⁿ toⁿga: chief leggings

xitháthage / xithá watháge: whole eagle headdress

táhiⁿwagthoⁿ: roach / deer-tail headdress

táhiⁿwagthoⁿ uthí'ae: roach spreader

hazízige: stretchy fabric / bandage made of stretchy fabric

móⁿzeukoⁿt^{h}oⁿ / áuthisnoⁿ: silver cuffs / armbands

noⁿbéibik^{h}a (ubét^{h}oⁿ) : handkerchief (folded)

unóⁿzhiⁿ xépa / itháthisoⁿde: vest

niúkigthaziⁿ: mirror board

watháge: headdress / hat

nushnóⁿha: otterskin / dragger

nushnóⁿhapagthe: otter turban

hímoⁿgthe: cane / dance stick

tehéupagthe: buffalo-horn hat

wét^{h}iⁿ: hatchet

nisúde: whistle

niní úzhiha: tobacco bag

iⁿdéagani / weágani: fan

núsi áxthade: bandolier beads

móⁿge ágthoⁿ: breastplate

síⁿde: tail

Wa'ú Wáthaha: Women's

háwat^{h}e: buckskin dress

weágashke: safety pin

wat^{h}é: dress

hiⁿbé / hiⁿbéuk^{h}ethiⁿ: moccasins

Umóⁿhoⁿ wat^{h}é snéde: long dress

Umóⁿhoⁿ hiⁿbé: Umóⁿhoⁿ moccasins

móⁿshoⁿ: feather

noⁿbéuthixtha: ring

xithá móⁿshoⁿ: eagle feather

úwiⁿ: earrings

xithá: eagle plume

wágthoⁿ: pin / brooch

híthoⁿwiⁿ: garters

wanóⁿp'iⁿ: choker / necklace

ípithage: belt / sash

wáyiⁿ: blanket / shawl / robe

unóⁿzhiⁿ: shirt / blouse

wáyiⁿshnaha: broadcloth / apron

híⁿska: beadwork

gazóⁿdeikoⁿte: Umóⁿhoⁿ braid ties

páhiⁿbatʰe: quillwork

noⁿbéibikʰa: handkerchief

paúthishiⁿ: neck scarf

tezhíⁿhiⁿde: finger weave

táxtiha: deer hide / buckskin

móⁿze gatámoⁿ / móⁿze gamóⁿthe: bells

4.15 SEWING PHRASES: WABÁTʰE UTHÁ

Translation: Donna Morris Parker; elicitation/
transcription: Vida Woodhull Stabler.

wáku zhiⁿga: needle

wahóⁿ: thread

Wahóⁿ-thoⁿ oⁿʼí-a, wapátʰe kóⁿbtha: Give
me the spool of thread, I want to sew.

Wahóⁿ-thoⁿ gítha, wapátʰe kóⁿbtha: Pass
around the spool of thread, I want to sew.

Wahóⁿ-thoⁿ wíuga iⁿdádoⁿ-a?: What color
is the thread?

Wáku zhiⁿga-kʰe íthathe-a?: Did you find
the needle?

Wáku zhiⁿga-kʰe itháthe: I found the
needle.

Wáku zhiⁿga-kʰe ithátha-mazhi: I didn't
find the needle.

Wahóⁿ-thoⁿ wáku zhiⁿga-kʰe-di uthísnoⁿ:
Pull the thread through the needle.

Wahóⁿ-thoⁿ wáku zhiⁿga-kʰe-di uthísnoⁿ
pasí-thoⁿ kóⁿtʰoⁿ: Pull the thread
through the needle and tie it at the head.

Ákikʰihida, égithe zháthakihe-te: Be
careful, don't poke yourself. (literally
"Watch out for yourself or you might
stab yourself.")

Thipʰí-xchi wabátʰa: Sew right.

Wabátʰe-tʰe údoⁿ gáxa: Make your sewing
nice.

Waxíⁿha-kʰe ebé thiʼí-a?: Who gave you
the material?

Wikóⁿ-akʰa waxíⁿha-kʰe oⁿgíʼi: My
grandmother gave me the material.

Thi iⁿdádoⁿ íⁿshkaxe-ta?/Thi iⁿdádoⁿ
íⁿshkaxe-taniⁿkshe-a?: What are you
going to make for me?

Watʰé snéde wíⁿ akípaxe kóⁿbtha: I want
to make an Umóⁿhoⁿ long dress for
myself.

Cultural Note

Umóⁿhoⁿ women believe that when sewing or
making something you should do so with good
thoughts and feelings. You put all the good into
the clothing you are making.

There are Umóⁿhoⁿ women considered to be
gifted seamstresses. An Umóⁿhoⁿ dress, appliqué
skirt, shirt, or blouse made by one of the seamstresses is highly prized. The services of these
women are sought after by relatives and the community. This gifted group of women have their
choice of those for whom they will sew.

There are actions to avoid and considerations
that affect behaviors when sewing. A woman
who is pregnant or with child would not use
thread or sinew. Another consideration is the
proper placement and holding of anything sharp,
such as scissors or a knife. Always pass scissors
or any sharp object by placing pointed end away
from the other person. You can also place the
sharp object down on a table with the pointed
end away from the person who will pick it up.

4.16 THE FIRST UMÓⁿHOⁿ POWWOW PRINCESS: MÍⁿDASHOⁿTHIⁿ (GERINE WOODHULL DAVIDSON)

This account was told to Vida Woodhull Stabler to share with the Umóⁿhoⁿ people.

In 1941 I was seventeen years old and living and working in Omaha with my sister. I remember this time because World War II was going on. It was Powwow time back home in Macy and as usual we were looking forward to going home. I had no idea that this day would hold a totally new and exciting experience for me.

My dad (George Woodhull Sr.) usually picked us up at the bus stop, but this time was different. Instead, we were greeted by our relative Bernard Springer, who informed us that our dad had asked him to pick us up. Bernard drove us to the Powwow grounds and to our family campsite.

My Aunt Lizzie came out of her tent, came to me, took my hand, and led me inside the tent. I had taken great care to curl my hair with paper strips, as I wanted to look my best for Powwow. To my surprise they combed my hair and tried to smooth my reluctant curls. Soon my hair was in two braids.

I was scared and still didn't know exactly what I was being prepared for. I was captive to my Aunt Lizzie, and it was clear she was in charge. My mother peeked in. I asked her, "Iⁿdádoⁿ gáxai-a?" ("What are they doing?") She said, "Góⁿ xthíazhi gthíⁿ-a!" ("Keep quiet. Sit still.") So I listened, sat, and did what she said.

My aunt and Bernard were rushing and I could hear the drums in the distance. Next thing I knew they were putting a buckskin dress on me. Next, the beaded moccasins were on my feet. I knew I was done when they added a feather to the back of my headband. Little by little I realized I was being prepared for the arena.

The MC came and asked if we were ready. So they both brought me out of the tent and took me to the arena. We entered from the East side of the arena. The singers sang a slow song. Bernard said, "Go in the arena, slowly walk around and turn to the people and smile." Regina Lawry was behind me. We had known each other from boarding school. There were three or four other girls but I don't remember their names. The other contestants were eliminated by using a feather held over their heads. Those with the strongest cheers remained in the contest.

It came down to Regina and me. The people started whistling and clapping. We stopped on the southwest side of the arena. Regina and I stood together. A man came to me and lifted a feather over my head. He did the same to Regina. At first we both received the same amount of applause from the audience. They said we should go around the arena again. Wow, there was clapping whistling, and even car honking. Regina also received cheers from the crowd. I begin to think how I was home on my Umóⁿhoⁿ reservation.

They put the feather over on my head and the noise from the audience grew. The people clapped their hands and hollered. The people whistled and honked the car horns. The MC asked the crowd not to make so much noise because there was another person to consider, but the crowd kept it up. The MC announced that I was the First Powwow Princess. Since this was the first time, there was no crown or blanket given to me. The Wáxe people kept taking pictures of me for a long time. My aunt Lizzie had the biggest smile on her face. They announced over the loudspeaker that I was the daughter of George Woodhull Sr. and Fannie Woodhull. My dad and mom were so proud. My mom cried.

I didn't know what to think. I finally realized what had happened and that I was the First Umóⁿhoⁿ Princess. My sisters, Christine, Irene, Mary Jane, and Eunice, were so happy and kept saying, "My sister is the first Umóⁿhoⁿ Princess!" That's the way it was. That's how I became Princess.

4.17 ZOO: WANÍTA TÍ-ATA THÉ-WATHE

Translation: Marcella Woodhull Cayou; transcription: Vida Woodhull Stabler.

Cultural Note

The land we live on once provided a natural habitat for animals and other creatures to grow and roam free. The buffalo once thrived on our land. The United States government promoted the killing of the buffalo nearly to extinction. Buffalo were seen as blocking the passage of the railroad, and also as an obstacle to progress, by people with different perspectives on how to use our land. This is only one example. Encroachment on our land has had a serious impact on the future of animal life on our lands.

We know that animals need food and water to survive and thrive. Umóⁿhoⁿ people believe, from a spiritual sense, that if we are good stewards of the land, it will in turn provide what we need. Talk with our children about the animals that roam free on our lands. The four-legged deer, fox, coyote, beaver, muskrats and more, the fish, the turkey and other feathered ones need clean soil that grows the plants feeding the critters that they eat for sustenance. Those that live in the water need clean water, and they too serve a purpose. It will be a hard life when we can only see our relatives the animals in a zoo atmosphere.

Directions

Break down each word in the Umóⁿhoⁿ Íye sentences that follow. Write the English equivalent underneath each Umóⁿhoⁿ word. This will help you see how a sentence is structured.

Waníta tí-kʰe-ta thé-wathe.

Óⁿba Wésatoⁿ kʰé waníta tí-ta oⁿgáthe-taoⁿgatʰoⁿ.

Óⁿba Wésatoⁿ kʰé waníta tí wóⁿgabanoⁿ oⁿgáthe-taoⁿgatʰoⁿ.

Answer Key.

Waníta tí- kʰe- ta thé- wathe.
animal house the to go let's

Óⁿba Wésatoⁿ kʰé waníta tí- ta
day fifth c'mon animal house to
oⁿgáthe- taoⁿgatʰoⁿ.
we go we will

Óⁿba Wésatoⁿ kʰé waníta tí
day fifth c'mon animal house
wóⁿgabanoⁿ oⁿgáthe- taoⁿgatʰoⁿ.
we look on we go we will

4.18 GROCERY SHOPPING: PAHÓⁿGA ÚTHIWIⁿ TÍ-ATA OⁿGÁTHAI-TʰE

Translation: Donna Morris Parker and Marcella Woodhull Cayou; elicitation/transcription: Vida Woodhull Stabler.

Úthiwiⁿ tí-ta oⁿgátha. Áwata oⁿgáthe-ta?

We're going to the store. Where are we going?

Iⁿdádoⁿ bthíwiⁿ-tamiⁿkʰe? Iⁿdádoⁿ oⁿthíwiⁿ?

What am I going to buy? What should we buy?

Wathátʰe áhigi oⁿthíwiⁿ-taoⁿgatʰoⁿ. Moⁿkóⁿsabe bthíwiⁿ-tamiⁿkʰe.

We're going to buy a lot of food. I'm going to buy coffee.

Ánoⁿ íthawai-a? Móⁿzeska áhigi-áchoⁿ.

How much does it cost? It's too much money.

Umóⁿe-tʰe ánoⁿ íthawai-a? Úmakʰa thizá/ga./Úmakʰa-tʰe thizá/ga.

How much do the groceries cost? Take the cheapest.

Ebé móⁿzeska athíⁿ? Wagóⁿze-akʰa móⁿzeska athíⁿ.

Who has money? Teacher has the money.

Zhoⁿmóⁿthiⁿ-kʰe thizá/ga. Úzhi-thoⁿ athíⁿ-moⁿthiⁿ-a/ga.

Get / grab / take the grocery cart. Carry the bag.

Wéuzhi-tʰe agímoⁿthiⁿ-a/ga. Wéuzhi-tʰe thizá/ga.

Go get the basket and bring it back here. Get / grab / take the basket.

Gátʰe: Shéhi-ta.

It's right here (where I'm gesturing). It's over there.

Íⁿbaha/ga. Xátha itʰétha/ga.

Show me. Put it back.

Tagáxthixthi hébe zhiⁿga. Uíkoⁿ moⁿthíⁿ-a/ga.

Small package of hamburger. Go help him/her.

Thiwíⁿ-a/ga. Íⁿthiwiⁿ-a/ga.

Buy it. Buy it for me.

Wathígthoⁿ gáxai-a/ga. Oⁿthíshtoⁿ.

Make up your minds. We're done.

Kúkusi-kʰe páda/ga. Kúkusi apáde kóⁿbtha.

Butcher the hog. I want to butcher a hog.

Cultural Note

There have been numerous occasions when working with our Elders when they mention how "easy" it is now to acquire food and water compared to when they were young. Back then, much planning took place to ensure that enough food was stored to carry the family through the winter months. The family worked together as a unit to put food on the table. Today you will still hear comments about how "food is hard to come by."

4.19 SWEET DRINKS: NÍSKITHE

Translation: Donna Morris Parker; elicitation/ transcription: Vida Woodhull Stabler.

Óⁿbathe nískithe-tʰe oⁿgáxe-taoⁿgatʰoⁿ: Today we will make a sweet drink.

Awíⁿoⁿwa shkóⁿna?: Which one (kind) do you want?

Ígazhoⁿzhoⁿ/ga: Shake it.

Nískithe ígahi-tʰe thishíba/ga: Open the sweet drink mix.

Níuzhi-tʰe-di uzhí-a/ga: Put it in the pitcher.

Zhoⁿní-tʰe thizá/ga: Get the sugar.

Zhoⁿní-tʰe dúba uzhí-a/ga: Add some of the sugar.

Níuzhi-tʰe-di zhoⁿní-tʰe uzhí-a/ga: Put the sugar in the pitcher.

Ní dúba thizá/ga níuzhi-tʰe-di uzhí-a/ga: Take some water and put it in the pitcher.

Tehé toⁿga-kʰe thizá/ga: Get the big spoon.

Nískithe-tʰe uthúgahi-a/ga: Stir the sweet drink.

Níuthatoⁿ thizá/ga: Get a cup.

Nískithe-tʰe níuthatoⁿ-tʰe-di uzhí-a/ga: Pour the sweet drink in the cup.

Shetʰóⁿ-noⁿ thatóⁿzhi-a/ga: Don't drink it yet.

Shetʰóⁿ-noⁿ thatóⁿ-bazhii-a/ga: Don't drink it yet. (spoken to more than one)

Noⁿhéba/ga thatóⁿzhi-a/ga: Wait, don't drink it.

Noⁿhébai-a/ga thatóⁿ-bazhii-a/ga: Wait, don't drink it. (spoken to more than one)

Nískithe níuthatoⁿ-tʰe-di utházhi-a?: Did you pour the sweet drink in the cup?

Dúba uázhi: I poured some in.

Uázhi: I poured it in.

Núxe wíⁿ thizá/ga nískithe-tʰe-di ugthóⁿ/ ga: Take an ice cube and put it in the sweet drink.

Núxe uthágthoⁿ?: Did you put ice in?

Uágthoⁿ bthíshtoⁿ: I already put it in.

Nískithe-tʰe oⁿthátoⁿ-taoⁿgatʰoⁿ: We will drink the sweet drink.

Wóⁿgithe nískithe-tʰe thatóⁿi-a/ga: Everybody drink the sweet drink.

Nískithe-tʰe dúba ukízhi-a/ga uhá thétha/ga: Pour yourself some of the sweet drink and pass it on.

4.20 BANANA SPLITS: WAXTÁTHIGUZHE MÁSNE

Translation: Marcella Woodhull Cayou and Alice Freemont Saunsoci; elicitation/transcription: Vida Woodhull Stabler.

Ebé núxe bawégthi xtáthe-a?: Who likes ice cream?

Núxe bawégthi xtáthathe-a?: Do you like ice cream?

Núxe bawégthi iⁿdádoⁿ?: What kind of ice cream is it?

Núxe bawégthi házi xtáathe: I like grape ice cream.

Núxe bawégthi wiwíta-tʰe ska: My ice cream is the vanilla one.

Waxtáthiguzhe-kʰe thizhábai-a/ga: Peel the banana.

Wiⁿdétʰoⁿ máxoⁿi-a/ga: Cut it in half.

Waxtáthiguzhe-kʰe másnai-a/ga: Split the banana.

Zhoⁿní snúsnu uzhíi-a/ga: Put syrup on.

Whipcream íthizhoⁿzhoⁿ: Shake the whipped cream.

Táge shkóⁿna?: You want nuts?

Édi áthi'ai-a/ga: Sprinkle them there.

Zhoⁿní áthi'ai-a/ga: Sprinkle on the candy.

Ukíkoⁿ/ga: Help yourself.

núxe bawégthi: ice cream

sézi: orange

waxtáthiguzhe: banana

nóⁿpa: cherry

tehéxthu'a-égoⁿ: ice-cream cone

zíshabe / shabe: chocolate

núxe bawégthi tehé: ice-cream scoop

ska: vanilla

tehéxthu'a: ice-cream scoop

nóⁿpatu: blueberry / blue raspberry (flavoring)

uxpébuta: bowl

séziniuzhi: pineapple

zhoⁿní snúsnu ázhi-thoⁿthoⁿ: different kinds of syrup

házi: grape

táge / óⁿzhiⁿga: nuts / peanuts

zhápa: bubblegum

Xtáathe: I like it.

pézhitu: lime

Xtáatha-mazhi: I don't like it.

4.21 FUNERARY SAYINGS: WAT'É-KʰE WAGÍXE-TʰE-SHTI UTHÁ

Translation: Marcella Woodhull Cayou; elicitation/transcription: Vida Woodhull Stabler.

Cultural Note

There is much ceremony that takes place during the passing of an Umóⁿhoⁿ relative here at home. It is best to ask your family Elders about their beliefs regarding this time.

Sayings

thiézhuba-tʰe: respect

wat'é dóⁿbe: viewing the body / paying respects

Ébthiezhuba: I gave respect to her/him.

Wat'é dóⁿbe bthé: I'm going to pay respects.

Théniezhuba-a?: Did you give respect to her/him?

Wat'é dóⁿbe né-a?: Did you go to pay respects?

Gíthiezhuba/ga: Give respect to her/him.

Wat'é dóⁿbe né-te: You could go pay respects.

Wat'é dóⁿbe né-ta: You all could go pay respects.

Íⁿthiezhuba. or **Oⁿgu íⁿthiezhuba:** We gave respect to her/him.

Wat'é dóⁿbe oⁿgátha: We're going to pay respects.

Wat'é dóⁿbe thé-wathe: Let's go pay respects.

Wakóⁿda: Creator/God

Wakóⁿda Izhíⁿge: Jesus ("God's son")

Tha'é-wigithe: I pity you, my relative.

  Tha'é-oⁿthagithe: You pitied me, relative.

  Tha'é-wagitha/ga: Show your relatives kindness. / Pity your relatives.

Washkóⁿ: Try hard. (female speaker)

Washkóⁿ-ga hó: Try hard. (male speaker)

Wáiⁿ oⁿgáthiⁿ oⁿgátʰi: We brought a blanket (to give you).

Zhuóⁿthigthe oⁿgthíⁿ-taitʰé: We're going to sit here with you (for a while).

Iⁿdádoⁿ-shte zhiⁿgá-ma úwathagina-te. Íbahoⁿ góⁿtha: You should tell the children something about your relative. They want to know.

Wakʰéga áwa-tʰe-goⁿ thiⁿgé-a?: Was s/he ill? Why is s/he gone?

Éta-thishoⁿ oⁿgágthe-taoⁿgatʰoⁿ: We're going to go back (over that way).

Táp'ska xátha oⁿgágtha: We're going back to the school.

míxe: grave

Míxe ába'u-a/ga: Cover the grave with dirt (making a mound).

Oⁿgíxa: We buried our relative.

Ebé waxé?: Who is doing the burying?

Íⁿbashna/ga: Cut my hair for me.

  Éwipashna: I cut your hair for you.

  Máxe'a: S/he cut his/her hair short (traditional way).

  Thixé'a: S/he cut his/her hair short.

Noⁿzhíⁿha iⁿthíⁿgaha/ga: Comb my hair for me.

  Kʰé noⁿzhíⁿha íwigahe: Here, I'll comb your hair for you.

4.22 GRIEF IN OUR UMÓⁿHOⁿ COMMUNITY: ÚTʰIHA

Developed by the ULCC at UNPS and Vida Woodhull Stabler.

Cultural Note

When an Umóⁿhoⁿ passes on (leaves this world) there are many traditions involved. One of these takes place during the four days that the loved one is at home. During each meal, after a respected Elder prays, a small dish and cup are used to put out food and water. It is believed that the relative who has passed on will come to visit the people and places where s/he lived.

Teacher Note

We should be aware of the unique culture of our community and what occurs during the passing of Umóⁿhoⁿ relatives. Following is a list of activities, beliefs, and rituals taking place during this time.

Loved one lies "In State" for four days (at home or church).

The family has many responsibilities during this time.

Our children may miss up to four days of school due to a death in their family.

Extended Family involvement and participation: Family and Extended Family will stay with the relative lying in state, and a designated person will always be with the body.

No casual smoking at the final ceremony for the community at large.

Someone serving as the person In Charge takes care of all activities, food preparation, prayers, cup and saucer, spiritual aspects.

Wake or Native American Church; sacrifice a night of sleep.

Many community members support the family with food, gifts, money, and helping out with their presence.

Fire (specific clans) / Porch Light Left On; Cars in front of area.

State of Mourning: Hair Cut, Standing Back from Cultural Doings.

Annual memorials to remember; memorial dish prepared during special occasions.

Belief: Our relative returns to the "Place of Many Campfires" to be with all the relatives who have passed before.

Belief: Our relatives visit places they have been over their lifetime.

Emails are sent to staff to inform teachers when relatives may be missing school, as this will affect attendance.

Combing the Hair: ritual for breaking your mourning.

This is a brief explanation of what takes place and should *not* be thought of as a complete guide. Additional information will be added, and contributions are encouraged.

5.1 NAMES OF MONTHS

Transcription: Vida Woodhull Stabler.

> September: **Táxti moⁿnóⁿ'ai-kʰe**
> The moon when the deer paw the earth.
> October: **Táxti kigthígthoⁿi-kʰe**
> The moon when the deer rut.
> November: **Táxti hé baxóⁿi-kʰe**
> The moon when the deer shed antlers.

These names for months come directly from *The Omaha Tribe*, volumes 1 and 2, by Alice Fletcher and Francis La Flesche. There has been discussion concerning alternative or different ways to say a few of the names. The phrases are written as they appear in *The Omaha Tribe* with a few spelling updates to adapt them to the present orthography. When discussing existing names for months, one Elder said, "I stand to be corrected. Those were the Old People back then."

5.2 CHEERS FOR THE CHIEFS: NÍKAGAHI MOⁿTHÍⁿI-A/GA

Cheers elicited by: Umóⁿhoⁿ Íye II students Thomas Webster, Will Webster, Angel Aldrich, Tisha Webster, and Lawrence Webster, with teacher Vida Woodhull Stabler; Elders present: Marcella Woodhull Cayou and Alice Saunsoci. All phrases are to be used with the megaphone.

Football: *Tabé Sipá*

Marcella Woodhull Cayou.

> **Washkóⁿi-a/ga:** Try your best.
> **Níkagahi moⁿthíⁿi-a/ga:** Go Chiefs.
> **Utʰíⁿi-a/ga:** Hit 'em.
> **Hiⁿthékithe noⁿhégazhii-a/ga:** Hurry—run!
> **Uhóⁿge-tʰe kʰí góⁿthai-a/ga:** Try to get the goal! (literally "Try to come home to the end zone.")
> **Mási, Mási, wanóⁿoⁿi-a/ga!:** Macy, Macy, hear us!
> **Níkagahi, Níkagahi, Washkóⁿi-a/ga:** Chiefs, Chiefs, Try Hard!
> **Níkagahi, Níkagahi, Úhii-a/ga:** Chiefs, Chiefs, Win!
> **Tabé-thoⁿ weáhide noⁿtʰái-a/ga!** Kick the ball far!
> **Níkagahi oⁿthóⁿkizhu:** Chiefs we're proud of you. (literally "We're proud of the Chiefs")
> **Níkagahi-mashe oⁿthóⁿthikizhu:** Chiefs we're proud of you.
> **Níkagahi uhí-taama:** The Chiefs will win.
> **Wákʰithai-a/ga, Wákʰithai-a/ga, Uhíi-a/ga:** Fight, Fight, Win!

Volleyball

Marcella Woodhull Cayou.

Íwanoⁿthazhi Ut^{h}íⁿi-a/ga:

Tabé-thoⁿ ut^{h}íⁿi-a/ga: Hit the ball. Spike it!

Thip^{h}i shkádai-a/ga: Play right! (**Thip^{h}i** is pronounced **"thipi"** by some speakers.)

5.3 FALL PHRASES: TOⁿGÁXTHOⁿ UTHÁ

Translation: Marcella Woodhull Cayou and Donna Morris Parker; elicitation/transcription: Vida Woodhull Stabler; revision and annotation: Mark Awakuni-Swetland; orthography check: Bryan James Gordon.

Directions

Break down the following Umóⁿhoⁿ phrases. The English is provided.

Zhoⁿ'ábe-ama bíze uxpáthe.

The leaves are dry and falling.

Tiút^{h}oⁿnoⁿ zhoⁿ'ábe uxpáthe thibéxiⁿ-a/ga.

Rake the fallen leaves from the lawn (between the houses).

Usní-táthishoⁿ oⁿgátha.

Cool weather is coming. ("We are going toward the cold.")

Usní-táthishoⁿ oⁿgáthe-taoⁿgat^{h}oⁿ.

We will be going toward cold weather.

Móⁿhiⁿ, zhoⁿ'ábe-k^{h}e edábe oⁿthísihi-taoⁿgat^{h}oⁿ.

We are going to clear away the grass and leaves.

Mystery Sentences

Write the English equivalent under each Umóⁿhoⁿ word below on line provided.

Tabé sipá thashkáde xtáthathe-a? _____

_____

Óⁿba-t^{h}e sní. Unóⁿzhiⁿ úthanoⁿzhiⁿ-a? Unóⁿzhiⁿ únoⁿzhiⁿ-a/ga!

_____

_____

Words to Learn

wagthíshka kigthézha: box elder (bug) ("spotted-body bug"; they die off at this time)

tiíbabexiⁿ: broom ("used to uncover the house by pushing")

wébabexiⁿ: any kind of broom or brush ("tool for uncovering by pushing")

wéthibexiⁿ: rake ("tool for uncovering by hand")

Koⁿhá, waníshupe-taniⁿkshe-a?: Grandma, are you going to clean up?

Áoⁿ, gasóⁿthiⁿ tiút^{h}oⁿnoⁿ-thoⁿ wabthíshupe-tamiⁿk^{h}e: Yes, tomorrow I'm going to clean up in the hallway / yard.

Answer Key

Zhoⁿ'ábe-	ama	bíze	uxpáthe.
leaf	the	dry	fall

Tiút^ho^nno^n   **zho^n'ábe uxpáthe**
house between   leaf   fallen
thibéxi^n-a/ga.
rake

Usní- táthisho^no^ngátha.
cold   toward   we go

Usní- táthisho^no^ngáthe-   tao^ngat^ho^n.
cold   toward   we go   we will

Mo^nhí^n,   zho^n'ábe- k^he edábe
grass   leaf   the too
o^nthísihi- tao^ngat^ho^n.
we clear   we will

Tabé sipá thashkáde xtáthathe-a?
ball   toe   you play   you like
Do you like to play football?

Ó^nba- t^he sní. Unó^nzhi^n úthano^nzhi^n-a?
day   the cold   jacket   you wear
Unó^nzhi^n úno^nzhi^n-a/ga!
jacket   wear
It's cold today. Are you wearing a jacket?
   Wear a jacket!

Cultural Note

Vida Woodhull Stabler.

Umó^nho^n people noticed the many signs given by nature that spoke to the changes in weather and how those changes are reflected in our environment. Aunt Marcella Woodhull Cayou mentioned to me to notice "that the trees get dark and then lighter (in color)," and how the weather is "changeable, and sometimes people get sick." Grandma Donna Morris Parker had walnut trees in her yard. On one occasion, upon her invitation, I took the Umo^nho^n Language class to gather walnuts there. She told us a story about how squirrels helped themselves to the stored walnuts while the family waited for them to dry. There were shells here and there.

5.4 JUSTIN MCCAULEY'S COUGAR STORY: JUSTIN-AK^HA WANÍTA DÓ^NBAI-T^HE UGTHÁ GÓ^NTHA

Story: Justin McCauley; translation: Donna Morris Parker; elicitation/transcription: Vida Woodhull Stabler; orthography check and consolidation: Bryan James Gordon.

Justin- ak^ha ho^négo^nch^he to^ngáxtho^n
Justin   the   morning   fall
íkitha.   Édi   ho^nnó^npaze.
woke up   there   twilight
One early fall morning Justin woke up at dawn.

"Ó^nbathe táxti- tho^nk^ha uáne- tami^nk^he."
today   deer   the   I hunt   I will
"Today I am going to hunt deer."

"Hi^nbé-snede wiwíta,   unó^nzhi^n wiwíta,
boot   my   jacket   my
wahúto^nthi^n   wiwíta   kó^nbtha."
gun   my   I want

Unó^nzhi^n hi^nbé ágaha, wahúto^nthi^n
jacket   boot   gun
abthí^n   bthé-   tami^nk^he."
I take   with me   I will
"I want my boots, my jacket and my gun. I will take my jacket, boots and gun with me."

Justin moⁿzhóⁿ ábae wétugthoⁿ etá
Justin land hunt on truck his
ábaaze. Pahé- thoⁿ moⁿshíata noⁿshtóⁿ.
drove hill the up on top stopped
Justin drove his truck out to hunt on the land.
  He stopped up on top of a hill.

"Agthíⁿ, áakʰihide, anóⁿ'oⁿ."
"I sit, I watch, I listen."

Sabázhi, Justin- akʰa iⁿdádoⁿshtewoⁿ
suddenly Justin the something
dóⁿba, úthixide.
saw looking around
Suddenly while looking around, Justin
  saw something.

Noⁿbá, zí, iⁿshtá- kʰe,
two yellow eye the
ugáhoⁿnoⁿpaze, núga úthixide.
darkness male looking around
Two things, yellow, eyes, in the darkness, a
  male hunting.

Miídoⁿbe sátoⁿ xthabé gahá ithápe.
hour five tree on waited
He waits in the tree for five hours.

Waníta móⁿtanoⁿha- akʰa múgthoⁿ thé.
animal wild the go away went
Finally, the cougar runs away.

Justin- akʰá tanúka, táxti ábaa-bazhi,
Justin the meat deer didn't hunt
agtháthiⁿ-gthé-tatʰé
to bring his home with him
Justin didn't manage to hunt deer to bring
  it home with him

Umóⁿhoⁿ níkashiⁿga- thoⁿkʰa wa'í.
Umóⁿhoⁿ person the to give them
to give meat to the Umóⁿhoⁿ people.

Cultural Note

Vida Woodhull Stabler.

Our people tell stories of cougar sightings on our lands. Our timbers are a haven for wildlife, especially with ever-encroaching farmlands.

5.5 HOMECOMING FLOAT

This is a set of activities to be done over the course of two to three days leading up to homecoming.

Objectives

Practice phrases useful for encouraging teams.

- Prepare our Homecoming float.
- Review **bth-** verb pattern.
- Introduce the future tense.
- Commands to more than one.

Materials

Markers, construction paper (red, yellow, white), posterboard, scissors, pencils

Introduction.

Móⁿshoⁿ páagthoⁿ bthíxu- tamiⁿkʰe.
war bonnet I draw I will
I am going to draw a war bonnet.

Iⁿdádoⁿ níxu?

what   you draw

What are you drawing?

Today, we're going to start getting ready for homecoming, where we'll have a float. We need to encourage our team to do well, using Umóⁿhoⁿ Íye.

Lesson

We have large posterboards to decorate the sides of the van in which our Elders will ride. Practice sketching out a design for a poster for the van on construction paper. Put a phrase in Umóⁿhoⁿ Íye on your drawing that encourages our team to fight hard. The next day these pictures and phrases can be drawn onto posterboard and colored in with markers. These are to be placed on the van where the Elders ride during the parade. Also, some students will drum with Grandpa Rufus White on another float.

SOME OF THE PHRASES CREATED TO
GO ON THE POSTERS THIS YEAR WERE:

Níkagahi úhi-ta!: Win Chiefs! (hopeful)

Níkagahi-ama tabésipa íthigthoⁿ!: Chiefs are in charge of the football!

Níkagahi-máshe washkóⁿi-a/ga!: Try your best Chiefs!

Tabé-thoⁿ móⁿshi óⁿtha thétha/ga!: Throw the ball high!

Allen, Wakóⁿda-wathahoⁿi-a/ga!: Say your prayers, Allen! (opposing team's name)

Tabésipa wákii-a/ga!: Play football! (literally "play against them at football")

Xithá-ma oⁿgúna!: We're hunting the Eagles!

Washkóⁿi-ga hó!: All of you try hard! (male speaker)

Úhii-ga hó!: Beat 'em! (male speaker)

Conclusion

This week we practiced learning to show our spirit in Umóⁿhoⁿ and worked together to display our pride in our language. Let's try and use these phrases at the game!

Linguistic Notes

- **future tense:** When we are talking about something that will be done in the future, a helping verb follows the main verb and means "future tense."

  Móⁿshoⁿpaagthoⁿ bthíxu-**tamiⁿkʰe**.

  war bonnet   I draw   I will

  -**tamiⁿkʰe** is the "I" form of the future tense. It can be translated as "I am going to" or "I will." We will learn other forms of this at a later date.

- **bth- verbs continued:** We have acquired a new verb:

  Iⁿdádoⁿ **níxu?**

  what   you draw

  Níxu is the "you" form of "draw." How can we tell this? What is the sound that is in the "you" forms of **bth-** verbs?

  Answer: **n-**

Here is the pattern for **bth-** verbs:

I   **bth-**

you   **n-**

she/he   **th-**

If "you draw" is **níxu**, what is the "I" form?

According to the pattern, where the **n-** is in a "you" form, a **bth-** will be in the "I" form. This results in **bthíxu** "I draw."

Similarly, **n-** in the "you" form corresponds to **th-** in the "s/he" form. This means "s/he draws" is **thixú**.

These are the correct forms. So knowledge of the verb pattern, the "conjugation," allows us to complete a verb pattern from one form:

I draw it   **bthíxu**

you draw it   **níxu**

s/he draws it   **thixú**

- **commands to more than one:** When you tell somebody to do something, it is called a command. Commands do not have to be yelled or said condescendingly. This is just a term used to describe phrases telling somebody to do something, regardless of whether you ask them nicely or tell them roughly. We might also call it a "request" form instead of a "command" form.

- We have seen commands before in the lesson on passing on of a loved one. We noted that men put a sentence ending, "-*ga*," on commands.

- Commands change form based not only on who is speaking (male vs. female) but also on who is being spoken to. If we address more than one person, the form changes. We have the command:

Washkóⁿi-ga hó   All of you try hard!

- This is addressing an entire team — more than one person. If one were only telling one person to try hard, the sentence would be:

Washkóⁿ-ga hó!   Try hard!

- So, when giving a command to more than one, "-i" is added to the end of the verb:

Washkóⁿ-ga hó!   Try hard!

Washkóⁿi-ga hó!   All of you try hard!

- For a female speaker, the form is different:

Washkóⁿ!   Try hard!

Washkóⁿi-a!   All of you try hard!

Cultural Note

Our department, the Umóⁿhoⁿ Language and Culture Center, has participated in the UNPS parade on several occasions over the years. Grandson Rufus White and Wendy and Idell Grant sang while sitting on the back of a flatbed trailer as students walked alongside, displaying the Umóⁿhoⁿ cheers described. Candy or small items are thrown out to the spectators. It is common to see a decorated car with our Tribal Princess sitting elegantly on top of a Pendleton-clad hood, waving to the crowd.

5.6 CANDY ACTION: ZHO^{n}NÍ THAT^{h}É-WATHE

Translation: Donna Morris Parker; elicitation/transcription: Vida Woodhull Stabler.

No^{n}bé-t^{h}e-di zho^{n}ní áhigi bthíze uákizhi: I took many candies and put them in my hand.

Zho^{n}ní búta zhó^{n}zhi^{n}ga utháha wí^n níze-a?: Did you take a Tootsie Pop? ("round candy with stick attached")

Bthíze: I take it.

Níze-a?: Did you take it?

Thizá: S/he / they take it.

O^{n}thíza: We take it.

Thizá/ga: Take it.

Bthíshibe: I open it.

Níshibe-a?: Did you open it?

Thishíba: S/he / they open it.

O^{n}thíshiba: We open it.

Thishíba/ga: Open it.

Bthát^{h}e: I eat it.

Nát^{h}e-a?: Did you eat it?

That^{h}á: S/he / they eat it.

O^{n}thát^{h}a: We eat it.

That^{h}á/ga: Eat it.

Xtáathe: I like it.

Xtáthathe-a?: Do you like it?

Xtátha: S/he / they like it.

Xtáo^{n}tha: We like it.

Zho^{n}ní-t^{h}e o^{n}thá'i-a?: Did you give me the candy?

Zho^{n}ní wi'í: I gave you candy.

A'í: I gave it to her/him.

Wi'í: I gave it to you.

Awá'i: I gave it to them.

Tha'í: You gave it to her/him.

O^{n}thá'i: You gave it to me.

Wathá'i: You gave it to them/us.

'Í: S/he / they gave it to her/him.

'Í-a/ga: Give it to him/her.

O^n'í: S/he / they gave it to me.

O^n'í-a/ga: Give it to me.

Thi'í: S/he/they gave it to you.

Wa'í: S/he / they gave it to them / us.

Wa'í-a/ga: Give it to them / us.

O^n'í: We gave it to her/him.

O^{n}thí'i: We gave it to you.

O^{n}wó^n'i: We gave it to them.

5.7 TRIBAL COUNCIL PHRASES: GAHÍYE UTHÁ

Translation by Marcella Woodhull Cayou; elicitation/transcription by Vida Castro Woodhull

Gahíye Ugthí^n Pétho^{n}ba: Seven Tribal Council Seats

Gahíye Niáshi^{n}ga-ama: the Tribal Council Members, the Tribal Council (as a whole)

Gahíye/Gahíye Nudó^{n}ho^{n}ga: Chairperson

Gahíye Wénoⁿba/Gahíye Nudóⁿhoⁿga Wénoⁿba: Vice-Chairperson

Gahíye Niáshiⁿga umóⁿthiⁿkʰa thábthiⁿ téxi-xchi-áchoⁿ: A Tribal Council Member's three years are truly very hard.

Gahíye Niáshiⁿga umóⁿthiⁿkʰa thábthiⁿ úmakʰazhi-xchi: A Tribal Council Member's three years are not easy at all.

Óⁿbathe, Gahíye íye wóⁿganoⁿ'oⁿ oⁿgáthe-taoⁿgatʰoⁿ: Today we're going to go listen to the Council speak.

Nudóⁿhoⁿga thagthíⁿ, Umóⁿhoⁿ Tóⁿwoⁿgthoⁿ wethépahoⁿga moⁿníⁿ. Iⁿdádoⁿ-shte údoⁿ wagíkaxai-a. Washkóⁿ moⁿthíⁿi-a: Tribal Council Leader, you are a good leader for our Umóⁿhoⁿ people. Look for something good. Try hard for whatever your goals might be. (interpretive translation)

Sitting Chairman, you are leading the Umóⁿhoⁿ Nation. (All of you) do something good for us, your people. Continue to do your best. (literal translation)

Cultural Note

In the past, traditional Umoⁿhoⁿ leadership was held by chiefs supported by the different clan leaders and by the people, and through the unified beliefs held by the tribe as a whole.

In modern times the traditional organization and structure has evolved into selection of the Umóⁿhoⁿ Tribal Council seats by popular vote of enrolled Umóⁿhoⁿ people. The Umóⁿhoⁿ Tribal Council leadership consists of seven tribal leaders. The four executive officers consist of a chairperson, vice-chairperson, treasurer, and secretary. There are three additional members completing the Tribal Council membership of seven. This form of governance was promoted in 1933 by John Collier, commissioner of Indian Affairs, through the Indian Reorganization Act of 1934. Some Umóⁿhoⁿ tribal members believe this new system of governance falls short of meeting the ideals and the value system of past governance. However, all tribal members could vote to amend the constitution if or when it is necessary.

Today there are four Quarterly Stated Meetings held during the year (October, January, April, and July). They are a time to report business and program updates to the Umóⁿhoⁿ people as well as to hear tribal member concerns. The UNPS Umóⁿhoⁿ Language Classes routinely take the students to the Tribal Council Quarterly Stated Meetings. Recently, the UNPS Tribal Government class has also attended.

5.8 HALLOWEEN PHRASES

The phrases and words that follow were used to add to Halloween color sheets or connect the dots sheets.

Zhú etázhi: Frankenstein ("not his body")

Waxíⁿha niáshiⁿga uthíxide uíkoⁿ-a/ga: Help look for the rag man.

Wiⁿóⁿxchi théthudi átʰoⁿ uthúaki-watʰóⁿtʰoⁿ-a/ga: Connect the dots. (Literally "The first one is standing right here, then one after another.")

Wanóⁿxe: ghost

Wanóⁿxe-akʰa: the ghost

Wanóⁿxe-ama: the ghosts

Wanóⁿxe-akʰa é (pronounced **Wanóⁿxe-akʰé**): This is the ghost.

Wanóⁿxe-ama é (pronounced **Wanóⁿxe-amé**): These are the ghosts.

Kúheti: spooky house

Kúheti thixú-a/ga: Draw a haunted house.

Ebé théthudi gthíⁿ-a?: Who lives here?

Wahí niáshiⁿga: skeleton ("bone man")

Watʰóⁿ thábthiⁿ: three pumpkins

Watʰóⁿ dúba: four pumpkins

Didéshi gióⁿ: flying bat

Shóⁿtoⁿga niáshiⁿga: wolf man

Wa'ú piázhi: witch

Wa'ú piázhi iⁿdéugthoⁿ: witch mask

Wa'ú piázhi-akʰa moⁿkóⁿ piázhi uhóⁿ: The witch cooks bad medicine.

Iⁿgthóⁿga sábexti: really black cat

Zhoⁿní oⁿgúne oⁿgátha: We are hunting for candy.

Ebéshte uthúthixa?: Did anybody play tricks on you?

Oⁿwóⁿhi-bazhi: They didn't beat me.

Oⁿwóⁿthahi ní'a: You can't beat me.

Óⁿba wésatoⁿ pázeadi iⁿdádoⁿ shkáxe?: What did you do Friday night?

Íⁿ'utʰiⁿshti pʰí: I also went to handgame.

Iⁿdéugthoⁿ wachígaxe xtáatha-mazhi: I don't like masquerade dances.

Iⁿdéugthoⁿ wachígaxe xtáatha: I like masquerade dances.

Uáhi: I won.

Uáhi-mazhi: I didn't win.

Uáwakizhi wénoⁿba uhí: My relative won second place.

Zhoⁿní áwahi weágtha'e: I divided the candy between the two of them.

Mízhiⁿga ikʰáge wiwíta tí etá pʰí: I went to my girlfriend's house.

Óⁿkazhi mízhiⁿga ikʰáge wiwíta tí: No, my girlfriend's house.

Pahóⁿga: first

Ánoⁿ uthíhi-a?: How much did they beat you by?

Wáspeshti moⁿníⁿ-a?: And are you behaving?

Umóⁿthiⁿkʰa ánoⁿ éshte enégoⁿ?: How old do you think they might be?

Cultural Note

The Umóⁿhoⁿ community has a long tradition of hosting Masquerade dances and competitions around the Halloween holiday. It is an event highly anticipated by all ages of people. Most attend because they know it is a night filled with laughter. They come to look on, to hear the singers, and to watch the many comical characters come to life.

Those participating in the competition are secretive about their costumes. The competitions are held after the handgame or meal. Dressed as their characters, the competitors come prepared to dance throughout the evening festivities. They have the freedom to develop their character's persona. The masked ones often will not expose their identities until after the final judging (done by applause of onlookers) on the 1st, 2nd, and 3rd place position winners.

Winners sometimes receive a monetary award and candy is given to all.

It is a real joyful event with participation from all ages of Umóⁿhoⁿ people. The communities of Walthill, Lincoln, and Omaha have also incorporated masquerade competitions at their dances and handgames.

5.9 HALLOWEEN SILLY QUESTIONS AND ANSWERS

Translation: Donna Morris Parker; elicitation/ transcription: Vida Woodhull Stabler and Bryan James Gordon.

OBJECTIVES

· Students will become familiar with the Q&A format using familiar verb pairs.
· Students will break down Umóⁿhoⁿ sentences word by word to glean understanding of basic Umóⁿhoⁿ Íye structure.
· Students will identify verb patterns, both oral and written.

DIRECTIONS

Break down the Umóⁿhoⁿ Íye sentences that follow. Write the complete English sentence on the line provided.

Umóⁿhoⁿ Íye-kʰe
Complete English Sentence

Wamí nátoⁿ-noⁿ-a?

_____

Wamí-tʰe bthátoⁿ.

_____

Niáshiⁿga wánatʰe-noⁿ-a?

_____

Niáshiⁿga bthátʰe.

_____

Zhoⁿní shkóⁿna-a?

_____

Zhoⁿní kóⁿbtha.

_____

Noⁿshkí wahí-thoⁿ thashtóⁿbe-a?

_____

Noⁿshkí wahí-thoⁿ atóⁿbe.

_____

Tidéshi wamí-tʰe nátoⁿ-a?

_____

Tidéshi wamí-tʰe bthátoⁿ.

_____

Shóⁿtoⁿga níⁿ-a?

_____

Shóⁿtoⁿga bthíⁿ.

_____

Sí híⁿshkube aníⁿ-a?

_____

Sí híⁿshkube abthíⁿ.

_____

Sháge-kʰe thisnéde-a?

_____

Sháge-kʰe oⁿsnéde.

_____

Iⁿgthóⁿga sábe sátoⁿ wánatʰe-a?

_____

Iⁿgthóⁿga sábe sátoⁿ wábthatʰe.

_____

Wéthixthi noⁿba aníⁿ-a?

_____

Wéthixthi noⁿba abthíⁿ.

_____

Wanóⁿxe nóⁿwathape-a?

_____

Wanóⁿxe noⁿáwape.

_____

Wamí thithíta-tʰe bthádoⁿ kóⁿbtha.

_____

Wamí wiwíta-tʰe nádoⁿ shkóⁿna-a?

_____

Cultural Note

There was a time when our people ate foods provided by the land. These foods are no longer or rarely at our tables. Some of these foods would include rabbit, squirrel, and wild onions. We moved to a society reliant on canned goods, packed foods, and precut meats. There is a recent movement by the people to go back to planting gardens and eating more healthy foods. The preceding lesson aims to show that language learning can be fun and you can incorporate silly foods, as in this lesson.

5.10 HALLOWEEN DRAWING SCENE

OBJECTIVE

Students will "echo" new vocabulary. Students will draw the correct scene as commanded by an Elder.

MATERIALS

Small whiteboards and colored markers

COMMANDS

Nióⁿba-thoⁿ thixú-a/ga: Draw the moon.
Shóⁿtoⁿga thixú-a/ga: Draw a wolf.
Kúheti thixú-a/ga: Draw a scary house.
Wanóⁿxe thixú-a/ga: Draw a ghost.
Didéshi thixú-a/ga: Draw a bat.
Ukígthiske thixú-a/ga: Draw a spider.
Wa'ú píazhi thixú-a/ga: Draw a witch.
Watʰóⁿ thixú-a/ga: Draw a pumpkin.

HALLOWEEN SCRIPT

Nu Gthóⁿthiⁿ: Wathátʰe wiwíta íⁿnoⁿsha.

man crazy: He took my food from me.

Nú Píazhi: Apíbthe-tamiⁿkʰe.

man bad: I will go get it.

Nú Gthóⁿthiⁿ: Tóⁿthiⁿ-ga, tóⁿthiⁿ-ga! Noⁿpeóⁿhi!

man crazy: Run, run, I'm hungry.

Nú Píazhi: Witóⁿbe, witóⁿbe!

man bad: I see you. I see you.

Nú Gthóⁿthiⁿ: Watháthe-wathe!

man crazy: Let's eat.

5.11 PIN THE BONE ON THE SKELETON GAME

OBJECTIVE

Students will "echo" new vocabulary spoken by an Elder. Students will identify and perform appropriate commands for game play.

ACTIVITY

First, an Elder or Wagóⁿze will go over the names for the various body parts. Then the body or body outline will be hung up in the hall. In turn, each student is blindfolded and spun. (**Kigthísoⁿtha-a/ga**, "Turn around." **Noⁿshtóⁿ-a/ga**, "Stop.") They are given a paper bone or rubber body part and have to say what they have in Umóⁿhoⁿ Íye (example: **Noⁿshkí wahí abthíⁿ**, "I have a skull."). The student will then try to pin (tape) it in the correct place. Hints such as **moⁿshíadi**, "higher," **paháshi**, "toward the top," and **híde**, "lower" can be given.

MATERIALS

Paper skeleton bones, life-size drawing of a person or outline of a person, rubber body parts, blindfold

BONE NAMES

siⁿdéhi wahí: pelvic bone

noⁿshkí wahí: skull

tethítiⁿ wahí/thítiⁿ wahí: rib cage

zhíbe wahí: leg bones

sí wahí: foot bones

noⁿbé wahí: hand bones

á wahí: arm bones

Q: **Wahí-tʰe iⁿdádoⁿ-a?:** What is a **wahí**?

A: **Wahí** is **Umóⁿhoⁿ** for "bone."

OTHER GAME PLAY PHRASES

Dóⁿbazhi-a/ga: Don't look.

Iⁿshtá égaxada/ga: Cover his/her eyes.

Iⁿshtá thibtha/ga: Open eyes.

5.12 FLAG PLEDGE

Translation: Marcella Woodhull Cayou, Rufus White, Alice Freemont Saunsoci, and Winona Mitchell Caramony; transcription/elicitation: Austin Kaaihue and Creighton Saunsoci (Umóⁿhoⁿ Íye II students) and Vida Woodhull Stabler; curriculum and video design: Vida Woodhull Stabler.

Haská- thoⁿ égoⁿ-xti ébthiezhuba.
flag   the   truly   I respect it
I truly respect the flag.

Moⁿzhóⁿ níuthoⁿda gthúba gá- thoⁿ- di,
land   continent whole this the   in
Throughout this entire land (from coast
   to coast),

Wakóⁿda   gáxa,   moⁿzhóⁿ- thoⁿ-
Wakóⁿda   made it   land   the
di   údoⁿ   oⁿgthíⁿ.
in   good   we sit
made by Wakóⁿda, we live well in the
   land.

*History of the Umóⁿhoⁿ Pledge of Allegiance
at the Umóⁿhoⁿ Nation Public School*

The Umóⁿhoⁿ Pledge of Allegiance was requested by Violet Catches of the Pierre Indian Learning Center and was created for the students and staff of Umóⁿhoⁿ Nation Public School and the Umóⁿhoⁿ students of Pierre Indian Learning Center. The following Elders were gathered in the Umóⁿhoⁿ Language Center to create the UNPS Pledge of Allegiance: Marcella Woodhull Cayou, Rufus White, and Alice Freemont Saunsoci. Others present were: Winona Mitchell Caramony and Vida Woodhull Stabler.

The first public saying of the Umóⁿhoⁿ Pledge of Allegiance was performed by Umóⁿhoⁿ Language I students on Friday, April 4, 2003, during "Circle-Up." The following young men participated in this event: Thomas Edward Webster, Will Webster, and Raymond Sheridan. They recited the Umóⁿhoⁿ Pledge from their Hearts and Minds.

The verb **ébthiezhuba** is the "I" form of **gíthiezhuba** "to have respect for." This verb conjugates both the **gí-** "for" prefix and the **thi-** stem prefix, so its conjugation is unusual: **théniezhuba** "you respect," **ébthiezhuba** "I respect," **íⁿthiezhuba** "we respect," **gíthiezhuba** "s/he / they respect."

The word **níuthoⁿda** usually means "island." Its two parts are **ní** "water," and **uthóⁿda** "in the middle of." It is used here to refer to a great big island—the entire American continent. This word can be pronounced in various ways. The stress can be on **niúthoⁿda** instead of **níuthoⁿda**, and the last two vowels can sometimes switch to **níuthadoⁿ** depending on speaker preference.

5.13 CORN REMOVAL, STUDENT WORKSHEET

Translation: Donna Morris Parker and Marcella Woodhull Cayou; elicitation/transcription: Vida Woodhull Stabler; orthography check: Bryan James Gordon.

Cultural Note

Vida Woodhull Stabler.

Our Úmoⁿhoⁿ Language (UL) class was gifted white corn in 2008 by a descendant of the LaFlesche/Farley family (Elmer Blackbird/Dave Farley). Their contribution allowed me to plant the corn that would allow the two Elder relatives to teach our children how to process white corn into **washóⁿge** on an annual basis. Pat Phillips helped plant the second year. Our UL students would harvest the corn in later years upon their return for the new school year. We prayed as we planted the seed and gave thanks as we harvested. The most fruitful harvest came when we depended solely on prayer, rain, and sun.

Remove Corn from Cob

Marcella Woodhull Cayou.

> I remove the white corn: **Wahábe ská-kʰe bthíshpi.**
>
> You remove the yellow corn: _____ zí-kʰe _____.
>
> She removes the red corn: **Wa'ú-akʰa wahábe** _____ -kʰe _____ .
>
> We remove the blue corn: _____ -kʰe _____ .
>
> We will all sift the corn: **Wahábe-tʰe wóⁿgithe múzhoⁿ-taoⁿgatʰoⁿ.**

Remove Corn from Cob

Donna Morris Parker.

> We remove it: **Oⁿthízhu.**
>
> > I remove it: _____ .
> >
> > You remove it: _____ .
> >
> > S/he / they remove it: _____ .

Wóⁿgithe wahába oⁿthízhu noⁿbé-ge oⁿthídazha: We all took the corn off the cob and blistered our hands.

Wahábe bthízhu noⁿbé-tʰe bthídazhe: I took the corn off the cob and blistered my hands.

I raised it: **Bthízhutʰoⁿ.**

We planted and raised the corn: **Wahábe-tʰe oⁿgúzhi oⁿthízhutʰoⁿ.**

The woman blistered her hands:

_____ -akʰa _____ -tʰe _____ .

I blistered my little toe by walking: **Sipá zhiⁿga-tʰe anóⁿdazhe.**

5.14 CORN REMOVAL, TEACHER HANDOUT

Translation: Donna Morris Parker and Marcella Woodhull Cayou; elicitation/transcription: Vida Woodhull Stabler; orthography check: Bryan James Gordon.

Cultural Note

Vida Castro Woodhull.

It is important to note that on one occasion an Elder said she was not allowed to touch red corn. For this reason, when sample corn is brought in for the students to handle, consideration should be given to such restrictions. At the start of this lesson, check the students' prior knowledge by asking them if their family plants a garden and ask them to share with the other relatives.

Remove Corn from Cob

Marcella Woodhull Cayou.

I remove the white corn: **Wahábe ská-kʰe bthíshpi.**

You remove the yellow corn: **Wahábe zí-kʰe níshpi.**

She removes the red corn: **Wa'ú-akʰa wahábe zhíde-kʰe thishpí.**

We remove the blue corn: **Wahábe tú-kʰe onthíshpi.**

We will all sift the corn: **Wahábe-tʰe wóngithe múzhon-taongatʰon.**

Remove Corn from Cob

Donna Morris Parker.

I remove it: **Bthízhu.**

You remove it: **Nízhu.**

S/he / they remove it: **Thizhú.**

We remove it: **Onthízhu.**

Wóngithe wahába onthízhu nonbé-ge onthídazha: We all took the corn off the cob and blistered our hands.

Wahábe bthízhu nonbé-tʰe bthídazhe: I took the corn off the cob and blistered my hands.

I raised it: **Bthízhutʰon.**

We planted and raised the corn: **Wahábe-tʰe ongúzhi onthízhutʰon.**

The woman blistered her hands: **Wa'ú-akʰa nonbé-tʰe thidázha.**

I blistered my little toe by walking: **Sipá zhinga-tʰe anóndazhe.**

5.15 COLORING ACTIVITY FOR FOOD O' PLENTY: TEHÉXTHU'A

Translation: Donna Morris Parker; elicitation/transcription: Vida Woodhull Stabler; orthography check: Bryan James Gordon.

Objective

Students will listen for the singular and plural verb forms and respond appropriately as guided by their Wagónze.

Discuss the impact of farming, chemicals, hybrid seeds, and deforestation on our lands and landscape.

Activity: Listen and Do (Command, Question and Answer, Singular and Plural)

- MATERIALS: Horn of Plenty coloring sheet and colors; *Uses of Plants by the Indians of the Missouri River Region* by Melvin R. Gilmore; *The Omaha Tribe*, volumes 1 and 2, by Alice Fletcher and Francis La Flesche.

ELDER/TEACHER PHRASES
UMÓNHON PHRASES—
SINGULAR (THEN PLURAL)

Color the pumpkin orange.

Watʰón-thon séziegon ugá-a/ga (ugái-a/ga).

Did you color the pumpkin orange?

Watʰóⁿ-thoⁿ séziegoⁿ uthága-a (uthágai-a)?

I (we) colored the pumpkin orange.

Watʰóⁿ-thoⁿ séziegoⁿ uága (oⁿgúga).

Color the corn yellow.

Wahába-kʰe zí ugá-a/ga (ugái-a/ga).

Did you color the corn yellow?

Wahába-kʰe zí uthága-a (uthágai-a)?

I (we) colored the corn yellow.

Wahába-kʰe zí uága (oⁿgúga).

Color the grape purple.

Házi-tʰe háziegoⁿ ugá-a/ga (ugái-a/ga).

Did you color the grape purple?

Házi-tʰe háziegoⁿ uthága-a (uthágai-a)?

I (we) colored the grape purple.

Házi-tʰe háziegoⁿ uága (oⁿgúga).

Color the leaves green.

Zhóⁿʼabe-tʰe pézhitu ugá-a/ga (ugái-a/ga).

Did you color the leaves green?

Zhóⁿʼabe-tʰe pézhitu uthága-a (uthágai-a)?

I (we) colored the leaves green.

Zhóⁿʼabe-tʰe pézhitu uága (oⁿgúga).

Color the acorns brown.

Óⁿzhiⁿga-thoⁿ zíshabe ugá-a/ga (ugái-a/ga).

Did you color the acorns brown?

Óⁿzhiⁿga-thoⁿ zíshabe uthága-a (uthágai-a)?

I (we) colored the acorns brown.

Óⁿzhiⁿga-thoⁿ zíshabe uága (oⁿgúga).

Color one apple red.

Shé wíⁿ zhíde ugá-a/ga (ugái-a/ga).

Did you color one apple red?

Shé wíⁿ zhíde uthága-a (uthágai-a)?

I (we) colored one apple red.

Shé wíⁿ zhíde uága (oⁿgúga).

Color the other one green.

Óⁿma-thoⁿ pézhitu ugá-a/ga (ugái-a/ga).

Did you color the other one green?

Óⁿma-thoⁿ pézhitu uthága-a (uthágai-a)?

I (we) colored the other one green.

Óⁿma-thoⁿ pézhitu uága (oⁿgúga).

What color do you want to color the basket?

Sáhiⁿ-thoⁿ úgaxe iⁿdádoⁿ uthága shkóⁿna?

I want to color the basket brown.

Sáhiⁿ-thoⁿ zíshabe uága kóⁿbtha.

Cultural Note

Discuss the bounty of plants that once grew naturally on our lands (wild tea, plums, sage, various berries, and more).

5.16 THANKSGIVING DAY FOODS: WATHÁTʰE TOⁿGA ÓⁿBATHE

Translation: Marcella Woodhull Cayou and Donna Morris Parker; transcription/elicitation: Vida Woodhull Stabler; spellcheck: Bryan James Gordon.

Lesson: Placemats for the Table

OBJECTIVE

Students will design their own placemats to take home for use when sitting at the table.

MATERIALS

Construction paper (bigger sized), vocabulary document, markers, Placemat Foods Situational Quick Sheet

Vocabulary

EAT, BTH- VERB PATTERN

I	bth	bthát^{h}e
you	n	nát^{h}e
s/he / they	th	that^{h}á
we	o^{n}th	o^{n}thát^{h}a

UMÓ^{N}HO^N ÍYE WÁTHAHO^N-A/GA: TALK UMÓ^{N}HO^N WHEN YOU PRAY

Dadího / Dadíha Wakó^{n}da, ó^{n}bathe o^{n}thíthaho^n, wathát^{h}e údo^{n}xti o^{n}thát^{h}a wíbthaho^n.

Father, Creator (God), this day, we thank you, I thank you for the very good food we ate.

TANÚKA

zizíka: turkey

tanúka s'áthe: ham

wazhí^{n}ga zhézhi: fried chicken

SHEÚZHEGTHO^N

wat^{h}ó^n sheúzhegtho^n: pumpkin pie

shé sheúzhegtho^n: apple pie

taspó^n sheúzhegtho^n: cherry pie

házi sheúzhegtho^n: raisin pie

nó^{n}patu sheúzhegtho^n: blueberry pie

tanúka ígahi sheúzhegtho^n: mincemeat pie

WATHÁT^{H}E ÁZHI-THO^{N}THO^N

nú basnúsnu: mashed potatoes

wahába: corn

núskithe: sweet potatoes

taspó^n: cranberries

wamúska íkigthahi: stuffing

hi^{n}bthí^{n}ge waníde: green bean casserole

ubískabe: to stuff it (the turkey)

Upískabe / uwápiskabe "I stuffed it," **ushpískabe / utháshpiskabe** "you stuffed it," **ubískaba** "she/he/they stuffed it," **o^{n}gúbiskaba** "we stuffed it"

waxthá íkigthahi: salad

waníde: gravy

washí^{n}zhegtho^n: frybread

wamó^{n}ska buta: yeast buns

WASKÍTHE

waskíthe ázhi-tho^{n}tho^n íkigthahi: fruit salad

wamó^{n}ska skíthe: cake

waskíthe gashkó^{n}shko^n: jello

Gashkóⁿshkoⁿ means "move something repeatedly by hitting it," referring to how when you bump jello it wiggles for a while.

NÍSKITHE

ní gatúshi / nískithe: pop
téska moⁿzé ní: milk
moⁿkóⁿ sabe: coffee
sézi ní: orange juice

Cultural Note

During the Thanksgiving Day holiday the Umóⁿhoⁿ Tribal Council distributes a frozen turkey and side dishes to each community Elder. A turkey is also given to families in the communities of Macy, Walthill, and the local urban areas of Omaha, Lincoln, and Sioux City. As with the other holidays, prayer takes place and often a memorial dish is set out to acknowledge a loved one.

5.17 SET THE FOOD OUT: WATHÁT^HE-T^HE ÁWA-TA IT^HEÁTHE-A?

Translation: Donna Morris Parker and Marcella Woodhull Cayou; transcription: Vida Woodhull Stabler.

DIRECTIONS

Circle the placement word (or word part) in each UL sentence following. Break the sentence down by writing an English translation underneath the Umóⁿhoⁿ words. Number 10 is already broken down for you.

MATERIALS

This activity uses the plastic foods used in food vocabulary practice.

Cultural Note

It is the Umóⁿhoⁿ Way, "Umóⁿhoⁿ Ushkoⁿ-t^he," to place food in the center of the gathering or circle at any Umóⁿhoⁿ doings or ceremonial activity. There is a reason for this placement. You will notice a nice-sized cloth or tablecloth placed on the ground or floor first. The food will be placed on top as directed by the designated person (usually the man or woman in charge).

Sentences

1. **Waskíthe gashkóⁿshkoⁿ ágthiⁿ sabe gahá it^hétha/ga:** Place the jello on the black chair.

2. **Taspóⁿ zhoⁿbtháska híde it^hétha/ga:** Place the cranberries on the floor.

3. **Zizíka unéthe gahá ithóⁿtha/ga:** Put the turkey on the stove.

4. **Waxtá íkigthahi sniúzhi-t^he-di it^hétha/ga:** Put the salad in the refrigerator.

5. **Wat^hóⁿ-thoⁿ wáthat^he kigthá-ta ithóⁿtha/ga:** Place the pumpkin under the table.

6. **Waníde wáthat^he gahá it^hétha/ga:** Put the gravy on the table.

7. **Nú basnúsnu-tʰe uxpé toⁿga-tʰe-di itʰétha/ga:** Put the mashed potatoes and gravy on the big plate.

8. **Washíⁿzhegthoⁿ-tʰe néxe-tʰe-di itʰétha/ga:** Put the frybread in the frypan.

9. **Házi sheúzhegthoⁿ sniúzhi-tʰe-di itʰétha/ga:** Put the raisin pie in the refrigerator.

10. **Nóⁿpatu sheúzhegthoⁿ wáthatʰe gahá ithóⁿtha/ga:** Put the blueberry pie on the table.

    blueberry   pie   table   on top
    place it   (REQUEST)

11. **Núskithe-tʰe uxpé buta-tʰe-di uzhí-a/ga:** Add the sweet potato in to the bowl.

12. **Míxa-kʰe thizá/ga, shíshige úzhi-tʰe-di óⁿtha/ga:** Put the duck in the trash.

13. **Shé-thoⁿ wáthatʰe-thoⁿ-di ithóⁿtha/ga:** Put the apple on the table.

14. **Tanúka s'áthe-thoⁿ uxpé-thoⁿ-di ithóⁿtha/ga:** Put the ham on the plate.

15. **Shé sheúzhegthoⁿ thizá/ga, úzhioⁿhe-kʰe-di ugthóⁿ-a/ga:** Put the apple pie in the oven.

5.18 THANKSGIVING COLOR SHEET PHRASES: WAGTHÁBAZE UGÁ

Translation: Marcella Woodhull Cayou; elicitation/transcript: Vida Woodhull Stabler.

zizíka iⁿdé: turkey face

Zizíka gítha-bazhi: The turkeys are not happy.

Zizíka úthixide noⁿzhíⁿ: The turkey is standing there looking around.

Zizika-akʰa íⁿbe-thoⁿ thixáda noⁿzhíⁿ: The turkey fluffed out his feathers.

Wáxe zhiⁿga wathátʰe ázhi-thoⁿtho sáhi úzhi athíⁿ: The little White child has a rush basket filled with different kinds of food.

Wáxe mízhiⁿga wamúske skíthe athiⁿ ai: The little White girl is bringing cake.

sáhi shé ugípi: a basket full of apples

Wahába wíⁿ atóⁿbe: I see one ear of corn.

Watʰóⁿ-thoⁿ wíuga ázhithoⁿtho ugá-a/ga: Color the pumpkin all different colors.

Házi-tʰe ugá-a/ga: Color the grapes.

Watʰóⁿ toⁿga wíⁿ atóⁿbe: I see one big pumpkin.

5.19 THANKSGIVING DAY VERBS, "I LIKE" AND "I DON'T LIKE": XTÁATHE, XTHÁATHA-MAZHI

Translation: Marcella Woodhull Cayou and Donna Morris Parker; elicitation: Vida Woodhull Stabler; revisions: UNL Umóⁿhoⁿ Íye class; consolidation: Bryan James Gordon.

Student Handout

DIRECTIONS

Break down the Umóⁿhoⁿ Íye phrases that follow. Write the English sentence to the right of the Umóⁿhoⁿ Íye sentence.

Zizíka bthátʰe xtáathe:

_____

Nuskíthe bthátʰe xtáathe:

_____

Wamóⁿske ubískabe thatʰé xtátha:

_____

Watʰóⁿ sheúzhegthoⁿ thatʰé xtátha-bazhi:

_____

Zizíka sihí thatʰé xtátha-bazhi:

_____

Zizíka iⁿshtá thatʰé xtátha-bazhi:

_____

Nú basnúsnu waníde edábe thatʰé xtátha:

_____

Watʰóⁿ thatʰé xtháatha-mazhi:

_____

Taspóⁿ bthátʰe xtáathe:

_____

Zizíka pahí thatʰé xtátha-bazhi:

_____

Answer Key

Zizíka bthátʰe xtáathe.
turkey   I eat   I like
I like to eat turkey.

Nuskíthe   bthátʰe   xtáathe.
sweet potato I eat   I like
I like to eat sweet potatoes.

Wamóⁿske ubískabe thatʰé   xtátha.
bread   kneaded s/he eats s/he likes
S/he likes eating kneaded bread (dinner
   rolls, cowboy bread, biscuits).

Watʰóⁿ   sheúzhegthoⁿ thatʰé xtátha-bazhi.
pumpkin pie   to eat s/he does not like
S/he does not like eating pumpkin pie.

Zizíka sihí thatʰé xtátha-bazhi.
turkey foot to eat s/he does not like
S/he does not like eating turkey feet. (An
   earlier transcription of the audio has
   Zizíka sihí thatʰé xtáatha-mazhi, "I
   do not like to eat turkey feet.")

Zizíka iⁿshtá thatʰé xtátha-bazhi.
turkey eye   to eat s/he does not like
S/he does not like eating turkey eyes. (An
   earlier transcription of the audio has
   Zizíka iⁿshtá thatʰé xtáatha-mazhi, "I
   do not like to eat turkey eyes.")

Nú   basnúsnu waníde edábe thatʰé   xtátha.
potato mashed   gravy   also   s/he eats s/he likes
S/he likes eating mashed potatoes with gravy.

Watʰóⁿ   thatʰé xtháatha-mazhi.
pumpkin to eat   I do not like
I don't like to eat squash or pumpkins.

Taspóⁿ   bthátʰe   xtáathe.
cranberry I eat   I like
I like to eat cranberries.

Zizíka pahí thatʰé xtátha-bazhi.
turkey neck to eat   s/he does not like
She/he does not like to eat turkey necks.
   (An earlier transcription of the audio
   has **Zizíka pahí thatʰé xtáatha-mazhi,**
   "I do not like to eat turkey necks.")

5.20 THANKSGIVING BINGO, TODAY IS TURKEY DAY: ZIZÍKA ÓⁿBATHE

Translation: Marcella Woodhull Cayou; elicitation: Umóⁿhoⁿ Language II students Wynton Miller, Tyson Miller, Chantel Freemont, Lupita Moreno, and Skylar Sheridan, with Vida Woodhull Stabler; orthography check and consolidation with "Thanksgiving Day Bingo Match Phrases": Bryan James Gordon.

OBJECTIVE

Students will be able to identify and match the correct bingo picture space to cover when the UL phrase is called out by the caller.

MATERIALS

Bingo game cards, calling cards

Phrases

1. **Wa'ú zizíka uthóⁿ atóⁿbe:** I see a woman holding a turkey breast.

2. **Nú zizíka uthóⁿ atóⁿbe:** I see a man holding a turkey.

3. **Wa'ú zizíka toⁿga uthóⁿ atóⁿbe:** I see a woman holding a big turkey.

4. **Zizíka waníde uthóⁿ atóⁿbe:** I see a turkey and gravy.

5. **Nú noⁿba gítha, watháthe-taakʰa:** The two men are happy because they are going to eat.

6. **Watʰóⁿ-thoⁿ atóⁿbe:** I see the pumpkin.

7. **Nú noⁿba zizíka thatʰé awátoⁿbe:** I see two men eating a turkey.

8. **Zizíka-tʰe móⁿgthe noⁿzhíⁿ atóⁿbe:** I see the turkey standing.

9. **Watʰóⁿ séziegoⁿ atóⁿbe:** I see an orange pumpkin.

10. **Wa'ú zizíka uthóⁿ atóⁿbe:** I see the woman holding the turkey.

11. **Watʰóⁿ wióⁿxchi atóⁿbe:** I see one pumpkin.

12. **Sakʰíba-thoⁿ-di shénuzhiⁿga wíⁿ noⁿzhíⁿ:** There's a young man standing next to it.

13. **Zizíka-tʰe moⁿshóⁿ-tʰe thixáde noⁿzhíⁿ:** The turkey is fanning its feathers.

14. **Watʰoⁿ-thoⁿ íⁿde gíthexti atóⁿbe:** I see a pumpkin with a really happy face (a jack-o-lantern).

15. **Watʰóⁿ-thoⁿ íxaxti atóⁿbe:** I see the pumpkin really laughing.

16. **Niáshiⁿga wíⁿ oⁿdóⁿba:** There's somebody looking at me.

17. **Niáshiⁿga xáde ígahi atóⁿbe:** I see a man mixed out of hay (a scarecrow).

18. **Zhoⁿ'ábe ázhi-thoⁿthoⁿ atóⁿbe:** I see a lot of different kinds of leaves.

19. **Zhoⁿ'ábe gahíthe atóⁿbe:** I see blowing leaves.

20. **Zizíka wachígaxe atóⁿbe:** I see a dancing turkey.

21. **Tehéxthua-kʰe watʰóⁿ waskíthe edábe ázhi-thoⁿthoⁿ ugípi:** I see a buffalo horn (of plenty) filled with different kinds of squash and fruit.

22. **Watʰóⁿ noⁿba ázhi-thoⁿthoⁿ wahábe edábe atóⁿbe:** I see two different kinds of squash and corn too.

23. **"Watʰóⁿ sheúzhegthoⁿ bthátʰe-tʰe uáhita-mazhi," á:** She said, "I can't wait to eat pumpkin pie."

24. **Níkashiⁿga wa'ú-akʰa wathátʰe wáxe wa'ú-thiⁿkʰe 'í:** The Indian woman gave food to the White woman.

25. **Wahába wíⁿ atóⁿbe:** I see an ear of corn.

26. **Watháge watʰóⁿ shé edábe atóⁿbe:** I see a hat, a pumpkin, and an apple.

27. **Zizíka wathágé thagé atóⁿbe:** I see a turkey in a hat.

Cultural Note

Vida Woodhull Stabler.

Bingo has long been a favored form of entertainment among Umóⁿhoⁿ people, as are many other games of chance. Bingo is played at the Nursing Home, at UNPS school community nights, and at local churches and casinos. Long ago and occasionally even now, people still use trinkets, other items, and decorated boxes of prepared food as the winning gift instead of money when playing games of chance. Nowadays people decorate cakes for cake walks or sell 50/50 chances to raise money at a fundraising event.

5.21 THANKSGIVING
FILL-IN-THE-BLANKS HANDOUT

Translation: Marcella Woodhull Cayou.

Activity

Using the other Thanksgiving materials, fill in the blanks with twelve foods you want to eat.

Say aloud, _____ **bthátʰe kóⁿbtha,** "I want to eat_____."

1. _____
   bthátʰe kóⁿbtha.
2. _____
   bthátʰe kóⁿbtha.
3. _____
   bthátʰe kóⁿbtha.
4. _____
   bthátʰe kóⁿbtha.
5. _____
   bthátʰe kóⁿbtha.
6. _____
   bthátʰe kóⁿbtha.
7. _____
   bthátʰe kóⁿbtha.
8. _____
   bthátʰe kóⁿbtha.
9. _____
   bthátʰe kóⁿbtha.
10. _____
    bthátʰe kóⁿbtha.
11. _____
    bthátʰe kóⁿbtha.
12. _____
    bthátʰe kóⁿbtha.

Additional Sentences

Wathátʰe údoⁿ gthúba ázoⁿdi ázhoⁿ: The food was so good everybody's falling asleep all over each other.

Weóⁿnoⁿde ázhoⁿ kóⁿbtha, nóⁿde íⁿudoⁿ: I'm so full I want to sleep, my heart is good.

5.22 BIRDS GO SOUTH.

Wazhíⁿga-	**ama**
bird	the (more than one)
moⁿshté-ta	**agthá.**
to the warm	they go back
Usní-	**taak^{h}a.**
it is cold	it will

The birds are going south for the winter.
  It will be cold.

Cultural Note

Notice that the Umóⁿhoⁿ name for the month of February, **Míxa toⁿga mí agthíi-k^{h}e**, refers to the month "When the geese come home."

Winter: Mágashude

6.1 NAMES OF MONTHS

Transcription: Vida Woodhull Stabler.

December: **Wasábe zhiⁿga ídai-kʰe**

The moon when the little black bear is born.

January: **Hóⁿga Umúbthii-kʰe**

The moon when the snow drifts into the tents of the Hóⁿga.

February: **Míxa toⁿga mí agthíi-kʰe**

The moon when the geese come home.

These names for months come directly from *The Omaha Tribe*, volumes 1 and 2, by Alice Fletcher and Francis La Flesche. There has been discussion concerning alternative or different ways to say a few of the names. The phrases are written as they appear in *The Omaha Tribe* with a few spelling updates to adapt them to the present orthography. When discussing existing names for months, one Elder said, "I stand to be corrected. Those were the Old People back then."

6.2 CLOTHING AND WEATHER: HÁTHE, USNÍ

From: "Fall Phrases" by Marcella Woodhull Cayou, Donna Morris Parker, and Susan Freemont; "Seasonal Weather Terms" by Marcella Woodhull Cayou and Donna Morris Parker; "Morning Routine Commands" by Marcella Woodhull Cayou and Donna Morris Parker; "Clothing Items"; "New & Old Game"; "Shíⁿgazhiⁿga Everyday Phrases"; and "Stuffed Bear Phrases"; transcription/elicitation: Vida Woodhull Stabler.

Usní-doⁿshte: Whenever It's Cold Weather

Háthe shtíde áthaha/ga: Dress warm. / Put on warm clothes.

wáiⁿ: blanket / shawl / robe

Wáiⁿ míⁿ: I'm wearing a robe.

Wáiⁿ zhíⁿ-aʔ: Are you wearing a blanket?

Wáiⁿ ʔíⁿ wachʰígaxe: She's dancing in a shawl.

haxúde: woolen robe

paúthishiⁿ: scarf / headwrap

núde ígatoⁿtha: scarf / necktie (the kind that's rolled around to catch sweat)

Núde ígatoⁿtha móⁿ: I'm wearing a scarf.

nudúbetʰoⁿ: scarf / neckwrap

noⁿbéuthishiⁿ: gloves / mittens

Noⁿbéuthishiⁿ ʔóⁿ/ga: Put on your mittens.

unóⁿzhiⁿtoⁿga / unóⁿzhiⁿ: jacket / coat

Unóⁿzhiⁿ uánoⁿzhiⁿ: I'm wearing a jacket.

Óⁿba-tʰe sní, unóⁿzhiⁿ uthánoⁿzhiⁿ-aʔ: It's a cold day, are you wearing a jacket?

Unóⁿzhiⁿ-thoⁿ unóⁿzhiⁿ-a/ga. / Unóⁿzhiⁿ-thoⁿ giʔóⁿ/ga: Put on your coat.

Unóⁿzhiⁿtoⁿga ígazhoⁿzhoⁿ: S/he shook off her coat.

unó^{n}zhi^{n}ha: hide jacket

watháge: hat

Watháge-tho^n thagái-a/ga: Put on your hats.

Watháge btháge: I'm wearing a hat.

Watháge ska náge-a?: Are you wearing a white hat?

sáhi^n watháge: knit cap (named for reeds)

watháge zízige: knit cap (stretchy)

Sáhi^n watháge thaga: S/he put on a knit cap.

unó^{n}zhi^n zízige: sweater (stretchy knit)

Unó^{n}zhi^n zízige uáno^{n}zhi^n: I'm wearing a sweater.

Unó^{n}zhi^n zízige-tho^n o^{n}thó^{n}shtide: The sweater keeps me warm.

unó^{n}zhi^n xépa: vest

hi^{n}bé snéde: boots

Neúthiso^n dá-tho^n shnahá-tho^n-di núzo^n mó^n: I went skating on the slippery, frozen lake.

Xewó^{n}ge: There's light frost on the ground.

Má-ak^{h}a násko^n, ní-ak^{h}a ga'é no^{n}zhí^n: The snow is melting, it's raining dripping water.

Shtíde, núxe-ama násko^n ga'é no^{n}zhí^n: It's warm and the icicles are melting and raining drops.

Ásni: It's cool.

Sní. / Usní: It's cold.

Ó^{n}ba-ama chéshka athá: The days are getting shorter.

Míxa-ama mo^{n}shté-atathiso^n gi'ó^n agthá: The ducks are flying back south.

Ó^{n}ba-ak^{h}a wagthája: The weather snuck up.

Ó^{n}ba-t^{h}e ázhi égo^n: The weather is a little different.

Usní-ak^{h}a at^{h}í, masó^n aí: The cold weather is here, snow is coming.

Usní-ama agí: Cold days are coming back.

Zho^{n}ábe-t^{h}e ugá ázhi-tho^{n}tho^n: The leaves are different colors.

Zho^{n}ábe bíze-ama gahítha: The dry leaves are drifting in the wind.

Zho^{n}ábe bíze uxpáthe: Dry leaves are falling.

Usní é-tathiso^n o^{n}gátha: We're going toward winter.

Usní-tathiso^n o^{n}gáthe-tao^{n}gat^{h}o^n: We're going to head toward winter.

Wagthíshka-k^{h}e gthézha: Dead box elders.

Tushníge, usní-tait^{h}é: There's a rainbow, it'll be cold.

Minéthe, usní-tait^{h}é: There's a sundog, it'll be cold.

Máthe úmak^{h}a: It could snow.

Máthe-ak^{h}a aí. / Máthe-ak^{h}a agí: Snow is coming.

Máthe-taak^{h}a-ama: They say it's going to snow.

No^{n}zhí^n má ígahi: There's a mix of rain and snow.

Tadé-ak^{h}a sní-ácho^n: The wind is very cold.

Hó^{n}di ó^{n}ba-ak^{h}a zizígtha: Last night it sleeted.

Má-tʰe í-thoⁿthoⁿ: Snow is coming slowly.

Zigthíⁿgthiⁿ: It's heavy freezing rain.

Hóⁿsni: It's a clear, cold winter night.

Hóⁿdi áshi-ta agthíⁿ kʰi Níkanoⁿxe-tʰe atóⁿbe: Last night I sat outside, and I saw the Northern Lights.

tushníge / níkanoⁿxe: Northern Lights

Núxe-áchoⁿ: It's very icy.

Má uxpáthe: Snow is falling.

Má skíge-kʰe pásihi: I shovel the heavy snow.

Úhe-kʰe shnahá: The roads are slick.

Pézhe ubíxage: There's a heavy (killing) frost on the plants.

Shúdemoⁿhoⁿ pézhe ubíxage: There's a freezing fog on the plants.

Wíugoⁿba ubíxage: There's frost on the windows.

Cultural Note

The coming of winter brings with it an opportunity to practice activities specifically done in winter. The telling of our Hígoⁿ stories happens only after the first snowfall that covers the ground. It is said a Grandfather would tell these stories that teach life lessons about good Umóⁿhoⁿ behavior. Often children would fall asleep while the story was being told. They would ask to hear the story again the next night in hopes of being able to stay awake to hear how the story unfolds. Hígoⁿ stories are put away with the coming of spring (Mépahoⁿga).

Cold days require hard work by the young men and boys. They are responsible for keeping the home in firewood and water for cooking and warmth. For the young girls it was traditionally a time for them to learn sewing, beading, and other necessary life skills from the Grandmother and Mothers. Extended family members are ever present in the Umóⁿhoⁿ family to help too. Tedious handwork was done during wintertime. As in the past, there are numerous duties involved to keep home life functioning. Again, reminiscing about past times leads to the Elders telling us that life is easy for us today. In our culture it is important to do good work with our hands. Today shoveling a path to your door, clearing snow drifts away from your car, and working to keep the propane tank full are all ways to strive to contribute to the family unit.

6.3 SELF-INTRODUCTIONS: ADDITIONAL PHRASES AND TISHA WEBSTER'S EXAMPLE

Tisha "Thátawesa" Webster Ebé-tʰe Ukígtha.

Ebé bthíⁿ-tʰe uwíbtha-tamiⁿkʰe: I will tell you who I am.

Izházhe wiwíta-tʰe Tisha Webster: My name is Tisha Webster.

Iⁿdádi wiwíta-akʰa Daniel J. Webster Jr: My father is Daniel J. Webster Jr.

Íⁿnoⁿha wiwíta-akʰa Debra M. Cayou: My mother is Debra M. Cayou.

Thátada shémizhiⁿga bthíⁿ: I am a young lady of the Thátada ("sitting left of Hóⁿga") Clan.

Wazhíⁿga moⁿtʰánaha ithátʰa-mazhi-noⁿmoⁿ: I don't touch wild birds.

Umóⁿhoⁿ Tápuska-ta bthé-noⁿmoⁿ: I go to Umóⁿhoⁿ Nation Public School.

Umóⁿthiⁿkʰa thé íthishethoⁿ uéhe: It's my last year.

Wagóⁿze wiwíta-akʰa Wikóⁿ Marcella Woodhull Cayou: My teacher is my grandmother.

Add-Ons of Other Important or Student-Requested Self-Introduction Phrases

Umóⁿthiⁿkʰa ánoⁿ níⁿ-a?: How many years old are you?

Umóⁿthiⁿkʰa _____ bthíⁿ: I'm _____ years old.

Águdi thagthíⁿ-a?: Where do you live?

Umóⁿhoⁿ Tí-thoⁿdi agthíⁿ / Mási Tóⁿwoⁿgthoⁿ-thoⁿdi agthíⁿ / Umóⁿhoⁿ Tí-thoⁿ uágthiⁿ / Mási Tóⁿwoⁿgthoⁿ-thoⁿ uágthiⁿ: I live in Macy.

Iⁿsh'áge Tóⁿwoⁿgthoⁿ-thoⁿta agthíⁿ. or **Iⁿsh'áge Tóⁿwoⁿgthoⁿ-thoⁿ uágthiⁿ:** I live in Walthill.

Hidé-ata agthíⁿ: I live down bottom / I live in Decatur / I live by the creek.

Usní-atathishoⁿ agthíⁿ: I live out north.

Mí íthe-thoⁿ-tathishoⁿ agthíⁿ: I live out west.

Táp'ska águdi uthéhe-noⁿ-a? / Águdi táp'ska né-noⁿ-a? / Águdi táp'ska shí-noⁿ-a?: Where do you go to school?

or **Águdi wabthágaze ánade-noⁿ-a?:** Where do you take classes / read books?

Umóⁿhoⁿ Táp'ska uéhe-noⁿmóⁿ / Umóⁿhoⁿ Táp'ska bthé-noⁿmóⁿ /

Umóⁿhoⁿ Táp'ska pʰí-noⁿmóⁿ: I go to UNPS.

or **Umóⁿhoⁿ Táp'ska wabthágaze ábthade:** I read books / take classes at UNPS.

or **Umóⁿhoⁿ Táp'ska wagóⁿze pʰí-noⁿmóⁿ:** I go to learn at UNPS.

Umóⁿthiⁿkʰa thé _____ uéhe. (wéshoⁿka: 9th; wégtheboⁿ: 10th; agthíⁿwiⁿ: 11th; íthishethoⁿ: 12th, literally "by which to finish up"): I'm going into my _____th year.

Wagóⁿze wiwíta-ama _____: My teachers are _____.

Example: **Wagóⁿze wiwíta-ama Witóⁿshka Rufus White, Wikóⁿ Susan Freemont, Marcella Cayou, Donna Morris Parker. Íⁿchoⁿ uthíkie-taama:** My teachers are Nephew Rufus White and Grandmothers Susan Freemont, Marcella Cayou, and Donna Morris Parker. Now they will talk to you.

Iⁿdádoⁿ shkáxe xtáthathe-a?: What do you like to do?

Pahé móⁿshi-kʰeta gasnú gi'óⁿ pʰí xtáathe, wasékoⁿ-achoⁿ: I liked when I went skiing in the mountains, real fast.

Tabé sipá shkáde xtáathe: I like to play football.

Tabé ugásnoⁿ shkáde xtáathe: I like to play basketball.

Wikʰáge kinóⁿnoⁿge ugthíⁿ kúwiⁿxe xtáathe: I like to ride around in my friend's car.

Hóⁿadi iⁿdádoⁿ shkáxe?: What did you do last night?

6.4 BASKETBALL PHRASES: TABÉ UGÁSNOⁿ SHKÁDAI-TᴴE ÚWATHA

Translation: Donna Morris Parker and Marcella Woodhull Cayou; transcription/elicitation: Vida Woodhull Stabler.

> **Hóⁿ óⁿma-tʰedi, shénuzhiⁿga-ama tabé ugásnoⁿ úhi-bazhi:** The other night the young men didn't win the basketball game.
>
> **Údoⁿ oⁿshkáda. Núzhiⁿga-ama shkóⁿ waσσσsékoⁿ shóⁿ úhi-bazhi:** We played well. The boys moved fast, but still they lost.
>
> **Óⁿma-tathishoⁿ wáxe núzhiⁿga-ama moⁿshíadi-noⁿ:** The other side, the white boys were tall for the most part.
>
> **Shénuzhiⁿga-ama tabé ugásnoⁿ shkáde thipʰi-áchoⁿ:** The young men know how to play basketball.
>
> **Washkóⁿ iⁿwíⁿgoⁿtha:** We want them to try their best.
>
> **Tabé ubázu-ta óⁿtha théthai-a/ga:** Throw the ball in the corner.
>
> **Oⁿ'í-a/ga:** Give it to me.
>
> **Óⁿtha gítha/ga:** Throw it to me. ("Throw it back this way.")
>
> **Ugásnoⁿ thétha/ga:** Make a basket.
>
> **Óⁿkʰihida/ga:** Guard me.
>
> **Thábthiⁿ gáxa/ga:** Make a three-pointer.
>
> **Noⁿshnáha:** S/he slipped.
>
> **Gashnóⁿ:** S/he missed.
>
> **Gashí-ata óⁿtha thétha:** S/he threw it out of bounds.

Cultural Note

Historically, Umóⁿhoⁿ people played a game called **Tabégasí** "Stick Ball." It was last played by the students at UNPS during the reenactment of the "Last Buffalo Hunt" in 1999. Today boys' and girls' basketball at both Umóⁿhoⁿ Nation Public School and Walthill Public School have become the sporting events most heavily attended by the Umóⁿhoⁿ community. During the 2016 school year both schools went to the district and state basketball championships.

6.5 CEREMONIAL BALL TOSS: TABÉ ÓⁿTHA THÉTHA

Vida Woodhull Stabler. See also *The Omaha Tribe* by Fletcher and La Flesche.

"May I have your attention please! Before the start of a ball game between the Earth and Sky divisions of the Umoⁿhoⁿ tribe, a man from the Kóⁿze Clan has the Right to start the game. He would toss the Game Ball into the air to begin the game. Tonight, we are going to honor our culture and history by practicing the traditional Ceremonial Ball Toss. Jeremy Gilpin will start the game by tossing the Starting Ball to one of the Referees officiating tonight's game. Wíbthahoⁿ."

6.6 GLOBE TOSS GAME: ÁWA-KᴴE-TA NÉ-A?

Translation: Donna Morris Parker; elicitation/transcription: Vida Woodhull Stabler.

Directions

This game is played using a blow-up globe ball. Students listen to the following phrases before gameplay. Introduce basic phrases and practice them before enriching with other phrases.

óⁿbathe: today

Áwa-kʰe-ta né-a? (Áwaxta né-a?): Where are you going?

Óⁿbathe áwa-kʰe-ta né-a?: Where are you going today?

sidádi: yesterday

Áwa-kʰe-ta shí-a?: Where did you go?

Sidádi áwa-kʰe-ta shí-a?: Where did you go yesterday?

Atʰóⁿ-di thagthí-a?: When did you get back?

Sidádi agthí: I got back yesterday.

gasóⁿthiⁿ: tomorrow

Gasóⁿthiⁿ áwa-kʰe-ta né-taniⁿkshe-a?: Where will you go tomorrow?

Atʰóⁿ-ki thagthí-ta?: When will you get back?

Atʰóⁿ-ki thagthé-ta?: When are you going home?

Gasóⁿthiⁿ hóⁿ-ki agthí-tamiⁿkʰe: I'll be back tomorrow night.

Gasóⁿthiⁿ kinóⁿnoⁿge buta-kʰe uágigthiⁿ bthé-tamiⁿkʰe: Tomorrow I'll ride in my Volkswagen bug.

Sháoⁿ Tóⁿwoⁿgthoⁿ Nishúde Thégi-thishoⁿ-ta bthé-tamiⁿkʰe: I will go to South Sioux City. ("this side of the Missouri River from Sioux City")

Macy-ta bthé-tamiⁿkʰe. / Umóⁿhoⁿ Tí-ta bthé-tamiⁿkʰe. / Mási Tóⁿwoⁿgthoⁿ-ta bthé-tamiⁿkʰe: I will go to Macy.

Umóⁿhoⁿ Tóⁿwoⁿgthoⁿ-ta pʰí: I went to Omaha.

Nítoⁿga masóⁿthiⁿ bthé-tamiⁿkʰe: I'm going overseas.

Moⁿzhóⁿ weáhide-xti bthé-tamiⁿkʰe: I'm going far away.

New Zealand-ta móⁿde uágthiⁿ bthé-tamiⁿkʰe: I'm going to New Zealand by boat.

Cultural Note

It was during World War I and World War II, as Umóⁿhoⁿ people enlisted into the service, that they made tracks in other parts of the world. Even today, being in service to our country has taken many Umóⁿhoⁿ warriors across the waters into other countries. One example is King Stabler, a WWII veteran, who made his home in New Zealand after the war. His family resides there still.

6.7 CONJUGATION ACTIVITY: "MÚZHOⁿ THISHTÓⁿ"

Translation: Donna Morris Parker and Marcella Woodhull Cayou; transcription/elicitation: Vida Woodhull Stabler; additions: Rufus White; worksheet: Bryan James Gordon and Vida Woodhull Stabler.

Fill in the blanks following the pattern for these two verbs.

One verb follows the **a-** verb pattern; the other follows the **bth-** verb pattern. Some blanks have been provided.

Add the breakdown under each word.

The "Good English" translation has been provided.

> **Múthazhoⁿ-a?:** Did you finish sifting corn in the wind already?
>
> **Múoⁿzhoⁿ oⁿthishtoⁿ:** We already finished sifting corn in the wind.
>
> _____: I already finished sifting corn in the wind.
>
> _____: S/he / they already finished sifting corn in the wind.

Answer Key

> I finished sifting the corn in the wind: **Wahábe-tʰe múazhoⁿ bthíshtoⁿ.**
>
> Did you finish sifting the corn in the wind?: **Wahábe-tʰe múthazhoⁿ níshtoⁿ-a?**
>
> S/he/they finished sifting the corn in the wind: **Wahábe-tʰe múzhoⁿ thishtoⁿ.**
>
> We finished sifting the corn in the wind: **Wahábe-tʰe múoⁿzhoⁿ oⁿthishtoⁿ.**

Following is an extended use of "sift" when sifting flour for frybread. The example sentences were provided by Marcella Woodhull Cayou in 2005.

I sift: **Muázhoⁿ**
> **Wamóⁿska xude muázhoⁿ.**

You sift: **Múthazhoⁿ**
> **Wamóⁿska xude tʰe múthazhoⁿ-a?**

S/he / they sift: **Múzhoⁿ**
> **Wamóⁿska xude tʰe múzhoⁿ.**

We sift: **Oⁿgu muóⁿzhoⁿ**
> **Wóⁿgithe wamóⁿska xude tʰe oⁿgu muóⁿzhoⁿ.**

Cultural Note

Discuss the considerations given to "wind" regarding the planting and growth of traditional "white corn" (predominant winds, weather, neighboring fields). Discuss effects of wind on tall stalks. Discuss use of cloth used for corn sifting; tell story of how it was done in past.

6.8 WALNUT AND CORN MUSH STORY: TÁGE WASHÓⁿGE ÍUTHA

Story: Rufus White and Marcella Woodhull Cayou; elicitation/transcription: Vida Woodhull Stabler; additions: Donna Morris Parker.

Introductory Questions to Lead into the Story

> **Negihá, táge íutha- tʰe shi**
> Uncle walnut story the again
> **uáwagitha uthákihi-a?**
> you tell us yours can you?
> Uncle, could you tell us your walnut story again?

Koⁿhá táge bahí-noⁿ-di iⁿdádoⁿ
Grandma walnut shen she gathers what
ígaxe-noⁿ-a?
she makes with it?
When Grandma picks walnuts, what does
she make with them?

Story.

Táge uthéwiⁿ-oⁿtha úzhiha-thoⁿ-di
walnut we gathered in the burlap sack
oⁿgúzhi.
we put in
We gathered the walnuts and put them
into the burlap sack.

Táge há-thoⁿ oⁿthísihi. Táge-thoⁿ
walnut the skin we clear the walnut
oⁿgáxixixa. Oⁿgátuba.
we smash open we pound fine
We peeled off the shells. We cracked
them open. We pounded them into
little pieces.

Koⁿhá-akʰa táge-thoⁿ thizá.
Grandma the walnuts take
Grandma took the walnuts.

Táge-tʰe wéuzhi uzhí.
the walnuts container put in
She put the walnuts in a container.

Koⁿhá-akʰa táge-tʰe washóⁿga-tʰe
Grandma the walnuts the corn mush
ígahi.
mixed with
Grandma mixed the walnuts with corn
mush.

Koⁿhá-akʰa táge-tʰe waskíthe
Grandma the walnuts in the fruit
gashkóⁿshkoⁿ-tʰe uzhí.
that jiggles when you shake it put it
She also put the walnuts in jello.

Bonus Phrase

Wahába-tʰe bthípʰe noⁿtúba/ga.
the corn powder grind it
Grind the corn fine.

6.9 "DECK THE HALLS": WÍUGA NÁKOⁿ TʰIGTHÁGTHA

Translation: Donna Morris Parker; transcription/elicitation: Vida Woodhull Stabler.

Wíuga nákoⁿ tʰigthágtha: Colored
flashing lights.

Deck the halls with boughs of holly.

. . . Fa-la-la-la-la

Wóⁿgithe gíthe moⁿthíⁿi-a/ga: Everybody
go along happy.

Tis the season to be jolly.

. . . Fa-la-la-la-la

Háthe síni aníⁿ-ge gi'óⁿi-a/ga: Wear the
best-looking clothes you have.

Don we now our gay apparel.

. . . Fa-la-la-la-la

Nóⁿde gíudoⁿ waóⁿ noⁿzhíⁿi-a/ga: With
happy hearts all stand singing.

Troll the ancient Yuletide carol.

. . . Fa-la-la-la-la, la la la la.

Cultural Note

Christmas has become a part of the community holiday culture. The act of gift giving and sharing is a strong part of Umó^{n}ho^n culture. Sharing of food takes place at nearly every event and all doings. Gifts given at cultural events include blankets, shawls, and other handmade or purchased items. We honor and show respect for others by not showing up "emptyhanded." Our presence and the giving of ourselves by helping to support one another is most valued in Umó^{n}ho^n culture.

6.10 WHAT DID NED EAT?: NED I^{n}DÁDO^n THAT^{h}É-A?

Students practice **Wémo^{n}xe / Edégitho^n** "Question and Answer" using the é "s/he/they" form of the verb **that^{h}é** "eat" while playing a game. Because the game is full of new noun vocabulary, the Umó^{n}ho^n Íye I students are allowed to say the noun in English until they master the verb conjugation. Umó^{n}ho^n Íye II students will elicit and document and use nouns while playing the game.

> **Ned i^{n}dádo^n that^{h}é-a?:** What did Ned eat?
>
> **Ned_____that^{h}á:** Ned ate
> _____.
>
> **Ned zho^{n}gthíshka that^{h}a:** Ned ate ants.
>
> **Ned wagthíshka that^{h}a:** Ned ate worms / bugs.
>
> **Ned wéta zhézhi that^{h}a:** Ned ate fried eggs.
>
> **Ned tabé zhíde that^{h}a:** Ned ate a red ball.
>
> **Ned hí that^{h}a:** Ned ate teeth.

Ned no^{n}xíde wéthisihi that^{h}a: Ned ate a Q-Tip.

Ned kúk'si shí^n-xchi that^{h}a: Ned ate a fat little pig.

Ned gthébe that^{h}a: Ned ate vomit.

Ned i^{n}chó^{n}to^{n}ga that^{h}a: Ned ate a rat.

Ned tébi'a that^{h}a: Ned ate a frog.

Ned théze that^{h}a: Ned ate a tongue.

Ned uthígtheze that^{h}a: Ned ate a screw.

Ned ukígthiske that^{h}a: Ned ate a spider.

Ned waníta hé no^{n}ba that^{h}a: Ned ate an animal with two horns.

Ned wahí that^{h}a: Ned ate bones.

Ned no^{n}xíde that^{h}a: Ned ate an ear.

Ned sí that^{h}a: Ned ate a foot.

Ned no^{n}bé that^{h}a: Ned ate a hand.

Ned didéshi that^{h}a: Ned ate a bat.

Ned i^{n}shtási that^{h}a: Ned ate an eye pupil (a toy where the pupil rolls around).

Ned pá that^{h}a: Ned ate a nose.

Ned i^{n}chó^{n}ga wathát^{h}e uséso^n that^{h}a: Ned ate moldy cheese.

Ned mó^{n}xe mo^{n}shíadi níashi^{n}ga that^{h}a: Ned ate an angel.

Extensions

> **Ned gasó^{n}thi^n i^{n}dádo^n that^{h}é-tathi^{n}k^{h}e-a?:** What is Ned going to eat tomorrow?
>
> **Ned gasó^{n}thi^n_____that^{h}é-taak^{h}a:** Ned is going to eat_____ tomorrow.

Ned sidádi iⁿdádoⁿ thatʰé-a?: What did
  Ned eat yesterday?

Ned sidádi_____thatʰá: Ned ate
  _____yesterday.

Cultural Note

It is proper protocol for an Umóⁿhoⁿ to take
their own dishes and soup bucket. Often people
return home from a doings carrying **úthashte**,
for those who stayed home.

7.1 NAMES OF MONTHS

Transcription: Vida Woodhull Stabler.

> March: **Pénishka mí etái-kʰe**
>> Little frog moon.
> April: **Mí eátoⁿ thiⁿge-kʰe**
>> The moon in which nothing happens.
> May: **Mí wá'ai-kʰe**
>> The moon in which they plant.

These names for months come directly from *The Omaha Tribe*, volumes 1 and 2, by Alice Fletcher and Francis La Flesche. There has been discussion concerning alternative or different ways to say a few of the names. The phrases are written as they appear in *The Omaha Tribe* with a few spelling updates to adapt them to the present orthography. When discussing existing names for months, one Elder said, "I stand to be corrected. Those were the Old People back then."

7.2 FIRST THUNDER: LAWRENCE COOK-AKʰA MÉPAHO^NGA UTHÁI-TʰE

Story: Lawrence Cook; documentation: Vida Woodhull Stabler.

This story was told by Mr. Lawrence Cook, Iⁿshtáⁿsoⁿda Clan Elder, to Vida Castro-Woodhull while Mr. Cook worked as a Language Elder at Umóⁿhoⁿ Nation Public School (1999-2002). He wants the Umóⁿhoⁿ children to

be told this story after First Thunder in anticipation of springtime. Just after First Thunder, Uncle would come into work early. He would tell me that he took care of things. He said, "I went up on the hill to offer a prayer on behalf of our people." He would make prayers for our Umóⁿhoⁿ people for a good year to come. The following was written just as he told me—in his voice:

God created heavens and earth. When he finished he gave us life. Everything comes from the great creation that God made called heaven. He made life for the people.

Our people knew that they had to do, since they knew of these things. The people received a covenant. Christ was to be born and go forth. At times there would be certain times of the year called seasons. At certain times, the people noticed a month coming with warm days. In particular the month of May. When the white people came, they brought their calendar. During April or May there is the blessing of rain, that comes from above. They will see a change. There will be trees getting buds and leaves, flowers coming out. Umóⁿhoⁿ's call it Mépahoⁿga. Údoⁿ.

I believe it is a time for water to baptize the land. To bless the land with holy water. Soon the trees or plants grow from the blessing of the holy water.

The people noticed fruit and food was brought forward to nourish the creation on earth. Through that one life, there were birds, seeding of beans, wild potatoes, and more.

This was the sign of warm weather. There would be sunny days. Therefore the people were thankful. The forefathers would go upon the high hills to be close to the heavens. They would give a word of thanks to the heavenly father. They would give thanks for the good of life that we received on this earth. Our people, they noticed and saw this. They knew they received a blessing in this great life from the creator. They were thankful. When springtime came, when the thunder came, they gave a word of thanks. That there be life here and ever after for the people.

Clan Rites

The Iⁿshtásoⁿda division, spoken of as "the Sky people," had charge of those rites by which supernatural aid was sought and secured. The rites committed to the gentes composing this division were all connected with the creation and the maintenance on the earth of all living forms.— *The Omaha Tribe*, vol. I, pp. 196

The rites pertain to the sky, to the power which descends to fructify the earth. The response of the earth is typified by the abounding life as seen in the worms, insects and small burrowing creatures living in the earth.— *The Omaha Tribe* vol. 1, p. 186

For additional reading pertaining to Rites of Thunder regarding Wézhiⁿshte and Thátada Clans participation at First Thunder, additional reading can be found in the resource, *The Omaha Tribe*, vol. 1, pp. 142–143.

At my request, Orville Aldrich wrote this story about his past memory of "Macy Day":

Every year in the spring time a "Macy Day" would take place. People would be cleaning up their yards before hand. We used to have the place we called the "Athletic Field" located in the middle of the village. Everyone would come out and watch. The weather seemed to cooperate . . . maybe 65 degrees. All age groups would participate in running events; sprints, long distance race, marbles, tug of war, softball throw, softball game and horseshoe tournament. There was a good feast for everyone, I remember one time, they had buffalo meat. Maybe someone would put on a War Dance and Handgame. It was a good day to celebrate "Macy" and the new spring time. I could see it happening today . . . maybe some of the older people will recall this event . . . and start it up again.— Orville Aldrich

7.3 RAINSTICK ACTIVITY WITH WEATHER TERMS

Translation: Marcella Woodhull Cayou and Donna Morris Parker; elicitation/transcription: Vida Woodhull Stabler.

This activity reinforces weather terms and builds on prior knowledge about Mépahoⁿga. You will need weather terms, a rainstick, a blank calendar page and various materials for making weather sounds and sights: tin foil, pan, wooden spoon, flashlight, fan, white paper pieces, sunglasses, orange ball, etc. Go around the room asking your neighbor **Ó^{n}ba-t^{h}e eyó^n-a?** "What kind of day is it?" S/he replies with **Ó^{n}ba-t^{h}e** _____, filling in the word from the index card. Act out the term so the class can recognize and reinforce its meaning.

Ó^{n}ba-t^{h}e eyó^n-a?: How is the day?

Ó^{n}ba-t^{h}e ámo^{n}xpi: The day is cloudy.

Ó^{n}ba-t^{h}e usní: The day is cold.

Ó^{n}ba-t^{h}e no^{n}zhí^n: The day is raining.

Ó^{n}ba-t^{h}e nák^{h}ade: The day is hot.

Ó^{n}ba-t^{h}e shúdemo^{n}ho^n: The day is foggy.

Ó^{n}ba-t^{h}e údo^n: The day is good.

Ó^{n}ba-t^{h}e píazhi: The day is bad.

Ó^{n}ba-t^{h}e ásni: The day is cool.

tushníge: rainbow

Mo^{n}gáshuda: There's blowing dust.

tadó^{n}he: whirlwind/sudden gust

tadésagi: windy

Ó^{n}ba-t^{h}e áthixude: The day is gray / overcast.

zhído^n: dew

mási: hail

Mó^{n}xe-k^{h}e kétha: The sky is clear.

kétha-ácho^n: very bright

Thió^{n}ba: Lightning flashes.

I^{n}gthó^{n}hut^{h}o^n: Thunder roars.

Ó^{n}ba-t^{h}e tí^n: The day is humid.

Bring in a rainstick. Ask if anyone knows what it is. Tip it over, now do they know? What does it sound like? Explain that it is a rainstick. Allow each to try it, saying **Ó^{n}ba-t^{h}e no^{n}zhí^n** after it sounds. Show the students the proper way to handle the rainstick. Put out the various weather materials. Pair up students and ask them to create a kind of weather using these materials and any others they see in the classroom (ex. lights). The other students must guess in Umó^{n}ho^n Íye what the weather noise is. Write it on calendars.

Ó^{n}ba Xube / Ó^{n}ba Waxúbe: Sunday

Ó^{n}ba Xube Thishto^n / Ó^{n}ba Waxúbe Thishto^n: Monday

Ó^{n}ba Wéno^{n}ba: Tuesday

Ó^{n}ba Wéthabthi^n: Wednesday

Ó^{n}ba Wéduba: Thursday

Ó^{n}ba Wésato^n: Friday

Hithái: Saturday

sidádi: yesterday

ó^{n}bathe: today

gasó^{n}thi^n: tomorrow

Cultural Note

Discuss the I^{n}shtáso^{n}da Clan and rites pertaining to springtime, when the rains come. When there is no rain or a dry period for an extended amount of time exists, what types of things are jokingly said within the Umó^{n}ho^n community.

7.4 SPRING TREE ORNAMENTS

Translation: Marcella Woodhull Cayou; elicitation/transcription: Vida Woodhull Stabler.

Lesson: Decorating the Spring Tree

OBJECTIVE

Students will learn basic words for bugs, birds, and flower while creating an art project for the spring tree as guided by Wagóⁿze.

MATERIALS

This lesson requires the use of the tree sitting in the language classroom, construction paper, colors or markers, paper clips or yarn to hang

Cultural Note

Review Mépahoⁿga by going on a walk with the students prior to this activity. They can build on the vocabulary by observing other evidence of springtime.

Vocabulary

Izházhe thithíta-tʰe baxú-a/ga / Izházhe-tʰe gipáxu-a/ga: Write your name.

Mépahoⁿga: springtime

xthabé: tree

Wagthíshka thixú-a/ga: Draw a bug.

Wazhíⁿga thixú-a/ga: Draw a bird.

Waxchá thixú-a/ga: Draw a flower.

Wagthíshka-thiⁿkʰe zí ugá/ga: Color the bug yellow.

Wazhíⁿga-thiⁿkʰe tú ugá/ga: Color the bird blue.

Waxchá-thoⁿ zhíde ugá/ga: Color the flower red.

Wagthíshka-thiⁿkʰe thisá/ga: Cut out the bug.

Wazhíⁿga-thiⁿkʰe thisá/ga: Cut out the bird.

Waxchá-thoⁿ thisá/ga: Cut out the flower.

Wahóⁿ-kʰe thisá/ga: Cut the yarn.

Weáthaskabe-kʰe 'óⁿ/ga: Use the tape.

Xthabé-tʰe-di ubátʰi ithóⁿtha/ga: Hang it in the tree.

Níshtoⁿ-a?: Are you done?

Noⁿzhíⁿ-a/ga: Stand.

Mázi xthabé-ta moⁿthíⁿ-a/ga: Go to the cedar / pine tree.

Wáthatʰe-ta moⁿthíⁿ-a/ga: Go to the table.

7.5 EASTER PHRASES

Translation: Marcella Woodhull Cayou; elicitation/transcription: Vida Woodhull Stabler; consolidated from "Easter Phrases" and "Easter Bulletin Phrase"; consolidation/orthography check: Bryan James Gordon and Patricia Philips.

Mépahoⁿga Wakóⁿda Izhíⁿge gáxa.
spring   Wakóⁿda His Son made it
Spring/Mépahoⁿga, Wakóⁿda's Son did it.

Sáhiⁿ wéta ugá ugípi uzhí.
basket egg dyed fill   put it in
Fill a basket with dyed eggs.

Phrases Elicited to Go Along with Elementary Coloring Sheets

Wéta ugá: Dye the egg.

Wéta waxchá ugá: Dye the egg with a flower.

moⁿshtíⁿga gíthe: happy bunny

kipáda-zhiⁿga kipáshizhe: shivering hatchling

moⁿshtíⁿga hiⁿthékitha: rabbit in a hurry

moⁿshtíⁿga wéta dóⁿbe gthíⁿ: rabbit looking at eggs

moⁿshtíⁿga móⁿshoⁿ ábaxoⁿ: rabbit with a feather in its fur

wazhíⁿga íⁿbe gabthá: chicken fanning its tailfeathers

moⁿshtíⁿga íxa: laughing bunny

wéta ugá xthabé: Easter Tree ("colored-eggs tree")

7.6 DYEING EASTER EGGS

Translation: Rufus White, Marcella Woodhull Cayou, and Donna Morris Parker; elicitation/transcription: Vida Woodhull Stabler; orthography check: Bryan James Gordon.

OBJECTIVE

Practice listening, understanding, and repeating commands by the Elders. Creating new sentences of their own.

MATERIALS

Hard-boiled eggs, egg-dye kit, candy, water, index cards with instruction commands written on them

Noun Vocabulary

wéta: egg

wiúga: dye/color

úzhi: bag/container

ní: water

zhoⁿní: candy

thithíta: yours

tehé: spoon

wiwíta: mine

niúthatoⁿ: cup

Verb Vocabulary

xtáathe: I like (it)

xtáthathe: you like (it)

thatʰá: s/he / they eat (it)

thishíba: s/he / they open (it)

bashóⁿtha: s/he / they pour (it) out

uzhí: s/he / they add / put (it) in

uthúgahi: s/he / they mix (it) together

ugthóⁿ: s/he / they put (something round) in (it)

ithápa: s/he / they wait for (it)

Activity

The students are going to dye eggs through the step by step instruction of the Elder. First, the Elder teacher will review the vocabulary, and next introduce the new vocabulary (oral and written). As the eggs are dyeing, students will eat the candy and create their own sentences, using their prior verb knowledge. Examples are, "I like my egg," "Do you like my red egg,"

"He's eating candy," "Let's eat three green eggs." Example: **Wéta pézhitu thábthiⁿ atóⁿbe**.

Cultural Note

Discuss traditional colors used by Umóⁿhoⁿ people and what they represent. Discuss the plants that were used to make the colors, influences from nature. Discuss uses of color on clothing and use of paint during dance.

Student Handout

Break down the following Umóⁿhoⁿ Íye sentences. The "good English" translation is provided. How is **word order** different in Umóⁿhoⁿ Íye?

> **Zhoⁿní xtáthathe-a?:** Do you like candy?
>
> **Zhoⁿní-thoⁿ thithíta:** The candy is yours.
>
> **Úzhiha-thoⁿ thishíba/ga:** Open the bag.
>
> **Niúthatoⁿ bashóⁿtha/ga:** Pour out your cup.
>
> **Ní-tʰe niúthatoⁿ-tʰedi uzhí-a/ga:** Pour water in your cup.
>
> **ní shtáge:** warm water
>
> **Wiúga-tʰe niúthatoⁿ-tʰedi uzhí-a/ga:** Put the dye in the cup.
>
> **Ní-tʰe uthúgahi-a/ga:** Stir the water.
>
> **Wéta- thoⁿ tehé- kʰedi ugthóⁿ/ga.**
> egg   the   spoon the in put it in
> Put the egg in the spoon.
>
> **Wéta ní-   tʰedi uzhí-a/ga.**
> egg   water the in put it in
> Put the egg in the water.
>
> **Wéta ní-tʰedi ugá-tʰithe:** The egg starts to dye in the water.

Wéta ní-tʰe ugthóⁿ/ga, ugákʰitha/ga: Put the egg in the water and dye it.

Ithápa/ga: Wait for it.

Noⁿhéba/ga: Wait.

Wéta- tʰe gashíbe thizá/ga.
egg   the   out of it take it
Take the eggs out.

Wiúga iⁿdádoⁿ uthága?: What color did you dye it?

Zhoⁿní thatʰá/ga: Eat the candy.

7.7 HUNTING EGGS: WÉTA ÍTHATHE-A?

Translation: Marcella Woodhull Cayou and Donna Morris Parker; elicitation/transcription: Vida Woodhull Stabler; orthography check: Bryan James Gordon.

Directions

After students have colored the eggs, the eggs will be hidden around outside. Prior to playing the game, students will practice "hunting/finding" phrases.

Phrases

> **Gasóⁿthiⁿ wéta-tʰe gthúba áanoⁿxthe-tamiⁿkʰe:** I'll hide all the eggs tomorrow.
>
> **Uné moⁿthíⁿi-a/ga:** Go find them.
>
> **Áshita águdishte áanoⁿxthe:** I hid them all around outside.
>
> **Wíⁿ íthathe-tʰedi móⁿzeska wi'í-tamiⁿkʰe:** If you find one I'll give you money.
>
> **Thénoⁿ ázhi:** This much and more.

Wéta ázhi, wébaxu wi'í-tami^{n}k^{h}e: Another egg, I'll give you a pencil.

Wéta-t^{h}e áno^n íthathe-a?: How many of the eggs did you find?

Wi gthébo^n itháthe: I found ten.

Dúak^{h}a é dúba ítha: This person here found four.

Wó^{n}githe-o^{n}thi^{n}k^{h}e gthébo^n pétho^{n}ba o^{n}thó^{n}tha: Altogether we found seventy.

Káshi unái-a/ga: Keep looking.

Cultural Note

Marcella Woodhull Cayou and Donna Morris Parker.

Many Umó^{n}ho^n families lived outside of Macy in the country. Many of the homes had chickens and a rooster. The chickens provided eggs and meal for the families to eat. Chickens and stewing hens were often donated for cultural "doings" such as handgame, feasts, and other gatherings. Chickens were butchered and the meat was used to make soup. Many meals offered fried chicken in addition to soup and this tradition continues on to this day.

A Tribal Program will host an Easter Egg Hunt for the local communities. All the children are invited to join in on the hunt for eggs. There are categories based on ages.

7.8 EGG SALAD SANDWICHES/DEVILED EGGS: WÉTA WAMÓ^{N}SKA UBÍSKABE/ WÉTA UZÍ ÍGAHI

Egg salad sandwiches translation: Donna Morris Parker and Marcella Woodhull Cayou; elicitation/transcription: Vida Woodhull Stabler. Deviled eggs translation: Marcella Woodhull Cayou; elicitation/transcription: Vida Woodhull Stabler; orthography check: Bryan James Gordon.

Verb Vocabulary

thizá/ga: take it

máshpashpa/ga: chop it up in little pieces

uhó^n/ga: cook it

íkigthahi-a/ga: mix it together

gaxíxa/ga: crack it apart

dúba uzhí-a/ga: add some more

thizhába/ga: peel it

ábishnaba/ga: spread it on

áthi'a/ga: sprinkle it on

umásno^n/ga: slice it in half

bashíbe thizá/ga: take/push it out

uthúgahi-a/ga: stir it

Wéta wamúska ubískabe o^{n}gáxe-tao^{n}gat^{h}o^n:
We will make egg-salad sandwiches.

1. **Wéta thizá/ga:** Take an egg.
2. **Wéta há-tho^n thizhába/ga:** Remove the shell.
3. **Máshpashpa/ga. Zhi^{n}gá-xchi máshpashpa:** Chop it. Chop it into small pieces.
4. **Wawégahi dúba uzhí-a/ga:** Add some mayonnaise.
5. **Wiúkiho^n, niskíthe áthi'a/ga:** Sprinkle on some salt and pepper.
6. **Uthúgahi-a/ga:** Stir it.

7. **Wamúska-thoⁿ wéta ábishnaba/ga:** Spread it on the bread.

8. **Wéta-thoⁿ shéthiⁿkʰe í-a/ga:** Give him/her an egg.

9. **Shéthiⁿkʰe wéta wíⁿ tha'í-a?:** Did you give him/her an egg?

10. **Wóⁿgithe athíⁿ gíi-a/ga:** Bring all of it.

11. **Koⁿhá/Koⁿhó/Thikóⁿ-thiⁿkʰe wéta wíⁿ gíthizhaba/ga:** Peel an egg for Grandma.

Deviled Eggs

1. **Wéta-thoⁿ umásnoⁿ/ga:** Slice the egg in half.

2. **Weta-thoⁿ uzí bashíbe thizá/ga:** Push the egg yolk out.

3. **Wawégahi dúba uzhí-a/ga:** Add some mayonnaise.

4. **Kukúmi ní dúba uzhí-a/ga:** Add pickle juice.

5. **Uthúgahi-a/ga:** Stir it.

6. **Wéta uzí-thoⁿ xátha wéta ská-thoⁿdi uzhí-a/ga:** Put the yolk back into the eggwhite.

7. **Wóⁿgithe wéta-thoⁿ oⁿthátʰe-taoⁿgatʰoⁿ:** We will all eat the eggs.

7.9 MUSHROOM SEARCH: TENÍXA UGTHÉZHE OⁿGÚNAI-TʰE

Translation: Marcella Woodhull Cayou; elicitation/transcription: Vida Woodhull Stabler; orthography check: Bryan James Gordon.

Directions

Fill out the blanks with the **a-** verb pattern. The "she/he/they" form and "command/request" form are provided. Fill in the spaces with the correct forms. Prior to the fieldtrip to the timbers, play the Hide **"Ánoⁿxtha"** Game with the paper mushrooms. Find in Mushroom Student Worksheet and Games section.

Uné: Search

_____

I search for it.

_____

You search for it.

Uná._____

S/he / they search for it.

_____

We search for it.

Uná/ga._____

Search for it.

Unái-a/ga._____

Search for it. (spoken to more than one)

Directions

Break down the phrases below. The first one is done for you. Notice the word order.

Uxthábe-kʰe-ta thé-wathe.
Timbers the to let's go

Teníxa-ugthézhe uné thé-wathe: Let's go search for mushrooms.

_____

Óⁿthe íyai-a/ga: Speak softly.

_____

Thahéga-bazhi íya-bazhíi-a/ga: Don't talk loud.

Biíza-bazhii-a/ga, teníxa-ugthézhe shpáaze-ta: Don't make noise by shuffling your feet around, you'll scare off the mushrooms.

Teníxa-ugthézhe áhigi oⁿthóⁿtha: We found many mushrooms.

Óⁿbathe, teníxa-ugthézhe oⁿthóⁿtha-bazhi: Today, we didn't find mushrooms.

Cultural Note

Marcella Woodhull Cayou and Donna Morris Parker; additions: Patricia Phillips.

Discuss best way to harvest mushrooms (bag with holes for spores/best way to keep them growing, leave bottom part of stem in the ground)

Dress appropriately: Long sleeves/pants, head cover (ticks)

Give thanks or make offering for any food provided by Wakóⁿda

Behavior in the timbers: quiet or they hide from you

Identification of additional plants this time of year: gooseberries, raspberries and poison ivy.

While on the fieldtrip, also discuss oral teachings and traditional cure for poison ivy.

Look for gooseberries in June and raspberries in July

7.10 MUSHROOM WORKSHEET AND GAMES 1

Consolidated from "Mushroom Season" and "Mushroom Assessment"; orthography check: Bryan James Gordon.

Objectives

Students will learn culturally appropriate behavior when hunting for morel mushrooms. (Quiet.) Students will discuss where morel mushrooms can be found (timbers and sand). Students will discuss the science of what mushrooms need to grow, and that they are spores.

Vocabulary

uxthábe teníxa ugthézhe: timber mushrooms

Nishúde teníxa ugthézhe: river mushrooms

Uthíxida/ga: Look around for it.

Itháthe: I found it.

Xthíazhi gthíⁿi-a/ga: Sit quietly.

Úzhi thizá/ga: Take a bag.

Zhóⁿzhiⁿga aníⁿ-a?: Do you have a stick?

Ánoⁿ íthathe-a?: How many did you find?

Game: Teníxa "Ugthézhe Unái-a/ga!

- MATERIALS: Set of 50 laminated "mushrooms," spore bag.

  The teacher hides the mushrooms, and students try to find as many as they can. In good weather hide them outside and set a perimeter of where mushrooms can be found.

Game: Check for Understanding

Divide into teams. One team is the **Uxthábe Teníxa Ugthézhe**, and the other side is the **Nishúde Teníxa Ugthézhe**. Compete for points by answering questions. Kindergarteners may play pretending to be mushrooms.

Student Worksheet

1. Place the letter of the correct English translation next to the Umóⁿhoⁿ word.

   _____ **teníxa-ugthézhe**   a shirt

   _____ **unóⁿzhiⁿ**   b hat

   _____ **níⁿdushiⁿ**   c tick

   _____ **wathíbaba**   d cards

   _____ **wathage**   e pants

   _____ **hímoⁿgthe**   f cane

   _____ **táthazapa**   g mushrooms

2. Translate the following Umóⁿhoⁿ sentences into English:

   a: **Zhíde uáne** (used when playing UNO):

   _____.

   b: **Teníxa-ugthézhe uáne:**

   _____.

7.11 MUSHROOM WORKSHEET AND GAMES 2

Translation: Marcella Woodhull Cayou; elicitation/transcription: Vida Woodhull Stabler; orthography check: Bryan James Gordon.

Cultural Note

There is so much anticipation within the tribe around this time of year. Everyone takes notice of the warmer days and rainfall. Once there are a couple of very warm days, you'll find cars parked along tribal lands as people begin to head for the timber. Enrolled tribal members may hunt mushrooms on tribal lands. Many tribal members own land where they are able to hunt.

Directions

Break down the Umóⁿhoⁿ phrases and put the "Complete English Sentence" translation on the line to the left. Translate the English phrases into Umóⁿhoⁿ Íye.

Teníxa-   ugthézhe oⁿgúne   oⁿgáhi.
buffalo stomach striped   we search we went
We went to search for morel mushrooms.

_____

Teníxa-ugthézhe oⁿgúne oⁿgáthe-taoⁿgatʰoⁿ.

_____

teníxa-ugthézhe

_____ **bíze**

_____ **uxthábe**

Ithátha-mazhi.

Hégazhi itháthe teníxa-ugthézhe.

_____**Áhigi**
íthathe-a?

They already picked them. _____ **Bahí**
thishtóⁿ.

The mushrooms are disappearing.

They're gone._____
Teníxa-ugthézhe-ama kigthíshenoⁿ.

_____

I want mushrooms.

_____

I like mushrooms.

_____

I don't like mushrooms.

_____

I don't have mushrooms.

_____

I have mushrooms.

_____

I see mushrooms.

_____

I ate mushrooms.

Activity: Teníxa-Ugthéze Ékʰigoⁿ

Students will match cards related to mushroom hunting using the verbs for "search for," "I found," and "I didn't find."

Activity: Wiⁿóⁿxchi

Students will play UNO, saying [color] **uáne** "I'm searching for [color]," when they have to hunt for a card from the deck. Example: **Pézhitu uáne** "I'm searching for green."

Activity: Mushroom Phrases

Make up a "mushroom phrase" and translate it into Umóⁿhoⁿ Íye. You will need to work with Grandma or Wagóⁿze to complete the transcription work.

7.12 FRIED MUSHROOMS: TENÍXA UGTHÉZHE ZHÉZHI

Translation: Donna Morris Parker; elicitation/transcription: Vida Woodhull Stabler; orthography check: Bryan James Gordon.

Lesson: Cooking Morel Mushrooms

OBJECTIVE

Students will learn to cook the morel mushrooms they found while hunting.

MATERIALS

Cooking implements, salt, flour and oil. (Optional: egg)

Cultural Note

Review with students the Umóⁿhoⁿ traditions they practiced while searching for morel mushrooms.

Teníxa Ugthézhe Zhézhi-a/ga: Fry Mushrooms.

1. **Wéta, téska moⁿzéni íkigthahi-a/ga:** Mix the egg and milk together.

2. **Teníxa ugthézhe-tʰe noⁿbáha máxoⁿ/ga:** Cut the mushrooms in two.

3. **Wégthi-tʰe uzhí-a/ga. Óⁿthe uzhí-a/ga:** Put the oil in. Add it slowly. (It might splatter.)

4. **Wégthi-tʰe nákʰade-a?:** Is the oil hot?

5. **Wamúske xúde-tʰedi ubídoⁿ/ga:** Dip it in the flour.

6. **Íbashoⁿtha/ga, názi:** Turn it over with the spatula, it's browned.

7. **Shi thenóⁿ dúba uzhí-a/ga:** Now add a few more.

8. **Thizá/ga:** Take them out.

9. **Wíⁿ ígaskoⁿtha/ga:** Try one.

Conversational Phrases/Words

1. **Újoⁿ bahí-a/ga:** Pick beautiful ones.

2. **tubáthe:** crumbled / powdery (from getting old)

3. **Teníxa ugthézhe wóⁿgithe tubáthe:** All the mushrooms are crumbling.

4. **ubísoⁿde:** crowded in / squeezed close together

Cultural Note

These phrases were elicited prior to cooking the mushrooms with the Umóⁿhoⁿ language students. In the preparation and cooking of mushrooms, often it is the Elder woman teaching the younger one about what to notice (condition) with mushrooms.

Condition and cleaning of mushrooms; storage in refrigerator

How to store mushrooms if not cooking right away (traditional drying)

How to cook mushrooms

How to be around hot grease

7.13. HOW THE UMÓⁿHOⁿ GOT THE CORN: TÉ-AKʰA UMÓⁿHOⁿ-MA WAHÁBA-TʰE WA'Í-BIAMA

Story: Clifford Wolfe Sr.; transcription: John Mangan for "Stories from Our Elders" booklet.

This morning I'm going to tell the story about the Indian corn (C. Wolfe, Sr. used 'squaw' corn too).

This little boy always went up the hill, and looking over the hill he saw a buffalo standing there. He was wondering why the buffalo was standing down there – he didn't move, he was just standing there facing south. So he watched it pretty near all day; the buffalo just stood there motionless, and he went home again.

The next day he came back and the buffalo was facing west. He was standing in the same place again. The boy was watching where the buffalo couldn't see him. He was facing west in the same spot. He went home again.

The next day he came back and looked over the hill again and here he was facing north. He watched it and the buffalo didn't move or anything. He just stood in the one place.

The fourth day he came up on the hill again, and this time the buffalo was facing east. As the old people say, everything is always east, where daylight comes from, where the morning star comes from. Life, they say, comes from the east. The buffalo was facing east.

The fifth day he went down there and the buffalo was gone, but he saw a plant there. So he went right down to see what it was. It was a corn plant growing. He kept watching it as it grew and finally an ear came out; he wanted to see what was inside that ear. It had husks on it, so he pulled them open and inside was Indian corn, squaw corn they call it. That's what the buffalo left for the Omaha tribe.

So he took that ear of corn home and showed it to his family. He said, "Look what I brought home." They were wondering what it was, this corn. They took the kernels, and next spring they planted some to see what it would do. And it grew again and each one of the plants had ears. It's shaped like a war dancer today, with that head-dress and everything. It even looks like a human itself; it has ears.

So they took some and put some in the fire, turned it over, and made parched corn, and it was good to eat, and when they dried it they ground it and made bread out of it. And that's how the Omaha people found out that corn was good. Ever since then, wherever they go, they have the corn.

Nú-akʰa wahába uzhí thizhútʰoⁿ, wahába ukʰéthiⁿ. [Donna Morris Parker] 'The man planted and grew the Indian corn.'

wahába ukʰéthiⁿ 'Indian corn'
moⁿshté-atathishoⁿ 'southwards' ['towards the warm']
mí ithé-tathishoⁿ 'westwards' ['towards the sunset']
usní-atathishoⁿ 'northwards' ['towards the cold']
itʰáxa-tathishoⁿ 'northwards' ['towards the headwater']
mí éthoⁿbe-tathishoⁿ 'eastwards' ['towards where the sun appears']
óⁿba í-thoⁿtathishoⁿ 'eastwards' ['towards the coming day']
wahába hí 'corn plant / corncob / cornstalk'
wáxoⁿ há / wahába há 'corn husk'
wahába sída 'hard [ripe] ear of corn'
wahába shtóⁿga 'soft [unripe] ear of corn'
watʰóⁿzi skíthe 'sweet corn'
thigá 'to husk the corn'
thishpí 'to shell the corn'
wathítube 'cornbread'
wanáxi 'parched corn'
uthísoⁿ 'to roast / parch the corn'
waníde 'corn mush'

7.14 PUT UP THE TIPI: TIMÓ^NGTHE

Translation: Rufus White and Donna Morris Parker; elicitation/transcription: Vida Woodhull Stabler.

Vocabulary

The general word for "tipi" is **tísoⁿthe**. The other common word **timóⁿgthe** refers to the erected tipi after it is put up.

tísoⁿthe: whitened tipi

timóⁿgthe: tipi standing up

házhiⁿga/wékoⁿtʰoⁿ: rope

tíha: canvas

tíshi: pole

tesíⁿde ugáshke: lifting pole

tiúthugadoⁿ: stakes

tíshuthoⁿ/tíhuthoⁿ: sticks used to weave the front flap

tíhukoⁿ/shúde íhe: smoke hole / chimney

títhumoⁿhoⁿ: woven part above door

tíha ugábthiⁿtha: smoke flaps

tí ágaxada: door cover

áthiaze: open (the door cover) onto the poles

koⁿtʰóⁿ: tie

thimóⁿgthe: raise

uthíshoⁿ: go around

thisáda: straighten

gadóⁿ: hammer / pound

basnóⁿ: push (stick) through

íⁿʼe wétʰiⁿ: hammer

thibthá: spread door cover open

thidíⁿdiⁿ: pull hard

thidóⁿ: pull hard

thisóⁿtha: twist

tinóⁿde: tipi wall

ubázhiⁿ: adjust

tiúthipʰu zhiⁿga: sweat lodge / wigwam

ugábthi: (snow / smoke) blow back into the tipi

ugáshke: hang from

ugáxthuge: hammer a hole in

unéthe: fireplace

upé: enter

utí: pitch tipi just for overnight

épaze: pitch tipi for a few nights

wahóⁿ: strike and move tipi

tizhébe ugthóⁿ: dew cloth

moⁿthíⁿ tí: earth lodge

zhoⁿthóⁿha tí: bark lodge

zhóⁿ waxága tí: brush lodge

xáditi: grass lodge

tináze: back of the tipi

tiútʰoⁿna: hallway / walkway between tipis

Wágazhi-ge: Directive Sequence

Wóⁿgithe tísoⁿthe-tʰe agímoⁿthiⁿi-a/ga: Everybody go get the tipis.

Wóⁿgithe tíshi agímoⁿthiⁿi-a/ga. Dúda agígii-a/ga: Everybody go get the tipi poles and bring them here.

Tíshi-tʰe agíthe-wathe: Let's all go get the poles.

Tíshi koⁿtóⁿi-a/ga, thip^{h}í: Tie the (3) poles together. Tie them right.

Tíshi-t^{h}e thimóⁿgthai-a/ga: Raise the tipi poles.

Tíha thibthái-a/ga: Open the canvas.

Tíha-thoⁿ uthísho^n it^{h}éthai-a/ga: Put the canvas up around them.

Házhiⁿga-k^{h}e tísoⁿthe-t^{h}e uthísho^{n}i-a/ga: Go around the tipi with the rope.

Tíshi-t^{h}edi koⁿtóⁿi-a/ga: Tie the rope to the tipi pole.

Tísoⁿthe-t^{h}e thisádai-a/ga, it^{h}éthai-a/ga: Straighten and tighten the tipi canvas, put it up right.

Tiúthugadoⁿ-t^{h}e tóⁿde-k^{h}edi ugádo^{n}i-a/ga: Pound the stakes into the ground.

Tiúthugadoⁿ-t^{h}e thip^{h}í gadó^{n}i-a/ga: Hammer the stakes tight.

Tíshuthoⁿ uthó^n/ga: Hold the stick(s) that will be used for weaving.

Tizhébe-t^{h}e paháshi-tho^{n}di shúde íhe-t^{h}e zhó^{n}zhi^{n}ga-t^{h}e ubásno^{n}i-a/ga: Weave the sticks right above the door where smoke can pass through.

Cultural Beliefs for Putting Up Tipi

Whatever you do, start from the EAST.

Why? Move with the Sun.

Damper: directs the wind, go with the wind (know direction of wind damper is light, keeps rain out to keep fire dry)

Smoke hole: leave space at bottom of tipi, wind can interfere with the fire, also light damper effect

Three Poles: represent Orphan and Parents, leaning and sharing

Stakes: start from the door (east and go around)

Tíso^{n}the Zhi^{n}ga Gáxe: Making Little Tipis

MATERIALS: Model **tíha** "canvas," twine, skewers, glue gun, paint, and other decoration if desired

Using model **tíha**, determine the minimum diameter of the base.

Math enrichment: In Umóⁿho^n Íye determine the radius and use to create bases by compass.

Using model **tíha**, create **tíha** for students.

Art enrichment: Students may choose to decorate their **tíha**.

Have Elder instruct students on proper construction of **timóⁿgthe**.

7.15 KICKBALL: TABÉ NO^{N}T^{H}Á

Translation: Marcella Woodhull Cayou and Donna Morris Parker; elicitation/transcription: Vida Woodhull Stabler.

Lesson: Kickball at the Park

OBJECTIVE

Students will practice speaking recurring kickball phrases prior to playing the game. Each will be required to speak them while in position of 1st, 2nd, and 3rd bases, pitching and throwing as observed by Wagóⁿze.

MATERIALS

Kickball, bases, and coin

*Ebé Íkikoⁿ?: Who Is Playing
Against Whom?*

**Nudóⁿhoⁿga edi thashkáde-ama, ebé
níⁿi-a?:** The captains who are playing,
who are you?

**Tabé thashkáde-ama watháwa/ga, ánoⁿ
aníⁿi-a?:** Count how many of you are
playing, how many do you have?

Thégi shuthé: You're on this side. (Over
here goes to you.)

Thégi-thishoⁿ gí-a/ga: You're on this side.
(Come over this way.)

Thégi-thishoⁿ noⁿzhíⁿ gí-a/ga: You're on
this side. (Come stand over this way.)

Shéhi-ta shuthé: You're on that side. (Over
there goes to you.)

Shéhi-ta noⁿzhíⁿ moⁿthíⁿ-a/ga: You're on
that side. (Go stand over that way.)

Óⁿma-tathishoⁿ uéhe: I'm going to the
other side.

Óⁿma-tathishoⁿ noⁿzhíⁿ moⁿthíⁿ-a/ga:
Go stand on the other side.

*Wéthawa Zhiⁿga-thoⁿ Gamóⁿshi Thétha-wathe:
Let's Toss the Coin.*

Ebé wéthawa zhiⁿga athíⁿ-a?: Who has a
coin?

Wéthawa zhiⁿga gamóⁿshi thétha/ga:
Throw the coin up.

Awíⁿoⁿwa-tathishoⁿ shkóⁿna?: Which
side do you want?

Noⁿshkí-tathishoⁿ kóⁿbtha: I want heads
side.

Síⁿde-tathishoⁿ kóⁿbtha: I want tails side.

*Íye Tabé Noⁿtʰá Íshkade-ge: Phrases with Which
to Play Kickball*

Tabé-thoⁿ ganóⁿga/ga: Roll the ball.

**Tabé-thoⁿ gasnú-a/ga / Tabé-thoⁿ gasnú
thétha/ga:** Slide the ball.

Tabé-thoⁿ noⁿtʰá/ga: Kick the ball.

Tabé-thoⁿ uthóⁿ/ga: Catch the ball.

Tabé-thoⁿ óⁿtha thétha/ga: Throw the ball.

gashíbe: out of bounds

Gashí-ata óⁿtha thétha/ga: Throw it out of
bounds.

Gastákʰi thétha: S/he kicked it out of
bounds. (flung too far / fly ball)

**Gashíbe gastákʰi thétha./Gashíbe
noⁿstákʰi thétha:** S/he kicked it out of
bounds.

Tóⁿthiⁿ-a/ga: Run.

Wasékoⁿ noⁿhégazhi-a/ga: Run fast.

Wasékoⁿ noⁿhéga-bazhii-a/ga: Run fast.
(spoken to more than one)

Moⁿthíⁿ-a/ga: Go.

**Weáhide gastákʰi thétha/ga / Weáhide
noⁿstákʰi thétha/ga:** Knock it real far.

Tabé-thoⁿ dúda óⁿtha gítha/ga: Throw the
ball over here to me.

**Tabé-thoⁿ mízhiⁿga-thiⁿkʰe óⁿtha thétha/
ga:** Throw the ball to the girl.

Núzhiⁿga-thiⁿkʰe tabé-thoⁿ ítʰiⁿ-a/ga: Hit the boy with the ball.

Tabé-thoⁿ ítʰiⁿ-a/ga: Hit her / him with the ball.

Noⁿhégazhi, utʰíⁿ-a/ga: S/he's running, hit her/him.

Tabé thashkáda wóⁿdoⁿ íkikawiⁿthai-a/ga: Both teams of ball players switch sides.

Wi bthé-tamiⁿkʰe: My turn. (I will go.)

Náze-ta noⁿzhíⁿ-a/ga, noⁿhégazhi agí: Stand back, s/he's running home.

Íwanoⁿthazhi noⁿtʰá/ga: Kick it hard.

Gashnóⁿ: S/he missed him/her.

Núzhiⁿga-thiⁿkʰe tháshnoⁿ: You missed the boy.

7.16 EARTH DAY/MOTHER EARTH: ÍⁿNOⁿHA TÓⁿDE

Translation: Marcella Woodhull Cayou and Rufus White; transcription/elicitation: Vida Woodhull Stabler.

Cultural Note

Let's be aware of how we treat our Mother Earth. She is sacred. Here are a few ways that incorporate Umóⁿhoⁿ values to help guide our behavior:

Use your traditional ways by carrying your dishes to all doings. Never throw any packages from pop bottles, candy, chips or gum down on our mother or in our springs. Use trash cans for waste.

Carry your own bags to the grocery store to carry your food home.

Refill water or beverage in a water bottle instead plastic water bottles.

When you harvest from our earth, give thanks for what she provides (offering).

Respect the land of our ancestors.

Íⁿnoⁿha Moⁿzhóⁿ: Mother Earth

Moⁿzhóⁿ Ákʰihide-tʰe: Taking Care of Umóⁿhoⁿ Lands

Moⁿzhóⁿ Údoⁿ Ithóⁿthai-ga: Keep Umóⁿhoⁿ Land Beautiful. (spoken by male)

Kigthíezhubai-a/ga: Respect yourselves.

Moⁿzhóⁿ-thoⁿ: the Earth

Moⁿzhóⁿ usíhi gthíⁿ: The earth is clean.

Tíutʰoⁿna thisíhi shíshige bahí-a/ga: Pick up trash, clean your yard.

Kigthízhai-tʰe: No more litter on the ground. (literally "It must have washed itself.")

7.17 STANDING BEAR SPEECH: MAⁿCHʰÚ NAZHIⁿ ÍYA-BIAMA

Translation: Marcella Woodhull Cayou and Donna Morris Parker; transcription/elicitation: Vida Woodhull Stabler and K. Chavarria (Umóⁿhoⁿ Íye III). The request for the translation of this speech was made by music teacher John Mangan to Vida Woodhull Stabler. With the help of Elders Marcella Woodhull Cayou and Donna Parker, the speech was translated from English to Umóⁿhoⁿ Íye. Standing Bear's speech was taught to John Mangan, who in turn taught it to a student to render at the Standing Bear Awards presentation at the Nebraska State Capitol in 2008.

That hand is not the color of yours, but if I pierce it, I shall feel pain. If you pierce your hand, you also feel pain. The blood that will flow from mine will be the same color as yours. I am a man. The same God made us both. —MaⁿchʰúNazhiⁿ / Chief Standing Bear, Páⁿka Tribe, interpreted by IⁿshtáThioⁿba / Susette LaFlesche Tibbles, Umóⁿhoⁿ Tribe

Noⁿbé-tʰe wíuga-tʰe eóⁿkigoⁿzhi: Our hands are not the same color.

Zhákihe-ki oⁿníye-tamiⁿkʰe: If I pierce mine I will feel pain.

Noⁿbé-tʰe zháthakihe-ki thiníye-taniⁿkshe: If you pierce your hand you will feel pain.

Wamí-akʰa nóⁿgai-tʰe-di-ki wíuga eóⁿkigoⁿ-taóⁿgatʰoⁿ: When the blood floods we will be the same color.

Nú bthíⁿ: I am a man.

Wakóⁿda-akʰa ékigoⁿ wáxa: God made us the same.

Cultural Note

Umóⁿhoⁿ Elder Susan Freemont was a past recipient of the Standing Bear Award. As she stood there, wrapped in a star quilt blanket, and addressed the assembled crowd, she made an impromptu decision to sing "Twinkle, Twinkle

Little Star" (which she had translated earlier that year for the children). She called me up to sing with her. Everyone knew she was well deserving of the acknowledgment. —Vida Woodhull Stabler

7.18 MOTHER'S DAY PHRASES: IHÓⁿ ÓⁿBA ÍYE-GE

Translation: Marcella Woodhull Cayou; elicitation/transcription: Vida Woodhull Stabler.

Cultural Note

It is important to discuss with our children that we can have many "Mothers." One example to teach is that a woman could be called "Mother" by any of her sister's children.

Directions

These phrases are used to make Mother's Day cards with the students.

Happy Mother's Day!

Óⁿbathe Ihóⁿ   Óⁿba- tʰe, gíthe
today   Mother Day   the happy
moⁿthíⁿ-a/ga.
walk

Today is Mother's Day, be happy.

Ihóⁿ   Óⁿba- tʰe   gítha/ga!
Mother   Day   the   be happy

Happy Mother's Day!

Íⁿnoⁿha   Óⁿba- tʰe   gítha/ga!
my Mother Day   the   be happy

Ihóⁿ Óⁿba Íye-ge: Mother's Day Phrases

Eyóⁿ níⁿ hó, noⁿhó?: How are you, Mother? (male voice)

Noⁿhá/Noⁿhó, xcháwigithe: Mother, I love you, my own.

Óⁿbathe nóⁿde wiwíta wi'í: Today I give you my heart.

Noⁿhá/Noⁿhó, úwashkoⁿ oⁿthá'i: Mother, you give me strength.

Wisíthe moⁿbthíⁿ: I'm thinking of you.

Oⁿthíthahoⁿ: We thank you.

Card-Making Instructions

Wagthábaze wíⁿ thizá/ga: Take a paper.

Wiⁿdéthoⁿska betʰóⁿ/ga: Fold it in half.

Waxchá thixú-a/ga, shi waníta-shti thixú-a/ga: Draw a flower, and draw an animal too.

Izházhe gipáxui-a/ga: Write your names.

7.19 FLOWER POTS AND FLOWER PLANTING: WAXCHÁ ÚZHI

Translation: Marcella Woodhull Cayou and Donna Morris Parker; elicitation/transcription: Vida Woodhull Stabler; consolidated from "Flower Pot: Elder Script," "Flower Pot Handout," "Flower Pot Waxtá Úzhi," and "Flower Planting Part 2"; consolidation: Bryan James Gordon; linguistic notes: Ardis Eschenberg.

Activity

Students plant flower seeds as directed by the Wagóⁿze or Elder according to the Elder Script that follows in Umóⁿhoⁿ Íye. Then they break down the phrases on a worksheet by giving word-for-word translations under each Umóⁿhoⁿ word.

Cultural Note

It's appropriate to teach the children to say a word of prayer to acknowledge Wakóⁿda when planting. Our creator provides all that we need.

OBJECTIVES

Cultural practice of flower planting. Reinforcements of verbs **'í** "give," **uzhí** "put in," **thizé** "take," and **uhá théthe** "pass around." Introduction of postposition **-di** "in." Investigation of properties of Umóⁿhoⁿ nouns vs. verbs via the word **uzhí** "put in" vs. **úzhi** "container."

MATERIALS

Seeds, dirt, containers (cups or milk cartons), water, markers, pencils

Vocabulary

hí: plant

zháhi: stem

zhóⁿ'abe: leaf

hí: roots

waxchá-tʰe: the flowers

waxchá-thoⁿ: the flower

sí: seed

xthabé: tree

moⁿthíⁿkʰa: dirt

Elder Script

At the appropriate times, teach students their lines in the script:

Wíⁿ thizá/ga, uhá thétha/ga: Take one and pass it around.

Waxchá sí-tʰe noⁿbá thizá/ga, uhá thétha/ga: Take two of the flower seeds and then pass them around.

Gathering dirt:

1. **Tehé toⁿga-kʰe thizá/ga:** Take the big spoon.
2. **Moⁿthíⁿkʰa-kʰe moⁿ'á/ga:** Dig up some dirt.

Planting flowers in pots together in class (spoken to group)

This script contains some slight variations on the directions from the various documents we consolidated into this script.

3. **Wéuzhi-tʰe thizái-a/ga:** Get the cartons.

Teach the students their new phrase as they pass around cartons, tapes, cups, etc..

4. **Weáthaskabe thizái-a/ga:** Get tape.
   or **Weáthaskabe wíⁿ thizái-a/ga:** Take a tape.
5. **Izházhe gipáxui-a/ga:** Write your name.
   or **Izházhe-kʰe gipáxui-a/ga.**
6. **Niúthatoⁿ-tʰedi ábiskabai-a/ga:** Stick it onto the cup.

7. **Moⁿthíⁿkʰa-tʰe thizái-a/ga:** Take the dirt.
   or **Moⁿthíⁿkʰa-tʰe dúba thizái-a/ga:** Take some of the dirt.
8. **Moⁿthíⁿkʰa-tʰe wéuzhi-tʰedi uzhíi-a/ga:** Add the dirt into the carton.
   or **Wéuzhi-tʰedi moⁿthíⁿkʰa-tʰe uzhíi-a/ga.**
   Moⁿthíⁿkʰa-tʰe dúba uzhíi-a/ga.
   Moⁿthíⁿkʰa-tʰe wéuzhi-tʰedi wiⁿdétʰoⁿ ák'soⁿde uzhíi-a/ga: Fill the carton a little over halfway with the dirt.
   or **Moⁿthíⁿkʰa-tʰe wéuzhi-tʰedi wiⁿdétʰoⁿ ák'soⁿde itʰéthai-a/ga uzhíi-a/ga.**
9. **Niúthatoⁿ-tʰe ugípi uzhíi-a/ga:** Fill the cup.
10. **Waxchá sí noⁿbá thizái-a/ga:** Take two flower seeds.

Teach the students their new phrase at this point as they pass the seeds around.

11. **U'úde noⁿbá gáxai-a/ga:** Make two holes.
12. **Waxchá sí-tʰe édi uzhíi-a/ga:** Add the flower seeds there.
13. **Waxchá sí-tʰe ágaxadai-a/ga:** Cover the flower seeds.
14. **Ní-tʰe júba uzhíi-a/ga:** Add a little water.
    Ní-tʰe júba-xchi uzhíi-a/ga: Add just a little bit of water.
15. **Shóⁿ:** That's all.

Student Assessment

Izházhe wiwíta-t^he_____

Óⁿbathe_____

Directions

Break down the Mystery Phrases, Additional Phrases, and Flower-Planting Directions that follow.

Mystery Phrases

Q: **Ebé tha'í-ta?**

A: **Timíha/Timího a'í-tamiⁿk^he.**

Q: Who are you going to give it to?

A: I'm going to give to my aunt.

Additional Phrases

Áshi thé-wathe: Let's go outside.

Miéthoⁿbe-thoⁿtáthishoⁿ moⁿthíⁿi-a/ga: Walk east.

Flower-Planting Directions

1. **Tehé toⁿga-k^he thizá/ga:** Take the big spoon.
   _____

2. **Moⁿthíⁿk^ha-k^he moⁿ'á/ga:** Dig up some dirt.
   _____

3. **Wéuzhi-t^he thizái-a/ga:** Get the cartons.
   _____

4. **Weáthaskabe wíⁿ thizái-a/ga:** Take a tape.
   _____

5. **Izházhe-k^he gipáxui-a/ga:** Write your name.
   _____

6. **Niúthatoⁿ-t^hedi ábiskabai-a/ga:** Stick it onto the cup.
   _____

7. **Moⁿthíⁿk^ha-t^he dúba thizái-a/ga:** Take the dirt / Take some of the dirt.
   _____

8. **Moⁿthíⁿk^ha-t^he wéuzhi-t^hedi uzhíi-a/ga:** Add the dirt into the carton.
   _____

9. **Niúthatoⁿ-t^he ugípi uzhíi-a/ga:** Fill the cup.
   _____

10. **Waxchá sí noⁿbá thizái-a/ga:** Take two flower seeds.
    _____

11. **U'úde noⁿbá gáxai-a/ga:** Make two holes.
    _____

12. **Waxchá sí-t^he édi uzhíi-a/ga:** Add the flower seeds there.
    _____

13. **Waxchá sí-t^he ágaxadai-a/ga:** Cover the flower seeds.
    _____

14. **Ní-t^he júba-xchi uzhíi-a/ga:** Add just a little bit of water.
    _____

15. **Shóⁿ:** That's all.
    _____

Linguistic Notes:
Postpositional Phrase, Noun vs. Verb

In English we have **prepositions**—words like *in* or *for* that come before a noun or a noun phrase. Umó^{n}ho^n Íye has a similar set of words, but they come *after* nouns, so they are called **postpositions**. Consider the following phrase:

wéuzhi-t^{h}edi: in the container

Wéuzhi "container" is the noun in this phrase. As we have learned, **-t^{h}e** is the article "the." So what is the **-di** left on the end? What kind of word is it, and what is its meaning? It is a postposition, and it means "in."

> What is the order of words in a postpositional phrase in Umó^{n}ho^n Íye?

wéuzhi-t^{h}edi

noun-article-postposition

> What is the order of words in a postpositional phrase in English?

in the container

preposition-article-noun

It is exactly the opposite of Umó^{n}ho^n Íye!

7.20 DINING-OUT SCRIPT

Translation: Marcella Woodhull Cayou; elicitation/transcription: Vida Woodhull Stabler.

Waiter/Waitress Script

> **Wathát^{h}e gína/ga:** ask her/him for food
> **Ó^{n}ba-t^{h}e údo^n:** It's a good day.

That^{h}í-t^{h}e údo^n: It's good you're here.

I^{n}dádo^n nát^{h}e shkó^{n}na?: What do you want to eat?

I^{n}dádo^n ázhi shkó^{n}na?: What else do you want? ("Do you want anything else?")

I^{n}dádo^n náto^n shkó^{n}na?: What do you want to drink? ("Do you want anything to drink?")

Patron's Script

> **No^{n}pehi:** S/he is hungry.
> **Tagáxthixthi, washí^n, i^{n}chó^{n}ga wathát^{h}e-shti bthát^{h}e kó^{n}btha:** I want to eat a bacon cheeseburger.
> **Nú zhézhi-shti kó^{n}btha:** I also want French fries.
> **Sézi s'áthe nískithe btháto^n kó^{n}btha:** I want to drink lemonade.

Interpreter's Script

IYÉSKA: INTERPRETER

> **Dúak^{h}a tagáxthixthi, washí^n, i^{n}chó^{n}ga wathát^{h}e-shti that^{h}é gó^{n}tha:** This person wants to eat a bacon cheeseburger.
> **Waxthá íkigthahi-shti that^{h}é gó^{n}tha:** S/he also wants to eat a salad.
> **Coke tható^n gó^{n}tha:** S/he wants to drink a Coke.

Script While Waiting to Eat

> **Ithápe gthí^n:** They're sitting there waiting.
> **Wazhíde ágaxto^n thizá/ga:** Get the ketchup.

Washíⁿ ágaxtoⁿ thizá/ga: Get the mustard.

Noⁿbéibikʰa wíⁿ-thoⁿthoⁿ wa'í-a/ga: Give each one a napkin.

Niúthatoⁿ-tʰe núxe wiⁿdétʰoⁿ-tʰedi uzhí-a/ga: Fill the cup halfway with ice. ("Cup" may also be said as **niíthatoⁿ**.)

They've Brought the Food:
Wathátʰe tʰe Wéthiⁿ Atʰiⁿ

Wathátʰe-tʰe athíⁿ-atʰi: The food has arrived. / S/he brought the food.

Ebé etá?: Whose is it?

Tagáxthixthi, washíⁿ, iⁿchóⁿga wathátʰe, ebé etá?: Whose is the bacon cheeseburger?

Tagáxthixthi ebé ná?: Who asked for the hamburger?

Wazhíⁿga zhézhi ebé etá?: Whose is the fried chicken / chicken strips?

Wathátʰai-a/ga!: Eat!

Niskíthe-tʰe úha-thetha/ga: Pass the salt (around the circle).

Niskíthe-tʰe úha-githa/ga: Pass the salt back around to me.

7.21 WHAT WILL YOU DO IN THE SUMMER?: MOⁿSHTÉ-KI IⁿDÁDOⁿ SHKÁXE-TANIⁿKSHE?

Translation: Marcella Woodhull Cayou; elicitation/transcription: Vida Woodhull Stabler.

Lesson: Summertime

OBJECTIVES

- Review future tense forms
- Discuss plans for the summer
- Review weather

Introduction

The weather is changing all the time lately, especially today. How many words can you think of to describe today's weather?

Cultural Note

Many tribal members look to summer as a time to travel to different powwows or other ceremonies. There are many dances and ceremonies to go to locally as well as others you would have to travel a ways to get to. Many Umóⁿhoⁿ people invest in tents and outdoor cooking implements in order to get the full camping out experience.

Activity: What Are You Going to Do This Summer?

WÉMOⁿXE-GE: QUESTIONS

Moⁿshté-ki iⁿdádoⁿ shkáxe-taniⁿkshe?: What will you do this summer?

Moⁿshté-ki áwa-kʰ-ta né-taniⁿkshe?: Where will you be going this summer?

Moⁿshté-ki thahína né-taniⁿkshe?: Will you go swimming this summer?

EDÍYE-GE: ANSWERS

Moⁿshté-ki tabé ashkáde-tamiⁿkʰe: This summer I will play ball.

Áwa-kʰʼ-ta bthá-mazhi-tamiⁿkʰe: I won't be going anywhere.

Ahíbtha bthé-tamiⁿkʰe: I will go swimming.

Linguistic Note: Double-Conjugating Verb hithá: bathe

The verb **hithá** "bathe / swim" has the **a-** verb pattern in front, and the **bth-** verb pattern in the end:

Ahíbtha: I bathe / swim.

Thahína: You bathe / swim.

Oⁿhítha: We bathe / swim.

Hithá: S/he / they bathe / swim.

With the formal ending **-i**, **hithá** transforms into our word for Saturday — **Hithái** "they bathe."

7.22 GRADUATION PHRASES

Translation: Marcella Woodhull Cayou; elicitation/transcription: Vida Woodhull Stabler.

Cultural Note

Educational achievement or graduation is celebrated within the Umóⁿhoⁿ community for all levels of schooling from Head Start to higher level institutions. Celebrations include dinners or feasts, handgame, Gourd Dance, or War Dance. Sometimes all are done in one event. These events are "made" for the honoree.

Údoⁿ shkáxa, uthágashibe wóⁿgithe: All of you graduating did well.

Thanóⁿ, gashíbe né-taniⁿkshe: You're getting older, so it's time for you to go out there. / You matured, you'll go out of here.

Umóⁿhoⁿ Táp'ska-ta uéhe: I go to UNPS.

Umóⁿthiⁿkʰa thé íthishethoⁿ uágashibe-tamiⁿkʰe: This year is my last one, and I'm going to graduate.

Wathígthoⁿ-ta oⁿgáthe-taoⁿgatʰoⁿ: We're going to Quiz Bowl competition.

Wikʰáge wiwíta kinóⁿnoⁿge ugthíⁿ kúwiⁿxe xtáathe: I like to ride around in my friend's car.

Táp'ska moⁿbthíⁿ, awáshkoⁿ-xti, wagthábaze áthade bthíshtoⁿ kóⁿbtha. Uágashibe kóⁿbtha: I'm a student, I'm really trying hard, because I want to finish my assignments. I want to graduate.

gashíbe: out from

ugáshibe: graduate / pass through

shéthoⁿ: finished / completed

thishéthoⁿ: finish / complete / graduate

íthishethoⁿ: used to finish / complete / graduate

Additional Resources 8

8.1 WRITING SYSTEM EXTENSION, HOW IT IS WRITTEN IN UMÓⁿHOⁿ: UMÓⁿHOⁿ ÍYE-TʰE ÁWATʰEGOⁿ BAXÚ-NOⁿ

Common Complications and Issues in Applying the UNPS Spelling System

This extension builds on our Writing System Quick Sheet in chapter 1, lesson 1.1. Please begin your exploration and practice there, not here.

Although our spelling system is a simple "mapping" between Umóⁿhoⁿ sounds and letters, Umóⁿhoⁿ Íye is not as simple as the spelling system, so there are many issues that come up and can cause confusion or even disagreement about how to spell a word. Here we bring up some of the most frequent issues and provide advic—not necessarily rules—on how to deal with them.

Slashes

Umóⁿhoⁿ request/command verbs end in an -**a** sound for female speakers, and a -**ga** sound for male speakers. Because these verbs are so important in our curriculum we adopt a shorthand use of the slash symbol—/—to show where this male/female difference is. Some request/command forms end in -**a/ga**, which shows that female speakers pronounce the -**a** and male speakers pronounce -**ga** instead. Other request/command forms end in /**ga** without the -**a** before it. This is because these are verbs that

end in **e**, **a** or **oⁿ** where the female -**a** sound is already built into the verb ending, so that female speakers just say the verb up to the slash symbol and males still add the -**ga**. Examples:

FEMALE/MALE ENDINGS:
ENGLISH TRANSLATION

Baxú-a/ga: Write it.

Baxúi-a/ga: All write it.

Áthada/ga: Read it.

Áthadai-a/ga: All read it.

Dóⁿba/ga: Look at it.

Dóⁿbai-a/ga: All look at it.

Ugádoⁿ/ga: Hammer them in.

Ugádoⁿi-a/ga: All hammer them in.

Our example of a verb ending in **e** was **dóⁿbe**. You will never see **e/ga** at the end of a verb, because the final **e** always becomes **a** in request/command form.

Word Breaks and Dashes

The UNPS spelling system does not have hard rules on where to put spaces and dashes. Linguistically, there are issues of both meaning and rhythm to consider in figuring out whether a phrase has one or more words in it. But practically we believe the intuition of speakers and learners in our community is good enough. Still we try to be consistent in departmental documentation and curriculum.

There are a few cases of words that we separate when they add separate meanings to a phrase but combine together when they have a shared combined meaning. Names are a good example: if we want to write the words for "big elk," we write **óⁿpʰoⁿ toⁿga**, but if we want to write the name Big Elk, we write **ÓⁿpʰoⁿToⁿga**. Similarly, "to hit stones" is **íⁿ'e utʰíⁿ**, but "handgame" is **íⁿ'utʰíⁿ**.

We use the hyphen or dash to show separate words or word parts that are "said together." This "said together" basically means that we do not hear speakers pausing ever between these parts. Some words whose parts are "said together" in this way include **údoⁿ-xti** "truly good," **újoⁿ-xchi** "truly beautiful," **nákadách** (full spelling **nákʰade-átashoⁿ**) "very hot," **athé-noⁿ** "s/he goes regularly," **Wikóⁿ-akʰa** "my Grandmother," and many more.

Sometimes we skip the dash when two parts come together so often that we think of them as a single part. Examples include **iⁿdádoⁿshte** "something," and the future markers like **-tamiⁿkʰe** "I will." Even though **-ta** and **-miⁿkʰe** are both endings that can come up with dashes, when they come together we don't put a dash between them. There is one ending—final **-i**—that we never spell with a dash at all. In our curriculum this ending will be most familiar from plural requests like **noⁿzhíⁿi-a/ga** "stand up." It also comes up a lot in storytelling and formal speaking and before certain other endings like **-ki**.

"Said together" usually (but not always) also means that only one of the parts has a stressed on-beat (the heaviest, most melodic vowel sound in the word). When this is the case, we only spell one of the parts with an accent mark, as in **thípi-gaxe** "to do a good job."

Not every case of two words or word parts coming in contact works the same way. Some speakers have different habits, and some situations make different demands. It is good to be flexible about word divisions and dashes, paying attention to the sound, as in the following examples that can go more than one way, depending on where the stressed on-beat is:

SOUNDS LIKE → SPELLING WITH DASHES →
ENGLISH TRANSLATION

Wióⁿthoⁿmoⁿxa/ga →
  Wi-óⁿthoⁿmoⁿxa/ga → Ask me!
Wioⁿthóⁿmoⁿxa/ga →
  Wí oⁿthóⁿmoⁿxa/ga → Ask me!
Oⁿguíⁿwiⁿtha → **Oⁿgú-iⁿwiⁿtha** →
  We told him
Oⁿguiⁿwíⁿtha → **Óⁿgu iⁿwíⁿtha** →
  We told him

These pairs don't seem to have any different meanings; they just depend on how tightly the speaker "chunked" the parts together.

There is one final group of verbs where we regularly use dashes. Verbs like **xtáthe** "love"—or **shuthéthe** "send to you"—often wind up with a lot of additions between the main part of the verb and the final **-the**. We usually follow the rule that if the whole word is more than three syllables, we use a dash to break up the main verb part from all the additions, grouping the additions together with the final -**the**. Examples:

Xcháwithe: I love you.

Xchaó^{n}thathe / Xchá-o^{n}tháthe: You love me.

Mó^{n}z'ska uthéwi^{n}-athe: I gathered money.

Mó^{n}z'ska uthéwi^{n}-wathák^{h}ithe: You raised money for us.

Gthí^{n}k^{h}itha: She seated him.

Gthí^{n}-o^{n}thák^{h}ithe: You seated me.

Variable Vowels

Just as fluent speakers can find many ways to say what's on their minds, they also have different ways of pronouncing the same word, different shades of pronunciation of the same sound, and Umó^{n}ho^{n} writers have different ways of writing down those variations they hear or speak.

Let's think about variation in vowel pronunciation before we move on to variation in writing. This is a common area of difficulty, because Umó^{n}ho^{n} Íye divides up the "vowel space" in the mouth in a very different way than English.

Vowels are inexact things. We may say that Umó^{n}ho^{n} Íye has six vowels, while American English has as many as twenty-one, depending on regional and ethnic dialects. But both use the same mouth to divide up into these vowels.

Think about a vowel as a tiny dartboard permanently taking up some part of the mouth. When speakers pronounce that vowel, they aim at the dartboard, and they always hit it because they're fluent. But they don't always hit the same part of the dartboard. Sometimes they aim high, sometimes they aim low. Sometimes they aim high but hit low instead because they were swallowing or excited.

Also, and this is even more important, the dartboards overlap. Hitting one part of the *e* dartboard sounds exactly the same as hitting one part of the *i* dartboard—because in that part the two overlap. And part of the overlap is set in stone by the language itself. Umó^{n}ho^{n} Íye and English have different overlaps. English vowel dartboards are very small compared to Umó^{n}ho^{n} vowel dartboards, because speakers have to squeeze up to twenty-one of them into the same mouth where an Umó^{n}ho^{n} speaker only needs six. So our English-dominant ear may hear an Umó^{n}ho^{n} speaker pronounce the same vowel five times and hear it as five different vowels, because it hit a different English dartboard each time.

We have to train ourselves to ignore the English dartboards, or we'll constantly be thinking we heard the wrong vowel. It helps to understand when vowels are "weakened," or "centralized." This is actually something similar to what happened historically in English. We learn in school that the *a* in *ago*, the *o* in *parrot*, the *i* in *pencil*, etc., are all more or less the same sound. This is because these "weak" vowels, which are not pronounced with a heavy beat, all historically were gradually moved away from the outside parts of their dartboards and toward the middle of the mouth. Eventually in English they fell off their original dartboards altogether, and now we consider them a separate vowel all their own. In Umó^{n}ho^{n} Íye these vowels are still on their original dartboards, but they are in the part closest to the middle of the mouth.

So there are two hard questions we need to answer before we can understand this: (1) when do Umón̄hón̄ vowels get "weaker," and (2) what do "weak" vowels sound like in Umón̄hón̄ Íye? The first answer is "off-beats." Umón̄hón̄ Íye is a rhythmic language with a one-two-one-two rhythm. Each syllable is its own beat. Two vowels that come together may sometimes combine into a single beat; other times they do not. The first or second beat of a word is usually the strongest. We mark the strongest beat with an accent mark over the vowel in our writing system. Every other beat after a strong beat is an "on-beat," but the beats in between are "off-beats," and their vowels are "weak" or sometimes even disappear entirely as in **táp'ska** "school," **món̄z'ska** "money," or **áchon̄** "very/ extremely" (from **átashon̄**).

Finally, here is a table of examples of Umón̄hón̄ words with "weak" vowels, as a basic guide to the sound. Of course real learning of sound cannot come from a printed page, but this table may help:

VOWEL → HOW THE WEAK VOWEL SOUNDS (EXAMPLES FOLLOW EACH)

u → like *o* in *goes* or *u* in *flu* or *u* in *put*

tápuska: school

Uáwathagikon̄: You helped us.

Bthíwagazu: I fixed it.

on̄ → like *un* in *undo* or *ong* in *song* or even like *a* in *Anita*

mon̄á: ravine / bluff

Shénon̄: That's all.

Égon̄: It's that way. / That's true. / Like that.

gthébon̄: ten

hén̄gon̄chʰe: morning

úshk'udon̄: good ways / kind/polite

a → like *a* in *father* or *a* in *Anita*, sometimes even like *e* in *bed*

Íya He spoke.

Aí: She's coming.

Égazeze: side by side

iyéska: interpreter

e → in between *e* in *Las Vegas* and *e* in *bet*

Eáton̄-a?: What's going on?

kishte: even if

agudíshte: wherever / somewhere

Itháe I speak.

Éshte 'ón̄: She's being silly / doing whatever.

in̄ → like *ing* in *sing* or *ean* in *mean* or *ain* in *rain*

win̄ón̄xchi: just one

niáshin̄ga: person / Indian

ugábthin̄tha: smoke flaps

thábthin̄: three

i → like *i* in *pizza* or *sit*

thiádi: your father

házi: grape

házini: grape juice / alcohol

wiúga: color / dye

Giáxa/ga: Do it to him/her.

Common Confusions from Weak Vowels

Weak **u** is often spelled **o** or **a** (as in "tápaska" instead of **tápuska** "school," or "móⁿzhoⁿ" instead of **muóⁿzhoⁿ** "we sift it").

Weak **i** and **iⁿ** are often spelled **e** (as in "weóga" instead of **wiúga** "color," "weóⁿxchi" instead of **wiⁿóⁿxchi** "just one," "íthai-ki" instead of **íthae-ki** "when you speak").

Weak **oⁿ** and **a** sound almost exactly the same, which is why we see spellings like "úshkuda" instead of **úshk'udoⁿ** "good ways," and why it can be hard to learn a good way of saying words like **oⁿáze** "shade / umbrella."

Weak **e** usually sounds similar to **i** and so is often spelled that way (as in "iⁿdádoⁿshti" instead of **iⁿdádoⁿshte** "something"), but in certain contexts weak **e** may go a different way and sound more like **a**, which is confusing since final **e** and **a** are related anyway.

Another issue we won't cover here, but which is worth mentioning, is that there are "strong" versions of the vowels, too—versions where speakers aim for the outside part of their dartboard instead of the middle of the mouth. These vowels come before "strong consonants": **p t ch k**, **pʰ tʰ chʰ kʰ**, **p' t' s sh**, and sometimes **x**. Listen to the vowels before these consonants and notice how they sound "stronger" than your ordinary vowel.

We prefer the spellings we have put in bold here over the ones in quotes. This does not mean other spellings are wrong; it just means the UNPS spelling system tries to preserve consistent spelling even when the vowel lands on an off-beat and sounds different.

Variable Consonants

Two groups of consonants give English-dominant speakers the same "dartboard" problem as the vowels: the "weak" consonants **b d j g** and the "strong" consonants **p t ch k**. English speakers have a hard time hearing the difference between these, and just like the vowels, these consonants are not always pronounced exactly the same way by fluent speakers. We know that the English **p t ch k** sounds are represented in Umóⁿhoⁿ Íye by **pʰ tʰ chʰ kʰ**. And if we are able to get over that difficulty, we are still left with the difference between these other sets of four. Here are some rules and exceptions to help you:

The "weak" consonants **b d j g** are usually voiced. You can hold your hand to your voicebox and feel it vibrate when you pronounce these sounds, especially when they are in the middle of a word.

But at the beginning of a long phrase or sentence, many speakers do not voice these sounds.

The "strong" consonants **p t ch k** are usually extra long. You can feel the "tension" as you hold your tongue or lips together for up to half a second–much longer than you would close them for a "weak" consonant. This applies especially when these sounds are in the middle of a word.

But at the beginning of a long phrase or sentence it is impossible to hear whether a sound like this is extra long, whether the speaker pronounces it that way or not.

So your hardest sounds to recognize and write will be those at the beginning of a phrase or sentence. Maybe you write "bahé" instead of **pahé** "hill," "bíki'oⁿ" instead of **píki'oⁿ** "fix yourself," "píze" instead of **bíze** "dry," "padíⁿ" instead of **badíⁿ** "to shovel." (This last one is especially tricky since **pádiⁿ** means "I shovel.") All these examples are problems between **b** and **p**, because these are far and away the hardest sounds for an English ear to distinguish, but we can have a hard time with **g** and **k** too—for example, writing "gúwiⁿxe" instead of **kúwiⁿxe** "go around," "kóⁿchʰe" instead of **góⁿchʰe** "after a little while / a little later / in a little bit," "Goⁿhó" "Grandmother" (male term of address) instead of **Koⁿhó**, "gúk'si" instead of **kúk'si** "pig," or "gáxe" instead of **káxe** "crow." Even **d** and **t** can be hard, as in **táshe** "bud / swelling; milkweed bud," which is often spelled "dáshe" or "dáshi." Be patient with yourself and learn tricks for asking and looking up clues when you can't hear the difference.

One other issue is the "softening" of the breathy consonants **pʰ tʰ chʰ kʰ** and the throat-jump consonants **p' t'**. This often happens on the same off-beats as the weak vowels (although not always—it depends on the speaker). This "softening" just means that these consonants are pronounced like an ordinary strong consonant **p t ch k** and drop the extra ʰ or '. The word for "fox" may be pronounced either **tíkʰa** or **tíka**, the word for "dirt / earth" either **moⁿthíⁿkʰa** or **moⁿthíⁿka**, the word for "five" either **sátoⁿ** or **sátʰoⁿ**, the word for "necklace" either **wanóⁿp'iⁿ** or **wanóⁿpiⁿ**, the word for "elk" either **óⁿpʰoⁿ** or **óⁿpoⁿ**. Some words, like **thipʰí**, may get their

on-beat moved when they conjugate or attach to a neighboring word, and this can cause the same effect: "do it right" is more likely to come out **thipi-gáxa/ga** instead of **thipʰí gáxa/ga**, and "I learned it" is more likely to come out **bthípi** than **bthípʰi**. *Both spellings are acceptable, and both should be provided in dictionaries and similar documentation where possible.*

Abbreviations

Sometimes an Umóⁿhoⁿ word or phrase can be shortened. Fluent speakers, when they are having conversations with each other, sometimes shorten even more words. There are also some words and phrases that are so common that nearly everybody shortens them. At the Umóⁿhoⁿ Language and Culture Center we often give two spellings for words like this:

FULL VERSION → SHORTENED VERSION → ENGLISH TRANSLATION

úshkoⁿ údoⁿ → **úshk'udoⁿ** → good ways / kind / polite

Údoⁿ shkáxe → **Úd'shkaxe** → You did good (spoken to one person)

móⁿzeska → **móⁿz'ska** or **móⁿ'ska** → money

Dropping the First of Two Vowels

When two vowels come together, the first one is often not pronounced. This is the most common change you'll notice in fluent conversations. In the Umóⁿhoⁿ Language and Culture Center spelling system we usually try to spell these phrases and words with both vowels unless the first one was really never pronounced by any speaker who has worked here.

When the first vowel is nasal and the second vowel is oral, the nasality is sometimes kept around even though the first vowel disappeared.

FULL VERSION → SHORTENED VERSION → ENGLISH TRANSLATION

Xchaó^{n}thathe-a? → **Xchó^{n}thathe-a?** → Do you love me?

O^{n}wó^{n}that^{h}e o^{n}gáthe-táo^{n}gat^{h}o^n → **O^{n}wó^{n}that^h o^{n}gáthe-tó^{n}gat^{h}o^n** → We're going to eat.

Thitígo^n-ak^{h}a agthí → **Thitígak^h agthí** → Your grandfather is back.

Tabé-tho^n ugthó^n-a → **Tabé-th ugthá.** or **Tabé-th ugthó^n** → Put the ball in there. (spoken by female)

miído^{n}be → **mído^{n}be** → clock / hour

hó^{n}adi → **hó^{n}di** → last night

uthuákiwat^{h}o^{n}t^{h}o^n → **uthákiwat^{h}o^{n}t^{h}o^n** → one after the other / in line

witígo^n-ak^{h}a → **witígak^h / witígo^{n}k^h** → my grandfather

No^{n}bé i^{n}wí^{n}t^{h}i^n-a/ga → **No^{n}bi^{n}wí^{n}t^{h}i^n-a/ga** → Clap for me.

do^{n}shteó^n → **d'shtó^n** → maybe / or

Stressing Either of Two Vowels

STRESS ON FIRST VOWEL → STRESS ON SECOND VOWEL → ENGLISH TRANSLATION

Uzhí-a → **Uzhi-á** → Fill it. (spoken by female)

wéahide → **weáhide** → far away

nío^{n}ba → **nió^{n}ba** → moonlight

wí^{n}o^{n}xchi → **wi^{n}ó^{n}xchi** → just one

ushté-ama → **ushte-áma** → the rest of them

níashi^{n}ga → **niáshi^{n}ga** → person

Gthí^n-a → **Gthi^n-á** → Sit (spoken by female)

wíuga → **wiúga** → color / dye

wí^{n}o^{n}wa → **wi^{n}ó^{n}wa** → which one

Two Vowels Combining to Form a Third

When two vowels come together, usually they either share a stress or drop the first one, as earlier mentioned. But at other times they combine into a third, different vowel—even a vowel that is not a typical Umó^{n}ho^n vowel, like **e^n**!

COMBINED VOWEL → HISTORICAL SOURCE

hé^{n}go^{n}ch^{h}e: morning → **hó^n-égo^n-t^{h}e:** when it's like night

no^{n}béda: twin → **no^{n}bá ída:** born as two

Even though these words are fused together with their changed vowel, some of them can still work like a full phrase. **No^{n}béda** can work like a verb even though the verb **ída** is no longer clearly heard in it: **No^{n}béthida?** "Are you twins?" **No^{n}bédawatha** "She had her twins."

Two Words Getting Their Own Stress or Not

When a word is pronounced all by itself—as Elder speakers sometimes do for us in elicitation—it has stress on the same place nearly all the time. When it comes after another word and the two are closely tied together and form a unit, it might lose that stress and just follow the stress pattern of the first word. When it loses that stress, we spell it with no stress mark. When it has its own stress, we spell it with a stress mark. For example, the phrase for "dice" can be pronounced as two independent words, **kúge zhiⁿgá** "little boxes," really emphasizing the literal meaning of each part. Alternatively, the second word can just follow the same beat as the first, and then we spell it **kúge zhiⁿga.** Sometimes the two words even combine into a single word, which we spell with no space and just one stress mark. For example, **kúge zhiⁿga** can combine into **kúg'zhiⁿga.**

TWO STRESSES →
ONE STRESS, ONE WORD →
ENGLISH TRANSLATION

hí wéthizha → **hiwéthizha** → toothpaste

óⁿba itháugthe → **óⁿbithaugthe** → all day / every day

íⁿ'e utʰíⁿ → **íⁿ'utʰíⁿ** → handgame (literally "hit stone")

wéta ázhi → **wét-azhi** → another egg

Óⁿba Xubé → **Óⁿba-Xube** → Sunday

óⁿpʰoⁿ toⁿgá → **ÓⁿpʰoⁿToⁿga** → Big Elk

Interchangeable a and e

There are a lot of Umóⁿhoⁿ words that sometimes end in **a** and sometimes end in **e**. There is no one easy rule for this. Sometimes it's a gram-matical issue, where a verb will have one ending in some situations and another ending in the others. The rules for this are complicated, and sometimes even the rules have variations and exceptions. Sometimes it's just speaker choice, where a meaning like "corn" might be expressed either as **wahába** or **wahábe**. Don't get tripped up if you hear it one way one time and another way another time. But also don't just give up and assume either one is fine. If you hear it both ways then you know both are fine. But try to figure out the pattern when it comes to verbs. The Umóⁿhoⁿ Language and Culture Center has a long list of verb patterns involving final **e** and **a**, and our list gets longer all the time.

Nasalized Sounds

When the sounds **a e i u th** are near a nasal sound **m n oⁿ iⁿ**, they change and become more nasal. This can affect the spelling. We try to keep things closer to their basic spelling if the word is built out of smaller parts, but there's nothing wrong with a changed, more nasal-looking spelling.

"BASIC" SPELLING → "NASAL" SPELLING →
ENGLISH TRANSLATION

ithóⁿtha → **iⁿnóⁿtha** → put away

Awáhoⁿ'e → **Awáhoⁿiⁿ** → I prayed.

thiⁿgé → **niⁿgé** → none / have none / gone / without

náthiⁿge → **nóⁿniⁿge** → burnt down

íⁿthiⁿge → **íⁿniⁿge** → deceased to me / gone for me

Uáne → Owóⁿniⁿ → I searched for it

múathikʰoⁿ → móⁿoⁿthikʰoⁿ → fallen over in a flood / shot down

Múoⁿzhoⁿ → Móⁿoⁿzhoⁿ → We wind-sifted it

Akízhu moⁿbthiⁿ → Akízhoⁿ moⁿbthíⁿ → I'm feeling proud.

Washkóⁿi-a/ga → Washkóya / Washkóiⁿga → Do your best.

Ishtíⁿthiⁿkʰe → Ishtínikʰe → Monkey

Because the same nasal vowel can sound different depending on whether it's "weak" or "strong," as we saw earlier, there are some words where the "nasal" spelling seems to have two different vowels that are really the same one! And because a non-nasal vowel can become nasal when it is near a nasal sound, we also get words that sound as though they have the same vowel, even though they are really not the same.

"BASIC" SPELLING → "NASAL" SPELLING → ENGLISH TRANSLATION

Hí-thoⁿ égahe-noⁿmoⁿ → Hí-na égahe-noma → I comb her fur.

Íⁿthiwiⁿ. → Íⁿthiⁿwiⁿ / Íⁿniwiⁿ / Íniwi. → She bought it for me. (Íⁿniwiⁿ with a strong **n** sound is "You bought it for me.")

Dropping th

When **th** comes in certain words it can sound so soft that we don't even hear it. This affects words like **wóⁿgithe** "every / everybody," **umóⁿthiⁿkʰa**

"year," and **wahóⁿthishige** "orphan," which are sometimes spelled **wóⁿgie**, **umáikʰa** / **umóikʰa**, **wahóⁿishige**.

Adding w and y

After **oⁿ** and **u** a **w** sound is sometimes added before another vowel. After **e i iⁿ** a **y** is sometimes added. This spelling is optional.

"BASIC" SPELLING → OPTIONAL SPELLING → ENGLISH TRANSLATION

íe → íye → speak

íⁿ'utʰiⁿ → íⁿyutʰiⁿ → handgame

E'óⁿ-a? → Eyóⁿwa? → How is it?

Wahóⁿ'a → Wahóⁿwa or Wahóⁿ → They prayed.

u'éthoⁿba → uwéthoⁿba → where it appears

sú'e → súwe → loud rain

8.2 UMÓⁿHOⁿ RESOURCE LIST

This is a limited selection mostly made up of resources we use regularly to help us with our curriculum development. More complete lists of Umóⁿhoⁿ resources may be found on the Umóⁿhoⁿ Language and Culture Center resources page at the Umóⁿhoⁿ Nation Public School website (https://sites.google.com/a/unpsk-12.org/ushkon /resources), the online texts page at UNL's Umóⁿhoⁿ Indian Heritage site (http://omahatribe .unl.edu/etexts/), and in Michael Tate's bibliography (following). Additional resources include the cultural and linguistic documentation by Mark Awakuni-Swetland and others in this volume.

Awakuni-Swetland, Mark. *Dance Lodges of the Omaha People: Building from Memory*. New York: Routledge, 2001; repr., Lincoln: University of Nebraska Press, 2008.

Chase, Hiram. *O Mu Hu W B GRa Za: The Chase System of Reading and Recording the Omaha and Other Indian Languages*. Pender NE: Republic Press, 1897.

Clay, Mary, Bertha Wolfe, and Clifford Wolfe Sr. *Stories from our Elders*. Macy NE: Macy Public Schools, n.d.

Cook, Thurman. *HeadStart Dictionary*. Macy NE: Omaha Nation Head Start, 1982.

Dorsey, James Owen. *The Ƈegiha Language* [The Speech of the Omaha and Ponka Tribes of the Siouan Linguistic Family of North American Indians]. Contributions to North American Ethnology vol. 6. Washington DC: Government Printing Office, 1890. https://archive.org/details/ldpd_8627114_000.

———. *Omaha and Ponka Letters*. Bureau of American Ethnology Bulletin 11. Washington DC: Government Printing Office, 1891. https://archive.org/details/omahaandponkale00dorsgoog.

Fletcher, Alice Cunningham. *Historical Sketch of the Omaha Tribe of Indians in Nebraska*. Washington: Judd and Detweiler, 1885.

Fletcher, Alice Cunningham, and Francis La Flesche. *The Omaha Tribe*. Vol. 1. Bureau of American Ethnology 27th Annual Report, 1905–6. Washington DC: Government Printing Office, 1911; repr., Lincoln: University of Nebraska Press, 1992.

———. *The Omaha Tribe*. Vol. 2. Bureau of American Ethnology 27th Annual Report, 1905–6. Washington DC: Government Printing Office, 1911; repr., Lincoln: University of Nebraska Press, 1992. (Note: The 1992 reprinting does not include the list of allotments and original owners from the 1911 printing. Many of the resources listed are available in our department, our school's library, or online.)

Fletcher, Alice Cunningham, Francis La Flesche, and John Comfort Fillmore. *A Study of Omaha Indian Music*. Peabody Museum Papers vol. 1. Salem MA: Salem Press, 1904.

Freemont, Susan, and Vida Castro Woodhull. *Umóⁿhoⁿ Language and Culture Center Elementary Language Program Booklet and CD series 1*. Macy NE: Umóⁿhoⁿ Language and Culture Center, Umóⁿhoⁿ Nation Public School, 2005.

Freemont, Susan, Eugene Pappan, Francine Cayou, Vida Castro Woodhull, Pat Phillips, and Mihusa Stabler, with help from Thornton Media. *Omaha Basic*. iOS App. 2013. https://itunes.apple.com/us/app/omaha-basic/id705614006.

French, Suzanne (Luzathin). *The Baby Eagles. Xithazhi Ahigi* [Xithá ázhi áhigi]. Macy NE: Macy Public Schools, 1989.

Giffen, Fannie Reed. *Oo-mah-ha Ta-wa-tha (Omaha City)*. Lincoln: Giffen, 1898; repr., Charleston: Nabu Press, 2010.

Hastings, Dennis (Íⁿ'aska), and Margery Coffey. *Omaha History, Culture, Language: A Workbook for the Faculty and Staff of the Umóⁿhoⁿ Nation Public Schools*. Macy NE: Omaha Tribal Historical Research Project, 2007.

Jimmy and Blackie: Jimmy ke-egoⁿ çabeaka shena [Jimmy ké égoⁿ Sábe-ak^ha shénoⁿ]. Macy NE: Macy Public Schools, n.d.

La Flesche, Francis. "Death and Funeral Customs among the Omaha." *Journal of American Folklore* 2, no. 4 (1889): 3–11. http://www.sacred-texts.com/nam/pla/dfco/dfco00.htm.

———. *Ke-ma-ha: The Omaha Stories of Francis La Flesche*. Edited by James W. Parins and Daniel F. Littlefield Jr. Lincoln: University of Nebraska Press, 1995.

———. *The Middle Five: Indian Boys at School*. Boston: Small, Maynard and Company, 1900;

repr. *The Middle Five: Indian Schoolboys of the Omaha Tribe*, Lincoln: University of Nebraska Press, 1978.

———. "Omaha Bow and Arrow Makers." *Annual Report of the Board of Regents of the Smithsonian Institution*, 478–94. Washington: Government Printing Office, 1927.

La Flesche, Susette. *A Philadelphia Christmas Tree in Nebraska: An Indian Woman's Letter*. Omaha Agency, 1879.

La-Ta-We-Sah [Thátʰa Wes'a / Eunice Woodhull Stabler]. *La-Ta-We-Sah (Woman of the Bird Clan): Her Poetry and Prose*. Macy NE: Macy School Press, 1989.

Parker, Arnold Jr. (Tawainge). *The Day Blackie Had Puppies*. Macy NE: Macy Public Schools, 1989.

Parker, Brian. *Carlos in the Print Shop: Carlos wabáxu gaxeke ti kidi* [Carlos wabáxu gáxe-kʰe tí-kʰe-di]. Macy NE: Macy Public Schools, n.d.

Parker, Ravae. *Susie*. Macy NE: Macy Public Schools, n.d.

Ridington, Robin, and Dennis Hastings (Íⁿ'aska). *Blessing for a Long Time: The Sacred Pole of the Omaha Tribe*. Lincoln: University of Nebraska Press, 1997.

Saunsoci, Alice, and Ardis Eschenberg. *500+ Verbs in Umoⁿhoⁿ (Omaha): Doing Things in the Umoⁿhoⁿ Way*. Lexington: CreateSpace Independent Publishing Platform, 2016.

Stabler, Elizabeth, Carol Marshall, and J. Travis Rouse. *Omaha Language Workbook*. Unpublished, 1977.

Stabler, Elizabeth, and Mark J. Swetland. *Umoⁿhoⁿ iye of Elizabeth Stabler: A Vocabulary of the Omaha Language with an Omaha to English Lexicon*. Macy: John Mangan Printing, 1991.

Stabler, Eunice Woodhull [La-Ta-We-Sah]. *How Beautiful the Land of My Forefathers*. Wichita: Stabler, 1943.

Stabler, Hollis D. *No One Ever Asked Me: The World War II Memoirs of an Omaha Indian Soldier*. Edited by Victoria Smith. Lincoln: University of Nebraska Press, 2005.

Tate, Michael L. *The Upstream People: An Annotated Research Bibliography of the Omaha Tribe*. Metuchen: Scarecrow Press, 1991.

Parker, Arnold Jr. [Tawaiⁿge]. *Jimmy and Blackie at Christmas: Jimmy çabe Wakoⁿda Izhiⁿga oⁿba Ide Tidi* [Jimmy Sábe Wakóⁿda Izhíⁿge Óⁿba Ída-tʰe-di]. Macy NE: Macy Public Schools, 1987.

———. *The Little Indian: Niashinga ukethiⁿ zhiⁿga* [Niáshiⁿga ukʰéthiⁿ zhiⁿga]. Macy NE: Macy Public Schools, 1987.

United States Library of Congress Umóⁿhoⁿ Collections. https://www.loc.gov/collections/omaha-indian-music/index/contributor/?c=150&st=list.

8.3 ULCC GLOSSARY IN MACY STANDARD ORTHOGRAPHY: UMÓⁿHOⁿ TO ENGLISH

á: arm

ábaaze: drive

ábae: hunt; hunting

ábanoⁿ: gaze; watch

ába'u: cover the grave with earth; make a mound

ábaxoⁿ: place upright on (as a feather in hair)

ábaxu: write down; write on

ábazu: point at

ábishnabe: spread on

ábiskabe: stick onto something

ábitʰe: touch

ábixe: boil

áchoⁿ: extremely; too much; very (see átashoⁿ)

ágaha: on top; outside

ágapuga: mat

ágashke: buckle; button; fasten one bit of clothing to another

ágaxade: close; cover

ágaxtoⁿ: pour on; topping on food

ágazhi: command; tell someone to do something

agtháthiⁿ: have one's own

ágthiⁿ: chair; ride (as a horse); seat; sit on

agthíⁿ sátoⁿ: fifteen

agthíⁿwiⁿ: eleven

agthóⁿgamoⁿge: blackberry; raspberry

águdi: where?

águdishte: somewhere

áhigi: a lot; many; numerous

áhigi-áchoⁿ: a lot

áhigi thipʰí: learn a lot

aíathe: be gone away; leave

aíatha: left

-akʰa: the (living singular, main actor)

áki: play against

ákigthaha: one on top of the other

ákʰihide: guard; watch

ákikʰihide: watch out for oneself

ákisoⁿde: little beyond the mark

ákithe: fight

-ama: the (living plural, main actor)

ámoⁿxpi: cloudy; overcast

ámusni: pour (water) on to cool something

ánoⁿ: how many?

ánoⁿ'oⁿ: listen to

ánoⁿse: close or lock; locked; turn off

ánoⁿ'u: stash underground

ánoⁿxthe: hide

Áoⁿ: yes

ápathage: headland

áshiata: outside

áshitathishoⁿ: on the outside

ásni: cool

astúhi: elbow

áta: best; highest

átashoⁿ: extremely; too much; very (see áchoⁿ)

áthade: call; read; recite

áthaha: smear on; wear

áthaskabe: glue to

áthiaze: open the door cover of a tipi onto
the poles

áthi'e: sprinkle on

athíⁿ: have; have something at hand

áthiⁿ: ridge

áthixude: gray day; overcast

átʰoⁿ: stand on

atʰóⁿ: when?

atʰóⁿ-di: when? (past)

atʰóⁿ-ki: when? (future)

atʰóⁿ-kizhi: if (future)

atʰóⁿshte: sometimes

áuthisnoⁿ: armband; silver cuff

awagí: where did you come from?

á wahí: arm bones

áwata: where to (is someone going)?

awatʰégoⁿ: how? explain this; what does it
mean?

áxibe: bracelet

ázhi: different; other

ázhi-thoⁿthoⁿ: different kinds; various

ázhoⁿ: fall asleep on; sleep on

ázoⁿde: together on

báaze: scare

bahé: push or shove

bahí: collecting; gather; pick up

bahóⁿhoⁿ: rolling hilly land

bamóⁿshi: lift; press (a weight)

baníuski: burp; hiccup

banúski: burp; hiccup

basása: divided

bashéthoⁿ: eliminate; lay down one's hand
to win; pay off a debt

bashíbe: push out

bashná: buzz somebody; give a real close
haircut; shave; shave off

bashóⁿthe: dump; pour out

basíhi: clear by shovelling

basníde: shuffle or deal out (cards)

basnóⁿ: push a pole through a loop; put a
spit through food to roast it; skewer

basnúsnu: mash or mashed

batʰé: sew; stitch

batúshi: elderberry

baxú: sharp rocky peak; write

bazú: round peak

bibíze: dry; mop; wipe

bibtháze: bust (a water balloon or a blister)

bigúde: rub; scrub

biíze: make noise by shuffling feet around

bikʰá: wipe

bimóⁿshi: pull upward

bispóⁿ: press

bíze: dry

bizhú: rub

bóⁿ: scream; yell

bóⁿ thahégazhi: scream; yell

bthípe: powder

bthóⁿ: odor; smell

búta: round

chéshka: short

d'shtoⁿ: or

dá: frozen

didéshi: bat (the animal)

-doⁿ: during the time of

doⁿ: while

dóⁿbe: see

doⁿshteóⁿ: maybe; or

dúba: four; some

dúba-thoⁿthoⁿ: four at time

dúde: this way

é: say

Eábaha: Camp Crier

Éabaha: Master of Ceremonies

eátoⁿ: what's going on?; what's the matter?; why?

ebé: who?

edábe: also; too

ede: but

edégithoⁿ: answer

edéshe: what did you say?

edi: exist; then; there

edíye thékʰithe: answer her/him

éduatʰoⁿ: next

égashke: button for someone; fasten for someone; pin on for someone; velcro for someone

égaxade: cover somebody's (e.g. eyes)

égazeze: side by side

égipʰe: I said it to somebody

égishe: you said it to somebody

égithoⁿ: say it to somebody

égoⁿ: for that reason; I agree; It is so; like (similar to); like that; Mhm; so; therefore; Yes

-egoⁿ: having

ehé: I said it

éhi: lucky

éiⁿtʰe: if

ékigoⁿ: equal; matching; same

énoⁿ : that's all

eóⁿgithoⁿ: we said it to somebody

épe: wait for

eshé: you said it

eshóⁿ: close; close together; near

etá: her (possession); hers; his (possession); its; their; theirs

éta: in that direction; that way

éthe: kin; related; relative

ethégoⁿ: think something

éthoⁿba: appear

éthoⁿska: as big or tall as

etʰégoⁿ: must; required

étoⁿthiⁿ: forward

éwakʰe: refer to

éwazhiⁿnoⁿge: railroad; train

eyóⁿ: how?

gá: that exact one

Gá!: Here you go (word used when giving something to someone); Here!

gabíze: dry something in the open air

gabthá: bloom (a flower); open up; spread out (a bedsheet)

gach^{h}ách^{h}aki: clap

gach^{h}áki: clap once; slap someone; smack

gadí^{n}di^n: hard (as a hard throw)

gadó^n: hammer (action word); pound

gadúzhe: burst or pop a bladder-like thing like an egg, a blister, a water balloon or an overripe tomato

ga'é: dripping

gaétho^{n}be: appear (as the sun through clouds)

gahá: on; upon

gahé: comb someone's hair

gahíde: hurtling low

gahíthe: blowing or drifting in the wind

Gahíye Niashi^{n}ga: Tribal Council Member

Gahíye Nudó^{n}ho^{n}ga: Tribal Council Chair

Gahíye Nudó^{n}ho^{n}ga Wéno^{n}ba: Tribal Council Vice-Chair

Gahíye Ugthi^n Petho^{n}ba: seven Tribal Council seats

Gahíye Wéno^{n}ba: Tribal Council vice-chair

gakíze: get clear

gakúge: sound of something hollow falling; thump

gakúku: sound of drums beating

gamó^{n}shi: hurtling high

gamó^{n}shi théthe: toss

gamó^{n}the: lay down (cards)

ganó^{n}ge: roll (as a rock or dice)

gasáthu: rattle; shake a gourd

gasé: chop; cut (as a deck of cards)

gashíata: out of bounds

gashíbe: out

gashkó^{n}shko^n: moving repeatedly by force (as jello bouncing)

gashnó^n: miss (as when playing a game)

gashnúde: give up (a card)

gashnúde-k^{h}ithe: get somebody to give up (a card)

Gashúde: winter

gasíhi: clear up (the sky)

gaskí-ácho^n: breathless

gasnú: slide

gasnú gi'ó^n: ski

gasó^{n}the: slap down (cards)

gasó^{n}thi^n: tomorrow

gastáki: knock something and send it flying

gathí^{n}ge: get rid of by hitting (as the other team's sticks in Handgame)

gatúbe: pound fine; wreck

gatúshi: loud popping sound

gaxá: branch; tree branch

gáxe: do; make

gaxíxe: crack

gaxíxixe: crack open repeatedly

gazhí^n: blow one's nose

gazí: extend

gazó^{n}de íko^{n}te: Umo^{n}ho^n braid ties

-ge: the (nonliving scattered here and there)

gí: come; come back

gíbaha: show to

gíbashna: cut hair for

gíboⁿ: call someone over

gíku: invite someone

giná: ask for; collect a debt

agína: ask for one's own back

gíoⁿhe: flee from

gióⁿze: teach someone

gíshoⁿ: approves; happy; pleased

gisíthe: remember

gítha-bazhi: sad

gíthe: blissful; glad; happy

gíthiezhuba: have respect for

gíthisnu: move a piece on a boardgame for someone

gíthiwiⁿ: buy for someone

gíthizhabe: peel for someone

gíudoⁿ: feel good; glad; like (care for, take a liking to)

gíuzhawa: enjoy oneself; have fun

góⁿchʰe: later

góⁿki: and

góⁿtha: want; want to

gtháwasisige: encourage to be active

gthébe: vomit

gthéboⁿ: ten

gthí: arrive back here

gthíⁿ: sit

gthíⁿkʰithe: seat someone

gthóⁿthiⁿ: crazy

gubéhi: hackberry

há: hide; leather; skin

háhade: light (not heavy)

háshi: behind; last

háska: flag

háthe: clothes; clothing

háthe wéthizha: washing machine

háthukathiⁿ: bare; naked

háwatʰe: buckskin dress

haxúde: sheep; woolen robe

haxúde miⁿga: ewe

haxúde zhiⁿga: lamb

házhiⁿga: cord; rope; strap

házhiⁿga thidóⁿ: tug-of-war

házhiⁿga uóⁿsi: jump rope

házhiⁿga uóⁿsisi: jump rope

házi: grape

házi-egoⁿ: purple

házi sheúzhegthoⁿ: raisin pie

hazízige: Ace bandage; balloon; rubber; stretchy fabric

hazízige ni uzhi: water balloon

hazízige tabé: balloon

hé: antler; horn

hébe: part; part of; piece of

Hédewachʰi: Harvest Celebration; Pow-Wow

hégazhi: expensive

héⁿgachʰe: morning

héⁿgoⁿchʰa-xchi: early morning

héⁿgoⁿchʰe: morning

hé^{n}go^{n}ch^{h}e-ki: tomorrow morning

héskiba: goat

Hethúshka: warrior's dance originated by the Umo^{n}ho^n tribe

hí: plant; stalk; stem; tooth; trunk

híde: base; bottom; down; low

hídeata: bottomland; Decatur; down bottom

hímo^{n}gthe: cane; dance stick

hi^{n}bé : moccasin; shoe

hi^{n}bé ágaha: boots

hi^{n}béagahadi: overboots; rubber boots

hi^{n}béakigthaha: overboots; rubber boots

hi^{n}béko^n: shoelaces

hi^{n}békuwi^{n}xe: socks

hi^{n}bésnede: boots

hi^{n}bé uk^{h}éthi^n: moccasin

hi^{n}bthí^{n}ge waníde: green-bean casserole

hí^{n}shkube: hairy

hí^{n}ska: bead; beadwork

hi^{n}thékithe: hasten; hurry

hi^{n}xpé: cottonwood seed fluff (figurative); fluffy, fuzzy down feather of a bird

hítha: bathe; swim

Hithái: Saturday

hithé^{n}kithe: hurry

hítho^{n}wi^n: garters

hi-wéthizha: toothpaste

hó^n: night

hó^n-de : last night

hó^n-do^n: during the night; nighttime

hó^n-do^n háthe: pajamas

hó^n-do^n wáthaha: pajamas

ho^{n}égo^{n}ch^{h}e: morning

Hó^{n}ga umúbthi^{n}i-k^{h}e: January

hó^n-ki: tonight

ho^{n}nó^{n}paze: twilight

hó^{n}skaska: midnight

hú: voice

hugási: fish; go fishing

huhú: fish

huhú shnaha: seal

huhú to^{n}ga: whale

Húthuga: Tribal Circle

hút^{h}o^n: cry out

í: come; give; mouth

íbaho^n: know

íbaho^n thé: learn

íbaso^{n}tha: turn over (as food with spatula)

íbiski: next to

ído^{n}be: in the middle

ígadi: toilet paper

ígashno^n: rest

ígasko^{n}the: attempt; taste; try

ígazho^{n}zho^n: shake something

íhe: get through; pass

ihéthe: put it away by laying it flat

ihétho^{n}tho^n: happening suddenly over and over

Ihó^n: her/his Mother

Ihó^n Ó^{n}ba: Mother's Day

íkigthahi: mix together

íkigthaskoⁿthe: practice speaking; rehearse; try together

íkikawiⁿthe: swap; switch; trade places

íkikoⁿ: play against each other

íkinoⁿxthe: hide oneself

íkipahoⁿ-azhi: clueless; faint; pass out; unconscious

íkithe: wake up

íkitʰe : cheat

íkizhu: proud

íkoⁿthe: handle

íkoⁿtʰoⁿ: tie

ímoⁿxe: ask; ask a question

íⁿ: carry on one's back; packing

íⁿbe: bird tail

íⁿbehi: pillow

íⁿchʰoⁿ: just now; now

iⁿchʰóⁿga: mouse

iⁿchʰóⁿga toⁿga: rat

iⁿchʰóⁿga wathátʰe: cheese

iⁿdádoⁿ: what?

iⁿdé: face

iⁿdéagani: fan

iⁿdé íbikʰa: face towel

iⁿdéugthoⁿ: mask

iⁿdéugthoⁿ wachʰígaxe: masquerade dance

íⁿ'e: rock; stone

Íⁿ'e Moⁿshóⁿde: Hole-in-the-Rock

íⁿ'epa: diamonds (suit)

íⁿ'e ska: diamonds (suit)

Íⁿ'e U'úde: Hole-in-the-Rock

íⁿ'e wétʰiⁿ: hammer

iⁿgthóⁿga: cat

iⁿgthóⁿga gthezáza: leopard

iⁿgthóⁿga shíshige: cat litter

iⁿgthóⁿga zhiⁿga: kitten

iⁿgthóⁿhutoⁿ: thunder

iⁿgthóⁿ siⁿ snéde: cougar; mountain lion; panther; puma

Iⁿkésabe: Black Shoulder Clan; Buffalo (Black Shoulder) Clan

iⁿkʰéde: shoulder

Íⁿnoⁿha: my Mother

Íⁿnoⁿha Moⁿzhóⁿ: Mother Earth

Íⁿnoⁿha Tóⁿde: Mother Earth

ínoⁿpehi: make one hungry

ínoⁿse: cut off (as in a game)

ínoⁿshe: deprive of; take away

Iⁿsh'áge: male Elder

iⁿsh'áge: king (in cards)

Iⁿsh'áge Tóⁿwoⁿgthoⁿ: Walthill

iⁿshtá: eye

iⁿshtási: eye pupil

Íⁿ'utʰiⁿ: Handgame

ípithage: belt; sash

ít'athe: detest; dislike; loathe

ít'e: get killed by something (e.g. figuratively in cards)

ithábashna: scissors

Ithádi: her/his Father

ithágashke: buckle; pin

ithápe: wait for

itháthisoⁿde: vest

íthigtho^n: decide for; decide on; decision; idea; take charge of; thought

íthishetho^n: be the last one (e.g. last year in school); finish

íthishi: feed

íthizho^{n}zho^n: as a spray can; jar; shake (as a spray can)

ithó^{n}the: put or place something globular

it^{h}éthe: place; put; put away; set

itó^{n}thi^{n}adi: ancient; old

itó^{n}thi^{n}ata: in front

íutha: story

íutha-ithó^{n}thai-tho^n: bulletin board

íxa: laugh

íxa-thahégazhi: laugh out loud

íxazhi^{n}ga: smile

íye: language; speak; speech; talk; word

Iyébaha: Camp Crier; Master of Ceremonies

Iyék^{h}ithe: Camp Crier

íye sagí: loud speech

iyéska: interpreter

izházhe: name

júba-xchi: little bit

káshi: for a long time; long time

káxe: bustle; crow

ké: turtle

kétha: clear sky

ké to^{n}ga: snapping turtle; tortoise

K^{h}agé: Friend

K^{h}ágeso^{n}ga: Little Brother (male's)

K^{h}agézhi^{n}ga: Little Brother (female's)

-k^{h}e: the (nonliving horizontal or flat)

k^{h}é ___!: come and (followed by suggestion)

k^{h}íde: shoot; shoot at; shoot cards

-ki: if; when

kigthá: at the bottom; below; under

kigtházi: stretch (oneself)

kigthíazhi: change; transform oneself

kigthíbuta wach^{h}ígaxe: round-dance

kigthíhathukathi^n: get undressed; undress

kigthísheno^n: come to an end; disappear

kigthíso^{n}the: turn around; wheel

kigthíto^n: get ready

kigthíwashko^{n}to^{n}ga: get stronger

kigthízha: wash oneself; wash up

kigthó^{n}xe: bee

kinó^{n}no^{n}ge: automobile; car

kinó^{n}no^{n}ge buta: Volkswagen bug

kinó^{n}sada: jog; walk

kinó^{n}se: fall; stumble; trip

kinó^{n}shibe: get oneself out (of jail)

kinó^{n}xe: groundhog; prairie dog

kió^{n}ze: rest

kipáda: baby bird; chick; duckling; hatchling

kipáho^n: sit up

kipáshizhe: shiver

kipímo^{n}shi: do a push-up

-kishte: even if

-kizhi: whenever

kó^{n}si: dice; plum seed

kó^{n}t^{h}o^n: tie

Kúge: Big Center Drum

kúge: box; thousand

kúge wíⁿ: one thousand dollars

kúge zhiⁿga: dice

kúhe: scared; spooked

kúhe ti: spooky house

kukúmi: cucumber; pickle

kukúmi ní: pickle juice

kúkusi: hog; pig; swine

kúkusi miⁿga: sow

kúkusi zhiⁿga: piglet

kúwiⁿxe: spin around; turn around

-ma: the (living plural, not the main actor)

má'a: cottonwood

má'a toⁿga: cottonwood

Mágashude: winter

Mámatoⁿga!: Mother's big sister! (female speaking to)

Mámazhiⁿga!: Mother's little sister! (female speaking to)

máshpashpa: chop up into little pieces

mási: hail

Mási: Macy

másne: split by cutting

masóⁿ: snowflake

máthe: snow; snowing

máxoⁿ: cut with a knife

máxoⁿxoⁿ: cut in many pieces

mázi: cedar; evergreen tree; fir; pine; spruce

mémathe: spring snow

Mépahoⁿga: First Thunder; spring (season)

mí: month; sun

Mí eátoⁿ thiⁿgé-kʰe: April

mí éthoⁿbe: sunrise

miídoⁿbe: clock; time; watch

mí-ithé-tathishoⁿ: west

miká: raccoon

miká'e: star

miká'e íthawa: quarter dollar

miká'e wáiⁿ púga: star quilt

minéthe: sundog

mí-thoⁿ umóⁿshi: noon

mithúmoⁿshi: noon

mithúmoⁿshiadi: past afternoon

mithúmoⁿshi-ki: this (coming) afternoon; tomorrow afternoon

míthumoⁿshi wathatʰe: lunch; noon meal

mithúmoⁿshi-xti: exact noon; high noon

mithúmoⁿshi-zhiⁿga: just before noon

mí u'éthoⁿba-tathishoⁿ: east

Mí wá'ai-kʰe: May

Míwathixe: Daughter-in-Law

míxa: duck

míxa níkashiⁿga égoⁿ: penguin

míxa toⁿga: goose

Míxa toⁿga mí agthíi-kʰe: February

míxe: cemetery; grave

mízhiⁿga: girl

mízhiⁿga ikʰáge: girlfriend

moⁿá: bluff; ravine

moⁿchʰú: grizzly bear

mó^{n}da: bow; dart

mó^{n}de: bow; dart

mó^{n}dehi: bayonet; dart; lance; spear

mo^n'é: dig in earth

mó^{n}ga: skunk; skunk hand

mó^{n}ga gaxe: skunk an opponent

mo^{n}gáshude: dust devil; dust storm

Mó^{n}ga Úhe: Skunk Hollow

mó^{n}ge: chest (body part)

mó^{n}ge ágtho^n: breastplate

mó^{n}ge ithágashke: button (chest)

mó^{n}gthe: upright

Mo^{n}gthíxta: Blackbird Hill

mó^{n}hi: knife

mó^{n}hi^n: grass

mo^{n}kó^{n}sabe: coffee

mo^{n}kó^{n}sabe ígaxe: coffee pot

mo^{n}kó^{n}sabe niúthato^n: coffee cup

mo^{n}kó^{n}sabe úzhi: coffee can

mo^{n}shchí^{n}ga zhi^{n}ga: bunny

mó^{n}shi: above; high; high up

mo^{n}shíadi: tall

mó^{n}sho^n: feather; plume

mó^{n}sho^{n}pagtho^n: eagle tail-feather war bonnet

Mo^{n}shté: summer

mo^{n}shté: warm weather

mo^{n}shtí^{n}ga: rabbit

mo^{n}só^{n}thi^n: across; on the far side; side

mo^{n}só^{n}thi^{n}ha: half dollar

mo^{n}táno^{n}di: in the wild

mo^{n}thí^n: go; walk

mo^{n}thí^{n}ga: gopher

mo^{n}thí^{n}k^{h}a: earth; soil

mo^{n}thí^n tí: earth lodge

mo^{n}thí^{n}xude: groundhog; prairie dog

mo^{n}thó^n: steal

mó^{n}t^{h}ano^{n}ha: wild

mó^{n}t^{h}ata: in; inside; underneath

mó^{n}t^{h}e: in; inside

mó^{n}xe: sky

mó^{n}xeatathisho^n: toward the sky

mó^{n}xe mo^{n}shíadi níashi^{n}ga: angel

mo^{n}xpí: cloud

mó^{n}ze bet^{h}ó^{n}t^{h}o^n: tin foil

mó^{n}ze gamó^{n}the: bells

mó^{n}ze gasása: metal dish rack

mó^{n}ze gatámo^n: bells

mó^{n}ze i^{n}shtugtho^n: eyeglasses

mó^{n}ze íutha: phone; telephone

mó^{n}zemo^n: bullet; shot

mó^{n}zepe: hatchet; spades (suit)

mó^{n}zeska: dollar; money; silver

mó^{n}zeska úzhi: purse

mó^{n}zeska wí^{n}bthuga: silver dollar

mó^{n}zeskige: weight (for exercise)

mó^{n}ze ubét^{h}o^n: tin foil

mó^{n}ze unéthe: stove

mó^{n}ze úzhi: can; tin can

mó^{n}ze wao^n: cassette deck; CD player; radio

mó^{n}ze wéthishibe: can opener

moⁿzhóⁿ basása: piece of land

moⁿzhóⁿ níuthoⁿda: continent

moⁿzhóⁿ waxúbe: sacred grounds

múathikoⁿ: tilted or fallen by flooding or shooting

múgthoⁿ: stray off; wander away

múpa: strong (coffee or cider)

múzhawa: loud gunshot

múzhoⁿ: sift; strain out

ná: ask for; beg

nákʰade: heat; hot

nákoⁿ: light (action word)

náskoⁿ: melt; thaw

náze: behind; in back of

néxe: bladder; kettle; skillet

néxe-shuga-wézhegthoⁿ: cast-iron skillet

ní: water

niádi-wakóⁿda: hippopotamus

niáshiⁿga: person

niáshiⁿga wawéxaxa: joker (in cards)

niáshiⁿga xáde ígahi: scarecrow

níde : cooked; done (cooked); ripe

nígatushi: pop (in a pop can)

nihá: snail

Níkagahi: Chief

Níkanoⁿxe: Northern Lights

níkashiⁿga: person; Indian

ník'shiⁿga: person; Indian

Ník'shiⁿga Ukʰéthiⁿ: Indian

niⁿdágthe: diaper

níⁿde ágthoⁿ: diaper

níⁿde uthíshi: pants

níⁿdushi: pants

níⁿdushi-móⁿtʰe: shorts; underwear

niⁿdúthishi: pants

niⁿdúthishi-móⁿtʰe: shorts; underwear

niní: tobacco

niní úzhiha: tobacco bag

nióⁿba: moon

Nishúde: Missouri River

ní skithe: Kool-Aid; pop (sweet beverage)

niskíthe: salt

nístu: backward

nisúde: whistle

níta: alive; live

nithátoⁿ: drinking fountain

ní-tʰe thixtóⁿ: faucet

nítoⁿga: ocean; sea

niúbixoⁿ: mist

niúkigthaziⁿ: mirror; mirror board

níuski: burp; hiccup

níuthadoⁿ: island

niúthatoⁿ: cup

niúthishoⁿ: lake

níuthoⁿda: island

níuzhi: pitcher

níxa: belly; stomach

Niyé-thiⁿge Tí: Wellness Center

nóⁿ: adult; grown up; habitually; regularly ; routinely

Nóⁿ: Elder

Nóⁿ-ama: the Old People

noⁿbá: two

noⁿbáha máxoⁿ: cut in two

noⁿbá-thoⁿthoⁿ: two at a time

noⁿbé: hand

noⁿbéhi: finger

noⁿbé íbikʰa: hand towel; handkerchief; napkin

noⁿbéshka: fist

noⁿbéuthishi: gloves; mittens

noⁿbéuthixthoⁿ: ring

noⁿbé wahí: hand bones

noⁿdázhe: get blisters (on foot) by walking

nóⁿde: heart; hearts (suit)

nóⁿde gíudoⁿ: content; happy

NóⁿdeMóⁿze: Iron Heart

nóⁿde údoⁿ: good-hearted

nóⁿgethe: run a machine

noⁿhébe: wait

noⁿhégazhi: dance excessively; kick excessively; run excessively; walk excessively

nóⁿka: back (anat.)

noⁿ'óⁿ: hear

nóⁿpa: cherry; chokecherry

nóⁿpatu: blue raspberry (frozen treat flavor); blueberry

nóⁿpatu sheúzhegthoⁿ: blueberry pie

noⁿpéhi: hungry

noⁿshámoⁿ: loganberry

noⁿshkí: head (top and back or whole head, not the face)

noⁿshkí-tathishoⁿ: heads (in coin toss)

noⁿshkí wahí: skull

noⁿshnáha: slip (while walking)

noⁿshnóⁿ: miss (as in time)

noⁿshtóⁿ: dancing or kicking; stop running; walking

noⁿstáki: kick and send flying

noⁿtʰé: dance (as in Hethúshka); kick

noⁿtúbe: grind; mealy; milled

nóⁿxahi: backbone; spine

nóⁿxahi t'úsa: camel

nóⁿxe: glass

nóⁿxeskazhi: dizzy; woozy

nóⁿxe wamúske skithe úzhi: cookie jar

noⁿxíde: ear; hearing; internal ear

noⁿxíde wéthisihi: Q-Tip

Nóⁿ-xti: aged; Elder; mature

Nóⁿ-xti-ama: the Old People

nóⁿze: fence

noⁿzhíⁿ: rain; stand

noⁿzhíⁿha: hair of the head; scalp

noⁿzhíⁿ ubixoⁿ: mist

noⁿzhíⁿ unoⁿzhiⁿ: raincoat

nú: man; potato

nú basnúsnu: mashed potatoes

nubthóⁿ: perfume

núde: neck; throat

núde ígatoⁿtha: necktie; scarf

Nudóⁿhoⁿga: Man in Charge

nudúbetʰoⁿ: neckwrap; scarf

Nugé: summer

Nugé Moⁿshte: summer

núka: wet

nushnóⁿha: dragger; otterskin

nushnóⁿhapagthe: otterskin turban

núsi áxthade: bandolier beads

núski: burp; hiccup

núskithe: sweet potato

núxe: ice

núxe bawégthi: ice cream

núxe bawégthi tehé: ice-cream scoop

núxe úzhi: icebox; refrigerator

nú zhézhi: French fries

núzhiⁿga: boy

núzoⁿ 'óⁿ: skate; sled

óⁿ: put on; use; wear

óⁿaze: shade (curtain)

óⁿba: day

óⁿba ída: birthday

óⁿba itháugthe: all day; every day

óⁿbathe: today

Óⁿba Waxúbe: Sunday

Óⁿba Wéduba: Thursday

Óⁿba Wénoⁿba: Tuesday

Óⁿba Wésatoⁿ: Friday

Óⁿba Wéthabthiⁿ: Wednesday

Óⁿba Xubé: Sunday

Óⁿba Xubé-thishtoⁿ: Monday

óⁿba zhíde: dawn

óⁿgu: us; we

óⁿhe: flee

Óⁿhoⁿ: yes

óⁿkʰithe: get somebody dressed

óⁿma: other one

óⁿpʰoⁿ: elk

Óⁿpʰoⁿ-hútʰoⁿi-kʰe: August

Óⁿpʰoⁿ Toⁿga Moⁿzhó: Big Elk Park

óⁿtha théthe: throw; throw away

óⁿthe : calm; careful; casual; gentle; lenient; relaxed; slow

óⁿthinoⁿ: almost

Oⁿwóⁿzhiⁿpi-mazhi: I'm angry

óⁿxtiwathe: praiseworthy

óⁿzhiⁿga: acorn; hazelnut; peanut

pá: bitter; head; nose

páde: butcher; cut up

paháshi: above; on top

paháshi-ta: upstairs

pahé: hill

pahé zúbe: hilltop

páhi: neck

páhiⁿ: porcupine; quillwork

páhiⁿbatʰe: quillwork

pahóⁿga: ahead; before; first; in front

pánuhu: owl

pasí: head or top tip of a pole or a needle

pasiáta watʰátʰe: giraffe

pasóⁿ: bald eagle

páta: in front

patháge: dead-end bluff

paúthishiⁿ: headwrap; scarf

páze: evening; twilight

pázeadi: yesterday evening

páze-ki: this evening

péde: fire; match (for starting a fire)

péde náxthi^n: match (for starting a fire)

Pénishka mí etái-k^{h}e: March

pethá bthi^n: eight

pétho^{n}ba: seven

péxe: gourd; rattle

péxeha: gourd rattle

péxeha to^{n}ga: gallon container

pézhe: grass; moss; plants; vegetation

pézhitu: green; lime (literally 'green')

pézi: gooseberry

p^{h}í: again

p^{h}úga: puffy

piázhi: bad; rancid; ugly

pí'o^n: fix; repair

pízi ugtho^{n}ge: chicken gizzard

sabázhi: suddenly; unexpectedly

sábe: black

sagígi: faster; harder

sáhi: basket; burlap; cattail; woven straw

sáhi watháge: knit cap

sak^{h}íba: beside; next to

sát^{h}o^n: five

sáto^n: five

sebé-xchi: neatly dressed

sézi: orange (fruit)

sézi-ego^n: orange (color)

sézi ní: orange juice

séziniuzhi: pineapple

sézi s'áthe: lemon

sézi s'áthe ní skíthe: lemonade

shábe: chocolate (literally 'brown'); dark

sháge: claw; hoof; nails; talons

Sháo^n Tó^{n}wo^{n}gtho^n Nishúde-thégi-thisho^n: South Sioux City

shápe: six

shápe no^{n}ba: twelve

shé: apple; that

shéhi : that over there

shémizhi^{n}ga: young woman

Shéno^n : that's all I have to say

shénuzhi^{n}ga: jack (in cards); young man

shé sheúzhegtho^n: apple pie

shet^{h}ó^{n}no^n: still; yet

sheúzhegtho^n: apple pie; pie; pizza

shi: again

shígthe: dip; serve

shí^n: chubby; fat

shí^{n}ga waséso^n: doll

shí^{n}gazhi^{n}ga: baby; child; doll; small child; toddler

shinó^{n}de: knee

shí^{n}udo^n: dog

shínudo^n: dog

shínudo^n zhi^{n}ga: puppy

shíshige: dust; garbage; litter; trash

shíshige úzhi: garbage can; trash container

shkáde: play

shkó^n: move; movement

shkúbe: deep; thick

shnábe: dirty

shnahá: slippery; smooth

shó^n: that's all / we're done

shó^{n}ge: horse

shó^{n}ge gthéze: zebra

shó^{n}ge mi^{n}ga: mare

shó^{n}ka: nine

shó^{n}sho^n: always; continually; still

shó^{n}to^{n}ga: wolf

shó^{n}to^{n}ga niáshi^{n}ga: wolf man

shó^{n}zhi^{n}ga: foal

shtáge: lukewarm

-shti: also; too

shtíde: warm

-shto^n: always doing

shú: prairie chicken

shúde íhe: chimney; smoke hole for a tipi

shúdemo^{n}ho^n: foggy

shugá zhi^{n}ga: dime

sí: foot; seed

sidádi: yesterday

sígthe: footprints; track; trail

sihí: foot

sí íkashe: catch one's foot

sikó^n: ankle

sí^{n}de: tail; taildancer

sí^{n}dehi: back of the hips

si^{n}déhi wahí: pelvic bone

sí^{n}de-tathisho^n: tails (in coin toss)

sí^{n}ga: squirrel

sí^{n}gthe: cricket

sipá: toe

sipázhi^{n}ga: little toe

síthe: think about

sí wahí: foot bones

ská: vanilla (ice cream); white

skída: saddle or notch between bluffs

skíge: heavy

skíthe: sweet

snéde: long; tall

sní: cold (an object)

sníshtage: lukewarm

sníuzhi: refrigerator

snó^{n}sno^n: bottomland; flatland; prairie

snó^{n}sno^n thi^{n}ge: hilly (with no flat places); rough (with no flat places)

só^n: bright; light (color); pale

su'é: loud sound of pouring rain

tá: dried meat; meat

tabé: ball

Tabégasi: Stickball

tabéhi: ball plant

tabé íshkade: ball game

tabé no^{n}t^{h}á: kickball

tabé sipá: football

tabé úgasno^n: basketball (hoop)

tadé: wind

tadésagi: windy

tadésagi to^{n}ga: tornado

tadó^{n}he: dust devil; whirlwind

tadó^{n}he to^{n}ga: tornado

tagáxthixthi: hamburger; sausage

táge: chestnut; walnut

tágeha: walnut shell

táhiⁿwagthoⁿ: deer-tail headdress; roach

táhiⁿwagthoⁿ uthí'ae: roach spreader

taní: broth; soup

taní uzhi: bowl

tanúka: fresh meat; meat

tanúka ígahi sheúzhegthoⁿ: mincemeat pie

tanúka s'áthe: ham

tápuska: classroom; school

táshe: bud; lump; swelling

táshi: bud; lump; swelling

tashníⁿga: chipmunk

tashtáde: waist

taspóⁿ: cranberries

taspóⁿ sheúzhegthoⁿ: cherry pie

táthazapa: tick

táxti: deer

táxtiha: buckskin; deer hide

Táxti hé baxóⁿi-kʰe: November

Táxti kigthígthoⁿi-kʰe: October

Táxti kigthíxai-kʰe: October

Táxti moⁿnóⁿ'ai-kʰe: September

té: bison; buffalo

t'é: dead; die (pass away)

tébi'a: frog

téga: new

tehé: buffalo horn; spoon

tehé toⁿga: serving spoon

tehé upágthe: buffalo-horn hat

tehé uzhi: drawer (for silverware)

tehé xthu'a: Food o' Plenty; Horn of Plenty; ice-cream scoop

tehé xthu'a égoⁿ: ice-cream cone

tehé zhiⁿga: small spoon

Té hútʰoⁿi-kʰe: July

teníxa ugthézhe: morel mushrooms

teníxa ugthézhe zhézhi: fried mushrooms

Tenúga míga unái-kʰe: June

tesíⁿde ugáshke: lifting pole for a tipi

téska: cattle; cow

téska míⁿga: cow

téska moⁿzé ni: cow's milk

téska núga: bull

téska zhiⁿga: calf

téthawe: banana

tethítiⁿ wahí: rib cage

téxi: difficult

tezhíⁿhiⁿde: finger weave

thábthiⁿ: three

thabthízhe: fell by gnawing

thadíⁿdiⁿ: loud yelling

tha'éthe: pity; show kindness to; take pity on

tha'étʰewathe: humble; pitiful

tha'éwathe: kind

thagé: put on (head); wear (on head)

thahégazhi: speak loudly or excessively

thanóⁿ: spouse

thashpé: bite off a piece

thashtóⁿ: stop eating or drinking; stop singing; stop talking

thasníⁿ: devour; swallow

thastúbe: lick; taste

tháta: left (side)

thátatathishoⁿ: on the left side

thatʰé: eat

thatóⁿ: drink

thatóⁿga: loud singing

thaxtá: bite

thaxthúde: choke on food

thé: go

thégoⁿ: like this

thénoⁿ: again; another

théthe: send; throw

théthudi : around here; here; in this area

théwathe: Let's go!

théze: tongue

thí: you

thi'á: can't; fail

thibéni: bend

thibthá: open (eyes); spread open

thibúta: make round by hand

thidázhe: get blisters

thidíⁿdiⁿ: pull hard

thidóⁿ: pull

thidúzhe: bust

thi'é: side (body part)

thiézhube: respect

thigthíze: electricity; lightning fork

thigthíze uzhégthoⁿ: microwave (oven)

thigthíze wíuhoⁿ: electric skillet; microwave (oven)

thihíde: lower (a bucket or a shade)

thihóⁿ: lift something easily handled

thikúge: make a hollow sound pulling a wagon or a sled

thikúwiⁿxe: spin (a wheel); turn (a doorknob or a faucet handle)

thimóⁿgthe: put up (as a tipi); raise (as a tipi)

thimóⁿshi: elevate; lift; raise up into the air

thíⁿ: be

-thiⁿ: the (living singular moving, not the main actor)

thinákoⁿ: turn on the lights

thinázhi: turn off

thiⁿgé: gone; lacking; none; not exist; run out (as food)

-thiⁿkʰe: the (living singular, not the main actor)

thinóⁿge: roll; start something rolling; turn on

thióⁿba: lightning; lightning flash

thipʰí: good at; know; learn; skilled

thípi gáxe: do a good job

thip'íⁿp'iⁿze: blink (eyes)

thip'íⁿze: close (eyes)

thipúxe: fold in (as a leg)

thisáda: straighten out (as an arm or fabric)

thisáthu: rattle; shake a gourd

thisé: clip (hair); cut

thishíbe: open

thishpí: remove kernels from the cob by hand

thishtóⁿ: done; finished; let (a bird) go; release (a prisoner) thishúpa: put everything in its proper place

thisíhi: clean (action word); straighten up (the house)

thisnú: drag; move (as a piece in a board game); pull; tow

thisónthe: turn over; twist (as a rope)

thíta: dove; pigeon

thithíta: your; yours

thítin: rib

thítin wahí: rib cage

thitúshi: snap (fingers)

thitútushi: snap (fingers) multiple times

thi'ú: scratch

thiwágazu: examine; look hard; recognize; set straight

thiwín: buy; purchase

thixáde: spread (as fingers or tailfeathers)

thixón: break

thixú: draw; mark; sketch

thizé: pick up; take

thizhá: wash

thizhábe: peel

thizhádon: spread the fingers

thizhú: remove corn from the cob by hand

thizhúthon: grow (a plant); raise (bring to maturity)

thizú'e: lying down stretched out

-thon: the (nonliving round, bundled, hanging)

-thonkha: the (living plural, not the main actor)

thonzha: but; however; nevertheless

thúton: straight

-the: the (nonliving standing or group)

thí: arrive here

thigthágtha: coming and going; flashing

thithé: start to

-thon: the (living standing, not the main actor)

Thigthíze-tí: Electric House / Electric Company (in real-estate board game)

tí: building; house

tí ágaxada: door cover for a tipi

tibábexin: broom

tibábexin-non: sweeper

tibáxiatha: elephant

tibúta: jail

tíha: canvas

tíha ugábthintha: smoke flaps for a tipi

tíha uthón: sticks used to weave the front flap of a tipi

tíhukon: chimney; smoke hole for a tipi

tíhuthon: sticks used to weave the front flap of a tipi

tí íbabexin: broom

tiísonthe: tipi

tíka: fox

timóngthe: tipi (when already up)

tín: dewy; humid; moist

tináze: back of the tipi

tinónde: wall of a tipi

tíshi: pole for a tipi

tíshi uthón: sticks used to weave the front flap of a tipi

tíshuthoⁿ: sticks used to weave the front flap of a tipi

títhumoⁿhoⁿ: woven part above the door of a tipi

tí ugípi: full house

tiúpe: visit

tiúthipu: sweat lodge

tiúthugadoⁿ: stakes for a tipi

tiútʰoⁿnoⁿ: hallway; lawn; open space between houses or rooms; pathway; room

tí wéthisihi: vacuum cleaner

tizhébe: door

tizhébe ugthóⁿ: tipi liner

tízhiⁿga: bathroom; outhouse

tóⁿde: ground

tóⁿdeata: uphill

tóⁿdeatathishoⁿ: toward the ground

toⁿgá: big

Toⁿgáxthoⁿ: autumn; fall (season)

tóⁿthiⁿ: run

tóⁿwoⁿgthoⁿ: clan; town

tú: blue

tubáthe: crumbled; powdery

t'úse: humpbacked

tushníge: rainbow

ubásnoⁿ: put on (as a ring)

ubátʰi: hang up

ubázhiⁿ: adjust

ubázu: corner

ubésniⁿ: sense something

ubétʰoⁿ: fold; wrap

ubídoⁿ: dip into

ubískabe: fill with; stuff with

ubísoⁿde: crowded in; people pressed together; squeezed close together

ubíxage: killing frost

ubíxoⁿ: blow up (as a balloon); mist; sprinkle

ubúde: in pieces

uchʰízhe: brush (underbrush, brushy thicket); forest with lots of little trees; thicket; weedy

údoⁿ: good

udóⁿbe: appearance

uéthoⁿba: where (something) appears

ugá: color; dye; paint (something)

ugábthiⁿ: blowing back into the tipi (as snow or smoke)

ugáhoⁿnoⁿpaze: darkness

ugáshibe: graduate

ugáshke: fasten; hang from; tie (as a horse)

ugáshoⁿ: journey; travel

ugásnoⁿ: lasso; make a basket; throw a loop over something

ugásnoⁿ théthe: make a basket (in basketball)

ugáspe: depression or indentation (as on a bed where somebody sat)

ugátigthoⁿ: ace (in cards)

úgaxe: color

úgaxeshkoⁿshkoⁿ: television; TV

ugáxthuge: hammer a hole into

ugípi: full

ugthí^n: place where you sit or live

ugthó^n: contain; put into

uhé: go along; pass; path; road; street

úhe: stairstep; step

uhéat^{h}o^n: bridge; ladder; stairway; viaduct

uhí: beat (in game); win

uhítazhi: anxious; can't wait; eager

uhó^n: cook

úho^n: cook (things)

uhó^{n}ge: boundary; end; goal; limit

úho^n tí: kitchen

úho^n tí ukígthizha: kitchen sink

úho^n wagthábaze: cookbook

uhúthe: attract

uíhe: attend (go to regularly); follow or join someone

uíshte: left to someone

uítha: tell someone

uít^{h}i^n: hit for (as in clapping for somebody)

újo^n: beautiful; pretty

uk^{h}éthi^n: common; normal; simple

ukiáwat^{h}o^{n}t^{h}o^n: standing in a line

ukíe: converse; have a conversation with someone

ukígthiske: spider

ukígthiski: spider

ukígthizha: sink (as in kitchen)

ukíhi: able to do something; can

ukízhi: kin; relative

úmak^{h}a: cheap; easy

umásno^n: slice in half

umó^{n}e: food for travel; groceries; provisions

Umó^{n}ho^n: Umo^{n}ho^n (describing word); Umo^{n}ho^n person

Umó^{n}ho^n Tí: Macy

Umó^{n}ho^n Tó^{n}wo^{n}gtho^n: Omaha

Umó^{n}ho^n Wá'ai: Tribal Farm

umó^{n}thi^{n}ka: year

umúto^{n}thi^n: turn on the water in a sink

unágo^{n}ba: bright or glowing; light up; shine

unáhe tí: firehouse

uné: look for; search for; seek

unéthe: fireplace; hearth; stove

unézhe tí: bathroom

unézheti wagthábaze: toilet paper

unézheti wéthisihi: toilet brush

unó^{n}shto^n: parking; rest stop; station

unó^{n}zhi^n: jacket; put on; shirt; wear (on torso)

unó^{n}zhi^{n}ha: hide jacket

unó^{n}zhi^n mó^{n}t^{h}e: undershirt

unó^{n}zhi^n xépa: vest

unó^{n}zhi^n zízige: sweater

u'ó^{n}he: baby board; baby on baby board

uó^{n}si: jump

uó^{n}sisi: jump repeatedly

uó^{n}si-tho^{n}tho^n: jump up and down

uó^{n}thi^{n}ge: free

upé: crawl into or enter a house

up'útho^n: steamy

uséso^n: moldy

úshkade: field (for playing sports); game; park

úshkoⁿ: customs; ways

úshk'udoⁿ: good ways; kind; kindness

ushté: left over; remaining; rest (of something)

usíhi: clean (descriptive word for a space); clear

usní: cold (temperature)

Usní: winter

uspé: sink (as a boat); valley

uthá: tell (the news)

úthashte: leftover food taken home from a doings or feast (prayed over)

úthashte úzhi: container for food

uthátʰe tí: dining room

uthéwiⁿ: gather or assemble themselves

uthéwiⁿkʰithe: raise money for somebody

uthéwiⁿthe: gather; gather or assemble people; raise (as money)

uthíbthoⁿ: smell something

uthídoⁿ: latch; lock

uthígtheze: screw

uthíshoⁿ: go around the outside of something

uthísnoⁿ: put on a necktie or a fanbelt; thread a needle

úthiwiⁿ tí: shop; store

uthíxide: look around

Úthixide Thétha Moⁿzhóⁿ: Lookout Point

uthíxpathe: drop

uthízoⁿ: down the middle (in Handgame); in the middle

uthóⁿ: catch; grab; hold

uthúakiwatʰoⁿtʰoⁿ: in line

Uthúama: Sorry (as said in the board game)

uthúbidoⁿ: dip into; push down

uthúgahi: mix in; stir

uthúshi: between (players); facing a crowd; in front

utʰíⁿ: hit

utʰóⁿnoⁿ: aisle

utʰónoⁿ: path; room; space in the middle of a building or village; walkway

utóⁿ: leggings; wear (on legs)

utóⁿ toⁿga: chief leggings

u'úde : full of holes; holes; tattered

úwachʰigaxe: dance arena

úwashkoⁿ: strength

úwiⁿ: earrings

úwiⁿgazoⁿde: sidestitch choker

uxpáthe: fall

uxpé: dish; plate

uxpé basása: divided plate

uxpé íbikʰa: dishtowel

uxpé íthizha wéthihide: dishwasher

uxpé ugá'u'ude: strainer

uxpé úgthe: cupboard

uxpé ukígthizha: kitchen sink

uxpé úzhi: cabinet; cupboard; dish rack

uxthábe: bushes; forest; out in the woods; timbers; trees

úzhawa: doings; festivities; fun; having a good time; pleasure

uzhégthoⁿ: oven

uzhéoⁿhe: oven; stove

úzhi: bag; container

uzhí: fill; full; loaded; put in

úzhi kúge: shelf

úzhioⁿhe: oven

uzhóⁿ: bed

uzhóⁿiti: hotel

uzhóⁿti: bedroom

uzí: egg yolk

wabáhi: graze

wabásada: ironing board

wábatʰe: appliqué; ribbonwork

wabáxte: bundle for supplies

wabthágaze: paper

wachʰígaxe: dance

Wachʰígaxe Tí: Alfred Gilpin Building

wachʰíninika: butterfly

wagáxe: bill; credit advance; loan; rent; tax

wágazhi: command

wagóⁿze: teacher

wagthábaze: book; paper

wagthábaze shuga: cardboard

wagthábaze úzhi: packet (as of sugar)

wagtháde: creep up

wagtháje: creep up

wágthe: counter (kitchen)

wagthíshka: bug; crawling things; reptile; worm

wagthíshka hi duba: alligator

wagthíshka kigthézha: box elder bug

wagthíshka sihí dúba: alligator

wagthíshka zhiⁿga: bug

wágthoⁿ: brooch; medallion; pin; slide

wahába: corn

wahábe: corn

wahí: bone

wahí niáshiⁿga: skeleton

wahóⁿ: strike camp and move tipi; thread; yarn

wahútoⁿthiⁿ: gun

wa'íⁿ: backpack; load; packing

wáiⁿ: blanket; robe; shawl

wáiⁿgthabe: shawl

wáiⁿshnaha: apron; broadcloth

Wajépa: Camp Crier

wakʰéga: ill; sick

wákʰihide: paying attention

Wakóⁿda: God

Wakóⁿda Izhíⁿge: Jesus

Wakóⁿda Wathahoⁿ Niáshiⁿga Iⁿshʼáge: Old Mission

wáku: awl; fork

wákuzhiⁿga: needle; pin

wamí: blood

wamóⁿske: bread

wamóⁿske buta: bun (bread); roll (bread)

wamóⁿske íbibthaska: rolling pin

wamóⁿske íkigthahi: stuffing

wamóⁿske shuga: cowboy bread

wamóⁿske skíthe: cake

wamóⁿske ubískabe: stuffing

wamóⁿske xude: flour

wamóⁿske xude úzhi: flour canister

wamúske: bread

wanágthe: domesticated; livestock

wanáxoⁿxoⁿ: firefly

wanáxude ígaxe: toaster

waníde: gravy

waníta: animal; four-legged animal

waníta moⁿtʰanoⁿha: wildcat

waníta nóⁿka t'úsa: camel

waníta tí: zoo

waníta wáxa: lion

wanítʰe: miserly; stingy

wanóⁿ'oⁿ: hearing; listening

wanóⁿp'iⁿ: choker; necklace

wanóⁿshe: whipman

wanóⁿxe: spirit

wáoⁿ: sing

waóⁿ wathize: cassette; CD; record; recording (sound)

Wapʰígthe: Spirit Plate

wasábe: black bear

Wasábe zhiⁿga ídai-kʰe: December

wasékoⁿ: fast; speedy

washíⁿ ágaxtoⁿ: mustard

washíⁿzhegthoⁿ: frybread

washkóⁿ: do one's best; make an effort; try hard

washkóⁿ thiⁿgé: weak

washkóⁿtoⁿga: strong

washóⁿga: corn mush

washtáge: tame

wasísige: clever; energetic; frisky; full of life; go-getter; lively; spry; tough

waskíthe: berries; dessert; fruit; melon; pudding; sweets

waskíthe ázhi-thoⁿthoⁿ íkigthahi: fruit salad

waskíthe gashkóⁿshkoⁿ: jello

wasníde: late; slow

wáspa: behave properly

watháge: cap; hat; headdress

watháge zízige: knit cap

wáthaha: clothes

wathátʰe: food; meal

wáthatʰe: table

wathíbaba: card; playing card

wathígthoⁿ: mind

wathígthoⁿ wasékoⁿ: computer

wathíshnazhi: out of sight

wathítʰoⁿ: work

wathíze: someone who receives help

Wathíze Tí: Social Services Building

watʰé: dress; skirt

watʰé moⁿtʰe: underskirt

watʰé snede: long Umoⁿhoⁿ dress

watʰíninika: butterfly

watʰóⁿ sheúzhegthoⁿ: pumpkin pie

wa'ú: woman; queen (in cards)

wa'ú piazhi: witch

Wa'úzhiⁿga: female Elder

wawégahi: baking powder; frosting; mayonnaise

wawégahi úzhi: baking powder can; frosting can

wawégaxe: wave to

wawéshi: paycheck

wawéxaxa: joker (in cards)

wawíugahi: baking powder; frosting

wawíugahi úzhi: baking powder can; frosting can

waxchá: flower

Wáxe: White (descriptive term for ethnicity or race); White person

Wáxe Íye: English

Wáxe izházhe: English name

waxí^{n}ha: cloth; fabric; material; paper

waxí^{n}ha nágo^{n}ba: ribbon

waxí^{n}ha niáshi^{n}ga: rag man

waxpáthi^n: poor

waxpáthi^n wagáxe: poor tax (real estate board game)

waxtá: flower

waxtáhi: houseplant; plant

waxtá thigúzhe: banana

waxtá thiguzhe másne: banana split

waxthá: milkweed; broccoli; cabbage

waxthá íkigthahi: salad

waxthá mo^{n}t^{h}ano^{n}ha: milkweed

Waxthá Taní: milkweed soup

waxthá táshe: milkweed bud

wazéthe tí: hospital; Carl T. Curtis Health Center

wazhíde: buffalo berry; tomato

wazhíde ágaxto^n: ketchup

wazhí^{n}ga: chicken; bird; winged ones

wazhí^{n}ga í^{n}be gabthá: peacock

wazhí^{n}ga mi^{n}ga: hen

wazhí^{n}ga nuga: rooster

wazhí^{n}ga to^{n}ga ó^{n}sagi: ostrich

wazhí^{n}ga to^{n}ga ó^{n}sagi-kipáda: ostrich chick

wazhí^{n}ga zhézhi: fried chicken

wazhí^{n}ga zhíbe-snéde: ostrich

wazhí^{n}ga zhi^{n}ga: birdie

wazhí^{n}ga zhi^{n}ga ut^{h}í^n: badminton; racquetball

wazhí^{n}piazhi: angry

wéagani: fan

wéagashke: safety pin

wéahide: far away

wéathaskabe: paste; tape

weáthaskabe: tape

weáthitabe: potholder

wébabexi^n: broom; brush

wébashnade: tongs

wébaso^{n}tha: spatula

wébaxu: chalk; marker; pen; pencil

wébaxuni: pen

wéganazhi: fire extinguisher

wégazu: straight

wégo^{n}ze: amount; gallon; measure

wégthi: grease; lard; oil

wégthi úzhi: grease can

Wehéd!: Awesome!; Excellent!

wéki'o^n: jewelry

wéko^{n}t^{h}o^n: rope

wémoⁿxe: question

wénoⁿde: full (from eating)

wés'a: snake

wéshi: ante; pot (in gambling); prize; wager

wéta: egg

wéta há: eggshell

wéta ská: eggwhite

wéta uzí: egg yolk

wéta wamoⁿske ubískabe: egg-salad sandwich

wéta zhézhi: fried eggs

wéthawa: counter; nickel

wéthawa zhíde: penny

wéthawa zhiⁿga: coin

wéthibexiⁿ: rake

wéthihide: appliance; machine; tool; utensil; weight (for weighing something down or exercise)

wéthihoⁿ: any tool used to lift with

Wéthihoⁿ Thihóⁿ Tí: Four Hills of Life Building ("weightlifting house")

wéthishibe uthóⁿ: keyring

wéthitega: soap

wéthitega úzhi: soapbox

wéthitʰoⁿ: right (side)

wéthitʰoⁿtathisho: on the right side

wéthixthi: brain

wétʰiⁿ: club; clubs (suit); hatchet; striker; tomahawk

wétʰiⁿ zázade: racket

wétugthoⁿ: truck

wéuzhi: carton; container

wézhezhi: frying pan; skillet

wí: I; me

Wíbthahoⁿ: thank you

Wihé: my (female's) female friend; my (female's) Little Sister

Wihézhiⁿga: my (female's) Little Sister

Wihóⁿga: my (male's) Sister-in-Law

Wikóⁿ: my Grandmother

wíⁿ: one

wíⁿbthuga: one dollar

wiⁿdénoⁿ: half amount

wiⁿdéthoⁿska: half of a thing

wiⁿdétʰoⁿ: half length

Winégi: my Uncle (mother's brother)

Winísi: my (male's) son or daughter; my (male's) son or daughter

wiⁿóⁿxchi: one

Wishí'e: my (female's) Brother-in-Law

Wishíkoⁿ: my (female's) Sister-in-Law

Witáhoⁿ: my (male's) Brother-in-Law

Witígoⁿ: my Grandfather

Witími: my Aunt (father's sister)

Witíni: my Daughter-in-Law

Witínu: my (female's) Big Brother

Witóⁿde: my Son-in-Law

Witóⁿge: my (female's) Little Sister; my (male's) Sister

Witóⁿshka: my (male's) Nephew (sister's son)

Witúshka: my (female's) Nephew (brother's son)

Witúshpa: my Grandchild

Witúzho^{n}ge: my (female's) Niece (brother's daughter)

wíubesni^n: senses

wíuga: coloring; dye; paint (activity); paint (liquid)

wíugo^{n}ba: window

wíugo^{n}ba ithágaxade: curtain

wíuhe: follow (as in tracks or prints)

wíuho^n: cake pan; cooking pot; pan; pot

wíuzhi: basket

wiwíta: mine; my

Wizhí^{n}ge: my Son

Wizhí^{n}the: my (male's) Big Brother

Wizhó^{n}ge: my Daughter

Wizhó^{n}the: my (female's) Big Sister

wó^{n}do^n: both

wó^{n}githe: all; each; everybody

xáde: fodder; grass (tallgrass, hay); hay

xádeata: into the grass or prairie

xáde mo^{n}ko^n: tea

xáditi: grass lodge

xátha: back (as in going back home)

xáthe: back (as in going back home)

xcháthe: love

Xcháwigithe: I love you

-xchi: really

xé: bluff; bury; mountain

xéki: foot of a bluff

xékigtha: foot of a bluff

xeút^{h}o^{n}nadi: between bluffs; floodplain

xéwo^{n}ge: dew; frost

xithá: eagle; golden eagle

xithá mó^{n}sho^n: eagle feather

xitháthage: whole eagle headdress

xitháwathage: whole eagle headdress

xó^n: broke; broken; out of money

xó^{n}xo^n: squint

xtáthe: like (care for, take a liking to); love

xthá: skinny; thin

xthabé: tree

xthabéata: into the timbers

xthíazhi: quiet; silent

xthítu: brutal; bullying; cruel; mean

xthu'á: empty; hollow

-xti: really; very

xúde: gray

xu'é: soft; steady sound

xúka: sing (in Ceremony); singer (in Ceremony)

Xúka Nudó^{n}ho^{n}ga: Head Singer

za'é: noise

zhábe: beaver

zháhe: stab

zháhi: houseplant; stem of a plant

zhápa: bubblegum

zhápe: chewing gum; gum

zheátigtho^n: breechcloth

zhézhi: fry

zhíbe: leg (esp. the lower leg)

zhíbe wahí: leg bones

zhíde: red

zhído^n: dew

zhí-egoⁿ: pink

zhiⁿgá: little; small; young

zhóⁿ: sleep

zhoⁿ'ábe: leaf

zhoⁿbtháska: board; floor

zhoⁿbtháska áshkade: board game

zhoⁿbtháskaska: whiteboard

zhóⁿ gáxe: pretend to sleep

zhoⁿgthíshka: ants

zhoⁿmóⁿthiⁿ: cart; limo; wagon

zhoⁿmóⁿthiⁿ wanóⁿmoⁿshi: elevator

zhoⁿní: candy; maple syrup; sugar

zhoⁿní buta zhóⁿzhiⁿga utháha: Tootsie Pop

zhoⁿní snúsnu: syrup

zhoⁿní úzhi: sugar canister

zhoⁿní zízige: taffy

zhoⁿthóⁿha tí: bark lodge

zhoⁿ waxága tí: brush lodge

zhóⁿxude: juneberry

zhóⁿzhiⁿga: stick

zhóⁿzi: mulberry

zhú: flesh; skin

Zhú etázhi: Frankenstein

zhúgthe: accompany; together

zí: yellow

zigthiⁿgthiⁿ: heavy freezing rain

zíshabe: brown; chocolate (literally 'brown')

zizígthe: sleet

zizíka: turkey

8.4 ULCC GLOSSARY IN MACY STANDARD ORTHOGRAPHY: ENGLISH TO UMÓ^{n}HO^n

able to do something: ukíhi

above: mó^{n}shi; paháshi

accompany: zhúgthe

ace (in cards): ugátigtho^n

Ace bandage: hazízige

acorn: ó^{n}zhi^{n}ga

across: mo^{n}só^{n}thi^n

adjust: ubázhi^n

adult: nó^n

again: p^{h}í; shi; théno^n

aged: Nó^n-xti

ahead: pahó^{n}ga

aisle: ut^{h}ó^{n}no^n

Alfred Gilpin Building: Wach^{h}ígaxe Tí

alive: níta

all: wó^{n}githe

all day: ó^{n}ba itháugthe

alligator: wagthíshka hi duba; wagthíshka sihí dúba

almost: ó^{n}thino^n

a lot: áhigi; áhigi-ácho^n

also:-shti; edábe

always: shó^{n}sho^n

always doing:-shto^n

amount: wégo^{n}ze

ancient: itó^{n}thi^{n}adi

and: gó^{n}ki

angel: mó^{n}xe mo^{n}shíadi níashi^{n}ga

angry: wazhí^{n}shte

animal: waníta

ankle: sikó^n

another: théno^n

answer: edégitho^n

answer her/him: edíye thék^{h}ithe

ante: wéshi

antler: hé

ants: zho^{n}gthíshka

anxious: uhítazhi

any tool used to lift with: wéthiho^n

appear: étho^{n}ba

appear (as the sun through clouds): gaétho^{n}be

appearance: udó^{n}be

apple: shé

apple pie: shé sheúzhegtho^n; sheúzhegtho^n

appliance: wéthihide

appliqué: wábat^{h}e

approves: gísho^n

April: Mí eáto^n thi^{n}gé-k^{h}e

apron: wái^{n}shnaha

arm: á

armband: áuthisno^n

arm bones: á wahí

around here: théthudi

arrive back here: gthí

arrive here: t^{h}í

as a spray can: íthizho^{n}zho^n

as big or tall as: étho^{n}ska

ask: ímo^{n}xe

ask a question: ímo^{n}xe

ask for: giná; ná

ask for one's own back: agína

attempt: ígaskoⁿthe

attend (go to regularly): uíhe

at the bottom: kigthá

attract: uhúthe

August: Óⁿpʰoⁿ-hútʰoⁿi-kʰe

automobile: kinóⁿnoⁿge

autumn: Toⁿgáxthoⁿ

Awesome!: Wehéd!

awl: wáku

baby: shíⁿgazhiⁿga

baby bird: kipáda

baby board: u'óⁿhe

baby on baby board: u'óⁿhe

back (anat.): nóⁿka

back (as in going back home): xátha; xáthe

backbone: nóⁿxahi

back of the hips: síⁿdehi

back of the tipi: tináze

backpack: wa'íⁿ

backward: nístu

bad: piázhi

badminton: wazhíⁿga zhiⁿga utʰíⁿ

bag: úzhi

baking powder: wawégahi; wawíugahi

baking powder can: wawégahi úzhi; wawíugahi úzhi

bald eagle: pasóⁿ

ball: tabé

ball game: tabé íshkade

balloon: hazízige; hazízige tabé

ball plant: tabéhi

banana: téthawe; waxtá thigúzhe

banana split: waxtá thiguzhe másne

bandolier beads: núsi áxthade

bare: háthukathiⁿ

bark lodge: zhoⁿthóⁿha tí

base: híde

basket: sáhi; wíuzhi

basketball (hoop): tabé úgasnoⁿ

bat (the animal): didéshi

bathe: hítha

bathroom: tízhiⁿga; unézhe tí

bayonet: móⁿdehi

be: thíⁿ

bead: híⁿska

beadwork: híⁿska

beat (in game): uhí

beautiful: újoⁿ

beaver: zhábe

bed: uzhóⁿ

bedroom: uzhóⁿti

bee: kigthóⁿxe

before: pahóⁿga

beg: ná

be gone away: aíathe

behave properly: wáspa

behind: háshi; náze

bells: móⁿze gamóⁿthe; móⁿze gatámoⁿ

belly: níxa

below: kigthá

belt: ípithage

bend: thibéni

berries: waskíthe

beside: sak^{h}íba

best: áta

be the last one (e.g. last year in school): íthishetho^n

between (players): uthúshi

between bluffs: xeút^{h}o^{n}nadi

big: to^{n}gá

Big Center Drum: Kúge

Big Elk Park: Ó^{n}p^{h}o^n To^{n}ga Mo^{n}zhó^n

bill: wagáxe

bird: wazhí^{n}ga

birdie: wazhí^{n}ga zhi^{n}ga

bird tail: í^{n}be

birthday: ó^{n}ba ída

bison: té

bite: thaxtá

bite off a piece: thashpé

bitter: pá

black: sábe

black bear: wasábe

blackberry: agthó^{n}gamo^{n}ge

Blackbird Hill: Mo^{n}gthíxta

Black Shoulder Clan: I^{n}késabe

bladder: néxe

blanket: wái^n

blink (eyes): thip'í^{n}p'i^{n}ze

blissful: gíthe

blood: wamí

bloom (a flower): gabthá

blowing back into the tipi (as snow or smoke): ugábthi^n

blowing or drifting in the wind: gahíthe

blow one's nose: gazhí^n

blow up (as a balloon): ubíxo^n

blue: tú

blueberry: nó^{n}patu

blueberry pie: nó^{n}patu sheúzhegtho^n

blue raspberry (frozen treat flavor): nó^{n}patu

bluff: mo^{n}á; xé

board: zho^{n}btháska

board game: zho^{n}btháska áshkade

boil: ábixe

bone: wahí

book: wagthábaze

boots: hi^{n}bé ágaha; hi^{n}bésnede

both: wó^{n}do^n

bottom: híde

bottomland: hídeata; snó^{n}sno^n

boundary: uhó^{n}ge

bow: mó^{n}da; mó^{n}de

bowl: taní uzhi

box: kúge

box elder bug: wagthíshka kigthézha

boy: núzhi^{n}ga

bracelet: áxibe

brain: wéthixthi

branch: gaxá

bread: wamóⁿske; wamúske

break: thixóⁿ

breastplate: móⁿge ágthoⁿ

breathless: gaskí-áchoⁿ

breechcloth: zheátigthoⁿ

bridge: uhéatʰoⁿ

bright: sóⁿ

bright or glowing: unágoⁿba

broadcloth: wáiⁿshnaha

broccoli: waxthá

broke: xóⁿ

broken: xóⁿ

brooch: wágthoⁿ

broom: tí íbabexiⁿ; tibábexiⁿ; wébabexiⁿ

broth: taní

brown: zíshabe

brush: wébabexiⁿ

brush (underbrush, brushy thicket): uchʰízhe

brush lodge: zhoⁿ waxága tí

brutal: xthítu

bubblegum: zhápa

buckle: ágashke; ithágashke

buckskin: táxtiha

buckskin dress: háwatʰe

bud: táshe; táshi

buffalo: té

Buffalo (Black Shoulder) Clan: Iⁿkésabe

buffalo berry: wazhíde

buffalo horn: tehé

buffalo-horn hat: tehé upágthe

bug: wagthíshka; wagthíshka zhiⁿga

building: tí

bull: téska núga

bullet: móⁿzemoⁿ

bulletin board: íutha-ithóⁿthai-thoⁿ

bullying: xthítu

bun (bread): wamóⁿske buta

bundle for supplies: wabáxte

bunny: moⁿshchíⁿga zhiⁿga

burlap: sáhi

burp: baníuski; banúski; níuski; núski

burst or pop a bladder-like thing like an egg, a blister, a water balloon or an overripe tomato: gadúzhe

bury: xé

bushes: uxthábe

bust: thidúzhe

bust (a water balloon or a blister): bibtháze

bustle: káxe

but: ede; thoⁿzha

butcher: páde

butterfly: wachʰíninika; watʰíninika

button: ágashke

button (chest): móⁿge ithágashke

button for someone: égashke

buy: thiwíⁿ

buy for someone: gíthiwiⁿ

buzz somebody: bashná

cabbage: waxthá

cabinet: uxpé úzhi

cake: wamóⁿske skíthe

cake pan: wíuho^n

calf: téska zhi^{n}ga

call: áthade

call someone over: gíbo^n

calm: ó^{n}the

camel: nó^{n}xahi t'úsa; waníta nó^{n}ka t'úsa

Camp Crier: Eábaha; Iyébaha; Iyék^{h}ithe; Wajépa

can: mó^{n}ze úzhi; ukíhi

can't: thi'á

candy: zho^{n}ní

cane: hímo^{n}gthe

can opener: mó^{n}ze wéthishibe

can't wait: uhítazhi

canvas: tíha

cap: watháge

car: kinó^{n}no^{n}ge

card: wathíbaba

cardboard: wagthábaze shuga

careful: ó^{n}the

Carl T. Curtis Health Center: Wazéthe Tí

carry on one's back: í^n

cart: zho^{n}mó^{n}thi^n

carton: wéuzhi

cassette: waó^n wathize

cassette deck: mó^{n}ze wao^n

cast-iron skillet: néxe-shuga-wézhegtho^n

casual: ó^{n}the

cat: i^{n}gthó^{n}ga

catch: uthó^n

catch one's foot: sí íkashe

cat litter: i^{n}gthó^{n}ga shíshige

cattail: sáhi

cattle: téska

CD: waó^n wathize

CD player: mó^{n}ze wao^n

cedar: mázi

cemetery: míxe

chair: ágthi^n

chalk: wébaxu

change: kigthíazhi

cheap: úmak^{h}a

cheat: íkit^{h}e

cheese: i^{n}ch^{h}ó^{n}ga wathát^{h}e

cherry: nó^{n}pa

cherry pie: taspó^n sheúzhegtho^n

chest (body part): mó^{n}ge

chestnut: táge

chewing gum: zhápe

chick: kipáda

chicken: wazhí^{n}ga

chicken gizzard: pízi ugtho^{n}ge

Chief: Níkagahi

chief leggings: utó^n to^{n}ga

child: shí^{n}gazhi^{n}ga

chimney: shúde íhe; tíhuko^n

chipmunk: tashní^{n}ga

chocolate (literally 'brown'): shábe; zíshabe

chokecherry: nó^{n}pa

choke on food: thaxthúde

choker: wanó^{n}p'i^n

chop: gasé

chop up into little pieces: máshpashpa

chubby: shíⁿ

clan: tóⁿwoⁿgthoⁿ

clap: gachʰáchʰaki

clap once: gachʰáki

classroom: tápuska

claw: sháge

clean (action word): thisíhi

clean (descriptive word for a space): usíhi

clear: usíhi

clear by shovelling: basíhi

clear sky: kétha

clear up (the sky): gasíhi

clever: wasísige

clip (hair): thisé

clock: miídoⁿbe

close: ágaxade; eshóⁿ

close (eyes): thip'íⁿze

close or lock: ánoⁿse

close together: eshóⁿ

cloth: waxíⁿha

clothes: háthe; wáthaha

clothing: háthe

cloud: moⁿxpí

cloudy: ámoⁿxpi

club: wétʰiⁿ

clubs (suit): wétʰiⁿ

clueless: íkipahoⁿ-azhi

coffee: moⁿkóⁿsabe

coffee can: moⁿkóⁿsabe úzhi

coffee cup: moⁿkóⁿsabe niúthatoⁿ

coffee pot: moⁿkóⁿsabe ígaxe

coin: wéthawa zhiⁿga

cold (an object): sní

cold (temperature): usní

collect a debt: gína

collecting: bahí

color: ugá; úgaxe

coloring: wíuga

comb someone's hair: gahé

come: gí; í

come and (followed by suggestion): kʰé
____!

come back: gí

come to an end: kigthíshenoⁿ

coming and going: tʰigthágtha

command: ágazhi; wágazhi

common: ukʰéthiⁿ

computer: wathígthoⁿ wasékoⁿ

contain: ugthóⁿ

container: úzhi; wéuzhi

container for food: úthashte úzhi

content: nóⁿde gíudoⁿ

continent: moⁿzhóⁿ níuthoⁿda

continually: shóⁿshoⁿ

converse: ukíe

cook: uhóⁿ

cook (things): úhoⁿ

cookbook: úhoⁿ wagthábaze

cooked: níde

cookie jar: nóⁿxe wamúske skithe úzhi

cooking pot: wíuhoⁿ

cool: ásni

cord: házhi^{n}ga

corn: wahába; wahábe

corner: ubázu

corn mush: washó^{n}ga

cottonwood: má'a; má'a to^{n}ga

cottonwood seed fluff (figurative): hi^{n}xpé

cougar: i^{n}gthó^n si^n snéde

counter: wéthawa

counter (kitchen): wágthe

cover: ágaxade

cover somebody's (e.g. eyes): égaxade

cover the grave with earth: ába'u

cow: téska; téska mí^{n}ga

cowboy bread: wamó^{n}ske shuga

cow's milk: téska mo^{n}zé ni

crack: gaxíxe

crack open repeatedly: gaxíxixe

cranberries: taspó^n

crawling things: wagthíshka

crawl into or enter a house: upé

crazy: gthó^{n}thi^n

credit advance: wagáxe

creep up: wagtháde; wagtháje

cricket: sí^{n}gthe

crow: káxe

crowded in: ubíso^{n}de

cruel: xthítu

crumbled: tubáthe

cry out: hút^{h}o^n

cucumber: kukúmi

cup: niúthato^n

cupboard: uxpé úgthe; uxpé úzhi

curtain: wíugo^{n}ba ithágaxade

customs: úshko^n

cut: thisé

cut (as a deck of cards): gasé

cut hair for: gíbashna

cut in many pieces: máxo^{n}xo^n

cut in two: no^{n}báha máxo^n

cut off (as in a game): íno^{n}se

cut up: páde

cut with a knife: máxo^n

dance: wach^{h}ígaxe

dance (as in Hethúshka): no^{n}t^{h}é

dance arena: úwach^{h}igaxe

dance excessively: no^{n}hégazhi

dance stick: hímo^{n}gthe

dancing or kicking: no^{n}shtó^n

dark: shábe

darkness: ugáho^{n}no^{n}paze

dart: mó^{n}da; mó^{n}de; mó^{n}dehi

Daughter-in-Law: Míwathixe

dawn: ó^{n}ba zhíde

day: ó^{n}ba

dead: t'é

dead-end bluff: patháge

Decatur: hídeata

December: Wasábe zhi^{n}ga ídai-k^{h}e

decide for: íthigtho^n

decide on: íthigtho^n

decision: íthigtho^n

deep: shkúbe

deer: táxti

deer hide: táxtiha

deer-tail headdress: táhiⁿwagthoⁿ

depression or indentation (as on a bed where somebody sat): ugáspe

deprive of: ínoⁿshe

dessert: waskíthe

detest: ít'athe

devour: thasníⁿ

dew: xéwoⁿge; zhídoⁿ

dewy: tíⁿ

diamonds (suit): íⁿ'e ska; íⁿ'epa

diaper: niⁿdágthe; níⁿde ágthoⁿ

dice: kóⁿsi; kúge zhiⁿga

die (pass away): t'é

different: ázhi

different kinds: ázhi-thoⁿthoⁿ

difficult: téxi

dig in earth: moⁿ'é

dime: shugá zhiⁿga

dining room: utháthe tí

dip: shígthe

dip into: ubídoⁿ; uthúbidoⁿ

dirty: shnábe

disappear: kigthíshenoⁿ

dish: uxpé

dish rack: uxpé úzhi

dishtowel: uxpé íbikʰa

dishwasher: uxpé íthizha wéthihide

dislike: ít'athe

divided: basása

divided plate: uxpé basása

dizzy: nóⁿxeskazhi

do: gáxe

do a good job: thípi gáxe

do a push-up: kipímoⁿshi

dog: shíⁿudoⁿ; shínudoⁿ

doings: úzhawa

doll: shíⁿga wasésoⁿ; shíⁿgazhiⁿga

dollar: móⁿzeska

domesticated: wanágthe

done: thishtóⁿ

done (cooked): níde

do one's best: washkóⁿ

door: tizhébe

door cover for a tipi: tí ágaxada

dove: thíta

down: híde

down bottom: hídeata

down the middle (in Handgame): uthízoⁿ

drag: thisnú

dragger: nushnóⁿha

draw: thixú

drawer (for silverware): tehé uzhi

dress: watʰé

dried meat: tá

drink: thatóⁿ

drinking fountain: nitháToⁿ

dripping: ga'é

drive: ábaaze

drop: uthíxpathe

dry: bibíze; bíze

dry something in the open air: gabíze

duck: míxa

duckling: kipáda

dump: bashó^{n}the

during the night: hó^n-do^n

during the time of:-do^n

dust: shíshige

dust devil: mo^{n}gáshude; tadó^{n}he

dust storm: mo^{n}gáshude

dye: ugá; wíuga

each: wó^{n}githe

eager: uhítazhi

eagle: xithá

eagle feather: xithá mó^{n}sho^n

eagle tail-feather war bonnet: mó^{n}sho^{n}pagtho^n

ear: no^{n}xíde

early morning: hé^{n}go^{n}ch^{h}a-xchi

earrings: úwi^n

earth: mo^{n}thí^{n}k^{h}a

earth lodge : mo^{n}thí^n tí

east: mí u'étho^{n}ba-tathisho^n

easy: úmak^{h}a

eat: that^{h}é

egg: wéta

egg-salad sandwich: wéta wamo^{n}ske ubískabe

eggshell: wéta há

eggwhite: wéta ská

egg yolk: uzí; wéta uzí

eight: pethá bthi^n

elbow: astúhi

Elder: (female) Wa'úzhi^{n}ga; (male) I^{n}sh'áge; (both genders) Nó^n; (both genders) Nó^n-xti

elderberry: batúshi

Electric House / Electric Company (in real-estate board game): Thigthíze-tí

electricity: thigthíze

electric skillet: thigthíze wíuho^n

elephant: tibáxiatha

elevate: thimó^{n}shi

elevator: zho^{n}mó^{n}thi^n wanó^{n}mo^{n}shi

eleven: agthí^{n}wi^n

eliminate: bashétho^n

elk: ó^{n}p^{h}o^n

empty: xthu'á

encourage to be active: gtháwasisige

end: uhó^{n}ge

energetic: wasísige

English: Wáxe Íye

English name: Wáxe izházhe

enjoy oneself: gíuzhawa

equal: ékigo^n

even if:-kishte

evening: páze

evergreen tree: mázi

everybody: wó^{n}githe

every day: ó^{n}ba itháugthe

ewe: haxúde mi^{n}ga

exact noon: mithúmo^{n}shi-xti

examine: thiwágazu

Excellent!: Wehéd!

exist: edi

expensive: hégazhi

extend: gazí

extremely: áchoⁿ; átashoⁿ

eye: iⁿshtá

eyeglasses: móⁿze iⁿshtugthoⁿ

eye pupil: iⁿshtási

fabric: waxíⁿha

face: iⁿdé

face towel: iⁿdé íbikʰa

facing a crowd: uthúshi

fail: thi'á

faint: íkipahoⁿ-azhi

fall: kinóⁿse; uxpáthe

fall (season): Toⁿgáxthoⁿ

fall asleep on: ázhoⁿ

fan: iⁿdéagani; wéagani

far away: wéahide

fast: wasékoⁿ

fasten: ugáshke

fasten for someone: égashke

fasten one bit of clothing to another: ágashke

faster: sagígi

fat: shíⁿ

faucet: ní-tʰe thixtóⁿ

feather: móⁿshoⁿ

February: Míxa toⁿga mí agthíi-kʰe

feed: íthishi

feel good: gíudoⁿ

fell by gnawing: thabthízhe

fence: nóⁿze

festivities: úzhawa

field (for playing sports): úshkade

fifteen: agthíⁿ sátoⁿ

fight: ákithe

fill: uzhí

fill with: ubískabe

finger: noⁿbéhi

finger weave: tezhíⁿhiⁿde

finish: íthishethoⁿ

finished: thishtóⁿ

fir: mázi

fire: péde

fire extinguisher: wéganazhi

firefly: wanáxoⁿxoⁿ

firehouse: unáhe tí

fireplace: unéthe

first: pahóⁿga

First Thunder: Mépahoⁿga

fish: hugási; huhú

fist: noⁿbéshka

five: sátʰoⁿ; sátoⁿ

fix: pí'oⁿ

flag: háska

flashing: tʰigthágtha

flatland: snóⁿsnoⁿ

flee: óⁿhe

flee from: gíoⁿhe

flesh: zhú

floodplain: xeút^{h}o^{n}nadi

floor: zho^{n}btháska

flour: wamó^{n}ske xude

flour canister: wamó^{n}ske xude úzhi

flower: waxchá; waxtá

fluffy, fuzzy down feather of a bird: hi^{n}xpé

foal: shó^{n}zhi^{n}ga

fodder: xáde

foggy: shúdemo^{n}ho^n

fold: ubét^{h}o^n

fold in (as a leg): thipúxe

follow (as in tracks or prints): wíuhe

follow or join someone: uíhe

food: wathát^{h}e

food for travel: umó^{n}e

Food o' Plenty: tehé xthu'a

foot: sí; sihí

football: tabé sipá

foot bones: sí wahí

foot of a bluff: xéki; xékigtha

footprints: sígthe

for a long time: káshi

forest: uxthábe

forest with lots of little trees: uch^{h}ízhe

fork: wáku

for that reason: égo^n

forward: éto^{n}thi^n

four: dúba

four at time: dúba-tho^{n}tho^n

Four Hills of Life Building ("weightlifting house": Wéthiho^n Thihó^n Tí

four-legged animal: waníta

fox: tíka

Frankenstein: Zhú etázhi

free: u'ó^{n}thi^{n}ge

French fries: nú zhézhi

fresh meat: tanúka

Friday: Ó^{n}ba Wésato^n

fried chicken: wazhí^{n}ga zhézhi

fried eggs: wéta zhézhi

fried mushrooms: teníxa ugthézhe zhézhi

Friend: K^{h}agé

frisky: wasísige

frog: tébi'a

frost: xéwo^{n}ge

frosting: wawégahi; wawíugahi

frosting can: wawégahi úzhi; wawíugahi úzhi

frozen: dá

fruit: waskíthe

fruit salad: waskíthe ázhi-tho^{n}tho^n íkigthahi

fry: zhézhi

frybread: washí^{n}zhegtho^n

frying pan: wézhezhi

full: ugípi; uzhí

full (from eating): wéno^{n}de

full house: tí ugípi

full of holes: u'úde

full of life: wasísige

fun: úzhawa

gallon: wégo^{n}ze

gallon container: péxeha toⁿga

game: úshkade

garbage: shíshige

garbage can: shíshige úzhi

garters: híthoⁿwiⁿ

gather: bahí; uthéwiⁿthe

gather or assemble people: uthéwiⁿthe

gather or assemble themselves: uthéwiⁿ

gaze: ábanoⁿ

gentle: óⁿthe

get blisters: thidázhe

get blisters (on foot) by walking: noⁿdázhe

get clear: gakíze

get killed by something (e.g. figuratively in cards): ít'e

get oneself out (of jail): kinóⁿshibe

get ready: kigthítoⁿ

get rid of by hitting (as the other team's sticks in Handgame): gathíⁿge

get somebody dressed: óⁿkʰithe

get somebody to give up (a card): gashnúde-kʰithe

get stronger: kigthíwashkoⁿtoⁿga

get through: íhe

get undressed: kigthíhathukathiⁿ

giraffe: pasiáta watháthe

girl: mízhiⁿga

girlfriend: mízhiⁿga ikʰáge

give: í

give a real close haircut: bashná

give up (a card): gashnúde

glad: gíthe; gíudoⁿ

glass: nóⁿxe

gloves: noⁿbéuthishi

glue to: áthaskabe

go: moⁿthíⁿ; thé

goal: uhóⁿge

go along: uhé

go around the outside of something: uthíshoⁿ

goat: héskiba

God: Wakóⁿda

go fishing: hugási

go-getter: wasísige

golden eagle: xithá

gone: thiⁿgé

good: údoⁿ

good at: thipʰí

good-hearted: nóⁿde údoⁿ

good ways: úshk'udoⁿ

goose: míxa toⁿga

gooseberry: pézi

gopher: moⁿthíⁿga

gourd: péxe

gourd rattle: péxeha

grab: uthóⁿ

graduate: ugáshibe

grape: házi

grass: móⁿhiⁿ; pézhe

grass (tallgrass, hay): xáde

grass lodge: xáditi

grave: míxe

gravy: waníde

gray: xúde

gray day: áthixude

graze: wabáhi

grease: wégthi

grease can: wégthi úzhi

green: pézhitu

green-bean casserole: hiⁿbthíⁿge waníde

grind: noⁿtúbe

grizzly bear: moⁿchʰú

groceries: umóⁿe

ground: tóⁿde

groundhog: kinóⁿxe; moⁿthíⁿxude

grow (a plant): thizhútʰoⁿ

grown up: nóⁿ

guard: ákʰihide

gum: zhápe

gun: wahútoⁿthiⁿ

habitually: noⁿ

hackberry: gubéhi

hail: mási

hair of the head: noⁿzhíⁿha

hairy: híⁿshkube

half amount: wiⁿdénoⁿ

half dollar: moⁿsóⁿthiⁿha

half length: wiⁿdétʰoⁿ

half of a thing: wiⁿdéthoⁿska

hallway: tiútʰoⁿnoⁿ

ham: tanúka s'áthe

hamburger: tagáxthixthi

hammer: íⁿ'e wétʰiⁿ

hammer (action word): gadóⁿ

hammer a hole into: ugáxthuge

hand: noⁿbé

hand bones: noⁿbé wahí

Handgame: Íⁿ'utʰiⁿ

handkerchief: noⁿbé íbikʰa

handle: íkoⁿthe

hand towel: noⁿbé íbikʰa

hang from: ugáshke

hang up: ubátʰi

happening suddenly over and over:
    ihéthoⁿthoⁿ

happy: gíshoⁿ; gíthe; nóⁿde gíudoⁿ

hard (as a hard throw): gadíⁿdiⁿ

harder: sagígi

Harvest Celebration: Hédewachʰi

hasten: hiⁿthékithe

hat: watháge

hatchet: móⁿzepe; wétʰiⁿ

hatchling: kipáda

have: athíⁿ

have a conversation with someone: ukíe

have fun: gíuzhawa

have one's own: agtháthiⁿ

have respect for: gíthiezhuba

have something at hand: athíⁿ

having: -egoⁿ

having a good time: úzhawa

hay: xáde

hazelnut: óⁿzhiⁿga

head: pá

head (top and back or whole head, not the face): noⁿshkí

headdress: watháge

headland: ápathage

head or top tip of a pole or a needle: pasí

heads (in coin toss): noⁿshkí-tathishoⁿ

Head Singer: Xúka Nudóⁿhoⁿga

headwrap: paúthishiⁿ

hear: noⁿ'óⁿ

hearing: noⁿxíde; wanóⁿ'oⁿ

heart: nóⁿde

hearth: unéthe

hearts (suit): nóⁿde

heat: nákʰade

heavy: skíge

heavy freezing rain: zigthiⁿgthiⁿ

hen: wazhíⁿga miⁿga

her (possession): etá

her/his Father: Ithádi

her/his Mother: Ihóⁿ

here: théthudi

Here!: Gá!

Here you go (word used when giving something to someone): Gá!

hers: etá

hiccup: baníuski; banúski; níuski; núski

hide: ánoⁿxthe; há

hide jacket: unóⁿzhiⁿha

hide oneself: íkinoⁿxthe

high: móⁿshi

highest: áta

high noon: mithúmoⁿshi-xti

high up: móⁿshi

hill: pahé

hilltop: pahé zúbe

hilly (with no flat places): snóⁿsnoⁿ thiⁿge

hippopotamus: niádi-wakóⁿda

his (possession): etá

hit: utʰíⁿ

hit for (as in clapping for somebody): uítʰiⁿ

hog: kúkusi

hold: uthóⁿ

Hole-in-the-Rock: Íⁿ'e Moⁿshóⁿde; Íⁿ'e U'úde

holes: u'úde

hollow: xthu'á

hoof: sháge

horn: hé

Horn of Plenty: tehé xthu'a

horse: shóⁿge

hospital: wazéthe tí

hot: nákʰade

hotel: uzhóⁿiti

house: tí

houseplant: waxtáhi; zháhi

how?: eyóⁿ

how? explain this: awatʰégoⁿ

however: thoⁿzha

how many?: ánoⁿ

humble: tha'étʰewathe

humid: tíⁿ

humpbacked: t'úse

hungry: no^{n}péhi

hunt: ábae

hunting: ábae

hurry: hi^{n}thékithe; hithé^{n}kithe

hurtling high: gamó^{n}shi

hurtling low: gahíde

I: wí

I agree: égo^n

ice: núxe

icebox: núxe úzhi

ice cream: núxe bawégthi

ice-cream cone: tehé xthu'a égo^n

ice-cream scoop: núxe bawégthi tehé; tehé xthu'a

idea: íthigtho^n

if:-ki; éi^{n}t^{h}e

if (future): at^{h}ó^n-kizhi

ill: wak^{h}éga

I love you: Xcháwigithe

in: mó^{n}t^{h}ata; mó^{n}t^{h}e

in back of: náze

Indian: Ník'shi^{n}ga Uk^{h}éthi^n

in front: itó^{n}thi^{n}ata; pahó^{n}ga; páta; uthúshi

in line: uthúakiwat^{h}o^{n}t^{h}o^n

in pieces: ubúde

inside: mó^{n}t^{h}ata; mó^{n}t^{h}e

internal ear: no^{n}xíde

interpreter: iyéska

in that direction: éta

in the middle: ído^{n}be; uthízo^n

in the wild: mo^{n}táno^{n}di

in this area: théthudi

into the grass or prairie: xádeata

into the timbers: xthabéata

invite someone: gíku

Iron Heart: Nó^{n}deMó^{n}ze

ironing board: wabásada

I said it: ehé

I said it to somebody: égip^{h}e

island: níuthado^n; níutho^{n}da

It is so: égo^n

its: etá

jack (in cards): shénuzhi^{n}ga

jacket: unó^{n}zhi^n

jail: tibúta

January: Hó^{n}ga umúbthi^{n}i-k^{h}e

jar: íthizho^{n}zho^n

jello: waskíthe gashkó^{n}shko^n

Jesus: Wakó^{n}da Izhí^{n}ge

jewelry: wéki'o^n

jog: kinó^{n}sada

joker (in cards): niáshi^{n}ga wawéxaxa; wawéxaxa

journey: ugásho^n

July: Té hút^{h}o^{n}i-k^{h}e

jump: uó^{n}si

jump repeatedly: uó^{n}sisi

jump rope: házhi^{n}ga uó^{n}si; házhi^{n}ga u'ó^{n}sisi

jump up and down: uó^{n}si-tho^{n}tho^n

June: Tenúga míga unái-k^{h}e

juneberry: zhó^{n}xude

just before noon: mithúmoⁿshi-zhiⁿga

just now: íⁿchʰoⁿ

ketchup: wazhíde ágaxtoⁿ

kettle: néxe

keyring: wéthishibe uthóⁿ

kick: noⁿtʰé

kick and send flying: noⁿstáki

kickball: tabé noⁿtʰá

kick excessively: noⁿhégazhi

killing frost: ubíxage

kin: éthe; ukízhi

kind: tha'éwathe; úshk'udoⁿ

kindness: úshk'udoⁿ

king (in cards): iⁿsh'áge

kitchen: úhoⁿ tí

kitchen sink: úhoⁿ tí ukígthizha; uxpé
    ukígthizha

kitten: iⁿgthóⁿga zhiⁿga

knee: shinóⁿde

knife: móⁿhi

knit cap: sáhi watháge; watháge zízige

knock something and send it flying: gastáki

know: íbahoⁿ; thipʰí

Kool-Aid: ní skithe

lacking: thiⁿgé

ladder: uhéatʰoⁿ

lake: niúthishoⁿ

lamb: haxúde zhiⁿga

lance: móⁿdehi

language: íye

lard: wégthi

lasso: ugásnoⁿ

last: háshi

last night: hóⁿ-de

latch: uthídoⁿ

late: wasníde

later: góⁿchʰe

laugh: íxa

laugh out loud: íxa-thahégazhi

lawn: tiútʰoⁿnoⁿ

lay down (cards): gamóⁿthe

lay down one's hand to win: bashéthoⁿ

leaf: zhoⁿ'ábe

learn: íbahoⁿ thé; thipʰí

learn a lot: áhigi thipʰí

leather: há

leave: aíathe

left (side): tháta

left over: ushté

leftover food taken home from a doings or
    feast (prayed over): úthashte

left to someone: uíshte

leg (esp. the lower leg): zhíbe

leg bones: zhíbe wahí

leggings: utóⁿ

lemon: sézi s'áthe

lemonade: sézi s'áthe ní skíthe

lenient: óⁿthe

leopard: iⁿgthóⁿga gthezáza

let (a bird) go: thishtóⁿ

Let's go!: théwathe

lick: thastúbe

lift: bamóⁿshi; thimóⁿshi

lifting pole for a tipi: tesíⁿde ugáshke

lift something easily handled: thihóⁿ

light (action word): nákoⁿ

light (color): sóⁿ

light (not heavy): háhade

lightning: thióⁿba

lightning flash: thióⁿba

lightning fork: thigthíze

light up: unágoⁿba

like (care for, take a liking to): gíudoⁿ;
    xtáthe

like (similar to): égoⁿ

like that: égoⁿ

like this: thégoⁿ

lime (literally 'green'): pézhitu

limit: uhóⁿge

limo: zhoⁿmóⁿthiⁿ

lion: waníta wáxa

listening: wanóⁿ'oⁿ

listen to: ánoⁿ'oⁿ

litter: shíshige

little: zhiⁿgá

little beyond the mark: ákisoⁿde

little bit: júba-xchi

Little Brother (female's): Kʰagézhiⁿga

Little Brother (male's): Kʰágesoⁿga

little toe: sipázhiⁿga

live: níta

lively: wasísige

livestock: wanágthe

load: wa'íⁿ

loaded: uzhí

loan: wagáxe

loathe: ít'athe

lock: uthídoⁿ

locked: ánoⁿse

loganberry: noⁿshámoⁿ

long: snéde

long time: káshi

long Umoⁿhoⁿ dress: watʰé snede

look around: uthíxide

look for: uné

look hard: thiwágazu

Lookout Point: Úthixide Thétha Moⁿzhóⁿ

loud gunshot: múzhawa

loud popping sound: gatúshi

loud singing: thatóⁿga

loud sound of pouring rain: su'é

loud speech: íye sagí

loud yelling: thadíⁿdiⁿ

love: xcháthe; xtáthe

low: híde

lower (a bucket or a shade): thihíde

lucky: éhi

lukewarm: shtáge; sníshtage

lump: táshe; táshi

lunch: míthumoⁿshi wathatʰe

lying down stretched out: thizú'e

machine: wéthihide

Macy: Mási; Umóⁿhoⁿ Tí

make: gáxe

make a basket: ugásnoⁿ

make a basket (in basketball): ugásnoⁿ théthe

make a hollow sound pulling a wagon or a sled: thikúge

make a mound: ába'u

make an effort: washkóⁿ

make noise by shuffling feet around: biíze

make one hungry: ínoⁿpehi

make round by hand: thibúta

man: nú

Man in Charge: Nudóⁿhoⁿga

many: áhigi

maple syrup: zhoⁿní

March: Pénishka mí etái-kʰe

mare: shóⁿge miⁿga

mark: thixú

marker: wébaxu

mashed potatoes: nú basnúsnu

mash or mashed: basnúsnu

mask: iⁿdéugthoⁿ

masquerade dance: iⁿdéugthoⁿ wachʰígaxe

Master of Ceremonies: Éabaha; Iyébaha

mat: ágapuga

match (for starting a fire): péde; péde náxthiⁿ

matching: ékigoⁿ

material: waxíⁿha

mature: Nóⁿ-xti

May: Mí wá'ai-kʰe

maybe: doⁿshteóⁿ

mayonnaise: wawégahi

me: wí

meal: watháтʰe

mealy: noⁿtúbe

mean: xthítu

measure: wégoⁿze

meat: tá; tanúka

medallion: wágthoⁿ

melon: waskíthe

melt: náskoⁿ

metal dish rack: móⁿze gasása

Mhm: égoⁿ

microwave (oven): thigthíze uzhégthoⁿ; thigthíze wíuhoⁿ

midnight: hóⁿskaska

milkweed: waxthá; waxthá moⁿtʰanoⁿha

milkweed bud: waxthá táshe

milkweed soup: Waxthá Taní

milled: noⁿtúbe

mincemeat pie: tanúka ígahi sheúzhegthoⁿ

mind: wathígthoⁿ

mine: wiwíta

mirror: niúkigthaziⁿ

mirror board: niúkigthaziⁿ

miserly: wanítʰe

miss (as in time): noⁿshnóⁿ

miss (as when playing a game): gashnóⁿ

Missouri River: Nishúde

mist: niúbixoⁿ; noⁿzhíⁿ ubixoⁿ; ubíxoⁿ

mittens: noⁿbéuthishi

mix in: uthúgahi

mix together: íkigthahi

moccasin: hi^{n}bé ; hi^{n}bé uk^{h}éthi^n

moist: tí^n

moldy: uséso^n

Monday: Ó^{n}ba Xubé-thishto^n

money: mó^{n}zeska

month: mí

moon: nió^{n}ba

mop: bibíze

morel mushrooms: teníxa ugthézhe

morning: hé^{n}gach^{h}e; hé^{n}go^{n}ch^{h}e;
    ho^{n}égo^{n}ch^{h}e

moss: pézhe

Mother Earth: Í^{n}no^{n}ha Mo^{n}zhó^n; Í^{n}no^{n}ha
    Tó^{n}de

Mother's big sister! (female speaking to):
    Mámato^{n}ga!

Mother's Day: Ihó^n Ó^{n}ba

Mother's little sister! (female speaking to):
    Mámazhi^{n}ga!

mountain: xé

mountain lion: i^{n}gthó^n si^n snéde

mouse: i^{n}ch^{h}ó^{n}ga

mouth: í

move: shkó^n

move (as a piece in a board game): thisnú

move a piece on a boardgame for someone:
    gíthisnu

movement: shkó^n

moving repeatedly by force (as jello
    bouncing): gashkó^{n}shko^n

mulberry: zhó^{n}zi

must: et^{h}égo^n

mustard: washí^n ágaxto^n

my: wiwíta

my (female's) Big Brother: Witínu

my (female's) Big Sister: Wizhó^{n}the

my (female's) Brother-in-Law: Wishí'e

my (female's) female friend: Wihé

my (female's) Little Sister: Wihé;
    Wihézhi^{n}ga; Witó^{n}ge

my (female's) Nephew (brother's son):
    Witúshka

my (female's) Niece (brother's daughter):
    Witúzho^{n}ge

my (female's) Sister-in-Law: Wishíko^n

my (male's) Big Brother: Wizhí^{n}the

my (male's) Brother-in-Law: Witáho^n

my (male's) Nephew (sister's son):
    Witó^{n}shka

my (male's) Sister: Witó^{n}ge

my (male's) Sister-in-Law: Wihó^{n}ga

my (male's) son or daughter: Winísi

my (male's) son or daughter: Winísi

my Aunt (father's sister): Witími

my Daughter: Wizhó^{n}ge

my Daughter-in-Law: Witíni

my Grandchild: Witúshpa

my Grandfather: Witígo^n

my Grandmother: Wikó^n

my Mother: Í^{n}no^{n}ha

my Son: Wizhí^{n}ge

my Son-in-Law: Witó^{n}de

my Uncle (mother's brother): Winégi

nails: sháge

naked: háthukathiⁿ

name: izházhe

napkin: noⁿbé íbikʰa

near: eshóⁿ

neatly dressed: sebé-xchi

neck: núde; páhi

necklace: wanóⁿp'iⁿ

necktie: núde ígatoⁿtha

neckwrap: nudúbetʰoⁿ

needle: wákuzhiⁿga

nevertheless: thoⁿzha

new: téga

next: éduatʰoⁿ

next to: íbiski; sakʰíba

nickel: wéthawa

night: hóⁿ

nighttime: hóⁿ-doⁿ

nine: shóⁿka

noise: za'é

none: thiⁿgé

noon: mí-thoⁿ umóⁿshi; mithúmoⁿshi

noon meal: míthumoⁿshi wathatʰe

normal: ukʰéthiⁿ

Northern Lights: Níkanoⁿxe

nose: pá

not exist: thiⁿgé

November: Táxti hé baxóⁿi-kʰe

now: íⁿchʰoⁿ

numerous: áhigi

ocean: nítoⁿga

October: Táxti kigthígthoⁿi-kʰe; Táxti kigthíxai-kʰe

odor: bthóⁿ

oil: wégthi

old: itóⁿthiⁿadi

Old Mission: Wakóⁿda Wathahoⁿ Niáshiⁿga Iⁿsh'áge

old woman: wa'úzhiⁿga

Omaha: Umóⁿhoⁿ Tóⁿwoⁿgthoⁿ

on: gahá

one: wíⁿ; wiⁿóⁿxchi

one dollar: wíⁿbthuga

one on top of the other: ákigthaha

one thousand dollars: kúge wíⁿ

on the far side: moⁿsóⁿthiⁿ

on the left side: thátatathishoⁿ

on the outside: áshitathishoⁿ

on the right side: wéthitʰoⁿtathishoⁿ

on top: ágaha; paháshi

open: thishíbe

open (eyes): thibthá

open space between houses or rooms: tiútʰoⁿnoⁿ

open the door cover of a tipi onto the poles: áthiaze

open up: gabthá

or: d'shtoⁿ; doⁿshteóⁿ

orange (color): sézi-egoⁿ

orange (fruit): sézi

orange juice: sézi ní

ostrich: wazhíⁿga toⁿga óⁿsagi; wazhíⁿga zhíbe-snéde

ostrich chick: wazhíⁿga toⁿga óⁿsagi-kipáda

other: ázhi

other one: óⁿma

otterskin: nushnóⁿha

otterskin turban: nushnóⁿhapagthe

out: gashíbe

outhouse: tízhiⁿga

out in the woods: uxthábe

out of bounds: gashíata

out of money: xóⁿ

out of sight: wathíshnazhi

outside: ágaha; áshiata

oven: uzhégthoⁿ; uzhéoⁿhe; úzhioⁿhe

overboots: hiⁿbéagahadi; hiⁿbéakigthaha

overcast: ámoⁿxpi; áthixude

owl: pánuhu

packet (as of sugar): wagthábaze úzhi

packing: íⁿ; wa'íⁿ

paint (activity): wíuga

paint (liquid): wíuga

paint (something): ugá

pajamas: hóⁿ-doⁿ háthe; hóⁿ-doⁿ wáthaha

pale: sóⁿ

pan: wíuhoⁿ

panther: iⁿgthóⁿ siⁿ snéde

pants: níⁿde uthíshi; níⁿdushi; niⁿdúthishi

paper: wabthágaze; wagthábaze; waxíⁿha

park: úshkade

parking: unóⁿshtoⁿ

part: hébe

part of: hébe

pass: íhe; uhé

pass out: íkipahoⁿ-azhi

past afternoon: mithúmoⁿshiadi

paste: wéathaskabe

path: uhé; utʰónoⁿ

pathway: tiútʰoⁿnoⁿ

paycheck: wawéshi

paying attention: wákʰihide

pay off a debt: bashéthoⁿ

peacock: wazhíⁿga íⁿbe gabthá

peanut: óⁿzhiⁿga

peel: thizhábe

peel for someone: gíthizhabe

pelvic bone: siⁿdéhi wahí

pen: wébaxu; wébaxuni

pencil: wébaxu

penguin: míxa níkashiⁿga égoⁿ

penny: wéthawa zhíde

people pressed together: ubísoⁿde

perfume: nubthóⁿ

person: niáshiⁿga; níkashiⁿga; ník'shiⁿga

phone: móⁿze íutha

pickle: kukúmi

pickle juice: kukúmi ní

pick up: bahí; thizé

pie: sheúzhegthoⁿ

piece of: hébe

piece of land: moⁿzhóⁿ basása

pig: kúkusi

pigeon: thíta

piglet: kúkusi zhiⁿga

pillow: íⁿbehi

pin: ithágashke; wágthoⁿ; wákuzhiⁿga

pine: mázi

pineapple: séziniuzhi

pink: zhí-egoⁿ

pin on for someone: égashke

pitcher: níuzhi

pitiful: tha'étʰewathe

pity: tha'éthe

pizza: sheúzhegthoⁿ

place: itʰéthe

place upright on (as a feather in hair): ábaxoⁿ

place where you sit or live: ugthíⁿ

plant: hí; waxtáhi

plants: pézhe

plate: uxpé

play: shkáde

play against: áki

play against each other: íkikoⁿ

playing card: wathíbaba

pleased: gíshoⁿ

pleasure: úzhawa

plume: móⁿshoⁿ

plum seed: kóⁿsi

point at: ábazu

pole for a tipi: tíshi

poor: waxpáthiⁿ

poor tax (real estate board game): waxpáthiⁿ wagáxe

pop (in a pop can): nígatushi

pop (sweet beverage): ní skithe

porcupine: páhiⁿ

pot: wíuhoⁿ

pot (in gambling): wéshi

potato: nú

potholder: weáthitabe

pound: gadóⁿ

pound fine: gatúbe

pour (water) on to cool something: ámusni

pour on: ágaxtoⁿ

pour out: bashóⁿthe

pouting: wazhíⁿshte

powder: bthípe

powdery: tubáthe

Pow-Wow: Hédewachʰi

practice speaking: íkigthaskoⁿthe

prairie: snóⁿsnoⁿ

prairie chicken: shú

prairie dog: kinóⁿxe; moⁿthíⁿxude

praiseworthy: óⁿxtiwathe

press: bispóⁿ

press (a weight): bamóⁿshi

pretend to sleep: zhóⁿ gáxe

pretty: újoⁿ

prize: wéshi

proud: íkizhu

provisions: umóⁿe

pudding: waskíthe

puffy: p^{h}úga

pull: thidó^n; thisnú

pull hard: thidí^{n}di^n

pull upward: bimó^{n}shi

puma: i^{n}gthó^n si^n snéde

pumpkin pie: wat^{h}ó^n sheúzhegtho^n

puppy: shínudo^n zhi^{n}ga

purchase: thiwí^n

purple: házi-ego^n

purse: mó^{n}zeska úzhi

push a pole through a loop: basnó^n

push down: uthúbido^n

push or shove: bahé

push out: bashíbe

put: it^{h}éthe

put a spit through food to roast it: basnó^n

put away: it^{h}éthe

put everything in its proper place: thishúpa

put in: uzhí

put into: ugthó^n

put it away by laying it flat: ihéthe

put on: ó^n; unó^{n}zhi^n

put on (as a ring): ubásno^n

put on (head): thagé

put on a necktie or a fanbelt: uthísno^n

put or place something globular: ithó^{n}the

put up (as a tipi): thimó^{n}gthe

Q-Tip: no^{n}xíde wéthisihi

quarter dollar: miká'e íthawa

queen (in cards): wa'ú

question: wémo^{n}xe

quiet: xthíazhi

quillwork: páhi^n; páhi^{n}bat^{h}e

rabbit: mo^{n}shtí^{n}ga

raccoon: miká

racket: wét^{h}i^n zázade

racquetball: wazhí^{n}ga zhi^{n}ga ut^{h}í^n

radio: mó^{n}ze wao^n

rag man: waxí^{n}ha niáshi^{n}ga

railroad: éwazhi^{n}no^{n}ge

rain: no^{n}zhí^n

rainbow: tushníge

raincoat: no^{n}zhí^n uno^{n}zhi^n

raise (as a tipi): thimó^{n}gthe

raise (as money): uthéwi^{n}the

raise (bring to maturity): thizhút^{h}o^n

raise money for someone: uthéwi^{n}k^{h}ithe

raise up into the air: thimó^{n}shi

raisin pie: házi sheúzhegtho^n

rake: wéthibexi^n

rancid: piázhi

raspberry: agthó^{n}gamo^{n}ge

rat: i^{n}ch^{h}ó^{n}ga to^{n}ga

rattle: gasáthu; péxe; thisáthu

ravine: mo^{n}á

read: áthade

really: -xchi; -xti

recite: áthade

recognize: thiwágazu

record: waó^n wathize

recording (sound): waó^n wathize

red: zhíde

refer to: éwakʰe

refrigerator: núxe úzhi; sníuzhi

regularly: noⁿ

rehearse: íkigthaskoⁿthe

related: éthe

relative: éthe; ukízhi

relaxed: óⁿthe

release (a prisoner): thishtóⁿ

remaining: ushté

remember: gisíthe

remove corn from the cob by hand: thizhú

remove kernels from the cob by hand:
   thishpí

rent: wagáxe

repair: pí'oⁿ

reptile: wagthíshka

required: etʰégoⁿ

respect: thiézhube

rest: ígashnoⁿ; kióⁿze

rest (of something): ushté

rest stop: unóⁿshtoⁿ

rib: thítiⁿ

ribbon: waxíⁿha nágoⁿba

ribbonwork: wábatʰe

rib cage: tethítiⁿ wahí; thítiⁿ wahí

ride (as a horse): ágthiⁿ

ridge: áthiⁿ

right (side): wéthitʰoⁿ

ring: noⁿbéuthixthoⁿ

ripe: níde

roach: táhiⁿwagthoⁿ

roach spreader: táhiⁿwagthoⁿ uthí'ae

road: uhé

robe: wáiⁿ

rock: íⁿ'e

roll: thinóⁿge

roll (as a rock or dice): ganóⁿge

roll (bread): wamóⁿske buta

rolling hilly land: bahóⁿhoⁿ

rolling pin: wamóⁿske íbibthaska

room: tiútʰoⁿnoⁿ; utʰónoⁿ

rooster: wazhíⁿga nuga

rope: házhiⁿga; wékoⁿtʰoⁿ

rough (with no flat places): snóⁿsnoⁿ thiⁿge

round: búta

round-dance: kigthíbuta wachʰígaxe

round peak: bazú

routinely: noⁿ

rub: bigúde; bizhú

rubber: hazízige

rubber boots: hiⁿbéagahadi;
   hiⁿbéakigthaha

run: tóⁿthiⁿ

run a machine: nóⁿgethe

run excessively: noⁿhégazhi

run out (as food): thiⁿgé

sacred grounds: moⁿzhóⁿ waxúbe

sad: gítha-bazhi

saddle or notch between bluffs: skída

safety pin: wéagashke

salad: waxthá íkigthahi

salt: niskíthe

same: ékigoⁿ

sash: ípithage

Saturday: Hithái

sausage: tagáxthixthi

say: é

say it to somebody: égithoⁿ

scalp: noⁿzhíⁿha

scare: báaze

scarecrow: niáshiⁿga xáde ígahi

scared: kúhe

scarf: núde ígatoⁿtha; nudúbetʰoⁿ;
    paúthishiⁿ

school: tápuska

scissors: ithábashna

scratch: thi'ú

scream: bóⁿ; bóⁿ thahégazhi

screw: uthígtheze

scrub: bigúde

sea: nítoⁿga

seal: huhú shnaha

search for: uné

seat: ágthiⁿ

seat someone: gthíⁿkʰithe

see: dóⁿbe

seed: sí

seek: uné

send: théthe

senses: wíubesniⁿ

sense something: ubésniⁿ

September: Táxti moⁿnóⁿ'ai-kʰe

serve: shígthe

serving spoon: tehé toⁿga

set: itʰéthe

set straight: thiwágazu

seven: péthoⁿba

seven Tribal Council seats: Gahíye Ugthiⁿ
    Pethoⁿba

sew: batʰé

shade (curtain): óⁿaze

shake (as a spray can): íthizhoⁿzhoⁿ

shake a gourd: gasáthu; thisáthu

shake something: ígazhoⁿzhoⁿ

sharp rocky peak: baxú

shave: bashná

shave off: bashná

shawl: wáiⁿ; wáiⁿgthabe

sheep: haxúde

shelf: úzhi kúge

shine: unágoⁿba

shirt: unóⁿzhiⁿ

shiver: kipáshizhe

shoe: hiⁿbé

shoelaces: hiⁿbékoⁿ

shoot: kʰíde

shoot at: kʰíde

shoot cards: kʰíde

shop: úthiwiⁿ tí

short: chéshka

shorts: níⁿdushi-móⁿtʰe; niⁿdúthishi-
    móⁿtʰe

shot: móⁿzemoⁿ

shoulder: iⁿkʰéde

show kindness to: tha'éthe

show to: gíbaha

shuffle or deal out (cards): basníde

sick: wakʰéga

side: moⁿsóⁿthiⁿ

side (body part): thi'é

side by side: égazeze

sidestitch choker: úwiⁿgazoⁿde

sift: múzhoⁿ

silent: xthíazhi

silver: móⁿzeska

silver cuff: áuthisnoⁿ

silver dollar: móⁿzeska wíⁿbthuga

simple: ukʰéthiⁿ

sing (in Ceremony): xúka

singer (in Ceremony): xúka

singing: wáoⁿ

sink (as a boat): uspé

sink (as in kitchen): ukígthizha

sit: gthíⁿ

sit on: ágthiⁿ

sit up: kipáhoⁿ

six: shápe

skate: núzoⁿ 'óⁿ

skeleton: wahí niáshiⁿga

sketch: thixú

skewer: basnóⁿ

ski: gasnú gi'óⁿ

skilled: thipʰí

skillet: néxe; wézhezhi

skin: há; zhú

skinny: xthá

skirt: watʰé

skull: noⁿshkí wahí

skunk: móⁿga

skunk an opponent: móⁿga gaxe

skunk hand: móⁿga

Skunk Hollow: Móⁿga Úhe

sky: móⁿxe

slap down (cards): gasóⁿthe

slap someone: gachʰáki

sled: núzoⁿ 'óⁿ

sleep: zhóⁿ

sleep on: ázhoⁿ

sleet: zizígthe

slice in half: umásnoⁿ

slide: gasnú; wágthoⁿ

slip (while walking): noⁿshnáha

slippery: shnahá

slow: óⁿthe ; wasníde

smack: gachʰáki

small: zhiⁿgá

small child: shíⁿgazhiⁿga

small spoon: tehé zhiⁿga

smear on: áthaha

smell: bthóⁿ

smell something: uthíbthoⁿ

smile: íxazhiⁿga

smoke flaps for a tipi: tíha ugábthiⁿtha

smoke hole for a tipi: shúde íhe; tíhukoⁿ

smooth: shnahá

snail: nihá

snake: wés'a

snap (fingers): thitúshi

snap (fingers) multiple times: thitútushi

snapping turtle: ké toⁿga

snow: máthe

snowflake: masóⁿ

snowing: máthe

so: égoⁿ

soap: wéthitega

soapbox: wéthitega úzhi

Social Services Building: Wathíze Tí

socks: hiⁿbékuwiⁿxe

soft: xu'é

soil: moⁿthíⁿkʰa

some: dúba

someone who receives help: wathíze

sometimes: atʰóⁿshte

somewhere: águdishte

Sorry (as said in the board game): Uthúama

sound of drums beating: gakúku

sound of something hollow falling: gakúge

soup: taní

South Sioux City: Sháoⁿ Tóⁿwoⁿgthoⁿ
  Nishúde-thégi-thishoⁿ

sow: kúkusi miⁿga

space in the middle of a building or village:
  utʰónoⁿ

spades (suit): móⁿzepe

spatula: wébasoⁿtha

speak: íye

speak loudly or excessively: thahégazhi

spear: móⁿdehi

speech: íye

speedy: wasékoⁿ

spider: ukígthiske; ukígthiski

spin (a wheel): thikúwiⁿxe

spin around: kúwiⁿxe

spine: nóⁿxahi

spirit: wanóⁿxe

Spirit Plate: Wapʰígthe

split by cutting: másne

spooked: kúhe

spooky house: kúhe ti

spoon: tehé

spouse: thanóⁿ

spread (as fingers or tailfeathers): thixáde

spread on: ábishnabe

spread open: thibthá

spread out (a bedsheet): gabthá

spread the fingers: thizhádoⁿ

spring (season): Mépahoⁿga

spring snow: mémathe

sprinkle: ubíxoⁿ

sprinkle on: áthi'e

spruce: mázi

spry: wasísige

squeezed close together: ubísoⁿde

squint: xóⁿxoⁿ

squirrel: síⁿga

stab: zháhe

stairstep: úhe

stairway: uhéatʰoⁿ

stakes for a tipi: tiúthugadoⁿ

stalk: hí

stand: nonzhín

standing in a line: ukiáwathonthon

stand on: áthon

star: miká'e

star quilt: miká'e wáin púga

start something rolling: thinónge

start to: thithé

stash underground: ánon'u

station: unónshton

steady sound: xu'é

steal: monthón

steamy: up'úthon

stem: hí

stem of a plant: zháhi

step: úhe

stick: zhónzhinga

Stickball: Tabégasi

stick onto something: ábiskabe

sticks used to weave the front flap of a tipi: tíha uthón; tíhuthon; tíshi uthón; tíshuthon

still: shethónnon; shónshon

stingy: waníthe

stir: uthúgahi

stitch: bathé

stomach: níxa

stone: ín'e

stop eating or drinking: thashtón

stop running: nonshtón

stop singing: thashtón

stop talking: thashtón

store: úthiwin tí

story: íutha

stove: mónze unéthe; unéthe; uzhéonhe

straight: thúton; wégazu

straighten out (as an arm or fabric): thisáda

straighten up (the house): thisíhi

strainer: uxpé ugá'u'ude

strain out: múzhon

strap: házhinga

stray off: múgthon

street: uhé

strength: úwashkon

stretch (oneself): kigtházi

stretchy fabric: hazízige

strike camp and move tipi: wahón

striker: wéthin

strong: washkóntonga

strong (coffee or cider): múpa

stuffing: wamónske íkigthahi; wamónske ubískabe

stuff with: ubískabe

stumble: kinónse

suddenly: sabázhi

sugar: zhonní

sugar canister: zhonní úzhi

summer: Monshté; Nugé; Nugé Monshte

sun: mí

Sunday: Ónba Waxúbe; Ónba Xubé

sundog: minéthe

sunrise: mí éthonbe

swallow: thasní^n

swap: íkikawi^{n}the

sweater: unó^{n}zhi^n zízige

sweat lodge: tiúthipu

sweeper: tibábexi^n-no^n

sweet: skíthe

sweet potato: núskithe

sweets: waskíthe

swelling: táshe; táshi

swim: hítha

swine: kúkusi

switch: íkikawi^{n}the

syrup: zho^{n}ní snúsnu

table: wáthat^{h}e

taffy: zho^{n}ní zízige

tail: sí^{n}de

taildancer: sí^{n}de

tails (in coin toss): sí^{n}de-tathisho^n

take: thizé

take away: íno^{n}she

take charge of: íthigtho^n

take pity on: tha'éthe

talk: íye

tall: mo^{n}shíadi; snéde

talons: sháge

tame: washtáge

tape: weáthaskabe; wéathaskabe

taste: ígasko^{n}the; thastúbe

tattered: u'úde

tax: wagáxe

tea: xáde mo^{n}ko^n

teacher: wagó^{n}ze

teach someone: gió^{n}ze

telephone: mó^{n}ze íutha

television: úgaxeshko^{n}shko^n

tell (the news): uthá

tell someone: uítha

tell someone to do something: ágazhi

ten: gthébo^n

thank you: Wíbthaho^n

that: shé

that exact one: gá

that over there: shéhi

that's all: éno^n

that's all / we're done: shó^n

that's all I have to say: Shéno^n

that way: éta

thaw: násko^n

the (living plural, main actor):-ama

the (living plural, not the main actor):-ma;
   -tho^{n}k^{h}a

the (living singular, main actor):-ak^{h}a

the (living singular, not the main actor):
   -thi^{n}k^{h}e

the (living singular moving, not the main
   actor):-thi^n

the (living standing, not the main actor):
   -t^{h}o^n

the (nonliving horizontal or flat):-k^{h}e

the (nonliving round, bundled, hanging):
   -tho^n

the (nonliving scattered here and there):
   -ge

the (nonliving standing or group):-tʰe

their: etá

theirs: etá

then: edi

the Old People: Nóⁿ-ama; Nóⁿ-xti-ama

there: edi

therefore: égoⁿ

thick: shkúbe

thicket: uchʰízhe

thin: xthá

think about: síthe

think something: ethégoⁿ

this (coming) afternoon: mithúmoⁿshi-ki

this evening: páze-ki

this way: dúde

thought: íthigthoⁿ

thousand: kúge

thread: wahóⁿ

thread a needle: uthísnoⁿ

three: thábthiⁿ

throat: núde

throw: óⁿtha théthe; théthe

throw a loop over something: ugásnoⁿ

throw away: óⁿtha théthe

thump: gakúge

thunder: iⁿgthóⁿhutoⁿ

Thursday: Óⁿba Wéduba

tick: táthazapa

tie: íkoⁿtʰoⁿ; kóⁿtʰoⁿ

tie (as a horse): ugáshke

tilted or fallen by flooding or shooting:
  múathikoⁿ

timbers: uxthábe

time: miídoⁿbe

tin can: móⁿze úzhi

tin foil: móⁿze betʰóⁿtʰoⁿ; móⁿze ubétʰoⁿ

tipi: tiísoⁿthe

tipi liner: tizhébe ugthóⁿ

tipi (when already up): timóⁿgthe

toaster: wanáxude ígaxe

tobacco: niní

tobacco bag: niní úzhiha

today: óⁿbathe

toddler: shíⁿgazhiⁿga

toe: sipá

together: zhúgthe

together on: ázoⁿde

toilet brush: unézheti wéthisihi

toilet paper: ígadi; unézheti wagthábaze

tomahawk: wétʰiⁿ

tomato: wazhíde

tomorrow: gasóⁿthiⁿ

tomorrow afternoon: mithúmoⁿshi-ki

tomorrow morning: héⁿgoⁿchʰe-ki

tongs: wébashnade

tongue: théze

tonight: hóⁿ-ki

too:-shti; edábe

tool: wéthihide

too much: áchoⁿ; átashoⁿ

tooth: hí

toothpaste: hi-wéthizha

Tootsie Pop: zhoⁿní buta zhóⁿzhiⁿga
  utháha

topping on food: ágaxto^n

tornado: tadésagi to^{n}ga; tadó^{n}he to^{n}ga

tortoise: ké to^{n}ga

toss: gamó^{n}shi théthe

touch: ábit^{h}e

tough: wasísige

tow: thisnú

toward the ground: tó^{n}deatathisho^n

toward the sky: mó^{n}xeatathisho^n

town: tó^{n}wo^{n}gtho^n

track: sígthe

trade places: íkikawi^{n}the

trail: sígthe

train: éwazhi^{n}no^{n}ge

transform oneself: kigthíazhi

trash: shíshige

trash container: shíshige úzhi

travel: ugásho^n

tree: xthabé

tree branch: gaxá

trees: uxthábe

Tribal Circle: Húthuga

Tribal Council Chair: Gahíye Nudó^{n}ho^{n}ga

Tribal Council Member: Gahíye Niashi^{n}ga

Tribal Council Vice-Chair: Gahíye
Nudó^{n}ho^{n}ga Wéno^{n}ba

Tribal Council vice-chair : Gahíye Wéno^{n}ba

Tribal Farm: Umó^{n}ho^n Wá'ai

trip: kinó^{n}se

truck: wétugtho^n

trunk: hí

try: ígasko^{n}the

try hard: washkó^n

try together: íkigthasko^{n}the

Tuesday: Ó^{n}ba Wéno^{n}ba

tug-of-war: házhi^{n}ga thidó^n

turkey: zizíka

turn (a doorknob or a faucet handle):
thikúwi^{n}xe

turn around: kigthíso^{n}the; kúwi^{n}xe

turn off: áno^{n}se; thinázhi

turn on: thinó^{n}ge

turn on the lights: thináko^n

turn on the water in a sink: umúto^{n}thi^n

turn over: thisó^{n}the

turn over (as food with spatula): íbasho^{n}the

turtle: ké

TV: úgaxeshko^{n}shko^n

twelve: shápe no^{n}ba

twilight: ho^{n}nó^{n}paze; páze

twist (as a rope): thisó^{n}the

two: no^{n}bá

two at a time: no^{n}bá-tho^{n}tho^n

ugly: piázhi

Umo^{n}ho^n (describing word): Umó^{n}ho^n

Umo^{n}ho^n braid ties: gazó^{n}de íko^{n}te

Umo^{n}ho^n person: Umó^{n}ho^n

unconscious: íkipaho^n-azhi

under: kigthá

underneath: mó^{n}t^{h}ata

undershirt: unó^{n}zhi^n mó^{n}t^{h}e

underskirt: wat^{h}é mo^{n}t^{h}e

underwear: ní^{n}dushi-mó^{n}t^{h}e; ni^{n}dúthishi-
mó^{n}t^{h}e

undress: kigthíhathukathiⁿ

unexpectedly: sabázhi

uphill: tóⁿdeata

upon: gahá

upright: móⁿgthe

upstairs: paháshi-ta

us: óⁿgu

use: óⁿ

utensil: wéthihide

vacuum cleaner: tí wéthisihi

valley: uspé

vanilla (ice cream): ská

various: ázhi-thoⁿthoⁿ

vegetation: pézhe

velcro for someone: égashke

very:-xchi;-xti; áchoⁿ; átashoⁿ

vest: itháthisoⁿde; unóⁿzhiⁿ xépa

viaduct: uhéatʰoⁿ

visit: tiúpe

voice: hú

Volkswagen bug: kinóⁿnoⁿge buta

vomit: gthébe

wager: wéshi

wagon: zhoⁿmóⁿthiⁿ

waist: tashtáde

wait: noⁿhébe

wait for: épe; ithápe

wake up: íkithe

walk: kinóⁿsada; moⁿthíⁿ

walk excessively: noⁿhégazhi

walking: noⁿshtóⁿ

walkway: utʰónoⁿ

wall of a tipi: tinóⁿde

walnut: táge

walnut shell: tágeha

Walthill: Iⁿshʼáge Tóⁿwoⁿgthoⁿ

wander away: múgthoⁿ

want: góⁿtha

want to: góⁿtha

warm: shtíde

warm weather: moⁿshté

warrior's dance originated by the Umoⁿhoⁿ
    tribe: Hethúshka

wash: thizhá

washing machine: háthe wéthizha

wash oneself: kigthízha

wash up: kigthízha

watch: ábanoⁿ; ákʰihide; miídoⁿbe

watch out for oneself: ákikʰihide

water: ní

water balloon: hazízige ni uzhi

wave to: wawégaxe

ways: úshkoⁿ

we: óⁿgu

weak: washkóⁿ thiⁿgé

wear: óⁿ; áthaha

wear (on head): thagé

wear (on legs): utóⁿ

wear (on torso): unóⁿzhiⁿ

Wednesday: Óⁿba Wéthabthiⁿ

weedy: uchʰízhe

weight (for exercise): mó^{n}zeskige

weight (for weighing something down or exercise): wéthihide

Wellness Center: Niyé-thi^{n}ge Tí

we said it to somebody: eó^{n}githo^n

west: mí-ithé-tathisho^n

wet: núka

whale: huhú to^{n}ga

what?: i^{n}dádo^n

what did you say?: edéshe

what does it mean?: awat^{h}égo^n

what's going on?: eáto^n

what's the matter?: eáto^n

wheel: kigthíso^{n}the

when:-ki

when?: at^{h}ó^n

when? (future): at^{h}ó^n-ki

when? (past): at^{h}ó^n-di

whenever:-kizhi

where?: águdi

where (something) appears: uétho^{n}ba

where did you come from?: awagí

where to (is someone going)?: áwata

while: do^n

whipman: wanó^{n}she

whirlwind: tadó^{n}he

whistle: nisúde

white: ská

White (descriptive term for ethnicity or race): Wáxe

whiteboard: zho^{n}btháskaska

White person: Wáxe

who?: ebé

whole eagle headdress: xitháthage; xitháwathage

why?: eáto^n

wild: mó^{n}t^{h}ano^{n}ha

wildcat: waníta mo^{n}t^{h}ano^{n}ha

win: uhí

wind: tadé

window: wíugo^{n}ba

windy: tadésagi

winged ones: wazhí^{n}ga

winter: Gashúde; Mágashude; Usní

wipe: bibíze; bik^{h}á

witch: wa'ú piazhi

wolf: shó^{n}to^{n}ga

wolf man: shó^{n}to^{n}ga niáshi^{n}ga

woman: wa'ú

woolen robe: haxúde

woozy: nó^{n}xeskazhi

word: íye

work: wathít^{h}o^n

worm: wagthíshka

woven part above the door of a tipi: títhumo^{n}ho^n

woven straw: sáhi

wrap: ubét^{h}o^n

wreck: gatúbe

write: baxú

write down: ábaxu

write on: ábaxu

yarn: wahóⁿ

year: umóⁿthiⁿka

yell: bóⁿ; bóⁿ thahégazhi

yellow: zí

yes: Áoⁿ; égoⁿ; Óⁿhoⁿ

yesterday: sidádi

yesterday evening: pázeadi

yet: shetʰóⁿnoⁿ

you: thí

young: zhiⁿgá

young man: shénuzhiⁿga

young woman: shémizhiⁿga

your: thithíta

yours: thithíta

you said it: eshé

you said it to somebody: égishe

zebra: shóⁿge gthéze

zoo: waníta tí

Part 2

Lessons from the Omaha Language Class
at the University of Nebraska–Lincoln

Cultural Lessons 9

Mark Awakuni-Swetland, Wagǫ́ⁿze Ūthiɣide

9.1 WHAT IS CULTURE? WHAT IS LANGUAGE?

Sooner or later all of us use the term *culture* in our walk of life. Phrases such as "Indian culture," "Omaha culture," and "hip-hop culture" express many different things depending upon the context of the conversation. A single definition of the term is difficult, but we can consider the following as our working model: culture is the beliefs, customs, practices, and social behavior of a particular nation or people passed on from generation to generation by learning.

The term *society* is often used interchangeably with the term *culture*. For our purposes, society can be considered to be the various modes of interaction among people. Society is the visible expression of, and is guided by, the underlying cultural concepts. So we can talk about social organization, subsistence strategies, economic strategies, warfare, rituals, and settlement patterns as parts of a group's society. A way to remember this difference is to say that culture

is the concepts of the group while society is the structures or actions of the group.

We can consider some of the characteristics of culture. The first important characteristic of culture is that it is learned. Culture is not inherited. The color of our eyes and texture of our hair is genetically determined. Culture is learned through socialization in the family,

FIG. 5. (*top left*) Drum Circle by Jacob Smith.

FIG. 6. (*above*) Flag Raising by Jacob Smith.

245

from peers, superiors, the community at large, and institutions.

Culture is symbolic and includes both verbal and non-verbal symbols. Language is a symbol system and it is essential to the maintenance and perpetuation of culture. Some symbols are universal; some are culturally specific. Information and ideas are presented in symbolic ways. For example, flags, gestures, and icons hold symbolic meaning that can vary between cultures. We will examine language in greater detail in a moment.

Culture is general and all-encompassing. It covers everything seen, heard, and experienced by humans. It includes even the smallest details of life, such as which hand to extend when greeting someone or whether it is acceptable to belch in public.

Culture is specific; that is to say it is associated with a specific language and a set of beliefs and behaviors. Hence we can talk about "American culture," "Omaha culture," and "Washington Beltway culture."

Culture is shared with relatives, neighbors, and the community. There is no culture-of-one. Culture is patterned. By that we mean it is scheduled, periodic, seasonal, cyclical, and often based on what is happening in the universe or surrounding environment. Events usually follow a pattern, so we all know what to expect at a birthday party, powwow, or handgame.

Culture is used creatively. There is usually an "ideal" or "perfect world" culture. Investigation and observation can often uncover the actual "practiced" or "real" culture. For example, in the Omaha ideal culture, clan membership is described as patrilineal (traced through the father's lineage). In practice, however, there are many examples where clan membership is matrilineal (traced through the mother's lineage) or jumps a generation and crosses to the mother's mother's clan. This may indicate the working of an even deeper ideal culture value of "inclusion" that outranks the ideal culture value of patrilineal clan membership.

Culture is not static or set in stone. Some parameters of culture may not change easily. For example, the practice of polygamy or the use of the death penalty may be slow to change. Other parameters are more pliable and can change quickly. For example, when I was adopted by Charles and Elizabeth Stabler (see Awakuni-Swetland contributor biography) and then named into the I^{n}k^{h}ésabe, Black Shoulder Buffalo Clan, as a young boy, buffalo and beef head meat became taboo to me. My white parents immediately quit serving beef tongue at our family dinners, much to the delight of my brothers and sisters, who never really liked eating beef tongue.

Culture can be both adaptive and maladaptive. Culture adapts as environmental conditions change. So as group size increases, there may be a shift from hunting and gathering to reliance upon agriculture. Other changes may appear to solve a short-term problem but create new problems for the future. For example, some subarctic Indigenous peoples used to practice female infanticide. Additional baby girls would be killed if there were insufficient male hunters or game animals to feed another person. While solving the immediate problem of survival in a harsh environment, years later it would lead to a shortage of marriageable females for the higher population of surviving males.

Now that we understand the concept of culture, let us consider the primary vehicle by which culture is transmitted to the next generation: language. Language is a system for the communication, in symbols, of any kind of information. A symbol is any sound, gesture, object, behavior, or idea with a meaning assigned to it by a group of people. Humans are capable of teaching and using a complex symbol system, passed on through enculturation (the process by which a society's culture is passed on from one generation to the next). Therefore symbolic communication is the mode of transmitting cultural ideas. Language is part of culture (shared concepts). It is essential to the maintenance and perpetuation of culture.

Culturally specific symbols are ideas, things, and values with special meaning in a single culture. While languages differ from each other as message systems based on culture, language itself is a unifying factor of humanity. We can say that language is the most critical factor that makes us "human."

All languages share several defining characteristics. Language has semantic universality. It is a communication system that can convey information on all aspects of life, places, events, and properties. Language can place events in the past, present, and future.

Human language is infinitely productive. Messages can be continuously expanded without losing efficiency. For example, I can say: I went / I went home / I went home after the game / I went home after the game to eat supper / I went home after the game to eat supper before going to the movie / . . .

Language also has the property of displacement. Communication can occur regardless of whether the sender or receiver has immediate sensory contact with whatever the message refers to. Therefore I can describe a person to you without that person being present, or give you directions to a location that you have never seen. The infinite productivity and displacement qualities of human language are what separate humans from the call system of primates and other animals. The ability to speak is species specific.

Humans are genetically determined to have the ability to speak but do not inherit the particular language that they will speak after birth. The ear, mouth, tongue, and brain are examples of a genetic predisposition for language. The universal grammar (UG) is a genetically transmitted blueprint for language, a basic linguistic plan in the human brain. Fundamental similarities in all of the world's languages support the theory of a universal innate grammar. The actual language a person speaks depends upon exposure. The UG can be envisioned as a limited set of options. As babies are exposed to a target language they will automatically match what is being heard to the UG options. For example, let us take two twin babies and separate them at birth. One baby is raised in an Omaha-speaking home. The other is raised in an English-speaking home. The first baby will grow up speaking only Omaha, which has a subject-object-verb word order. The identical twin will grow up speaking only English, which has a subject-verb-object word order. It is all about the environment in which we live, not the particular genes that make up our body.

Communication in humans includes spoken language, signs, color systems, hieroglyphics, and writing. There are numerous modes of writing and symbolizing a language. Some examples relevant to Omaha include the various orthographies (writing systems) used by James Owen Dorsey in the late nineteenth and early twentieth centuries, the Fletcher and La Flesche system, the current Umóⁿhoⁿ Nation and University of Nebraska–Lincoln system, the NETSIOUAN computer-friendly system, and all the personal orthographies of Omaha tribal members past and present.

Words create an image in the mind. Language is often combined with gestures. Emotions can also be conveyed through gestures. Body language can include posture, the physical space between sender and receiver, and whether there is eye contact.

Linguistic Anthropology is the study of language as it relates to humans. It has three broad areas of interest. Descriptive Linguistics involves the construction of any single language, its rules, presentation, and iconography. Practitioners develop metalinguistic terms that give them the ability to talk "about" the language.

Historical Linguistics reconstructs the history of contemporary and ancient languages and may compare multiple languages. This approach is useful in studying the migration patterns of humans. Historical linguists develop a language family tree as a visual reconstruction of the chronology of change and division in related languages. The further apart two languages appear on the tree represents the greater differences between the two languages. Practitioners may attempt to reconstruct a "proto" language from which a family tree theoretically evolved. Of interest to Omaha language students is the reconstruction of a Proto-Siouan language from which the whole of the Siouan language family has emerged over time.

Sociolinguistics is focused on how language is used within the cultural group, within segments of society, and in code-switching. Code-switching refers to shifting between formal and informal forms of speech, and between distinct ethnic or social group languages. For example, when meeting a buddy on the playground I might informally say, "Howzit goin'?" Meeting an adult or teacher I would be more formal and say, "How are you?"

This textbook explains many of the structural components of language, such as phonemes, phonetics, morphemes, grammar, vocabulary or lexicon, accent, tone, pacing, and dialect. The dual goals of this textbook are to develop the speaker's competence (what a speaker must *know* about the language in order to speak and understand it), and performance (what a speaker actually says, the *use* of speech in social situations).

Today the Omaha and Ponca languages are considered to be two distinct languages. Historically they were a single language. Today many people prefer to describe Omaha and Ponca as dialects or separate languages. The purpose of this textbook is not to try to settle that debate, since the distinction may hinge more upon political identity and distinctive writing systems rather than degrees of mutual intelligibility.

In considering how we translate Omaha to English to Omaha, we can note that all languages are translatable. The ease of translation depends upon similarities in morpheme inventory, grammar, and environment. Variations in culture, behavior, and language illustrate adaptations to unique environments. Therefore translations may not have a one-to-one equivalency. It may take more or fewer words to translate something adequately between languages. That is part of what makes studying a language a dynamic activity.

9.2 FIRST CATCH, FIRST FRUITS

A growing child learns many core values by observing adult behavior. Many adults will present their "first catch fish," "first hunt meat," or "first harvest fruits" to someone else. The recipient may be an Elder or a person in poor health. This practice models to younger community members the importance of being generous—not stingy.

Such acts of food sharing are highly prized. The person receiving the gift of food serves as a witness to the generosity of the giver. By receiving the gift he or she acknowledges the giver's skills at food acquisition. This also reinforces the feeling that the giver has received proper upbringing by the giver's family and clan.

This practice sometimes extends to non-food items. When people master the skills to make or craft something, such as tying a shawl or making a piece of beadwork, they will often present the first completed item to the person who taught them the skill, as a token of respect and gratitude.

9.3 HOW TO ASK SOMEONE FOR HELP

From an Umóⁿhoⁿ perspective, as we go through life we often need to ask someone for help. For example, we need the help of our Elder speakers in learning the language. We need to ask skilled artisans for help in learning how to make or acquiring vital material culture objects. We often ask experienced people for guidance in learning appropriate behavior and for help in organizing our social activities. Unlike in the mainstream U.S. culture, these requests cannot always be divided into strictly secular needs (daily life) or ritual situations (ceremonial life).

For Umóⁿhoⁿ people the process of asking for help takes several cultural values into account.

FIG. 7. (*top left*) Grandfather and Grandson Fishing by Jacob Smith.

FIG. 8. (*above*) Entering the Dance Arena in a Good Way by Jacob Smith.

1. The person asking for help recognizes a lack of personal knowledge, skills, or authority in this particular case.

2. The person being asked is recognized by the community as being an appropriate authority with knowledge and skills that can address this particular issue or need.

3. Certain knowledge and social roles are gendered and described as nú ūshkoⁿ tʰe (men's customs) or wa'ú ūshkoⁿ tʰe (women's customs).

4. Knowledge, skills, and duties may be proprietary in nature.

5. Requests for knowledge, skills, or other help are best asked for in a formal face-to-face meeting at the Elder's or mentor's home; not by telephone, letter or e-mail, or during a casual encounter in public.

6. Nothing in the world is "free," so the person asking for help should be prepared to compensate the person being asked.

7. An Umóⁿhoⁿ teaching is to not say "no" to a person's request if you are an appropriate authority, even if the request might be inconvenient to your own personal schedule.

8. Consideration of who helped you in the past has an impact on the decision about whom you might ask in the future. An Umóⁿhoⁿ teaching is to return to the same fireplace (i.e., Native American Church altar) that has been previously used by you or your family. This linkage between families and a particular NAC fireplace can span generations and predates the NAC. A complementary teaching is that the fireplace should be administered by a person who is not too closely related to the family. This means that the minister will be a little distant from whatever crisis (death, illness) is affecting the family and thus able to offer advice unclouded by emotions.

In the Umóⁿhoⁿ community the general expectation is that the person wanting knowledge or a particular skill will become self-aware and take the first steps in the quest for help of their own free will. A possible explanation for this approach is that since the seeker is already personally motivated, the transfer of knowledge will be undertaken with greater attentiveness and effectiveness. The seeker is less likely to be disappointed by early setbacks and will value and protect the knowledge or skill for future generations.

A Secular Request

How the actual interaction of the seeker and the knowledgeable person proceeds may vary depending upon each person's personal character, prior experience, and the nature of the request. For a relatively simple secular example, let us say that you wish to have a pair of moccasins made for your grandchild so that he can begin dancing in the arena. You do not know how to make the moccasins. By asking dancers, family members, and friends in the community you learn the names of one or more known moccasin makers. You learn through the experiences of others about which moccasin maker is the best crafts person and most reliable.

You call that person and arrange a home visit. When you travel to the moccasin maker's home you might take along a small gift (a sack of groceries including a piece of meat is always appreciated) to show your serious intentions. After a period of casual conversation you bring up the reason for your visit. You describe your desire for a pair of moccasins so that your grandchild can dance. You acknowledge the moccasin maker's reputation in the community. You ask if the moccasin maker will pity you and help out by making the desired item. The moccasin maker will deliberate on your request and may describe the current work schedule, ask who will provide the materials, ask what the expected delivery date is, and perhaps hint at possible compensation. A moccasin maker who feels unable to fulfill your request will usually suggest an alternate crafts person.

A deal is struck after all the details are discussed and agreed upon. After a period of casual conversation you take your leave. A reputable artisan will make every effort to complete the requested job on time. Any arrangements for compensation should be honored in a timely manner. When the grandchild uses the moccasins for the first time in the arena it is appropriate to honor the maker again by publicly presenting a gift (monetary or material goods). This acknowledges and reinforces the person's skills to the community.

A Ritual Request

Additional steps are taken in the case of requests for ritual assistance and the transfer of privileged or proprietary skills and knowledge. Nú ūshko^n t^{h}e (men's customs) or wa'ú ūshko^n t^{h}e (women's customs) are central concepts because religious rituals and many skills and ritual knowledge are in the male domain. The presentation of a gift of tobacco is expected for most requests for ritual help. The often repeated teaching of Umó^{n}ho^n people is that "the tobacco always comes first." In other words, the tobacco helps to initiate the request, carries the ritual leader to his appointed day, aids in the completion of the request, and safeguards the person and his family throughout the process. Tobacco is in the male domain and as a general rule is not presented to men by women or presented to women. If a widow or female head of household needs to make a ritual request, she will ask a male relative (son, nephew, brother) to carry the tobacco, make the presentation, and speak on her behalf. Public speaking, like tobacco, is in the male domain.

Building upon the moccasin example given earlier, let us propose that you now wish to sponsor a handgame and war dance to honor the birthday of your grandchild. You have taken care of asking for help in acquiring moccasins for the dance. Now you need to ask someone to come and officiate at the event, offer a word of prayer for your grandchild, and take care of distributing the food your family will gather for the communal feast.

If your family has a long-standing relationship with a minister in the Native American Church and you wish to have a cedar smoke blessing (an NAC ritual) for your grandchild, you will most likely think of that husband-wife team to fill the "Man-in-Charge" role. This is not a totally binding rule. You might consider some other NAC couple well admired by the community and able to perform the expected duties (e.g., able to travel and help cook). If you do not expect a cedar smoke blessing, you can consider asking any respected married couple in the community. As with the moccasin inquiry, you will ask family and friends for advice in selecting a Man-in-Charge.

With that decision made, you contact the man and arrange a formal visit when he and his wife are at their home. Anywhere from a week to a few months prior to the event is the usual time for the visit. A man who has received a tobacco offering will usually not accept any other tobacco-requests until the first request has been concluded. If you are female, you will enlist the aid of a male relative to accompany you. Following the same protocols as described earlier, you will bring a small gift. After some casual conversation, you, or your male relative, will state the reason for the visit and present the tobacco. There are variations to the actual presentation based upon the individual's experiences and teachings.

Up through the late 1970s, Bull Durham™ brand loose tobacco was routinely rolled into a paper cigarette by the supplicant and then presented. Other brands of loose tobacco have become popular after Bull Durham™ production declined and became hard to acquire. Supplicants who are unfamiliar with the technique of rolling cigarettes may simply present the papers and tobacco, or commercially manufactured cigarettes of the brand smoked by the person they are asking help from. In some cases the presenter may provide corn husk cigarette wrappers similar to those used in NAC meetings.

The tobacco is accepted with thanks. The man will often recount some previous experiences that illustrate his authority or ability to fulfill the request for aid. This may include telling about prior ritual connections to your family. If the presented tobacco is unrolled, the man will prepare the cigarette while telling his story. When completed, he will light the cigarette and offer a short prayer for the success of the proposed activity. He will acknowledge the visiting family, his own family, and pray for the health and well-being of the community. Depending upon his teachings, he may offer the cigarette to his wife to take four ritual puffs. He may offer the cigarette to you or your male spokesperson to take four ritual puffs. At the conclusion of his prayer he will put out the cigarette and keep the remaining tobacco safe. The visit concludes with further discussion of the event details. The wife of the Man-in-Charge is often included in this discussion as she may be called upon to do the cooking and will want to know what the planned menu will be.

The man with the tobacco will often save the remaining quantity of tobacco to make daily prayers for success leading up to the day of your event. Some Elders have described the tobacco as a "messenger" that helps to carry the man to the appointed event and return him safely home again. On the day of the event the Man-in-Charge and his wife will perform the duties that were requested during the presentation of tobacco. If the man is a minister in the NAC, he will perform a cedar smoke blessing for the honoree (your grandchild in this case) and the sponsors (you and your family). Depending upon his teachings, the Man-in-Charge may already have returned the unsmoked part of the cigarette that you presented to Wakkónda (the Creator) by placing it on the ground in some special place near his home. Or he will return it to the hot coals of his fireplace during the cedar smoke blessing.

As the sponsor of the handgame and war dance event you will want to make a presentation of gifts to supporters, visitors, and people in need. Those individuals you asked to serve in various capacities, such as the Man-in-Charge, should be honored with gifts and public thanks. For descriptions of how a handgame or other event is organized, and the giveaway practice, see sections 2.28, 9.10, and 9.13.

9.4 KNIFE AND FIRE

In many regions of the world it is not uncommon for cooks to slice food such as potatoes, vegetables, and meat directly into the frying pan on the stove or over the fire. The tip of the knife is often used to stir the cooking food. Likewise many boys play a knife throwing game, sometimes called mumblety-peg, in which a pocket knife is flipped toward the ground. The goal is to have it stick upright into the earth or a wooden surface close to a target. Both behaviors are acceptable in many parts of the mainstream U.S. culture. Such behaviors would be considered grossly inappropriate by many traditional Umóⁿhoⁿ families.

Many Umóⁿhoⁿ people hold the knife and the fire in high, sacred regard. Prior to the introduction of commercially manufactured metal knives, all cutting tools had to be laboriously crafted from flint or similar natural materials. The very act of acquiring a good stone knife meant much work and sacrifice, either to make your own knife or to have the necessary material wealth to trade with a knife craftsman. The knife was used for many tasks, including food preparation, butchering, ritually preparing tobacco for smoking, cutting a child's hair, and defensive warfare. The Iⁿkʰésabe Clan was charged with using the knife to cut wooden drum sticks for singers as well as cutting and shaping long-handled paddles for stirring soup and long-handled forked sticks for extracting meat from the boiling soup kettle.

The fire is held sacred and treated with great respect. Fire is an ancient gift to the people and holds spiritual power. It is acknowledged as an animate being assisting the Umóⁿhoⁿ people in their daily struggle to survive. People bring their prayers to the fire. It protects us from the cold, illuminates the darkness, and provides comfort around which we gather for family and ritual activities. It cooks our food. Fire assists us in fashioning our tools and implements of daily life. Used wisely, it helps drive the buffalo closer to our hunters and provides new green grass for our horses.

When we build a fire on a camping trail it marks the place that we call home. The Elders routinely admonish us not to scatter our ashes around the landscape. By that they mean to say that we should always strive to return to the same camping place in the future. We see this in practice at the annual Umóⁿhoⁿ powwow at Macy and other annual powwow gatherings around the region. Having once established a campsite and fireplace, a family will strive to return to the same site each successive year. The fire marks not only our home for this particular occasion but also a promise to return again. For some, the laying of a fire in a hearth establishes a sense of ownership and the intent to occupy.

This is the case with the fireplace at the Lincoln Indian Center. The oldest Native American

Church minister residing in Lincoln was asked by the Lincoln Indian Center Board of Directors to bless the grounds with cedar smoke at their groundbreaking ceremony on August 17, 1978. Grandpa Charles Stabler Jr. established a small fireplace from which he gathered hot coals to make his blessing prayer. After the blessing was completed and the dignitaries and community members departed, Grandpa Charlie urged that the fireplace be permanently marked and remembered. Grandpa never called this an "Umóⁿhoⁿ-only" fireplace, reserved only for the Umóⁿhoⁿ people living in Lincoln. He said that future prayers and blessings would flow from this fireplace for the benefit of the entire multi-tribal Lincoln Indian community. He compared this fireplace to the one in the center of a family's home. It served all of the purposes noted above: prayer, cooking, comfort, and family togetherness.

Fires to be used for cooking feast food or for use in the Native American Church rituals are usually laid out and watched over by responsible young men. Such was the case of the Lincoln Indian Center fireplace. This is an example of nú ūshkoⁿ or "men's customs." Daily home cooking fires are laid out and maintained by women as an example of waʔú ūshkoⁿ or "women's customs." Children are taught not to play with the fire, to throw sticks or rubbish into the fire, or to run around the fire.

In many families the bundle keepers (people in charge of particular bundles of sacred objects) and NAC roadmen (ministers) are leaders who demonstrate their respect for the role that the knife and the fire play in both ritual and survival. Such individuals will not place or use the knife on or near the fireplace. Sometimes this has been explained as a mutual display of respect toward both the fire and the knife. Today the modern stove has replaced daily cooking over an open fire. The restriction about knives has been extended to include modern gas and electric appliances. Many Umóⁿhoⁿ families do not have medicine bundles or NAC instruments in their homes. However, they choose to follow the knife restriction as a demonstration of their respect for their relatives who are ritual bundle keepers and NAC roadmen.

One story tells of a man whose family returned late at night from a feast with a pile of dirty dishes. In the haste to clean the dishes that evening some plates were stacked on the stove next to the sink. As the dish washer pulled the dirty dishes from the stove it was discovered that a knife was lying on a plate with the bones of a chicken wing. A few days later the person who had inadvertently placed the dishes with the knife on the stove suffered a broken arm. The explanation for the cause of the injury was that the knife restriction had not been respected. The association of the knife with the wing bones shaped the punishment.

9.5 THE SPIRIT WORLD

The Umóⁿhoⁿ worldview describes a fluid connection between the natural world and the supernatural world. A deep discussion of Umóⁿhoⁿ spirituality is not considered by Elders to be appropriate in a textbook. It is a topic that is reserved for the Umóⁿhoⁿ Elders to teach and explain. However, it is useful for students to understand a few basic concepts related to the Umóⁿhoⁿ view of the supernatural. While most Umóⁿhoⁿ people have adopted varying degrees of mainstream Christian beliefs, many continue to acknowledge and interact with the supernatural world through animism: the belief that things in the world are animate (alive) and have souls.

As discussed in other lessons, the Umóⁿhoⁿ people acknowledge the existence of spirits of deceased relatives and other supernatural beings. Elders describe a set of proper behaviors that should be practiced when a person encounters a spirit. First and foremost, do not get scared and run away! Unlike in the American popular culture and Hollywood movies, Umóⁿhoⁿ spirits are not commonly aggressive or life threatening. Instead, it is often reported that the spirit is bringing a valuable teaching or message to the person. By standing your ground and not giving in to the desire to run away, you prove your worthiness for the information that the spirit wishes to give.

One story tells of a man walking home from a handgame many years ago. He was on a country road late at night outside Macy. He heard someone walking up behind him in the dark. When the person came very close the man turned to see who it might be. The other person was dressed in old time Indian clothes (deer skin big shirt and leggings), and his feet were not touching the ground as he walked. At that point the man realized that the other person was a spirit.

The man ran away in fear. The spirit pursued him relentlessly until the man arrived at his country home and barred the door. The spirit knocked on the door a few times but finally gave up and departed without a word spoken. Over the years, several Elders recounted this story. At the end of the story they often suggested that if the man had controlled his fear he might have

gained some valuable knowledge that the spirit was bringing. Instead, he lived the rest of his life in misery and fear.

An important point of this brief discussion about spirits in the Umóⁿhoⁿ worldview is that most spirits are known to the people. They are not some unnamed terror that haunts us for malicious reasons. They are our own relatives. Many Umóⁿhoⁿ people report encountering spirits of departed relatives in their home. A deceased companion sometimes returns to check on the condition of the surviving wife or husband. A parent or grandparent may return to see a child or grandchild.

While the encounters may initially be startling, most are seen as a gentle reminder of a life that has been lost from this world. Sometimes the visitation is interpreted to be a warning of a problem or calamity coming in the near future. In many of those cases the future problem or tragedy is not specifically named. Elders have regularly reported that they would speak to a spirit. They would reassure the deceased relative that all was well with the family and not to worry. At that point the spirit would usually depart.

Other stories tell of Umóⁿhoⁿ families moving into old homes or apartments and experiencing recurring visits by spirits. Sometimes the spirit is a baby who died in the home. The baby might be heard crying in an upstairs room. Other spirits might be of persons who died in a tragic manner in or near the home. They may appear at some place in the home or be heard moving about in an otherwise empty room. In any case, many Umóⁿhoⁿ families will ask a respected man to come and make a prayer for the safety of the home and family. A cup of water might be used to sprinkle the house as a blessing. A Native American Church minister may use cedar smoke to bless the home and family. Every effort is made to ease the concerns of the spirit and wish it a good journey into the next world.

Another Umóⁿhoⁿ practice is to prepare a small dish of food for the spirit. It is thought that the spirit may simply be lonesome or longing for human food and thus returns to the home where he or she ate when alive. Any adult can prepare this dish any time when the family is having a regular meal. A short prayer is offered for the comfort of the spirit, and the food is poured outside on the ground. This practice of pouring out food is further described in a lesson related to food (see section 9.6).

Nightmares

We have all had them at some time in our life. Deep in sleep we suddenly enter into a scary world that seems to trap us forever. Perhaps we are slowly falling, being chased by some terrifying thing, or being required to repeat some difficult task. When we finally shake ourselves awake we may be trembling and short of breath. We have just had a nightmare. Umóⁿhoⁿ people are no different from people around the world. We all can experience a nightmare.

Nightmares are different from other times of dreams and visions. They are often of a disturbing or uncomfortable situation or activity. The sleeper feels helpless to change the direction of the dream or to get free of its grip and wake up immediately. Nightmares can occur due to various reasons. Children who watch a scary television show or Hollywood horror movie often experience the same story in their dreams. A tragic event in life, such as a car crash or loss of a parent, can spawn nightmares. Anxiety about some ongoing or upcoming situation can cause people of all ages to experience restless sleep and nightmares.

Umóⁿhoⁿ people have strategies to cope with nightmares. Each family may use any number of methods to cause the nightmares to end or to turn aside the disturbing outcome that is presented in the dream. As a young boy I was experiencing several nights of a recurring bad dream. My grandmother, Elizabeth Saunsoci Stabler, recommended that I get out of bed the next time it happened. She said I should fill a cup with water and walk outdoors into the night air. I was to place the cup on the ground and face east. Grandma urged me to make a prayer—to talk to Wakkóⁿda. I was to describe the nightmare and request that Wakkóⁿda turn it away from me. I could drink a bit of the water and pour the rest onto the ground as an offering. Then I should return to bed. In every case this ritual reduced the recurrence of the nightmare or stopped it outright.

Grandma Elizabeth recalled seeing her own grandparents dealing with a period of nightmares in a different way. They were living in a country home west of Macy at the time. Elizabeth's Elder relative went into the nearby cornfield and cut down several stalks of corn. Small bundles of the stalks were tied to the outside four corners of the home. Grandma Elizabeth said that the stalks remained hanging for several days until the wind, rain, and sun had worn them away. She could not explain why the cornstalks were used, but she reported that her relative afflicted with the repeated nightmare recovered.

There may be other Umóⁿhoⁿ family remedies for nightmares. What seems apparent from the two remedies described here is that the Umóⁿhoⁿ attitude about nightmares and encounters with spirits are similar. Both are experiences that should not be run away from. Both may be the bringers of potential knowledge — or not. Regardless of the reason for a visit by a spirit or a nightmare, they should be treated with thoughtful respect.

9.6 FOOD AND THE SPIRITS

Umóⁿhoⁿ people are deeply attached to family. The Umóⁿhoⁿ concept of what constitutes a "family" is more complex and inclusive than the mainstream American practice. It is for this reason that a death reaches far beyond the nuclear family and touches the lives of distant kin. As part of the mourning process many Umóⁿhoⁿ families sponsor some sort of memorial activity for the deceased on the anniversary of his or her death. It is believed that the spirit of the deceased may return and linger nearby during this time. The family may sponsor a Native American Church prayer service, memorial handgame, or some other social activity. All of these include a feast. The most common practice is just to have the memorial feast. These are usually held during the middle of the day and rarely after dark. Many families repeat this sacrifice annually for four years following their loved one's death.

During the feast the deceased person is remembered and often humorous stories are shared. The family tries to acknowledge and honor those who have helped them during the difficult time. Often there is a giveaway of material goods. The most important gift is the food provided to the assembled family, friends, and community. The menu will include foods that the deceased person enjoyed during life. For this reason the final meal is often described as "the food the deceased relative left behind."

All the food for the feast is brought out to the middle of the circle. A man is asked to pray over the food. He, or his female relative, will take a small dish the size of a coffee cup saucer and fill it with food for the spirit of the deceased. For this reason, the feast is often referred to as "the separation of food," because the feeding of the spirit is the primary goal of the meal. The prepared dish is called wappígthe. Umóⁿhoⁿ people will place up to four small pieces of each food on the dish. Others will choose only a few key items such as meat and bread. Water is the preferred drink placed in the tiny cup that accompanies the plate. The teaching of this action is that all life on earth depends upon water to survive. However, some families use coffee or other soft drinks that the deceased preferred during life.

After a brief prayer, the Man in Charge will cedar smoke the wappígthe dish and carry it outdoors. He will pour the contents on the ground, often near the base of a tree used repeatedly for such purposes. The pouring out of food is not without some risks. Umóⁿhoⁿ people believe that the spirit of the deceased may be lingering nearby waiting for the food. Other spirits may also gather due to the presence of the food being offered. The man pouring out the food is cautioned to not look around, and to keep his attention focused on going to the designated place and returning. Men who have looked around while walking outdoors with the food often report seeing the spirits of their own deceased relatives gathered in a group. For this reason the people waiting inside are encouraged to sit quietly while the man is outside.

After the man completes his task he returns to the feast area. The empty dish is returned to the family for use at the next year's memorial feast. If it is the fourth and final feast, they are directed to destroy the dish. This indicates the end of the memorial cycle. Keeping the dish as a memento could cause another relative to die in order to use the same dish again. The Man in Charge will use the cedar smoke to bless the remaining food, the family of the deceased, the memorial cake, and the assembled crowd. Then he and his wife will direct the distribution of the remaining food to the people in attendance. (Sometimes the Man in Charge gives another person a cup of water to pass all the way around the circle. The person asked is usually someone else who sits in the prayer meeting and attends the Native American Church; it is an honor to be asked to help by the Man in Charge.)

Again, people are encouraged to carry their own dishes to the memorial feast. It relieves the sponsors from the added expense of providing paper goods such as plates, bowls, cups, and spoons. Elder Bertha McCauley Wolfe described how in her younger days a funeral was held at a family member's country home. Mourners arriving without dishes used plates and cups from the family's pantry. Because the family did not own enough plates to serve everyone, the people were fed in shifts. After the first group finished eating the dirty dishes were washed and reused for the rest of the crowd. Today it is more commonly the case that the sponsors will provide disposable dinnerware for the entire gathering.

Eating in the Dark

The Umónhon people value food and food sharing. They are also thoughtful about the feelings of the spirits of departed kin. In Umónhon cosmology we believe that the spirits of departed kin can be drawn back to our world from time to time. The spirits of the people who died in certain horrific ways, or who were not properly buried, may linger around us. They appear most often after dark. They are especially drawn to food because it was their source of earthly sustenance throughout their life. For this reason Umónhon people prefer to eat before the sun goes down in the evening. Many Elders such as Old Man Charles Stabler explained it this way: "I want to be able to see with whom I am eating." In other words, people eating outdoors after dark may not be aware that spirits have entered the circle to join the feast. In the winter time when the days are short it is difficult to have the evening meal before sunset. Out of respect for the feelings of these spirits, Old Man Charlie would first close the curtains over the windows so as to not tantalize any would-be visitors from the spirit realm. Most Umónhon leaders of social and ritual functions strive to eat the evening meal while the sun is in the sky. In the case of the Lincoln Indian Club, the curtains are closed if the sun has set prior to sharing the evening meal.

A related practice of many Elder Umónhon is the admonition to not bring food into the bedroom. Many of us have experienced the midnight munchies. We raid the refrigerator and bring the food back to bed. Several Elders commented that this was discouraged in earlier days as it could lure spirits into the house.

As well, they described the practice of laying

a knife across any uneaten food or beverage left unattended. This deters spirits from partaking of the food. Food left uncovered will be "eaten" by the spirits who consume the life-giving essence in the food needed by humans to survive.

Whistling in the Dark

Many Umóⁿhoⁿ people believe that spirits move about during the nighttime hours. These may be spirits of deceased kin, animal beings, or other supernatural beings. It is generally believed that such spirits are benevolent, meaning no harm to the living. Some spirits appear to the living to remind their kindred of unfinished obligations, to foretell some future event, or to offer some form of power. People who died violently, such as being struck by lightning, or were improperly buried, are described as very lonely spirits. They may return to the home and vicinity that they frequented in life. They often whistle out of loneliness. For this reason the Umóⁿhoⁿ people discourage whistling after dark as it imitates and disrespects the lonely spirits.

9.7 ARRIVING AT AND LEAVING AN UMÓⁿHOⁿ CAMPSITE

In the past the Umóⁿhoⁿ people traveled to find seasonally available foods to augment their garden produce. This required them to leave their earth lodge village and move across the landscape with their buffalo hide tipis. Camp sites were selected with care in order to fulfill the needs of the travelers for water, pasturage, and firewood. When possible, defensive campsites were chosen to protect the people from enemy

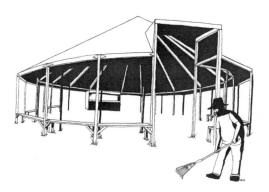

FIG. 9. Getting the Dance Grounds Ready by Jacob Smith.

attacks. For this reason, favorite campsites were revisited when the Umóⁿhoⁿ people traveled through the same area.

The tradition of returning to the same campsite year after year continues today. While the Umóⁿhoⁿ people no longer trek to hunt buffalo on the western Great Plains, many families regularly travel by automobile to festivities and powwows throughout the region. Some families carry tents, bedding, cooking gear, and other equipment for the weekend or longer encampment. Traditional Umóⁿhoⁿ campers try to return to the same good campsite used on previous visits.

There is a code of behavior that many Umóⁿhoⁿ people practice when arriving at or departing from a campsite. Before the sponsors of the powwow or event open the campgrounds to visitors and vendors, a respected man is asked to make a tobacco offering and pray for the success and safety of the event. Many individual families repeat this ritual before their own tents are erected. An Elder male in the family or group will make a tobacco offering and pray.

A family's camp was traditionally centered

at the fireplace with one or more tents nearby. In earlier days the powwow sponsors distributed quantities of staple foods such as meat, eggs, potatoes, flour, coffee, and sugar to families with a fireplace at their campsite. The women would gather firewood and cook meals as in the old buffalo hunting camps. The tents served as sleeping quarters and dressing rooms for dancers. Elders and young children would often take naps during the heat of the day. Visitors would come to the camp to share stories and eat with the family.

At the conclusion of the powwow the event sponsors would ask the same respected man to offer a closing prayer before dismissing the dancers from the arena. When the individual camps were packed away and the family was ready to depart, another ritual took place. The Elder male in the family could often be seen standing by the cold ashes of the family's fireplace. He would make a small tobacco offering and pray for a safe journey home. He would thank the fire for providing the warmth, light, and comfort enjoyed by the family. As a final act, he might softly call out

FIG. 10. Lightning Storm by Miya Kobayashi.

the Umóⁿhoⁿ names of each of the children who had been at the camp. He would talk to the spirits of the children who might still be playing around the campsite. Even though the physical children might be sitting in the family car waiting to leave, the man would call their spirits, asking them to come home too. In this way the spirit and the flesh are reunited and the children do not unexpectedly sicken or die.

Today few Umóⁿhoⁿ people maintain a fireplace, cook, or camp in the same manner that their grandparents did. Fewer people erect a camp when traveling to powwows, preferring to stay in motels or at the homes of nearby friends and relatives. However, the practice of returning to the same campsite remains especially strong during the annual Umóⁿhoⁿ powwow held at Macy during the full moon of August. The descendants of old time powwow campers strive to erect their tents in the same location as their ancestors did year after year. The tents are still used for sleeping and as dressing rooms for dancers. However, few people make the effort to maintain a fireplace and cook meals at their camp.

Establishing a fireplace, "unéthe," at a campsite is a visible symbol that the person intends to occupy and use the area. Umóⁿhoⁿ people did not claim ownership of land in the same way that Euro-American immigrants did. However, it was understood that if a person, family, or tribe claimed a piece of land, then it was theirs for as long as they used it. This is similar to the land tenure system of communal societies worldwide. The fireplace serves as a marker of intent to use. Umóⁿhoⁿ people return to the same campsite in order to renew that marker.

As noted earlier, there is a fireplace on the

grounds of the Lincoln Indian Center. Established by Elder Charles Stabler Jr. on August 11, 1978, for the groundbreaking ceremonies, it remains an active symbol for the Lincoln Indian community. It is used regularly to provide coals for cedar blessings; to cook food for feasts, funerals, and memorial dinners; and to focus the prayers of community members from many tribes.

9.8 FIRST THUNDERS

In eastern Nebraska the first Thunders are heard anytime from late February through April. Elders, bundle keepers, Native American Church staff keepers and other spiritually motivated people often walk outdoors — usually to a nearby elevated hill — to pray. They make tobacco offerings to Wakkónda and the Thunder beings using a pipe or rolled cigarette. They give thanks for the continuing good health and harmony of their family and tribe. Many times they return home soaking wet from the early spring rains. Doctoring bundles or other sacred packs may be opened by their owners and ritually fed. This is generally seen as a joyous time. After learning of the introduced concept of "New Year's," some Omaha people consider hearing the first Thunders to be the Omaha equivalent of the "New Year."

The first Thunders signal a reawakening of life after the cold winter sleep. They mark the return of migratory animals and birds, the emergence of early spring edible plants, and the hope of continuing life.

Traditionally minded Umónhon people observe several other practices during thunderstorms. The mirrors in the house will be covered during a lightning storm. One explanation for this action is to prevent accidentally "capturing" the lightning in the glass. This possibly comes from the respect given to old-time Umónhon doctors. Some of these men and women would use a piece of reflective crystal, glass, or metal during curing ceremonies. Warriors also used reflective materials to communicate across distances with other members of the war party.

Children often want to run around outdoors playing during a rainstorm. Instead they are encouraged to sit quietly indoors during thunderstorms. Elders say this is a sign of respect to the Thunder beings who are sending life-giving water.

9.9 THE FOUR HILLS OF LIFE

Umónhon people refer to the "Four Hills of Life" as a way to teach our children about the changes they will experience as they travel their path through life. In the educational video *We Are One: Umónhon*, the mother's brother (uncle) illus-

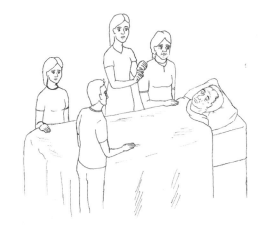

FIG. 11. Family Members Around the Deathbed of an Elder Relative by Miya Kobayashi.

FIG. 12. Closed Casket in a Community Hall by Miya Kobayashi.

FIG. 13. Graveside Scene, with Elder Male Standing at the Head/West and Facing the Casket to Offer a Final Prayer, by Miya Kobayashi.

FIG. 14. Folding of the Flag with an Honor Guard by Miya Kobayashi.

trates this concept to his son and nephew by making a line of four small earthen mounds on the floor of the earth lodge. Pointing to the first hill, he describes this as the time of infancy when the mind and character of the child are not yet formed. The second hill represents the age of adolescence or youth. It is a time when children know right from wrong, and have a developing sense of themselves and their place in the tribe. The third hill represents adulthood and the responsibilities thereof. The fourth hill is the age of the Elder, who can look back and reflect upon life's experiences.

Mainstream American culture uses a more rigid standardized age system to measure expectations of a child's progress and development. The mainstream public school is a good example of how this system of expectations works. All children reaching age five are expected to be ready to begin kindergarten. Ideally they continue to develop mentally, physically, and emotionally and are advanced one grade each year. Twelfth grade high school graduates are routinely all at or near age eighteen.

The Umónhon people recognize that we all develop at our own pace. That is why movement from one hill to the next is not predetermined by some set standard of ages. In the pre-reservation days, children participating in the Turning of the Child ceremony could be within a wide range of ages. The same held true for adolescents who developed their social and survival skills at different ages and entered into adult status. There is no evidence that a child's late development was seen as a negative condition. Parents, grandparents, and community members know that each person is worthy of respect and nurturing, regardless of physical or mental age.

FIG. 15. Pallbearers Filling in the Grave, with Other Men Ready to Assist by Miya Kobayashi.

The spaces or valleys between hills are considered times of transition. The traditional Turning of the Child ceremony and the cutting of the boy's hair dedicating him to the Thunders and the protection of the tribe are in the first valley. Successful hunting of the first buffalo or related acts of self-sacrifice and bravery for boys, and the display of physical maturity together with appropriate childcare and home maintenance skills for girls, signal the movement from the second hill of adolescence to the third hill of adult status and greater responsibility. A life full of modeling good character, together with gaining many life experiences and skills, marks the transition to Elder status and the respect that it entails. Some Umóⁿhoⁿ describe the treasured ideal life having a gentle descent beyond the fourth hill into the valley of eternal rest.

A funeral is very complex in Omaha society. The illustrations provided here depict only a few selected scenes of funeral events. In these illustrations, the deceased person is a retired veteran.

9.10 GENEROSITY AND GIFT GIVING

The Giveaway

Umóⁿhoⁿ people value generosity and thoughtfulness. Whenever there is a joyous occasion, such as a birthday, anniversary, the safe return of a relative from the armed services, or other achievement in life, we want to share the good news with the community. For this and many other reasons a family will sponsor a "giveaway." A giveaway describes the giving of gifts to friends, relatives, and visitors on behalf of the honoree's achievement. But it is much more than just the presentation of gifts. Often a giveaway is part of a larger social event. A family gathers and prepares food to share, organizes a dance or handgame for entertainment, and asks a respected person to make prayers for the well-being of the honoree, family, and community.

By attending such an event and accepting the food offered, community members and friends acknowledge the occasion and the accomplishments of the honoree. People attending these events often bring gifts to share among the community. Monetary donations received during the course of the dance or handgame are given to the honoree at the end of the event. Everyone shares in the food that has been provided, and for many Umóⁿhoⁿ people this represents the most important gift that can be given. The food is blessed and considered nourishing for both the body and spirit. Leftover food is distributed and taken home so that none is wasted.

The giving of gifts at a giveaway follows some regular patterns. Respected people are asked to serve in various capacities for the dance or handgame. In nearly every case there will be a man who has been asked to fulfill the spiritual role at the event. He is called the Man-in-Charge, and is accompanied by his wife or another female relative. A handgame will also have a male "Head Singer" and a male "Master of Ceremonies" or M C.

For a war dance there may be a male "whip-man" and his four male "taildancers" or just a "head man dancer." There will also be a "head woman dancer," and a head singer. The M C will be the spokesman for the event. A gourd dance will often add two more staff members: a "head boy dancer" and a "head girl dancer." If there are any powwow or social club royalty (princesses) present, they are acknowledged as well.

Through the course of the activity each of the staff will call for a "special" song to be rendered for him or her. Usually the song belongs to the staff member, that person's family, or a close relative. They and their family and supporters will join in the dance. On rare occasions the dancing family will carry a basket full of pieces of wrapped penny candy or small coins. As they dance they scatter these items toward the crowd. Children scramble to collect the treats. At the end of the song each staff person conducts a small giveaway. They usually acknowledge the other staff members chosen for the occasion, including the honoree and singers, with gifts. They may acknowledge visitors from other tribes or persons who have traveled great distances to attend the event. In many cases they take the opportunity to give gifts to individuals or groups who have been personally helpful to them and their family in the past.

At the end of the event the sponsoring family requests a song. They conduct the final giveaway. In turn, they acknowledge the staff who have been asked to fulfill the ritual roles for the

event. Other people in attendance are recognized as well. Cash can be given as a gift to the honoree, placed on the drum, or left on the table for the sponsoring organization. It is a common gift in these cases. Gifts of material goods represent more forethought and feeling and are commonly presented to the staff and others.

Besides recognizing the named staff of the event and the honoree, there are other guidelines for an Umó^{n}ho^n giveaway. Many Elders have said that it is best to give gifts to people in need, visitors from other tribes, orphans, the elderly, widows, and those suffering from illness. Giving to one's own close family member in a public giveaway is not encouraged. It has been suggested that if someone wishes to give a gift to a very close relative, it is best to do it on the side and out of public view. This admonition comes from the viewpoint that proper Umó^{n}ho^n people readily share with their own relatives as part of life. Thus giving to one's own close relative is, in fact, the same as giving to one's self.

A range of material goods are seen at social events and giveaways. Pendleton™ wool blankets are one of the Umó^{n}ho^n gold standard items for gifts to men. Finely woven colorful Mexican serapes are a close second choice. The more coarsely woven Mexican bed blankets are next, followed by inexpensive polyester bed blankets. Personal toiletries and other useful items in a basket, bowl, or bag often accompany a blanket gift.

Fine broadcloth wool blankets or shawls with satin ribbon decorations, beadwork, and fringes are the Umó^{n}ho^n gold standard items for gifts to women. Any woman wishing to dance in the arena should wear a shawl to be considered properly attired. Gabardine or wool dance shawls with knotted fringes are the next in line, followed by lighter weight cloth shawls. Many kinds of embellishments can be made to a woman's shawl. Layers of satin ribbons sewn into a complex decorative strip are highly prized. A second row of knots in the fringe or the addition of glass trade beads in the fringe add to the aesthetic value. As with the men, additional items such as hand towels and kitchen or household items often accompany a shawl gift. Today, the star quilt has emerged as another gold standard gift appropriate for both men and women.

As recently as the 1970s, occasionally some families would conclude a giveaway by placing items on the ground around the drum in the arena. Pieces of calico material for ribbon shirts, hand towel sets, sacks of coffee and sugar, enamelware dishes, glassware, and other household items would be laid in the arena circle. The family would have the MC invite anyone in the crowd to come out and choose a gift. The recipients would retrieve an item and then shake the hands of the honoree and family.

Gift giving is not reserved only for festive occasions. Umóⁿhoⁿ people sacrifice and have giveaways at funerals and annual memorial feasts. The most important teaching offered here is that generosity, self-sacrifice, and thinking about the needs of others are primary and persistent values of the Umóⁿhoⁿ people.

Gift Giving When Visiting a Home

Umóⁿhoⁿ people love to visit friends and relatives. When coming to a person's home for the first time, the visitor often brings a gift to mark the occasion. The gift is seldom very large or expensive. A sack of groceries is always welcome, especially including some meat. It is common to include a small household or personal item that the visitor knows will be appreciated and useful.

In most cases the visitor is asked to share some coffee or a meal with the host. When the visitor is ready to depart, the host or hostess gives a small parting gift. Homegrown vegetables, homemade cookies, and other useful items are common gifts. Perhaps the visitor has admired some small article in the house, such as a potted plant or photograph. That item would be given to the visitor as a happy reminder of the first visit. In subsequent visits, the exchange of gifts is not as formalized but is still routinely practiced.

When Someone Admires Your Personal Property

When a person admires a material object that you have, it is an indication that he or she desires to have it. This usually involves items of jewelry, clothing, and other small household or personal objects. The generous Umóⁿhoⁿ person would immediately make a gift of the item to the admirer. For the giver, retaining ownership of the object would not be considered as important as the act of generosity. The giver's thoughtfulness and self-sacrifice brings prestige and community admiration to the giver.

On the other hand, those persons who habitually admire other people's property for the sole purpose of receiving gifts are not well favored. They are often described as being too lazy to acquire their own goods by their own labors. Therefore it is important to be mindful of how we compliment people about their personal property. We do not want our polite admiration to be mistaken as a veiled attempt to receive an undeserved gift.

FIG. 16. Sharing Food by Miya Kobayashi.

FIG. 17. Getting Coffee by Jacob Smith.

9.11 CARRYING DISHES TO A FEAST

We know that our cultural values and the practices (behaviors) they express cover every aspect of our lives. They range from the smallest details, such as how to practice proper personal hygiene, to large-scale community activities, such as powwows and funerals. When we consider the complexity of human culture, it is obvious that this textbook can only touch on a very few of the modern cultural practices of the Umóⁿhoⁿ people. Many of the cultural topics described in this volume were suggested by the Elder contributors. They said they want our children to carry on these valued traditions.

In earlier lessons we learned about the high value Umóⁿhoⁿ people place on food sharing. Elders tell us that it is a sign of respect toward the sponsors of the feast that we bring our own dishes. They remind us that since we know we are going to eat, we should come prepared with our dishes. As late as the 1970s it was common to see everyone carrying dishes and lawn chairs to a feast, dance, or powwow. Men would sometimes be teased for "carrying the dishes" for someone, usually considering this a public display of affection for a new girlfriend.

Dishes were most often carried in a cloth bundle tied together by knotting the diagonal corners. Some women used a picnic basket or other rigid container. The man in charge of the feast would tell the gathered people to "get out your dishes" when it was time to bring out the food and place it in the center of the floor. Women would untie their bundles and distribute enamelware plates, bowls, and cups to family members. A spoon, fork, cloth napkin, and a salt shaker were usually included. A bucket or container for soup was a standard item. A knife was optional. An extra set of dishes would often be included in the bundle to accommodate unexpected visitors to the feast. Single young men would often be seen "borrowing" a dish from relatives.

Some social clubs used to have a sergeant-at-arms check that all members had a complete set of dishes. Members who arrived late, had forgotten dishes, or lacked specified items in their dish bundle would be punished by having to perform some humorous task. Typical punishments included women having to dance to a fast war dance song and giving the male war whoop. Men would dance while wearing a woman's shawl and would give the female "lulu" (a non Omaha-specific sound of pride during dancing, as in victory or celebration). All offenders accepted their punishment with much merriment.

The food is served to the gathered people, but no one begins eating until the Man in Charge gives permission to "go ahead and eat." Waiting to eat shows respect to the servers. It is impolite to be eating in front of someone who cannot eat but must struggle with the heavy containers of food until all have been served. Everyone eats together in the same manner that families eat together at home.

Food is shared to all in attendance. Servers are instructed to try to portion the food so that all can receive a bite to eat. The food is passed out by the server. Members of the audience should not reach into the food container and help themselves. This is considered very rude. Whenever food is distributed in such a self-service way there is never enough for all in attendance.

One time a young boy was helping to serve food at a small birthday meal in Lincoln. When he finished his duties and returned to his seat, he discovered that someone had placed a hot dog bun on his plate without a hot dog. Looking to his immediate right, he saw that the family next to him, who had been served before him, had helped themselves to two or three hot dogs for each plate. That family had disrespected the sponsors by being greedy and thoughtless. They disrespected the young boy who had sacrificed himself to serve them but who received no portion of the hot dogs. For this reason the servers are asked to control the portion size of whatever they are serving so that everyone gets the same amount of food. The Elders tell us that the goal of attending a feast is not to "get filled up."

Looking at it from another perspective, Elders tell us not to refuse any offer of food at a feast, even if our plate is full, or the item is something we do not normally eat. Refusal of food is considered disrespectful. The food has been blessed with a prayer and represents the humble gift of the feast sponsors. Just a mouthful is said to be enough to satisfy our hunger.

After everyone has been served, the Man in Charge invites people to help themselves to the remaining food that has been returned to the center of the floor. He tells people to "get out your soup buckets." The extra food can be taken home to be shared with other family members. Leftover food is called "ūthashte," the remainder of something done with the mouth (food). For many families living on a fixed income, ūthashte becomes very important when other food sources have been exhausted near the end of the pay cycle.

Today it is increasingly rare to see younger Umó^{n}ho^n people carrying dishes to a feast. Even Elders are now coming without dishes. Several Elders in the community suggest that this movement away from carrying dishes may originate with the Native American Church. Men who attend the all-night prayer services may not want to be burdened with carrying their own dishes. To accommodate this behavior, prayer meeting sponsors may have started the custom of providing paper plates for the congregation.

Posters and flyers announcing social activities and feasts usually ask people to "bring dishes and chairs." These pleas are regularly ignored. The feast sponsors are now expected to provide Styrofoam plates and plastic utensils. This is an additional expense for the sponsors who are already providing the food. Another burden is the mountain of waste the sponsors must dispose of after the event.

A few Elders and the more traditionally minded younger people continue to carry dishes. They recognize the value of carrying dishes because hard plastic or enamelware dishes are sturdier than Styrofoam plates and bowls. Old-time metal lard buckets as soup containers have given way to plastic freezer bags or plastic containers with lids.

Today the expectation of appropriate behavior, such as carrying dishes and arriving at an activity on time, has become more difficult to enforce. It seems that people are now very quick to take offense at anyone appearing to comment on their inappropriate or non-traditional behavior. Social clubs have become reluctant to enforce traditional rules of behavior. They ignore the shifting behaviors in order to avoid confrontations. Respected Elders in the community no longer step forward to share their teachings on such matters for fear of verbal abuse or other kinds of retaliation from the family of the individual whose behavior is being questioned. In the face of such negative responses, it is unclear how these traditional practices might survive into the next generations.

9.12 STORYTELLING

The Umóⁿhoⁿ people have a rich oral tradition full of stories about mythic heroes, tricksters, other supernatural beings, historic persons, and important events. Preserved and passed down through the generations, these hīga stories represent an important collection of historical and cultural knowledge. In the late nineteenth century many of these stories were recorded by James Owen Dorsey from Elder fluent speakers. Dorsey wrote the story in the Umóⁿhoⁿ language as he heard it from the storyteller. He translated the story into English so that others could enjoy the tales of mystery and wonder. Dorsey compiled many of the stories into a single volume called the *The Çegiha Language*, printed in 1890. Students are encouraged to locate a copy of this book and explore this treasure trove of Umóⁿhoⁿ literature.

Mythic beings come in various forms. The Umóⁿhoⁿ people have several heroes whose interactions with animals and people cause things to happen. These include the Orphan, Rabbit, Monkey, and Coyote. Monkey and Coyote are also tricksters. They can change their appearance to fool people. Many animal beings appear in the stories, including Red Bird, Beaver, Elk, Crayfish, Raccoon, Buzzard, and Bear, to name a few.

Other supernatural beings enter the stories of our heroes. The Sun, the Male Winter, a Giant, and the Devouring Hill are some of the characters who challenge Rabbit and Monkey. Another type of supernatural being has its own wondrous adventures. Two Faces and the Twin Brothers, the Thunders, Corn Woman, and the Big Turtle teach us many good lessons.

Not all heroes are supernatural beings. Historic humans including Háxige, Hiⁿx̌péagthe, Ishíbazhi, and Wabáskaha have many interesting adventures. Historic Umóⁿhoⁿ warriors such as

Ppathíⁿ noⁿppazhi, Mawádoⁿthiⁿ, and Kkáǧenoⁿ-ba tell of their valorous battles and raids against enemy tribes. Stories such as these capture the history of the Umóⁿhoⁿ people through time.

Many of the stories mentioned are no longer actively told today. However, Umóⁿhoⁿ story-telling remains a strong cultural practice. More recent historic events that influence the tribe, a clan, a family, or an individual circulate through the community. Tales of the early reservation days, the building of allotment homes, going to boarding schools, and riding horses and wagons to travel to visit neighbors or nearby towns are numerous. Many stories told by families relay information about grandparents, veterans, and other relatives. Through the telling and retell-ing of such stories, memories of deceased rel-atives and their individual characters are kept alive and vivid for the younger generations.

A new collection of supernatural beings has emerged to mix with older beings such as Water Monster and Trickster. They all offer good teach-ings about appropriate Umóⁿhoⁿ behavior and values. Modern stories tell about the Little Peo-ple who inhabit the thick timbered bluffs of the Missouri River area. Deer Woman and Big Foot (also known as the Hairy Man) are sighted from time to time. The giant Snake that lives in the Missouri River bottom land and the Monkey Faced Owl have both evolved and flourished since the early twentieth century. These and other stories are not limited to the reservation communities. Many families in far-flung urban areas enjoy the telling and hearing of these tales. In turn, the tales of the urban Umóⁿhoⁿ experi-ences drift back to the reservation.

Storytelling Protocols

The Umóⁿhoⁿ are a storytelling people. At any gathering or on any occasion stories are shared. Some stories recall recent events, while other stories describe the adventures of mythic heroes and supernatural beings. Many stories have a lesson or cultural value that is transmitted to the listener. Stories are used to teach young and old alike. Even the most tragic stories contain humorous passages. Stories are the repository of countless generations of Umóⁿhoⁿ wisdom and knowledge. Telling a story is the equivalent of opening the door to the library of the Umóⁿhoⁿ universe.

Because of the power associated with the spoken word, Umóⁿhoⁿ people are careful about when they tell certain stories. Tales about ani-mals, and perhaps some mythic beings, are called hīga. They were routinely told only during the long winter nights. Telling such sto-ries during the summer could have serious con-sequences. One Umóⁿhoⁿ explanation for this practice takes into consideration the feelings of the animals that are the characters of the sto-ry. Elders have said that since the animals have migrated away or are hibernating in the winter, they cannot hear the stories that are being told about them. If they were to overhear the sto-ries the animals might become angry or embar-rassed and run away. This would result in the Umóⁿhoⁿ people starving due to poor hunting.

A second explanation of the winter-time-only rule for such stories involves the snake and snow. Snakes are reported to be quite curi-ous whenever stories are being told. They will gather in large numbers to hear a good story.

By telling certain types of stories in the winter when the snakes are asleep, the problem of having snakes congregate around your home is solved. Recall that the power of the spoken word is very strong, so telling stories reserved for the winter time out of season may cause it to snow.

Stories that describe current events, family history, historic events, and other supernatural or mythic beings can be told at any time. Ghost stories are popular during the late fall as people begin to celebrate the Halloween season. Love stories and stories of unrequited love start appearing in the spring as social clubs host Valentine's Day festivities. Stories from the powwow trail are told and retold at powwow camps throughout the summer.

Storytelling and storytellers are worthy of our respect. Umónhon people place a high value on good oratorical skills. To be soft spoken and to choose words that are thoughtful and appropriate to the occasion are important elements of Umónhon culture. Personal boastfulness is discouraged. Proper pronunciation of words is greatly admired. Many people are hesitant to rise and speak in front of a crowd for fear of mispronouncing a word, choosing an inappropriate way to explain something, or overlooking some critical element in their speech. Public speaking is in the realm of men. A man who is skilled in the oratorical arts will be regularly invited to stand and speak or to tell stories to a gathering of people. Today such men serve as master of ceremonies for public functions. They are asked to stand and speak on the behalf of others in public.

Visitors to the home are often encouraged to share their stories after eating a meal with the family. The act of sharing food with someone is a sign of the desire by the giver to hear a story or gain knowledge. Elder women and men can tell stories in the privacy of the family home. Young people are encouraged to withhold interruptions out of respect for the storyteller. It is from these stories that our children learn how the world works and how the Umónhon people fit into the universe.

9.13 THE OMAHA HANDGAME: ÍNʔUTʰÍN, "STRIKE THE STONE"

A Beginner's Guide to Playing the Game

The Omaha handgame is a guessing game in which a team tries to hide two small stones or shells in their hands from the opposing team. It is from this action that the Omaha name for the game, ínʔutʰín, or "strike the stone" (ínʔe stone, utʰín "to strike it") is derived. The score is kept using eight tally sticks. A team winning all eight sticks is declared the winner of the game. Members of the losing team after each game have to dance while shaking gourd rattles and then pay a penalty. A team winning four games is declared the winner of the match.

FIG. 18. Handgame Pros by Jacob Smith.

The handgame is a popular activity that has been played by the Omaha people for many generations. Anecdotal information suggests that the handgame may have come from the Otoe tribe. Some attribute the game to the Kiowa; however, this may be a confusion between the gourd dance portion of the handgame with the warrior society gourd dance of the Kiowa tribe. There are some similarities to the formal protocols of the Omaha handgame and the Pawnee Ghost Dance handgame, as described by Alexander Lesser in *The Pawnee Ghost Dance Handgame* (University of Wisconsin Press, 1978).

The Omaha handgame is a secular (social) activity, but it has sacred elements and protocols (code of behavior). Many Elder relatives have contributed to my learning how to behave at handgames, including my adoptive grandparents, Charles and Elizabeth Stabler, and their kin: Clyde and Lillian Sheridan Jr., Oliver and Mae Saunsoci Sr., John and Suzette Turner, Lillian Wolf, Mary Clay, Mary Lieb Mitchell, and Carrie Drum, all now deceased. They were quite clear in their teachings. They said:

Handgame players should bathe, comb their hair, and dress nicely for the game. Players should avoid eating leftovers prior to handling the stone since greasy hands may cause the stone to fall. If you are chosen as a feather-carrier, never lay the feather down (even between games) and never allow it to fall on the floor. Players should arrive at the handgame on time and take their seat on whichever side they choose to support. No one should switch sides once the match has begun. Losers should not run away from the penalty gourd, but rather accept the penalty gourd gladly and dance as best as they can. Players should be a good sport, even if their side is losing. Everyone should support their teammates and opponents alike when they are dancing with the penalty gourds by dancing with them and offering them a gift to help pay the penalty. Players should be generous to the singers at the drum who provide the lively music that makes the game so enjoyable. Everyone can show their respect to the drum by walking clockwise around the drum when crossing the open floor area. Everyone should respect the scorekeepers for the important tasks they perform. No one should leave the handgame until the gathering is dismissed by the Man in Charge. Children should be kept seated with their family or sent outdoors to play. Parents will have to pay a penalty to the sponsors if their children walk between the feather-carrier and the people hiding stones. As with other Omaha social activities, to show respect to the bereaved family a handgame will be postponed or cancelled if there is a death in the community and the body is still unburied.
—Compiled in consultation with Elders

In no way do these protocols diminish the enjoyment of this animated social hour. Friendly rivalries often flourish between social clubs or groups and among competing players.

Handgame can be played in any space large enough to accommodate the players and singers. In past years the Lincoln Indian Club routinely played handgame in a club member's home in Lincoln, Nebraska. All the furniture was removed from a room so that players could sit on the floor along facing walls. Singers sat off to one corner, leaving the middle of the floor open for the movement of the feather-carrier. A scorekeeper was selected from each side to watch the tally sticks. If a drum was lacking, early club members would improvise, using an empty cardboard box to keep time to the hand-game songs.

Today the Lincoln Indian Club regularly plays handgame at the Lincoln Indian Center or, when weather permits, in the adjacent William Canby Powwow Arena. At Macy most handgames are played in the Alfred Gilpin Community Building. Other handgame sites include the Native American Church Hall, Small Arena at the pow-wow grounds, Umóⁿhoⁿ Nation Public School Gymnasium, and the Carl T. Curtis Health Education Center.

A handgame can be initiated by a person, family, or group. They are the "sponsors." The purpose of the handgame may be any number of things: to honor someone on a birthday or anniversary, to mark an achievement, or to honor a soldier returning from service (the "honoree"); to celebrate a holiday (Christmas, Mother's Day, etc.); or as a fundraiser for the sponsoring club. If a deceased relative was an avid handgame player, a family might sponsor memorial handgames on the anniversary of the person's death over the course of the four-year mourning period.

The sponsors set the time and place of the handgame and invite—or challenge—other social clubs to come and play. It was common in the past for sponsors to provide a game wager, particularly when social clubs competed. Today some sponsors continue to provide a game wager, usually twenty dollars or more. Stone-carrier and feather-carrier prizes are normally provided. Prizes may be smaller or absent if the event was advertised as a "hard-time handgame"

sponsored as a fundraiser for an individual or family having suffered any sort of crisis.

The sponsors select a man and woman to serve as scorekeepers, a head singer, and a Master of Ceremonies (always a male) and provide food for a communal feast after the game.

The floor arrangements are similar in the Gilpin building at Macy and at the Lincoln Indian Center. A table is set at the north end of the rectangular space for the scorekeepers and the MC with his microphone. The head singer with his drum and helpers sit in a circle at the center of the room. The room is divided down the middle from north to south, forming a "west side" team and an "east side" team. Unlike other tribes, who have set teams with everyone else being spectators, anyone in the room is an eligible player in the Omaha handgame. In Lincoln the sponsors (and honoree) sit on the west side. Invited clubs sit on the east side. Non-member spectators can sit on the side they choose to support.

The selection of the man and woman scorekeepers is the responsibility of the sponsors. This is a highly honored position and is accepted with dignity. In small, informal games, a man from the sponsoring team and a woman from the opposing team can be asked to sit at the table. More often, a husband and wife are selected ahead of time to keep score. The husband represents the sponsoring team. The male is referred to as the Man in Charge.

Today the husband and wife are often Native American Church members. The chosen male is usually an ordained minister. At the conclusion of the handgame he offers a cedar smoke blessing for the sponsors, honoree, and all in attendance. He also asks a blessing on the food. His wife may be called upon to assist the sponsors in cooking the meal. She is in charge of directing the distribution of the food and assuring that everyone gets something to eat.

If the Man in Charge is not an ordained minister in the NAC, he offers a prayer for the food without a cedar blessing. If the woman is his wife, she is in charge of the food distribution. If the woman was selected from the east side team, she is not expected to distribute the food. The sponsors may distribute the food while both scorekeepers remain seated at the head table during the meal.

The handgame "sticks" are provided by the sponsors or by the Man in Charge. The game pieces are usually carried in a small, homemade wooden box the size of a bread box. Before the game begins the Man in Charge and his wife arrange the game pieces on the table. A piece of cloth is spread on the table. The eight counter sticks are lined up in the center of the cloth. Sticks are often ⅜- to ½-inch wooden dowels approximately 10 to 12 inches long. Sometimes the eight sticks are beaded or otherwise ornamented on one end so that four are of one color and four of another color. If so, they are arranged so that each team has its own color.

The gourd rattles are placed on either side of the counter sticks, one for each scorekeeper. Today, the rattles are usually of the wooden maraca type available from music supply stores and Mexican arts and crafts dealers. One set of rattles in use today for child players is made from large aluminum salt shakers. Rattles made from natural gourds are not commonly used today, but several sets are known to exist as cherished family heirlooms. The wooden handles may be plain or carved with designs.

An eagle feather is placed on the table on the outer side of each gourd for each team. Feathers are approximately 12 inches long and usu-

ally come from the body rather than the tail or wing. Often the body of the eagle feather is narrowed by trimming and the end is lengthened by inserting a small stick in the base of the quill and covering it with leather for a better grip.

Dropping the feather is cause for losing the game and ending the match. The sponsors call a combat veteran from the crowd to pick up the feather and return it to the head table. Dropping the feather requires a penalty be paid to the sponsors and veteran by the guilty party. The sponsors will have to sacrifice (pay a penalty) if they want to resume the game or start a new match.

Some handgame sets from the early twentieth century do not have eagle feathers. It was difficult to obtain feathers, as evidenced in the Hethúshka war dance regalia of the period using pheasant and other non-eagle feathers. In the case of the handgame, an alternate instrument was sometimes used. Two "markers" were made using the same materials as the counter sticks. They were cut an inch or two longer and embellished with additional beadwork and leather fringe. They were treated with the same respect as the eagle feather.

Two small pieces of bone, plastic hair pipe, glass pebbles, stones, or cowry shells are laid near the feathers for each side. These are the stones to be hidden. Dropping the stone is cause for losing the team's turn.

When the singers have taken up their positions and the sponsors indicate their readiness, the Man in Charge formally announces the beginning of the handgame. He describes the reason for the handgame. He indicates the wager, if any, placed on the table in front of the handgame sticks, the prizes for the best feather-carriers on each side, and a prize for the stone-carriers. He then tells the head singer that they will play for four games. That means they will play until one team has won four games. Depending upon how the play proceeds, this could require a total of seven games. Four games is the normal number played. If the games end quickly with a score of 4-0, sometimes the sponsors or challengers provide a new wager (sacrifice) and call for another two games.

The singers render the handgame "starting song." The song is considered mandatory. There is a story of a handgame played at Macy at which the assembled singers did not know the starting song. Everyone waited for nearly an hour as the singers searched their collective memories for the song. Finally, an Elder singer arrived at the building. He joined the singers and started the appropriate song.

Most scorekeepers wait until the song is completed before distributing the stones and feathers. Other scorekeepers start moving before the song ends so that play can proceed more quickly. After circling the drum, the scorekeepers give one stone to an experienced player on their team to act as the "stone-carrier" for the entire match. On the west side the feather and second stone are to be given to the honoree or ranking officer of the sponsoring group, and on the east side they are to be given to the ranking officer of the challenging group. They become the "feather-carriers" for the first game.

The singers begin a fast-paced handgame song. The stone-carriers on each side join their team's feather-carrier and all walk around the drum before having a face-off in front of the scorekeepers' table. This is the "coin toss" to see which side gets to hide the stones first. Each team's feather-carrier and stone-carrier stand in front of the team, facing the opposing side.

The sponsoring team, or the winner of the previous game, always goes first. While holding the feather in one hand, the west side feather-carrier hides his or her single stone behind the back. When ready, both clenched fists are presented to the east side feather-carrier. The hands can be moved in a rhythmic motion with the beat of the drum to confuse the opponent. Using the feather as a pointer, the east side feather-carrier indicates a left side or right side guess. The west side feather-carrier indicates whether the guess "caught" or "struck" the stone, or "missed" it, by opening both hands. Now the east side feather-carrier hides the stone and the west side feather-carrier guesses. Regardless of whether the east side feather-carrier caught or missed the first guess, he or she always gets to hide the stone.

If each side "caught" the other, or each side "missed" the other, then it is a stalemate and there is another round of guessing. If the east side "caught" the west side, but the west side "missed" the east side, the stones go to the east side to start the game. If the east side "missed" the west side, but the west side "caught" the east side, the stones go to the west side to start the game. Sometimes there are ten or more rounds of guessing between the feather-carriers before actual play can begin. This often sparks some jokes from the MC about letting the rest of the people play, too.

When the feather-carriers have determined which side will start, they give their stones to the teams' stone-carriers. The stone-carriers now have two stones each. A stone-carrier signals to the singers to stop singing by waving a hand back and forth in a downward sweeping motion. The singers begin a new handgame song while the stone-carrier on the side that gets to hide first distributes one stone each to two team members.

On the west side, the stone-carrier chooses the first two people seated on the south side of the room on their team. On the east side, the stone-carrier chooses the first two people seated on the north side of the room on their team—often their team's scorekeeper and another nearby person. As the game proceeds, the stone-carriers continue to select players by moving clockwise through their team.

There are mixed feelings about allowing young children to play handgame. The concern is that they will drop the stone, which loses that team's turn. Children as young as the elementary grades are encouraged to play in Lincoln, although they are cautioned to be attentive and not to drop the stone. In the late 1980s the children at Macy Public School were taught how to play handgame as part of their Omaha language and culture class. They challenged the unbeatable Macy Senior Citizens to play handgame at the end of the school year. The Elders were flabbergasted when the children "skunked" the senior citizens by winning four games in a row.

The chosen players accept the stones. They stand to hide the stones behind their backs and usually move to stand side by side if they were seated far apart. When ready, they bring their clenched hands out in front and move their arms in rhythm to the fast-paced drumming. Team members are encouraged to clap in time with the drum to add to the confusion for the opposing team's feather-carrier.

The opposing team's feather-carrier and stone-carrier circle the drum clockwise and approach the stone-hiders. The feather-carrier tries to guess which hands hold the stones in a single play. The feather is used to indicate one of four possible combinations.

With the stone-hiders standing side by side, if the guess is the two inside hands, the feather is pointed down toward the floor between the players.

If the guess is the two outside hands the feather is grasped in the middle of its length and held horizontally in front of the feather-carrier.

If the guess is the two left hands the arm is extended toward that side and the feather clearly pointed to the players' left (the feather-carrier's right side).

If the guess is the two right hands the arm is extended toward that side and the feather clearly pointed to the players' right (the feather-carrier's left side).

Therefore the possible guesses are: inside, outside, players' left, or players' right.

The players must show their hands after a guess is made. If both stones are "struck" or "caught," the stone-carrier waves down the singers to stop the song, and the play goes to the opposing team. If one player successfully hides the stone, the stone-carrier raises one arm overhead to indicate one point won for the hiding team. The stone-carriers serve as the eyes for the scorekeepers and can settle minor disputes about the outcome of the guessing. That is why stone-carriers are chosen for their experience in playing handgame. The scorekeeper for the hiding team will claim one of the opponent's counter sticks, hold it overhead briefly for all to see, and then place it on the outside of the gourd rattle. The MC keeps up a running commentary on the movement of the sticks. Ideally, the MC remains a neutral party and encourages both sides to do their best. If both players successfully hide their stones, two arms are held overhead by the stone-carrier, and two points are taken by the scorekeepers. If only one player won the point, that player will hide the stone again. The player whose stone was caught does not hide in this second round. If the remaining player is successful in hiding in the second round, another point is won, and the sidelined player is now redeemed to hide in the third round. A round is over when the feather-carrier catches both the stones. The stone-carrier waves to the singers to stop the song, and a new song is started for the opposing team. Each turn of play is marked by a new handgame song.

Play goes back and forth between the teams, with players being chosen in a clockwise order for each team. After everyone has had a chance to play, the stone-carriers are free to pick randomly among their team members. Singers are eligible players for the side of the drum they are sitting on, although some people do not think it is appropriate to divert the head singer from his duties at the drum. The game is over when one team has successfully won all eight counter sticks. The scorekeeper for the victorious side raises and shakes the rattle to close the game. The feather-carrier from the losing side retrieves one stone from the stone-carrier and returns feather and stone to the table. The feather-carrier from the winning side retrieves one stone from the stone-carrier and keeps feather and stone for the start of the next game.

In an especially hard-fought game that hinges on a single point, the feather-carrier may relinquish the feather to another team member to make the decisive guess. If the new feather-carrier makes the correct guess and saves the game, that player keeps the feather and continues to play. If the new person ultimately wins the game, that player keeps the feather for the next game. If the new person mis-guesses and loses the game, the feather is returned to the original feather-carrier, who returns it to the head table.

It is considered a stroke of exceptional good fortune, or divine intervention, when a feather-carrier wins four games in a row. While not a requirement, this occasion is often marked by the winning feather-carrier giving away or pledging money or material goods to some future social activity of the sponsoring club.

After each game the singers render two round dance songs. All the women are invited to dance. Wearing a dance shawl is considered appropriate attire when dancing in street clothes. Males can round dance, too. This is an opportunity to stand up and stretch legs, use the rest room, or go outdoors to smoke. At or near the end of the second round dance song the scorekeeper from the victorious team takes both rattles from the table and distributes them to two players on the losing team. Normally there is little difficulty in passing out the gourds, as most people anticipate receiving it in the case of their team's loss. Receiving the gourd is usually seen as an honor. However, sometimes it becomes a comic affair. Some female losers may try to "hide out" in the women's rest room until after the round dancing is over to avoid the penalty gourds. Several elderly male scorekeepers are known to have waited patiently outside the rest room for a particular woman to exit. It has been reported that one Elder male scorekeeper walked into the rest room to present the gourd. Scorekeepers have been known to wait near the building entrance to catch a particular smoker who had gone outdoors to avoid getting the gourds.

Visitors, non-Indians, and individuals known to be good dancers are often the target for the penalty gourds. It is all meant to be in good fun.

The singers render an appropriate war dance song or family song. Players with the gourds dance clockwise around the drum. Supporters, friends, and relatives from both teams often dance behind the gourd dancers. They place a dollar or two into the hands of each gourd dancer. At the end of the song the two gourd dancers go to the head table. Usually the older of the two dancers approaches the MC first to express some thoughts about the day's event, the happiness at getting the gourd and the opportunity to dance, to wish the sponsors or honoree good fortune, and to thank the friends and relatives who helped with gifts to pay the penalty. The MC announces all this to the crowd, adding culturally appropriate words that express the gourd dancer's thoughts.

The dancer counts the money in hand and must decide how to pay the penalty. The dancer can add a few dollars and return all the money with the gourd to the table. The table money goes to the sponsors or the honoree. The dancer can split the money and place some on the table and take the rest and place it on the drum for the singers. The money is placed on the drum in front of the head singer's chair. If the dancer has some additional material gift to present to the sponsors, honoree, or a visitor, the presentation can be made at this time. After shaking hands with both scorekeepers, the gourd dancer is free to circle the drum and sit down. After both gourds have been returned, the sponsors or honoree walk around the arena and shake hands with the gourd dancers for their generosity.

This concludes the first game. The scorekeepers rearrange the sticks and gourds back to their starting positions. The MC announces the score while the scorekeeper from the losing side circles the drum and hands out the feather and stone to a new team member for the next game.

Both feather-carriers and stone-carriers circle the drum and face off again to determine which side hides the stone first. When it is the winning side's turn to hide the stones, the stone-carrier always starts with the last two players who won the previous game. It is hoped that their good luck will last from the previous game. That is why it is very important that all participants remain in their seats and are able to play when called upon.

If the first game ended before everyone on the team had a chance to play, the stone-carriers pick up where they left off and proceed to choose players in a clockwise manner. If all team members have played previously, the stone-carrier can pick and choose pairs of players at random.

The activity continues with rounds of handgame, round dance, and gourd dancing until one team has won four games. If the score is tied 3–3, with only one game remaining, an additional song is sung after the dance with the gourds. This is a giveaway song, sometimes called the "tie-breaker" song. This provides people who may not otherwise have received the gourd a final opportunity to get up and dance in order to participate in the giveaway. After the song is rendered the dancers ask the MC to relay their thoughts to the assembled crowd. Gifts may be presented to the sponsors, honoree, visitors, or the drum. Sometimes pledges of support for some future event are made. When this is concluded, the final game to determine the match winner begins.

At the conclusion of the handgame cycle, the scorekeepers usually dance with the penalty gourds. An appropriate honor song is rendered, and the crowd stands out of respect. Often many of the players join in the dance with the scorekeepers to show their support. At the end of the song the Man in Charge usually speaks on behalf of the female scorekeeper and himself. He thanks the sponsors for the honor of watching the sticks. He thanks the members of both teams for being good sports and accepting the gourds that he and the female scorekeeper passed out. He makes gifts to the sponsors, honoree, and/or the drum as part of the sacrifice for taking the gourds.

If the event is a fundraiser or a hard-time handgame, the eight counter sticks may be passed out in addition to the two gourds following each game. Or they can be passed out following the final game to anyone who has not received the gourds. In some cases, the scorekeepers pass out the sticks to their own team members rather than the opposing team. The sticks serve as an additional way to gather donations for whatever the fundraising cause happens to be.

At the conclusion of the handgame the Man in Charge announces the winners, often accompanied by thunderous applause from the victors. He recounts the efforts of the feather-carrier(s) from the losing side and awards the feather prize to the person with the most games won, or to the feather-carrier of the final game if the side had no winning games. He also awards the prize to the losing side's stone-carrier.

Next, he recounts the exploits of the winning team's feather-carrier(s) and awards the prize to the feather-carrier who won the most games, or the final game won if all other feather-carriers had single scores. If there are two feather-carriers, each winning two games, the prize goes to the feather-carrier winning the decisive game. He also awards the prize to the winning side's stone-carrier. Feather-carrier prizes are often fruit baskets or similar items. Stone-carrier prizes may be smaller versions of the feather-carrier prizes, or small monetary gifts.

The handgame sticks, gourds, feathers, and stones are returned to their box. This formally indicates the end of the handgame portion of the social hour. The money that comes to the table with the gourds is counted and announced to the crowd, then handed over to the sponsors or honoree.

A meal is always served at a handgame. If the handgame is still underway at sundown, the sponsors may suspend the game in order to eat before dark. The break will be made after the gourd dance and before the beginning of the next game. The eagle feather from the losing side will already have been returned to the table. The feather-carrier from the winning side may choose to keep the feather in his or her possession or return it to the head table for safe keeping during the meal.

Eating after dark is of concern especially in the Lincoln case. The community room at the Lincoln Indian Center has multiple windows without blinds or curtains. Handgame sponsors are keenly aware of the approaching darkness and the inability to cover the windows after dark. The covering of windows reflects the Omaha belief that the spirits of deceased relatives are attracted to food. Covering the windows is a sign of respect to avoid "teasing" the spirits by eating in front of them. The handgame resumes after the meal is finished, the food has been cleared away from the arena, and the singers have rendered an appreciation song. The Gilpin building at Macy does not have external windows, so it is possible to continue play until the match is over regardless of the approach of darkness. The meal is served after the match game.

This recognition of the spirits and their attraction to earthly food may be the explanation of an old tradition. In handgames of the past, it was reported that the Man in Charge would pour out a small ladleful of soup on the ground. This was explained as an offering to the spirits of all the deceased relatives. This honorable practice has not been witnessed in the past several decades.

Other activities may be incorporated into the handgame. Food basket raffles, 50/50 raffles, cake walks, and other diversions may be inserted between the gourd dance and start of the next game. Other diversions include having people wearing eye-glasses dance, selected males dancing to a fast-paced contest song while wearing a woman's shawl, or couples dancing as pairs trying to hold a potato pressed between their foreheads. This is not a universal practice. Some handgame organizers view the traditional protocols as being too sacred for such secular diversions. However, most people see handgame as a primarily social event that allows other light-hearted amusements to be embedded into the handgame rounds.

Moving the Sticks

Depending upon the teachings and experiences of the individual scorekeepers, there may be more than one way to move the counter sticks. The predominant Omaha method appears to be always first to take the sticks from between (inside) the two gourd rattles. The following illustrations show the stick movement rules when you take the inside sticks first.

Round one: Both EAST side stone-hiders avoid being caught and win two points. The EAST side scorekeeper takes two sticks from the WEST side's inside pile and places them on the EAST side of their team's gourd. Both EAST side stone-hiders get caught in the next play and lose the round. The play goes to the WEST side.

Round two: The WEST side stone-hiders avoid being caught and win two points. The WEST side scorekeeper takes two sticks from the EAST side's inside pile and places them on the WEST side of the gourd. Both WEST side stone-hiders get caught in the next play and lose the round. The play goes back to the EAST side.

Round three: The EAST side stone-hiders avoid being caught and win two points. The EAST side scorekeeper takes two more sticks from the WEST side's remaining inside pile and places them on the EAST side of the gourd.

One of the EAST side stone-hiders gets caught and is temporarily out of the game. The

FIG. 19. Handgame start (*below, top*). Starting formation after the feathers and stones have been distributed.

FIG. 20. (*below, bottom*) Round one scorekeeper table.

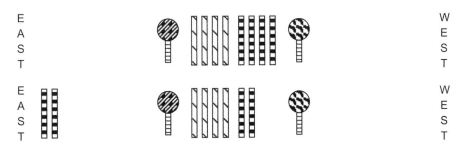

other EAST side stone-hider avoids being caught and wins one point. The EAST side scorekeeper takes one point from their own inside pile and places it on the EAST side of the gourd.

The remaining EAST side stone-hider again avoids being caught and wins one point. The EAST side scorekeeper takes one point from their own remaining inside pile and places it on the EAST side of the gourd. The other EAST side stone-hider who was sidelined is redeemed and now eligible to play.

Both EAST side hiders avoid being caught and win two points. The EAST side scorekeeper takes two sticks from the WEST side's winnings and places them on the EAST side of the gourd. The EAST side now has all eight sticks. The EAST side scorekeeper raises and shakes the rattle to indicate winning the game.

In this method, the winning point is always be the last available stick drawn from the inside or from the opponent's winnings.

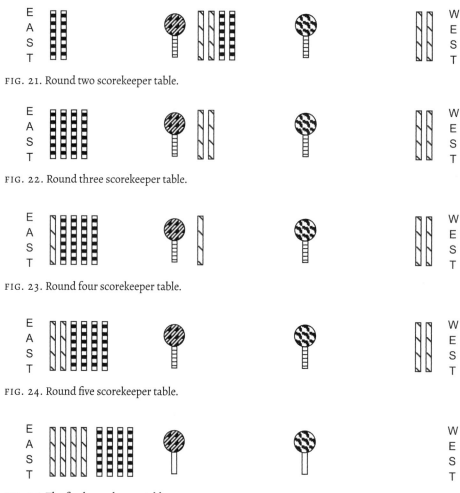

FIG. 21. Round two scorekeeper table.

FIG. 22. Round three scorekeeper table.

FIG. 23. Round four scorekeeper table.

FIG. 24. Round five scorekeeper table.

FIG. 25. The final scorekeeper table.

10.1 WELCOME

The UNL grammar section stands somewhere between a college introductory language textbook and a grammatical treatise. In its first incarnation, in the spring of 2007, it was intended to be a grammatical guide upon which skeleton Mark and Vida would build the real textbook. As work progressed, however, it soon *became* the textbook for UNL. Rather windy at first, it was tightened up to comply with Mark's suggestion that we trim it back into simple rubrics for easy learning. This gave us our formula of illustrative tables with explanatory bullet points. The remainder of each lesson was filled out with vocabulary and five exercise sections. Part A provided ten sentences to be translated from Omaha to English, and part B gave ten more sentences to be translated from English to Omaha. Parts C, D, and E were for imaginative classroom exercises along the lines of the "Ttígaxe" immersion exercises we had been experimenting with for a number of years.

The original plan was for twelve chapters of nine lessons each, to be covered at the rate of one per day, with a chapter quiz every second week. This book would be the core of the first college year, six chapters for twelve weeks per semester. We commenced writing for our fourth Omaha class cohort of 2007–8, three bright and diligent students. Writing and teaching a lesson a day, we made good progress for the first semester through chapter 5. In the middle of the

following semester we set it aside and reverted to other activities. We taught two more cohorts after that and made a few revisions, but we never continued beyond chapter 6. Chapters 7 through 10 have been written in the past two years to complete the project and cover the essentials of Omaha grammar. In fact, five chapters per semester seems more realistic than six, and this conforms nicely with the five credit hours per semester that are standard for first-year language courses at the University of Nebraska–Lincoln.

It should be emphasized that the UNL grammatical lessons in part 2, unlike the UNPS section making up part 1, are not based directly on sentences elicited from native speakers. Our focus has been on grammatically analyzing the language to understand its system in a way that would allow a second language learner to speak it in any context with a morpheme-level understanding of what they are saying. Our approach is therefore experimental rather than cautiously empirical. We, the students of Omaha, have made up our Omaha sentences, to be reviewed by our native speakers, who either pass each sentence or help us correct it. But the sentences are from the imaginations of outsiders and are not necessarily reflective of what people native to the language and culture ever actually say. Our method has its benefits for learning to use the language again in an open-ended way that allows us to say what we will, but it has its risks of potential distortion as well. With that caveat in mind, we have always striven for accuracy and have maintained an ethic of correcting ourselves immediately whenever we find ourselves in error. We sincerely hope that our grammatical analysis and the supporting sentences in this book do justice to the Omaha language and to the people who have spoken it as their native language.

10.2 SIOUAN LANGUAGES

Omaha belongs to a large family of related languages called *Siouan*. Its closest relative is *Ponca*, which probably split off from Omaha some three hundred years ago, around 1700. Omaha and Ponca are essentially the same language. They are perhaps about as similar to each other as British English is to American English. The Poncas lived just to the northwest of the Omahas in northeastern Nebraska, until most of them were removed to Oklahoma in the 1870s.

Next most closely related are *Osage*, from central Missouri, and *Kaw*, or *Kansa*, from eastern Kansas. These two languages are more closely related to each other than to Omaha-Ponca. They would be only partially comprehensible to a speaker of Omaha, perhaps as a speaker of Scottish English would be to a speaker of American English.

A bit further away again is *Quapaw*, from eastern Arkansas. These five languages — Quapaw, Osage, Kaw, Omaha, and Ponca — make up a group that we call *Dhegihan* (pronounced "*lay*-ghee-han").

Dhegihan is one of three or four groups that make up *Mississippi Valley Siouan*, or MVS for short.

The *Dakotan* branch of MVS is the Sioux proper, and includes *Santee (Dakota)*, *Yankton*, *Teton (Lakota)*, *Assiniboine*, and *Stoney*. This is a widespread group that dominated the northern Plains from Minnesota to Montana, and from

FIG. 26. Dhegihan family tree.

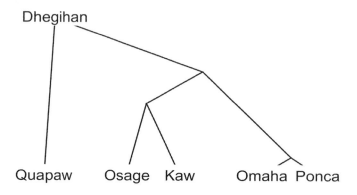

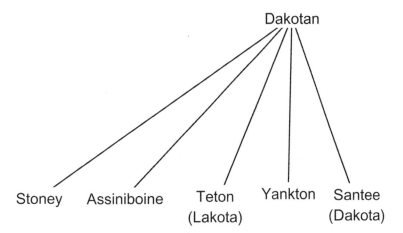

FIG. 27. Dakotan family tree.

northern Nebraska into Canada. It may have originated in southern Minnesota.

An Omaha speaker and a Dakotan speaker would probably not be able to understand each other's speech without learning the other's language, but they would find many of their basic words to be the same or very similar. This would be much like the case of a speaker of English matched with a speaker of German, Dutch, or Swedish.

MVS also includes *Ho-Chunk* (*Winnebago*) and *Chiwere*, which are usually considered to be most closely related to each other. *Chiwere* includes *Iowa* and *Otoe*, which are about as close as Omaha and Ponca, as well as *Missouria*, originally from the St. Louis area around the mouth of the Missouri River, which is thought to have been closely related to these. The Iowas and Otoes ranged over Iowa, southern Minnesota, and eastern Nebraska.

For several centuries up until the mid-nineteenth century, the Omahas seem to have maintained a particularly close social relationship with them. *Ho-Chunk*, from eastern Wisconsin, is more distantly related to Chiwere. One group of this tribe was displaced, and eventually moved into the northern part of the Omaha reservation in Nebraska in the nineteenth century, where they still live today.

These branches make up Mississippi Valley Siouan, which is the largest portion of the Siouan language family.

Siouan includes three other language groups besides MVS. In the northwest, around the upper Missouri in Montana and North Dakota are *Crow* and *Hidatsa*, which are fairly closely related. Also on the Missouri River, just downstream from the Hidatsa, are the *Mandan*. Mandan may be somewhat intermediate between *Crow-Hidatsa* and MVS. In the east are several related languages, the last native speakers of which lived about a century ago. In the Appa-

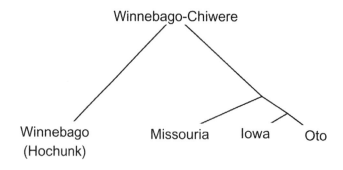

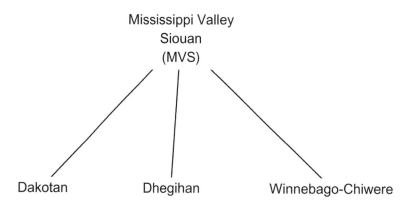

FIG. 28. Winnebago-Chiwere family tree (*top*).

FIG. 29. Family tree of Mississippi Valley Siouan (MVS) (*bottom*).

lachians of western Virginia were *Tutelo* and *Saponi*, on the lower Mississippi was *Ofo*, and on the Gulf coast, just east of the mouth of the Mississippi, was *Biloxi*. These languages are grouped together as *Southeastern Siouan*.

An Omaha speaker and a Crow speaker not only would not be able to understand each other, but they would not even find very many of their words to be obviously similar.

Catawba and *Yuchi* are two languages that were spoken around the Appalachians of North and South Carolina and that were related more distantly to Siouan and to each other. Beyond these, no other languages are really known to be related to Omaha or to the other Siouan languages.

Siouan is one of the great language families of North America. It occupies the central part of the continent, ranging from the Appalachians to the Rockies, and from the Gulf coast to the northern Plains in Canada. The habitat of Siouan-speaking peoples has generally been

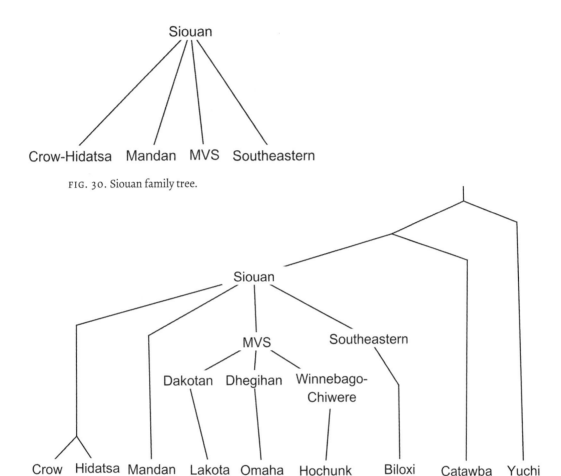

FIG. 30. Siouan family tree.

FIG. 31. Family tree of Siouan, Catawba and Yuchi, with sample languages.

plains, prairie, and deciduous forest. They are seldom found far from the great interior rivers, such as the Ohio, Missouri, and the Mississippi. They do not seem to have extended across the Rockies, nor far into the arid Southwest or the coniferous forest to the north. Their original homeland may have been around the central Appalachians, close to the headwaters of the Ohio and Tennessee rivers, near where Catawba,

Yuchi, Tutelo, Saponi, and originally Ofo lived in more recent times.

Siouan has been surrounded by several other great language families. To the northeast is *Algonquian*, which includes Ojibwe, Ottawa, Potawatomi, Cree, Delaware, Menominee, Meskwaki, and many others. The entire eastern subarctic of Canada is Algonquian speaking as well as most of the Great Lakes area and

FIG. 32. Siouan and neighboring language families of North America.

the northeast coast. The Cheyenne, Arapaho, and Blackfoot languages of the western Plains are also Algonquian, though perhaps more distantly related to the northeastern ones. In the mountains of New York state and parts of the Appalachians farther south is *Iroquoian*, which includes Huron, Mohawk, Seneca, Oneida, and Cherokee, among others. In the southeast, from Georgia and Florida westward along the Gulf coast states, is *Muskogean*, which includes Creek, Seminole, Alabama, Chocktaw, and Chickasaw. Extending up the Plains from the south, from Louisiana and Texas to South Dakota, is *Caddoan*, which includes Caddo, Wichita, Pawnee, and Arikara. To the west and southwest is *Uto-Aztecan*, which includes Shoshoni, Comanche, Ute, Hopi, the Nahuatl language of the pre-Hispanic Mexican empire, and many others. To the northwest is *Athabaskan (Dene)*, which includes the interior languages of the subarctic region of western Canada and Alaska as well as Navaho and Apache in the American Southwest.

Siouan is the most centrally situated native language family in North America, and Omaha and its Dhegiha relatives in historical times have been languages of people who lived near the geographical center of Siouan. This introduction to the relatives and neighbors of Omaha sets the context for the study of Omaha itself.

10.3 OMAHA SOUNDS:
ORAL VOWELS AND H

Letter	Pronounced	Letter Name
a	a as in "father"	a
e	like ey in "hey"	e
i	like ee in "fee"	i
o	like o in "go"	o
u	like oo in "too"	u
h	like h in "home"	ha

- The Omaha language has its own set of sounds. Some of these sounds are like sounds in English. Others are different. We use a special alphabet for the sounds of Omaha.

- In English we cannot always tell how a word is pronounced by looking at how it is spelled. The same letter may be pronounced differently in different words, and different letters are sometimes pronounced the same way. In our Omaha alphabet, we don't want to allow this. We will have one letter for every sound. That way, we will know how to pronounce any word we see.

- Each letter has a name by which we call it when we spell. In English the letter names have changed in the way they sound. In most languages, the letter *a* is pronounced "ah" as in "father"; *e* is pronounced "ey" as in "hey"; *i* is pronounced "ee" as in "see"; *o* is pronounced "o" as in "go"; and *u* is pronounced "oo" as in "too." This is the way we pronounce them in Omaha.

- Language sounds are either *vowels* or *consonants*. Vowels are the full-voiced sounds that are made with the mouth open. The letters *a, e, i, o,* and *u* are vowels. Consonants are the sounds made by muffling the voice. They separate the vowels. The letter *h* is a consonant. We will name it "ha."

- We speak by alternating vowels and consonants to make a rhythm: muffled, full-voice, muffled, full-voice; consonant, vowel, consonant, vowel. Each cycle of consonant and vowel is called a *syllable*. Some syllables are louder or higher-pitched than others. We mark these with an accent over the vowel.

Vocabulary

á: arm

há: leather, hide

hé: horn, antler

hí: tooth

hú: voice

huhú: fish

í: mouth

íha: lips

FIG. 33. hé: horn, antler. Figures 33–102 and 104–210 by Barbara Salvatore.

FIG. 34. huhú: fish

Speaking Practice

A. The instructor reads the vocabulary words aloud, noting their meanings, and also spelling the word out loud and writing it on the board. The students repeat the words aloud as a group and repeat the spelling.

B. The instructor goes through the words again, having each student repeat a word, spell it out loud, and tell what it means. The instructor corrects the student's pronunciation.

C. The instructor goes through the words randomly, asking each student the Omaha word for the English meaning. The student also spells the word.

D. The instructor again goes through the words randomly, asking each student the Omaha word for the English meaning. This time the instructor asks the question in Omaha using the construction: "_____," Umóⁿhoⁿ īe tʰe awatʰégoⁿ? What is the Omaha word for "_____"? The instructor also uses an Omaha command to have them spell the word: Wabáx̣u kʰe āthada ga! (if the instructor is a man) or Wabáx̣u kʰe āthada a! (if the instructor is a woman), "Spell it!" Example:

Instructor: Sam, "fish," Umóⁿhoⁿ īe tʰe awatʰégoⁿ? ("Sam, what is 'fish' in Omaha?")

    Sam: Huhú.

    Instructor: Wabáx̣u kʰe āthada ga!

    Sam: Ha, u, ha, u.

E. The students form small groups of about two to four. In each group the students take turns quizzing their partners on randomly chosen vocabulary words, both in Omaha to English and in English to Omaha. They also quiz each other on how to spell the Omaha word out loud.

10.4 OMAHA SOUNDS: NASALS

Letter	Pronounced	Letter Name
ε^n	like ε, the sound in "pet", but nasalized	ε^n
i^n	like i, but nasalized	i^n
o^n	variously between a, o, and u, but nasalized	o^n
m	like m in "man"	mi
n	like n in need	ni

· Some language sounds are made through the nose. These sounds are called *nasals*.

· Nasals can be consonants or vowels. English and Omaha both have the nasal consonants *m* and *n*. The *m* is made by closing your lips and letting the sound out through your nose, while *n* is made by closing the front of your mouth with the front of your tongue and letting the sound out through your nose.

· A nasal vowel is made by letting the sound flow out through your nose as well as your mouth. An oral vowel lets the sound out through your mouth only, not the nose. The vowels we met in the last lesson were all oral vowels.

- We have no vowels that are distinctively nasal in English, but in Omaha we have between two and four. The sound of i^n is pronounced like i, but is nasalized. There seem to be two or three sounds like the nasalized versions of a, o, and perhaps the sound of u in "but." These are often treated as a single sound, written as o^n for Omaha and a^n for Ponca. In this section we distinguish o^n, spoken with slightly rounded lips and sounding like a nasalized short o, and a^n, spoken without lip-rounding and sounding like a nasalized version of the u in "but" or "underwear." There seems to be at least one minimal pair, thihó^n, "lift it," vs. thihá^n, "your mother," that these sounds distinguish. There is also a very rare sound like the nasalized version of ɛ, the sound in "men." We write this as e^n.

- In Omaha the nasalization of a nasal vowel is very faint or absent when it comes at the end of a word with more than one syllable, and its syllable is unaccented. Thus, dí^{n}di^n, "tense," is pronounced more like dí^{n}di, and shínuda^n, "dog," is pronounced more like shínuda.

- The name of the Omaha tribe or language uses the a^n sound, and by our orthography would be written as Umá^{n}ha^n or Umá^{n}ha. However, since the spelling is generally established as Umó^{n}ho^n within the tribe, this is what we use in our lessons.

FIG. 35. hó^n: night

Vocabulary

áhi^n: wing

áo^n: yes

hí^n: body hair; animal hair

hó^n: night

ihá^n: a mother; his/her mother

má: snow

mé: spring (the season)

mí: sun

mó^{n}hi^n: knife

ní: water

nó^n: adult, grown up

nú: man

uhá^n: to cook

Umó^{n}ho^n: Omaha

FIG. 36. má: snow

FIG. 37. móⁿhiⁿ: knife

Speaking Practice

A. The instructor reads the vocabulary words aloud, noting their meanings, and also spelling the word out loud and writing it on the board. The students repeat the words aloud as a group and repeat the spelling.

B. The instructor goes through the words again, having each student repeat a word, spell it out loud, and tell what it means. The instructor corrects the student's pronunciation.

C. The instructor goes through the words randomly, asking each student the Omaha word for the English meaning. The student also spells the word.

D. The instructor goes through the words again randomly, asking each student the Omaha word for the English meaning. This time the instructor asks the question in Omaha using the construction: "_____," Umóⁿhoⁿ īe tʰe awatʰégoⁿ? What is the Omaha word for "_____"? The instructor also uses an Omaha command to have students spell the word: Wabáx̣u kʰe áthada ga! (if the instructor is a man) or Wabáx̣u kʰe áthada a! (if the instructor is a woman), "Spell it!" Example:

> Instructor: Sam, "Omaha," Umóⁿhoⁿ īe tʰe awatʰégoⁿ? ("Sam, what is 'Omaha' in Omaha?")
>
> Sam: Umóⁿhoⁿ.
>
> Instructor: Wabáx̣u kʰe áthada ga!
>
> Sam: U, mi, oⁿ, ha, oⁿ.

E. The students form small groups of about two to four. In each group the students take turns quizzing their partners on randomly chosen vocabulary words, both in Omaha to English and in English to Omaha. They also quiz each other on how to spell the Omaha word out loud.

10.5 OMAHA SOUNDS: STOPS

Letter	Pronounced	Letter Name
k	like k in "skate"	ka
p	like p in "spike"	pe
t	like t in "stun"	te
b	like b in "ban"	be
d	like d in "dog"	de
g	like g in "go"	ge
k^h	like k in "keep"	ka-ha
p^h	like p in "pat"	pe-ha
t^h	like t in "too"	te-ha
kk	like k in "skate," but longer and tenser	ka-dí^{n}di^n
pp	like p in "spike," but longer and tenser	pe-dí^{n}di^n
tt	like t in "stun," but longer and tenser	te-dí^{n}di^n

- Some consonants stop the speech sound completely by closing both the mouth and the nasal passage. These sounds are called *stops*.

- Stops vary according to where the mouth is closed. The three easiest places to close your mouth are at the lips (*labial* closure), between the front of the tongue and the front of the mouth (*alveolar* closure), and between the back of the tongue and the back of the mouth (*velar* closure). Labial consonants are *m, b* and *p*; *n, d* and *t* are alveolar consonants; *g, k,* and the *ng* (ŋ) sound in "singing" are velar consonants.

- Stops also vary according to the manner in which they are made. In English, we distinguish two series: the voiced stops *b, d* and *g*; and the voiceless stops *p, t* and *k*. The voiceless stops are usually *aspirated*, which means that a puff of air comes out with them. The voiceless stops are not aspirated when they are preceded by *s*. The voiced stops are never aspirated.

- In Omaha, we distinguish several series of stops. First is the *simple* series p, t and k. These occur only when they are preceded by s or some similar consonant.

- The second is the *voiced* series b, d and g. These are like the sounds in English. They do not occur with another consonant except for th.

- Third is the *tense* series pp, tt and kk. These stops are unlike anything in English. They are neither voiced nor aspirated, but are pronounced with more tension than the others, and they are held longer. These sounds were originally either stops coming before an accented syllable or two consonants together. We call these [stop]-dí^{n}di^n.

- Fourth is the aspirated series p^h, t^h and k^h. These are pronounced with a puff of breath like the English p, t and k when they stand alone in front of a vowel. We write them with a raised h, and call them [stop]-ha.

	Labial	Alveolar	Velar	
Simple	**p**	**t**	**k**	voiceless, unaspirated, untense; only found after a consonant like **s**
Voiced	**b**	**d**	**g**	voiced, unaspirated, untense; found alone or followed by **th**
Tense	**pp**	**tt**	**kk**	tense, voiceless, unaspirated; double consonant, found alone
Aspirated	**p^h**	**t^h**	**k^h**	aspirated, voiceless, untense; stop + **h**, found alone

Vocabulary

bóⁿ: to scream, yell

dúba: four

gióⁿ: to fly

hiⁿbé: shoe, moccasin

iⁿdé: face

kʰí: arrive back there

kké: turtle

migá: female (animals only)

móⁿga: skunk

noⁿbá: two

noⁿbé: hand

núde: throat, neck

nugá: male (animals only)

óⁿba: day

óⁿpʰaⁿ: elk

ppá: head; nose

ppé: forehead

ppí: liver

tʰí: arrive here

tté: buffalo

ttí: house, building

ttú: blue

Speaking Practice

A. The instructor reads the vocabulary words aloud, noting their meanings, and also spelling the words out loud and writing them on the board. The students repeat the words aloud as a group and repeat the spelling.

B. The instructor goes through the words again, having each student repeat a word, spell it out loud, and tell what it means. The instructor corrects the student's pronunciation.

C. The instructor goes through the words randomly, asking each student the Omaha word for the English meaning. The student also spells the word.

D. The instructor goes through the words again randomly, asking each student the Omaha word for the English meaning. This time the instructor asks the question in Omaha using the construction: "_____," Umóⁿhoⁿ íe tʰe

FIG. 38. kké: turtle

FIG. 39. móⁿga: skunk

FIG. 40. tté: buffalo

awat^hégoⁿ? What is the Omaha word for
"_____"? The instructor also uses an
Omaha command to have students spell
the word: Wabáx̣u k^he áthada ga!
(if the instructor is a man) or Wabáx̣u
k^he áthada a! (if the instructor is a
woman), "Spell it!"

E. The students form small groups of about
two to four. In each group the students
take turns quizzing their partners on
randomly chosen vocabulary words,
both in Omaha to English and in English
to Omaha. They also quiz each other on
how to spell the Omaha word out loud.

10.6 OMAHA SOUNDS: FRICATIVES

Letter	Pronounced	Letter Name
s	like s in "sit"	sa
sh	like sh in "ship"	she
x̌	like ch in "Bach"	x̌u
ṣ	like s but muted	sa-shtóⁿga
ṣh	like sh but muted	she-shtóⁿga
x̣	like x̌ but muted and farther back	x̣a
z	like z in "zoo"	ze
zh	like si in "Asia"	zhu

· Some consonants restrict the speech
breath so as to produce a hissing or
buzzing sound. These sounds are called
fricatives.

· Like stops, fricatives vary according
to where the mouth is closed and the
manner in which they are made. In
English, we have *f, th* as in "think," *s* and

sh in the voiceless fricative series, and
v, th as in "this," *z* and *zh* as the voiced
fricative series.

	Alveolar	Alveolo-Palatal	Velar	
Forced	s	sh	x̌	voiceless, forceful
Muted	ṣ	ṣh	x̣	semivoiced, lax
Voiced	z	zh		voiced

· Omaha seems to have three series
of fricatives. First is the *forced* series,
including the strong, voiceless sounds s
and sh as in English.

· Second is the *voiced* series, which has
the clear, voiced sounds z and zh as in
English.

· Third is the *muted* series, which includes
the sounds ṣ and ṣh. These sounds are
pronounced weakly, without much
force, and it is hard to tell if they are
voiced or not. The two sounds ṣ and ṣh
occur regularly before n, and sometimes
after a nasal vowel. They do not appear
anywhere else. We call them s-shtóⁿga
and sh-shtóⁿga. Shtóⁿga means "soft" in
Omaha.

· Omaha also makes fricatives in the back
of the mouth where k and g are made.
English does not do this, but other
languages such as German and Spanish
do. These sounds are not hard to make.
You simply start to make a k, but don't
quite hit it. Done forcefully, this makes
a x̌. If lax or muted, it makes a x̣; x̣ also
seems to be made a little farther back in
the mouth than x̌, and x̣ may be either
voiced or muted. (For linguistically

experienced students, we are using x̌ here to represent the voiceless velar fricative usually written as /x/, and x̣ to represent what might be the voiced velar fricative /ɣ/.)

- Unlike ṣ and ṣh, x̣ can occur alone in environments that are not nasal. In consonant clusters, x̌ occurs before both simple stops and th.

Vocabulary (a)

móⁿshoⁿ: feather, plume

móⁿze: metal (esp. iron)

sábe: black

sagí: hard

sí: foot

síⁿde: tail

sóⁿ: pale, distant white

shábe: dark

shág̣e: nails, claw, hoof, talons

shé: apple

shínuda: dog

shóⁿge: horse

shugá: thick

zí: yellow

Vocabulary (b)

izházhe: name

noⁿzhíⁿ: to stand

noⁿzhíⁿha: head hair, scalp

uzhóⁿge: road

zhábe: beaver

zhíbe: leg, lower leg

zhiⁿgá: small, young

zhóⁿ: wood

Vocabulary (c)

moⁿzéni: milk

nuṣhnáⁿ: otter

ṣní: cold (an object)

ṣhnábe: dirty

uṣní: it's cold (ambient temperature)

FIG. 41. shínuda: dog

FIG. 42. shóⁿge: horse

Vocabulary (d)

baxú: to write

míxa: duck, goose

xáde: hay, fodder

xé: to bury

xubé: holy, sacred

xúde: gray

xúga: badger

xagé: to cry, weep

FIG. 43. míxa: duck

FIG. 44. xúga: badger

Speaking Practice

A. The instructor reads the vocabulary words aloud, noting their meanings, and also spelling each word out loud and writing it on the board. The students repeat the words aloud as a group and repeat the spelling.

B. The instructor goes through the words again, having each student repeat a word, spell it out loud, and tell what it means. The instructor corrects the student's pronunciation.

C. The instructor goes through the words randomly, asking each student the Omaha word for the English meaning. The student also spells the word.

D. The instructor goes through the words randomly again, asking each student the Omaha word for the English meaning. This time the instructor asks the question in Omaha using the construction: "_____," Umóⁿhoⁿ íe tʰe awatʰégoⁿ? What is the Omaha word for "_____"? The instructor also uses an Omaha command to have students spell the word: Wabáxu kʰe áthada ga! (if the instructor is a man) or Wabáxu kʰe áthada a! (if the instructor is a woman), "Spell it!"

E. The students form small groups of about two to four. In each group the students take turns quizzing their partners on randomly chosen vocabulary words, both in Omaha to English and in English to Omaha. They also quiz each other on how to spell the Omaha word out loud.

10.7 OMAHA SOUNDS: AFFRICATES

Letter	Pronounced	Letter Name
č	like ch in "exchange"	če
j	like j in "just"	jútta
čʰ	like ch in "chimp"	če-ha
čč	like ch in "exchange", but longer and tenser	če-díⁿdiⁿ

· Sometimes a stop is released as the corresponding fricative. Such consonants are called *affricates*.

· Omaha has one series of affricates. These are made in about the same place as the

English sounds *ch* and *j* in "church" and "judge." These sounds are simply a *t* or *d* stop that is released as a *sh* or *zh* fricative.

- The Omaha affricate č/j series is closely related to its t/d series. The affricates are relatively rare, and most of them seem to be derived from alternate words that have the corresponding t/d stop. The affricate version of the word is often an endearing diminutive version of the regular word.

- Note that č can be either simple (č), aspirated (čʰ), or tense (čč), just like any other voiceless stop. These are pronounced differently, though for English speakers it might be hard to perceive that at first.

Vocabulary

čččéshka: short

íⁿčʰoⁿ: now, just now

iⁿčʰóⁿga: mouse

maⁿčʰú: grizzly bear

shínuja: puppy

FIG. 45. maⁿčʰú: grizzly bear

Speaking Practice

A. The instructor reads the vocabulary words aloud, noting their meanings, and also spelling the words out loud and writing them on the board. The students repeat the words aloud as a group and repeat the spelling.

B. The instructor goes through the words again, having each student repeat a word, spell it out loud, and tell what it means. The instructor corrects the student's pronunciation.

C. The instructor goes through the words randomly, asking each student the Omaha word for the English meaning. The student also spells the word.

D. The instructor goes through the words randomly again, asking each student the Omaha word for the English meaning. This time the instructor will ask the question in Omaha using the construction: "_____," Umóⁿhoⁿ ie tʰe awatʰégoⁿ? What is the Omaha word for "_____"? The instructor also uses an Omaha command to have them spell the word: Wabáx̣u kʰe āthada ga! (if the instructor is a man) or Wabáx̣u kʰe āthada a! (if the instructor is a woman), "Spell it!"

E. The students form small groups of about two to four. In each group the students take turns quizzing their partners on randomly chosen vocabulary words, both in Omaha to English and in English to Omaha. They also quiz each other on how to spell the Omaha word out loud.

10.8 OMAHA SOUNDS: SEMIVOWELS AND LEDH

Letter	Pronounced	Letter Name
w	like w in wow	wau
th	like l in "long" changing to th in "this"	tha

- Some sounds are intermediate between consonants and vowels. *High vowels* such as *i* and *u* are made with the mouth nearly closed. When these sounds are made next to other vowels, they restrict the speech breath and act like consonants. When i acts as a consonant, it is like the hard y sound in English. When u acts as a consonant, it is like the w sound. Vowel type sounds that act as consonants are called *semivowels*.

- Omaha has the semivowel *w*, which is about the same as in English. It does not have the y sound, however, except for the sound that occurs automatically to our ears when the vowel i is followed by another vowel. Hence, we do not include y in the Omaha alphabet.

- In place of y, Omaha has a special sound all its own, which we will call *ledh* in English. (The dh in "ledh" is pronounced like the voiced th in "this" or "breathe.") Ledh is traditionally written th because some people thought it sounded like the voiced th, or *edh*, in English words like "the" or "these." Other people think it sounds like an *l*. In fact, it seems to be made by flipping the tongue rapidly and smoothly from *l* to *edh*. It is a very common sound in Omaha, and it takes practice to learn to make it correctly.

Vocabulary

gthêbo^n: ten

gthedó^n: hawk

gthí^n: to sit

i^{n}gthó^{n}ga: cat

mo^{n}thí^n: to walk

x̌ithá: eagle

thattó^n: to drink

thâbthi^n: three

that^{h}é: to eat

skíthe: sweet

ttó^{n}thi^n: to run

wasábe: black bear

wāx̌e: white person, non-Indian

wazhí^{n}ga: bird, chicken

wí^n: one

FIG. 46. i^{n}gthó^{n}ga: cat

FIG. 47. x̌ithá: eagle

FIG. 48. wazhí^{n}ga: bird

Speaking Practice

A. The instructor reads the vocabulary words aloud, noting their meanings, and also spelling the words out loud and writing them on the board. The students repeat the words aloud as a group and repeat the spelling.

B. The instructor goes through the words again, having each student repeat a word, spell it out loud, and tell what it means. The instructor corrects the student's pronunciation.

C. The instructor goes through the words randomly, asking each student the

Omaha word for the English meaning. The student also spells the word.

D. The instructor goes through the words randomly again, asking each student the Omaha word for the English meaning. This time the instructor asks the question in Omaha using the construction: "_____," Umóⁿhoⁿ íe tʰe awatʰégoⁿ? What is the Omaha word for "_____"? The instructor also uses an Omaha command to have them spell the word: Wabáx̣u kʰe āthada ga! (if the instructor is a man) or Wabáx̣u kʰe āthada a! (if the instructor is a woman), "Spell it!"

E. The students form small groups of about two to four. In each group the students take turns quizzing their partners on randomly chosen vocabulary words, both in Omaha to English and in English to Omaha. They also quiz each other on how to spell the Omaha word out loud.

10.9 OMAHA SOUNDS: GLOTTALS

Letter	Pronounced	Letter Name
ʔ	glottal stop; like the consonant in "uh-oh"	ʔáʔa
pʔ	glottal stop released right after p	pe-ʔáʔa
tʔ	glottal stop released right after t	te-ʔáʔa
sʔ	glottal stop released right after s	sa-ʔáʔa
shʔ	glottal stop released right after sh	she-ʔáʔa

• The ultimate stop consonant is simply to close the vocal cords. This stops the

speech sound altogether in the throat. We call this sound a *glottal stop*. This is the sound in "uh-oh", or the sound that replaces *t* in "mountain" or "bitten."

• Omaha uses the glottal stop as a regular speech sound, which we write as ʔ and call ʔáʔa (pronounced "uh-uh").

• Omaha also combines the glottal stop with oral stops and fricatives. This is the case for *p, t, s* and *sh*, in which the glottal stop may immediately follow them with no intervening vowel. We treat these combinations as separate letters in Omaha. This gives us five glottal letters.

Vocabulary

ʔuʔúde: hole, tattered

iⁿshʔáge: old man

mikkáʔe: star

sʔáthe: sour

tʔé: dead, to die

ttébiʔa: frog

wanóⁿpʔiⁿ: necklace

waʔú: woman

wésʔa: snake

FIG. 49. ttébiʔa: frog

Speaking Practice

A. The instructor reads the vocabulary words aloud, noting their meanings, and also spelling the words out loud and writing them on the board. The students repeat the words aloud as a group and repeat the spelling.

B. The instructor goes through the words again, having each student repeat a word, spell it out loud, and tell what it means. The instructor corrects the student's pronunciation.

C. The instructor goes through the words randomly, asking each student the Omaha word for the English meaning. The student also spells the word.

D. The instructor goes through the words randomly again, asking each student the Omaha word for the English meaning. This time the instructor asks the question in Omaha using the construction: "_____," Umónhon īe tʰe awatʰégon? What is the Omaha word for "_____"? The instructor also uses an Omaha command to have students spell the word: Wabáx̣u kʰe āthada ga! (if the instructor is a man) or Wabáx̣u kʰe āthada a! (if the instructor is a woman), "Spell it!"

E. The students form small groups of about two to four. In each group the students take turns quizzing their partners on randomly chosen vocabulary words, both in Omaha to English and in English to Omaha. They also quiz each other on how to spell the Omaha word out loud.

10.10 CONSONANT CLUSTERS

fricative	stop	ledh

· Omaha consonants are sometimes combined in *clusters*. There are only a few special ways in which this can occur,

and these take a definite order. Only two consonants can be in a cluster. A fricative comes before a stop, n, or a ledh. A stop comes before a ledh.

forced fricative			simple stop
	p	t	k
s	sp	st	sk
sh	shp	sht	shk
x̌	x̌p	x̌t	

· A forced, voiceless fricative comes before a simple stop. There seems to be no x̌k cluster.

· In a fricative + stop combination, both elements are voiceless. Stops are never tense, aspirated, voiced or glottalized, and fricatives are never voiced or muted.

fricative	ledh/n
	th
ṣ	ṣn
ṣh	ṣhn
x̌	x̌th

· A fricative comes before ledh.

· When the fricative is s or sh, the ledh changes to n and the s or sh is muted to ṣ or ṣh.

· When the fricative is x̌, the ledh remains ledh and the x̌ remains x̌.

voiced stop	ledh
	th
b	bth
g	gth

· A voiced stop comes before ledh. This occurs only with b and g. There is no dth cluster.

Vocabulary

bthóⁿ: smell, odor

gthedóⁿ: hawk

moⁿshtíⁿge: rabbit

ská: white

skíthe: sweet

ṣní: cold

shnábe: dirty

shtóⁿga: soft

uẋpé: dish, plate

ẋthá: skinny, thin

FIG. 50. moⁿshtíⁿge: rabbit

Speaking Practice

A. The instructor reads the vocabulary words aloud, noting their meanings, and also spelling the words out loud and writing them on the board. The students repeat the words aloud as a group and repeat the spelling.

B. The instructor goes through the words again, having each student repeat a word, spell it out loud, and tell what it means. The instructor corrects the student's pronunciation.

C. The instructor goes through the words randomly, asking each student the Omaha word for the English meaning. The student also spells the word.

D. The instructor goes through the words randomly again, asking each student the Omaha word for the English meaning. This time the instructor asks the question in Omaha using the construction: "_____," Umóⁿhoⁿ íe tʰe awatʰégoⁿ? What is the Omaha word for "_____"? The instructor also uses an Omaha command to have students spell the word: Wabáẋu kʰe āthada ga! (if the instructor is a man) or Wabáẋu kʰe āthada a! (if the instructor is a woman), "Spell it!"

E. The students form small groups of about two to four. In each group the students take turns quizzing their partners on randomly chosen vocabulary words, both in Omaha to English and in English to Omaha. They also quiz each other on how to spell the Omaha word out loud.

10.11 VOWEL LENGTH AND ACCENT

Normal Vowel	Accented Short Vowel	"Long" Vowel	Circumflex Vowel
a	á	ā	â
e	é	ē	ê
i	í	ī	î
u	ú	ū	û
iⁿ	íⁿ	īⁿ	îⁿ
oⁿ	óⁿ	ōⁿ	ôⁿ

· Spoken Omaha has a characteristic pattern of rising and falling pitch. In general, the pitch of the voice rises at the beginning of a phrase and then falls toward the end. This may happen several times in the course of a sentence.

- Some Omaha vowels are longer than others, so that two different words may be distinguished according to how long a vowel is held. Originally, these may have been places where there were two separate vowels next to each other that have since merged into one.

- In each word or phrase, there is normally one syllable that is most prominent. It is marked by being spoken more loudly or at a higher pitch than other syllables around it, and it serves as a landmark for the listener trying to recognize words and phrases from a series of syllables. We call this the *accented* syllable.

- Theoretically, the second syllable of a word is the one that takes the accent. However, there are many exceptions to this rule, because in many cases the first two syllables have merged into one. This means that the first two vowels have merged into one long vowel, which retains the accent that was originally on the second of those two vowels. In this case, we hear the accent on what is now the *first* syllable. By this time, the merged vowel itself may no longer actually be held longer.

- Vowel length is significant in Omaha only some of the time. Length difference seems most likely to be retained when it is required to distinguish two different words that would otherwise sound the same.

- The interaction of vowel length, pitch contour and accent is complicated, and we do not understand it very well. In the UNL section of this book, we use one of three symbols to mark the accented vowel.

- If we use an *acute* accent (e.g., á), it means that we assume the vowel to be a basic "short" vowel, with no special history and no distinctive pronunciation.

- If we use a *macron* (e.g., ā), it means that we believe it to be historically composed of two original vowels so that it is, or was once, pronounced long. In this case, the vowel will take the accent if it is either the first or second syllable of the word. A number of verb prefixes are like this, and it will help us to recognize them.

- We also use a macron to distinguish between words when a native speaker of Omaha has indicated that the two words are distinguished in speech by the length of that vowel. This distinction is often hard for us to hear.

- Finally, certain vowels seem to have a marked rising and falling intonation, which sometimes distinguish them from a similar sounding word with a short vowel. We write them with a *circumflex* accent (e.g., â). In general, circumflex vowels can be considered definitely long.

Vocabulary

āgthi^n: chair, seat

āthade: read, recite

hô^{n}de: last night

mô^{n}de: bow (for shooting arrows)

níde: butt

FIG. 51. āgthi^n: chair

nîde: cooked, done

nóⁿde: wall

nôⁿde: heart

thâbthiⁿ: three

ūdaⁿ: good

ûjaⁿ: pretty

FIG. 52. nôⁿde: heart

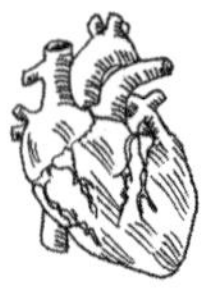

Speaking Practice

A. The instructor reads the vocabulary words aloud, noting their meanings, and also spelling the words out loud and writing them on the board. The students repeat the words aloud as a group and repeat the spelling.

B. The instructor goes through the words again, having each student repeat a word, spell it out loud, and tell what it means. The instructor corrects the student's pronunciation.

C. The instructor goes through the words randomly, asking each student the Omaha word for the English meaning. The student also spells the word.

D. The instructor goes through the words randomly again, asking each student the Omaha word for the English meaning. This time the instructor asks the question in Omaha using the construction: "_____," Umóⁿhoⁿ īe tʰe awatʰégoⁿ? What is the Omaha word for "_____"? The instructor also uses an Omaha command to have them spell the word: Wabáx̣u kʰe āthada ga! (if the instructor is a man) or Wabáx̣u kʰe āthada a! (if the instructor is a woman), "Spell it!"

E. The students form small groups of about two to four. In each group the students take turns quizzing their partners on randomly chosen vocabulary words, both in Omaha to English and in English to Omaha. They also quiz each other on how to spell the Omaha word out loud.

11.1 NOUNS: "WHO" AND "WHAT"

	Noun Question	Noun Answer	
Who is it?			
(casually)	**Ebé?**	**Bill.**	Bill.
(seriously)	**Ebé a?**	**Ttesóⁿwiⁿ.**	It is Ttesóⁿwiⁿ.
What is it?			
(casually)	**Idādoⁿ?**	**Hiⁿbé.**	A shoe.
(seriously)	**Idādoⁿ a?**	**Wēbax̣u.**	It is a pencil.
What is "arm" in Omaha?	"Arm", **Umóⁿhoⁿ** **īe tʰe awatʰégoⁿ?**	**"Á".**	It is "á".
What is "sí" in English?	**"Sí", wāx̌e īe tʰe awatʰégoⁿ?**	"Foot".	It is "foot".

- A word that answers a question like "What?" or "Who?" is called a *noun*.

- In Omaha, a noun can stand alone as a complete sentence. This can be as an answer to a Who? or What? question just as in English, or it can be an independent comment. In either case, it means "It is [noun]," where the "It is" is implied.

- To ask for the identity of a person, use the question word ebé, "who."

- To ask for the classification of something, use the question word idādoⁿ, "what."

- To ask for the meaning or explanation of something, use the question word awatʰégoⁿ. This is the word we use to ask for the translation of a word from one language to another. We first quote the

known word that we want translated, then tell the target language into which we want it translated with [ethnicity] īe tʰe, and then ask awatʰégoⁿ?, "What does it mean?" or "What does it translate to?"

Vocabulary: Classroom Objects

āgthiⁿ: chair

hiⁿbé: shoe

miīdoⁿbe: clock; watch

nóⁿde: wall

ttizhébe: door

wāthatʰe: table

wagthábaze: book, paper

wēbax̣u: pen, pencil, chalk

īe tʰe: the language

FIG. 53. miīdoⁿbe: clock

Vocabulary: ebé: who?

idādoⁿ: what?

awatʰégoⁿ: explain this; what does it mean?

Vocabulary: Ethnicity

Umóⁿhoⁿ: Omaha

wāx̌e: white, non-Indian

Heshpaiúni: Hispanic; Mexican

Shaóⁿ: Sioux; D/Lakota

Húttoⁿga: Winnebago

Vocabulary: Language

Umóⁿhoⁿ íe tʰe: the Omaha language

wāx̌e íe tʰe: the English language

Heshpaiúni íe tʰe: the Spanish language

Shaóⁿ íe tʰe: the Sioux language

Húttoⁿga íe tʰe: the Hochunk language

Speaking Practice

A. The instructor reads the vocabulary words aloud, noting their meanings, and also spelling the words out loud and writing them on the board. The students repeat the words aloud as a group and repeat the spelling. The instructor goes through the words again, student by student, commanding them—for example: Susan, "miīdoⁿbe" á ga! Susan will say the word. Then he tells Susan to spell it: Wabáx̌u kʰe āthada ga! Finally, he will have her give the translation: Wāx̌e íe tʰe awatʰégoⁿ?

B. The instructor goes through the words randomly, asking each student the Omaha word for the English meaning: Brian, "door," Umóⁿhoⁿ íe tʰe awatʰégoⁿ? Brian also spells the word.

C. The instructor walks around the students, standing next to, and perhaps placing a hand on the head or shoulders of one student and asking another: Naomi, níkkashiⁿga dúakʰa, ebé a? "Who is this person?" Naomi should tell the name of the other student if she knows it. If she doesn't know the other student's name, she should ask that student: Izházhe thithítta tʰe idādoⁿ? The other student should answer: Izházhe wiwítta tʰe Tim. Naomi should then reply to the instructor: Tim.

D. The instructor points out various classroom items, asking each student in turn: Idādoⁿ? The student should identify the item by its Omaha name.

E. The students form small groups of about three or four. In each group the students take turns quizzing their partners on items in the classroom (Idādoⁿ?) and on the names of their classmates (Níkkashiⁿga shêakʰa, ebé a? "Who is that person?"). They should be able to answer with a single name or Omaha noun. If they forget, they can ask the person's name, or they can ask someone the Omaha translation of the English word using Umóⁿhoⁿ íe tʰe awatʰégoⁿ?

11.2 VERBS: WHAT IS SOMEONE DOING?

	Verb Question	Verb Answer	
What's s/he doing?	**Idādoⁿ gāx̌e a?**	**Noⁿzhíⁿ.**	S/he's standing.

· A word that tells what someone is doing is called a *verb*.

· In Omaha a verb can stand alone as a complete sentence, without needing a subject in front of it as in English. The subject is implied. This is the Omaha way of saying that he, she or it is doing something.

- To ask what someone is doing, use Idādo^n gāχe a?

- To ask what a particular subject is doing, add ak^{h}á after the subject noun: Wagō^{n}ze ak^{h}á, idādo^n gāχe a? "The teacher, what is he doing?" Alice ak^{h}á idādo^n gāχe a? "What is Alice doing?"

- To ask about a particular subject out of a group, you can use shêak^{h}a for "that one" or dúak^{h}a for "this one." For example, Núzhi^{n}ga dúak^{h}a idādo^n gāχe a? "This boy, what is he doing?" Táppuskazhi^{n}ga shêak^{h}a idādo^n gāχe a? "What is that student doing?"

- The four verbs for "sit," "stand," "walk," and "lie (down)" are very important in Omaha. We will concentrate especially on learning these in this lesson.

Vocabulary: Verbs

gthí^n: sit

gió^n: fly

zhō^n: lie (down)

mo^{n}thí^n: walk

no^{n}zhí^n: stand

thattó^n: drink

uó^{n}sisi: jumping

FIG. 56. núzhi^{n}ga: boy, young man

FIG. 57. mīzhi^{n}ga: girl, young woman

FIG. 58. shénuzhi^{n}ga: boy, little boy

FIG. 59. shémizhi^{n}ga: girl, little girl

Vocabulary: Nouns

nú: man

wa'ú: woman

núzhi^{n}ga: boy, young man

mīzhi^{n}ga: girl, young woman

shénuzhi^{n}ga: boy, little boy

shémizhi^{n}ga: girl, little girl

shí^{n}gazhi^{n}ga: little child

shié: baby

i^{n}sh'áge: old man, male Elder

wa'úzhi^{n}ga: old woman, female Elder

wagō^{n}ze: teacher

wagáχtho^n: assistant

ttáppuskazhi^{n}ga: student, pupil

FIG. 54. nú: man

FIG. 60. shí^{n}gazhi^{n}ga: little child

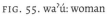

FIG. 55. wa'ú: woman

FIG. 61. shié: baby

Speaking Practice

A. The instructor reads the vocabulary words aloud, noting their meanings, and also spelling the words out loud and writing them on the board. The students repeat the words aloud as a group and repeat the spelling. The instructor goes through the words again, student by student, commanding them; for example: Emma, "mīzhiⁿga" á ga! Emma will say the word. Then he will tell Emma to spell it: Wabáx̣u kʰe āthada ga! Finally, he will have her give the translation: Wāx̌e īe tʰe awatʰégoⁿ?

B. The instructor goes through the words randomly, asking each student the Omaha word for the English meaning: Bruce, "walk," Umóⁿhoⁿ īe tʰe awatʰégoⁿ? Bruce also spells the word.

C. The instructor invites an assistant to do other things besides just sit. The wagáx̌thoⁿ models such activities as standing, walking, lying down, and perhaps even drinking, jumping and flying. While doing so, the instructor asks the students, first as a group and then individually: Wagáx̌thoⁿ akʰá idādoⁿ gāx̌e a? The students should answer: Moⁿthíⁿ, or Gióⁿ, or whatever is appropriate.

D. The instructor invites more volunteers to model the different verbs. As they do, the instructor points them out to other students and asks them, for example, what that young man is doing:

Núzhiⁿga shêakʰa idādoⁿ gāx̌e a? The student asked should give the correct Omaha answer.

E. The students form small groups of about two or three. Each student or group illustrates one of the verbs. Partners in a group will ask each other what some person in another group is doing, either by name or by [noun] shêakʰa. If the person asked doesn't know, s/he will approach and ask a partner: Mīzhiⁿga dúakʰa idādoⁿ gāx̌e a? The partner should be able to answer, and the inquirer reports back to the one who asked: Uóⁿsisi. "She's jumping."

11.3 ADJECTIVES: STATIVE VERBS

	Explanation Question	**Adjective Answer**	
How is it?			
(casually)	Eóⁿ?	Ūdaⁿ.	Good.
(seriously)	Eóⁿ a?	Ttoⁿgá.	It's big.

- A word that describes a noun is called an *adjective*.

- In Omaha, an adjective can stand alone as a complete sentence. In this case, it simply says that the person or thing we are talking about is big, or whatever. In Omaha we call adjectives *stative verbs*.

- To ask for an explanation about a situation or thing, use the question word eóⁿ, "how."

Vocabulary: Stative Verbs (Adjectives)

sābe: black

ská: white

shábe: dark

só^n: pale, white

zhĩde: red

zí: yellow

ttú: blue

FIG. 62. gthéze: striped

xŭde: gray

gthéze: striped

gthézhe: spotted

ūda^n: good

ppiâzhi: bad, evil, ugly

tto^{n}gá: big

zhi^{n}gá: small

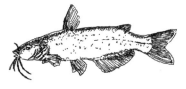

FIG. 63. gthézhe: spotted

Vocabulary: Question Words

eó^n: how?

Speaking Practice

A. The instructor reads the vocabulary words aloud, noting their meanings, and also spelling the words out loud and writing them on the board. The students repeat the words aloud as a group and repeat the spelling. The instructor goes through the words again, student by student, commanding them, for example:

FIG. 64. tto^{n}gá: big

Sam, "xŭde" á ga! Sam will say the word. Then he will tell Sam to spell it: Wabáxu k^{h}e āthada ga! Finally, he will have Sam give the translation: Wāxe ĩe t^{h}e awat^{h}égo^n?

FIG. 65. zhi^{n}gá: small

B. The instructor goes through the words randomly, asking each student the Omaha word for the English meaning: Theresa, "striped," Umó^{n}ho^n ĩe t^{h}e awat^{h}égo^n? Theresa also spells the word.

C. The instructor tacks up pieces of colored construction paper on the walls, and perhaps draws illustrations on the board, of big and little, and good and bad, and points to these, asking the students: Duát^{h}e eó^n a? "How is this?" or Shêt^{h}e eó^n a? "How is that?" The students reply by giving the appropriate stative verb.

D. The instructor points out various classroom items, asking each student in turn: Idādo^n? (Idādo^n a?) The student should identify the item by its Omaha name. Eó^n? (Eó^n a?) The student should tell its color, or something else about it.

E. The students form small groups of about three or four. In each group the students take turns quizzing their partners on items in the classroom (Idādo^n?) and their characteristics (Eó^n a?).

11.4 NUMBERS: "HOW MANY"

	Number Question	Number Answer	
How many are there? (casually) (seriously)	Ānoⁿ? Ānoⁿ a?	Thâbthiⁿ. Sáttoⁿ.	Three. There are five.

- A word that gives a count of things is called a *number*. In Omaha, numbers come after the things they count.

- To ask for a number, use the question word ānoⁿ, "how many."

- The basic framework is the set 1–10, as in English.

- 12 is sháppenoⁿba, "two sixes."

- The other numbers from 11 to 19 are of the form agthíⁿ-plus the number to be added to 10. Thus, 11 is agthíⁿwiⁿ, 13 is agthíⁿthabthiⁿ, 14 is agthíⁿduba, and so on.

- The "tens" numbers from 20 to 90 are counted as the number of tens. Thus, 20 is gthêboⁿnoⁿba, 30 is gthêboⁿthâbthiⁿ, 90 is gthêboⁿshóⁿkka, and so on.

- The other numbers from 21 to 99 are formed as the "tens" number, plus-kkiédi-, plus the number to be added to the "tens" number. Thus, 21 is gthêboⁿnoⁿba-kkiédi-wiⁿ, 75 is gthêboⁿppéthoⁿba-kkiédi-sáttoⁿ, and so on.

- The word for "hundred" is gthêboⁿhíⁿwiⁿ.

- The word for a "thousand" is kkúge, "box," from the boxes of 1,000 silver dollars delivered by the United States government to meet treaty obligations.

Vocabulary: Question Words

ānoⁿ: how many?

Vocabulary: Numbers

wiⁿóⁿx̌či: one

noⁿbá: two

thâbthiⁿ: three

dúba: four

sáttoⁿ: five

sháppe: six

ppéthoⁿba: seven

ppethâbthiⁿ: eight

shóⁿkka: nine

gthêboⁿ: ten

agthíⁿwiⁿ: eleven

sháppenoⁿba: twelve

gthêboⁿhíⁿwiⁿ: hundred

kkúge: box, thousand

FIG. 66. wiⁿóⁿxči: one

FIG. 67. noⁿbá: two

FIG. 68. thâbthiⁿ: three

FIG. 69. dúba: four

FIG. 70. sáttoⁿ: five

FIG. 71. sháppe: six

FIG. 72. ppéthoⁿba: seven

FIG. 73. ppethâbthiⁿ: eight

FIG. 74. shóⁿkka: nine

FIG. 75. gthêboⁿ: ten

Speaking Practice

A. The instructor recites the numbers from 1 to 10 aloud, spelling each one out loud and writing it on the board. The students repeat them aloud as a group and repeat the spelling. The instructor goes through them again, student by student, commanding them, for example: Mikki, "shóⁿkka" á ga! Mikki will say the number. Then he will tell Mikki to spell it: Wabáxu kʰe āthada ga! Finally, he will have her give the translation: Wãx̌e īe tʰe awatʰégoⁿ?

B. The instructor goes through the words randomly, asking each student the Omaha word for the English meaning: Mike, "ten," Umóⁿhoⁿ īe tʰe awatʰégoⁿ? Mike also spells the word.

C. The instructor holds up a certain number of fingers and drills the class: Ānoⁿ a?

D. The instructor makes sets of various classroom items, asking each student in turn: Idādoⁿ? The student should identify the item by its Omaha name. Ānoⁿ a? The student should tell how many are in the set.

E. The students form small groups of about three or four. In each group the students take turns quizzing their partners on the number of fingers they are holding up or on the number of items of particular types in the classroom.

11.5 UNITARY UTTERANCES

	Men	Women
Hello!	**Ahó!**	(none)
Good-bye!	(none)	(none)

- Only men say Ahó!, "Hello!", to each other. Women seem to have no word for hello.
- It seems there is no word for goodbye in Omaha.

We are done (with this activity)!	**Shóⁿ!**
I am finished (speaking).	**Shénoⁿ.**

- To declare the end of a meeting or activity, say Shóⁿ!
- To let people know you are done speaking, say Shénoⁿ.
- Both men and women use these expressions.

Yes.	**Óⁿhoⁿ.** / **Áoⁿ.**
No.	**Áⁿkkazhi.**

- Both men and women use these terms.
- Óⁿhoⁿ probably does not exist in modern Omaha. It is found in nineteenth-century Omaha and Ponca texts collected by James Owen Dorsey.

	Men	Women
Hey there!	**Dúda!**	**Dúda!**

- Dúda! is used most commonly, by both men and women, to get attention or call to someone.

	Men	Women
Yes? What?	**Hó.**	**Há.**

- If someone calls on you in class, or tries to get your attention by saying Dúda!, you reply by saying Hó if you are a man, or Há if you are a woman, to let the person know you are paying attention.

Groan of internal pain	**Ōⁿoⁿ–hōⁿoⁿ–hōⁿoⁿ–!**
Groan of pain due to an external injury, e.g., bumping your arm	**Ōⁿoⁿ–nōⁿoⁿ–nōⁿoⁿ–!**
Cry when burned: Ouch-ouch-ouch!	**Í–čči–čči–!** (older form) **Í–ji–ji–!** (newer form)

- These are used by both men and women. Both were recorded in the nineteenth century and are still used today.

- One of our speakers (Emmaline Walker Sanchez) tells us that the voiced version of the cry of being burned is more common today. The change may be to avoid confusion with an obscenity that would occur if the aspirated form were used.

- The insertion of a hyphen between syllables marks the preceding syllable as being drawn out as an emotional utterance.

	Men	Women
Yikes! Eek!	**Wá!**	**Íⁿ!**
Startled, as by a sudden sound	**Bá!**	none

- Both Wá! and Íⁿ! are uttered forcefully and then quickly cut off.

- Íⁿ! is emphatically feminine. One of our younger speakers remembers boys teasing each other when she was a child: Íⁿ á ga! "Say 'Íⁿ!'!"

- Bá! is used primarily by men as when startled by a sudden sound, or upon hearing something said that is unexpected. Like Wá! and Íⁿ!, Bá! is uttered forcefully and then quickly cut off.

- In modern practice, some women have begun to use Bá!.

	Men	**Women**
Direct surprise	**Būu–hūu–!**	**Hī̆iⁿ–thāa–!**
Hearing surprising news	**Būu–hūu–!**	**Híⁿiⁿ–!**

- Women use Hī̆iⁿ–thāa–! when they directly encounter something that surprises them, and Híⁿiⁿ–! with a rising voice when they hear surprising news. Men use Būu–hūu–! in either case.

	Men	**Women**
Are you kidding me??!!	**Ttená!**	**Ēe–!**
Wow! Check this out! I can't believe this surprise!	**Bushéam!**	**Bushéam!**

- Ttená! is an old expression, recorded from the nineteenth century, that is still recognized by our speakers today.

- Ēe–! is expressed with a rising tone of voice.

- Bushéam! is the modern contraction of the formal form Bushêama.

	Men	**Women**
Baloney!	**Wúx̆!**	none
Baloney!	**Ēe–shtoⁿna!**	**Ēe–shtoⁿna!**

- Wúx̌! is used by men only to say "You're pulling my leg!". The vowel is like the vowel in "book."

- Eē–shto^{n}na! is used by both men and women, though in recent years younger men have begun to avoid it because the initial Eē– is thought to sound feminine. The voice tone on this Eē– is held very flat, unlike the rising tone of the women's surprised disbelief expression described earlier. This expression seems to be a recent coinage in the community and was very popular in the middle twentieth century. One of our speakers thought it was coined in the early 1960s, but an older speaker later recalled having heard it as early as the 1940s. Eē–shto^{n}na! is a very good-humored expression, releasing tension and causing people to break up into laughter.

	Men	Women
@#$%!!	**(X̌āa–īi–!)**	**Ī–thīi–!**

- Women use Ī–thīi–! to express extreme exasperation.

- In the nineteenth century, men used X̌āa–īi–! This does not seem to be used any more; none of our speakers seems to recognize it.

Vocabulary

UNITARY UTTERANCES

Ahó!: Hello! (male)

Áo^n: Yes.

FIG. 76. Eē–shto^{n}na! Baloney!

Bá!: Startled, as by a sudden sound (male)

Bushéam!: Wow! Check this out! I can't believe this unexpected surprise!

Būu–hūu–!: Direct surprise (Male)

Būu–hūu–!: Hearing surprising news (male)

Dúda!: Hey! Hey there!

Eē–!: Are you kidding me?! (female)

Eē–shto^{n}na!: Baloney!

Há: Response to being hailed: Yes? What? (female)

Hí^{n}i^n–!: Hearing surprising news (female)

Hī^{n}i^n–thāa–!: Direct surprise (female)

Hó: Response to being hailed: Yes? What? (male)

Í–ččí–ččí!: Cry when burned: Ouch-ouch-ouch! (older form)

Í–ji–ji–!: Cry when burned: Ouch-ouch-ouch! (newer form)

Í^n!: Startled fright: Yikes! Eek! (female)

Ī–thīi!: Exasperation! (female)

Á^{n}kkazhi: No.

Ó^{n}ho^n: Yes.

Ō^{n}o^n–hō^{n}o^n–hō^{n}o^n–!: Groan of internal pain

Ō^{n}o^n–nō^{n}o^n–nō^{n}o^n–!: Groan of pain due to an external injury

X̌āa–īi–!: Exasperation! (male, nineteenth century)

Shéno^n: I am finished (speaking).

Shóⁿ!: We are done (with this activity)!

Ttená!: Startled fright: Yikes! Eek! (male)

Wúx̌!: Baloney! (male)

Speaking Practice

A. The instructor reads the vocabulary words aloud, noting their meanings, and also spelling the words out loud and writing them on the board. The students repeat the words aloud as a group and repeat the spelling. The instructor goes through the words again, student by student, getting them to say the words with feeling and explain how they would be used.

B. The instructor goes through the words randomly, asking each student to explain the implication of each Omaha unitary utterance and then repeat the utterance with feeling. Whenever called upon, a student should respond appropriately with Hó or Há. If a student's mental focus is directed elsewhere, the instructor should get the student's attention by calling, for example: Pete, dúda!

C. The instructor describes various scenarios in which students might find themselves and then asks: Edéshe tte? "What should you say?" The student should reply with the appropriate Omaha unitary utterance.

D. The students form small groups of about three or four. In each group the students take turns quizzing their partners by describing situations that might call for an Omaha unitary utterance and challenging the partner to give the correct expression: Edéshe tte?

E. The instructor passes out one set of cards with students' names on them, and another with situations described. Students drawing their own name should call on another student to trade, using Dúda! Then the students each call on the student whose name they have drawn, and give them the situation on the card. The other student should reply with the appropriate Omaha unitary utterance. If the first student doesn't yet know the other student named, the first step is to call, for example: John Jones, ebé a? "Who is John Jones?" John Jones answers: Wí é bthíⁿ. "That's me."

11.6 USEFUL OMAHA EXPRESSIONS

- Thatʰí tʰe ūdaⁿ means "It is good that you have arrived." Our speakers have indicated that it may be used as well to say "You're welcome" in reply to "Thank you."

| Thank you. | **Wíbthahoⁿ.** |
| You are welcome. | **Thatʰí tʰe ūdaⁿ.** |

| Do you want some? | **Dūba shkōⁿna?** |
| No, thanks, I have enough. | **Shóⁿbthegoⁿ.** |

	Men	**Women**
Good luck! Do well!	**Washkóⁿ ga (ho)!**	**Washkóⁿ a!**
You did well.	**Ūdaⁿ shkáx̣e.**	**Ūdaⁿ shkáx̣e.**

Vocabulary

Dūba shkōⁿna?: Do you want some?

Shóⁿbthegoⁿ: No, thanks, I have enough.

Thatʰí tʰe ūdaⁿ: You are welcome.

Ūdaⁿ shkāẋe: You did well.

Washkóⁿ a!: Do well! Good luck! Be strong!
(Female speech)

Washkóⁿ ga (ho)!: Do well! Good luck! Be
strong! (Male speech)

Wíbthahoⁿ: Thank you.

Speaking Practice

A. The instructor reads the vocabulary
expressions aloud, noting their
meanings, and also spelling them out
loud and writing them on the board. The
students repeat the expressions aloud
as a group and repeat the spelling. The
instructor goes through the expressions
again, student by student, getting them
to say the phrases with feeling and
explain how they would be used.

B. The instructor goes through the
expressions randomly, asking each
student to explain the implication of
each and then repeat it with feeling.
Students called upon should respond
appropriately with Hó or Há.

C. The instructor describes various
scenarios in which students might find
themselves and then asks: Edéshe tte?
"What should you say?" The student
should reply with the appropriate Omaha
expression.

D. The students form small groups
of about three or four. In each group
the students take turns quizzing their
partners by describing situations that
might call for an Omaha expression,
and challenging the partners to give the
correct expression: Edéshe tte?

E. The instructor passes out one
set of cards with students' names on
them and another set with situations
described. Students drawing their own
names should call on another student
to trade, using Dúda! Then the students
each call on the student whose name
they have drawn and give them the
situation on the card. The other student
should reply with the appropriate
Omaha expression.

11.7 NOUN-NOUN WORD ORDER

Modifying Noun	Head Noun	Modifying Noun	Head Noun
apple	tree	**shé**	**hí**
turtle	head	**kké**	**ppá**
buffalo	horn	**tté**	**hé**

- A noun can be described or qualified
by another word. When this happens,
we say that the describing or qualifying
word *modifies* the noun.

- A noun can be modified by another
noun. The main noun that actually refers
to the thing is called the *head* noun, as
opposed to the modifying noun, which
tells what kind the head noun is. Thus,
an apple tree is a tree that bears apples,

a turtle head is the head of a turtle, and a buffalo horn is a horn of the buffalo kind. If we were to turn these around, the meaning would change. A tree apple might be an apple found in trees, a head turtle would be a leader of turtles, and a horn buffalo would be a buffalo of the kind that has horns.

· In both Omaha and English, the modifying noun comes first and the head noun comes after it. The result is a new noun that is a modified version of the head noun.

Vocabulary: Nouns

hí: stalk, stem, trunk, tree, tooth

shé: apple

shé hí: apple tree

ní: water, liquid

shéni: apple cider

zhóⁿ: wood

FIG. 77. shé: apple

FIG. 78. shé hí: apple tree

zhoⁿní: wood water, maple syrup, sugar, candy

kké: turtle

ppá: head

kképpa: turtle head, the playing card suit of diamonds

tté: buffalo, bison

hé: horn, antler

ttehé: buffalo horn, spoon

há: skin, hide

mikká: raccoon

FIG. 79. ttehé: spoon

FIG. 80. mikká: raccoon

mikkáha: raccoon skin

ppéde: fire

ppedéni: fire water, whiskey, hard liquor

moⁿsé: breast, udder

moⁿzéni: milk

ttéska: cow

ttéskamoⁿzéni: cow's milk

síⁿde: tail

ttesíⁿde: buffalo tail; Ttesíⁿde–an Omaha clan

FIG. 81. ttéska: cow

kkóⁿde: plum

kkóⁿde hí: plum tree

kkóⁿde ní:
plum juice

nóⁿppa:
chokecherry,
cherry

FIG. 82. nóⁿppa: cherry

nóⁿppa hí: cherry tree

nóⁿppa ní: cherry juice

Speaking Practice

A. The instructor reads the vocabulary words aloud, noting their meanings, and also spelling the words out loud and writing them on the board. The students repeat the words aloud as a group and repeat the spelling. The instructor goes through the words again, student by student.

B. The instructor goes through the words randomly, asking each student the Omaha word for the English meaning.

C. The students take a few minutes to look at the tree names listed in Fletcher and La Flesche's *The Omaha Tribe*, pp. 106–7. How many end in –hí?

D. The instructor passes out small offerings of candy, apple cider, milk, and possibly cherry or plum juice, asking each student, for example: Shéni dūba shkōⁿna? The student answers either: Hó/Há, shéni dūba kkoⁿbtha, if they want some, or Shóⁿbthegoⁿ, if they don't want any. After the instructor has gone around once, the offerings are passed around from student to student, each student asking if the next one wants any.

E. The students form small groups of about two or three. In each group the students take turns quizzing their partners on possible noun-noun combinations that they may make up themselves. They should especially try using animal names and parts, such as "head," "horn," "hide," "tail," and "tooth" (hí). Example:

"Raccoon tail," Umóⁿhoⁿ īe tʰe awatʰégoⁿ?

The quizzed student should respond: Mikkásiⁿde, ebthégoⁿ. "I think it's mikkásiⁿde."

11.8 NOUN–STATIVE VERB WORD ORDER

Adjective	Head Noun		Head Noun	Adjective
white	metal		**mōⁿze**	**ská**
big	turtle		**kké**	**ttoⁿga**
flat	water		**ní**	**btháska**

- A noun can be modified by an adjective (stative verb). When this happens in English, we put the adjective (stative verb) *in front of the noun*. In Omaha, it is the reverse: the adjective (stative verb) *follows the noun*.

Number	Head Noun		Head Noun	Number
one	woman		**waʔú**	**wiⁿ**
three	turtles		**kké**	**thâbthiⁿ**
five	deer		**ttáx̌ti**	**sáttoⁿ**

• A number can be used with a noun to tell how many there are. In English we put the number *in front of the noun*, but in Omaha we put it *after the noun*.

Vocabulary: Nouns

gahíge: chief

gthedóⁿ: hawk

hé: horn, antler

ishtá: eye

kkāx̣e: crow

kké: turtle

FIG. 83. ishtá: eye

maⁿčʰú: grizzly bear

mōⁿge: breast, chest

mōⁿze: metal, iron

ní: water, liquid

noⁿbé: hand

nóⁿkka: back

óⁿpʰaⁿ: elk

sí: foot

FIG. 84. óⁿpʰaⁿ: elk

sháge: nail, hoof, claw, talon

tté: buffalo

wasábe: black bear

zhóⁿ: wood

FIG. 85. wasábe: black bear

Vocabulary: Stative Verbs (Adjectives)

btháska: flat

x̌ūde: gray

ská: white

sóⁿ: pale, white

ṣnéde: long, tall

shábe: dark

shtóⁿga: soft

ttoⁿgá: big, large, great

zhīde: red

zhiⁿgá: small, young

FIG. 86. Óⁿpʰaⁿ-ttoⁿga: Big Elk

Omaha Names

Clan names follow the personal names.

Gahíge-ṣnede: Tall Chief (Iⁿkʰésabe)

Gahíge-zhiⁿga: Young Chief (Iⁿkʰésabe)

Gthedóⁿ-qude: Gray Hawk (Tháttada)

Gthedóⁿ-zhiⁿga: Little Hawk (Tháttada)

Hé-shabe: Dark Antler (Wézhiⁿshte)

Hé-shtoⁿga: Soft Antler (refers to new antler growth; Wézhiⁿshte)

Ishtá-duba: Four Eyes (Tháttada)

Ishtá-ska: White Eyes (Tháttada)

Kkax̣é-noⁿba: Two Crows (Hóⁿga)

Kké-ttoⁿga: Big Turtle (Tháttada)

Maⁿčʰú-noⁿba: Two Grizzly Bears (Hóⁿga)

Móⁿge-shabe: Dark Breast (refers to dark colored breast of elk; Wézhiⁿshte)

Móⁿge-ttoⁿga: Big Chest (Iⁿkʰésabe)

Moⁿgé-zi: Yellow Breast (Tháttada)

Móⁿge-zhide: Red Breast (Tháttada)

Noⁿbé-duba: Four Hands (Tháttada)

Nóⁿkka-x̌ude: Gray Back (Tháttada)

Óⁿpʰaⁿ-ska: White Elk (Wézhiⁿshte)

Óⁿpʰaⁿ-ttoⁿga: Big Elk (Wézhiⁿshte)

Óⁿpʰaⁿ-zhiⁿga: Young Elk (Wézhiⁿshte)

Ppóⁿkka-soⁿ: Pale Ponca (Iⁿkʰésabe)

Sí-x̌ude: Gray Foot (Tháttada)

Sí-ttoⁿga: Big Foot (Tháttada)

Sháge-noⁿba: Two Hoofs (refers to cloven hoofs; Iⁿkʰésabe)

Sháge-ska: White Claws (Tháttada)

Tte-sóⁿ: White Buffalo (Tháttada)

Wasábe-zhiⁿga: Young Black Bear (Tháttada)

Zhoⁿ-sóⁿ: White Wood (Hóⁿga)

Speaking Practice

A. The instructor reads the vocabulary nouns and stative verbs aloud, noting their meanings, and also spelling the words out loud and writing them on the board. The students repeat the words aloud as a group and repeat the spelling. The instructor goes through the words again, student by student.

B. The instructor goes through these words randomly, asking each student the Omaha word for the English meaning.

C. The instructor reads the Omaha names aloud, noting their meanings. The students repeat the names aloud as a class. The instructor then goes through the names randomly, asking each student the English meaning of the name.

D. The instructor invites students who have Omaha names to share these with the class. Do the names follow the pattern of [Noun][Adjective] or [Noun][Number]?

E. The students form small groups of about two or three. In each group the students take turns quizzing their partners on possible noun-adjective or noun-number combinations that they may make up themselves. They should especially try using animal names and parts, such as "head," "horn," "hide," "tail," and "tooth" (hí). Example:

"Big bear," Umóⁿhoⁿ īe tʰe awatʰégoⁿ?

The quizzed student should respond: Maⁿčʰú ttóⁿga, ebthégoⁿ. "I think it's maⁿčʰú ttóⁿga."

11.9 NOUN–ACTIVE VERB WORD ORDER

Verb	Head Noun		Head Noun	Verb
flying	boat		moⁿdé	gióⁿ
standing	bear		maⁿčʰú	noⁿzhíⁿ
makes	earth		moⁿthíⁿkka	gāx̌e

- A noun can be modified by a verb. When this happens in English, we put the verb *in front of the noun*. In Omaha, the verb *follows the noun*.

Vocabulary: Nouns

gthedóⁿ: hawk

kkáx̣e: crow

kké: turtle

mí: sun, moon

mikká: raccoon

maⁿčʰú: grizzly bear

moⁿdé: boat

moⁿx̌pí: cloud

moⁿthíⁿkka: earth

mōⁿze: metal, iron

noⁿzhīⁿ: rain

óⁿpʰaⁿ: elk

ppasóⁿ: bald eagle

síⁿde: tail

tté: bison, buffalo

ttóⁿwoⁿ: town, village

x̌ithá: eagle

Vocabulary: Active Verbs

bahá: show

gāx̣e: make, do

gióⁿ: fly

moⁿthíⁿ: walk

noⁿzhíⁿ: stand

FIG. 87. moⁿdé: boat

thihóⁿ: lift

thihí: scare up, as a bird

x̣agé: cry

Supplementary Vocabulary

iháⁿ: mother

ugíne: look for one's own

uhóⁿge: end (of a line)

x̌tāwathe: loves them

Omaha Names

Clan names follow the personal names.

Dúba-moⁿthiⁿ: Four Walking (Iⁿkʰésabe)

Gthedóⁿ-moⁿthiⁿ: Walking Hawk
(Iⁿkʰésabe)

Gthedóⁿ-thihí: Scares Up Hawk (Ttappá)

Iháⁿ-ugine: Looks for Its Mother
(Iⁿgthézhide)

Kkáx̣e-baha: Exhibits Crow (Tháttada)

Kkax̣é-gioⁿ: Flying Crow (Hóⁿga)

Kke-báha: Turtle Showing Itself (Ttappá)

Kké-gax̣e: Turtle Maker (Tháttada)

Kke-thíhi: Scares Up Turtle (Tháttada)

Mí-moⁿthiⁿ: Walking Moon (Iⁿshtásuⁿda)

Mikká-x̣age: Crying Raccoon (Ttappá)

Moⁿx̌pí-moⁿthiⁿ: Walking Cloud
(Iⁿshtásuⁿda)

Moⁿthíⁿkka-gax̣e: Earth Maker (Omaha
clan)

Móⁿze-baha: Shows Metal (Ttappá)

Noⁿzhíⁿ-moⁿthiⁿ: Rain Walker (Tháttada)

Óⁿpʰaⁿ-noⁿzhiⁿ: Standing Elk (Wézhiⁿshte)

Ppasóⁿ-noⁿzhiⁿ: Standing Bald Eagle (Tháttada)

Xithá-gaxe: Eagle Maker (Ttappá)

Xithá-gioⁿ: Flying Eagle (Ttappá)

Síⁿde-thihoⁿ: Lifts Tail (Ttesíⁿde)

Ttóⁿwoⁿ-gaxe: Village Maker (Mothíⁿkkagaxe)

Tté-moⁿthiⁿ: Walking Buffalo (Iⁿgthézhide)

Uhóⁿge-moⁿthiⁿ: Walks at the End of the Line (Iⁿgthézhide)

Uhóⁿge-noⁿzhiⁿ: Stands at the End of the Line (Iⁿgthézhide)

Waʔú-xtáwathe: Loves Women (Ttesíⁿde)

Speaking Practice

A. The instructor reads the vocabulary nouns and active verbs aloud, noting their meanings, and also spelling the words out loud and writing them on the board. The students repeat the words aloud as a group and repeat the spelling. The instructor goes through the words again, student by student.

B. The instructor goes through these words randomly, asking each student the Omaha word for the English meaning.

C. The instructor reads the Omaha names aloud, noting their meanings. The students repeat the names aloud as a class. The instructor then goes through the names randomly, asking

each student the English meaning of the name.

D. The instructor invites students who have Omaha names to share these with the class. Do the names follow the pattern of [Noun][Verb]?

E. The students form small groups of about two or three. In each group the students take turns quizzing their partners on possible noun-verb, noun-adjective, or noun-number combinations that they may make up themselves.

11.10 VERB CHAINING

Subject	Head Verb	Verb		Verb	Head Verb
she	wants	to drink it		**thattóⁿ**	**gōⁿtha**
he	can	walk		**moⁿthíⁿ**	**ukkíhi**
she	sits	writing		**baxú**	**gthíⁿ**

· A series of verbs can sometimes be chained together. When this occurs, one verb is the *head verb*. The head verb applies to the subject immediately. Other verbs modify the head verb by describing or limiting the domain of its action.

· In English the head verb comes first, and any modifying verbs follow it in a chain. In Omaha, the order is reversed. The head verb comes last, and any modifying verbs precede it in the reverse of the order they would appear in an English sentence.

· In English the modifying verbs in the chain are usually introduced by the little word "to," as in "to walk," "to hear," and so forth. In Omaha, there is no "to" word. The basic verbs are simply placed one after another.

- Omaha verbs that end in -e in the dictionary form will end in -e when they precede other verbs. When they are the head verb at the end of the sentence, however, they will usually end in -a.

  For example:

  Ígasko^{n}the gō^{n}tha. = "He <u>wants to try it</u>."

  but

  Gáx̣e ígasko^{n}tha. = "He <u>tried to make it</u>."

- A verb chain can sometimes be longer than just two verbs.

  For example:

  Bax̣ú ukkíhi gō^{n}tha. = "He <u>wants to be able to write</u>."

Vocabulary: Active Verbs

gō^{n}tha: want, want to

ígasko^{n}the: try, attempt

thippí: be good at

thiʼá: cannot, fail to

ukkíhi: can, be able to

uthíʼage: be unwilling, be reluctant

Speaking Practice

A. The instructor reads the vocabulary verbs aloud, noting their meanings, and also spelling the words out loud and writing them on the board. The students repeat the words aloud as a group and repeat the spelling. The instructor goes through the words again, student by student.

B. The instructor goes through these words randomly, asking each student the Omaha word for the English meaning.

C. The instructor makes Omaha sentences using verb chaining. The students tell the meaning in English. The instructor then makes English sentences with verb chaining, which the students have to translate into Omaha.

D. The instructor goes around the class having students make up sentences in Omaha, using verb chaining. The instructor has to translate them.

E. The students form small groups of about two or three. In each group the students take turns quizzing their partners on possible verb chains that they may make up themselves.

Demands and Ablaut

12.1 COMMANDS:
THE PARTICLES A AND GA

	Verb	Command Particle	Attention Particle
Woman speaking:	**Gthí^n**	**a!**	
Man speaking casually:	**Gthí^n**	**ga!**	
Man speaking formally:	**Gthí^n**	**ga**	**ho!**

- To tell someone to do something in Omaha, we place a command particle, a or ga, after the verb.

- Women use the command particle a. Men use the particle ga.

- If a man is speaking formally, trying to get attention in a group setting, he will add the stressing and attention-getting particle ho after the command particle ga. Only men can use ho.

- When writing the command particle in lessons we use the convention of [command] a/ga!. A student should use the command particle for his/her gender. The exclamation point does not imply a raised voice or excitement. It is used in these lessons to serve as a sign that the preceding a or ga is a command marker and nothing else.

Vocabulary

gthí^n: sit (down)

no^{n}zhí^n: stand (up)

gí: come (here), come back

mo^{n}thí^n: go, walk

thattó^n: drink it

āgazhi: command, tell someone to do something

īe t^{h}e: the word

baxú: write it

Speaking Practice

A. Read the following command sentences aloud. Then translate each sentence into English and tell who said it. If the speaker is a man, tell whether he is speaking formally or casually. Example:

Mo^{n}thí^n a!: Go! (woman speaking)

No^{n}zhí^n ga!: Stand up! (man speaking casually)

Gí ga ho!: Come here! (man speaking formally)

1. Gthí^n a!

2. Gí a!

3. Mo^{n}thí^n ga!

4. No^{n}zhí^n a!

5. Gthí^n ga ho!

6. Gí ga!

7. No^{n}zhí^n ga ho!

8. Gthí^n ga!

9. Mo^{n}thí^n a!

10. Mo^{n}thí^n ga ho!

B. The instructor (wagōⁿze) has each
student give a command in Omaha.
The student should give the command
with the appropriate command particle.
The instructor will do as commanded.
Example:

Wagōⁿze: Joe, tell me to go.

Joe: Moⁿthíⁿ ga! or Moⁿthíⁿ ga ho!

Wagōⁿze [walking away]: Ūdaⁿ shkāxe.
Mary, tell me to sit down.

Mary: Gthíⁿ a!

Wagōⁿze: Ho! or Ha! [Sits down.]

C. The students pair up. They command
their partners to come, sit down,
stand up, and go. The partners do as
commanded.

D. The instructor has each student
command some other student to do
something, using the verb āgazhi.
Example:

Wagōⁿze: Sally, Mike noⁿzhíⁿ āgazhi ga
ho! ("Sally, tell Mike to stand up!")

Sally: Ha. Mike, noⁿzhíⁿ a!

Mike: Ho! [Stands up.]

E. The instructor has each student come
forward and write a word on the board,
using the verb baxú. Example:

Wagōⁿze: Stan, gí ga ho!

Stan: Ho! [Comes forward.]

Wagōⁿze: "Moⁿthíⁿ" īe t^he baxú ga!

Stan: Ho! [Writes the word "moⁿthíⁿ."]

Ttígaxe

The students count from 1 to no more than 10
in Omaha. (If there are more than 10 students
in the class, the class is subdivided into two or
more groups as necessary.) This will be the order
in which they take their turns. The instructor
then puts the class in ttígaxe mode, in which
no English may be spoken, by saying: Ttígaxe
oⁿgátha tta! Then the students take turns, in
order of their numbers, giving each other commands. The person commanded should do as
instructed. If, for any reason, someone cannot
execute or does not understand the command,
the student may demur by saying: Bthí'a ("I can't
do it"). At the end of the period, the instructor
takes the class out of ttígaxe mode by announcing: Ttígaxe shóⁿ ppāxe! ("I put an end to
ttígaxe!").

12.2 COMMANDS: ABLAUT

	Verb	Command Particle
Plain form of verb ending in -**e**:	**thizé**	
Woman speaking:	**thizá**	**!**
Man speaking:	**thizá**	**ga!**

· When the plain form of a verb ends in -e,
this -e will change to -a in a command.

· This change from -e to -a is called
ablaut (pronounced *ahp*-lout). Ablaut
occurs before several types of particles,
including command particles.

· When a woman is giving a command
using a verb that normally ends in -e,
there is no separate command particle.
The command is signaled by the ablaut

to -a alone. The male command uses the command particle ga as well as the ablaut: -a ga.

· Verbs ending in any of the other five vowels, -i, -iⁿ, -u, -oⁿ or -a, do not change their endings, and are followed by the particle a for a female command.

Vocabulary: -e Active Verbs

āthade: recite it, read it

shkāde: play

dóⁿbe: see it, look

é: say it

gāxe: make it, do it

ígaskoⁿthe: try it, attempt it

itʰéthe: put away

thatʰé: eat it

thizé: take it, pick it up

uné: look for it, seek it, search for it

uthíxide: look around (for something)

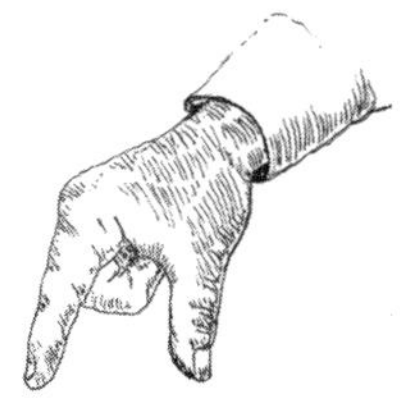

FIG. 88. thizé: take it, pick it up

Vocabulary: Miscellaneous

āshiatta: outside

wabáxu kʰe: the letters

wagthábaze: books, notes, papers

Speaking Practice

A. Read the following command sentences aloud. Then translate the sentence into English and tell who said them. If the speaker is a man, tell whether he is speaking formally or casually. Example:

Thatʰá!: Eat it! (woman speaking)

Gāxa ga!: Make it!/Do it! (man speaking casually)

Thizá ga ho!: Take it! (man speaking formally)

1. Á!

2. Dóⁿba ga ho!

3. Thatʰá ga!

4. Gāxa!

5. Uná!

6. Ígaskoⁿtha ga!

7. Uthíxida ga!

8. Thizá!

9. Āshiatta shkāda!

10. Wagthábaze itʰétha ga ho!

B. The instructor (wagōⁿze) has each student give a command in Omaha. The student should give the command with the appropriate command particle. The instructor will do as commanded. Example:

Wagōⁿze: Loren, tell me to look for it.

Loren: Uná ga! or Uná ga ho!

Wagōⁿze: Ūdaⁿ shkáxe. Ann, tell me to look around for it.

Ann: Uthíxida!

Wagōⁿze: Ho! or Ha! [Looks all around.]

C. The students pair up. Students command their partners to come, sit down, stand up, and go. The partners do as commanded.

D. The instructor has each student command some other student to do something, using the verb āgazhi. Example:

Wagōⁿze: Ginnie, Jake thatʰé āgazhi ga ho! ("Ginnie, tell Jake to eat it!")

Ginnie: Ha. Jake, thatʰá!

Jake: Ho! [Eats the treat the instructor has provided.]

E. The instructor has each student stand up and say a word, using the verb é. Example:

Wagōⁿze: Dan, noⁿzhíⁿ ga ho!

Dan: Ho! [Stands up.]

Wagōⁿze: "Shkāde" á ga!

Dan: Ho! "Shkāde."

Wagōⁿze: Wíbthahoⁿ. Gthíⁿ ga!

12.3 PLURAL COMMANDS: I AND ABLAUT

Command to One Person

	Verb	Command Particle
Plain Form of Verb:	moⁿthíⁿ	
Woman:	moⁿthíⁿ	a!
Man:	moⁿthíⁿ	ga!

Command to One Person, -e Verb

	Verb	Command Particle
Plain Form of Verb:	thizé	
Woman:	thizá	!
Man:	thizá	ga!

Command to More Than One Person

	Verb	Augment	Command Particle
Plain Form of Verb:	moⁿthíⁿ		
Woman:	moⁿthíⁿ	i	a!
Man:	moⁿthíⁿ	i	ga!

Command to More Than One Person, -e Verb

	Verb	Augment	Command Particle
Plain Form of Verb:	thizé		
Woman:	thizá	i	a!
Man:	thizá	i	ga!

· To command one person, the command particle follows the verb. To command more than one person, the particle i is placed after the verb and before the command particle.

· We will call this particle the *augment* i particle, because it takes the original thought and *augments* it, by adding extra actors or actions to the base idea. A plural command is like a command to one person, plus some other people as well.

· Like the command particle, the augment i also causes an immediately preceding verb ending in -e to ablaut to -a.

· Women sometimes seem to use the augment even when speaking to only one person when the verb ends in -a, either naturally or by ablaut. This is probably to avoid the confusion of "losing" the command particle when it is the same as the ending vowel of the verb. This habit may have arisen recently, in the twentieth century, as it does not seem to be recorded in nineteenth-century texts.

Vocabulary

wôⁿgithe: all, everyone

zhoⁿbtháska: board

zhoⁿbtháskasabe: blackboard

zhoⁿbtháskaska: whiteboard

Speaking Practice

A. Read the following command sentences aloud. Translate each sentence into English. Describe the gender of the speaker making the command, and whether the command is to one person or several. Example:

Thattóⁿ i a!: Drink it! (woman speaking to several people)

Gāxa i ga ho!: Make it!/Do it! (man speaking formally to a group)

Ígaskoⁿtha ga!: Try it! (man speaking casually to one person)

1. Gāxa i a!

2. Gthíⁿ i ga!

3. Thizá!

4. "Wíbthahoⁿ" á i ga ho!

5. Uthíxida i a!

6. Ĩe tʰe é ígaskoⁿtha i ga!

7. Ní tʰe thattóⁿ ga!

8. Gióⁿ moⁿthíⁿ i a!

9. Wabáxu kʰe āthada i a!

10. Wagthábaze itʰétha i ga ho!

B. Translate the following sentences into Omaha. Assume you are speaking to a single person.

1. Try it!

2. Eat it!

3. Look for it!

4. Stand up!

5. Lie down!

6. Take the water!

7. Write the word!

8. Look at the blackboard!

9. Go play outside!

10. Try to read it!

C. Translate the sentences in B again. This time assume you are speaking to a group of people.

D. The instructor has each student command some other student, or the entire class, to do something, using the verb āgazhi. To command the entire class, address them as wôⁿgithe. Example:

Wagōⁿze: Steve, wôⁿgithe uthíxide āgazhi ga ho! ("Steve, tell everyone to look around!")

Steve: Ho. Wôⁿgithe, uthíxida i ga!

Classmates: Ho!/Ha! [They all look around.]

E. The students will break into small groups of about three or four, and will take turns commanding each other to command one student or the entire group.

12.4 QUESTIONS: A WITH NO ABLAUT

	Verb	Question Particle	
	Thattóⁿ	**a?**	Did he drink it?
-e Verb:	**Thatʰé**	**a?**	Did he eat it?

- To ask what someone does or did in Omaha, we place a question particle, a, after the verb. Both men and women use this particle.
- The question particle does not cause a preceding -e verb to ablaut.
- We do not raise the pitch of our voice to ask a question in Omaha as we do in English; a question sounds just like a statement. For a woman using a verb that does not end in -e, asking whether someone did something may be indistinguishable from telling someone to do it. Example:

Gthíⁿ a?: Is s/he sitting?

sounds the same as

Gthíⁿ a!: Sit!

Vocabulary

ímoⁿx̱e: ask (a question)

íbahoⁿ: know something

noⁿshtóⁿ: stop (walking, etc.)

thippí: be good at something

x̌tāthe: like, love

uthíʼage: refuse, be reluctant to do it

thax̌tá: bite it

ūzhiha: bag, pack, backpack, purse

FIG. 89. ūzhiha: bag (Omaha style)

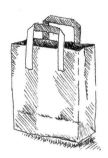

FIG. 90. ūzhiha: bag (grocery sack)

Speaking Practice

A. Read the following question sentences aloud. Then translate the sentences into English. Examples:

Moⁿthíⁿ a?: Is s/he walking? Did s/he walk?

Shkāde a?: Is s/he playing? Did s/he play?

Thax̌tá a?: Did she bite him?

1. Uthíx̱ide a?
2. Noⁿzhíⁿ a?
3. Ttí gāx̱e a?
4. Ttí tʰe dóⁿbe a?
5. Wēbax̱u uné a?
6. Īe tʰe é a?
7. Ūdaⁿ moⁿthíⁿ a?
8. Umóⁿhoⁿ īe tʰe íbahoⁿ a?
9. Ttōⁿthiⁿ noⁿshtóⁿ a?
10. Ūzhiha thoⁿ itʰéthe a?

B. Translate the following sentences into Omaha.

1. Does she hear it?

2. Does he want it?

3. Did he try it?

4. Is she sitting?

5. Did he sleep well?

6. Is he playing outside?

7. Does he love her?

8. Does she know Omaha?

9. Is he good at writing Omaha?

10. Did she refuse to do it?

C. The instructor asks each student yes/ no questions about someone else. The student responds with Áo^n or Á^{n}kkazhi.

D. The instructor has each student ask some other student a question about a third student, using the verb ímo^{n}xe. Example:

Wagō^{n}ze: Susan, Duane shó^{n}ge uná i t^{h}e Dan ímo^{n}xa ga! ("Susan, ask Dan if Duane is looking for a horse!")

Susan: Ha. Dan, Duane shó^{n}ge uné a?

Dan: Á^{n}kkazhi. [Dan decides without asking Duane.]

E. The students break into small groups of about three or four and take turns asking each other questions about a third person.

12.5 THIRD-PERSON STATEMENT OF ACTION: ABLAUT FOR DECLARATION

Nineteenth Century

He drank it.

	Verb	Augment	Emphatic Particle
	thattó^n		
Woman Making Statement:	**Thattó^n**	**i**	**he.**
Man Making Statement:	**Thattó^n**	**i**	**ha.**

-e Verb

He ate it.

	Verb	Augment	Emphatic Particle
	that^{h}é		
Woman Making Statement:	**That^{h}á**	**i**	**he.**
Man Making Statement:	**That^{h}á**	**i**	**ha.**

Twentieth Century

He drank it.

	Verb
	thattó^n
Woman Making Statement:	**Thattó^n.**
Man Making Statement:	**Thattó^n.**

-e Verb

He ate it.

	Verb
	that^{h}é
Woman Making Statement:	**That^{h}á.**
Man Making Statement:	**That^{h}á.**

- In the nineteenth century, a statement narrating a third party's action was made with the sequence: [Verb] [i] [Emphatic Particle]. For women, the emphatic particle was he. For men, it was ha. If the verb ended in -e, it ablauted to -a.

- In the twentieth century, the [i] [Emphatic Particle] was generally dropped, leaving only the verb. If the verb was an -e verb, however, it retained its ablaut to -a.

- When actions are conceived as states, or ongoing actions rather than events, there was never an i particle and -e verbs end in -e. This form may be used for the present tense or things that have just happened as well as for ongoing actions in the past that set the scene for something else.

Vocabulary

thi'á: fail, be unable

nā: ask for it

thawá: count them

FIG. 91. moⁿkkóⁿsabe: coffee

moⁿkkóⁿsabe: coffee

wamóskeshuga: cowboy bread

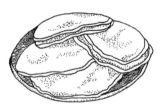

FIG. 92. wamóskeshuga: cowboy bread

Speaking Practice

A. Read the following third person statements aloud. Then translate the sentences into English. Examples:

Íbahoⁿ: S/he knows it.

X̱agá: S/he cried.

Āgthiⁿ tʰe doⁿbá: S/he saw the chair.

1. Gthíⁿ.
2. Noⁿóⁿ.
3. Thi'á.
4. X̌tātha.
5. Thizá.
6. Uthíx̱ida.
7. Wēbax̱u tʰe thawá.
8. Āshiatta shkāda.
9. Ūdaⁿ moⁿthíⁿ.
10. Zhoⁿbtháskasabe dóⁿbe ígaskoⁿthe gthíⁿ.

B. Translate the following sentences into Omaha.

1. He wants it.
2. He stopped walking.
3. She looked for the pen.
4. She bit the apple.
5. He asked for the book.
6. She said the word.
7. He refused to put away the backpack.
8. She knows how to spell the word.
9. They're drinking the coffee.
10. She can't make cowboy bread.

C. The instructor asks each student yes/ no questions about someone else. The student responds with Áoⁿ or Áⁿkkazhi. If the answer is Áoⁿ, the student restates the instructor's question as a statement.

D. The instructor has each student command some other student to do something. The student then asks a third student what the commanded student is doing. The third student answers with the appropriate statement. Example:

> Wagōⁿze: Sara, Elaine zhoⁿní kʰe thizé āgazhi ga! ("Sara, tell Elaine to take the candy bar!")
>
> Sara: Ha. Elaine, zhoⁿní kʰe thizá! [Elaine takes the candy bar.] Brad, Elaine idādoⁿ gāx̣e a?
>
> Brad: Zhoⁿní kʰe thizá.

E. The students break into small groups of about three or four and take turns performing exercise D, making up their own commands without the aid of the instructor.

12.6 NEGATION: ABLAUT BEFORE "NOT"

Third-Person Statement

Plain Verb		Verb	Negative Particle	
thattóⁿ		**Thattóⁿ**	**bazhi.**	She didn't drink it.
thatʰé		**Thatʰá**	**bazhi.**	She didn't eat it.

- To declare that somebody did *not* do something, we place the negating particle bazhi after the verb.

- If speaking about a specific past non-action, an -e verb ablauts to -a before the negating particle bazhi. If the non-action declared is an ongoing state or general fact, the -e apparently stays -e before declarative bazhi.

Negative Command to One Person

Plain Verb		Verb	Negating Particle	Command Particle	
thihóⁿ		**Thihóⁿ**	**azhi**	**a/ga!**	Don't lift it!
thizé		**Thizá**	**azhi**	**a/ga!**	Don't take it!

- To command a single person not to do something, we place the negating particle azhi between the verb and the command particle.

- In a command, a preceding -e verb ablauts to -a before the negating particle azhi. In this case, the ablaut -a and the initial a- of azhi merge into a single vowel in speech. Thus, Shkāda azhi ga!, "Don't play!", is pronounced, and might be written, as Shkādazhi ga!

Negative Command to More Than One Person

Plain Verb		Verb	Negating Particle	Augment	Command Particle	
íx̌ax̌a		**Íx̌ax̌á**	**bazhi**	**i**	**a/ga!**	Don't laugh!
x̣agé		**X̣agá**	**bazhi**	**i**	**a/ga!**	Don't cry!

- To command a group of people not to do something, we place the negating particle bazhi followed by the augment i between the verb and the command particle.

- In commands, this bazhi also causes -e verbs to ablaut to -a.
- In commands, the difference between azhi and bazhi is that azhi is used for commanding a single person not to do something, and bazhi is used for commanding multiple people. In making statements in the third person, bazhi is a sentence-level negative declarative, while azhi may be used otherwise within the sentence.
- Omaha does not seem to use negative questions like: "Don't you want it?" or "Didn't he read it?" All questions are apparently asked straight up, as "Do you want it?" or "Did he read it?"

Vocabulary

ābaxu: write it down
ābitte: touch it
badóⁿ: push it
ié: speak
izházhe: name
thidóⁿ: pull it
thihóⁿ: lift it

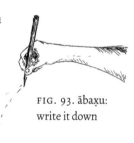

FIG. 93. ābaxu: write it down

FIG. 94. badóⁿ: push it

Speaking Practice

A. Read the following question sentences aloud. Then translate the sentence into English. Examples:

Noⁿzhíⁿ bazhi: S/he didn't stand.

Shkāda azhi a!: Don't play! (woman speaking to one person)

Ní tʰe thattóⁿ bazhi i ga!: Don't drink the water! (man speaking to a group)

1. Uthíxidá bazhi.
2. Gthíⁿ bazhi.
3. Thippí bazhi.
4. Thaxtá azhi a!
5. Ĩe tʰe á azhi ga!
6. Wāthatʰe kʰe badóⁿ azhi a!
7. Wãxe ĩe tʰe iá bazhi i ga ho!
8. Uóⁿsisi āgazhi bazhi i a!
9. Izházhe tʰe ímoⁿxa bazhi i a!
10. Izházhe tʰe íbahoⁿ bazhi.

B. Translate the following sentences into Omaha.

1. Don't say it!
2. She didn't want it.
3. He didn't refuse.
4. Don't sleep!
5. Don't go running!
6. He didn't try to speak Omaha.
7. She didn't like him.
8. Don't lift the table!
9. He didn't speak English well.
10. Don't touch it!

C. The instructor asks each student yes/no questions about what someone else did. The student responds with Áoⁿ or Áⁿkkazhi and then restates the question as a positive or negative statement, as appropriate.

D. The instructor has each student command a second student not to do something. The first student then asks a third student: Idādoⁿ gāx̣e a?, to which that third student replies that the second student is not doing what the first said not to do (unless the second is in fact doing it!). Example:

> Wagōⁿze: Tim, Kyle gióⁿ moⁿthíⁿ azhi tʰe āgazhi ga! ("Tim, tell Kyle not to go flying!")
>
> Tim: Ho. Kyle, gióⁿ moⁿthíⁿ azhi ga! [Kyle refrains from flapping his arms.]
>
> Ruth, Kyle akʰá idādoⁿ gāx̣e a?
>
> Ruth: Gióⁿ moⁿthíⁿ bazhi.

E. The students break into small groups of about three or four and take turns performing exercise D, making up their own commands without the help of the instructor.

12.7 THE POTENTIAL PARTICLE TTE

Suggestion of a Possibility

Verb	Potential Particle	
Thax̌tá	tte.	He might bite.
X̣agé	tte.	She might cry.

- To suggest a possibility, we use the potential particle tte after the verb.

- This potential particle does not cause a preceding -e verb to ablaut.

Prediction Acknowledging a Free Agent

Verb	Potential Particle	Positional	
Thatʰé	tta	akʰa.	He'll probably eat it.
Zhōⁿ	tta	akʰa.	She'll probably sleep.
Máthe	tta	akʰa.	It'll probably snow.

- To constrain the possibility, we generally add a *positional* particle after the potential particle tte. This positional particle causes the potential particle to ablaut to tta.

- To predict what someone is going to do in the future, we use the positional akʰa.

- These positionals imply that the action is uncertain, as it is predicated on the free will of the actor.

- Predictions about the weather also use akʰa, because the weather is a free agent.

- In colloquial speech the potential particle and the positional are run together and the final vowel is generally dropped. They will sound more like ttakʰ.

Vocabulary

gasóⁿthiⁿ: tomorrow

óⁿbathe: today

sidādi: yesterday

thastúbe: lick it

uthá: tell

Speaking Practice

A. Read the following sentences aloud.
Then translate the sentences into
English. Examples:

Gthíⁿ tte: S/he might sit down.

Uthíxide tte: S/he might look around.

Thastúbe tta akʰa: S/he will probably
lick it.

1. Thippí tte.

2. Thiʔá tte.

3. Wēbax̣u thizé tte.

4. Ní tʰe thattóⁿ tta akʰa.

5. Ímoⁿx̣e tta akʰa.

6. Izházhe tʰe uthá tte.

7. Uóⁿsisi āgazhi tta akʰa.

8. Wāx̌e īe tʰe ié tta akʰa.

9. Wāthatʰe kʰe badóⁿ tte.

10. Móⁿgasiⁿde kʰe thidóⁿ tta
akʰa.

B. Translate the following sentences
into Omaha.

1. He might take it.

2. She will probably eat it.

3. He might look for it.

4. She will probably say it.

5. He will probably fail.

6. He will probably drink the
coffee.

7. She may order him to speak
English.

8. He will probably put the
backpack away.

9. He may try to make a house.

10. She might be able to pick up the
table.

C. The instructor gives each student a
command. Before a student responds,
the instructor asks a second student
what the first will do. The second student
responds appropriately. Example:

Wagōⁿze: Jessica, shé thoⁿ thatʰá ga!
George, Jessica akʰa, idādoⁿ gāx̣e
tte? ("Jessica, eat the apple! George,
what do you suppose Jessica will
do?")

George: Shé thoⁿ thatʰé tta akʰa.

D. The instructor goes around the room
having each student command another
student to do something and asking a
third what that student is likely to do, as
the instructor did in exercise C.

E. The students break into small groups
of about three or four and take turns
performing exercise D, making up their
own commands without the help of the
instructor.

12.8 THE HEARSAY PARTICLE SET BI AMA

Statement of Hearsay

Plain Verb	Verb	Hearsay Particle	
noⁿʔóⁿ	**Noⁿʔóⁿ**	**bi ama.**	S/he supposedly heard it.
dóⁿbe	**Doⁿbá**	**bi ama.**	S/he supposedly saw it.

- To make a statement about something
we have heard about, without taking
direct responsibility for the truth of the

claim, we use the hearsay particle set bi ama.

- The bi ama hearsay particle set smoothly covers the cases where in English we would clumsily have to say "allegedly," "supposedly," or "they say," as in "They say Rabbit killed a giant," or "Supposedly, Susan worked at a store last summer," or "That boy allegedly broke into the judge's house."

- The particle bi in bi ama causes a preceding -e verb to ablaut.

- The particle bi can also occur by itself. When it does, it implies that the preceding clause is supposed, or hypothesized, but not necessarily true.

- The particle ama can also occur without bi. With or without bi, ama implies that the foregoing sentence is hearsay, the way the story goes.

Negative Statement of Hearsay

Plain Verb		Verb	Negative Particle	Hearsay Particles	
thattón		Thattón	bazhi	bi ama.	S/he supposedly didn't drink it.
thatʰé		Thatʰá	bazhi	bi ama.	S/he supposedly didn't eat it.

- To make a negative statement of hearsay, we place the negative particle bazhi between the verb and bi ama.

Vocabulary

āshka: in a little while

Speaking Practice

A. Read the following question sentences aloud. Then translate the sentences into English. Examples:

Zhōⁿ bi ama: It is said that s/he slept.

Shóⁿge uná bi ama: S/he was looking for a horse, they say.

Uthíʾaga bazhi bi ama: Supposedly s/he didn't refuse.

1. Āshiatta gthíⁿ bi ama.

2. Noⁿzhíⁿ bi ama.

3. Ié thippí bi ama.

4. Ní tʰe thattóⁿ bi ama.

5. Ímoⁿxa bi ama.

6. Ígaskoⁿtha bazhi āgazhi bi ama.

7. Āshka bi ama.

8. Wagthábaze kʰe itʰétha bazhi bi ama.

9. Izházhe tʰe uthá bazhi bi ama.

10. Móⁿgasiⁿde kʰe thidóⁿ ígaskoⁿtha bi ama.

B. Translate the following sentences into Omaha.

1. He supposedly bit it.

2. She supposedly knew.

3. They were playing, they say.

4. She didn't say it, they say.

5. Everyone wrote it, they say.

6. He couldn't lift the table, they say.

7. It is said she wanted to speak Winnebago.

8. He supposedly saw the black backpack.

9. He didn't count the trees, they say.

10. It is said she wanted to be able to make cowboy bread.

C. The instructor tells each student something another student did yesterday, as a matter of fact. A third student asks the student the instructor addressed what that student did yesterday. The student who heard it from the instructor tells what was heard, using the bi ama form. Example:

Wagōⁿze: Melanie, sidādi Kelsie akʰa zhoⁿní kʰe thatʰá. ("Melanie, yesterday Kelsie ate the candy bar.")

Tyler: Melanie, sidādi Kelsie akʰa idādoⁿ gāxe a?

Melanie: Zhoⁿní kʰe thatʰá bi ama.

D. The instructor has one student keeping eyes covered while a second student performs a chosen action. Eyes still covered, the first student asks a third student what the second student did. The third student describes the action as a matter of fact. The instructor asks the first student what the second student did, and the student who hasn't actually seen it replies using the bi ama form.

E. The students break into small groups of at least four and take turns performing exercise D, making up their own commands without the help of the instructor.

12.9 SIGNALING DEMAND IN ENGLISH AND OMAHA

- *Undirected Utterance*: a general broadcast of emotional state; a cry or expletive
- *Directed Utterance*: a verbal demand made upon a targeted listener
- *Unitary Demand*: a single word or set phrase that communicates the entire demand within the situation; a word like Hello!, Hey!, Sorry!, or Goodbye!
- *Sentence*: a directed series of words that conveys a concept along with the demand
- *Concept*: the part of the sentence that tells the listener what the speaker is talking about; this includes most nouns, verbs, adjectives, and other words and phrases that reference things in the real world
- *Demand*: the part of the sentence that signals what the speaker wants the listener to do with the concept; a demand might be a command, a statement, or a question, but a concept without a demand is not a complete sentence. To signal demand, English makes some basic postulates about a sentence:

It has a *subject,* to which the rest of the sentence relates as a predicate. The subject is a noun phrase.

It has a *head verb,* which links the predicate to the subject.

There are two types of verbs: *lexical* and *auxiliary.* Lexical verbs refer to the action of real world entities. Auxiliary verbs describe the mode or restrictions on their action as these relate to the current discussion. We sometimes call these "helping verbs."

How to Construct an English Sentence

Statement:	[Subject] + [Head Verb] + [rest of sentence]
Yes-No Question:	[Auxiliary Head Verb] + [Subject] + [verb] + [rest of sentence]
Command:	[Lexical Head Verb] + [rest of sentence]

Statement:	[Ryan] + [sat] + [at the table].
Yes-No Question:	[Did] + [Ryan] + [sit] + [at the table]?
Command:	[Sit] + [at the table]!

How to Construct an Omaha Sentence

Declaration:	[Concept] + (i he/ha)	Gthí^n (i he/ha).	S/he sat.
Yes-No Question:	[Concept] + a	Gthí^n a?	Did s/he sit?
Command:	[Concept] + a/ga	Gthí^n a/ga!	Sit down!
Possibility:	[Concept] + tte	Gthí^n tte.	S/he might sit.
Expectation of Free Agent:	[Concept] + tta ak^{h}a	Gthí^n tta ak^{h}a.	S/he will sit.
Hearsay:	[Concept] + bi ama	Gthí^n bi ama.	S/he allegedly sat.

The English method relies on permutations of classes of concept words and is extremely complicated. The Omaha method is to use a special word for each type of demand and is quite simple.

Note that in Omaha, verbs always come after their nouns, whether these are subject or object. This is entirely different than in English, where object nouns normally come after their verb. Thus in English [The cat (subject noun)] [caught (transitive verb)] [the mouse (object noun)], but in Omaha [The cat (subject noun)] [the mouse (object noun)] [caught (transitive verb)].

Concept and Demand in English and Omaha

English:	[Demand] [Concept]	[(Drink)!][drink the water]	Drink the water!
Omaha:	[Concept] [Demand]	[Ní tʰe thattóⁿ][a/ga!]	Drink the water!

The English method establishes the demand at the beginning of the sentence and then elaborates on the concept. The Omaha method orients the listener to the concept first, and waits until the end to signal the demand.

Vocabulary

noⁿzhíⁿ: rain

shóⁿshoⁿ: still, continually

ukkíhi: be able to

Speaking Practice

A. Read the following sentences aloud. Then translate the sentences into English. Tell what kind of demand is conveyed and other implied details of communication.

  1. Umóⁿhoⁿ ié thippí gōⁿtha bi ama.

  2. Umóⁿhoⁿ īe tʰe baxú ígaskoⁿthe a?

  3. Áⁿkkazhi, thiʔá. Wēbaxu shóⁿshoⁿ uná.

  4. Wabáxu kʰe āthade tte.

  5. Umóⁿhoⁿ wabáxu kʰe íbahoⁿ bazhi.

  6. Wāxe wagthábaze āthade ukkíhi.

  7. Āshka Umóⁿhoⁿ ié thippí tta akʰa.

  8. Wēbaxu wiwítta kʰe thizá ga!

  9. Izházhe tʰe uthá i a!

  10. Wāthatʰe kʰe badóⁿ bazhi i ga ho!

B. Translate the following sentences into Omaha.

  1. Is he running?

  2. She knows the name.

  3. Tomorrow it will likely rain.

  4. They say she refused.

  5. Take the coffee!

  6. She might play outside.

  7. Ask for the watch!

  8. Is she able to lift the blue bag?

  9. Don't tell him to jump!

  10. They say she was making cowboy bread.

C. The instructor goes around the room saying a sentence in Omaha to each student, to which the student should respond appropriately.

D. The instructor has each student take a turn at saying an Omaha sentence to another student as in exercise C, to which the second student should respond appropriately.

E. The students break into small groups of at least four and take turns performing exercise D, making up their own sentences without the help of the instructor.

Verb Conjugation

13.1 AFFIXED PRONOUNS: I AND YOU COMMON FORMS

Plain Verb	I-form: a + [Plain Verb]	You-form: tha + [Plain Verb]
no$^{n?}$ó^n	anó$^{n?}$o^n	thanó$^{n?}$o^n
no^{n}zhí^n	anó^{n}zhi^n	thanó^{n}zhi^n
gthí^n	agthí^n	thagthí^n
zhō^n	azhō^n	thazhō^n
ttó^n	attó^n	thattó^n
x̣agé	ax̣áge	thax̣áge

- To make a statement about an action that includes either the speaker or the listener, we attach an *affixed pronoun* to the front of the verb.

- To say that "I" did something, the usual affixed pronoun is a-. To say that "you" did it, the usual affixed pronoun is tha-.

- This works for verbs starting with nasal consonants (n), fricatives, tense or aspirated stops, or consonant clusters. It does not work for verbs starting with ledh, a free-standing voiced stop, or a vowel. We will discuss these situations in future lessons.

- In declarations, -e verbs do not ablaut in the I form or the you (singular) form. To say "I cry," we would say Ax̣áge. To say "you cry" talking to one person, we would say Thax̣áge.

- When we add an affixed pronoun to the front of a verb that has two or more syllables with the accent not on the first syllable, the accent is drawn forward so that it falls on the second syllable of the derived verb. Thus: no^{n}zhí^n, "to stand," becomes anó^{n}zhi^n, "I stand," with the accent moving up to stay on the second syllable.

- In Omaha there is no affixed pronoun representing third person subject. If you are talking about someone else only, who is neither speaker nor listener, the actor of the verb is never marked. The party that in English we would call "he," "she," "it," or "they" is simply assumed.

- When chaining verbs, each verb is appropriately conjugated. Thus to ask "Why are you crying?", we would say: Awádi thax̣áge thagthí^n? Here, "you" is the subject of both verbs in the chain, so both verbs are conjugated with an affixed tha-. Literally, this asks: "Why you-cry you-sit?"

Vocabulary: Nouns

wanó^{n}x̣e: ghost

Vocabulary: Verbs

gthí^n: sit

niúoⁿ: swim

noⁿtʰé: kick

noⁿzhíⁿ: stand

noⁿʾóⁿ: hear

nuzóⁿ: skate, sled

shkáde: play

ttóⁿ: have characteristically

ttóⁿthiⁿ: run

x̌é: bury

x̌thíⁿ: growl

x̣agé: cry

zúde: whistle

zhōⁿ: lie down, sleep

FIG. 95. niúoⁿ: swim

FIG. 98. x̣agé: cry

Question Words

awádi: why?

Speaking Practice

A. Read the following sentences aloud. Then translate the sentences into English. (Note: egoⁿ after a noun means "like." Wanóⁿx̣e egoⁿ means "like a ghost." Also, kkōⁿbtha is the "I" form of gōⁿtha, "want" or "want to.") Examples:

Āshiatta azhōⁿ: I'm sleeping outside.

Wazhíⁿga thanóⁿʾoⁿ?: Do you hear birds?

Eáttoⁿ thax̣áge a?: Why are you crying?

1. Āgthiⁿ tʰe thagthíⁿ.

2. Aníuoⁿ.

3. Anóⁿtʰe anóⁿshtoⁿ.

4. Ní tʰe thanóⁿʾoⁿ a?

5. Āshiatta thashkāde.

6. Ttéska kʰe ax̌é.

7. Maⁿx̌ʰú egoⁿ thax̌thíⁿ.

8. Wanóⁿx̣e egoⁿ thazúde.

9. Móⁿzeska attóⁿ.

10. Anúzoⁿ kkōⁿbtha.

FIG. 96. ttóⁿthiⁿ: run

FIG. 97. x̌thíⁿ: growl

B. Translate the following sentences into Omaha.

    1. Do you hear it?

    2. I hear it.

    3. Are you standing outside?

    4. Did you stop running?

    5. Are you sleeping?

    6. I am sleeping well.

    7. Did you bury the skunk?

    8. No, I buried the rabbit.

    9. Today I am playing.

    10. I am whistling.

C. The instructor tells each student to do something, using one of the verbs in today's list. The student does it. The instructor then asks what the student is doing. The student answers using the "I" form. Example:

    Wagō^{n}ze: Jason, no^{n}zhí^n ga.

    [Jason stands up.]

    Wagō^{n}ze: Idādo^n shkáx̣e a? ("What are you doing?")

    Jason: Anó^{n}zhi^n.

D. The instructor then acts out a verb for each student, asking the student what the action is. The student answers using the you form. Example:

    Wagō^{n}ze [lying down]: Deb, idādo^n ppāx̣e a? ("What am I doing?")

    Deb: Thazhō^n.

E. The students break into small groups of at least four and take turns performing exercises C and D among themselves,

making up their own activities without the help of the instructor.

13.2 AFFIXED PRONOUNS: I AND YOU FOR LEDH VERBS

Plain Verb	I-form:	You-form:
th-	**bth-**	**n-**
thí^n	**bthí^n**	**ní^n**
thattó^n	**bthátto^n**	**nátto^n**
athí^n	**abthí^n**	**aní^n**

- If a verb starts with ledh (th-), then the I- or you- affixed pronoun combines tightly with it. The "I" form adds b in front (bth-), and the "you" form changes the ledh to n (n-).

- In this case, an extra syllable is not actually added because there is no vowel intervening between the affixed pronoun and the beginning of the verb. However, there was a vowel here in the past. This is shown by the fact that a second-syllable accent in a verb with more than one syllable is drawn forward to the first syllable of the verb, just as it would be in the case of the common forms. Thus the accent of thattó^n is on the second syllable, but for the I- and you- forms bthátto^n and nátto^n it falls on the first syllable.

- Generally, for verbs that start with the vowels a-, u-, or i-, the affixed pronoun is placed on the first consonant after the initial vowel. Thus, uné, "to seek," becomes uáne, "I seek," and utháne, "you seek." Similarly, athíⁿ, "to have," becomes abthíⁿ, "I have," and aníⁿ, "you have."

- The verb moⁿthíⁿ places the affixed pronoun after the initial moⁿ-. Thus: moⁿbthíⁿ, "I walk," and moⁿníⁿ, "you walk."

Vocabulary: Verbs

athíⁿ: have, at hand

ethégoⁿ: think

moⁿthíⁿ: walk

thaxtá: bite it

thastúbe: lick it

thatʰé: eat it

thattóⁿ: drink it

thawá: count it

thiʾá: fail

thidóⁿ: pull it

thihóⁿ: lift it

thíⁿ: be (a member of)

thippí: be expert at

thizé: take it

ukkíhi: be able to

uné: seek

uthíʾage: refuse

uthíxide: look around

FIG. 99. moⁿthíⁿ: walk

Speaking Practice

A. Read the following sentences aloud. Then translate the sentences into English. Examples:

Umóⁿhoⁿ bthíⁿ: I am an Omaha.

Ní tʰe nattóⁿ a?: Did you drink the water?

Bthíhoⁿ bthíʾa: I can't lift it.

1. Bthíze.
2. Nátʰe a?
3. Náwa níppi.
4. Nástube tte.
5. Ūdaⁿ moⁿbthíⁿ.
6. Wēbaxu kʰe ubthíxide.
7. Maⁿčʰú síⁿde kʰe náxta tte.
8. Áⁿkkazhi, btháxta ubthíʾage.
9. Nú níⁿ a? Waʾú níⁿ a?
10. Móⁿzeska sáttoⁿ abthíⁿ.

B. Translate the following sentences into Omaha.

1. I licked it.
2. You pulled it.
3. Are you looking around?
4. You should go to the board.
5. I'm good at skating.
6. I can't count the stars.
7. I refuse to look for the cat.
8. Do you have a pencil?
9. Can you whistle?
10. I can swim.

C. The instructor tells each student to do something, using one of the verbs in today's list. The student does it. The instructor then asks the student what the action is. The student answers using the "I" form. Example:

Wagōⁿze: Hillary, moⁿthíⁿ ga!

[Hillary walks away.]

Wagōⁿze: Idādoⁿ shkāx̣e a? ("What are you doing?")

Hillary: Moⁿbthíⁿ.

D. The instructor then acts out a verb for each student, asking the student what the action is. The student answers using the "you" form. Example:

Wagōⁿze [looking around]: Dave, idādoⁿ ppāx̣e a? ("What am I doing?")

Dave: Uníx̣ide.

E. The students break into small groups of at least four and take turns performing exercises C and D among themselves, making up their own activities without the help of the instructor.

13.3 AFFIXED PRONOUNS: I AND YOU FOR VERBS BEGINNING WITH SIMPLE STOPS

In the following three lessons we consider the forms for "I" and "you" when the verb in Siouan began with one of the four simple stops *[p], *[t], *[k], and *[ʔ], followed immediately by a vowel. (Asterisks before words, sounds, or morphemes mean that these are reconstructed for the ancient ancestral language, before it developed into historical Omaha.)

The rule in each of these four cases is parallel to the rule for tha (ledh). The affixed pronoun *wa- (I) or *ra- (you) was added to the front of the basic verb in Proto-Siouan (PSI, see What Is Language, chapter 9), drawing the accent forward if necessary. Then, in Mississippi Valley Siouan (MVS), the vowel of the affixed pronoun was lost, and the weak labial or alveolar consonant joined with the following simple stop of the basic verb to make a consonant cluster. Further phonetic simplification occurred from there. The symbol => indicates that the form at right is derived from the prefixes at left, and ~= means "approximately equals."

PSI "I"	=>	MVS "I"	PSI "you"	=>	MVS "you"
*wa-r-	=>	*w-r-	*ra-r-	=>	*r-r-
*wa-p-	=>	*w-p-	*ra-p-	=>	*r-p-
*wa-t-	=>	*w-t-	*ra-t-	=>	*r-t-
*wa-k-	=>	*w-k-	*ra-k-	=>	*r-k-
*wa-ʔ-	=>	*w-ʔ-	*ra-ʔ-	=>	*r-ʔ-

In each of these four cases, the *[w] sound for "I" coming before a simple stop or *[r] seems to have resulted in full labial closure, effectively */p/. The *[r] sound for "you," in the same environment, regularly became an alveolo-palatal fricative, effectively */š/ (*/sh/). This is exactly the same as what we saw for tha (ledh).

*w-r-	~=	*p-r-	*r-r-	~=	*sh-r-
*w-p-	~=	*p-p-	*r-p-	~=	*sh-p-
*w-t-	~=	*p-t-	*r-t-	~=	*sh-t-
*w-k-	~=	*p-k-	*r-k-	~=	*sh-k-
*w-ʔ-	~=	*p-ʔ-	*r-ʔ-	~=	*sh-ʔ-

I and You Forms of Voiced Stop Verbs

Plain Verb	**I-form:**	**You-form:**
b-, d-, g-	**pp-, tt-, kk-/pp-**	**shp-, sht-, shk-**
(simple stops, voiced)	(tense stops, voiceless)	(cluster: **sh** plus the simple stop, voiceless)
baxú	**ppáxu**	**shpáxu**
dónbe	**ttónbe/attónbe**	**shtónbe/thashtónbe**
gāxe	**ppāxe**	**shkāxe**
góntha	**kkónbtha**	**shkónna**

- If a verb starts with a voiced stop followed by a vowel, then the "I" form typically becomes a tense stop and the "you" form becomes a consonant cluster of sh- plus the plain (unvoiced) version of the voiced stop.

- In general, the tense stop for the "I" form should be the tense version of the voiced stop. Thus b- should become pp-, d- should become tt-, and g- should become kk-. This is almost always true for b- and d- verbs. One exception is bón, "yell, scream," which conjugates in the common way, as abón for "I scream" and thabón for "you scream."

- Note that for the consonant forms of "I" and "you," the accent is always on the first syllable of the verb, immediately following the fused cluster of affixed pronoun + initial consonant of basic verb. For the common forms, when nothing precedes them, the accent is always on the second syllable, because

a- and tha- do not demand the accent themselves.

- Dónbe, "to see," seems to be the only d-verb in Omaha that can be conjugated. In the nineteenth century it behaved as we might expect: ttónbe and shtónbe. In the twentieth century, however, it became *doubly inflected*; that is, the common form affixed pronouns were added to the front of these already inflected simple stop verbs, making attónbe and thashtónbe. Our modern speakers do not seem to recognize the older form as valid.

Vocabulary: Verbs

badí: push off, as snow with a shovel

badón: push

baxú: write

dónbe: see

gāxe: make, do

FIG. 100. baxú: write

Vocabulary: Nouns

ttízhiⁿga: outhouse, potty, small house

Speaking Practice

A. Read the following sentences aloud. Then translate the sentences into English. Examples:

Ppāx̣a mazhi: I did not do it.

Thashtóⁿbe a?: Did you see it?

Idādoⁿ shkāx̣e?: What are you doing?

1. Shóⁿ ppāx̣e.

2. Ĭe tʰe shpáx̣u tte.

3. Attóⁿba mazhi.

4. Dūba shkōⁿna?

5. Má kʰe íⁿčʰoⁿ ppádi.

6. Zūde wiwítta tʰe attóⁿba mazhi.

7. Móⁿga kʰe thashtóⁿbe (a)?

8. Áoⁿ. Móⁿga kʰe āshiatta ppádoⁿ.

9. Wāthatʰe tʰe shpádoⁿ tte.

10. Ttízhiⁿga tʰe āshiatta shkāx̣e tte.

B. Translate the following sentences into Omaha.

1. Do you see the badger?

2. Do you see the board?

3. Did you make some coffee?

4. Yesterday I pushed a grizzly bear.

5. Are you writing/did you write your name?

6. They say he wrote a book.

7. Kathleen, did you push off the snow?

8. I might build an outhouse.

9. Today I am making cowboy bread.

10. Did you write a book?

C. The instructor tells each student to do something, using one of the verbs in today's list. The student does it. The instructor then asks the student what the action is. The student answers using the "I" form. Example:

Wagōⁿze: Megan, zhoⁿbtháskasabe tʰe "Maⁿčʰú" ĭe tʰe āshpax̣u moⁿní tte.

[Megan walks to the blackboard and writes the word "Maⁿčʰú."]

Wagōⁿze: Idādoⁿ shkāx̣e a? ("What are you doing?")

Megan: Zhoⁿbtháskasabe tʰe "Maⁿčʰú" ĭe tʰe āppax̣u.

D. The instructor then acts out a verb for each student, asking the student what the action is. The student answers using the "you" form. Example:

Wagōⁿze [pushing on a table]: Darlene, idādoⁿ ppāx̣e a? ("What am I doing?")

Darlene: Wāthatʰe shpádoⁿ.

E. The students break into small groups of at least four and take turns performing exercises C and D among themselves, making up their own activities without the help of the instructor.

13.4 AFFIXED PRONOUNS: I AND YOU FOR VERBS BEGINNING WITH SIMPLE STOP G-

The rule for g- verbs is much more complicated. Sometimes the "I" form is kk-, but more often it is pp-. Verbs that start with gi- generally use the common form for both "I" and "you." Except for gāχe, verbs that start with ga- usually follow a special pattern of their own that we introduce later, in lesson 17.6.

Verbs Starting with g- that Take Their I Form in pp-

		Plain Verb	**I-form**	**You-form**
make, do		gāχe	ppāχe	shkāχe
not know how		gó^{n}zhi^{n}ga	ppó^{n}zhi^{n}ga	shkó^{n}zhi^{n}ga

- Some verbs that start with g- take the tense stop pp- for the "I" form. These include gāχe, "to make or do," and gó^{n}zhi^{n}ga, "to not know how to do something."

A Verb Starting with g- that Takes Its I Form in kk-

		Plain Verb	**I-form**	**You-form**
want		gō^{n}tha	kkō^{n}btha	shkō^{n}na

- With the verb gō^{n}tha, "to want," the initial g- transforms to the expected kk- in the "I" form rather than the more usual pp-. Note that this verb is doubly inflected, but differently than the way dó^{n}be is. Here, both syllables took an affixed pronoun: kkō^{n}btha, "I want it," and shkō^{n}na, "you want it."

Verbs Beginning with gi-

	Plain Verb	**I-form**	**You-form**
fly	gió^n	agió^n	thagió^n
remember	gisíthe	agísithe	thagísithe

- Verbs that begin with gi- generally take the common form.

The Doubly Inflected Verb "to try"

	Plain Verb	**I-form**	**You-form**
try	ígasko^{n}the	ithágasko^{n}bthe	íthagasko^{n}ne

- The verb ígasko^{n}the, "to try," is another doubly inflected verb, with one inflection relating to the th and the other relating to the initial í plus ga-: ithágasko^{n}bthe, "I try it," and íthagasko^{n}ne, "you try it."

Vocabulary: Nouns

ūgaχe: picture

Vocabulary: Verbs

gāχe: make, do

gió^n: fly

gisíthe: remember

gō^{n}tha: want

gó^{n}zhi^{n}ga: doesn't know how

ígasko^{n}the: try

Speaking Practice

A. Read the following sentences aloud. Then translate the sentences into English. Examples:

Agísitha mazhi: I don't remember.

Shkónzhinga a?: Do you not know how to do it?

Idādon gōntha?: What does he want?

1. Agíon bthíppi kkōnbtha.

2. Wamóskeshuga ppáxe agísithe kkōnbtha.

3. Hūttonga shpáxu shkónzhinga?

4. Ónpha n khe thagísithe a?

5. Wēbaxu náwa shkōnna?

6. Umónhon īe the ppāxu ppónzhinga.

7. Má-wasábe ppāxe the nástube shkōnna?

8. Thihán izházhe the thagísitha azhi.

9. Thagíon shkōnna?

10. Hinbé ppāxe ppónzhinga.

B. Translate the following sentences into Omaha.

1. I want to fly.

2. You pushed the chair.

3. I remember my school.

4. She doesn't know how to make cherry juice.

5. I don't want to kick the door.

6. I don't know how to whistle.

7. Do you remember it?

8. Do you not know how to swim?

9. She remembers flying.

10. Do you remember swimming?

C. The instructor tells each student to do something, using one of the verbs in today's list. The student does it. The instructor then asks the student what the action is. The student answers using the "I" form. Example:

Wagōnze: Ryan, zhonbtháskasabe the "Mančhú" ūgaxe shkāxe monnín tte.

[Ryan walks to the blackboard and draws a picture of a grizzly bear.]

Wagōnze: Idādon shkāxe a? ("What did you make?")

Ryan: Mančhú ūgaxe ppāxe.

D. The instructor then acts out a verb for each student, asking the student what the action is. The student answers using the "you" form. Example:

Wagōnze [running, flapping arms]: Dave, idādon ppāxe a? ("What am I doing?")

Dave: Thagíon.

E. The students break into small groups of at least four and take turns performing exercises C and D among themselves, making up their own activities without the help of the instructor.

13.5 AFFIXED PRONOUNS: I AND YOU FOR OLD GLOTTAL STOP VERBS AND "SAY"

I and You Forms of Old Glottal Stop Verbs

	Plain Verb (ˀ)-	I-form: m-	You-form: zh-
wear	íⁿ	míⁿ	zhíⁿ
do habitually	óⁿ	móⁿ	zhóⁿ
wound, hit with a shot	ú	??	??

- There are three very old verbs in Omaha that used to begin with a glottal stop. The glottal stop has been lost, but it caused the I- and you- forms to be made in a special way. All of these verbs now consist of a single vowel in the plain form. Two of these are nasal vowels, íⁿ and óⁿ. For these, the "I" form adds m- in front, and the "you" form adds zh-. These sounds are the result of combining the affixed pronoun with the original glottal stop and the following nasal vowel. The third old glottal stop verb, ú, has an oral vowel. Unfortunately, the speakers we have asked do not know of an "I" or "you" form for this verb.

The Verb "to say"

Plain Verb	3ʳᵈ Person Declaration	I-form	You-form
é	á	epʰé / ehé	eshé

- The verb é, "to say," is another verb that may have started with a consonant in the past but is reduced to a single vowel today in the plain form.
- When é is in a position that causes ablaut, it becomes simply á.

- The I- and you- forms of é were originally epʰé and eshé. Later, the "I" form became ehé.
- To ask "What did you say?" we say: Edéshe? To ask "What did I say?" we say: Edépʰe? This special construction preserves the original epʰé.

Vocabulary: Verbs

é: say

íⁿ: wear, as a shirt

óⁿ: use; do, as habitual behavior

ú: hit with a shot, wound, get 'em

Vocabulary: Nouns

hiⁿbé: shoe, moccasin

unóⁿzhiⁿ: shirt

unóⁿzhiⁿshtoⁿga: jacket

unóⁿzhiⁿttoⁿga: coat

watʰé: skirt, dress

watháge: cap, hat

FIG. 101. hiⁿbé: shoe, moccasin

FIG. 102. watháge: hat

Vocabulary: Adverbs

no^n: regularly, routinely, habitually

Speaking Practice

A. Read the following sentences aloud. Then translate the sentence into English. Examples:

Hi^{n}bé zhí^n a?: Are you wearing shoes?

"Mo^{n}thí^n a!" eshé tte: "Walk!" you might say.

"Wathát^{h}a i a!" á, wa'ú ak^{h}a: "Eat!" the woman said to them.

1. "Ma^{n}č^{h}úska ú t^{h}e íbaho^n," eshé.
2. Wat^{h}é zhí^n no^n zhó^n.
3. Unó^{n}zhi^{n}shto^{n}ga t^{h}e mí^n.
4. Mīzhi^{n}ga thi^{n}k^{h}e wat^{h}é zhīde í^n thi^{n}k^{h}e thashtó^{n}be a?
5. "Mō^{n}zeska kkúge wi^n bthíze." Edép^{h}e a?
6. Hi^{n}bé sábe t^{h}e zhí^n t^{h}e o^n'í ga!
7. Watháge zhiégo^n í^n no^n.
8. Edéshe?
9. I^{n}sh'áge ak^{h}a wasábe thi^{n}k^{h}e ú.
10. "Shó^{n}ge t'é wiwítta k^{h}e shpádo^n íthagasko^{n}ne tte," ehé.

B. Translate the following sentences into Omaha.

1. I want to wear a snake-skin jacket.
2. Did he wound the dog?
3. What did I say?
4. "Go to the board!" I said.
5. I am trying to wear the long jacket.
6. She said, "I want to slap his dirty face."
7. That's baloney!
8. Yesterday, you tried to take the pair of white shoes.
9. Today, you are wearing them.
10. Oh! What did you say?

C. The instructor tells each student something, using one of the verbs in today's list, and then asks the student what was said. The student answers using the appropriate form. Example:

Wagō^{n}ze: Alicia, watháge ûja^n zhí^n. Edép^{h}e? ("Alicia, you're wearing pretty shoes. What did I say?")

Alicia: Watháge ûja^n mí^n, eshé. ("You said I'm wearing pretty shoes.")

D. The instructor says something personal (in the first person) for each student and then asks the student what was said. The student answers using the appropriate form (in the second person). Example:

Wagō^{n}ze: Raj, ttáx̌ti ú ithágasko^{n}bthe no^n mo^n. Edép^{h}e? ("Raj, I'm always trying to hit the deer I'm shooting at. What did I say?")

Raj: Ttáx̌ti ú íthagasko^{n}ne no^n zho^n, eshé. ("You said you're always trying to hit the deer.")

E. The students break into small groups of at least four and take turns performing exercises C and D among themselves, making up their own activities without the help of the instructor.

13.6 AFFIXED PRONOUNS: WE

We Form of Verbs

Plain Verb	We-form
noⁿʔóⁿ	oⁿnóⁿʔoⁿ
thattóⁿ	oⁿtháttoⁿ
baxú	oⁿbáxu
athíⁿ	oⁿgáthiⁿ

- The "we" form of a verb is made by prefixing the affixed pronoun oⁿ(g)-. If the plain verb starts with a consonant, we simply add oⁿ- to the front. If the plain verb starts with a vowel, we generally add oⁿg-.

- The declarative we form of a verb that ends in -e usually ablauts to -a. This may originally have been only for cases where more than two people were included in "we." At least some of our speakers at present maintain that this ablaut always occurs, no matter how many people are included in "we."

- In modern Omaha the "we" form is often augmented by the word wôⁿgithe, meaning "everybody," or the word wôⁿdoⁿ, meaning "both."

Internally Inflected Verbs

Plain Verb	I-form	You-form	We-form
moⁿthíⁿ	moⁿbthíⁿ	moⁿníⁿ	oⁿmóⁿthiⁿ
gōⁿtha	kkōⁿbtha	shkōⁿna	oⁿgōⁿtha

- The we-affixed pronoun oⁿ(g)- is less tightly bound to the verb than the I- and you- forms are. Thus we generally find

oⁿ(g)- at the very beginning of a verb that might take internal I- and you- forms.

Vocabulary: Nouns

kkinóⁿnoⁿge (kʰe): car, automobile

móⁿshoⁿ: feather, plume

xithá: eagle

Vocabulary: Miscellaneous

FIG. 103. kkinóⁿnoⁿge: car by Jacob Smith

wiⁿ: one, a, an

wôⁿdoⁿ: both

wôⁿgithe: everyone, everybody

Speaking Practice

A. Read the following sentences aloud. Then translate the sentences into English. Examples:

Watháthe oⁿgōⁿtha: We want food.

Wazhíⁿga oⁿnóⁿʔoⁿ: We heard birds.

Oⁿgúthixida: We looked around.

1. Ūdaⁿ oⁿmóⁿthiⁿ.
2. Īe tʰe oⁿbáxu tte.
3. Shé ge oⁿtháwa.
4. Āshka oⁿshkāde tte.
5. Oⁿnóⁿzhiⁿ oⁿgōⁿtha.
6. Umóⁿhoⁿ īe tʰe oⁿthíppi kkōⁿbtha.
7. Oⁿthástube oⁿgúthiʾaga.
8. Kkinóⁿnoⁿge kʰe shpádoⁿ oⁿgōⁿtha.
9. Sidādi xithámoⁿshoⁿ wiⁿ oⁿthíza.
10. Wôⁿgithe wamóskeshuga oⁿgāxa.

B. Translate the following sentences into Omaha.

   1. We all see it.
   2. We two bit it.
   3. We pushed the car.
   4. We might sleep.
   5. We want to drink coffee.
   6. We lifted the bag.
   7. We couldn't lift the car.
   8. We are expert at swimming.
   9. We don't know how to write it in Omaha.
   10. In a little while, we'll stop walking.

C. The instructor commands all the students to do something. The students do it. The instructor then asks a student what the student is doing. The student answers using the "we" form. Example:

   Wagōⁿze: Wôⁿgithe noⁿzhíⁿ i ga ho!

   [The students all stand up.]

   Wagōⁿze [to Tamara]: Idādoⁿ shkāxa i a? ("What are you doing?")

   Tamara: Oⁿnóⁿzhiⁿ.

D. The instructor has one student command the class to do something, and another ask a third student what that student is doing.

E. The students break into small groups of at least four and take turns performing exercise D among themselves, making up their own activities without the help of the instructor.

13.7 PERSON AND NUMBER OF THE SUBJECT

Subject Conjugation of "make, do"

Plain Verb:	gāxe
3rd Person Declarative:	gāxa
I:	ppāxe
You-singular:	shkāxe
You-plural:	shkāxa
We:	oⁿgāxa

- The "you" form of a verb can be either singular or plural when used at the end of the sentence to declare a statement. If you are speaking about a single person, an -e verb ends in -e. But if you are speaking about more than one person, the -e verb ablauts to -a.

- We thus have about five person-number combinations in modern Omaha for the subject: I; you-singular; you-plural; we; and the third person (he, she, it, they).

- The distinction between you-singular and you-plural holds only for -e verbs. For all other verbs, there is only I, you, we, and third person.

FIG. 104. moⁿx̌pí: clouds

Vocabulary: Nouns

moⁿx̌pí: clouds

wéathatʰe: food

Speaking Practice

A. Read the following sentences aloud. Then translate the sentences into English. Tell who is the subject of each sentence (person and number). Examples:

Wéathatʰe shkō̄ⁿna: You want food.

Áⁿkkazhi. Shkáx̌e: No. You (sing.) did it.

Uníx̌ida: You (pl.) looked around.

1. Níppi.
2. Thashkáda.
3. Utháne.
4. Ppāx̌e tte.
5. Bax̌ú.
6. Ní tʰe náttoⁿ tte.
7. Wagthábaze ūzhiha oⁿthíza.
8. Kkinóⁿnoⁿge kʰe shpádoⁿ thanóⁿshtoⁿ tte.
9. Moⁿx̌pí thashtóⁿbe thagthíⁿ.
10. Wabáx̌u kʰe oⁿgáthade oⁿgúkkihi.

B. Translate the following sentences into Omaha.

1. You bit it.
2. You all refused.
3. They made cowboy bread.
4. We drank it yesterday.
5. You (sing.) refused.
6. I am able to lift a horse.
7. You couldn't push the car.
8. She wants to take the card.
9. Did he look for a chair yesterday?
10. Try to speak Omaha! (to one/to a group)

C. The instructor does something and may have several of the students do it as well. The instructor then asks a student what they are doing. The student answers using the you-singular form or you-plural form, as appropriate. Example:

Wagō̄ⁿze [writing on the board]: Jill, idādoⁿ ppāx̌e a?

Jill: Zhoⁿbtháskasabe tʰe shpáx̣u.

Wagōⁿze [standing]: Ho. Julian, Jason, Justin, Julia, noⁿzhíⁿ i ga ho!

Wagōⁿze [to John]: Idādoⁿ oⁿgáx̣a i a? ("What are we doing?")

John: Thanóⁿzhiⁿ.

D. The instructor has the students take turns leading the class as the instructor did in exercise C.

E. The instructor starts out as the leader of a conjugation bee, challenging each student to give the conjugated form of a verb. First, all the students stand up. If they fail (thiʔá), they must sit down. If they miss a second time, they must lie down. When they miss a third time, they must take over as the leader, challenging others, and the previous leader stands as one of those challenged. Example:

Wagōⁿze: Frank, "I looked around," Umóⁿhoⁿ īe tʰe awatʰégoⁿ?

Frank: Ubthíx̣ide.

Wagōⁿze: Ho. Francine, "we licked it," Umóⁿhoⁿ īe tʰe awatʰégoⁿ?

Francine: Bthíʔa. [Sits down.]

13.8 PERSON AND NUMBER: NEGATION

Negating Conjugation of "make, do"

	Verb	Negating Particle
3rd Person Declarative:	gáx̣a	bazhi
I:	ppāx̣a	mazhi
You-singular:	shkāx̣a	azhi
You-plural:	shkāx̣a	bazhi
We:	oⁿgáx̣a	bazhi

- To negate a verb, we add a negating particle after it. This particle is itself conjugated.

- The negating particle for the "I" form is always mazhi. In colloquial speech this particle is usually pronounced something like maṣh.

- For all other forms, we use bazhi where we would originally have i in the positive form, and azhi where we would not. When azhi is used, it combines tightly with the preceding verb, so that shkāx̣a azhi sounds like shkāx̣azhi.

- All versions of the negating particle allow a preceding -e verb to ablaut to -a when describing someone's past action.

Vocabulary: Verbs

nā: ask for, request, beg

Speaking Practice

A. Read the following sentences aloud. Then translate the sentences into English. Examples:

Kkōⁿbtha mazhi: I don't want it.

Nátʰazhi a?: Didn't you (sing.) eat it?

Oⁿgúna bazhi: We didn't look for it.

1. Thax̌tá bazhi.

2. Ashkāda mazhi.

3. Thanóⁿzhiⁿ azhi.

4. Wéathatʰe oⁿnā bazhi.

5. Thazhōⁿ bazhi.

6. Umóⁿhoⁿ ié āagazhi mazhi.

7. Ūzhiha thoⁿ oⁿthíhoⁿ oⁿthíʼa bazhi.

8. Āshiatta uáne moⁿbthíⁿ mazhi.

9. Wabáx̣u kʰe āshpax̣u shkóⁿzhiⁿga bazhi.

10. Umóⁿhoⁿ īe tʰe itháppahoⁿ mazhi.

B. Translate the following sentences into Omaha.

   1. Don't you want it?

   2. We are not able to make it.

   3. I didn't stop walking.

   4. We are not sitting outside.

   5. You (sing.) didn't try.

   6. I wasn't able to push the car.

   7. We don't want to swim.

   8. You are not expert at skating.

   9. We didn't tell him to write it down.

   10. I didn't see the red car.

C. The instructor asks each student if someone is doing/has done something. The student answers appropriately. Example:

   Wagōⁿze: Werner, azhōⁿ a?

   Werner: Áⁿkkazhi, thazhōⁿ azhi.

D. Each student then does the same as the instructor did in exercise C, asking another student a question, which that student must answer appropriately. Example:

   Werner: Dave, sidádi kkinóⁿnoⁿge wiⁿ shpádoⁿ a?

   Dave: Áⁿkkazhi, sidádi kkinóⁿnoⁿge ppádoⁿ mazhi.

E. The students break into small groups of at least four and take turns performing exercise D among themselves, making up their own questions for each other.

13.9 PATIENT-AFFIXED PRONOUNS

Patient-Affixed Pronoun Conjugation

	Affixed Pronoun		**Patient Conjugation of noⁿʔóⁿ**
3rd Person:	- (none)	he hears her	noⁿʔóⁿ
me:	óⁿ-	he hears me	óⁿnoⁿʔoⁿ
you:	thi-	he hears you	thinóⁿʔoⁿ
us:	wā-, -awa-	he hears us	wānoⁿʔoⁿ
them:	wa-	he hears them	wanóⁿʔoⁿ

- An object is someone or something that is on the receiving end of the verb's action. If "Arabelle kicked the rock," then the rock is the direct object of Arabelle's kicking action. If "Madelyn sees the tree frog," then the tree frog is the object of Madelyn's action.

- Omaha object pronouns are affixed to the front of the verb, just as the subject pronouns are. For Omaha, we call the direct object pronouns the *patient* pronouns.

- The third person singular patient, like the subject, takes no affixed pronoun. The default meaning of a plain transitive verb is: s/he [verb]s/ed him/her.

- The patient affixed pronouns include óⁿ-, "me"; thi-, "you"; and wā- or -awa-, "us"; just as the subject affixed pronouns include forms for "I," "you," and "we." In addition, we have a patient affixed pronoun wa-, which means animate "them." This type of "them" is used only for people and animals. We do not use an affixed pronoun when referring to multiple inanimate objects.

- The patient form of "me," ó^n-, is identical to the subject form of "we" that comes before consonants. Thus, o^{n}nó^n'o^n will mean "we hear him," while ó^{n}no^n'o^n means "he hears me."

- The "we" form affixed pronoun is normally wā-, but it may contain an extra a in some cases. In a special type of conjugation that we cover later in lesson 16.7, the "we" form is awa-. It is possible that the normal wā- was actually waa- originally, with separate a- and wa- elements reversed. Unlike the animate "them" form of wa-, the "us" form draws the accent.

Vocabulary: Transitive Verbs with Personal Objects

badó^n: push

no^n'ó^n: hear

no^{n}t^{h}é: kick

thax̌tá: bite

that^{h}é: eat

thidó^n: pull

thihó^n: lift

thizé: take

Vocabulary: Miscellaneous

égithe: it might happen, beware!

kki: if

Speaking Practice

A. Read the following sentences aloud. Then translate the sentences into English. Examples:

O^{n}bádo^n: He pushed me.

Thidó^{n}ba: She saw you.

Wāno^{n}t^{h}a bazhi: They didn't kick us.

1. O^{n}tháx̌tazhi a!
2. Ó^{n}that^{h}e tte.
3. Wāthiho^n.
4. Wanó^n'o^n a?
5. Thax̌áge thinó^n'o^n a?
6. Ttáx̌ti ak^{h}a wādo^{n}be a?
7. Égithe wanó^{n}t^{h}e tte.
8. Gasó^{n}thi^n, thithíze tte.
9. Égithe ma^{n}č^{h}ú wāthat^{h}e tte.
10. Égithe shínuda ak^{h}a ó^{n}thax̌ta tte.

B. Translate the following sentences into Omaha.

1. He didn't hear you.
2. Yesterday, she saw me.
3. The horse bit you.
4. He doesn't know how to push you.
5. He is able to lift you.
6. He kicked me.

7. Beware! He might see you.

8. Today, the car pulled us.

9. Did she take him?

10. I think he wants to eat them.

C. The instructor asks the students if someone is doing or has done something to them. The students answer using the "me" or "you" form, as appropriate. Example:

Wagōⁿze: Patty, thidóⁿbe a? ("Patty, did he see you?")

Patty: Áⁿkkazhi, óⁿdoⁿba bazhi. ("No, he didn't see me.")

D. Each student then does the same as the instructor did in exercise C, asking another student a question, which that student must answer appropriately.

E. The students break into small groups of at least four and take turns performing exercise D among themselves, making up their own questions for each other.

13.10 PATIENT-AFFIXED PRONOUNS FOR Ā-, Í-, AND U- VERBS

Verbs beginning with the prefixes ā-, í- and u- add complexity to the pattern for affixing the object pronouns.

Patient-Affixed Pronoun Conjugation: ā- Verbs

	Affixed Pronoun		**Patient Conjugation of an ā-Verb**
3rd Person:	- (none)	he touches her	ābitte
me:	óⁿ-	he touches me	āoⁿbitte
you:	thi-	he touches you	āthibitte
us:	wā-	he touches us	āwabitte
them:	wa-	he touches them	āwabitte

- For ā- verbs, all patient affixed pronouns are placed *after* the initial vowel ā-. Except for loss of accent, these are transparent.

Patient-Affixed Pronoun Conjugation: í- Verbs

	Affixed Pronoun		**Patient Conjugation of íbahoⁿ**
3rd Person:	- (none)	he knows her	íbahoⁿ
me:	oⁿthóⁿ-	he knows me	oⁿthóⁿbahoⁿ
you:	thi-	he knows you	íthibahoⁿ
us:	wā-, wé-	he knows us	íwabahoⁿ, wébahoⁿ
them:	wa-, wé-	he knows them	íwabahoⁿ, wébahoⁿ

- For í- verbs, the patient form of "me" is *í- + *oⁿ- => oⁿthóⁿ-, which is identical to the subject form of "we." (Here we use the symbol => to indicate that the form on the right is derived from the combination of the two prefixes on the left.) Thus oⁿthóⁿbahoⁿ might mean either "he knows me" or "we know it." Which one is meant has to be figured out from context.

- The thi-, "you" patient affixed pronoun is placed after the í-.

- The wā-, "us," and wa-, "them," slots appear each to have *two* accepted forms. One method is to put the affixed pronoun after the initial í-, which is transparent except for the loss of the accent. The other is to put the affixed pronoun in front of the í-, which yields *wa- + *í- => wé-.

Patient-Affixed Pronoun Conjugation: u- Verbs

	Affixed Pronoun		**Patient Conjugation of uné**
3rd Person:	- (none)	he seeks her	**uné**
me:	**ón-**	he seeks me	**onwónne (uónne)**
you:	**thi-**	he seeks you	**uthíne**
us:	**wā-**	he seeks us	**uwāne, ūne**
them:	**wa-**	he seeks them	**uwáne, ūne**

- For u- verbs, the ón-, "me," patient affixed pronoun placed after the initial vowel u- works out as u- + ón- => onwón- in pronunciation. In careful speech, the underlying uón- may also be acceptable.

- The thi-, "you," patient affixed pronoun is transparent and takes the accent after the word-initial vowel u-.

- The wā-, "us," and wa-, "them," forms each appear to have *two* accepted forms. One method is to put the affixed pronoun after the initial u-, which is transparent. The other puts the affixed pronoun in front of u-, which yields wa- + u- => ū-.

Vocabulary: Transitive Verbs with Personal Objects

ābitte: touch

āgazhi: command

íbahon: know

ímonxe: ask

thidón: pull

uhí: beat, win

uné: seek, search for

uthín: hit

Speaking Practice

A. Read the following sentences aloud. Then translate the sentences into English. Examples:

Onwóne: He searches for me.

Āthigazhi: She commanded you.

Uwāhi: They beat us.

1. Āthibitte, íthibahon gōntha, mónga akha.

2. Uthíne tte.

3. Uthíthin kki, uthíhi.

4. Indé thastúbe íthimonxe.

5. Onwónthin bazhi.

6. Ttaxti uníxide āthigazhi a?

7. Égithe uthíhon thitháthe tte.

8. Wôngithe onthónbahon bazhi.

9. Íthashpahon shkōna kki, íwamonxa ga!

10. Huhú dūba athín kki, uwáhon tte.

B. Translate the following sentences into Omaha.

1. If they touch you, scream!

2. They're looking for me.

3. Did the mouse touch you?

4. They want to hit us.

5. Did she tell you to sit down?

6. They don't know how to beat us.

7. After a little while, she went looking for them.

8. If he knows, he might hit me.

9. If he commands you, do it!

10. Yesterday, she tried to ask us.

C. The instructor asks the students if someone is doing or has done something to them. The students answer using the "me" or "you" form, as appropriate. Example:

Wagóⁿze: Patty, uthítʰiⁿ a? ("Patty, did he hit you?")

Patty: Áⁿkkazhi, oⁿwóⁿtʰiⁿ bazhi. ("No, he didn't hit me.")

D. Each student then does the same as the instructor did in exercise C, asking another student a question, which that student must answer appropriately.

E. The students break into small groups of at least four and take turns performing exercise D among themselves, making up their own questions for each other.

13.11 AGENT-TO-PATIENT AFFIXED PRONOUN COMBINATIONS

We now have two series of affixed pronouns: an agent series for "I," "you," and "we"; and a patient series for "me," "you," "us," and "them (animate)." Our task in this lesson is to learn how to combine them, so that we can say "I do it to you," "you did it to me," "we did it to them," and so forth.

Perhaps the most common of these is the "I do it to you" option. In this case only, the "I" and "you" pronouns have fused together into a single affixed pronoun, of which the original pieces are no longer distinguishable. This has happened with Omaha and other Mississippi Valley Siouan languages. For Omaha, the "I do it to you" affixed pronoun is wi-.

Plain Verb		I do it to 3rd		I do it to you	
noⁿóⁿ	hear	anóⁿoⁿ	I hear him	winóⁿoⁿ	I hear you
thidóⁿ	pull	bthídoⁿ	I pull her	wíbthidoⁿ	I pull you
badóⁿ	push	ppádoⁿ	I push it	wíppadoⁿ	I push you

- When we want to say "I do it to you," we use the affixed pronoun wi-. This pronoun combines both the agent "I" and the patient "you."

- When this wi- pronoun comes before a consonant—a consonant that changes to make the "I" form, such as th, b, or d—then that consonant makes the change in addition to having the wi- in front of it. In this case, the accent shifts forward to the wi-.

- When the wi- pronoun comes before a verb that uses the common pattern of a- to make the "I" form, the wi- simply replaces the a-, without drawing the accent to itself.

Combination	Elements	Compound	Example: noⁿóⁿ
I -> them	a- + wá-	awá-	awánoⁿoⁿ
you -> me	óⁿ- + tha-	oⁿthá-	oⁿthánoⁿoⁿ
you -> us	wā- + tha-	wathá-	wathánoⁿoⁿ
you -> them	wa- + tha-	wathá-	wathánoⁿoⁿ
we -> you	oⁿ(g)- + thi-	oⁿthí-	oⁿthínoⁿoⁿ
we -> them	oⁿ(g)- + wa-	oⁿwóⁿ-	oⁿwóⁿnoⁿoⁿ

- The other cases of agent-patient combinations simply combine two that we already know about (subject -> object).

- The order of combination seems to follow two rules: (1) If one affixed pronoun begins with a vowel and the other does not, then the one beginning with a vowel comes first. (2) Otherwise, the patient pronoun comes first, before the agent pronoun.
- The combinations "I do it to us" and "We do it to me" do not make much sense semantically, and there seems to be no known way of saying these things.

Vocabulary: Miscellaneous

kkáshi: for a long time

Speaking Practice

A. Read the following sentences aloud. Then translate the sentences into English. Examples:

Wibtháx̌ta: I bit you.

Onshpádon: You pushed me.

Onwónthiza: We took them.

1. Āwippitta mazhi.
2. Onthánon'on a?
3. Onthíthihon.
4. Ontháshtonbe (a)?
5. Kkáshi x̌agá (i) onwónnon'on.
6. Umónhon onthóne wāthanon'on a?
7. Égithe, onnáx̌ta kki wippádon tte.
8. X̌tāwithe.
9. Eátton wāthanonthe?
10. Nónzhin (i) kki watháshtonbe tte.

B. Translate the following sentences into Omaha.

1. I am able to hear you.
2. You were unable to lift us.
3. You tried to kick me.
4. We didn't bite you.
5. I wanted to hear them.
6. We don't know how to see them.
7. I want to look for them.
8. Do you want to eat them?
9. Are you trying to pull me outside?
10. If I see you, I may know you.

C. The instructor asks the students what they did in relation to their instructor. The students answer appropriately. Example:

Wagónze: DeAnna, ontháthihon uthákkihi a? ("DeAnna, are you able to lift me?")

DeAnna: Ánkkazhi, wibthíhon uákkihi mazhi. ("No, I can't lift you.")

D. Each student then does the same as the instructor did in exercise C, asking another student a question, which that student must answer appropriately.

E. The students break into small groups of at least four and take turns performing exercise D among themselves, making up their own questions for each other.

13.12 SUBJECT-AFFIXED PRONOUNS FOR STATIVE VERBS

Plain Stative Verb	tto^{n}ga	'big'
3rd Person Declarative	tto^{n}gá	's/he is big'
I Form	o^{n}ttó^{n}ga	'I am big'
You Form	thittó^{n}ga	'you are big'
We Form	wātto^{n}ga	'we are big'
They Form	wattó^{n}ga	'they are big'

- To use adjectives, or *stative verbs*, to describe personal categories like I, you, or we, we add the patient affixed pronoun rather than the agent affixed pronoun to indicate the subject. Thus, I use o^n- to describe myself, thi- to describe you, and wa- to describe us or them.

- Although most common stative verbs do not usually apply to people as a whole, they can be used to describe a part of a person. In this case, the part is stated first, and the appropriately conjugated stative verb is placed after it. For example:

    Sí t^{h}e o^{n}ṣnéde.   My feet are big.

- Don't actually use o^{n}ttó^{n}ga to describe your size. This could be seen as boasting, according to one of our Elder speakers (Alberta Grant Canby).

Vocabulary: Stative Verbs

bútta: round

ččéshka: short

nié: hurting, in pain

nítta: alive (active or stative)

nó^{n}kka: hurt, injured

sagí: hard

shtó^{n}ga: soft

ṣnéde: long

ṣní: cold

t'é: dead (active or stative)

thi^{n}gé: there is none, lacking

tto^{n}gá: big

uzhétha: tired, weary

zhi^{n}gá: small

Vocabulary: Body Parts

á (k^{h}e): arm

hí (k^{h}e): teeth

í (t^{h}e): mouth

íha: lips

i^{n}dé (tho^n): face

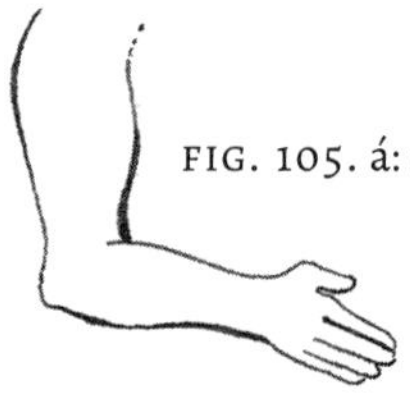

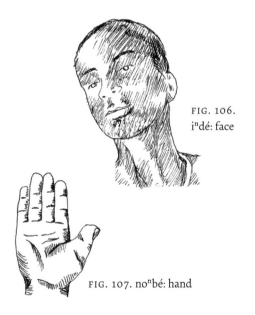

FIG. 105. á: arm

FIG. 106. i^{n}dé: face

FIG. 107. no^{n}bé: hand

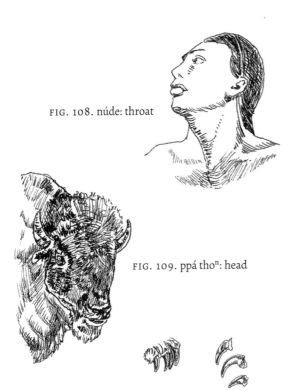

FIG. 108. núde: throat

FIG. 109. ppá thoⁿ: head

FIG. 110. shagé: nail, talon, hoof

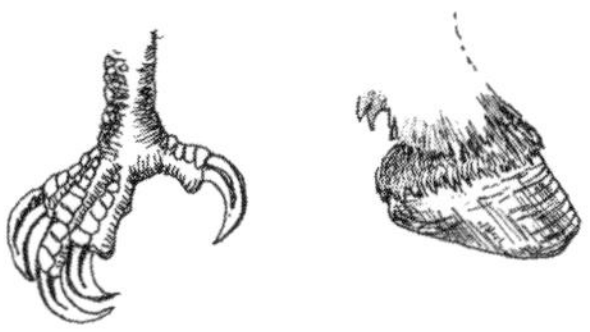

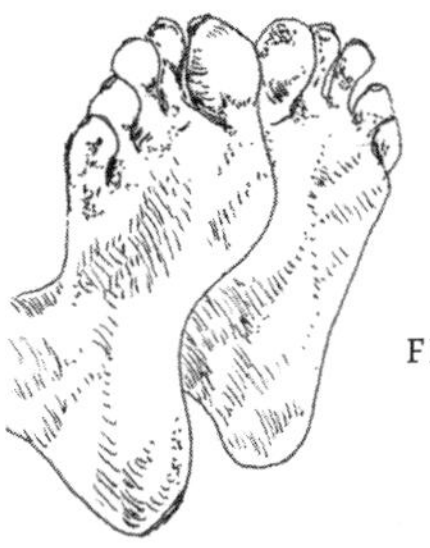

FIG. 111. sí: foot

iⁿkʰéde: shoulder

ishtá (thoⁿ): eye

nittá: (external) ear

noⁿbé (tʰe): hand

noⁿbéhi (tʰe): finger

noⁿshkí (thoⁿ): head (except face), jug, conk

noⁿxíde: ear (internal)

noⁿzhíⁿha: hair of head

núde: throat

ppá (kʰe): nose

ppá (thoⁿ): head (whole head including face)

ppé: forehead

sháge: nail

sí (kʰe): foot

théze: tongue

zhíbe: leg (upper part, thigh)

Speaking Practice

A. Read the following sentences aloud. Then translate the sentences into English. Examples:

Oⁿwóⁿzhetha: I'm tired.

Hiⁿbé thithíⁿge: You don't have shoes.

Noⁿbé tʰe wattóⁿga: They have big hands.

1. Thinóⁿkka.

2. Oⁿníe.

3. Wôⁿgithe waṣní.

4. Móⁿzeska oⁿthíⁿge.

5. Iⁿdé thoⁿ thibútta.

6. Oⁿtʼé shkōⁿna kki, atʼé kkōⁿbtha.

7. Oⁿnítta moⁿbthíⁿ.

8. Watháтʰe thithíⁿge kki, thatʼé tte.

9. Ishtá thoⁿ wattóⁿga, sháge tʰe waṣnéde.

10. Noⁿshkí thoⁿ oⁿsági tʰe ūdaⁿ.

B. Translate the following sentences into Omaha.

    1. Don't you have any money?

    2. My arms are long.

    3. I have a big nose.

    4. Are your ears cold?

    5. Are you tired?

    6. I want to live.

    7. We don't have water.

    8. If I'm injured, I might die.

    9. Do your teeth hurt?

    10. My eye has been hurting for a long time.

C. The instructor asks the students about themselves, using a stative verb. The students answer appropriately. Example:

Wagōⁿze: Howard, thinóⁿkka? ("Howard, are you hurt?")

Howard: Áⁿkkazhi, oⁿnóⁿkka mazhi. ("No, I'm not hurt.")

D. Each student then does the same as the instructor did in exercise C, asking another student a question, which that student must answer appropriately.

E. The students will break into small groups of at least four and take turns performing exercise D among themselves, making up their own questions for each other.

Pronouns and Positionals

14.1 INANIMATE POSITIONALS

The Four Inanimate Positionals in Omaha

k^he	'lying'
t^he	'standing'
tho^n	'globular'
ge	'scattered'

Use of the Four Inanimate Positionals

Noun	**Positional**	**Implication**
í^nʔe	k^he	the rock is lying, or there is a line of rocks
í^nʔe	t^he	a rock is standing upright, or is a cliff face, or a rock collection
í^nʔe	tho^n	the rock is a chunk with no particularly long dimension
í^nʔe	ge	a bunch of rocks are scattered randomly

- In Omaha, nouns are frequently followed by a particle called a *positional*.

- A positional after a noun implies something about its dynamic properties. In addition, it implies that we are talking about a particular entity that actually exists to manifest those properties. In this respect, it is comparable to the English article "the."

- Omaha has four positionals that refer to inanimate things. These are k^he, "lying," t^he, "standing," tho^n, "globular," and ge, "scattered."

Vocabulary: Nouns

házhi^nga: rope, strap, cord

hethúbazho^n: swing

í^nʔe: rock

mô^n: arrow

mô^nde: bow

mó^nzemo^n: bullet, shot

mo^nzhó^n: land

ní: water

FIG. 112. hethúbazho^n: swing

nú: potato

ppahé: hill

ppéde: fire

shé: apple

ttabé: ball

ttí: house, building

FIG. 113. mô^nde: bow, mô^n: arrow

ttó^nde: ground

uzhó^nge: path, road

wahútto^nthe: gun

wāi^n: robe, blanket, shawl

wēbaxu: pen, pencil, chalk, marker, writing implement

FIG. 114. nú: potato

wétta: egg

xthabé: tree

zhó^n: wood

zhó^nzhi^nga: stick

FIG. 115. wāiⁿ: robe, blanket, shawl

FIG.116. x̌thabé: tree

FIG. 117. ābazu: point at

FIG. 118. āne: climb

Vocabulary: Verbs

ābazu: point at

āne: climb

bahí: gather, pick up, collecting

íthe: find

thasníⁿ: swallow

(ishtá) thibthá: open (eyes)

(ishtá) thip'íⁿze: close (eyes)

uhé: pass, go along

uthá: tell

'í: give

Vocabulary: Miscellaneous

edādoⁿ: what (specific)

Speaking Practice

A. Read the following sentences aloud.
    Then translate the sentences into
    English. Examples:

    Shé ge bahí a!: Gather the (scattered)
    apples!

    Ttabé thoⁿ bthíze: I took the (round)
    ball.

    Wétta tʰe íthathe?: Did you find the
    (set of) eggs?

    Uzhóⁿge kʰe uhá ga!: Go along the
    trail.

    1. Móⁿzemoⁿ tʰe oⁿ'í ga!

    2. Wétta thoⁿ thasníⁿ.

    3. Ttí tʰe ttoⁿgá.

    4. Wēbax̌ú kʰe itháthe.

5. Ppahé ge oⁿgúha.

6. Zhóⁿ kʰe shpáhi kki, ppéde ppāxe uákkihi tte.

7. X̌thabé tʰe āane kkōⁿbtha mazhi. Ubthíʔage.

8. Ttabé thoⁿ wiʔí kki, thizá i ga ho!

9. Wahúttoⁿthe kʰe āoⁿbazu azhi ga!

10. Wāiⁿ zhīde thoⁿ thashtóⁿbe a?

B. Translate the following sentences into Omaha.

   1. I have the bullets.

   2. He gave me the gun.

   3. Follow the line of hills!

   4. He climbed the rope.

   5. We gathered up the arrows.

   6. Did you find the standing rock?

   7. What? Did you swallow the potato?

   8. I passed over the land for a long time.

   9. He took the stick and hit me.

   10. If the path is long, I may not find the tree.

C. The instructor, looking away, commands each student to look at something, and then asks what the student is looking at. The student answers appropriately, using a positional. Example:

Wagōⁿze: Henry, idādoⁿshti doⁿbá ga ho! ("Henry, look at something!")

[Henry looks at the door.]

Wagōⁿze: Idādoⁿ thashtóⁿbe a? ("What do you see?")

Henry: Ttizhébe tʰe attóⁿbe. ("I see the door.")

D. The students then take turns doing what the instructor did in exercise C, looking away and having another student look at something, then asking what that student is looking at. The other student should answer, using the appropriate positional.

E. The students break into small groups of at least two and take turns performing exercise D among themselves, making up their own questions for each other.

Ttígaxe: Twenty Questions

A number of known objects are laid out around the room. One student is "it," and the rest close their eyes. The one who is "it" wanders freely around the room and chooses an item. The other students take turns guessing what the item is, or asking questions or giving commands to the one who is "it," to narrow down the range of possibilities. They can ask any question but what the item is. Positionals should be used. When someone guesses correctly, that person is the next to be "it." Otherwise, if no one guesses correctly within twenty tries, the person who is "it" must tell what it is (using a positional), and the next person in order becomes "it." Example:

Cari ("it"): Wôⁿgithe ishtá thip'íⁿza i a!
("Everyone close their eyes!")

[Everyone else closes their eyes. Cari picks
the red apple.]

Cari: Edādoⁿ ebthégoⁿ tʰe uthá ígaskoⁿtha i
a! ("Try to tell what I'm thinking of!")

Ron: Snēde a?

Cari: Áⁿkkazhi, snēda bazhi.

Jack: Ābitta ga!

Cari: Ha. [Touches the apple.]

Ruth: Uẋpé tʰe a?

Cari: Áⁿkkazhi.

Mike: Bútta a?

Cari: Áoⁿ.

Patty: Shé tʰe a?

Cari: Awíⁿoⁿwoⁿ?

Patty: Shé ppézhittu tʰe.

Cari: Áⁿkkazhi.

Fred: Shé zhīde tʰe.

Cari: Áoⁿ. Thithítta.

14.2 ACTIVE SUBJECT POSITIONALS

The Two Active Subject Positionals

akʰá	'manifest'
amá	'positionally indefinite'

Use of the Two Subject Positionals

- The two subject positionals in Omaha
  are akʰá and amá. These are used for the
  subject of the sentence: the actor of the
  verb, or the party the sentence is about.

- These two positionals most commonly
  apply to people or animals. However, if
  an inanimate object does something, or
  is the thing the sentence is all about, it
  too can take the positionals akʰá or amá.

- The positional akʰá is used for a subject
  that is *manifest*. The subject will be
  clearly defined and in sight. In telling a
  story, akʰá is used for the party whose
  progress the listener is following. The
  positional amá is used for a subject that
  is not manifest. It is most commonly
  used for plural subjects, but can also
  be used for a single subject that is not
  present, and has not been seen for a
  while, so that the speaker does not know
  quite where that subject is. In a story,
  amá suggests that the subject has been
  out of sight of the narrator and listener,
  who have been following their own
  perspective on the story.

- The positional amá is felt by many
  modern speakers to indicate that the
  subject is plural. However, either amá
  or akʰá can refer to a plural subject. If
  we use akʰá, we mean a clearly defined,
  manifest set, with all members known,
  accounted for, and acting together as

Noun	Positional	Implication
mōⁿga	akʰá	the skunk is visible, or there is a collective group of skunks
mōⁿga	amá	the skunk is elsewhere, or there are various skunks around

a unit. We call this concept *collective* plurality. We use amá to indicate *distributive* plurality, by which we mean various individuals of no fixed number, all going their own way.

· Subjects using akʰá or amá usually come at the beginning of the sentence, before the verb or other nouns. Sometimes, however, particularly when telling stories using the bi ama demand particles, the subject is thrown to the end of the sentence, after bi ama.

FIG. 121. Ishtíthiⁿkʰe: Trickster, monkey

nú: man

nudóⁿhoⁿga: war chief; leader

núzhiⁿga: boy

shíⁿgazhiⁿga: baby, small child

waʼú: woman

waʼúzhiⁿga: old woman

Vocabulary: Nouns

héga: buzzard

ishtíthiⁿkʰe: Trickster; monkey

iⁿshʼáge: old man

mīzhiⁿga: girl

moⁿshtíⁿge: rabbit

niáshiⁿga: person

FIG. 119. héga: buzzard (in flight)

Vocabulary: Verbs

athé: go

agthé: s/he goes/went back

gí: come back

óⁿtha thétha: throw away

Vocabulary: Miscellaneous

égoⁿ: like, like that

egóⁿ: the foregoing having happened, . . .

kki: if; when the foregoing happened, . . .

FIG. 120. héga: buzzards (sitting)

Speaking Practice

A. Read the following sentences aloud.
   Then translate the sentences into
   English. Examples:

   Moⁿshtíⁿge akʰá athá bi ama: The
   rabbit was going, they say.

   Héga amá shóⁿge kʰe ítha i a?: Did the
   buzzards find the horse?

   "Í-jí-jí!" á biama Moⁿshtíⁿge akʰá:
   "Ouch-ouch-ouch!" said Rabbit.

   1. Núzhiⁿga akʰá xagé tte.

   2. Nú ttóⁿga akʰá uzhóⁿge kʰe
      uhá.

   3. Waʼú amá wamóskeshuga
      gáxe tta ama.

   4. Mīzhiⁿga akʰá uthá bi ama.

   5. Wāiⁿ gōⁿtha, waʼúzhiⁿga
      akʰá.

   6. Núzhiⁿga akʰá ttabé thoⁿ
      thizá i egóⁿ, óⁿtha thétha.

   7. Wéathatʰe thiⁿgé kki,
      shíⁿgazhiⁿga amá tʼé tta.

   8. Nudóⁿhoⁿga amá gí bi ama.

   9. Iⁿshʼáge akʰá moⁿkkóⁿsabe
      gōⁿtha kki, ʼí i ga ho!

   10. Núzhiⁿga akʰá moⁿthíⁿ kki,
       moⁿshtíⁿge amá uóⁿsisi athá.

B. Translate the following sentences
   into Omaha.

   1. The buzzard saw it.

   2. The boys gathered rocks.

   3. The rabbit tried to jump.

   4. "Yes," said Tom.

   5. The child ate the egg.

   6. When the boy saw the rope,
      he climbed the tree.

   7. Having drunk the water, the
      man lay down.

   8. The women want to gather
      plums tomorrow.

   9. The three girls pointed at
      the feather.

   10. The teachers tried to find the
       markers.

C. The instructor commands students
   or groups of students to do something
   and then asks another student what one
   of them is doing. The student answers
   appropriately, using an active subject
   positional. Example:

   Wagōⁿze: Lisa, wēbaxu kʰe thizá ga!
   ("Lisa, pick up the pencil!")

   [Lisa picks up the pencil.]

   Wagōⁿze: Rudy, Lisa akʰá idādoⁿ gáxe
   a? ("Rudy, what is Lisa doing?")

   Rudy: Lisa akʰá wēbaxu kʰe thizá.
   ("Lisa has picked up the pencil.")

D. The students then take turns doing
   what the instructor did in exercise C. The
   other students should answer, using the
   appropriate active subject positional.

E. The students break into small groups
   of at least two and take turns performing
   exercise D among themselves, making up
   their own questions for each other.

14.3 ANIMATE POSITIONALS

The Six Active Subject Positionals

thi^{n}k^{h}é	'sitting', singular
tho^{n}k^{h}á	'sitting', plural
ma	plural, distributive
k^{h}e	'lying', helpless
t^{h}o^n	'standing'
thi^n	'moving'

- Omaha has five more positionals that are applied to animate beings, as well as k^{h}e, which can be used for animate or inanimate objects.

- Of the five animate positionals, only thi^{n}k^{h}é is really common in modern Omaha. The others are either rare, or easily confused with other positionals, so they are hard to elicit. It is likely that they have been dropping out of use in the twentieth century.

- The positional thi^{n}k^{h}é originally may have meant "sitting." In historical Omaha, however, it refers generically to the object or recipient of an action, regardless of the being's posture. Like ak^{h}á, it probably carries the implication of being manifest.

- The positional tho^{n}k^{h}á is the plural of thi^{n}k^{h}é. It probably refers specifically to a small, closed, manifest set, as a collective plural, like the plural usage of ak^{h}á.

- The positional ma seems to imply a diffuse, distributive plurality, like the plural usage of amá. The difference is that ma does not imply that the beings are the topic or subject of the sentence or the actor of the verb.

- The positionals t^{h}o^n and thi^n are particularly rare and not well understood. Modern speakers may not recognize them at all. We do not use them much in this course.

- The positional k^{h}e is basically an inanimate term that is used with animate beings only for the case of "lying helpless." There seem to be just four situations when this applies: (1) for infants in arms; (2) for someone sound asleep; (3) for someone so sick or injured as to be unable to get up; and (4) for someone lying dead. If the person or animal is lying down, but is awake and able to move, we would use thi^{n}k^{h}é or ak^{h}á.

Vocabulary: Nouns

āgthi^n: chair

hó^{n}t'ega: fly

ithādi: father, his father

niáshi^{n}ga: person

níkkashi^{n}ga: people

nudó^n: warrior

wamóskeẋude: flour

FIG. 122. hó^{n}t'ega: fly

FIG. 123. wamóskeẋude: flour

FIG. 124. thix̌í: wake up

Vocabulary: Verbs

āgthiⁿ: to sit on, ride (as a horse)

í: coming

gí: come back

íx̌a: laugh

íx̌ax̌a: laughing; ridicule

ppáhoⁿ: get up

thix̌é: chase

thix̌í: wake up

zhōⁿt'e: sound asleep

Vocabulary: Miscellaneous

edādoⁿ: what (specific)

égoⁿ: like, like that

egóⁿ: the foregoing having happened, . . .

i: plural particle in commands; plural particle in verb statements; indicates "action" as contrasted with "state"

kki: if; when the foregoing happened, . . .

Speaking Practice

A. Read the following sentences aloud. Then translate the sentences into English. Examples:

Iⁿčʰóⁿga thiⁿkʰé doⁿbá: She saw the mouse.

Héga amá ttáx̌ti kʰe íthe tte: The buzzards might find the deer.

Shóⁿge thoⁿkʰá uwátʰiⁿ, bi ama: He struck the horses, they say.

1. Huhú kʰe ttóⁿ.

2. Wazhíⁿga thiⁿkʰé oⁿgúhoⁿ oⁿtʰátʰe shkōⁿna?

3. Iⁿgthóⁿga akʰá iⁿčʰóⁿga ma doⁿbá i kki, wiⁿ thiⁿkʰé thix̌á.

4. Mīzhiⁿga thiⁿkʰé utʰíⁿ bi ama, núzhiⁿga akʰá.

5. Íthashpahoⁿ shkōⁿna kki, waʔúzhiⁿga thiⁿkʰé ímax̌a a!

6. Nú akʰá núzhiⁿga thiⁿkʰé ttabé thoⁿ ʔí.

7. Wésʔa kʰe kkáshi tʔé. Ābitta bazhí i a!

8. Iⁿshʔáge zhōⁿtʔe kʰe ítha i kki, ithādi thiⁿkʰé thix̌í, mīzhiⁿga akʰá.

9. Gasóⁿthiⁿ núzhiⁿga shóⁿge tʰoⁿ āgthiⁿ ígaskoⁿthe tta akʰa.

10. Shaóⁿ níkkashiⁿga ma wadóⁿba i egóⁿ, nudóⁿ amá gí.

B. Translate the following sentences into Omaha.

1. I saw the buzzards.

2. The girl lifted the cat.

3. The boy pushed the two girls.

4. They all laughed at the old man.

5. Did you swallow the fly?

6. She wanted to know the old woman.

7. If you see the deer, give me the gun.

8. We pulled the (dead) cow.

9. Give the teacher the marker!

10. Don't point at the person!

C. The instructor commands students or groups of students to do something and then asks another student what one of them is doing. The student answers appropriately, using an animate positional. Example:

> Wagōⁿze: Kyle, Ellen thiⁿkʰé ābitta ga! ("Kyle, touch Ellen!")
>
> [Kyle touches Ellen.]
>
> Wagōⁿze: Duane, Kyle akʰá idādoⁿ gāx̣e a? ("Duane, what is Kyle doing?")
>
> Duane: Ellen thiⁿkʰé ābitta. ("He's touched Ellen.")

D. The students then take turns doing what the instructor did in exercise C. The other students should answer, using the appropriate active subject positional.

E. The students break into small groups of at least two and take turns performing exercise D among themselves, making up their own questions for each other.

14.4 ARTICLES

Singular Noun

Indefinite	I'm looking for a (any) horse.	**Shóⁿge uáne.**
Definite (introductory)	I'm looking for a (particular) horse.	**Shóⁿge wiⁿ uáne.**
Definite (well-known)	I'm looking for the horse.	**Shóⁿge thiⁿ uáne.**

Plural Noun

Indefinite	I'm looking for horses.	**Shóⁿge uáwane.**
Definite (introductory)	I'm looking for some horses.	**Shóⁿge dūba uáwane.**
Definite (well-known)	I'm looking for the horses.	**Shóⁿge ma uáwane.**

- We may distinguish three grades of "knownness" for nouns. First is the *indefinite* grade, in which the speaker has no particular one in mind. Second is the definite, introductory grade, in which the speaker is talking about a particular one and is introducing it to the listener, who has not heard about it until that moment. Third is the definite, well-known grade, which is a particular one that is presumed to be already known to the listener as well as the speaker.

- The Omaha positionals are sometimes called "articles," like the English word "the." Like "the," they indicate that it is a particular one that is referred to. This is because they convey positional information about the noun that would not be established if the noun itself were not established.

- The word wíⁿ, or "one," can be used much like English "a/an" to refer to a particular one that is being introduced to the listener. In this usage, it can also be considered an article rather than a number.
- For the indefinite grade, we do not normally use an article in Omaha. However, if an actual number is specified, it could still be indefinite.
- For the plural, we do not use an article in the indefinite grade, and we do use a positional for the definite, well-known grade. For the definite, introductory grade, we normally use dūba, "some," as the article in place of wíⁿ.

Vocabulary: Nouns

kkóⁿde: plum

shínuda: dog

shóⁿge: horse

ttáx̌ti: deer

wāiⁿ: robe, shawl, blanket

FIG. 125. ttáx̌ti: deer

Vocabulary: Verbs

uthá: tell it

Speaking Practice

A. Read the following sentences aloud. Then translate the sentences into English. Examples:

Wāiⁿ kkōⁿbtha: I want a robe (any will do).

Wāiⁿ wiⁿ kkōⁿbtha: I want a (particular) robe.

Wāiⁿ thoⁿ kkōⁿbtha: I want the robe.

1. Ttáx̌ti thashtóⁿbe kki, thawá a!
2. Āshiatta ttáx̌ti dūba awáttoⁿbe.
3. Ttáx̌ti thoⁿkʰá doⁿbá bi ama.
4. Mīzhiⁿga utʰíⁿ tte, núzhiⁿga akʰá.
5. Shínuda wíⁿ uátʰiⁿ ithágaskoⁿbthe kki, oⁿtháx̌ta.
6. Shóⁿge thiⁿkʰé utʰíⁿ bi ama, niáshiⁿga wíⁿ.
7. Iⁿshʼáge wíⁿ ttabé thoⁿ ítha.
8. Iⁿshʼáge akʰá ttabé wíⁿ ítha.
9. Núzhiⁿga wíⁿ amá ttabé íthe gōⁿtha bi ama.
10. Núzhiⁿga ttabé thinā kki, wíⁿ ʼí a!

B. Translate the following sentences into Omaha.

    1. Do you want a (any) plum?

    2. We rode a (particular) horse.

    3. I saw some horses.

    4. The rabbit kicked the ball, they say.

    5. The dogs bit the rabbit.

    6. She tried to see a (any) warrior.

    7. The cat chased a (particular) fly.

    8. Give me an (any) arrow!

    9. I don't know how to make a (any) bow.

    10. The person looked around for deer.

C. The instructor interacts with the students, ranging over grades of "known-ness." Example:

    Wagō^{n}ze: John, zho^{n}ní shkō^{n}na?

    John: Ho. [Takes a piece.] Zho^{n}ní wi^n bthíze.

    Wagō^{n}ze: Zho^{n}ní tho^n níze t^{h}e ūda^n.

D. The students then take turns doing what the instructor did in exercise C. Other students should answer, using the appropriate article, if any.

E. The students break into small groups of at least two and take turns performing exercise D among themselves, making up their own questions for each other.

14.5 FUTURE

Personal Future

		Verb	Future Marker	Derived from Positional
I will eat it.		bthát^{h}e	tta mi^{n}k^{h}e	< thi^{n}k^{h}é
you will eat it.		nát^{h}e	tta ni^{n}kshe	< thi^{n}k^{h}é
we will eat it.		o^{n}thát^{h}e	tta o^{n}gat^{h}o^n	< t^{h}o^n

- Intended future for the three persons, "I," "you," and "we," is indicated by the potential particle tte, ablauted and followed by a *conjugated* positional. For "I," the future marker is tta mi^{n}k^{h}e; for "you" it is tta ni^{n}kshe; and for "we" it is tta o^{n}gat^{h}o^n.

- In the "I" and "you" forms in modern Omaha, the final vowel is dropped or whispered, so that these forms sound like tta mi^{n}k^h and tta ni^{n}ksh. For the "we" form, the first two vowels merge together, so that it sounds like ttó^{n}gat^{h}o^n.

Volitional Future

		Verb	Future Marker	Derived from Positional
S/he will eat it.		that^{h}é	tta ak^{h}a	< ak^{h}á
They will eat it.		that^{h}é	tta ama	< amá

- The volitional future is used primarily for third person actors and describes the expectation that they will do something, of their own volition. Generally we use tta ak^{h}a for a single actor and tta ama for plural actors.

- In colloquial speech, the first two vowels are merged and the final vowel is dropped or whispered: ttak^h and ttam.

Constrained Future

	Verb	Future Marker	Derived from Positional
S/he must/should eat it.	thathé	tta tʰe	< tʰe
They must/should eat it.	thathé	tta i tʰe	< tʰe

- Omaha also has a *constrained* future form, for something that must or ought to happen. Here, the point is that the actor is constrained by necessity or expectations. This form uses tta tʰe in the singular and tta i tʰe in the plural. These again are normally used for the third person.

Vocabulary: Nouns

hīga: legend, traditional tale

Vocabulary: Verbs

bthé: I go

thaṣníⁿ: devour

FIG. 126.
thaṣníⁿ: devour

Speaking Practice

A. Read the following sentences aloud. Then translate the sentences into English. Examples:

Ithágaskoⁿbthe tta miⁿkʰe: I will try.

Oⁿníuoⁿ tta oⁿgatʰoⁿ: We will swim.

Ppáhoⁿ tta tʰe: He should get up.

1. Uwítʰiⁿ tta miⁿkʰe.
2. Íthaẋa tta niⁿkshe.
3. Ttáẋti wíⁿ thiẋé tta i tʰe.

4. Waʔúzhiⁿga amá thidóⁿbe kki, thithíẋe tta ama.
5. Shóⁿge tʰoⁿ ní ʔí tta tʰe, núzhiⁿga akʰá.
6. Āshiatta áshka bthé tta miⁿkʰe.
7. Wéathatʰe bthúga náṣniⁿ tta niⁿkshe.
8. Hīga oⁿgútha tta oⁿgatʰoⁿ.
9. Môⁿ ge íthe tta i tʰe.
10. Wôⁿgithe ishtá thipʔíⁿze tta i tʰe.

B. Translate the following sentences into Omaha.

1. You are going to win.
2. We are going to write it.
3. The old man should make a house.
4. I am going to pull the car.
5. The rabbits have to jump.
6. She will point at it.
7. You will cook it.
8. We are going to know Omaha.
9. Tomorrow I will be able to lift the deer.
10. The girls have to gather eggs.

C. The instructor interacts with the students, asking about their intentions. Example:

Wagōⁿze: Evelyn, idádoⁿ shkāẋe tta niⁿkshe?

Evelyn: Zhoⁿní bthátʰe tta miⁿkʰe.

D. The students then take turns doing what the instructor did in exercise C. Other students should answer, using the appropriate article, if any.

E. The students break into small groups of at least two and take turns performing exercise D among themselves, making up their own questions for each other.

14.6 DEMONSTRATIVES: THIS AND THAT

Free Demonstratives

thê	'this', toward the speaker; the aforementioned one
shê	'that', toward the listener, away from the speaker
shêhi	that over there, yon, away from both speaker and listener
gá	the one at the indicated location

Bound Demonstratives

du(a)-	this one right here
shu-	toward you
gu(a)-	away

- Words like "this" or "that" in English are called *demonstratives*. A demonstrative is used to help the listener locate a noun in physical or conceptual space by "pointing" at it.
- Omaha has two classes of demonstratives. The *free demonstratives* are a set of at least four that may stand alone as separate words, much as "this" and "that" can in English. The *bound*

demonstratives are a set of three that are always prefixed to another word.

- In physical space, demonstratives tend to use the speaker or listener as reference points. In English, "this" tells the listener to look toward the speaker, and "that" tells the listener to look away from the speaker. The archaic demonstrative "yon" tells the listener to look away from both the speaker and the listener.
- In conceptual space, demonstratives may refer to things that have been previously mentioned. In this case the flow of understanding and dialog replaces physical space, and a demonstrative used for physical space may be additionally used with a special meaning in conceptual space. "So this man (that I just mentioned) comes walking along . . ." or "You know, that guy I told you about yesterday . . ." are examples of this in English.
- In Omaha, usage of the demonstratives is complex. Most of the time, even the "free" demonstratives are bound to something else. We examine these situations in more detail in the next lesson. For this lesson, we look at just a few particular cases.
- The free demonstrative thê is probably the only one that is really free in practice. It is used to refer to someone we are talking about who is not present. It would precede the noun, as in thê niáshiⁿga akʰá, "this person I'm talking about."

Vocabulary: Nouns

shêhi t^{h}e no^{n}zhí^n: soldier(s) or traveler(s) in other lands; s/he/they was/were far away

shêhi t^{h}e gthí^n: people living somewhere else; s/he/they was/were living somewhere else

shí^{n}gazhi^{n}ga: small child; doll

Vocabulary: Verbs

at^{h}í: s/he arrived here

hátheze: come back safely from a place of danger

Vocabulary: Miscellaneous

dúda: attention getting word ("Hey!")

dúde: this way

dúdiha: over here (as a place to move)

eshó^n: close, close together

Gá!: Here! (used when giving something to someone)

gúdiha: away, over there (as a place to move)

thê: the one we are talking about, not present

thê t^{h}e no^{n}zhí^n: this is where s/he stood

thê t^{h}e gthí^n: this is where s/he sat, this was his/her place

thêthudi: here, around here, in this area

Speaking Practice

A. Read the following sentences aloud. Then translate the sentences into English. Examples:

Gá! Wi'í: Here! I give it to you.

Gúdiha mo^{n}thí^n a!: Get out of here!

Thê wa'ú ak^{h}á núzhi^{n}ga uná bi ama: This woman looked for the boy.

1. Mo^{n}zhó^n thêthudi ūda^n ebthégo^n.

2. Shêhi t^{h}e no^{n}zhí^n amá hátheze gí tta i t^{h}e.

3. Dúda! Shí^{n}gazhi^{n}ga dúde gí i a!

4. Shêhi t^{h}e gthí^n amá nudó^n wi^n at^{h}í.

5. Thêthudi thé t^{h}e no^{n}zhí^n.

6. Ma^{n}č^{h}ú ak^{h}á dúdiha mo^{n}thí^n tta ak^{h}á.

7. Eshó^n thagthí^n. Gúde mo^{n}ní^n tte.

8. Thêthudi hīga uthá tta ak^{h}a, wagō^{n}ze ak^{h}á.

9. Wāthat^{h}e thashtó^{n}be t^{h}e thê gthí^n.

10. Thê hó^{n}t'ega ak^{h}á gió^n bi ama.

B. Translate the following sentences into Omaha.

1. I have the card. Here, take it.

2. I don't want it. Get out of here!

3. The people over there (in another land) might die.

4. Teacher, come over here!

5. This girl (that I mentioned) lifted the doll.

6. The bird will fly over there.

7. Did you see the people living over there?

8. He was over there (in another land) for a long time.

9. This boy (mentioned in 8) came back safely.

10. Come closer! This is where he lay.

C. The instructor interacts with the students, telling them to come closer or move farther away. Example:

> Wagōⁿze: Eddie, dúdiha gí ga! ("Eddie, come over here!")

> Cathy, gúde moⁿthíⁿ ga! ("Cathy, go farther away!")

D. The students then take turns doing what the instructor did in exercise C. Other students should answer, using the appropriate article, if any.

E. The students break into small groups of at least two and take turns performing exercise D among themselves, making up their own questions for each other.

14.7 DEMONSTRATIVE PRONOUNS

Demonstrative + Positional Paradigm

	du(a)-	the-	she-	shehi-	ga-
-akʰá	dúakʰa	théakʰa	shêakʰa	shehíakʰa	gáakʰa
-amá	dúama	théama	shêama	shehíama	gáama
-thiⁿkʰé	duáthiⁿkʰe	théthiⁿkʰe	shêthiⁿkʰe	shehíthiⁿkʰe	gáthiⁿkʰe
-thoⁿkʰá	duáthoⁿkʰa	théthoⁿkʰa	shêthoⁿkʰa	shehíthoⁿkʰa	gáthoⁿkʰa
-ma	duáma	théma	shêma	shehíma	gáma
-thiⁿ	duáthiⁿ	théthiⁿ	shêthiⁿ	shehíthiⁿ	gáthiⁿ
-tʰoⁿ	duátʰoⁿ	thétʰoⁿ	shêtʰoⁿ	shehítʰoⁿ	gátʰoⁿ
-kʰe	duákʰe	thékʰe	shêkʰe	shehíkʰe	gákʰe
-tʰe	duátʰe	thétʰe	shêtʰe	shehítʰe	gátʰe
-thoⁿ	duáthoⁿ	théthoⁿ	shêthoⁿ	shehíthoⁿ	gáthoⁿ
-ge	duáge	thége	shêge	shehíge	gáge

- The most common use of demonstratives in Omaha is in combination with a positional. This usage is completely productive. All four free demonstratives and du(a)- combine with any positional. We call these combinations *demonstrative pronouns*. There are fifty-five in all.

- An Omaha demonstrative pronoun can be used alone in place of a noun, or it can be used together with a noun either preceding or following it. Thus to refer to a boy who is the manifest active subject right here, we have three possibilities for using a demonstrative pronoun, any one of which works as a complete noun phrase:

> dúakʰa: "this one"

> núzhiⁿga dúakʰa: "this boy"

> dúakʰa núzhiⁿga akʰá: "this here boy"

- When du(a)- is combined with either of the two active subject positionals akʰá or amá, the (a) is dropped and the accent is on the dú-. For all other positionals, which start with a consonant, the (a) is retained and takes the accent: duá-.

Vocabulary: Nouns

héga: buzzard, vulture

wéttaugthe: nest (for eggs)

Vocabulary: Verbs

athíⁿ gí: bring ("come back having")

athíⁿ moⁿthíⁿ: take ("go having")

gakkúwiⁿxe: circle, move in a spiral

kkíde: shoot, shoot at

ú: hit it, wound it (something that is shot at)

FIG. 127. athíⁿ moⁿthíⁿ: take ("go having")

FIG. 128. gakkúwiⁿxe: circling, going around in circles

Vocabulary: Stative Verbs

nóⁿkka: be hurt, be injured

xuíⁿ: smelly, stinky

Vocabulary: Miscellaneous

égoⁿ: so, therefore, for that reason, thereupon

Speaking Practice

A. Read the following sentences aloud. Then translate the sentences into English. Examples:

Shêtʰe dóⁿba ga!: Look at that!

Gáthoⁿ ttabé thoⁿ oⁿʔí ga!: Give me that there ball!

Núzhiⁿga shêhikʰe nóⁿkka: That boy lying over there is hurt.

1. Gátʰoⁿ āgthiⁿ ga!

2. Shêama waʔú amá shé bahí tta ama.

3. Shêhige wiⁿ shkōⁿna kki, thizá a!

4. Núzhiⁿga dúakʰa thêthudi niúoⁿ gōⁿtha.

5. Shêhitʰe xthabé tʰe thashtóⁿbe a?

6. Wéttaugthe shêthoⁿ athíⁿ āne gí moⁿthíⁿ ga!

7. Égoⁿ xthabé tʰe āna bi ama, thêakʰa núzhiⁿga akʰá.

8. Waʔúzhiⁿga shêakʰa dúdiha moⁿthíⁿ tta tʰe.

9. Wathíbaba gák^{h}e bthíze tta mi^{n}k^{h}e.

10. Duátho^n ūzhiha x̌uí^n tho^n gúdiha athí^n mo^{n}thí^n a!

B. Translate the following sentences into Omaha.

1. Here, take this arrow!

2. Point it at that bird!

3. The aforementioned boy took the arrow, they say.

4. If you do not know how to shoot, you will not be able to hit that deer.

5. This bear wants to eat you.

6. Those buzzards over there are circling.

7. Do you remember that old man?

8. Those (boys) shouldn't whistle.

9. We're going to push this car.

10. This (girl) wants that doll.

C. The instructor interacts with the students, using demonstrative pronouns to tell them to do things. Example:

Wagō^{n}ze: Helen, shêt^{h}e gthí^n ga! ("Helen, sit there!")

Alan, duák^{h}e thizá ga! ("Alan, take this [pencil]!")

D. The students then take turns doing what the instructor did in exercise C. Other students should answer, using the appropriate article, if any.

E. The students break into small groups of at least two and take turns performing exercise D among themselves, making up their own questions for each other.

14.8 EMPHATIC PRONOUNS

The Four Emphatic Pronouns

wí	*I*
thí	*you*
o^{n}gú	*we*
é	*he, she, it, they*

- Omaha has four emphatic pronouns, one for each of the four subject persons.

- An emphatic pronoun is used only to draw special attention to the subject to distinguish it from somebody else with whom the listener might confuse it. In English we would generally emphasize the subject pronoun in this situation. Thus, uáhi means "I won." If we said wí uahi, it would be like the English "*I* won" (not the other guy). Don't be tempted to use emphatic pronouns unless this sort of emphasis is intended. The English emphatic pronouns are given in *italics* for emphasis. The Omaha emphatic pronouns are given in regular type.

Vocabulary: Nouns

ttanúkka: meat, fresh meat

wahútto^{n}the: gun

Vocabulary: Verbs

niúoⁿ: swim

nuzóⁿ: skate

wíⁿkʰe: be true, tell the truth

Vocabulary: Miscellaneous

noⁿ: only

shti: too, also

Speaking Practice

A. Read the following sentences aloud. Then translate the sentences into English. Examples:

Thí shti nátʰe tte?: Why don't *you* eat it too?

Wí é bthíⁿ: It is I. (It's *me*.)

Shêakʰa niáshiⁿga akʰá, é waʼú: *That* person is a woman.

1. Oⁿgú oⁿgúhi tta oⁿgatʰoⁿ.

2. É shti ttanúkka thatʰé gōⁿtha.

3. Thí é níⁿ.

4. Wí shti anúzoⁿ ithágaskoⁿbthe tta miⁿkʰe.

5. É niúoⁿ bazhi. Oⁿgú oⁿníuoⁿ.

6. Wéttaugthe shêtʰe wí ithátʰe.

7. Wathíbaba gákʰe shkōⁿna azhi kki, wí bthíze tta miⁿkʰe.

8. Égoⁿ uná tʰe, é wíⁿkʰa bazhi.

9. Oⁿgú shti wagthábaze shêkʰe oⁿgáthade oⁿgóⁿzhiⁿga.

10. Thêakʰa niáshiⁿga akʰá thí é níⁿ a?

B. Translate the following sentences into Omaha.

1. *I* am the one who saw the buzzards.

2. *I* didn't do it; *you* did.

3. *It* was the gun that the aforementioned man took, they say.

4. *They* were the ones who shot at it; *we* didn't have a gun.

5. That man over there is the one who must do it.

6. That is the dog that bit him.

7. I am the only one who remembers that old man. *Those* (people) don't know him.

8. *We* will make cowboy bread; *you* will give them this meat.

9. *You* too can speak Omaha!

10. The one who wrote that is *I*.

C. The instructor accuses each student of doing something that another student is actually doing. The accused student corrects the instructor, pointing out who is actually doing it. Example:

Wagōⁿze: Stan, thazhōⁿ. ("Stan, you are sleeping.")

[Jeff is the one actually sleeping.]

Stan: Wíⁿthakʰa azhi. Wí azhōⁿ mazhi. Jeff akʰá, é zhōⁿ.

D. The students then take turns doing what the instructor did in exercise C. Other students should answer, using the appropriate article, if any.

E. The students break into small groups of at least two and take turns performing exercise D among themselves, making up their own questions for each other.

14.9 POSSESSIVE PRONOUNS

The Four Possessive Pronouns

wiwítta	my, mine
thithítta	your, yours
oⁿgútta	our, ours
ettá	his, her, hers, its, their, theirs

· Omaha has four *possessive pronouns*, one for each of the four subject persons, and corresponding to the four emphatic pronouns.

· These possessive pronouns function something like stative verbs. They are placed after the noun that is possessed.

· When used alone, possessive pronouns can declare whose turn it is in a game: Thithítta, "It's your turn."

· These possessive pronouns act much like stative verbs. They can be placed after a noun to modify it: moⁿkkóⁿsabe wiwítta, "my coffee." Or they can be used to declare a fact about it: Moⁿkkóⁿsabe tʰe wiwítta, "The coffee is mine." Or they

can stand alone as a declaration about something that is understood: Wiwítta, "It is mine."

Vocabulary: Verbs

moⁿthóⁿ: steal
íthe: find

Stative Verbs

ûǰaⁿ: pretty

FIG. 129.
ûǰaⁿ: pretty

Miscellaneous

hébe: part of, a piece of
íⁿčʰoⁿ: now, just now

Speaking Practice

A. Read the following sentences aloud. Then translate the sentences into English. Examples:

Kkinóⁿnoⁿge shêkʰe wiwítta: That car is mine.

Mōⁿzeska thithítta tʰe thizá ga!: Take your money!

Molly ettá: It's Molly's turn. (or: It's Molly's.)

1. Ttí oⁿgútta tʰe ttoⁿgá.

2. Iⁿgthóⁿga wiwítta thiⁿkʰé uáne.

3. Wagōⁿze thithítta thiⁿkʰé, wí é bthíⁿ.

4. Dúak^{h}a shó^{n}ge ak^{h}á wiwítta; shêhit^{h}o^n thithítta.

5. Gá! Wēbax̧u wiwítta k^{h}e wi'í.

6. Ttabé duátho^n ebé ettá?

7. Thí no^n shó^{n}ge thithítta t^{h}o^n āthagthi^n uthákkihi.

8. Mō^{n}zeska o^{n}gútta t^{h}e níze kki, níde thithítta k^{h}e anó^{n}t^{h}e tta mi^{n}k^{h}e.

9. Wéathat^{h}e thithítta t^{h}e wí shti hébe winā tte.

10. Shó^{n}ge shêhiak^{h}a wiwítta kki, é āagthi^n tta mi^{n}k^{h}e.

B. Translate the following sentences into Omaha.

1. This car is mine; that one is yours.

2. Now it is our turn.

3. It was my gun that the man took.

4. Did you find your money?

5. She's looking for her dog.

6. My name is _____. What is your name?

7. Your hands are pretty.

8. I want some of your cowboy bread too.

9. I am the only one who saw your horse.

10. This is my knife. I'm looking for my spoon.

C. The instructor asks each student who owns some item. The student responds appropriately. Example:

Wagō^{n}ze: Kay, ūzhiha shêtho^n ebé ettá? ("Kay, whose bag is that?")

Kay: Larry ettá.

D. The students then take turns doing what the instructor did in exercise C. Other students should answer, using the appropriate article, if any.

E. The students break into small groups of at least two and take turns performing exercise D among themselves, making up their own questions for each other.

15.1 POSTPOSITIONS

The Three Postpositions

-di	at the location
-tta	toward the location
-tʰoⁿ	from the location

- In English, *prepositions* are little words like "in," "on," "under," or "from" that come before a noun to use the noun as a point of reference for something else. *Postpositions* are the same thing, except that they come after the noun instead of before it. Omaha uses postpositions.

- While English has many prepositions, Omaha has only three common postpositions. These postpositions are: -di, meaning at, on or in the location; -tta, meaning to, toward, or in the direction of the location; and -tʰoⁿ, meaning from the location.

- -tʰoⁿ, "from," is often appended after one of the other two. This seems to have been normal in nineteenth-century Omaha, but our modern speakers have indicated that it is fine to use it alone.

- Postpositions may be appended directly to the generic third person emphatic pronoun e: edí, "right there, at that spot"; ettá, "toward that place"; edítʰoⁿ or ettátʰoⁿ, "from that place."

- The nouns ttí, "house," móⁿxe, "sky," and ttóⁿde, "ground," commonly tack the postposition directly to the noun. Other nouns normally require a positional first, which we discuss in section 15.2.

- Nouns that end in -i may add a light -a- before the postposition: ttíatta, "toward the house." Nouns that end in -e replace the e with -a: móⁿxadi, "in the sky"; ttóⁿdatta, "to the ground."

Vocabulary: Nouns

gāxa: tree branch

gthedóⁿ: hawk

móⁿxe: sky

ttí: house

ttóⁿde: the ground

FIG. 130. móⁿxe: sky

Vocabulary: Verbs

> atʰí: arrive here
>
> uppé: crawl in, enter
>
> ux̌páthe: to fall

Vocabulary: Miscellaneous

> edí: there, at the aforementioned location
>
> ettá: in that direction; his/hers/theirs
>
> gakkúwiⁿx̌e: circling, going around in circles
>
> shti: too, also
>
> théthudi: here, in this area

Speaking Practice

A. Read the following sentences aloud. Then translate the sentences into English. Examples:

> Ttíadi gthíⁿ: She's sitting in the house.
>
> Shêgedi gthíⁿ ga!: Sit by those scattered things!
>
> Gthedóⁿ wiⁿ móⁿx̌adi gióⁿ: A hawk was flying in the sky.

1. Ttóⁿdadi zhōⁿ.

2. Wazhíⁿga ama móⁿx̌adi thanóʾoⁿ a?

3. "Ettátʰoⁿ gí i a!" á bi ama iháⁿ akʰá.

4. Núzhiⁿga akʰá edí noⁿʾóⁿ azhi gthíⁿ bi ama.

5. Ttóⁿdatta dóⁿba i ga ho!

6. Móⁿx̌aditʰoⁿ uxpátha bi ama.

7. Wēbax̌u thithítta kʰe gátʰedi íthathe tte.

8. Thí shti théthudi gthíⁿ a!

9. Ttíatʰoⁿ ttóⁿdatta uóⁿsi.

10. X̌ithá akʰa móⁿx̌atta kkúwiⁿx̌e gióⁿ moⁿthíⁿ.

B. Translate the following sentences into Omaha.

1. Stand next to that (vertical thing)!

2. It arrived here from the sky.

3. It arrived here from the ground.

4. The mouse runs inside the house.

5. Are you able to pull that tree branch toward the ground?

6. The children will play there (at the aforementioned location).

7. The snake moves into the house.

8. They say she sits in the sky.

9. You too might look around for something here, in this area.

10. Do you see the airplane that is flying, circling skyward?

C. The instructor commands each student to go to, stand by, come from, or look toward some item in the room. The student responds appropriately. Then the students command one another in the same way. Example:

Wagõⁿze: Brett, ttóⁿdatta dóⁿba ga!
("Brett, look toward the ground!")

D. The instructor asks where certain things are. The students answer with reference to some standard location. Example:

Wagõⁿze: Courtney, mí thoⁿ āgudi a?
("Courtney, where is the sun?")

Courtney: Mí thoⁿ móⁿxadi noⁿzhíⁿ.
("The sun is in the sky.")

The students then take turns quizzing each other the same way.

E. The students then take turns asking for and exchanging information about where things are after the example of the instructor.

15.2 POSITIONALS AND POSTPOSITIONS

Postpositions Combined with Positionals

· Most commonly, postpositions are used with noun phrases that end in positionals.

· In this case, there is no -a- added to positionals ending in -iⁿ, and positionals ending in -e do not change to -a.

· A noun phrase that is the object of a postposition apparently does not take akʰá or amá.

FIG. 131.
wathíbaba:
playing card

Vocabulary: Nouns

inégi: his/her uncle

moⁿthíⁿkka: earth

niīthattoⁿ: cup

ttaní: soup

wathíbaba: playing card

nuṣhnáⁿ: otter

Vocabulary: Verbs

āne: to climb

uhé: pass

	-di	-tta	-tʰoⁿ	-di-tʰoⁿ	-tta-tʰoⁿ
kʰe	kʰe-di	kʰe-tta	kʰe-tʰoⁿ	kʰe-di-tʰoⁿ	kʰe-tta-tʰoⁿ
tʰe	tʰe-di	tʰe-tta	tʰe-tʰoⁿ	tʰe-di-tʰoⁿ	tʰe-tta-tʰoⁿ
thoⁿ	thoⁿ-di	thoⁿ-tta	thoⁿ-tʰoⁿ	thoⁿ-di-tʰoⁿ	thoⁿ-tta-tʰoⁿ
ge	ge-di	ge-tta	ge-tʰoⁿ	ge-di-tʰoⁿ	ge-tta-tʰoⁿ
thiⁿkʰe	thiⁿkʰe-di	thiⁿkʰe-tta	thiⁿkʰe-tʰoⁿ	thiⁿkʰe-di-tʰoⁿ	thiⁿkʰe-tta-tʰoⁿ
thoⁿkʰa	thoⁿkʰa-di	thoⁿkʰa-tta	thoⁿkʰa-tʰoⁿ	thoⁿkʰa-di-tʰoⁿ	thoⁿkʰa-tta-tʰoⁿ
tʰoⁿ	?	?	?	?	?
thiⁿ	?	?	?	?	?
ma	?	?	?	?	?

Speaking Practice

A. Read the following sentences aloud. Then translate the sentences into English. Examples:

X̌thabé tʰedi gthíⁿ: He's sitting in the tree.

Ttabé thoⁿdi gthíⁿ, hóⁿt'ega ama: The flies are sitting on the ball.

Zhoⁿbtháska kʰetta moⁿthíⁿ, á bi ama: She walked to the board, they say.

1. Mīzhiⁿga akʰa wahúttoⁿthe kʰetʰoⁿ ttóⁿthiⁿ moⁿthíⁿ.

2. Ttabé thoⁿtta uóⁿsisi.

3. Wathíbaba geditʰoⁿ wiⁿ thizá ga!

4. Izházhe thithítta tʰe thêkʰedi baχú ga!

5. Inégi thiⁿkʰédi gthíⁿ bi ama.

6. X̌thabé tʰedi āna bi ama, núzhiⁿga akʰa.

7. X̌thabé tʰetʰoⁿ ttóⁿdatta uχpátha bi ama.

8. Héga amá shóⁿge kʰetta gióⁿ tta ama.

9. Nóⁿde kʰetta thashtóⁿbe kki, miīdoⁿbe gátʰedi thashtóⁿbe tta niⁿkshe.

10. Ttizhébe shêhitʰetta moⁿthíⁿ a!

B. Translate the following sentences into Omaha.

1. The otter swam toward the turtle.

2. What is in your bag?

3. She stood by the door, they say.

4. Do you want to drink from the cup?

5. The card passes to the instructor.

6. Put the seed in the earth!

7. Rabbit will walk toward the soup, they say.

8. They sat at the table.

9. He went running over the land.

10. Go get a knife from the pack!

C. The instructor commands each student to go to, stand by, come from, or look toward some item in the room. The student responds appropriately. Then the students command one another in the same way. Example:

Wagōⁿze: Jeb, zhoⁿbtháskasabe tʰetta moⁿthíⁿ ga! ("Jeb, go toward the board!")

D. The instructor puts a number of props such as toy animals around the room and asks students where particular items are. The students answer with reference to some other item. Example:

Wagōⁿze: Becky, nuṣhnáⁿ tʰe āgudi a? ("Becky, where is the otter?")

Becky: Nuṣhnáⁿ tʰe maⁿčʰú tʰedi gthíⁿ. ("The otter is by the bear.")

The students then take turns quizzing each other the same way.

E. The instructor has the students bring him items from a sack. Example:

Wagóⁿze: Lyle, ūzhiha shêhikʰeditʰoⁿ uχpé wiⁿ athíⁿ gí moⁿthíⁿ ga ho! ("Lyle, go bring me a plate from that sack!")

The students then take turns having each other fetch things from the sack after the example of the instructor.

15.3 LOCATION NOUNS AND ADVERBS

Location Nouns

āshi	outdoors	āshiadi	āshiatta
eshóⁿ	near, very close	eshóⁿadi	eshóⁿatta
gahá	on, upon	gahádi	gahátta
háshi	behind	háshiadi	háshiatta
híde	down, bottom, base	hídadi	hídatta
ittóⁿthiⁿ	ahead, as in a race	ittóⁿthiⁿadi	ittóⁿthiⁿatta
kkóⁿge	near	kkóⁿgadi	kkóⁿgatta
móⁿshi	high up, above	móⁿshiadi	móⁿshiatta
moⁿsóⁿthiⁿ	across, on the far side	moⁿsóⁿthiⁿadi	moⁿsóⁿthiⁿatta
móⁿtʰe	in	móⁿtʰadi	móⁿtʰatta
náze	behind	názadi	názatta
óⁿma	other side (of a two-sided thing)	óⁿmadi	óⁿmatta
ppaháshi	above, on top	ppaháshiadi	ppaháshiatta
ppahóⁿga	before, ahead, in front	ppahóⁿgadi	ppahóⁿgatta
uthúshi	in front (facing a crowd)	uthúshiadi	uthúshiatta
wéahide	far away	wéahidadi	wéahidatta

- In English there are many different prepositions to express relationships more subtle than "located at," "toward," and "from." In Omaha these relationships are handled by *location nouns*.

- Location nouns refer to an absolute or relative position. Postpositions can be added to them to indicate location at or motion toward or from the position. When -di or -tta is added, a preceding -a- is added with them.

Demonstrative -thu Words

duáthu	here, this area close at hand	duáthudi
thêthu	here, this area	thêthudi
shêthu	there, that area	shêthudi
shêhithu	there, that area over yonder	shêhithudi
gáthu	there, that specified area	gáthudi

- For referring generally to an area, as with English "here" and "there," we use a demonstrative plus the root -thu. Most commonly, these forms have the postposition -di tacked to the end: "in this/that area." The -thu forms do not seem to take the postposition -tta.

Location Adverbs

ppamú	downhill
égaχe	surrounding, around the periphery
ídabe	in the middle (of a tribal circle)
gashíbe	out of (anything but a house)
akkíwatta	across, as in reaching across

- Some location words do not seem to take postpositions at all. We have found at least four location words to which our speakers do not accept the addition of postpositions, and a fifth, ending in -tta, for which they do not accept a root form without the -tta. We may call these forms *location adverbs*.

Vocabulary: Location Nouns

āshi: outdoors; outside

eshóⁿ: near; very close

gahá: on; upon

háshi: behind

híde: down; bottom; base; low

ittóⁿthiⁿ: ahead, as in a race

kkóⁿge: near

moⁿsóⁿthiⁿ: across; on the far side

móⁿshi: high up; above

móⁿtʰe: in; inside

náze: behind

ppaháshi: above; on top

ppahóⁿga: before; ahead; in front; first

uthúshi: in front (facing a crowd)

wéahide: far away

FIG. 132. āshi: outdoors, outside

FIG. 133. eshóⁿ: near, very close

FIG. 134. móⁿshi: high up, above

Vocabulary: Other Nouns

iháⁿ: his/her mother

moⁿthíⁿkka: earth

móⁿxe: sky

níshude: Missouri River

ppahé: hill

Wakkóⁿda: God

FIG. 135. móⁿtʰe: in, inside

Vocabulary: Verbs

hí, ahí: arrive there

íthe: find

théthe: send; throw

tʰí, atʰí: arrive here

uppé: crawl into; enter a house

Vocabulary: Miscellaneous

akkíwatta: across, as in reaching across the table

āttashoⁿ: very; too much (an intensifier)

égaxe: around, surrounding, around the periphery

gashíbe: out of (anything but a house)

gáthu: there, that specified area

ídabe: in the middle; e.g., of a tribal circle

ppamú: downhill

shêhithu: there, that area over yonder

shêthu: there, that area

thêthu: here, this area

-xti: very; really; real (an intensifier)

Speaking Practice

A. Read the following sentences aloud. Then translate the sentences into English. Examples:

Wāthatʰe gahádi noⁿzhíⁿ bazhi i a!: Don't stand on the table!

Ttí móⁿtʰatta uppá bi ama: She entered the house.

Gáthudi gthíⁿ ga!: Sit right in that area!

Edí ppamú oⁿmóⁿthiⁿ tta i tʰe: We have to walk downhill there.

1. Gúdiha moⁿthíⁿ i ga! Eshóⁿ āttashoⁿ thagthíⁿ.

2. Wāthatʰe égaxe gthíⁿ i ga ho!

3. Ittóⁿthiⁿatta moⁿthíⁿ bi ama, núzhiⁿga akʰá.

4. Mīzhiⁿga akʰa kkinóⁿnoⁿge móⁿtʰadi gthíⁿ.

5. "Shíⁿgazhiⁿga athíⁿ gashíbe gí a!" á bi ama, iháⁿ akʰá.

6. Xthabé ppaháshiatta āane kki, wéahidexti attóⁿbe uákkihi tte.

7. Níshude móⁿtʰadi niúoⁿ kki, moⁿsóⁿthiⁿatta hí ígaskoⁿthe tta akʰa.

8. Ppahóⁿgaxtidi Wakkóⁿda akʰa mōⁿxe kʰe, moⁿthíⁿkka kʰe gāxa bi ama.

9. Ppahé hídatta ní wiⁿ ítha bi ama, nú akʰá.

10. Kkóⁿgatta moⁿthíⁿ bi ama, nudóⁿ akʰá.

B. Translate the following sentences into Omaha.

1. Stand up front (facing the class)!

2. The girl walked behind.

3. They say he stood in the center (of the circle), speaking Omaha.

4. He looked behind him.

5. He threw the ball up high.

6. Omaha is spoken here.

7. They live on the other side.

8. Please look for my knife in that bag!

9. She reached across the table and picked up the card.

10. The leader should walk at the head of the line. Warriors should walk behind.

C. The instructor makes a question or a command for each student, using locative nouns or adverbs. The student responds appropriately. Example:

Wagṓⁿze: Chris, uthúshiatta moⁿthíⁿ ga! ("Chris, go stand in front.")

D. The students then take turns doing what the instructor did in exercise C. Other students should answer or do what they are commanded, as appropriate.

E. The students break into small groups of at least two and take turns performing exercise D among themselves, making up their own questions and commands for each other.

15.4 VERBS OF MOTION

The Four Basic Verbs of Motion

thé	go	hí	arrive there going, get there
í	come	tʰí	arrive here coming, show up here

- English uses the verbs "come" and "go" very frequently. Omaha does too but adds two more verbs of motion: "arrive here," tʰí, and "arrive there," hí.

- These verbs are not often used in their root form, except at the beginning of a verb chain:

Shêakʰa hí gṓⁿtha: That person wants to get there.

- The two verbs of arrival are used in commands only rarely, as it usually makes little sense to command someone to arrive.

- In commands, the verb í, "to come," is usually replaced by gí, which actually means "to come back." Either could be used in the nineteenth century, but our modern speakers seem to prefer gí ga! or gí a! The reason for this preference is probably that í, "come," could easily be confused with other words, such as the verb ʼí, "give."

- For a positive command, the verb thé, "to go," is usually replaced by the verb moⁿthíⁿ, "to walk." Thus we normally say: moⁿthíⁿ a/ga!, not thá a/ga!. For the negative of this command, "Don't go!", however, we do use the basic "go" verb: thá azhi a/ga!

- The "arrive there" verb, hí, is often used with a postpositional construction to mean arriving at or achieving a certain state or position, much as English uses the word "get." Thus, móⁿtʰatta hí would mean "get inside," and ittóⁿthiⁿatta hí would mean "get ahead," as in a race.

Vocabulary: Nouns

níxa: stomach; belly

ppahé: hill

Ppahé-watháhuni: The Devouring Hill

thinégi: your uncle

wahí: bone, bones

FIG. 136. wahí: bone

Vocabulary: Verbs

hí: arrive there

í: come

ígthebe: vomit it up

thahúni: devour, gobble up

thé: go

t^{h}í: arrive here

Vocabulary: Miscellaneous

he: marks a statement made by a female

no^n: regularly

tho^{n}di: when in the past

no^n tho^{n}di: whenever in the past

Speaking Practice

A. Read the following sentences aloud. Then translate the sentences into English. Examples:

   Edí thá bazhi i a!: Don't go there!

   Ttíatta gí ga!: Come to the house!

   Shínuda ak^{h}a í gō^{n}tha: The dog wants to come.

   1. Ppahó^{n}gatta thé gō^{n}tha, núzhi^{n}ga ak^{h}a.

   2. Ettát^{h}o^n í ukkíhi bazhi bi ama, nudó^n ama.

   3. Ppahé ppiâzhi k^{h}e edí tháazhi a!

   4. Niáshi^{n}ga ama edí hí no^n tho^{n}di watháhuni no^n i he.

5. Edí hí kki, "Ppahé-watháhuni, ó^{n}thahuni ga!" á bi ama, Mo^{n}shtí^{n}ge ak^{h}a.

6. Ppahé-watháhuni níx̣a mó^{n}t^{h}atta hí kki, Mo^{n}shtí^{n}ge ígtheba bi ama.

7. Égithe níkkashi^{n}ga ppahó^{n}ga hí ma t'é ma, wahí k^{h}e só^n k^{h}é ama.

8. Ttí ppaháshiatta hí ígasko^{n}tha i kki, thi'á.

9. Wagō^{n}ze ak^{h}a t^{h}í no^n tho^{n}di, uthúshiadi no^{n}zhí^n no^n.

10. Wahí k^{h}edi thé kki, Mo^{n}shtí^{n}ge Ppahé-watháhuni ak^{h}a thahúni tta ak^{h}a.

B. Translate the following sentences into Omaha.

   1. Did he try to go?

   2. Whenever the old men used to arrive there, the Devouring Hill would gobble them up.

   3. When your uncle gets here, we will eat.

   4. Don't go to where the pale white bones are lying!

   5. When the people arrived, the Devouring Hill said, "Come here!"

   6. When he got ahead, he screamed, "I win!"

   7. When she got to the base of the hill, she saw the deer.

8. He wanted to get here yesterday.

9. When the Rabbit got inside the Devouring Hill's belly, he saw its heart.

10. The boy didn't want to come.

C. The instructor commands each student to go or not to go somewhere, possibly using a word like azhi or ígaskoⁿthe after the verb of motion. The student may choose to do so or not, or may pretend to try and fail. The instructor then asks another student if the first student wants to do it, or tried to do it, or is able to do it, using an auxiliary like gōⁿtha, ígaskoⁿthe, ukkíhi, or gōⁿzhiⁿga, and the second student replies appropriately. Example:

Wagōⁿze: Ralph, ttizhébe tʰedi né tháazhi ga! ("Ralph, don't go to the door!")

[Ralph looks longingly at the door.]

Wagōⁿze: Angel, Ralph akʰa ttizhébe tʰedi thé gōⁿtha? ("Angel, does Ralph want to go to the door?")

Angel: Áoⁿ. Ralph akʰa ttizhébe tʰedi thé gōⁿtha. ("Yes. Ralph wants to go to the door.")

D. The students then take turns doing what the instructor did in exercise C.

E. The students break into small groups of at least three and take turns performing exercise D among themselves, making up their own commands and questions for each other.

15.5 VERBS OF MOTION WITH THE A- PREFIX

The Four Basic Verbs of Motion, with Liminal a-

athé	go		ahí	arrive there going, get there
aí	come		atʰí	arrive here coming, show up here

- Most commonly, each of these four basic verbs of motion appears with a prefixed a-. The exact meaning of this prefix is uncertain. We will call this the *liminal* a- prefix, on the theory that it may suggest a transition into the state implied by the verb of motion.

- The liminal a- forms of the verbs of motion are not used for commands. They are the normal forms used for statements and questions in the third person.

Vocabulary: Nouns

Ishtíthiⁿkʰe: Trickster; monkey

nudóⁿ: warrior

x̌thabé: tree

Vocabulary: Verbs

ahí: arrive there

aí: come

athé: go

atʰí: arrive here

Speaking Practice

A. Read the following sentences aloud. Then translate the sentences into English. Examples:

Athá bi ama, Moⁿshtíⁿge akʰa: The Rabbit left/was going along, they say.

Inégi wiwitta akʰa atʰí a?: Has my uncle arrived?

Nudóⁿ ama aí bi ama: The warriors were coming.

1. Ppamú athá bi ama, Moⁿshtíⁿge akʰa.

2. Ettátʰoⁿ aí bi ama, nudóⁿ ama.

3. Ittóⁿthiⁿatta athá bi ama, núzhiⁿga akʰa.

4. X̌ithá akʰa mōⁿshiatta athé tta akʰa.

5. Shíⁿgazhiⁿga ama hátheze atʰí.

6. X̌thabé tʰedi ahí i egóⁿ, uthíx̣ida.

7. Níshude mōⁿtʰadi niúoⁿ akʰa moⁿsóⁿthiⁿadi hátheze atʰí.

8. Wéahidatta athá bi ama, nudóⁿ akʰa.

9. Ppahé hídatta ppamú aí.

10. Nudóⁿ akʰa kkóⁿgatta ahí.

B. Translate the following sentences into Omaha.

1. He went to the end of the line.

2. The old man arrived there.

3. Your grandmother has arrived (here).

4. They say that Ishtíthiⁿkʰe was coming.

5. The girls left.

6. He reached the other side.

7. It went up toward the sky.

8. He got here yesterday.

9. That one should leave tomorrow.

10. The Rabbit got to the bottom of the hill.

C. The instructor commands each student to come or go somewhere, using locative nouns, adverbs, or postpositions. When the student has done what was requested, the instructor asks another student what that student has done. Example:

Wagōⁿze: Ryan, ídabe noⁿzhíⁿ ga! ("Ryan, stand in the center!")

[Ryan goes and stands in the center of the circle.]

Wagōⁿze: Carly, Ryan akʰa idādoⁿ gāx̣e a? ("Carly, what did Ryan do?")

Carly: Ryan akʰa ídabe athá. ("Ryan went into the center.")

D. The students then take turns doing what the instructor did in exercise C.

E. The students break into small groups of at least three and take turns performing exercise D among themselves, making up their own commands and questions for each other.

15.6 RETURN VERBS OF MOTION

The Basic Verbs of Motion, with Their "Returning" Counterparts

thé	go		gthé	go back, go home
í	come		gí	come back, come home
hí	get there		kʰí	get back there, arrive home going
tʰí	show up here		gthí	get back here, arrive home here
moⁿthíⁿ	walk, go		moⁿgthíⁿ	go back, scram

- Each of the four basic verbs of motion in Omaha has a counterpart that means to go/come back, or home. We may call these the *return motion* verbs. The verb for "walk," moⁿthíⁿ, which sometimes fills in for "go," also has a return motion form, moⁿgthíⁿ.
- The return motion verbs are generally formed by adding a simple velar stop (k or g) to the front of a basic verb of motion. This is a special case that we call the *vertitive* conjugational pattern.
- As with the basic verbs of motion, the return motion verbs also take the a-prefix form: agthé; agí; akʰí; agthí.
- The verbs of motion introduced here can be viewed as describing various stages in the return journey begun in section 15.5. The return trip may resume from "here," or resume from "there."
- From "here" the traveler sets out to return, "agthé," and eventually arrives back there, "akʰí." Alternatively, a person from "there" sets out to return, "agí," and finally arrives back here, "agthí."

Vocabulary: Nouns

niníba: pipe, peace pipe

ukkítte: tribe, nation, enemy

Vocabulary: Verbs

ʾíthe: talk about something

moⁿzhóⁿ ūdaⁿ gāx̣e: make peace

Vocabulary: Miscellaneous

āhigi: many, numerous

dūba: some

gthūba: all of it

kki: and it so happened that . . .

kkóⁿgex̌či: very close

moⁿshíattaha: further up

FIG. 137. dūba: some

FIG. 138. gthūba: all of it

Speaking Practice

A. Read the following sentences aloud. Then translate the sentences into English. Examples:

Moⁿgthíⁿ ga!: Go home!

Akʰí bi ama, ikkóⁿ akʰa: His grandmother reached home, they say.

Shíⁿgazhiⁿga wôⁿgithe gí i a!: All you kids, come back here!

Shínuda akʰa kkáshi agthí bazhi: The dog didn't come home for a long time.

1. "Uthá moⁿgthíⁿ i ga!" á bi ama, Ppóⁿkka ama.

2. Umóⁿhoⁿ ama edí athá bi ama, Ppóⁿkka ttí i thóⁿdi.

3. Moⁿzhóⁿ ūdaⁿ gāx̣e niníba athíⁿ agí bi ama.

4. Atʰí bi ama, āhigi ama.

5. Edí kkóⁿgex̌či ahí gōⁿtha bi ama.

6. Waíⁿ, ttíha, wéathatʰe gthūbax̌ti, ʾíⁿ agí bi ama.

7. Kki dūba agthí ama wéathatʰe gōⁿtha bi ama.

8. "Moⁿshíattahá moⁿgthíⁿ i ga!" á bi ama.

9. Ppáthiⁿ iⁿshʾáge ʾíthe akʰí bi ama.

10. Níkkashiⁿga athíⁿ akʰí bi ama, Ppáthiⁿ ama.

B. Translate the following sentences into Omaha.

   1. Has she come back?

   2. Go back where you came from!

   3. The old Ponca woman got home.

   4. The buzzards went back to the dead horse.

   5. When he finishes, he will come back.

   6. Having swum to the other side, he started back.

7. On his way back, the enemy were shooting at him.

8. They didn't hit him, and he arrived back safely.

9. When the warriors showed up, the enemy retreated.

10. All of the warriors arrived home safely.

C. The instructor commands each student to come or go somewhere, and then go back, using locative nouns, adverbs or postpositions. When the student has done what was requested, the instructor asks another student what that student has done. Example:

   Wagōⁿze: Ray, uthúshiatta noⁿzhíⁿ ga! ("Ray, stand up front!")

   [Ray goes and stands in front of the class.]

   Wagōⁿze: Ūdaⁿ shkāx̣e, āgthiⁿ tʰe gthí ga! ("Good. Return to your seat!")

   Wagōⁿze: Grace, Ray akʰa idādoⁿ gāx̣e a? ("Grace, what did Ray do?")

   Grace: Uthúshiatta noⁿzhíⁿ athá, āgthiⁿ tʰe agthí. ("He went and stood up front, and returned to his seat.")

D. The students then take turns doing what the instructor did in exercise C.

E. The students break into small groups of at least three and take turns performing exercise D among themselves, making up their own commands and questions for each other.

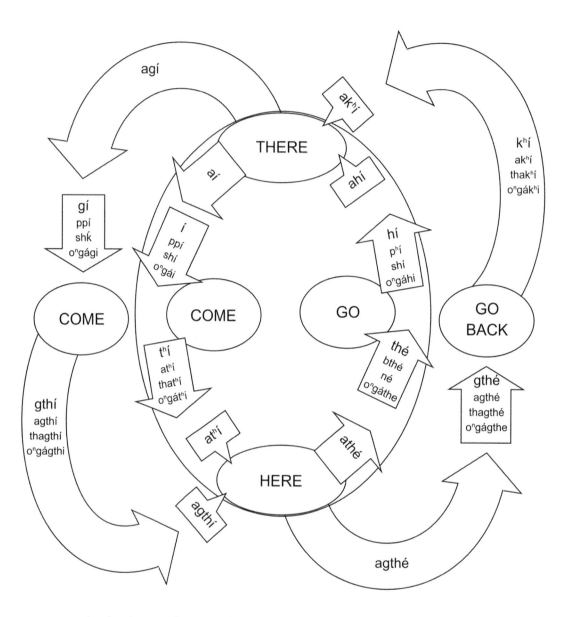

FIG. 139. Verbs of motion: *go* and *come*, *going back* and *coming back*. Note: The third person comes in two forms, with and without liminal a-. The I-, you-, and we- conjugations have only one form.

15.7 CONJUGATING VERBS OF MOTION

Conjugation of the Eight Verbs of Motion

Plain / 3rd Person	I-form	You-form	We-form
thé	bthé	né	oⁿgáthe
í	ppí	shí	oⁿgái
hí	pʰí	shí	oⁿgáhi
tʰí	atʰí	thatʰí	oⁿgátʰi
gthé	agthé	thagthé	oⁿgágthe
gí	ppí	shkí	oⁿgági
kʰí	akʰí	thakʰí	oⁿgákʰi
gthí	agthí	thagthí	oⁿgágthi

- Each of the eight basic and return verbs of motion in Omaha can be conjugated through the I-, you- and we- forms as well.

- The we- form is always based on the a- prefix form of the plain verb. It is formed as oⁿgá- + the plain form of the verb.

- The "go" verb thé is a ledh verb and conjugates as such for the I- and you- forms: bthé, "I go"; né, "you go." One of our speakers (Emmaline Walker Sanchez) has advised us that this verb is used only for present and future.

- The four verbs that begin with consonant clusters (including aspirated stops) in the plain form, tʰí, gthé, kʰí, and gthí, conjugate in the common pattern for I- and you-forms. For these, the I- form is formed by prefixing a-, and the you- form by prefixing tha- to the plain form.

- The remaining three verbs, í, hí, and gí, make their I- and you- forms in the consonant conjugation pattern by adding a labial consonant (p) for the I- form and an alveolar fricative consonant (sh) for the you- form. For the you- form, this works out to shí, shí, and shkí respectively, with no distinction between the forms for "you come" and "you arrive there." For the I- form, p + hí works out to pʰí, and p + gí works out to ppí. The original form for "I come" has been replaced by the one for "I come back," so the I- form of í is also ppí.

Vocabulary: Nouns

hāzi: grapes

Vocabulary: Stative Verbs

wasékkoⁿ: fast, speedy

FIG. 140. wasékkoⁿ: fast, speedy

Vocabulary: Miscellaneous

thóⁿzha: but, nevertheless

Speaking Practice

A. Read the following sentences aloud. Then translate the sentences into English. Examples:

Bthé tta miⁿkʰe: I'm going. I'm going to leave.

Atʰí: I've arrived. I'm here.

Thikkóⁿ thiⁿkʰeditʰoⁿ shkí a?: Have you come back from your grandma's?

Wôⁿgithe oⁿgágtha tta oⁿgatʰoⁿ: We're all going home.

1. Edí shóⁿge uáwane pʰí.

2. Thagthé a?

3. Moⁿzhóⁿ ūdaⁿ ppax̣e niníba abthíⁿ bthé kkōⁿbtha.

4. Né shkōⁿna thóⁿzha, hátheze shkí tte enégoⁿ?

5. Āshka oⁿgákʰi tta, ebthégoⁿ.

6. Waíⁿ, ttíha, wéathatʰe gthūbax̌ti, tha'íⁿ shkí wíttoⁿbe tʰe, ūdaⁿx̌ti.

7. Ppí kki, oⁿthóⁿshpahoⁿ tta niⁿkshe.

8. Né kki, moⁿkkóⁿsabe, zhoⁿní dūba aníⁿ shkí moⁿníⁿ tte.

9. Wasékkoⁿ moⁿbthíⁿ ppahóⁿgadi pʰí kki, iⁿsh'áge oⁿwóⁿkkie egóⁿ, háshiadi ppí.

10. Kkáshi wíttoⁿba mazhi egóⁿ, hátheze thagthí tʰe ūdaⁿ.

B. Translate the following sentences into Omaha.

1. Are you coming back tomorrow?

2. We will get there soon.

3. Do you want to go home?

4. We just left (coming back).

5. I will get there before you do.

6. On our way back, we saw one elk. (as said by a person who has just come home)

7. We are coming to pick grapes.

8. I got there, but I didn't see the Pawnees.

9. Whenever you get home, look around for the turtle!

10. Try to swim to the other side!

C. The instructor politely asks each student to come or go somewhere, and then go back, using locative nouns, adverbs, or postpositions. When the student has done what was requested, the instructor asks what that student has done. Example:

Wagōⁿze: Rosie, ppahóⁿgatta né tte. ("Rosie, why don't you go to the front of the line?")

[Rosie goes to the front of the line.]

Wagōⁿze: Ūdaⁿ shkāx̣e, háshiadi shkí tte. Idādoⁿ shkāx̣e? ("Good. Please come back to the end. What did you do?")

Rosie: Ppahóⁿgatta pʰí egóⁿ, háshiadi ppí. ("I went to the head of the line, and then came back to the end.")

D. The students then take turns doing what the instructor did in exercise C.

E. The students break into small groups of at least three and take turns performing exercise D among themselves, making up their own commands and questions for each other.

15.8 VERB CHAINING AND CONTINUATIVES

Continuatives

Meaningful Verb	Continuative Verb	
Íxa.		S/he laughed.
Íxa	**gthíⁿ**	S/he is laughing. / S/he sits laughing.

- In English we use the verb "to be" along with the -ing form of another verb to make the other verb *progressive*, meaning that the action is ongoing rather than a particular event. For example, we would say "He was smiling" or "She is washing the dishes" to set the scene or to tell that it is going on right now.

- In Omaha "to be" is not generally used for this. Instead, the progressive tense is signaled by chaining an appropriate verb of motion or verb of position to the main verb of interest. Thus in Omaha we would have to frame these sentences in such terms as "He arrived smiling" or "She is standing washing the dishes." We call a verb of motion or position used in this way a *continuative* verb.

- Different continuative verbs may be used to distinguish subtle differences in implication. Gthíⁿ suggests present activity or living situation, while moⁿthíⁿ is for more general states, like health. Noⁿzhíⁿ may be even more immediate than gthíⁿ, to describe a current standing activity.

Vocabulary: Nouns

unúshka: valley

wappé: weapon

wat'éthe: killer

wizhíⁿthe: my older brother (man speaking)

Vocabulary: Stative Verbs

thiⁿgé: lacking, none of

uzhí: full, loaded

wazhíⁿ ppíazhi: angry, in a bad mood

Vocabulary: Verbs

'óⁿhe: flee

ppáde: cut up, butcher

t'éthe: kill

wagtháde: creep up

wanóⁿse: surround/cut off/control a herd

wénoⁿxithe: attack them

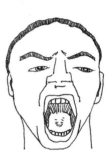

FIG. 141. wazhíⁿ ppíazhi: angry, in a bad mood

Vocabulary: Miscellaneous

de: but, when

égithe: after a while

kku'é: rushing forward, headlong

Speaking Practice

A. Read the following sentences aloud. Then translate the sentences into English. Examples:

Xagé noⁿzhíⁿ: He's crying. / He stands crying.

Uóⁿsisi aí: He was hopping. / He came hopping.

Ūdaⁿ moⁿbthíⁿ: I am fine. / I walk in wellness.

1. Wazhíⁿ ppíazhi gthíⁿ.

2. Umóⁿhoⁿ ama wanóⁿse gthíⁿ bi ama.

3. Unúshkadi ttezhíⁿga wiⁿ t'étha bi ama; ppáde noⁿzhíⁿ bi ama.

4. Shaóⁿ ama wagtháde aí bi ama, shóⁿge āgthiⁿ sháppex̌ti égoⁿ.

5. Wahúttoⁿthiⁿ uzhíazhi noⁿzhíⁿ bi ama, wizhíⁿthe tʰoⁿ.

6. Wénoⁿx̌itha i de, kku'é aí bi ama, Shaóⁿ ama.

7. Kku'é aí bi egóⁿ, t'éwatha bi ama, wappé thiⁿgé egóⁿ.

8. Égithe uthá agthí. "Umóⁿhoⁿ noⁿbá t'éwatha í," é uthá agthí.

9. Shaóⁿ ama 'óⁿhe agthá bi ama, wat'éthe ama.

10. Edí ahí égoⁿ, wa'íⁿ agthí.

B. Translate the following sentences into Omaha.

1. He's whistling.

2. He came running.

3. She's always in a bad temper.

4. My older brother was butchering the buffalo.

5. The warriors were charging forward to attack them.

6. A person arrived there to tell the news.

7. You're sitting pretty.

8. They came back carrying the three dead men.

9. The eagle is looking around.

10. They say the Sioux were camped in a valley to surround the buffalo herd.

C. The instructor has each student do something. While the student is doing it, the instructor asks another student what the activity is. The student responds, using a continuative verb. Example:

Wagōⁿze: Kent, uthúshiatta uthíx̌ide moⁿthíⁿ ga! ("Kent, go to the front and look around!")

[Kent goes to the front of the class and looks around.]

Wagōⁿze: Gary, Kent akʰa idādoⁿ gāx̌e a? ("Gary, what is Kent doing?")

Gary: Uthíx̌ide noⁿzhíⁿ. ("He's [standing] looking around.")

D. The students then take turns doing what the instructor did in exercise C.

E. The students break into small groups of at least three and take turns performing exercise D among themselves, making up their own commands and questions for each other.

15.9 POSITIONALS AS CONTINUATIVES

Continuatives

Meaningful Verb	Continuative Positional	
Gthín.		S/he sits/sat.
Gthín	**thinkhé.**	S/he is sitting.

- In section 15.8 we saw how verbs of position and verbs of motion could be used as continuatives, to imply that the action is ongoing. We can also use positionals after verbs in the same way. This principle can be used to convey an even more powerful and precise sense of the nature of the action. Using positionals in this way can perhaps be viewed as describing the scene or situation rather than narrating specific actions.

- When positionals are used after a verb, they occur in place of the particles i and bi. Therefore, an -e verb does not ablaut to -a before a positional, and bi ama after a positional is replaced simply by ama.

- In the nineteenth century the positionals akha and ama were sometimes changed to akhé and amé in this situation. Our speakers today recognize akhé but not amé. They tell us that akhé means that somebody is about to do something. The nineteenth-century usage may have had to do with identifying someone as an active party.

Vocabulary: Nouns

ingthónsinsnede: mountain lion

má: snow

niónba: moon

ttáppuskazhinga: student

ttéska: cow, domestic cattle

wamí: blood

Vocabulary: Verbs

hónbthe: dream

ídathe: be born

shkón: move around, be active

wégazhi: command them

FIG. 142. niónba: moon

FIG. 143. hónbthe: dream

Vocabulary: Miscellaneous

éwon: that's why, that's the reason, he's to blame

Speaking Practice

A. Read the following sentences aloud. Then translate the sentences into English. Examples:

Ẋagé noⁿzhíⁿ akʰa: He's crying. / He stands crying.

Uóⁿsisi í thiⁿ: He was hopping. / He came hopping.

Itʰádi akʰa zhōⁿ kʰe: Her father was lying asleep.

1. Uthíẋida bazhi gthíⁿ thoⁿkʰa.

2. Óⁿpʰaⁿ wiⁿ ahóⁿbthe; óⁿpʰaⁿ nugá ttoⁿgáẋči edí noⁿzhíⁿ akʰa.

3. Óⁿpʰaⁿ shêhiama ppahé hídeẋti uhé ama ama.

4. Nudóⁿ hoⁿga wénoⁿẋithe wégazhi akʰa éde, nudóⁿ wiⁿ uthíʾage tʰoⁿ.

5. Wahúttoⁿthiⁿ uzhíazhi kʰe; égoⁿ ʾóⁿhe agthé tta miⁿkʰe.

6. Ttéska tʾé kʰe. Héga dūba gakkúwiⁿẋe gióⁿ ama.

7. Ttáppuskazhiⁿga shêthiⁿkʰe wathíbaba uhí noⁿ gthíⁿ thiⁿkʰe.

8. Góⁿkki ttezhíⁿga ídatha bi kki, skáẋči tʰoⁿ ama.

9. "Míkkasi akʰé" á bi ama niáshiⁿga ama.

10. Má zhīdeẋti kʰe, Moⁿshtíⁿge wamí éwoⁿ.

B. Translate the following sentences into Omaha.

1. The warrior is lying dead.

2. They say the people were going around in circles.

3. She's sitting in the house.

4. A valley is on the other side of this mountain.

5. That mountain lion is about to make its move.

6. They killed him, they say. His gun was lying there empty.

7. The buffalo was standing there, very dark.

8. A woman is sitting there weeping.

9. A boy was going about playing with a ball.

10. The moon was very pale.

C. The instructor has each student do something. While the student is doing it, the instructor asks another student what the activity is. The student responds, using a positional as a continuative marker. Example:

Wagōnze: June, uthúshiatta uthíẋide moⁿthíⁿ ga! ("June, go to the front and look around!")

[June goes to the front of the class and looks around.]

Wagōnze: Barbara, June akʰa idádoⁿ gāẋe a? ("Barbara, what is June doing?")

Barbara: Uthíẋide tʰoⁿ. ("She's [standing] looking around.")

D. The students then take turns doing what the instructor did in exercise C.

E. The students break into small groups of at least three and take turns performing exercise D among themselves, making up their own commands and questions for each other.

15.10 DECLARATION OF EXISTENCE USING POSITIONALS

Declaration of Existence

Noun Phrase	"There"	Positional	
Ttizhébe t^he	**edí**	**t^he.**	There is a door.
Ón̄p^hon̄ win̄	**ededí**	**ak^ha.**	There is an elk.

- To declare the existence of an entity in English, we use the demonstrative "there" as the subject, together with a form of "to be" as the head verb, followed by a noun phrase that indicates the entity we are declaring: [There] [is] [a door], or [There] [is] [an elk]. This is a special usage that has nothing to do with the basic meaning of "there." It is employed to insert a new record into the database of the other person's mind. Compare this with the nearly identical sentences "There is *the* door," or "There is *the* elk," in which "there" is used in its usual way to point something out. We can also use "There is *a* door" or "There is *an* elk" in the same way, when we are on the spot pointing them out. But these forms, with emphasis on the noun, notably mean "There exists a door" or "There exists an

elk," which we say when we are in fact nowhere near the door or the elk.

- In Omaha the special "there exists" function is handled in a comparable way. As in English, a general demonstrative meaning something like "there" is used, and as in English, that "there" can also be used as a real demonstrative pointing to something that can be seen in the present situation.

- The "there" word used in Omaha is either edí or ededí. The latter term is felt by our speakers to be more precise or specific.

- To say "There is a . . ." in Omaha, first give the noun phrase, then the edí or ededí, and finally finish the sentence with a positional appropriate to the noun phrase.

- This usage, ending the sentence with a positional, may be considered a special case of state declaration using a positional to end the sentence, as introduced in section 15.9.

Vocabulary: Nouns

unúshka: valley

Vocabulary: Stative Verbs

waṣníde: slow

Vocabulary: Miscellaneous

égithe: after a while

FIG. 144. waṣníde: slow

Speaking Practice

A. Read the following sentences aloud. Then translate the sentences into English. Examples:

Ttizhébe tʰe edí tʰe: There is a door.

Wēbaxu wiⁿ ededí kʰe: There is a pencil (right there).

Waʔú dūba edí ama: There are some women.

1. Wagōⁿze akʰa edí akʰa.

2. Ttabé thoⁿ ededí thoⁿ.

3. Unúshka shêhíkʰedi óⁿpʰaⁿ dūba ededí ma.

4. Shaóⁿ nudóⁿ wiⁿ ededí thiⁿ.

5. Wahúttoⁿthiⁿ uzhí kʰe edí kʰe ama.

6. Ttáppuskazhiⁿga wôⁿgithe edí thoⁿkʰa.

7. Shóⁿge tʼé kʰe ededí kʰe.

8. Égithe "Ttáx̌tigikkidabi" izházhe athíⁿ akʰa ededí akʰa ama.

9. Kki ukkítte ma shínuda shti watʰátʰe noⁿ ma edí ma ama.

10. Égoⁿ shínuda waṣníde gáthudi edí bazhi ama.

B. Translate the following sentences into Omaha.

1. There's a mouse in the house.

2. There is food on the table.

3. There is a book in the bag.

4. There was a boy running away.

5. There is a house over there.

6. There is a person sitting there whistling.

7. There is a marker by the whiteboard.

8. There is a rock at the foot of the hill.

9. There are buzzards circling around above the dead horse.

10. They say there were people camped in a valley to surround buffalo.

C. The instructor points to something and asks each student what is there. The student answers appropriately. Example:

Wagōⁿze: Cory, shêthudi edādoⁿ edí akʰa? ("Cory, what's that over there?")

Cory: Niīthattoⁿ wiⁿ edí akʰa. ("There's a cup there.")

D. The students then take turns doing what the instructor did in exercise C.

E. The students break into small groups of at least three and take turns performing exercise D among themselves, making up their own commands and questions for each other.

Kinship and Causative Constructions **16**

16.1 GRANDPARENTS AND GRANDCHILDREN

	grandfather	grandmother	grandchild
his/her, the	**i-ttígo^n**	**i-kkó^n**	**i-ttúshpa**
my	**wi-ttígo^n**	**wi-kkó^n**	**wi-ttúshpa**
your	**thi-ttígo^n**	**thi-kkó^n**	**thi-ttúshpa**
female addressing	**ttigo^n-há**	**kko^n-há**	**ttushpa-há**
male addressing	**ttigó^n-ho**	**kko^n-hó**	**ttushpá-ho**

- Omaha has five basic ways of referring to a "relative." The first three are for talking *about* that person: my relative, your relative, or someone else's relative. The last two are for talking *to* that person, depending on whether the person speaking is male or female. We call the form of a word that is used for talking *to* a person the *vocative* form.

- Here the root word for "grandfather" is ttigo^n, the root word for "grandmother" is kko^n, and the root word for "grandchild" is ttushpa. In the vocabulary, kinship terms are usually listed as the root words, with a hyphen in front.

- These root words are never used alone. A person is a relative only with respect to someone else, and that relativity must be indicated in Omaha. Hence the hyphen.

- To show the relation when talking about a person, Omaha requires a prefix of *inalienable possession* before the kinship term. If you possess something "alienably," it means that you can give it away, like money, or a horse. Since you can't get rid of your relatives that easily, you possess them *inalienably*.

- The inalienable prefix for "my" relative is wi-. For "your" relative, it is thi-. For someone else's relative, or for, say, "a grandmother" in general, the inalienable possessive prefix is simply i-.

- In English we usually use a kinship term to address a relative of an older generation but not for relatives of our own generation or younger. We call our fathers "Dad," our mothers "Mom," our grandparents "Grandma" and "Grandpa," and our uncles and aunts "Uncle Bob" or "Aunt Betty," but we normally call our siblings, cousins, nephews, nieces, children, and grandchildren by their first name. In Omaha everyone is addressed by the appropriate kinship term, including relatives your own age or younger. The first name is not normally used for addressing anyone.

- To address someone in Omaha, you take the root kinship term and append a *vocative suffix* to it. In modern Omaha the vocative suffix is -há if you are female, and -ho if you are male. If you are female, the accent is always on that final -há. If you are male, the accent is always on the second syllable. If the root kinship word has only one syllable, like kkoⁿ, then the accent will be on the vocative suffix: kkoⁿhó. If it has two syllables, like ttigoⁿ, then the accent will be on the second syllable of the root: ttigóⁿho.

· In the nineteenth century it seems that both genders used -ha as the vocative suffix.

Vocabulary: Nouns

-kkoⁿ: grandmother

-ttigoⁿ: grandfather

-ttushpa: grandchild

FIG. 145. ikkóⁿ: grandmother

Vocabulary: Conjunctions and Adverbs

mégoⁿ: also, as well as

-shte: at all, ever, as in "whatever"

FIG. 146. ittúshpa: grandchild

Speaking Practice

A. Read the following sentences aloud. Then translate the sentences into English. Examples:

Thikkóⁿ ededí thiⁿkʰe: Your grandmother is right there.

Wittúshpá kʰe xagé shtoⁿ: My (infant) grandchild is always crying.

Ttigoⁿhá! Ttaní dūba thattóⁿ a!: Grandfather! Drink some soup!

1. Wamóskeshuga gāxa, thikkóⁿ akʰa.

2. "Umóⁿhoⁿ ié thippí, wittúshpa akʰa," á, ittígoⁿ akʰa.

3. Ittúshpa thanóʾoⁿ?

4. Ttigóⁿho! Moⁿkkóⁿsabe dūba shkōⁿna?

5. Thittígoⁿ thiⁿkʰe dóⁿbe ukkíhi, wittígoⁿ akʰa.

6. Shóⁿge ma sidādi thixá bi ama, thittúshpa akʰa.

7. Ttéskamoⁿseni thattóⁿ gōⁿtha, wikkóⁿ akʰa.

8. Kkoⁿhá! Thazhōⁿ a?

9. "Ttushpahá! Ānoⁿʾoⁿ a!" á, ikkóⁿ akʰa.

10. Ttushpáho! Ttanúkka thoⁿ thizá ga ho!

B. Translate the following sentences into Omaha.

1. Grandchild! Do you know how to swim?

2. His grandchild doesn't want to play outside.

3. Is your grandmother looking for the coat?

4. Grandfather! It is good that you are here.

5. Do you remember my grandchild?

6. The grandmother might eat the plum.

7. Your grandmother will come back tomorrow.

8. My grandfather is going on the summer buffalo hunt.

9. Grandmother! I don't see your dog!

10. How is your grandchild doing?

C. The instructor has the class divide themselves into two groups, the "grandparents" and the "grandchildren." Going around the room, students alternately declare themselves to be one or the other, using the appropriate Omaha term for their own gender. Example:

John: Ittígo^n. ("Grandfather.")

Mary: Ittúshpa. ("Grandchild.")

Jane: Ikkó^n. ("Grandmother.")

Jeff: Ittúshpa. ("Grandchild.")

Bill: Ittígo^n. ("Grandfather.")

Sally: Ittúshpa. ("Grandchild.")

D. The "grandchildren" sit back a little from the main circle and converse with their nearest "grandparents" to find out the name of the other one, as the grandparents inquire about the name of their other grandchild. To ask about people, point toward them with your lips. Example:

John [ittígo^n, speaking to Mary, pointing with his lips to Jeff]: Ttushpáho, wittúshpa izházhe t^{h}e idādo^n? ("Grandchild, what is my grandchild's name?")

Mary: Ttigo^{n}há, izházhe ettá t^{h}e Jeff. . . . Ttigo^{n}há, wikkó^n izházhe t^{h}e idādo^n? ("Grandfather, his name is Jeff. . . . Grandfather, what is my grandmother's name?")

John: Ttushpáho, thikkó^n izházhe t^{h}e Jane. ("Grandchild, your grandmother's name is Jane.")

E. The instructor has the "grandchildren" stand up and walk around their "grandparents." The grandchildren are on call to run errands for their grandparents, such as fetching small items from the table or bringing coffee or candy. In return, the grandchildren may beg quarters from their grandparents. In every case, the students address each other by the appropriate kinship term. Example:

Wagōⁿze: Ttushpáho wôgithe, noⁿzhíⁿ i ga ho! Thittígoⁿ, thikkóⁿ mégoⁿ, égaχe moⁿthíⁿ i ga ho! Edādoⁿshte thinā tʰe, égoⁿ shkāχe tta i tʰe. ("Grandchildren, all of you, stand up! Walk around your grandfathers and your grandmothers! Whatever they ask of you, you should do it.")

Jane: Dúda! Ttushpahá, gí a! ("Grandchild, come here!")

Mary: Kkoⁿhá, idādoⁿχti shkōⁿna? ("Grandmother, do you want something?")

Jane: Ttushpahá, moⁿkkóⁿsabe dūba athíⁿ gí moⁿthíⁿ a! ("Grandchild, go fetch me some coffee!")

Mary: Há, Kkoⁿhá. . . . Gá, gátʰe moⁿkkóⁿsabe tʰe. ("Yes, Grandmother. . . . Here. Here is your coffee.")

Mary: Kkoⁿhá, zhoⁿní kkōⁿbtha. Mikkáha aníⁿ a? ("Grandmother, I want some candy. Do you have a quarter?")

16.2 PARENTS AND CHILDREN

	father	mother
his/her, the	**i-thādi**	**i-háⁿ**
my	**iⁿdādi**	**íⁿ-naⁿha / íⁿ-naⁿho**
your	**thi-ādi**	**thi-háⁿ**
female addressing	**dadi-há**	**naⁿ-há**
male addressing	**dadí-ho**	**naⁿ-hó**

- Relationships between parents and children are particularly close and complex, and the kinship terms used between them are somewhat irregular in Omaha. The sets for "father," "mother," "son," and "daughter" need to be studied closely and memorized.

- The "father" term in Omaha is old, and the initial part of the root word has been reinterpreted. The original root was probably something like ādi. In the vocabulary we list "father" as ithādi, including the inalienable possessive prefix -i, since the root form is too ambiguous to use.

- For the "father" term, the inalienable possessive prefix for "my" is iⁿ- rather than wi-.

- The "mother" set is one of the very few that has two separate roots: generally haⁿ for talking about her, and naⁿ for talking to her.

- As for "father", the inalienable possessive prefix for "my" referring to one's mother is iⁿ- rather than wi-. In this case, however, the accent goes on the íⁿ-, and the root is taken as the appropriate vocative form. Thus if you are female, you address your mother as naⁿhá!, but talk about her as íⁿnaⁿha, "my mother." If you are male, you address her as naⁿhó!, but talk about her as íⁿnaⁿho, "my mother."

	son	daughter
his/her, the	**i-zhíⁿge**	**i-zhóⁿge**
my (female speaking)	**wi-zhíⁿge**	**wi-zhóⁿge**
(male speaking)	**wi-nísi**	**wi-nísi**
your (female addressed)	**thi-zhíⁿge**	**thi-zhóⁿge**
(male addressed)	**thi-nísi**	**thi-nísi**
female addressing	**(wi)-zhiⁿge-há**	**(wi)-zhoⁿge-há**
male addressing	**nisí-ho**	**nisí-ho**

- The main complexity in the sets for "son" and "daughter" is that in modern Omaha a man generally speaks of his children and addresses them as nisi. A woman speaks of them and to them as "son" and "daughter."

- Here, and in some other cases, speakers sometimes use the inalienable possessive prefix wi-, "my," in front of the term of address to say "My son" or "My daughter," rather than simply "Son!" or "Daughter!" Presumably, this softens the address and makes it more affectionate.

Vocabulary: Nouns

ithādi (-ādi): father

-haⁿ: mother

naⁿ-: mother (addressing)

-zhiⁿge: son

-zhoⁿge: daughter

-nisi: son or daughter (father speaking)

kkúge: box

FIG. 147. ihóⁿ: mother

Vocabulary: Verbs

ābae: go hunting

aíathe: gone away

uthóⁿ: hold, grab, arrest, catch

Speaking Practice

A. Read the following sentences aloud. Then translate the sentences into English. Examples:

Iⁿdādi akʰa ābae aíatha: My father is away hunting.

Íⁿnaⁿha akʰa é shti aíatha: My mother has gone away too.

Izhóⁿge thiⁿkʰe é noⁿ ttíadi gthíⁿ: Their daughter sits at home alone.

1. Dadihá! É zudé akʰa thí e níⁿ a?

2. Uzhéthe gthíⁿ izhóⁿge thiⁿkʰe.

3. Wasékkoⁿ ittóⁿthiⁿ athá, thinísi akʰa.

4. Moⁿsóⁿthiⁿadi ahí, íⁿnaⁿho akʰa.

5. Thiādi kʰe hóⁿbthe zhōⁿ.

6. Nisího! Moⁿgthíⁿ ga ho!

7. Nisího! Wittóⁿbe.

8. Winísi akʰa shínudattí gāxe tta tʰe.

9. Wizhíⁿge akʰa shóⁿge shêhithiⁿ thixé akʰa é thiⁿ kki, uthóⁿ tta akʰa.

10. Ithādi akʰa móⁿzeska ttóⁿ bi ama.

B. Translate the following sentences into Omaha.

1. Mother! I'm going to go. (female speaking)

2. Father! We are unable to push the big black car. (male speaking)

3. In a little while my father came laughing.

4. Your daughter will probably pull the skunk's tail. (addressing a female)

5. Who is your son? (addressing a female)

6. Son! What did I say? (female speaking)

7. My daughter is trying to speak Spanish.

8. "Do well!" the mother told her son.

9. Your mother counted twelve (scattered) cherry trees.

10. Mother! You might drink a little bit of water. (male speaking)

C. The instructor passes out a classroom item to each student and then has the class divide themselves into two groups, the "parents" and the "children." Going around the room, students alternately declare themselves to be one or the other, using the appropriate Omaha term for their own gender. Example:

Nick: Ithādi. ("Father.")

Megan: Izhóⁿge. ("Daughter.")

Sue: Iháⁿ. ("Mother.")

Gary: Izhíⁿge. ("Son.")

D. The "children" sit back a little from the main circle and converse with their nearest "parents" to find out what item the other one has, as the parents inquire the same about their other child. To ask about people, point toward them with your lips. Note that it is perfectly permissible in Omaha to have multiple mothers or multiple fathers. Example:

Sue [iháⁿ, speaking to Megan, pointing with her lips to Gary]: Zhoⁿgehá, wizhíⁿge akʰa idādoⁿ athíⁿ a? ("Daughter, what does my son have?")

Megan: Naⁿhá, thizhíⁿge akʰa ttehé wiⁿ athíⁿ. . . . Naⁿhá, iⁿdādi akʰa idādoⁿ athíⁿ a? ("Mother, your son has a spoon. . . . Mother, what does my father have?")

Sue: Zhoⁿgehá, thiādi akʰa kkúge wiⁿ athíⁿ. ("Daughter, your father has a box.")

E. The instructor has the "children" stand up and walk around their "parents." The parents have the children bring them items or give items to other parents. In every case the students address each other by the appropriate kinship term. Example:

Wagōⁿze: Nisího wôgithe, noⁿzhíⁿ i ga ho! Thiādi, thiháⁿ mégoⁿ, égaxe moⁿthíⁿ i ga ho! Edādoⁿshte thinā tʰe, égoⁿ ʔí i ga! ("Children, all of you, stand up! Walk around your fathers and your mothers! Whatever they ask of you, give it to them!")

Nick: Dúda! Nisího, gí ga ho! ("Child, come here!")

Gary: Hó! Dadího, idādoⁿx̌ti shkōⁿna? ("Yes. Father, do you want something?")

Nick: Nisího, thiháⁿ akʰa kkúge wiⁿ gōⁿtha, ebthégoⁿ. Égoⁿ duáthoⁿ ʔí ga ho! ("Child, I think your mother wants a box. So give her this one!")

Gary: Hó, Dadího. . . . Naⁿhó, kkúge wiⁿ shkōⁿna thoⁿ, Gá! gáthoⁿ wiʔí. ("Yes, Father. . . . Mother, the box you wanted, Here! I give it to you.")

Sue: Há, Zhiⁿgehá, égoⁿ kkōⁿbtha. Házhiⁿga shti athíⁿ gí moⁿthíⁿ a! ("Yes, Son, that's what I want. Get me some string too!")

16.3 SIBLINGS

	male's	female's
elder brother	**-zhiⁿthe**	**-ttinu**
younger brother	**-soⁿge**	**-soⁿge**
elder sister	**-ttoⁿge**	**-zhoⁿthe**
younger sister	**-ttoⁿge**	**-ttoⁿge**

· In English we have two kinds of siblings, distinguished only by their gender, as "brother" or "sister." Some languages such as Japanese distinguish four kinds of siblings, depending on whether they are younger or older than the reference person. Thus in Japan you might have an "elder brother," a "younger brother," an "elder sister," and a "younger sister," as four distinct classes of sibling.

· In Omaha and its Mississippi Valley Siouan relatives, up to eight different types of sibling may be recognized. In addition to distinguishing by the sibling's gender and by whether older or younger than the reference person, the reference person's own gender is also a factor. My relationship to my elder male sibling differs depending on whether I myself am male or female, and the kinship term I call him by may also differ accordingly.

· In Omaha only five distinct sibling categories are actually used: zhiⁿthe, zhoⁿthe, ttinu, soⁿge, and ttoⁿge.

· The zhiⁿthe and zhoⁿthe terms are used to refer to your elder sibling of the same gender you are. If you are male and have an elder brother, then he is your zhiⁿthe. If you are female and have an elder sister, then she is your zhoⁿthe.

· If you are female and have an elder brother, he is your ttinu.

· Your younger brother is your soⁿge, regardless of whether you yourself are male or female.

· If you are female, your ttoⁿge is your younger sister. If you are male, any sister you have is your ttoⁿge.

Vocabulary: Nouns

-zhiⁿthe: elder brother of a male

-zhoⁿthe: elder sister of a female

-ttinu: elder brother of a female

-soⁿge: younger brother

-ttoⁿge: sister of a male, younger sister of a female

umóⁿthiⁿkka: year

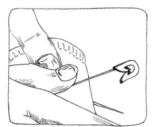

FIG. 148. wabátʰe: sewing

Vocabulary: Verbs

wabátʰe: sewing, to sew

zhūgthe: together, accompany, be with

Speaking Practice

A. Read the following sentences aloud. Then translate the sentences into English. Examples:

Izhíⁿthe ama ābae athá: His older brothers went hunting.

Wittínu akʰa é zhūgthe athá: My older brother went with him.

Wittóⁿge ttíadi wabátʰe gthíⁿ ama: My younger sisters sit at home sewing.

1. Núzhiⁿga akʰa ittóⁿge zhūgthe athá bi ama, wēahidatta.

2. Soⁿgehá! Maⁿčʰúska ānoⁿ a?

3. Ttigóⁿho! Thizhíⁿthe ama nishúde kkóⁿgadi noⁿzhíⁿ a?

4. "Wittóⁿge akʰa ǧthabé tʰe āna. Égoⁿ ppāx̱e ubthíʼage," á, núzhíⁿga akʰa.

5. Zhoⁿthehá! Wamóskex̌ude noⁿbé noⁿbá ttaní tʰe uázhi tta miⁿkʰe.

6. Ttoⁿgého! Thêakʰa atʰí bi ama.

7. Égithe, isóⁿge akʰa thinóⁿtʰe tte.

8. Thisóⁿge akʰa watʰátʰa bazhi.

9. "Wittóⁿge akʰa ux̌pé thoⁿ itʰétha," á, ikkóⁿ akʰa.

10. Ittínu akʰa ābae nóⁿ, ebthégoⁿ.

B. Translate the following sentences into Omaha.

1. Younger brother! What is it like outdoors today? (male addressing)

2. "My elder brother asked for the book," said the girl.

3. My younger sister has a puppy in her backpack.

4. His elder brother took the (round) ball.

5. "My elder sister was following the trail," said the woman.

6. Younger brother! How do you say "Superman" in Omaha? (female addressing)

7. Grandfather! Tell your elder sister to stand up!

8. Younger sister! Write your name! (male addressing)

9. The baby was carried by her elder sister.

10. My elder brother gathers the scattered bullets. (female speaking)

C. In this exercise the students are all brothers and sisters, and the instructor is their parent. The instructor goes around the class asking each student's age: Umónⁿthiⁿkka ānoⁿ aníⁿ a? The students will tell their age: Umóⁿthiⁿkka agthíⁿshoⁿkka abthíⁿ, or make up a more suitable one if their real age is too high for their counting knowledge. The two students sitting nearest then declare their relationship to the first student: Shêakʰa wizhóⁿthe akʰé ("This is my older sister") or Ttoⁿgehá, thizhíⁿgaẋči! ("Little sister, you're so young!") or Zhiⁿthého, thinóⁿatč! ("Elder brother, you're sure old!").

D. The instructor calls random pairs of the students to the front and asks one of them who the other one is. The one asked may first have to inquire again about the other one's age. Example:

Wagōⁿze: Nisího, shêakʰa ebé a? ("Child, who is this?")

Zoe [to Morton]: Umóⁿthiⁿkka ānoⁿ aníⁿ a? ("How old are you?")

Morton [to Zoe]: Umóⁿthiⁿkka gthêboⁿnóⁿba-kkiédi-sháppe abthíⁿ. ("I'm twenty-six.")

Zoe: Dadihá, thêakʰa thinísi, wittínu akʰé. ("Father, this is your son, my elder brother.")

E. Finally, the students mill about, speaking only in Omaha, all attempting to establish their sibling relationships with every other student in class.

16.4 UNCLES AND AUNTS, NIECES AND NEPHEWS

	mother's	father's
brother	-negi	ithādi (-ādi)
sister	-haⁿ/naⁿ-	-ttimi

- In English our father's brother is our "uncle," and our mother's sister is our "aunt." In Omaha and its Mississippi Valley Siouan relatives, this is not the case. In their perspective, our father and all his brothers form a set, each of whom is our "father." Likewise, our mother and all her sisters form another set, each of whom is our "mother." Our father's brother is also our "father," and our mother's sister is also our "mother."

- If you are a man, any child of one of your brothers is also your own son or daughter. If you are a woman, any child of one of your sisters is your own as well.

- Any child of either your "mother" or your "father" is also your own sibling. This means that many of the people we would call "cousins" in English would be our brothers and sisters in Omaha.

- These rules are recursive. This means that in Omaha you can have any number of brothers and sisters and sons and daughters and grandchildren that you never met before, even if you are an only child who has always been celibate.

- In Omaha, our "uncle," negi, is strictly our mother's brother. Our "aunt," ttimi, is strictly our father's sister. These terms apply very broadly too, however, since the scope of "mother," "brother," "father," or "sister" is practically unlimited.

- All male-line descendants of our "uncle," negi—his son or his son's son, for example—are also negi or "uncle" to us.

	uncle's	aunt's
nephew	**-tto^{n}shka**	**-ttushka**
niece	**-ttizho^n**	**-ttuzho^{n}ge**

- In English we have "nieces" and "nephews." In Omaha, we have four categories, depending on whether the niece or nephew is being viewed from the perspective of an uncle or an aunt.

Vocabulary: Nouns

i^{n}čh^{n}gawathathe: cheese, "mouse food"

-negi: "uncle," mother's brother

-ttimi: "aunt," father's sister

-tto^{n}shka: uncle's nephew

-ttushka: aunt's nephew

-ttizho^n: uncle's niece

-ttuzho^{n}ge: aunt's niece

Vocabulary: Verbs

ādo^{n}be: look at

āno$^{n'}$o^n: listen to

no^{n}ppéhi: hungry

thikkúthe: hurry

uhá^n: cook

Speaking Practice

A. Read the following sentences aloud. Then translate the sentences into English. Examples:

"Negího!" á bi ama, ittó^{n}shka ak^{h}a: "Uncle!" said his nephew.

Ittími thi^{n}k^{h}e no$^{n'}$ó^n, ittúzho^{n}ge ama: Her nieces heard their aunt.

Wittízho^n ama niúo^n thippí: My nieces are good at swimming.

1. Í^{n}čh$o^n shó^{n}ge wiwítta duáthi^{n}k^{h}e mo^{n}thó^n, thittízho^n ak^{h}a.

2. Dadího! Wahútto^{n}thi^n wiwítta k^{h}e uné mo^{n}thí^n ga ho!

3. Na^{n}há! Ppáho^n a!

4. Í^{n}na^{n}ha ak^{h}a xthabé t^{h}e thawá.

5. I^{n}čh^{n}gawathat^{h}e dūba aní^n kki, wittízho^n ak^{h}a égo^n íbaho^n gō^{n}tha.

6. Ithādi ak^{h}a thippí tte.

7. Thittó^{n}shka thi^{n}k^{h}e uníxide a?

8. Thihá^n wamóske ettá gāxe égo^n, ppó^{n}zhi^{n}ga.

9. Ttimího! Wétta ánoⁿ shpáhiⁿ
   a?

10. Negihá! Hīga wiⁿ uthá i a!

B. Translate the following sentences
   into Omaha.

   1. How is your aunt, your
      father's sister?

   2. Nephew! Come here! (uncle
      speaking)

   3. My mother's brother refuses
      to take his cup.

   4. Niece! Go fish for a card!
      (aunt speaking)

   5. The aunt's niece went
      fishing. "I did not get it," she said.
      "It's your turn."

   6. "I win!" said the aunt, the
      mother's sister.

   7. Aunt (father's sister)! Do you
      see that airplane far over there?

   8. "I don't see it," said the aunt.
      "Where is it?"

   9. Tomorrow we both might
      see it.

   10. "I want to sleep for a little
       while," said my father's brother.

C. In this exercise the students are
   again of two generations, counting off
   alternately. The first will be "uncle" or
   "aunt," depending on gender. The second
   will be the "niece" or "nephew" of that
   person. The third will be the "father" or
   "mother" of the second, the fourth the
   "niece" or "nephew" of the third, the

fifth the parent of the fourth, and so on.
To make an even number, the instructor
may fill in or not. The circle closes when
the first student declares parenthood
over the last, and then the declarations
go back around in the opposite direction,
as each person declares the detail of
relationship to the previous person.
Example:

Tom: Inégi. ("Uncle.")

Aleisha: Ittízhoⁿ. ("His niece.")

Wynn: Iháⁿ. ("Her mother.")

Tony: Ittúshka. ("Her nephew.")

Sam: Ithādi. ("His father.")

Conrad: Ittóⁿshka. ("His nephew.")

Beth: Iháⁿ. ("His mother.")

Kim: Ittúzhoⁿge. ("Her niece.")

Tom: Ithādi. ("Her father.")

Kim: Izhóⁿge. ("His daughter.")

Beth: Ittími. ("Her aunt.")

Conrad: Izhíⁿge. ("Her son.")

Sam: Inégi. ("His uncle.")

Tony: Izhíⁿge. ("His son.")

Wynn: Ittími. ("His aunt.")

Aleisha: Izhóⁿge. ("Her daughter.")

Tom: Inégi. ("Her uncle.")

D. The instructor goes around the circle,
   asking each student who it is sitting
   beside that student, until everyone is
   clear on their relationship. Example:

   Wagōⁿze [to Wynn, pointing with lips
   to Tony]: Ttushpáho, shêthiⁿkʰe ebé
   a? ("Grandchild, who is that sitting
   there?")

Wynn: Wittúshka. ("My nephew.")

E. The students of the younger generation pull their chairs out a bit from the table and interact with their parent and their aunt or uncle. Their parent tells them to look at their aunt or uncle and surmises that they are hungry. The child asks if the uncle or aunt is hungry, and the uncle or aunt says yes and tells what kind of food is favored. The niece or nephew promises to get it or cook it, and the uncle or aunt says to hurry. The child then goes to the item table to fetch the appropriate item symbol and deliver it to the parent's hungry sibling. Example:

Beth: Zhiⁿgehá, thinégi ādoⁿba! Noⁿppéhi, ebthégoⁿ. ("Son, look at your uncle! I think he is hungry.")

Conrad: Hó, Naⁿhó. Negího, noⁿppéthihi a? ("Yes, Mother. Uncle, are you hungry?")

Sam: Hó, Ttoⁿshkáho, noⁿppóⁿhi. Ttaní dūba kkōⁿbtha. ("Yes, Nephew, I'm hungry. I want some soup.")

Conrad: Hó, Negího. Ttaní dūba uáhoⁿ tta miⁿke. ("Yes, Uncle. I'll cook some soup.")

Sam: Thikkútha ga, Ttoⁿshkáho! Noⁿppóⁿhi āttashoⁿ. ("Hurry, Nephew. I'm extremely hungry.")

Conrad [goes to the item table to cook soup, and returns with it]: Gá, Negího. Gáthe ttaní tʰe. ("Here, Uncle. Here's the soup.")

16.5 SPOUSES AND IN-LAWS

	man's	woman's
wife	-gaх̌thoⁿ	
husband		égthoⁿge
father-in-law	-ttigoⁿ	-ttigoⁿ
mother-in-law	-kkoⁿ	-kkoⁿ
son-in-law	-ttoⁿde	-ttoⁿde
daughter-in-law	-ttini	-ttini
brother-in-law	-ttahoⁿ	-shiʔe
sister-in-law	-hoⁿga	-shikkoⁿ

- The "husband" term, égthoⁿge, is irregular. It does not take the prefixes of inalienable possession, but can be possessed as a normal noun; for example, as égthoⁿge wiwítta, "my husband." A husband, perhaps, can be gotten rid of.

- In Omaha your father-in-law and mother-in-law are called by the same name as your "grandfather" and "grandmother."

- Your "son-in-law" and "daughter-in-law" are the same, regardless of whether you are male or female.

- Remember that in traditional Omaha culture, mothers do not talk to sons-in-law, and fathers do not talk to daughters-in-law. These relations may be spoken about but are not directly addressed.

- There is an additional term, "mīwathiх̌e," for daughter-in-law. Our speakers have explained that a woman may use this term in directly addressing her daughter-in-law. Both men and women may say "mīwathiх̌e akʰa" when speaking about their daughter-in-law in her presence, or a woman may address her as "Mīwathiχe"; when the daughter-in-law is not present, they would instead say "wittíni akʰa" when speaking about her.

- What you call your "brother-in-law" or "sister-in-law" depends on what gender you are, as with brothers and sisters or nephews and nieces.

- In the cross-relationship of brother-in-law to sister-in-law, the two use the inalienable possessive "my" form, rather than the standard vocative suffix form, to address each other. Thus, a brother-in-law calls his sister-in-law "Wihóⁿga!" (*not* "Hoⁿgého!"), and a sister-in-law calls her brother-in-law "Wishíʼe!" (*not* "Shiʼehá!").

- Husbands and wives normally address each other as Iⁿshʼáge!, "Old Man!," and Waʼúzhiⁿ!, "Old Woman!," even if they are both young.

Vocabulary: Nouns

égthoⁿge: husband

mīwathiχe: my daughter-in-law

-gaχthoⁿ: wife

-ttigoⁿ: father-in-law

-kkoⁿ: mother-in-law

-ttoⁿde: son-in-law

-ttini: daughter-in-law

-ttahoⁿ: man's brother-in-law

-hoⁿga: man's sister-in-law

-shiʼe: woman's brother-in-law

-shikkoⁿ: woman's sister-in-law

Vocabulary: Verbs

uīkkoⁿ: help someone

Speaking Practice

A. Read the following sentences aloud. Then translate the sentences into English. Examples:

Égthoⁿge wiwítta akʰé: He is my husband.

"Wishíʼe!" á, wihóⁿga akʰa: "Brother-in-law!" said my sister-in-law.

Igáχthoⁿ akʰa ittígoⁿ dóⁿba bazhi: The wife didn't see her father-in-law.

1. Égthoⁿge wiwítta akʰa ābae athá.

2. Awíⁿoⁿwatta thé a, thittígoⁿ akʰa?

3. Ihóⁿga akʰa atʰí.

4. Wigáχthoⁿ akʰa uzhóⁿge kʰe uhá.

5. Shikkoⁿhá! Izházhe thithítta tʰe wabáχu kʰe āthada!

6. Thittóⁿde akʰa wagthábaze shúga baχú a?

7. Nudóⁿ akʰa gí kki, ikkóⁿ thiⁿkʰe ttanúkka thoⁿ ʼí.

8. Ttinihá! Kkinóⁿnoⁿge kʰe nóⁿgethe shkōⁿna?

9. Wittáhoⁿ akʰa uīkkoⁿ ukkíhi tte.

10. Ishíʼe akʰa íⁿʼutʰíⁿ nudóⁿhoⁿga thíⁿ tte.

B. Translate the following sentences into Omaha.

1. I know her sister-in-law.

2. Is that your mother-in-law, wearing the green shawl?

3. My sister-in-law is wearing the brown jacket. (male speaking)

4. Husband! Chase the rabbit!

5. His wife will return in a little while.

6. My father-in-law sang.

7. Brother-in-law! Is it you arriving here? (male speaking)

8. It's me, your son-in-law.

9. Daughter-in-law! Make soup!

10. Her brother-in-law keeps eating it.

C. In this exercise the students are again of two generations, counting off alternately. The first is "father-in-law" or "mother-in-law," depending on gender. The second is the "daughter-in-law" or "son-in-law" of that person. The third is the "father" or "mother" of the second, the fourth the "daughter-in-law" or "son-in-law" of the third, the fifth the parent of the fourth, and so on. To make an even number, the instructor may fill in or not. The circle closes when the first student declares parenthood over the last, and then the declarations go back around in the opposite direction, as each person declares the detail of relationship to the previous person. Example:

Tom: Ittígo^n. ("Father-in-law.")

Aleisha: Ittíni. ("His daughter-in-law.")

Wynn: Ihá^n. ("Her mother.")

Tony: Ittó^{n}de. ("Her son-in-law.")

Sam: Ithādi. ("His father.")

Conrad: Ittó^{n}de. ("His son-in-law.")

Beth: Ihá^n. ("His mother.")

Kim: Ittíni. ("Her daughter-in-law.")

Tom: Ithādi. ("Her father.")

Kim: Izhó^{n}ge. ("His daughter.")

Beth: Ikkó^n. ("Her mother-in-law.")

Conrad: Izhí^{n}ge. ("Her son.")

Sam: Ittígo^n. ("His father-in-law.")

Tony: Izhí^{n}ge. ("His son.")

Wynn: Ikkó^n. ("His mother-in-law.")

Aleisha: Izhó^{n}ge. ("Her daughter.")

Tom: Ittígo^n. ("Her father-in-law.")

D. The students of the younger generation pull their chairs out a bit from the table, and they alone count themselves off by sibling-in-law terms, starting from the first one who declares initially in reference to the first parent-in-law. Again, the count-off goes around the table once, then reverses and goes back around to the beginning. Example:

Tom: Ittígo^n. ("Father-in-law.")

Aleisha: Ittíni. ("His daughter-in-law.")

Tony: Ishí'e. ("Her brother-in-law.")

Conrad: Ittáho^n. ("His brother-in-law.")

Kim: Ihó^{n}ga. ("His sister-in-law.")

Aleisha: Ishíkko^n. ("Her sister-in-law.")

Kim: Ishíkko^n. ("His sister-in-law.")

Conrad: Ishíʼe. ("Her brother-in-law.")

Tony: Ittáhoⁿ. ("His brother-in-law.")

Aleisha: Ihóⁿga. ("His sister-in-law.")

E. The students of the younger generation attempt to find out if their parents-in-law are hungry or otherwise want something (a classroom item on the desk). If the parent-in-law is of the same sex, the younger person can ask directly. Otherwise, the younger person must ask a sibling-in-law who is the child of the parent-in-law to make the inquiry instead. The child then goes to the item table to fetch the appropriate item symbol for delivery to the parent-in-law. Remember never to speak or interact directly with a parent-in-law or child-in-law of the opposite sex.

16.6 CAUSATIVES: THE BASIC CONSTRUCTION WITH -THE

base word		causative form	
bīze	dry (state)	**bīze-the**	dry (action)
má	snow (noun)	**má-the**	it's snowing (action)
noⁿʔóⁿ	hear (action)	**noⁿʔóⁿ-the**	cause to hear (action)
nóⁿge	run (action)	**nóⁿge-the**	run or operate (action)
nóⁿkka	injured (state)	**nóⁿkka-the**	harm or injure (action)
ppāshude	bloody nose (state)	**ppāshude-the**	cause a bloody nose (action)
ppiâzhi	bad, rancid (state)	**ppiâzhi-the**	go rancid (action)
thaʼé	pitiful (state)	**thaʼé-the**	feel pity (action)
thé	go (action)	**thé-the**	send, cause to go (action)
tʼé	die (action)	**tʼé-the**	kill, cause to die (action)
ttóⁿ	have, possess (state)	**ttóⁿ-the**	acquire (action)
x̌óⁿde	bunch, pile (noun)	**x̌óⁿde-the**	gather into a pile (action)
x̌tā	loved, liked (state)	**x̌tā-the**	love or like (action)
zhiⁿgá	small, little (state)	**zhiⁿgá-the**	dwindle, reduce (action)

- A very important verb construction in Omaha is the *causative*. This is formed by appending the verbal ending -the to the end of a base word.

- The base word describes some state of affairs. Most commonly, this is a stative verb (adjective), which tells a quality. But sometimes it can be a noun or an active verb as well. "Snow" and "pile" are usually nouns, but we may also think of them as describing states, such as a snowy landscape, or autumn leaves being piled up in heaps. "Go," "run," and "hear" are usually active verbs, but they can be considered states as well, in the sense that something may be in motion, or that someone is listening to the speaker.

- The causative ending -the generally implies bringing the foregoing state of affairs into being. This can work in either of two ways. Either the state comes about on its own, or somebody does something to cause it. Thus, a shirt may be dry, bīze. But a wet shirt may dry out on its own, bīzethe, or your mom may cause it to become dry by running it through the drier. In this case, she bīzethe'ed the shirt. The causative does not distinguish between intransitive "The shirt dried" and transitive "Your mom dried the shirt." Similarly, zhiⁿgá, "small," is the base for the causative zhiⁿgáthe, meaning either intransitive "dwindle" (something becomes smaller on its own), or transitive "reduce" (someone actively makes it smaller).

- Some causatives may be only one or the other. Máthe, "it's snowing," is probably always intransitive, since it generally just happens, with nobody actually controlling it. Meat that is rancid is ppiâzhi, but if meat goes rancid, you would say ppiâzhithe. On the other hand, if the base word is already an active intransitive verb like "go," then its causative form will be a transitive verb implying that the action is brought about or governed by an agent. Thus, thé, "go," is the base for the causative théthe, "send" or "cause to go," in which somebody does something to cause the thing to go. The active intransitive verb nóⁿge means "run," in the sense that a car or machine runs (not people). It is the base for the transitive causative nóⁿgethe, "run," in the sense of "My father ran the baler."

- The causative construction is also used to describe expected *feelings* one has toward a state of affairs. Thus, if somebody is miserable and wretched, tha'é, then someone else may tha'éthe that person, feel pity for them.

Vocabulary: Nouns

má: snow

mábadi: snowplow

Nibtháska: Platte River

nihóⁿga: spring (of water)

Niskíthettoⁿwoⁿgthoⁿ: Lincoln (city of)

síⁿga: squirrel

FIG. 149. síⁿga: squirrel

ttáshka: acorn

xóⁿde: bunch, pile, heap

FIG. 150. ttáshka: acorn

Vocabulary: Stative Verbs

bīze: dry

nóⁿkka: hurt, injured

ppāshude: bloody nose

ppiâzhi: bad, ugly, evil, rancid

tha'é: miserable, wretched, pitiable

xtā: loved, liked

zhiⁿgá: small, little, young

Vocabulary: Active Intransitive Verbs

FIG. 151. xóⁿde: bunch, pile, heap

máthe: snowing

noⁿ'óⁿ: hear

nóⁿge: running (as a car or machine runs)

ppiâzhithe: go rancid

thé: go

t'é: die

ttóⁿ: have, possess

Vocabulary: Transitive Verbs

noⁿ'óⁿthe: cause to hear

nóⁿgethe: run or operate (a machine)

nóⁿkkathe: injure, cause injury

ppāshudethe: cause a nosebleed

tha'éthe: feel pity for

théthe: send, cause to go

t'éthe: kill, cause to die

ttón̄the: acquire

šón̄dethe: gather into a bunch

xtāthe: like, love

FIG. 152. xtāthe: like, love

Vocabulary: Transitive or Intransitive Verbs

bīzethe: dry out, cause to dry

zhin̄gáthe: dwindle, reduce

Speaking Practice

A. Read the following sentences aloud. Then translate the sentences into English. Examples:

Máthe tta akʰa: It's probably going to snow.

Thinégi non̄ʼón̄tha ga: Make sure your uncle can be heard.

Ttanúkka tʰe ppiâzhithe a?: Has the meat spoiled?

1. Nudón̄ akʰa tté thin̄ t'étha.

2. Ukkítte thin̄kʰé nón̄kkatha, Pón̄kka nú akʰa.

3. Shínuja thin̄kʰé thaʼétha.

4. Kkinón̄non̄ge zhīde kʰe nón̄ga.

5. Nihón̄ga shêhi bīzethe.

6. Nibtháska nishúde kʰe bīzetha bazhi i ga ho!

7. Niskíthettón̄won̄gthon̄tta eshón̄ mátha.

8. Mon̄zhón̄ bīze kʰe águdi a?

9. Ín̄nan̄ha akʰa gāxa ge xón̄dethe thizá.

10. Ebé ppāshudethe a?

B. Translate the following sentences into Omaha.

1. Rabbit acquired some money.

2. Did your mother dry your shirt?

3. The clouds piled up in the sky.

4. Don't pity the bad man!

5. The pile of acorns dwindled away.

6. It was the squirrels eating that reduced the pile of acorns.

7. Don't hit your younger brother and make his nose bleed!

8. If my elder sister is injured, he will feel pity for her.

9. Where exactly did it snow yesterday?

10. Since it snowed, he is running the snowplow.

C. The instructor goes around the table calling on students. The instructor says one of the preceding base words, and the student responds with the causative based on it. Example:

Wagōn̄ze: Bīze. ("Dry, adj.")

Lee: Bīzethe. ("Dry, v.")

Wagōn̄ze: T'é. ("Dead.")

Sharon: T'éthe. ("Kill.")

D. The instructor introduces four gestures to the class. Left hand lying on the table palm up means a state of affairs. Left elbow on table with hand up, palm facing chest, falling to the table with palm up means self-transition to the state. The same thing with right hand karate chopping left hand to the table means transitive transition to the state. Left hand on the table with the back of the open right hand against the forehead means psychic recognition of the state. Turns pass around the class with each student challenging the instructor with a state word while using the state gesture, and the instructor must respond with the appropriate causative and appropriate gesture. Example:

Amber: Má. [Left hand palm up on the table for snow on the landscape]

Wagóⁿze: Máthe. [Left hand drops to the table, as self-falling snow]

Jake: Xǒⁿde. [Left hand palm up on the table as a heap of something]

Wagóⁿze: Xǒⁿdethe. [Right hand chops left to the table to make the heap]

Brett: Tha'é. [Left hand palm up on the table as something pitiful]

Wagóⁿze: Tha'éthe. [Right hand against forehead as emotional reaction to the pitiful thing]

E. Students take turns going around the circle, each one challenging the student on the opposite side with one of the state words in this lesson, together with the state gesture. The student who is challenged must reply with the causative verb built on the state word, together with the appropriate action or reaction gesture. Some causatives may have more than one possible valid gesture.

16.7 CONJUGATION OF THE CAUSATIVE

Subject	Object	Affix	xtā-the	'to like, love'
3rd	3rd		xtā-the	s/he likes him/her
I	3rd	-a-	xtā-a-the	I like him/her
you	3rd	-tha-	xtā-tha-the	you like him/her
we	3rd	-oⁿ-	xtā-oⁿ-the	we like him/her
3rd	me	-oⁿ-	xtā-oⁿ-the	s/he likes me
3rd	you	-thi-	xtā-thi-the	s/he likes you
3rd	us	-awa-	xtā-awa-the	s/he likes us
3rd	them	-wa-	xtā-wa-the	s/he likes them
I	you	-wi-	xtā-wi-the	I like you
I	them	-a-wa-	xtā-a-wa-the	I like them
you	me	-oⁿ-tha-	xtā-oⁿ-tha-the	you like me
you	us	-wa-tha-	xtā-wa-tha-the	you like us
you	them	-wa-tha-	xtā-wa-tha-the	you like them
we	you	-oⁿ-thi-	xtā-oⁿ-thi-the	we like you
we	them	-oⁿ-wa-	xtā-oⁿ-wa-the	we like them

- In conjugating the causative, the final -the is treated as the proper verb. The affixed pronouns are attached immediately in front of -the, and the base word serves only as a qualifier, without any affixes of its own. This means that the conjugation is the same for all causatives.

- The preceding table shows the base forms of the conjugated verb. In actual use, the final -e will take -a grade ablaut in all cases where any other final -e verb would.

- Note that the I-form is a-the, not bthe. The you-form is tha-the, not ne.

- Although the causative-proper verb that is being conjugated starts with a ledh, /th/, it does not merge in front with the affixed pronouns for "I" and "you," as all other ledh verbs do. Early in Siouan history, it may have been shielded by some other initial sound, possibly an initial /h/, that has since dropped away. Thus, the causative conjugation is perfectly regular.

- Omaha recognizes four possible subjects, or agents: "I," "you," "we," and third person (he, she, it, and they). It recognizes five possible objects, or patients: "me," "you," "us," animate "them," and third person (him, her, it, and inanimate them). This means that twenty combinations are theoretically possible for a transitive verb. Some of these do not usually make much sense, such as "you do it to you," "I do it to us," "I do it to me," "we do it to me," and "we do it to us." Scratching from the list these reflexive scenarios, which Omaha handles in a different way, we are left with fifteen possible combinations for any transitive Omaha verb, which are shown in the preceding table.

- Usually, a word that ends in -the after a vowel is a causative. But there are exceptions. A number of common words end in the unrelated morpheme -the, meaning "go."

- Sometimes the causative form of a word may go full-circle, so that it simply becomes a new word of its own and is no longer a causative, even though it retains the causative ending. The active verb shó^{n}the, "spill," is probably an example of this. It looks and feels like a causative, but it actually conjugates at the front: ashó^{n}the, "I spill it," thashó^{n}the, "you spill it." It may once have been a causative that was later reanalyzed as a whole word in itself.

- A causative based on a stative verb may arc back to replacing that stative verb. If we have a stative verb wxy indicating the quality of being X-ish, then the causative wxy-the would mean that the X-ish state comes into being. But if it has come into being, then it is now there, and we are back to indicating the X-ish state, now designated by the new stative verb wxythe, understood as a whole word. This sort of development may be the origin of stative verbs like skíthe, "sweet," and s'ãthe, "sour."

- The accented syllable normally remains the same throughout the causative conjugation. If it is on the first syllable of the base word, or the base word has only one syllable, the accent will be on the first syllable in all forms. If it is on the second syllable, it will be on the second syllable in all forms.

Vocabulary: Nouns

hāthe: clothes, clothing

ttíuzhi: family, household

FIG. 153. hāthe: clothing

Vocabulary: Stative Verbs

skíthe: sweet

s'āthe: sour

Vocabulary: Active Verbs

shóⁿthe: spill

Speaking Practice

A. Read the following sentences aloud. Then translate the sentences into English. Examples:

Oⁿwóⁿtʰiⁿ kki, ppāshudeoⁿtha: When he hit me, he made my nose bleed.

Thinóⁿkka tʰe tha'éwithe: I pity you because you got hurt.

X̌tāwathathe a?: Do you like us?

1. Tha'éoⁿthathe.

2. Ppāshudeathe mazhi.

3. Thittígoⁿ akʰa théthudi théthithe a?

4. Nóⁿkkaoⁿthithe tte.

5. Tha'éawathe tta miⁿkʰe.

6. "X̌tāwithe noⁿ," waóⁿ wa'ú akʰa.

7. Ttéskamoⁿzéni s'áthe tʰe oⁿshóⁿtha.

8. Móⁿga thíⁿkʰe t'éthathe a?

9. Noⁿ'óⁿawathe kkōⁿbtha mazhi.

10. Hāthe ge x̌óⁿdeathe ubthóⁿ bīzeatha.

B. Translate the following sentences into Omaha.

1. We let them be heard.

2. She feels pity for me.

3. You injured them.

4. You are unable to injure me.

5. Rabbit spilled cherry juice, they say.

6. We sent him toward the house.

7. You sent us toward your uncle's place.

8. The whole family likes you.

9. I see your younger sister drying her hair.

10. He will like them.

C. The instructor goes around the class, challenging each student with a state word and an emphatic pronoun. The student should respond with the appropriate causative construction to have the party indicated by the pronoun actualize that state. Note that "wí" and "thí" will be reversed in the interaction. Example:

Wagōⁿze: T'é. Wí. ("Dead. I.")

Garrot: T'éthathe. ("You killed him.")

Wagōⁿze: Ttóⁿ. É. ("Possess. S/he.")

Violet: Ttóⁿtha. ("S/he acquired it.")

Wagṓⁿze: X̌óⁿde. Oⁿgú. ("Heap. We.")

Kat: X̌óⁿdeoⁿtha. ("We gathered it into a pile.")

Wagṓⁿze: Zhiⁿgá. Thí. ("Little. You.")

Shane: Zhiⁿgáathe. ("I reduced it.")

D. The instructor goes around the class again, challenging each student with a state word and two emphatic pronouns, using gestures with the pronouns. The first pronoun is the object pronoun, said with the left hand held palm up toward the speaker. The second is the subject pronoun, stated as the right hand karate-chops the left one down, or is raised with its back against the instructor's forehead. A third person subject will be é. A third person plural animate object, "them," will be é ama. Again, the student should respond with the appropriate causative construction to have the party indicated by the subject pronoun actualize that state upon the party of the object pronoun. Again, "wí" and "thí" will be reversed in the interaction.

E. The students form groups of about four to six, with a deck of cards, and play this as a game. One student is the dealer and deals out five cards each. The person to the dealer's left starts the game by challenging another student as in exercise D. In this game, the person challenged may put the response in the negative, in the future, or ask it as a question if preferred. If that student answers with the correct construction,

the answerer gets to put one card back in the deck, and the turn passes to that person. Otherwise, the challenger must challenge someone else with a different challenge. If all other students have failed on the challenger's turn, the challenger puts back a card and the turn passes next to the person on the challenger's left. If the challenger gives a semantically unreasonable challenge, such as má, or a wí-oⁿgú combination, the victim may respond: Oⁿthóⁿwoⁿxazhi a/ga!, "Don't trick me!," in which case the challenger must accept a card from the undeceived challengee. The first player to lose all cards is the winner.

16.8 THE DATIVE CAUSATIVE: -KʰITHE

wittígoⁿ noⁿ'óⁿ	my grandfather hears it.
wittígoⁿ noⁿ'óⁿ-the	s/he causes my grandfather to be heard.
wittígoⁿ noⁿ'óⁿ-kʰithe	s/he lets my grandfather hear it.

- The dative causative construction has -kʰi- in front of the basic causative -the.

- Affixed pronouns go directly in front of the -kʰithe. As with the basic causative, conjugation is completely regular.

- The base word of the dative causative should be an active verb. The meaning is that one person allows or makes it possible for another person do the verb, so that they do it. So if the base word is to "hear it," then the dative causative means that someone lets someone else hear it.

Vocabulary: Nouns

níabiẋe: beer

wakkóⁿdagi: water monster

Vocabulary: Active Verbs

noⁿʼóⁿ-kʰithe: allow to hear

ẋubékkithe: practice one's mysterious powers

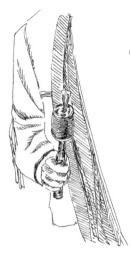

FIG. 154. ẋubé: holy, sacred, mysterious power

Vocabulary: Stative Verbs

ẋubé: holy, sacred, mysterious power

Speaking Practice

A. Read the following sentences aloud. Then translate the sentences into English. Examples:

Thikkóⁿ thiⁿkʰe thatʰé-kʰitha!: Let your grandmother eat!

Winísi akʰa noⁿʼóⁿ-oⁿkʰitha: My child let me hear it.

Núzhiⁿga ma shkāde-wathakʰithe tte: You might let the boys play.

1. Thizhóⁿthe noⁿʼóⁿ-thakʰithe.

2. Izhíⁿge é-kʰitha.

3. Núzhiⁿga thoⁿkʰa wakkóⁿdagi dóⁿbe-wakʰitha bi ama, niáshiⁿga ẋubé akʰa.

4. Unóⁿzhiⁿ bīzeathe-oⁿkʰitha.

5. Nóⁿkkathathe-thikʰithe.

6. Ppāshudeathe-oⁿthákʰithe.

7. Ttanúkka thatʰé-wakʰitha, shínuda thoⁿkʰa.

8. Wagōⁿze akʰa ttáppuskazhiⁿga thiⁿkʰe wagthábaze shúga tʰe dóⁿbe-kʰitha.

9. Shíⁿgazhiⁿga thiⁿkʰe moⁿshtíⁿgeha thoⁿ ābitte-akʰithe.

10. Égthoⁿge wiwítta thiⁿkʰe thaʼéthe-kʰithe.

B. Translate the following sentences into Omaha.

1. She lets us go.

2. He is letting the leader die.

3. The woman is letting her husband practice his mysterious powers.

4. She lets him love her.

5. Let it dwindle away!

6. Don't let him eat it!

7. I let you take the card.

8. You let her read it.

9. She wants to let her son hear Omaha.

10. My grandchild will not let the pile of leaves dwindle away.

C. The instructor goes around the class, challenging each student with an active verb sentence. The student replies by putting the sentence into the dative causative construction. Example:

Wagōⁿze: Dóⁿbe. ("S/he sees.")

Roy: Dóⁿbe-kʰithe. ("S/he allows him/her to see.")

Wagōⁿze: Níabiẖe thattóⁿ. ("S/he drinks beer.")

Nora: Níabiẖe thattóⁿ-kʰithe. ("S/he allows him/her to drink beer.")

D. The instructor again goes around the class, informing each student that someone wants to do something. The student commands the instructor either to allow it or not to allow it. Example:

Wagōⁿze: Gáthudi gthíⁿ gōⁿtha. ("She wants to sit there.")

Matt: Égoⁿ gáthudi gthíⁿ-kʰitha ga! ("So let her sit there!")

Wagōⁿze: Níabiẖe thattóⁿ gōⁿtha. ("He wants to drink beer.")

Ruth: Níabiẖe thattóⁿ-kʰitha azhi a! ("Don't let him drink beer!")

E. The instructor goes around the class, asking the students what they would like to do. A student will answer, and the instructor either allows or disallows it with a command. The student two seats away asks the one sitting next to the original student what the instructor did.

The one asked tells what the instructor allowed or didn't allow. Example:

Wagōⁿze: Lynn, idādoⁿ shkāẖe shkōⁿna? ("Lynn, what do you want to do?")

Lynn: Anóⁿzhiⁿ kkōⁿbtha. ("I want to stand up.")

Wagōⁿze: Hó, égoⁿ ga ho! ("Alright, do that!")

[Lynn stands up.]

Sue: Peter, idādoⁿ gāẖa, wagōⁿze akʰa? ("Peter, what did the teacher do?")

Peter: Lynn noⁿzhíⁿ-kʰitha. ("He let Lynn stand up.")

Wagōⁿze: Peter, idādoⁿ shkāẖe shkōⁿna? ("Peter, what do you want to do?")

Peter: Azhōⁿ kkōⁿbtha. ("I want to sleep.")

Wagōⁿze: Wúẖ! égoⁿ gāẖazhi ga! ("Baloney! don't do that!")

[Peter remains awake.]

Dave: Sue, idādoⁿ gāẖa, wagōⁿze akʰa? ("Sue, what did the teacher do?")

Sue: Peter zhōⁿ-kʰitha bazhi. ("He didn't let Peter sleep.")

16.9 THE CAUSATIVE OF POTENTIALITY: -WATHE

base word			causative form	
āgthe	bother, annoy		**āgthe-wathe**	annoying (quality)
dóⁿbe	see (response)		**dóⁿbe-wathe**	visible (quality)
gōⁿtha	want (response)		**gōⁿtha-wathe**	desirable (quality)
íhe	get through (road)		**ihethiʔa-wathe**	impassable (quality)
íshkoⁿ	move (something)		**íshkoⁿazhi-wathe**	immovable (quality)
íshte	ashamed (response)		**íshte-wathe**	shameful (quality)
ítʔathe	detest (response)		**ítʔathe-wathe**	detestible (quality)
íxa	laugh at (response)		**íxa-wathe**	comical (quality)
nóⁿppe	fear (response)		**nóⁿppe-wathe**	dangerous (quality)
óⁿ	use		**óⁿ-wathe**	usable (quality)
thatʰé	eat		**thatʰé-wathe**	edible (quality)
thé	go		**théthiʔa-wathe**	untraversable (quality)
uthúhi	reach		**uthúhithiʔa-wathe**	inaccessible (quality)
waxthí	scared (response)		**waxthí-wathe**	scary (quality)
xtāthe	like (response)		**xtāthazhi-wathe**	unlikable (quality)

- The causative of potentiality has -wa- in front of the basic causative -the.

- The causative of potentiality is much like the English suffix -able/-ible. Combined with the base word, it makes a stative verb indicating that something cries out for the response suggested by the base. So a grizzly bear might be said to be nóⁿppewathe, "scary" or "dangerous," something that calls forth the emotion of immediate fear, nóⁿppe. Something you can see, dóⁿbe, is visible, dóⁿbewathe, and something you can eat, thatʰé, is edible, thatʰéwathe. Something comical is laughable, íxawathe, from íxa, "laugh at."

- Causatives of potentiality seem to be stative verbs that are normally only used in the third person. We may not have to worry about conjugating them. If we do need to use them for "I" and "you,"

the fudge seems to be either emphatic pronoun plus causative of potentiality, or causative of potentiality plus conjugated form of thíⁿ. Thus, Wí íxawathe might be used for "I'm funny," or Āgthewathe níⁿ for "You're bothersome."

Vocabulary: Nouns

nóⁿppamoⁿttānoⁿha: chokecherries

wamóskeskithe: cookies

Vocabulary: Active Verbs

āgthe: bother, annoy

dóⁿbe: see

gōⁿtha: want

íhe: get through (a possibly blocked road or trail)

íshkoⁿ: move (something)

íshte: embarrassed, ashamed of something or someone

ítʔathe: loathe, dislike, detest

íxa: laugh at

nóⁿppe: fear an immediate threat

óⁿ: use

thatʰé: eat

thé: go

uthúhi: reach

waxthí: frightened, scared, in a phobic sense

xtāthe: like (something or someone)

Vocabulary: Stative Verbs

āgthewathe: bothersome, annoying, troublesome

dóⁿbewathe: visible

gōⁿthawathe: desirable

íhethiʼawathe: impassable

íshkoⁿazhiwathe: immovable

íshtewathe: embarrassing, shameful

ítʼathewathe: loathesome, detestible, despicable

íxawathe: comical

nóⁿppewathe: scary, dangerous

óⁿwathe: usable

thatʰéwathe: edible

théthiʼawathe: untraversable

FIG. 155. nóⁿppewathe: scary, dangerous

uthúhithiʼawathe: inaccessible

waxthíwathe: scary, potentially dangerous, as on a height

FIG. 156. thatʰéwathe: edible

xtāthazhiwathe: unlikable

Speaking Practice

A. Read the following sentences aloud. Then translate the sentences into English. Examples:

Uzhóⁿge kʰe íhethiʼawathe kʰe: The road is impassable.

Íⁿʼe shêthoⁿ íshkoⁿazhiwathe: That rock is immovable.

Égoⁿ éde, thêthoⁿ óⁿwathe, ebthégoⁿ: So it is, but I think this one is usable.

1. Maⁿčʰú akʰa nóⁿppewathe.

2. Thinégi akʰa íxawathe.

3. Thinégi íxawathe akʰa uóⁿsisi.

4. Tté shêhiama dóⁿbewatha.

5. Dóⁿbewatha bazhi.

6. Nóⁿwappewathe.

7. Nóⁿppamoⁿttānoⁿha thatʰéwatha.

8. Wamóskeskithe ettá thoⁿ thatʰéwatha bazhi.

9. Nóⁿppewathe bthíⁿ.

10. Thí nóⁿppewathe.

B. Translate the following sentences into Omaha.

1. Is this egg edible?

2. That (egg we have been talking about) is not edible.

3. You are visible.

4. The stars in the sky are visible.

5. The warriors are scary.

6. He is not funny.

7. Don't laugh! The story is scary.

8. If you eat it, it is edible.

9. The black bear is comical.

10. Is that whistling one a scary ghost?

C. The instructor challenges each student with a base word or construction. The student responds with the corresponding causative of potentiality. Example:

> Wagóⁿze: Dóⁿbe. ("S/he sees.")
>
> Randy: Dóⁿbewathe. ("It is visible.")
>
> Wagóⁿze: Uthúhi thi'á. ("S/he fails to reach it.")
>
> Cindy: Uthúhithi'awathe. ("It is inaccessible.")

D. The instructor asks each student a yes-no question using a base word. The student responds appropriately, using the corresponding causative of potentiality. Example:

> Wagóⁿze: Jeff, ttí ttoⁿga shkóⁿna? ("Jeff, do you want a big house?")
>
> Jeff: Áoⁿ. Ttí ttoⁿga góⁿthawathe. ("Yes. A big house is desirable.")
>
> Wagóⁿze: Jill, Jeff āthigthe a? ("Jill, is Jeff annoying you?")
>
> Jill: Áⁿkkazhi, Jeff āgthewathe bazhi. ("No, Jeff isn't annoying.")
>
> Wagóⁿze: Robert, wés'a wathíx̌thi a? ("Robert, are you afraid of snakes?")
>
> Robert: Áoⁿ, wés'a ama wax̌thíwatha. ("Yes, snakes are scary.")

E. The students form small groups of about two or three and take turns asking each other yes-no questions according to the pattern of exercise D.

16.10 CAUSATIVES AND KINSHIP

Subject	Object	Affix	kʰagé	man's male friend
3rd	3rd		i-kʰáge-the	he has him as a friend
I	3rd	-a-	i-kʰáge -a-the	I have him as a friend
you	3rd	-tha-	i-kʰáge -tha-the	you have him as a friend
we	3rd	-oⁿ-	i-kʰáge -oⁿ-the	we have him as a friend
3rd	me	-oⁿ-	i-kʰáge -oⁿ-the	he has me as a friend
3rd	you	-thi-	i-kʰáge -thi-the	he has you as a friend
3rd	us	-awa-	i-kʰáge -awa-the	he has us as friends
3rd	them	-wa-	i-kʰáge -wa-the	he has them as friends
I	you	-wi-	i-kʰáge -wi-the	I have you as a friend
I	them	-a-wa-	i-kʰáge -a-wa-the	I have them as friends
you	me	-oⁿ-tha-	i-kʰáge -oⁿ-tha-the	you have me as a friend
you	us	-wa-tha-	i-kʰáge -wa-tha-the	you have us as friends
you	them	-wa-tha-	i-kʰáge -wa-tha-the	you have them as friends
we	you	-oⁿ-thi-	i-kʰáge -oⁿ-thi-the	we have you as a friend
we	them	-oⁿ-wa-	i-kʰáge -oⁿ-wa-the	we have them as friends

- The kinship term kʰagé can mean a man's younger brother. Most often, however, it is used more freely to designate any male friend of a man. In modern usage at least, it may serve as the male friend of a woman as well. Unlike most other kinship terms, this one frequently stands alone. But like most of the others, it can take the prefixes of inalienable possession i-, wi-, and thi-, or -ho as a vocative suffix.

- In Omaha the basic causative construction can be used with kinship terms to state a kinship relationship objectively, as a relationship rather than simply naming the relative. The kinship term appears with the third person prefix of inalienable possession i-, and the basic causative ending -the is added after that.

- The kinship relationship indicated is transitive: it has a subject and an object. The relationship indicated is the relationship that the object is to the subject. Thus, "You are my mother" is the wrong way to think about it. The statement "Ihá^{n}withe" means "I have you as a mother." It's something I'm doing to you, not you to me. (Perhaps only a mother can appreciate this perspective.)

- The causative form of a kinship relationship is innately a transitive verb, but it can also be used as a noun to indicate the person whom you have as a relative. A term like ihá^{n}the could also be used to mean "the person I have as a mother."

- In the nineteenth century the United States government established its authority over Indian tribes by interpreting itself as their elder male relative. Thus the president of the United States and the symbol of its central government became their "Grandfather." In nineteenth-century Omaha the word for "president," or "American government," is ittígo^{n}tha i ak^{h}a, "the Grandfather," or "the one they have as a grandfather." Indian agents, or United States government officials, are ithāditha i ama, "fathers," or "the ones they have as fathers."

- Sometimes in informal or modern pronunciation, the -e- at the end of -k^{h}age- is dropped when it is immediately followed by a vowel in the causative form of a kinship relationship. So, ik^{h}ágeathe might sound more like ik^{h}ágathe. However, no vowels are dropped in formal speech.

- The term k^{h}agé by itself means specifically a male friend. The word for a female friend is wihé. The causative construction ik^{h}ágethe may be used for a friendship relationship of either gender.

Vocabulary: Nouns

ithāditha i: Indian agent

ittígo^{n}tha i: president of the United States

k^{h}agé: friend (male)

wihé: friend (female)

Wazhí^n-dathi^n: Washington, DC ("Drunken-Temper")

Speaking Practice

A. Read the following sentences aloud. Then translate the sentences into English. Examples:

Ittó^{n}geathe: I have her for a sister.

Na^{n}há! Izhó^{n}gethithe ak^{h}a wí é bthí^n!: Mother! I am the one who is your daughter!

Ittáho^{n}withe tta mi^{n}k^{h}e: I will have you as a brother-in-law.

1. Ik^{h}ágeawathe.

2. I^{n}sh'áge ik^{h}ágethe ak^{h}a gthí^n.

3. Ittó^{n}gewithe.

4. Wik^{h}áge ak^{h}a mo^{n}kkó^{n}sabe dūba gō^{n}tha tte.

5. K^{h}agého! Águdi thágthi^n a?

6. Ithāditha i ama ittígoⁿtha i thiⁿkʰe āwakkippe athá bi ama, Wazhíⁿdathiⁿ etta.

7. Ikʰágewathathe nā ga!

8. "Ppáthiⁿ āhigi ikʰágeoⁿwatha," á bi ama, Umóⁿhoⁿ gahíge akʰa.

9. Ikʰágewathathe ama hátheza atʰí bi ama.

10. Ikʰágewithe tʰe ūdaⁿ.

B. Translate the following sentences into Omaha.

1. Friends! Bring the soup!

2. Are you my friend?

3. We have you as a father.

4. Do you have her as a grandmother?

5. Supposedly the Indian agents counted the money.

6. The president will talk about it.

7. His friends felt pity for Rabbit, they say.

8. Is he your friend?

9. You might tell me the name of your new friend.

10. "You have me as a friend," said the Ponca man, they say.

C. The instructor challenges each student with a base kinship term. The student responds with the corresponding causative of kinship. Example:

Wagōⁿze: Soⁿge. ("Younger brother.")

Luke: Isóⁿgethe. ("S/he has him for a younger brother.")

Wagōⁿze: Ttuzhoⁿge. ("Niece, of a woman.")

Gwen: Ittúzhoⁿgethe. ("She has her for a niece.")

D. The instructor asks if each student has a particular kinship relationship with another student. The student responds affirmatively or negatively, according to whether this relationship applied in any of the 16.1–16.5 exercises. Example:

Wagōⁿze: Aleisha, Wynn iháⁿthathe a? ("Aleisha, do you have Wynn as a mother?")

Aleisha: Áoⁿ, iháⁿathe. ("Yes, I have her as a mother.")

Wagōⁿze: Bill, Jeff ittígoⁿthathe a? ("Bill, do you have Jeff as a grandfather?")

Bill: Áⁿkkazhi, ittígoⁿathe mazhi. ("No, I don't have him as a grandfather.")

E. The students form small groups of about two or three and take turns asking each other yes-no questions about their kinship relationships according to the pattern of exercise D.

17.1 THI- "BY HAND"

ázhi	other, different	thi-ázhi	changed
bīze	dry (quality)	thi-bīze	dry (make something dry)
bthāska	flat	thi-bthāska	flatten, deflate, let out the air
bthóⁿ	smell (have an odor)	thi-bthóⁿ	smell (sniff a rose)
gthéze	striped	thi-gthéze	streak, make stripes, stitch lines
ppaí	sharp	thi-ppaí	sharpen (a knife)
thiⁿgé	gone, none	thi-thiⁿge	demolish, tear down
thúttoⁿ	straight	thi-thúttoⁿ	straighten (an arrow or wire)
sagí	hard	thi-sági	harden, fortify
ská	white	thi-ská	whiten, bleach, make white
shíⁿ	fat, chubby	thi-shíⁿ	fatten up (a pigeon)
șhná	bald	thi-șhná	pluck (a chicken)
shtóⁿga	soft	thi-shtóⁿge	soften
ttéga	new	thi-ttéga	renew
ttoⁿgá	big	thi-ttóⁿga	enlarge, expand, increase, dilate
ūdaⁿ	good	thi-ūdaⁿ	make better, improve
ûjaⁿ	pretty	thi-ūjaⁿ	decorate
x̌óⁿ	broken	thi-x̌óⁿ	break

- Omaha uses *instrumental prefixes* to turn words indicating a condition into verbs of action. In the preceding table, stative verbs (adjectives) are turned into transitive verbs by adding the instrumental prefix thi-. This is functionally comparable to what the basic causative introduced in 16.6 does.

- The basic causative indicates a transition to the state implied by the base word. There may or may not be an actor who causes the transition, and how the transition takes place is unspecified. The information given is fairly general and vanilla.

- An instrumental prefix, on the other hand, suggests *how* the action takes place. The instrumental prefix thi-suggests that the action is implemented by means of someone's *hands*. "Hand" is the instrumentality suggested by thi-, though it is not always limited to this literally.

- Since state changes brought about by hands imply an agent controlling those hands and directing them intentionally to an end, thi- instrumental prefix verbs are usually transitive. They usually have a subject and a direct object.

- In general, the set of words built from instrumental prefixes is fairly fixed in modern Omaha. When we try to mix and match prefixes with base words (roots), our speakers tell us clearly whether the word exists or not. For them, the entire prefix + base construction is a single word. New words built with instrumental prefixes should be coined only by a fluent native speaker or if there is a clear need.

hébe	part, a portion	thi-hébe	decrease (volume or speed)
híde	bottom, base	thi-híde	lower (bucket), insult
mōⁿshi	up, overhead, above	thi-mōⁿshi	elevate, raise up in the air
nóⁿge	run	thi-nóⁿge	start something rolling

- Sometimes the base word is something other than a stative verb. In the preceding table we have a partitive noun (hébe), two location nouns (híde and moⁿshi), and an active verb (nóⁿge). Again, the instrumental prefix verb based on each of these is a transitive verb.

thi-ʔá	fail, can't do it
thi-béxiⁿ	sweep, rake
thi-bthá	unfold (a blanket), open (eyes or mouth)
thi-bthāze	tear (a page)
thi-dóⁿ	pull
thi-hí	scare up (game), scare away
thi-hóⁿ	lift, raise
thi-kkúwiⁿxe	turn (a doorknob, or a water faucet knob)
thi-nūshi	turn down, dim (a lamp, or the volume)
thi-ppí	skilled, good at doing something
thi-sé	cut, clip (hair)
thi-síhi	clean up (the house)
thi-skí	wring out (socks)
thi-ṣnú	drag, pull, tow
thi-sóⁿde	tighten (a washer)
thi-shpé	pinch off a piece
thi-shtóⁿ	done, finished; release (a prisoner), let go (a bird)
thi-xú	draw, sketch, mark
thi-zé	get, take, pick up, accept, receive
thi-zhá	wash

- Both the causative and instrumental prefixes are very old in Siouan. Some words have evolved their meaning as a unit, beyond the original elements of the compound.

- Many instrumental prefix verbs are so old that their base word no longer exists as an independent word. Sometimes we can reconstruct the meaning of the base word, as with thippí, "skilled," which is founded on an original stative verb ppí, meaning "good." This word no longer exists by itself in Omaha, but it is also found as part of ppiâzhi, "bad," or literally "not good." It still exists in other Siouan languages as well.

- Others are not so easy. Thizé is presumably a thi- word, but it is very old in Siouan. We may never be able to do more than speculate about the original meaning of zé.

- All thi- instrumental prefix verbs conjugate the same way, as ledh verbs. The affixed pronoun comes immediately before the instrumental prefix. The I-form is bthí-, the you-form is ní-, and the I-to-you form is wibthí-.

Vocabulary: Nouns

hébe: part, piece, portion of something

híde: base, bottom

mōⁿshi: up, overhead, above

thītta: dove, pigeon

wāthixoⁿ: toy

zizíkka: turkey

Vocabulary: Stative Verbs

āzhi: other, different

bīze: dry

bthāska: flat

bthóⁿ: odoriferous

gthéze: striped

ppaí: sharp

thiāzhi: changed

thippí: skilled, good at doing something

thiⁿgé: gone, there is none

thúttoⁿ: straight

sagí: hard

ská: white

shíⁿ: fat, chubby

ṣhná: bald

FIG. 157. zizíkka: turkey

shtóⁿga: soft

ttéga: new

ttoⁿgá: big, large

ūdaⁿ: good

ûjaⁿ: pretty

x̌óⁿ: broken

Vocabulary: Active Verbs

nóⁿge: run (a car or a machine, not a person)

thiʾá: fail, can't do it

thibéx̣iⁿ: sweep, rake

thibīze: make dry (we drink all the water from a bucket)

thibthá: unfold (a blanket), open (eyes or mouth)

thibthāska: flatten, deflate, let the air out

thibthāze: tear (a page from a Sears catalog for toilet paper)

thibthóⁿ: smell, sniff (a rose)

thidóⁿ: pull

thigthéze: streak, make stripes, stitch lines

thihébe: decrease (volume or speed)

thihí: scare up (game), scare away

thihíde: lower (a bucket); tease, taunt, seduce, put someone down

FIG. 158. thibéx̣iⁿ: sweep, rake

FIG. 159. thibthá: unfold (a blanket)

thihóⁿ: lift (something easily handled), raise

thikkúwiⁿx̌e: turn (a doorknob, or a water faucet knob)

thimōⁿshi: elevate, raise up into the air

thinūshi: turn down (the volume), dim (a lamp)

thinóⁿge: start something rolling

thippái: sharpen (a knife)

thithíⁿge: demolish, tear down, make off with all the coins

thithúttoⁿ: straighten (an arrow or wire)

thisági: harden, fortify

thisé: cut, clip (hair)

thisíhi: clean, straighten up (the house)

thiská: whiten, bleach out

thiskí: wring out (socks)

thiṣnú: drag, pull, tow

thisóⁿde: tighten (a washer)

thishíⁿ: fatten (a pigeon)

thiṣhná: pluck (a chicken)

thiṣhpé: pinch off a piece

thishtóⁿ: done, finished; release (a prisoner), let (a bird) go

thishtóⁿge: soften

thittéga: renew

thittóⁿga: enlarge, expand, increase, dilate

thiūdaⁿ: make better, improve

thiûjaⁿ: decorate

thix̌óⁿ: break

thix̣ú: draw, sketch, mark

thizé: get, take, pick up, accept, receive

thizhá: wash

FIG. 160. thiṣhpé: pinch off a piece

Speaking Practice

A. Read the following sentences aloud. Then translate the sentences into English. Examples:

Házhiⁿga kʰe thidóⁿ ga!: Pull the rope!

Moⁿbthíⁿ kki, moⁿshtíⁿge ma bthíhi: While walking, I scared up some rabbits.

Ishtá tʰe níbtha tte: Please open your eyes.

1. Waʔú akʰa hiⁿbé tʰe thigthéza.

2. Watʰé thithítta tʰe thiská a?

3. Zizíkka kʰe thiṣhná a!

4. Wizhóⁿge akʰa wāthixoⁿ tʰe thixóⁿ.

5. Thizhíⁿge akʰa ttabé thoⁿ thibtháska.

6. Ttaní uháⁿ tʰe thibthóⁿ.

7. Niáshiⁿga xubé akʰa noⁿbé wôⁿdoⁿ etta tʰe thimôⁿshi.

8. Thithúttoⁿ bi ama.

9. Móⁿhiⁿ tʰe thippái i ga ho!

10. Izhóⁿthe akʰa wāiⁿ kʰe thizhá kki, thiskí thibīze tta tʰe.

B. Translate the following sentences into Omaha.

1. Pull the chair!

2. His friend released the eagle.

3. She is skilled at cutting hair, they say.

4. The dog may scare away the skunk.

5. Don't open your eyes! (addressing one person)

6. Your mother may turn down the light.

7. His father should clean up the house.

8. When the warrior fortifies a door, the leader tears down a wall.

9. My grandchild is unable to sweep the leaves into a pile.

10. The old man made a sketch, then tore the page.

C. The instructor challenges each student with a base word from one of the first two tables in this chapter. The student responds with the corresponding "hand" instrumental prefix verb. While doing so, the student makes a grasping gesture. Example:

Wagóⁿze: Xóⁿ. ("Broken.")

George: Thixóⁿ. ("Break.") [said with a grasping gesture]

D. The instructor asks each student a question using a base word. The student responds appropriately, using the corresponding thi- instrumental prefix verb. Example:

Wagóⁿze: Wāthixoⁿ tʰe xóⁿ. Awádi? ("The toy is broken. Why?")

Shane: Wāthixoⁿ shêtʰe bthíxoⁿ. ("I broke that toy.")

Wagóⁿze: Awádi môⁿ kʰe thúttoⁿ a? ("Why is the arrow straight?")

Carol: Sidādi níthuttoⁿ egóⁿ. ("Because you straightened it yesterday.")

Wagóⁿze: Awádi thītta thiⁿkʰe shíⁿ?
("Why is the pigeon fat?")

Kyle: Wôⁿgithe oⁿthíshiⁿ. ("We all
fattened it.")

E. The students form small groups
of about two or three and take turns
asking each other questions that can
be answered using a thi- instrumental
prefix verb. The one asking gets to set
the scene, but the one answering gets to
choose who did it.

17.2 THA- "BY MOUTH"

bīze	dry (quality)	tha-bīze	drink dry; absorb
gthóⁿ	foul language	tha-gthóⁿ	cuss, say bad things
híde	bottom, base	tha-híde	taunt, jeer at
óⁿba	day, daylight	tha-óⁿba	talk all night until dawn
xubé	holy, sacred	tha-xúbe	praise
zhiⁿgá	little	tha-zhíⁿga	belittle

- Another very old instrumental prefix is
  tha-, which suggests that the action is
  implemented by means of someone's
  mouth. This covers activities like eating,
  drinking, biting, and speaking.

- As with thi- verbs, tha- instrumental
  prefix verbs are normally active and
  frequently transitive. Someone uses
  the mouth to produce the condition
  indicated by the base word.

- All tha- instrumental prefix verbs
  conjugate the same way, as ledh verbs.
  The affixed pronoun comes immediately
  before the instrumental prefix. The
  I-form is bthá-, the you-form is ná-, and
  the I-to-you form is wibthá-.

tha-ʔá	fail at eating, e.g. spit out something too hot
tha-dóⁿ	suck
tha-hóⁿ	thank someone, give thanks
tha-hūni	devour, gobble it all up, leaving no leftovers
tha-xtá	bite
tha-shpé	bite off a piece
tha-shtóⁿ	stop talking, singing, eating, or drinking
tha-ttóⁿ	drink
tha-tʰé	eat, chew
tha-xthí	nibble, e.g. picking meat off a chicken's neck
tha-xthúde	choke (on food)

- As with thi- verbs, many of the base
  words with the instrumental prefix tha-
  do not seem to exist independently.
  However, many of these base words are
  shared between the two instrumental
  prefixes, and that allows us to triangulate
  in on their meaning, just as we can for
  many Latin or Greek roots in English.
  Consider:

ʔa	fail	thi-ʔá	fail at doing	tha-ʔá	fail at eating
bīze	dry	thi-bīze	dry by hand	tha-bīze	drink dry
doⁿ	draw	thi-dóⁿ	pull by hand	tha-dóⁿ	pull by mouth
híde	base	thi-híde	debase by action	tha-híde	debase by speech
hoⁿ	high	thi-hóⁿ	lift up by hand	tha-hóⁿ	elevate by speech
ppi	good	thi-ppí	skilled at doing	tha-ppí	skilled at speaking
shpe	piece	thi-shpé	pinch off a piece	tha-shpé	bite off a piece
shtoⁿ	cease	thi-shtóⁿ	cease doing	tha-shtóⁿ	cease mouth action

- Comparing these two sets allows us
  to distill five more base words, in
  addition to ppi, that no longer exist
  independently. We now know that ʔa
  means "fail," doⁿ means "draw," "pull,"
  or "impel," shtoⁿ means to cease doing
  something, shpe refers a piece being
  taken off something, and hoⁿ probably
  means something like "elevated," a state

that can be brought about either by physically lifting an object with one's hands or by giving thanks to someone—the opposite of thahíde-ing them.

- We already know that híde means the base or bottom of something, but here we can see how that fundamental term can be used with instrumental prefixes to create new verbs meaning literally "to put someone down." If we thihíde someone, we insult them by our actions. If we thahíde them, we put them down by our speech.

Vocabulary: Nouns

gthóⁿ: bad language, name-calling

híde: base, bottom

óⁿba: day, daylight

Vocabulary: Stative Verbs

bīze: dry

x̌ubé: holy, sacred

zhiⁿgá: small, little

Vocabulary: Active Verbs

thaʔá: fail at eating; e.g., spit out something too hot

thabīze: drink dry, or absorb

thadóⁿ: suck

thagthóⁿ: cuss, say bad things

thahíde: taunt, tease, give someone a hard time, mess around with

thahóⁿ: thank someone, give thanks

thahūni: devour, gobble it all up, leaving no leftovers

thaóⁿba: talk all night, talk till daybreak, talk the night away

thappí: fluent, good at speaking, has learned the language

thaṣhpé: bite off a piece

thashtóⁿ: stop talking, singing, eating, drinking

thattóⁿ: drink

thatʰé: eat, chew

thax̌thí: nibble; e.g., picking meat off a chicken's neck

thax̌thúde: choke (on food)

thax̌tá: bite

thax̌úbe: praise

thazhiⁿga: belittle

Vocabulary: Time Words

hôⁿwidetʰoⁿ: midnight

Vocabulary: Unitary Utterances

Sabá!: Beware! (woman's command)

Speaking Practice

A. Read the following sentences aloud. Then translate the sentences into English. Examples:

Shkōⁿna kki, ttá hébe thashpá ga!: If you want, bite off a piece of dried meat!

Sabá! Thax̌thúdazhi a!: Be careful! Don't choke on it!

Wazhíⁿga kʰe náx̌thi thagthíⁿ a?: Are
you nibbling on the chicken?

1. Wôⁿdoⁿ oⁿtháoⁿba.

2. Umóⁿhoⁿ btháppi.

3. Mīkkasi akʰa wahí kʰe hébe
thaṣhpá i egóⁿ, thasníⁿ ígaskoⁿtha.

4. Égoⁿ thax̌thúda bi ama.

5. Mīkkasi akʰa thaʔá.

6. Thahūni bazhi i ga!

7. Nátʰe shkōⁿna kki, óⁿnahoⁿ tte.

8. Wíbthahoⁿ.

9. Oⁿthíthaxuba.

10. Wittúshpa thiⁿkʰe
btházhiⁿge mazhi.

B. Translate the following sentences
into Omaha.

1. The funny uncle teases his
nephew.

2. Rabbit was nibbling some
meat, they say.

3. "Stop eating the food!" his
grandmother told him.

4. It so happened that Rabbit
sucked many of the bones.

5. He must drink all of the milk.

6. If he drinks it dry, he will see
the bottom of the cup.

7. If the dog bites you, you
might cuss.

8. What do you want to drink?

9. Don't pinch it off! Bite it off!

10. We fluent speakers might
talk all night.

C. The instructor challenges each
student with a base word from the
first table in section 17.2. The student
responds with the corresponding
"mouth" instrumental prefix verb. While
doing so, students should place a hand
beside their face and flap their fingers
and thumb together and apart to make a
"talking mouth" gesture. Example:

Wagōⁿze: Gthóⁿ. ("Foul language.")

Connie: Thagthóⁿ. ("Cuss.") [said with
"mouth" gesture]

Wagōⁿze: Xubé. ("Holy.")

Loren: Thaxúbe. ("Praise.") [said with
"mouth" gesture]

D. The instructor asks each student a
question that can be answered with a
"mouth" word. The student responds
appropriately, using a tha- instrumental
prefix verb. Example:

Wagōⁿze: Nátʰe kki, náʔa? ("When you
ate it, did you spit it out?")

Mike: Áⁿkkazhi, gthúba btháhuni.
("No, I ate it all up.")

Wagōⁿze: Náoⁿba? ("Did you talk until
dawn?")

Aubrey: Hôⁿwidetʰoⁿ kki, oⁿtháshtoⁿ.
("We stopped at midnight.")

E. The students form small groups
of about two or three and take turns
asking each other questions that
can be answered using a tha- or thi-
instrumental prefix verb. Using the
corresponding gestures with them is
encouraged.

17.3 NOⁿ- "BY FOOT"

noⁿ-ʔá	fail at kicking; e.g., a soccer ball
noⁿ-bthízhe	knock someone down
noⁿ-óⁿba	walk, run, or dance all night until dawn
noⁿ-stáppi	prance or march, lifting knees high
noⁿ-ṣhnáha	slip while walking or running, or failure in plans
noⁿ-shtóⁿ	cease walking, running, dancing, or kicking
noⁿ-tʰé	kick
noⁿ-ẋpáthe	knock something over by kicking, or bumping into it while walking
noⁿ-zhíⁿ	stand

- The instrumental prefix noⁿ- typically suggests that the action involves someone's *feet.*

noⁿ-btháska	trample something flat; e.g., stomp an aluminum can
noⁿ-btháze	explode underfoot (balloon, milk carton, bubblepack), or a flat tire
noⁿ-thíⁿge	erode away
noⁿ-sági	harden by walking; e.g., a path to school or through snow
noⁿ-sé	cut; e.g., the grass
noⁿ-shábe	cast shade, shaded, or to make something dark by dirtying it
noⁿ-shpí	shell corn
noⁿ-ttóⁿze	bounce off something hard
noⁿ-ttúbe	grind up, milled
noⁿ-ẋtóⁿ	strain; e.g., pour out soup broth against a ladle

- However, noⁿ- is also used for actions directed against a solid *surface,* such as the ground. Some of these may still refer to feet against the ground, but others are abstractions of this concept. To shade something is to cast a shadow against a surface. Shelling corn was probably once

done by trampling on it, and grinding it is done against a flat millstone. Arrows bounce off your shield, and you strain your soup by pouring it out against the surface of your big spoon that holds the good stuff back. These all may be broad extensions of the basic concept of stamping against the ground with your feet.

- Another, and possibly completely different, meaning of noⁿ- may be the idea that an inanimate thing operates under its own power. Things that roll, and any kind of machinery, would fall under this meaning. Thus wagons, cars, lawnmowers, mills, and their effects are all governed by noⁿ- verbs.

- The words formed from the instrumental prefix noⁿ- are often active verbs, as with the thi- and tha- words. This applies particularly with the first set, which specify actions done by foot. But the second set, of actions directed against a surface, are often stative. Some of these can be either active or stative depending on context, since the same word that describes the action can also describe the result of that action. Thus, noⁿttúbe can refer either to the action of grinding corn or to the state of the corn being ground into meal.

- All noⁿ- instrumental prefix verbs conjugate the same way, as common verbs. The affixed pronoun comes immediately before the instrumental prefix.

ʔa	fail	thi-ʔá	fail at doing	noⁿ-ʔá	fail at kicking
bthaze	rip	thi-btháze	tear by hand	noⁿ-btháze	blow out
sé	cut	thi-sé	clip, cut	noⁿ-sé	mow grass
shtoⁿ	cease	thi-shtóⁿ	cease doing	noⁿ-shtóⁿ	cease foot action
ttūbe	grind	thi-ttúbe	grind by hand	noⁿ-ttúbe	mill
tʰe		tha-tʰé	chew, eat	noⁿ-tʰé	kick
ẋtoⁿ	pour	thi-ẋtóⁿ	pour by hand	noⁿ-ẋtóⁿ	strain

- Comparing the noⁿ- set with the previous two allows us to discover several more base words. It confirms that ʾa means "fail," and shtoⁿ means to cease doing something. It also shows that se means "cut," ttūbe means "grind" or "ground," x̌toⁿ means "pour," and bthaze refers to something being ripped or shredded, perhaps explosively. Additionally, we may have a base word tʰe in common for thatʰé, "chew" or "eat," and noⁿtʰé, "kick," though the meaning for this is harder to determine.

Vocabulary: Active or Stative Verbs

noⁿʾá: fail at kicking; e.g., a soccer ball

noⁿbtháska: flatten by trampling or stomping; e.g., an aluminum can

noⁿbtháze: explode underfoot (balloon, milk carton), or a flat tire

noⁿbthízhe: knock someone down (by running into them?)

noⁿóⁿba: walk, run, or dance all night until daybreak

FIG. 161. noⁿóⁿba: dance all night until daybreak

noⁿsági: harden by walking; e.g., a path to school or through snow

noⁿsé: mow, cut; e.g., grass

noⁿstáppi: prance (horses), march (cheerleaders), lifting knees high

noⁿshábe: shade, shaded

noⁿṣhnáha: slip (while walking)

noⁿshpí: shell corn

noⁿshtóⁿ: stop running, walking, dancing or kicking

noⁿthíⁿge: erode (ruts in a gravel road, or roadkill run over until gone)

noⁿttóⁿze: bounce off (of something hard, like a shield)

noⁿttúbe: grind up, milled, mealy

noⁿtʰé: kick

noⁿx̌óⁿ: break, broken (by foot)

noⁿx̌páthe: knock over by kicking, or bumping into it while walking

noⁿx̌tóⁿ: strain, pour out water against a ladle so the rice remains

noⁿzhíⁿ: stand

wačʰígax̌e: dance

Vocabulary: Nouns

kkinóⁿnoⁿgehazízige: car tire

moⁿhíⁿ: grass

móⁿzemoⁿ: bullet

wahába: corn

FIG. 162. noⁿshpí: shell corn

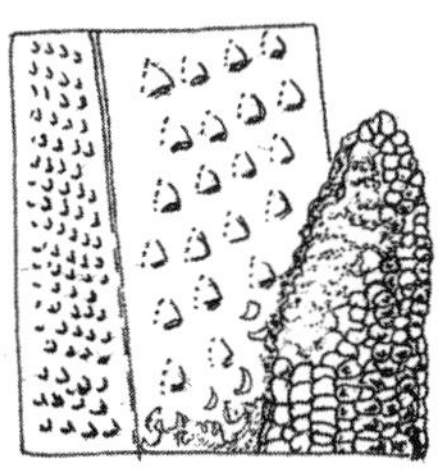

FIG. 163. noⁿttúbe: grind up, milled, mealy

FIG. 164. wahába: corn

Speaking Practice

A. Read the following sentences aloud. Then translate the sentences into English. Examples:

Sabá! Noⁿṣhnáhazhi a!: Careful! Don't slip!

Awádi thanóⁿstappi?: Why are you prancing?

Hó, moⁿhíⁿ kʰe anóⁿse tta tʰe: Yes, I should cut the grass.

1. Wačʰígaxe noⁿóⁿba bazhi i a!

2. Thanóⁿṣhnaha a?

3. Moⁿhíⁿ kʰe noⁿsá ga!

4. Ttóⁿthiⁿ noⁿshtóⁿ ga!

5. Máthe kki, uhé oⁿnóⁿsagi tta oⁿgatʰoⁿ.

6. Uhé kʰedi noⁿthíⁿge kʰe.

7. Móⁿzemoⁿ thoⁿ noⁿttóⁿza.

8. Ttabé ettá thoⁿ thanóⁿtʰe íthagaskoⁿne kki, thanóⁿˀa tta niⁿkshe.

9. Uxpé noⁿxóⁿ kʰe thiháⁿ thiⁿkʰe dóⁿbe kkōⁿbtha mazhi.

10. Ttaní thithítta thoⁿ thanóⁿxtoⁿ kki, thiūdaⁿ tte.

B. Translate the following sentences into Omaha.

1. He stood, shaded.

2. Grind up the corn!

3. The car tire is flat.

4. All the horses pranced.

5. You might shade the child.

6. He bumped into the table and knocked it down.

7. She knocked her younger sister down.

8. She gathered the scattered shelled corn into a pile.

9. Her friends danced all night until daybreak.

10. Don't stomp on my balloon! Deflate it by hand!

C. The instructor challenges the students with an appropriate base word, or a thi- or tha- verb that is built on the same base as one of the noⁿ-verbs. The students respond with the corresponding "foot" instrumental prefix verb. While doing so, they should lightly stamp their feet. Example:

Wagōⁿze: Bthāska. "Flat."

Ttáppuskazhiⁿga: Noⁿbthāska. ("Stomp flat.") [said with a stamp]

Wagōⁿze: Thashtóⁿ. ("Stop talking.")

Ttáppuskazhiⁿga: Noⁿshtóⁿ. ("Stop dancing.") [said with a stamp]

D. The instructor asks each student a question that can be answered with a "foot" word. The student responds appropriately, using a noⁿ- instrumental prefix verb. Example:

Wagōⁿze: Ttaní tʰe thanóⁿxtoⁿ a? ("Did you strain the soup?")

Brett: Áoⁿ, anóⁿxtoⁿ. ("Yes, I strained it.")

Wagóⁿze: Awádi wahába aníⁿ a? ("Why do you have corn?")

Paul: Gasóⁿthiⁿ anóⁿttube tta miⁿkʰe. ("I'm going to mill it tomorrow.")

E. The students form small groups of about two or three and take turns asking each other questions that can be answered using a noⁿ-, tha-, or thi- instrumental prefix verb. Using the corresponding gestures with them is encouraged.

17.4 BA- "BY PUSHING"

ba-ʔú	belch, burp
ba-ʔúde	puncture (a tire or a balloon), drill a hole (in wood)
ba-bīze	mop, make a floor dry, or dry something off with a towel
ba-dóⁿ	push
ba-há	display, show
ba-hé	shove; e.g., a person
ba-móⁿ	file
ba-níuski	hiccough
ba-nóⁿge	roll something by pushing it
ba-sáde	iron (clothes), press (clothes into a suitcase)
ba-sé	saw (wood), shear (sheep)
ba-sí	shoo, herd, drive (animals)
ba-ṣníde	deal out (cards), squirt (diarrhea)
ba-ṣnú	slide by pushing (furniture), reschedule (push the date forward)
ba-spóⁿ	poke, nudge
ba-shéthoⁿ	wipe out, eliminate, write off, pay off a debt; e.g., the restaurant tab
ba-shná	shave off, give a real close haircut, buzz somebody
ba-shóⁿthe	dump, pour out; e.g., your dirty dishwater outside
ba-thóⁿ	thrust up; e.g., with a broomstick to get those spider webs
ba-tʰé	sew
ba-x̌óⁿ	break off; e.g., an antler
ba-x̌thú	pierce; e.g., ears, nose, tongue, or belly button
ba-x̌té	shove into a bundle; e.g., a hay bale or suitcase, corner or corral
ba-x̌tóⁿ	pour; e.g., coffee, one vessel to another
ba-x̌ú	write
ba-zú	point (with a finger)
ba-zhíbe	poke; e.g., someone in the side while they're sitting there

- The instrumental prefix ba- suggests that the action is done by *pushing*.

- Usually pushing requires an actor. Most of these words would be used primarily as active verbs.

- The action of ba- verbs is directed *away from* the actor. This can be any sort of pushing or shoving motion, including self-expulsion of something from the body like a burp, pointing, poking, or piercing holes, pressing things together like ironing clothes or packing a suitcase, driving animals, dumping out water, or even more abstract actions like putting something out for display or pushing a date forward.

- The ba- words often cover actions you would do with *tools*.

- Actions of *sewing* and *writing* seem to take ba- regularly.

- The thi- instrumental prefix verbs sometimes pair with ba- verbs to reverse the action of the latter. Although thi- normally means any action that would be performed manually, it means *pulling*, or directing the action back to the actor when paired with a corresponding ba- verb. Thus, where ba-dóⁿ generically means "push," thi-dóⁿ generically means "pull." The base word doⁿ may not specifically mean "pull" after all, but rather any kind of forced motion toward or away from the actor.

- All ba- instrumental prefix verbs conjugate the same way, as simple stop b verbs. The affixed pronoun comes immediately before the instrumental prefix. The I-form is ppá-, the you-form is shpá-, and the I-to-you form is wippá-.

se	cut	**thi-sé**	clip, cut	**ba-sé**	shear, saw
t^{h}e	jab?	**no^n-t^{h}é**	kick	**ba-t^{h}é**	sew
x̣u	mark	**thi-x̣ú**	draw, sketch	**ba-x̣ú**	write

- Comparing the ba- set with the previous three gives us more insight into our base words. We see that "cutting" can be done in several different ways. Basic cutting by hand, like clipping a lock of hair, is thisé. But shearing sheep or sawing wood with the European sawing style of cutting on the push stroke, is basé, "cut by pushing." Cutting against the ground or with machinery, like mowing the lawn, is no^{n}sé. To that^{h}é, "eat" or "chew," and no^{n}t^{h}é, "kick," we can now add bat^{h}é, "sew." The meaning of the base word t^{h}e is still mysterious, but it might mean something like "jab" or "thrust," as teeth into food, a needle into hide, or feet into anything. We also discover the new base word x̣u, meaning "mark," in matching thix̣ú, "draw," with bax̣ú, "write."

Vocabulary: Nouns

nídushi: pants

wagáx̣e: debt

Vocabulary: Verbs

ba-ʾú: belch, burp

ba-ʾúde: puncture (a tire or a balloon), drill a hole (in wood)

ba-bīze: mop, make a floor dry, dry something off with a towel

FIG. 165. nídushi: pants

ba-dó^n: push

ba-há: display, show

ba-hé: shove; e.g., a person

ba-mó^n: file

ba-níuski: hiccup

ba-nó^{n}ge: roll something by pushing it

ba-sáde: iron (clothes), press (clothes into a suitcase)

ba-sé: saw (wood), shear (sheep)

ba-sí: shoo, herd, drive (animals)

FIG. 166. basí: shoo, herd, drive (animals)

ba-ṣníde: deal out (cards), squirt (diarrhea)

ba-ṣnú: slide by pushing (furniture), reschedule

ba-spó^n: poke, nudge

ba-shétho^n: wipe out, eliminate, write off, pay off a debt

ba-ṣhná: shave off, give a real close haircut, buzz somebody

ba-shó^{n}the: dump, pour out (e.g., your dirty dishwater) outside ba-thóⁿ: thrust up; e.g., with a broomstick to get those spider webs

ba-tʰé: sew

ba-x̌óⁿ: break off; e.g., an antler

ba-x̌thú: pierce; e.g., ears, nose, tongue, or belly button

ba-x̌té: shove into a bundle or bale, corral an animal

ba-x̌tóⁿ: pour out; e.g., coffee, one vessel to another

ba-x̣ú: write

ba-zú: point (with a finger)

ba-zhíbe: poke; e.g., someone in the side

Speaking Practice

A. Read the following sentences aloud. Then translate the sentences into English. Examples:

Zhoⁿbthāska kʰedi ededí shpáʔude tte: Please drill a hole in the board right there.

Awádi ní tʰe shpáshoⁿthe a?: Why did you dump out the water?

Oⁿbázhibazhi a!: Don't poke me!

1. Nídushi ettá kʰe basáde ígaskoⁿtha.
2. Bazú azhi a!
3. Íⁿʔutʰiⁿ basⱒú.
4. Winégi akʰa wagáx̣e bashéthoⁿ.
5. Ttáx̌tihe bax̌óⁿ bi ama.
6. Āshiatta ní tʰe bashóⁿtha ga!

7. Hax̌úde ma basé akʰa wí é bthíⁿ.
8. Íⁿʔe thoⁿ oⁿbánoⁿga, ppamú.
9. Nú ama ttéska thoⁿkʰa basí ukkíhi éde, tté ma bax̌té ukkíhi bazhi.
10. Iⁿshʔáge akʰa noⁿzhíⁿha ettá tʰe bashná azhi, ppá ettá kʰe bax̌thu azhi tta tʰe.

B. Translate the following sentences into Omaha.

1. Did the baby burp?
2. Don't pull! Push!
3. The little boy poked his elder sister.
4. Her sister-in-law sews beautiful shawls.
5. She might show one of her shawls.
6. It's your turn to deal the cards.
7. If you sweep it, I will mop it.
8. I think someone punctured the car tire.
9. Pour the coffee!
10. Are you the one who is hiccuping?

C. The instructor challenges the students with an appropriate base word, or a thi-, tha-, or noⁿ- verb that is built on the same base as one of the ba- verbs. The students respond with the corresponding "push" instrumental prefix verb. While doing so, they should make a gesture for "pushing" by thrusting the palm of their hand forward. Example:

Wagṓⁿze: Bīze. ("Dry.")

Ttáppuskazhiⁿga: Babīze. ("Mop it.") [said with the "push" gesture]

Wagṓⁿze: Thixú. ("Draw.")

Ttáppuskazhiⁿga: Baxú. ("Write.") [said with the "push" gesture]

D. The instructor asks each student a question that can be answered with a "push" word. The student responds appropriately, using a ba- instrumental prefix verb. Example:

Wagṓⁿze: Tom zhoⁿbthāska basé a? ("Did Tom cut the board?")

Nick: Áoⁿ, basá. ("Yes, he cut it.")

Wagṓⁿze: Awádi oⁿshpáhe a? ("Why did you shove me?")

Ryan: Oⁿshpázhibe egoⁿ, wippáhe. ("I shoved you because you poked me.")

E. The students form small groups of about two or three and take turns asking each other questions that can be answered using a ba- or other instrumental prefix verb. Using the corresponding gestures with them is encouraged.

17.5 BI- "BY PRESSURE" OR "BY BLOWING"

Verbs Using the Prefix bi- (*pu-), "by pressure, weight, or rubbing"

bi-béniⁿ	bend by weight or pressure
bi-bíde	mold (dough, clay or caulk)
bi-bīze	dry, mop
bi-bthāska	flatten, smash, deflate
bi-btháze	bust (a blister or a water balloon)
bi-bthízhe	fell; e.g., a tree by leaning against it)
bi-bthúga	flatten into a circular pattie between your hands; e.g., frybread dough
bi-bútta	make into a round ball between your hands; e.g., biscuit dough
bi-gīze	creak
bi-kʰá	wipe
bi-móⁿ	knead (bread)
bi-xóⁿ	break, broken by weight or pressure
bi-xtóⁿ	get fluid by pressing the button or lever; e.g., from a soda machine
bi-sáde	shake out, smooth out, straighten out; e.g., a sheet
bi-shéthoⁿ	destroy by weight or pressure; e.g., sit on a chair and it breaks
bi-shkí	wring out by kneading; e.g., on a washboard
bi-shnáha	sand, make smooth by rubbing

- The instrumental prefix bi- suggests that the action is done in one of several possible ways that generally involve some kind of *pressure*.

- Action by *weight* can take place when someone steps on, sits on, or leans against something. If you cause the metal chair legs to bend because you sat down in the chair, that is bibéniⁿ, where -beniⁿ is the base word meaning "bend." If you flatten something with your weight, that is bibthāska. If you lean against a tree and cause it to fall over, you have bibthízhe'd it (as opposed to knocking somebody down by running into the person, noⁿbthízhe). And if you step on a loose floorboard making it creak, that is bigíze.

- Action by *rubbing* or *kneading*, repetitive working of some material with your hands, is also signaled by bi-. This could mean wiping something dry or wiping up a mess, sanding something smooth, and especially any kind of action to shape dough or clay.

*Verbs Using the Prefix bi- (*pi-), "by blowing"*

bi-hīthe	blow away; e.g., by a person blowing on it
bi-hūttoⁿ	blow (a horn)
bi-χóⁿ	blow up (a balloon or mattress), blow out (a candle)

- Action by *air pressure* is signaled by bi- as well, though this actually seems to be a different instrumental prefix. Examples include biχóⁿ, to blow on a fire, to blow up something like a mattress or a balloon, or blow out a candle; bihíthe, to blow something away; and bihūttoⁿ, to blow a horn, where the base word hūttoⁿ means a loud cry or bellow as made by an animal.

- All bi- instrumental prefix verbs conjugate the same way, as simple stop b verbs. The affixed pronoun comes immediately before the instrumental prefix. The I-form is ppí-, the you-form is shpí-, and the I-to-you form is wippí-.

- Comparing the bi- set with the previous four gives us several more base words. It is apparent that shnaha means "smooth" or "slick," in reference to a solid surface. In contrast, we see that sade means "smooth," in the sense of fabric lying straight without wrinkles, which is a different kind of "smooth." Omaha distinguishes these two meanings, where English does not. The meaning of moⁿ is not so obvious, as "filing" seems hard to relate to "kneading." Perhaps the underlying sense is the idea of "shaping" an object into the form one wants.

Vocabulary: Nouns

nisūde: flute
noⁿdáze: blister
uzhóⁿ: bed
wamóskebimóⁿthishtoⁿ: dough
wanākkoⁿgthe: candle, lamp
weógoⁿbanoⁿχe: window glass

FIG. 167. nisūde: flute

FIG. 168. wanākkoⁿgthe: lamp

moⁿ	shape?	ba-móⁿ	file	bi-móⁿ	knead
sáde	smooth	ba-sáde	press smooth	bi-sáde	smooth out
shnaha	slick	noⁿ-shnáha	slip	bi-shnáha	sand smooth

Vocabulary: Verbs

bi-béniⁿ: bend by weight or pressure

bi-bíde: shape, mold (clay, dough, or caulk, not snow, wood or metal)

bi-bīze: dry, mop

bi-bthāska: flatten, smash, deflate

bi-btháze: bust (a water balloon or a blister)

bi-bthízhe: fell (e.g., a tree by leaning against it)

bi-bthúga: flatten (dough) into a circular pattie between one's hands

bi-bútta: make a round ball (of dough) between one's hands

bi-gize: creak

bi-híthe: blow away (as a person blowing on something)

bi-hūttoⁿ: blow (a horn)

FIG. 169. bihūttoⁿ: blow a horn

bi-kʰá: wipe

bi-móⁿ: knead (bread)

bi-sáde: shake out, smooth out, straighten out (e.g., a sheet)

bi-shéthoⁿ: destroy by weight (e.g., breaking a chair by sitting on it)

FIG. 170. bimóⁿ: knead bread

bi-shkí: wring out (water), wring out by kneading on a washboard

bi-ṣhnáha: sand, make smooth by rubbing

bi-xǒⁿ: break, broken

bi-xtóⁿ: get fluid from a dispensing machine

bi-x̱ōⁿ: blow up (balloon or mattress), blow out (candle)

FIG. 171. bix̱ōⁿ: blow out candles

Speaking Practice

A. Read the following sentences aloud. Then translate the sentences into English. Examples:

Wāthatʰe kʰe bikʰá a!: Wipe the table!

Bihūttoⁿ akʰa Roland akʰé a?: Is it Roland blowing the horn?

Watʰé kʰe ppísade-oⁿkʰitha!: Let me smooth out your skirt!

1. Āgthiⁿ tʰe bibéniⁿ azhi ga!

2. Wamóskebimóⁿthishtoⁿ thoⁿ bimóⁿ egóⁿ, bibída.

3. Weógoⁿbanoⁿx̱e tʰe shpíbize tte.

4. Ppíbthaska bthíʔa.

5. Bix̌tóⁿ ígaskoⁿtha!

6. Thittúshpa ama uzhóⁿ kʰe uóⁿsi bix̌óⁿ a?

7. Aóⁿ, bishéthoⁿ.

8. Wanākkoⁿgthe tʰe ppíx̱oⁿ.

9. Shúde kʰe bihītha ga!

10. Bigīze akʰa thí é níⁿ a?

B. Translate the following sentences into Omaha.

1. Wring it out!

2. I know how to knead dough.

3. Did your blister bust?

4. They say his grandfather felled the tree by leaning on it.

5. I smoothed out the blue blanket.

6. You might wipe that (table nearby).

7. The warriors rubbed their bows smooth.

8. Should they flatten the cookie dough into circular patties?

9. No, they should make it into round balls.

10. Did he blow the flute?

C. The instructor challenges the students with an appropriate base word or another instrumental prefix verb that is built on the same base as one of the bi- verbs. The students respond with the corresponding "weight" or "blowing" instrumental prefix verb. While doing so, they should make a gesture for "weight" by dropping the weight of their upper body supported by their arms on the table. If it is a "blowing" word, they should instead blow into their cupped hand after saying it. Example:

Wagōⁿze: Bamóⁿ. ("File it.")

Ttáppuskazhiⁿga: Bimóⁿ. ("Knead it.") [said with the "weight" gesture]

Wagōⁿze: Hūttoⁿ. ("Animal cry.")

Ttáppuskazhiⁿga: Bihūttoⁿ. ("Blow.") [and blow into their cupped hand]

D. The instructor asks each student a question that can be answered with a "weight" or "blowing" word. The student responds appropriately, using a bi-instrumental prefix verb. Example:

Wagōⁿze: Awádi āgthiⁿ tʰe xóⁿ a? ("Why is the chair broken?")

Half-troll: Āagthiⁿ kki, ppíxoⁿ. ("I broke it when I sat in it.")

Wagōⁿze: Zhoⁿbthāska shpíṣhnaha? ("Did you sand the board?")

Greg: Gasóⁿthiⁿ ppíshnaha tta miⁿkʰ'. ("I'll sand it tomorrow.")

E. The students form small groups of about two or three and take turns asking each other questions that can be answered using a bi- or other instrumental prefix verb. Using the corresponding gestures with them is encouraged.

17.6 GA- "BY FORCE"

ga-ʾá	fail; e.g., at chopping wood
ga-ʾé	dig a hole; e.g., to put your tomato plant in
ga-ʾóⁿsi	bounce; e.g., on a trampoline (not bouncing a ball)
ga-ʾúde	make a hole
ga-bīze	dry something; e.g., hang out laundry to dry in the air
ga-bízhe	shake, snap; e.g., blinking an eye, or shaking out a washrag
ga-bthá	open up, spread out (a bedsheet), bloom (flowers or trees)
ga-btháze	bust, by falling, like a ceramic cat's head
ga-bthóⁿ	make a stink by moving something spoiled through the air
ga-hé	comb (someone's hair)
ga-hīthe	blowing in the wind; e.g., leaves or grass, or drifting in the air
ga-hóⁿ	lift (something heavy, requiring more than one person)
ga-īⁿχe	wheeze (trying to draw breath when knocked out of wind)
ga-kkúge	thump (the sound of something hollow falling)
ga-ppāmoⁿgthe	lower the head to charge, like a bull
ga-thúzhe	slosh
ga-sáppi	lash, whip, snap a towel
ga-sáthu	rattle, shake a gourd
ga-sé	chop
ga-şné	frayed
ga-spé	settle out, like muddy water
ga-súde	trim, prune
ga-shūde	whiteout, blizzard, snowstorm, muddy water
ga-čʰákki	smack, slap someone up, clap
ga-wákʰega	nauseous from environment: seasick, carsick, rollercoaster
ga-wíⁿχe	tilt, bank, as a bird or an airplane
ga-χóⁿ	break by striking
ga-χábe	scrape, skin; e.g., a knee or an elbow from falling

- The instrumental prefix ga- is rich in meanings that suggest *impersonal force.*

- A typical sense of ga- is action performed by *striking,* usually with an implement.

Chopping wood or lashing someone with a whip or a wet towel are classical ga- activities. Destruction resulting from falling or crashing a car are also signaled by ga-. The idea here is kinetic energy converted to damage by impact.

- Another important meaning of ga- is that the action involves impersonal forces in the environment. The action of *wind, weather,* or *free water* fall into the ga- class of verbs. If you are gawákʰega, "seasick," "carsick," or nauseous from a rollercoaster ride, you are sick from environmental forces.

- Lifting something light and easy is thihóⁿ, lifting done by hand. But lifting something very heavy, like furniture or one end of a boat, is gahóⁿ, raising it despite a great weight. In this case, it seems that action taken *against* an external force is also ga-.

- Action that is reflexive or instinctive may also count as ga-. The opening of a bud to become a flower is gabthá, an inanimate thing spreading itself out on its own. But ga- can also be used for the blinking of an eye, the wheezing inhalation of breath after the wind has been knocked out of a person, or even for the standard bovine sequence of a bull lowering its head in readiness to charge. The sense here seems to be that the action is so automatic as to be an impersonal force, having no dependency on the conscious will of the actor.

gačʰákki	she slaps him
áčʰakki	I slap him
tháčʰakki	you slap him
wôⁿgithe oⁿgáčʰakki	we all slap him
óⁿačʰakki	she slaps me
thiáčʰakki	she slaps you
wāgačʰakki	she slaps us
wagáčʰakki	she slaps them
wiáčʰakki	I slap you
awágačʰakki	I slap them
oⁿtháčʰakki	you slap me
wāthačʰakki	you slap us
watháčʰakki	you slap them
óⁿthičʰakki	we slap you
oⁿthígačʰakki	we slapped you
oⁿwágačʰakki	we slap them

- The ga- instrumental prefix conjugates oddly. As with the previous five instrumental prefixes, the affixed pronoun comes in front of the ga-. But in this case, the initial consonant goes away in several of the common forms. To make the I-form, the ga- is replaced by accented á-. For the subject-you form, it is replaced by accented thá-, and for the I-to-you form it is replaced by wiá-. Our speakers have indicated that the we-to-you form alone comes in two different forms, depending on whether we are talking about present or past tense.

- Most of the ga- verbs are not transitive in a personal sense. The exception here is gačʰákki, "to slap someone up," a word that seems to be intrinsically hilarious.

Vocabulary: Verbs

ga-ˀá: fail; e.g., at chopping wood

ga-ˀé: dig a hole; e.g., to put your tomato plant in

ga-ˀóⁿsi: bounce; e.g., on a trampoline (not bouncing a ball)

ga-ˀúde: make a hole

ga-bīze: dry something; e.g., laundry, in the open air

ga-bízhe: snap, shake out (a washrag), blink (an eye)

ga-bthá: open up, spread out (a bedsheet), bloom (a flower)

ga-btháze: bust, by falling, like a ceramic cat's head

ga-bthóⁿ: make a stink by moving something through the air

ga-hé: comb (someone's hair)

FIG. 172. gabthá: bloom

ga-hīthe: blowing in the wind, like leaves or grass

ga-hóⁿ: lift (something heavy, like furniture)

ga-īⁿxe: wheeze, trying to draw breath

ga-kkúge: thump (the sound of something hollow falling)

ga-ppāmoⁿgthe: lower the head to charge, like a bull

ga-thúzhe: slosh

ga-sáppi: lash, whip, snap a towel

FIG. 173. gasáppi: lash

ga-sáthu: rattle,
shake a gourd

ga-sé: chop

ga-ṣné: frayed

ga-spé: settle out,
like muddy water

ga-súde: trim, prune

ga-shūde: whiteout,
blizzard, snowstorm,
muddy water

FIG. 174. gasáthu: rattle

ga-čʰákki: smack, slap someone up, clap

ga-wákʰega:
nauseous
from
environment:
seasick,
carsick, etc.

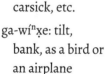

FIG. 175. gačʰákki: clap

ga-wíⁿẋe: tilt,
bank, as a bird or
an airplane

ga-ẋóⁿ: break by striking

ga-ẋábe: scrape, skin; e.g., a knee or an
elbow from falling

Speaking Practice

A. Read the following sentences aloud.
Then translate the sentences into
English. Examples:

Zhóⁿ tʰe gasá ga!: Chop the wood!

Wikkóⁿ akʰa óⁿačʰakki: My
grandmother slapped me up.

Thiáwakʰega?: Are you carsick?

1. Niáshiⁿga ẋubé akʰa
gasáthu.

2. Zhóⁿabe ge gahītha.

3. Ábthoⁿ.

4. Mé kʰedi waẋtá gabthá.

5. Ttenúga ttóⁿga akʰa
gappāmoⁿgtha bi ama.

6. Gashūde kʰedi attóⁿba
mazhi.

7. Zhóⁿ gasé ígaskoⁿthe éde
gaʔá.

8. Tháwakʰega a?

9. Shíⁿgazhiⁿga ama zhoⁿní
gthūba thatʰé kki, gaʔóⁿsisi.

10. Waʔúzhiⁿga akʰa gaⁿẋe
moⁿthíⁿ bi ama.

B. Translate the following sentences
into Omaha.

1. The boy wanted to dig a
hole, they say.

2. Did that aforementioned
boy make a hole?

3. Don't blink your eyes!

4. The water is sloshing.

5. She is pruning the apple
tree.

6. We all lifted something
heavy.

7. I didn't slap you.

8. Did you scrape your knee?

9. I combed my hair.

10. The drum fell with a thump.

C. The instructor challenges the students with an appropriate base word or another instrumental prefix verb that is built on the same base as one of the ga- verbs. The students respond with the corresponding "impersonal force" instrumental prefix verb. While doing so, they should make a gesture for "striking" by whapping a pen against their other hand. Example:

Wagōⁿze: Thiʼúde. ("Make a hole.")

Ttáppuskazhiⁿga: Gaʼúde. ("Make a hole.") [with the "striking" gesture]

Wagōⁿze: Kkúge. ("Box / drum.")

Ttáppuskazhiⁿga: Gakkúge. ("Thump.") [said with the "striking" gesture]

D. The instructor asks each student a question that can be answered with a "force" word. The student responds appropriately, using a ga- instrumental prefix verb. Example:

Wagōⁿze: Awádi xthabé tʰe ûjaⁿ a? ("Why is the tree beautiful?")

Molly: Ásude égoⁿ. ("Because I trimmed it.")

Wagōⁿze: Moⁿdé kʰe tháhoⁿ a? ("Did you heave up the boat?")

Joetta: Gákʰe Tim akʰa gahóⁿ. ("Tim heaved that up.")

E. The students form small groups of about two or three and take turns asking each other questions that can be answered using a ga- or other instrumental prefix verb. Using the corresponding gestures with them is encouraged.

17.7 NĀ- "BY FIRE"

nā-ʼa	fail at trying to burn or freeze something
nā-bize	dry by heat
nā-bthaze	explode
nā-bthoⁿ	smell of fire, incense, cooking, or anything else
nā-daze	sparking (car battery or flint), or cinders
nā-goⁿbe	bright, shining
nā-hegazhi	flare; fire spreading fast; burning pretty good; all lit up
nā-kkade	hot; heat
nā-kkoⁿ	light (noun)
nā-oⁿba	burn all night until daylight
nā-sabe	burnt black, scorched
nā-sade	ironed (clothes)
nā-sage	hardened by heat (stative verb)
nā-sagi	harden by heat (active verb)
nā-skoⁿ	melt; thaw
nā-shta	warm (water)
nā-tʼe	sunburn; die by electrication
nā-ttaze	shining in spots: rhinestones, planetarium, or a woodstove at night
nā-ttube	cooked so tender the meat just falls off the bones
nā-ttubthiⁿ	warped
nā-x̌thiⁿ	fire, flame, burn, as a house
nā-x̌ude	scorched, burnt, like toast
nā-x̌u	brand (cattle)
nā-zi	singe
nā-zhide	red hot (in a fire); ripe fruit that has turned red in the sun

- The instrumental prefix nā- implies the action of *fire, heat,* or *light.* Sometimes the idea of extreme temperature is extended to cover the action of *freezing* as well.

- The previous six instrumental prefixes, thi-, "by hand," tha-, "by mouth," noⁿ-, "by foot," ba-, "by pushing," bi-, "by pressure," and ga-, "by force," are conjugated with the affixed pronouns coming in front of them. These six are called *inner instrumentals* because they sit inside between the affixed pronouns and the base word.

- The inner instrumentals all have short vowels. They do not take the accent unless they are the second syllable. The "fire" instrumental prefix nā- historically has a long vowel, and it takes the accent even if it is the first syllable.

nā-a-x̣u	I brand him
nā-tha-x̣u	you brand him
nā-oⁿ-x̣u	we brand him
nā-oⁿ-x̣u	I got branded
nā-thi-x̣u	you got branded
nā-wa-x̣u	we got branded
nā-wa-x̣u	they got branded
nā-wi-x̣u	I brand you
nā-awa-x̣u	I brand them
nā-oⁿtha-x̣u	you brand me
nā-watha-x̣u	you brand us
nā-watha-x̣u	you brand them
nā-oⁿthi-x̣u	we brand you
nā-oⁿwa-x̣u	we brand them

- A nā- instrumental prefix verb is conjugated by putting the affixed pronouns *after* the instrumental prefix, directly against the base word. Unlike the inner instrumental prefixes we learned about earlier, the nā- is left out in the cold. For this reason, nā- is called an *outer instrumental*.

- Most nā- words do not apply to people, since fire is generally the actor, and since we usually do not like its actions to be applied to us. We only rarely need to conjugate them.

Vocabulary: Nouns

bashté: strawberry

hazízige: rubber

núx̣e: ice

shúde: smoke

waāthix̣oⁿ: toy

wēuhoⁿ: cooking pot

Vocabulary: nā- Verbs

nā-ʼa: fail at burning or freezing

nā-bize: dry something by heat

nā-bthaze: explode

nā-bthoⁿ: smell of fire, incense, or cooking

nā-daze: sparking (car battery or flint), cinders

nā-goⁿbe: bright, shining

nā-hegazhi: flare; spreading fire; burning well; all lit up

FIG. 176. nāgoⁿbe: bright, shining

FIG. 177. nāhegazhi: flare

FIG. 178. nākkoⁿ: light

nā-kkade: hot; heat

nā-kkoⁿ: light

nā-oⁿba: burn all night till dawn

nā-sabe: scorched, burnt black

nā-sade: ironed (clothes)

nā-sage: hardened by heat

nā-sagi: harden by heat

nā-skoⁿ: melt; thaw

nā-shta: warm (water)

nā-tʼe: sunburn; die by heat or electrocution

nā-ttaze: shiny in little spots, like stars in a planetarium

nā-ttube: cooked so tender the meat just falls off the bones

nā-ttubthiⁿ: warped

nā-x̌thiⁿ: fire, flame; burn

nā-x̌ude: scorched

nā-x̣u: brand (cattle)

nā-zi: singe

nā-zhide: red hot (in a fire); ripe fruit turned red in the sun

FIG. 179. nāx̌thiⁿ: fire, flame

Speaking Practice

A. Read the following sentences aloud. Then translate the sentences into English. Examples:

Hôⁿde ttí nāx̌thiⁿ bi amʼ: They say a house burned down last night.

Óⁿbathe nākkadʼatč: It's really hot today.

Zhoⁿbtháska thêkʰe nāttubthiⁿ: This board is warped.

1. Mí thoⁿ nāgoⁿbe.

2. Wamóskeshuga thithítta kʰe nāx̌uda.

3. "Nāwax̣u," á bi ama, ttéska ama.

4. "Nāwathax̣u shkóⁿzhiⁿga," á bi ama, tté ama.

5. Shêhithudi bashté ge nāzhide.

6. Nāthaʼa.

7. Mōⁿze kʰe nāasagi.

8. Mikkáʼe ge móⁿx̣adi nāttaze.

9. Nāoⁿthazi azhi.

10. Ttanúkka shêthoⁿ nāsage a? Nāttube a? Awíⁿoⁿwoⁿ?

B. Translate the following sentences into Omaha.

1. The fire is spreading fast.

2. It (this aforementioned fire) might burn all night until daylight.

3. The land might be burnt black.

4. Around here is the smell of fire.

5. I see the light right there, at that spot.

6. The cooking pot exploded.

7. This plastic toy is warped.

8. It's hot outside.

9. Since the ice melted, the water has warmed. Swim!

10. All around the boy the trees were burning.

C. The instructor challenges the students with an appropriate base word, or another instrumental prefix verb that is built on the same base as one of the nā- verbs. The students respond with the corresponding "fire" instrumental prefix verb. While doing so, they should make a gesture for "fire" by putting their palms up to warm them against an imaginary fire in front of them. Example:

Wagōⁿze: Sábe. ("Black.")

Ttáppuskazhiⁿga: Nāsabe. ("Scorched.") [said with the "fire" gesture]

Wagōⁿze: Noⁿsági. ("Harden by walking.")

Ttáppuskazhiⁿga: Nāsagi. ("Harden by heat.") [with the "fire" gesture]

D. The instructor asks each student a question that can be answered with a "fire" word. The student responds appropriately, using a nā- instrumental prefix verb. Example:

Wagōⁿze: Ttéska thoⁿkʰa nāwathax̣u? ("Did you brand the cattle?")

Gene: Áoⁿ, sidādi nāawax̣u. ("Yes, I branded them yesterday.")

Wagōⁿze: Bashté ge nāzhide a? ("Are the strawberries ripe?")

Sally: Áoⁿ, nāzhide. ("Yes, they're ripe.")

E. The students form small groups of about two or three and take turns asking each other questions that can be answered using a nā- or other instrumental prefix verb. Using the corresponding gestures with them is encouraged.

17.8 MĀ- "BY CUTTING"

mā-'e	slice, cut up; e.g., shaved or thin-sliced meat; whittle, carve
mā-gix̣e	carve, whittle; e.g., slice a roast, fruit, or other food
mā-se	cut
mā-ski	notch, or notches, as for a bowstring
mā-ttube	ground meat
mā-šoⁿ	cut with a knife; e.g., watermelon or bread
mā-x̣u	engrave, carve, notch

- The instrumental prefix mā- implies a *cutting* action, as with a knife.

mā-a-se	I cut it
mā-tha-se	you cut it
mā-oⁿ-sa	we cut it

- Like nā-, the instrumental prefix mā- has historically had a long vowel and takes the accent even if it is at the beginning.

- As with nā-, any affixed pronouns are placed after the instrumental prefix. Thus, mā- is also an outer instrumental.

Vocabulary: Nouns

bashté: strawberry

iⁿčʰóⁿgawathatʰe: cheese ("mouse food")

sákkathide: watermelon (old form)

sakkáid': watermelon (contraction)

watʰóⁿ: pumpkin, squash, melon

Vocabulary: mā- Verbs

mā-'e: slice thin; whittle, carve

mā-gix̣e: carve, whittle; cut meat, fruit or other food

FIG. 180. iⁿčʰóⁿgawathaᵗʰe: cheese

FIG. 181. sákkathide, sakkáidꞏ: watermelon

FIG. 182. watʰóⁿ: pumpkin

mā-se: cut

mā-ski: notches at the end of a bow for attachment of string

mā-ttube: ground meat

mā-x̌oⁿ: cut with a knife; e.g., watermelon or bread

mā-x̣u: engrave, carve, notch

Speaking Practice

A. Read the following sentences aloud. Then translate the sentences into English. Examples:

Házhiⁿga kʰe māase tta miⁿkʰ꞉ I'll cut the rope.

Iⁿčʰóⁿgawathaᵗʰe kʰe māx̌oⁿ ga!: Cut up the cheese!

Zhóⁿ māthax̣u shkō̄ⁿna?: Do you want to carve wood?

1. Sákkathide/sakkáidꞏ thoⁿ māx̌oⁿ a!

2. Sidādi māoⁿx̌oⁿ.

3. Thittízhoⁿ māx̣u.

4. Nudóⁿ akʰa móⁿde ettá kʰe māski māx̣u gisítha bi ama.

5. Māthax̣u kki, x̌thabé tʰe tꞌé tte.

6. Hébe wiⁿ māse a?

7. Māttube thoⁿ athíⁿ gí ga!

8. Shé dūba thizhá, māgix̣a.

9. Māse gō̄ⁿtha kki, môⁿhiⁿ íthe tta tʰe.

10. Watʰóⁿ thoⁿdi iⁿdé māthax̣u a?

B. Translate the following sentences into Omaha.

1. My father whittled a flute.

2. My younger sister engraved it.

3. Don't cut the cheese!

4. She found the ground meat.

5. I didn't slice the bread.

6. Your mother's brother (uncle) should slice the meat.

7. Do you know how to whittle wood?

8. Since you sliced the meat, we ate it.

9. Notch the stick!

10. She is cutting up the edible ripe strawberries.

C. The instructor challenges the students with an appropriate base word, or another instrumental prefix verb that is built on the same base as one of the mā- verbs. The students respond with the corresponding "cutting" instrumental prefix verb. While doing so, they should use a gesture for "cutting" by making a slicing motion with the edge of the right hand across the palm of the left hand. Example:

Wagṓⁿze: X̌óⁿ. ("Broken.")

Ttáppuskazhiⁿga: Māx̌oⁿ. ("Cut up.") [said with the "cutting" gesture]

Wagṓⁿze: Thix̣ú. ("Draw.")

Ttáppuskazhiⁿga: Māx̣u. ("Engrave.") [said with the "cutting" gesture]

D. The instructor asks each student a question that can be answered with a "cutting" word. The student responds appropriately, using a mā- instrumental prefix verb. Example:

Wagṓⁿze: Zhóⁿzhiⁿga kʰe māthagix̣e? ("Did you carve the stick?")

LuAnn: Áⁿkkazhi, Mark é māgix̣a. ("No, Mark carved it.")

Wagṓⁿze: Ttanúkka mā'e níppi a? ("Are you good at slicing meat thinly?")

Rob: Ttanúkka mā'e ppóⁿzhiⁿga. ("I don't know how to cut meat.")

E. The students form small groups of about two or three and take turns asking each other questions that can be answered using a mā- or other instrumental prefix verb. Using the corresponding gestures with them is encouraged.

17.9 MŪ- "BY SHOOTING"

mū-bix̣oⁿ	blow forcefully; e.g., with a bellows
mū-bthaze	explode; e.g., the gun barrel when firing the gun
mū-dada	aching pain; e.g., in the joints, or from falling off a bicycle
mū-gix̣e	make a furrow by shooting; e.g., a shell plowing across the ground
mū-gthoⁿ	stray, wander off from where someone expects you to be
mū-hatheza	come away with minimal injury from being shot at
mū-hega	wound slightly by shooting
mū-hegazhi	loud gunshot; kill many or wound seriously by shooting; run fast
mū-hithe	blow away; e.g., litter from corn with a wheat fan
mū-hoⁿ	shoot all day until nightfall
mū-kkoⁿ	fillip, tap lightly to loosen something, as the lid of a can
mū-kkuge	make a rumble by shooting an arrow against a hollow object
mū-ppa	strong (coffee or cider or peyote tea)
mū-sisi	shooting pain, as spasms in your stomach and innards
mū-s̱hnoⁿ	miss the mark when shooting
mū-x̌ta	peck with the head, as a woodpecker
mū-x̌toⁿ	flow; e.g., water from a water faucet
mū-x̣a	standing up, like ducks on the water, or the comb of a chicken
mū-x̣adoⁿ	bushy haired (person, sheep, or a scared cat)
mū-za	stick up, protrude, in precise order, like fenceposts
mū-zhoⁿ	winnow, sift, strain out

- The instrumental prefix mū- seems to be based on the concept of *shooting*, as with a bow and arrow. This concept extends outward in several ways.
- Any action that involves shooting a gun is mū-.
- A forceful *tapping* action, like a bird pecking or a man tapping a tobacco pouch to loosen the tobacco, is mū-.
- A *directed stream* of fluid, as from a bellows, a fan, or water shooting out of a faucet, is a mū- action.
- *Shooting sensations*, as pain or strong taste that seems to shoot right through you, can be described with mū-.
- Forcing something *through* something else, such as a strainer, is mū-.
- The idea of someone like a child wandering off from where they should be is expressed, perhaps rather humorously, as mūgtho^n, which may mean something like "shooting away in a dizzy-headed manner."

mū-a-ho^n	I shot till nightfall
mū-tha-ho^n	you shot till nightfall
mū-o^n-ho^n	we shot till nightfall

- In another dimension, mū- may derive from the image of shot arrows embedded and sticking up from the ground or a target. Several mū- words, including one also used for "plant fenceposts," are stative verbs that describe something standing up perpendicular to its substrate.

- Like nā- and mā-, the instrumental prefix mū- has historically had a long vowel and takes the accent even if it is at the beginning.
- As with nā- and mā-, any affixed pronouns are placed after the instrumental prefix. Thus, mū- is also an outer instrumental.

Vocabulary: Nouns

ttúska: woodpecker

Vocabulary: mū- Verbs

mū-biхo^n: blow forcefully, as with a bellows

mū-bthaze: explode (a gun, when fired)

mū-dada: aching pain

mū-giхe: make a furrow by shooting

mū-gtho^n: wander away, stray off

mū-hatheza: come away safe from being shot at

mū-hega: wound slightly by shooting

mū-hegazhi: loud gunshot; kill many or wound badly by shooting

mū-hithe: blow away, as with a fan

mū-ho^n: shoot all day until nightfall

mū-kko^n: fillip, tap to loosen something

mū-kkuge: make rumble by shooting against something hollow

mū-ppa: strong (coffee or cider or peyote tea)

mū-sisi: shooting pain in one's innards

mū-ṣhnoⁿ: miss the mark when shooting

mū-x̌ta: peck with the head, as a
   woodpecker

mū-x̌toⁿ: flow, like water from a water
   faucet

FIG. 183. mūx̌toⁿ: flow

mū-x̣a: standing up, like ducks on the
   water, or unruly hair

mū-x̣adoⁿ: bushy haired (person, sheep, or
   scared cat)

mū-za: stick up, protrude, in order, like
   fenceposts

mū-zhoⁿ: winnow, sift, or strain out

Speaking Practice

A. Read the following sentences aloud.
   Then translate the sentences into
   English. Examples:

   Iⁿsh'áge akʰa mūsisi gthíⁿ: The old
     man has pain in his innards.

   Mūhatheza atʰí, nudóⁿ akʰa: The
     warrior returned safely from battle.

   Iⁿgthóⁿga thiⁿkʰe mūx̣adoⁿ gthíⁿ: The
     cat is sitting with its fur on end.

   1. Kkíde mūṣhnoⁿ.

2. Ní kʰedi mūx̣a, mīx̣a ma.

3. Ppáthiⁿ nudóⁿ akʰa
   mūhatheza bi ama.

4. Ttúska akʰa x̌thabé tʰe
   mūx̌tax̌ta.

5. Shíⁿgazhiⁿga akʰa mūgthoⁿ
   bazhi.

6. Iⁿkʰéde kʰe mūoⁿdada.

7. Mūoⁿgix̣a.

8. Kkída bi ama, mūhegazhi.

9. Moⁿkkóⁿsabe mūppa dūba
   shkáx̣e tte.

10. Sidādi mūazhoⁿ éde,
    mūahitha mazhi.

B. Translate the following sentences
   into Omaha.

1. The old man wounded
   Rabbit slightly when he shot him.

2. I will make it rumble (by
   shooting an arrow at it).

3. I heard you shoot until
   nightfall.

4. The gun (barrel) exploded,
   they say.

5. The bushy-haired cat
   jumped.

6. Now water is flowing.

7. You blew forcefully.

8. I'm going to plant
   fenceposts.

9. Tap lightly right here!

10. They have aching pain in
    their hands.

C. The instructor challenges the students with an appropriate base word or another instrumental prefix verb that is built on the same base as one of the mū- verbs. The students respond with the corresponding "shooting" instrumental prefix verb. While doing so, they should use a gesture for "shooting" by jabbing the index finger of the right hand into the palm of the left hand. Example:

> Wagō^{n}ze: Hô^n. ("Night.")
>
> Ttáppuskazhi^{n}ga: Mūho^n. ("Shoot till dark.") [with a "shooting" gesture]
>
> Wagō^{n}ze: Bihíthe. ("Blow away.")
>
> Ttáppuskazhi^{n}ga: Mūhithe. ("Blow away.") [with the "shooting" gesture]

D. The instructor asks each student a question that can be answered with a "cutting" word. The student responds appropriately, using a mū- instrumental prefix verb. Example:

> Wagō^{n}ze: Rory ak^{h}a águdi a? ("Where's Rory?")
>
> Barbara: Rory ak^{h}a mūgtho^n athá. ("Rory wandered off.")
>
> Wagō^{n}ze: Ttážti thi^n thakkíde a? ("Did you shoot at the deer?")
>
> Dan: Áo^n, akkíde éde, mūashno^n. ("Yes, I shot at it, but I missed.")

E. The students form small groups of about two or three and take turns asking each other questions that can be answered using a mū- or other instrumental prefix verb. Using the corresponding gestures with them is encouraged.

18.1 THE WA- PREFIX

Detransitivizing wa-

ʔĭⁿ	*vt* carry (it)	wa-ʔĭⁿ	*vg* pack, freight | *n* sacred bundle
moⁿthóⁿ	*vt* steal (it)	wa-móⁿthoⁿ	*vg* steal, rob
nã	*vt* ask for (it)	wa-nã	*vg* ask for things, beg
ppáde	*vt* butcher (it)	wa-ppáde	*vg* butcher | *n* surgery
ppíʔoⁿ	*vt* repair (it)	wa-ppíʔoⁿ	*vg* fix, repair, maintain
sⁿãthe	*vt* smear (it)	wa-sⁿãthe	*vg* wax, polish
thatʰé	*vt* eat (it)	wa-thátʰe	*vg* eat | *n* food, meal
thawá	*vt* count (them)	wa-tháwa	*vg* count | *n* counting
thigá	*vt* take (it) apart	wa-thíga	*vg* shuck corn
thiwíⁿ	*vt* buy (it)	wa-thiwíⁿ	*vg* shop
thixú	*vt* draw (it)	wa-thíxu	*vg* draw | *n* drawing (activity)
thizhá	*vt* wash (it)	wa-thízha	*vg* wash clothes

- In English, a transitive verb (*vt*) requires the object to be stated explicitly, either the noun it acts upon or a pronoun, like "him," "her," "it," or "them." If no object is mentioned, then the verb is intransitive. Thus if "I ate pie," the verb "ate" is transitive, but if "I already ate," the verb is intransitive, because no object is stated. Omaha works differently. In Omaha a simple transitive verb implies a discrete object, whether or not the object is mentioned. If no object is mentioned, the object is assumed to be "him," "her," "it," or "them." Thus, "Kkóⁿde thatʰá" means "He ate plums," but if we simply say "Thatʰa,'" it means "He ate it," not "He ate."

- To turn a transitive verb into an intransitive verb in Omaha, we need to add the prefix wa- in front of it (*vg*, verb generalizer or detransitivized form of the verb). To say "He ate" in Omaha, we would say "Wathátʰa." In this case, wa- may serve as a generic noun used to reference an indefinite thing or things that we don't need to mention.

- Detransitivized wa- verbs are not necessarily intransitive, however, because they may be repurposed for a different type of object. Thus sⁿathe is a transitive verb that means to smear something, such as wax. If we add detransitivizing wa-, we get wasⁿathe, which means to smear generally, whether wax, grease, paint, or whatever. But if we want to wax the car, then we use this same word, detransitivized with respect to the substance smeared, yet transitive with respect to the object the substance is smeared upon.

- Further, verbs can be used as nouns to discuss their action. In this case a wa- prefix verb will indicate the general activity implied by the verb. Thus, if thawá means "count (them)", then watháwa means the activity of counting. If thixú means to draw or paint something, then wathíxu means the activity of drawing or painting. Similarly, wathízha could mean the activity of washing or doing the laundry as well as the verb meaning to wash a variety of things, and wathát^{h}e could mean the activity of eating. In contrast, if that^{h}é were used as a noun, it would refer to a single discrete action of eating something.

	wa-ppí'o^n	*vg* fix things	wa-thát^{h}e	*vg* eat
I-	a-wá-ppi'o^n	I fix things	wa-bthát^{h}e	I eat
you-	wa-thá-ppi'o^n	you fix things	wa-nát^{h}e	you eat
we-	o^n-wó^n-ppi'o^n	we fix things	o^n-wó^n-that^{h}e	we eat

- A detransitivizing wa- verb should have only a subject, not an object.
- When the base verb is one with a special consonant conjugation for I- and you-forms, this remains for them with a detransitivizing wa- verb, and the detransitivizing wa- is simply tacked to the front: bthát^{h}e, "I eat it," becomes wabthát^{h}e, "I eat."
- When the base verb conjugates in the common way, with a- for "I" and tha- for "you," the tha- still comes after the wa-, but the a- preceeds it. Thus, watháppi'o^n, "you fix things," but awáppi'o^n, "I fix things."
- For the we- form, the o^n- is always placed in front of the wa-. But the nasalization of the o^n- bleeds across the weak consonant /w/ to take over the following vowel. Thus the combination of o^n-wa-[baseverb] becomes o^{n}wó^n-[baseverb].

Nominalizing wa-

'í^n	*vt* carry (it)	wa-'í^n	*n* pack, sacred bundle
basé	*vt* saw (it)	wa-básé	*n* saw
bibthúga	*vt* flatten (dough)	wa-bíbthuga	*n* rolling pin
bthúga	*vs* round and flat	wa-bthúga	*n* hominy
mā̜xu	*vt* carve (it)	wa-mā̜xu	*n* carver
nītta	*vs* alive	wa-nītta	*n* animal
ppáde	*vt* butcher (it)	wa-ppáde	*n* incision
sábe	*vs* black	wa-sábe	*n* black bear
skíthe	*vs* sweet	wa-skíthe	*n* sweets, fruit, dessert, jelly
shí^n	*vs* fat, chubby	wa-shí^n	*n* fat (for cooking)
that^{h}é	*vt* eat (it)	wa-thát^{h}e	*n* food, meal
thawá	*vt* count (them)	wa-tháwa	*n* numbers
thixú	*vt* draw (it)	wa-thíxu	*n* drawing (the picture)
thizhá	*vt* wash (it)	wa-thízha	*n* laundry
t'éthe	*vt* kill (him)	wa-t'éthe	*n* killer
xága	*vs* prickly	wa-xága	*n* burr
zéthe	*vt* doctor (him)	wa-zéthe	*n* doctor
zhi^{n}ga	*vs* small	wa-zhí^{n}ga	*n* bird, chicken
zhīde	*vs* red	wa-zhīde	*n* tomato, ketchup, buffalo berry

- The wa- prefix can also be added to either an active or a stative verb to make a concrete noun. For the *detransitivizing* wa- discussed earlier, the noun-like wa- is used simply to extend the reach of the verb, which remains the head of the word as an action or an activity. But for *nominalizing* wa-, the generic wa- itself becomes the head of its own little noun phrase, with the attached verb serving to qualify it. Here a new noun is created by taking the blank noun wa- and adding a verb that specifies its diagnostic characteristic. Thus a black bear is wasábe, "the black one"; an animal is wanítta, "a being that is alive"; dessert is waskíthe, "the sweet thing"; a saw is wabáse, "the thing that saws"; a killer is watʔéthe, "one who kills"; laundry is wathízha, "stuff to be washed"; a doctor is wazéthe, "one who doctors"; and so on.

- Note that some of the words formed by nominalizing wa- are pronounced the same as their counterparts that are formed from detransitivizing wa-. Thus, waʔíⁿ means packing or freighting things as an activity when formed from detransitivizing wa-, but it means a backpack, "the thing carried on one's back," if built from nominalizing wa-. Watháthᵉe means "food" or "meal," "the thing eaten", if construed as nominalizing wa-, but "eat (things)" if construed as detransitivizing wa-. Detransitivizing wa- makes wathíx̣u mean "draw or paint (things)," but nominalizing wa- makes it mean the finished product: the drawing or painting as the thing drawn or painted. The two elements are the same in each case. The distinction depends on whether we consider the wa- to be the head noun with a verb qualifying it, or whether we consider the transitive verb to be the head of the construction with the wa- noun extending it by extrapolating the force of the verb to indefinite possible objects.
- Note too that Omaha also uses wa- for affixed pronouns meaning animate "them" and "us." These affixed pronouns may be considered specialized examples of detransitivizing wa-. Wanting a personal pronoun for these cases, this use of wa- may have developed to fill the gap, originally implying an indefinite set of people, whether or not including

ourselves, that would be acted upon by the verb.

- The wa- prefix is very old in Siouan. It stands as a completely vanilla noun marker. Its only limitation is that it must attach to a verb.

Vocabulary: Transitive Verbs

ʔíⁿ: pack, carry on one's back

basé: saw, cut by pushing

bibthúga: flatten (dough) by pressing

mā́x̣u: carve

moⁿthóⁿ: steal

nā: ask for, request

ppáde: butcher, slaughter, cut up

ppíʔoⁿ: fix, repair

ṣnáthe: smear, spread, paint, polish, butter

thathᵉé: eat

thawá: count

thigá: take apart (undo braids, or shuck corn)

thiwíⁿ: buy, purchase

thix̣ú: draw, sketch, mark

FIG. 184. thathᵉé: eat

thizé: get, take, pick up, accept, receive

thizhá: wash

tʔéthe: kill

zéthe: doctor, treat (a patient)

Vocabulary: Stative Verbs

bthúga: round and flat

nītta: living, alive

thúkkathiⁿ: bare skin, naked

sábe: black

sithúkkathiⁿ: barefoot

skíthe: sweet

shíⁿ: fat, chubby

x̌ága: prickly, twisty, gnarled

zhiⁿga: small, little, young

zhīde: red

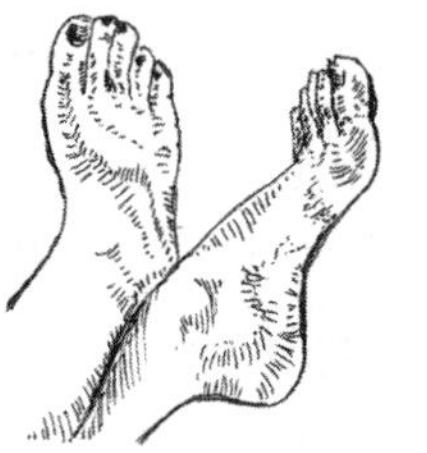

FIG. 185. sithúkkathiⁿ: barefoot

Vocabulary: Nouns

sṇá: scar

waʾíⁿ: backpack

wabáse: saw (the tool)

wabíbthuga: rolling pin

wabthuga: hominy

wamāx̌u: carver

wanītta: animal

wappáde: incision

wasábe: black bear

waskíthe: sweets, fruit, berries, melon, dessert, pudding, jelly

washíⁿ: fat (as for cooking)

watháthe: food, meal

watháwa: numbers

wathíx̌u: drawing or painting (the picture)

wathízha: laundry

FIG. 186. waskíthe: sweet

FIG. 187. wathíx̌u: drawing

watʾéthe: killer

wax̌ága: burr

wazéthe: doctor

wazhíⁿga: bird, chicken

wazhīde: tomato, ketchup, buffalo berry

Vocabulary: Miscellaneous

-shtoⁿ: always doing it

théwathe!: Let's go! (said to one other person)

Speaking Practice

A. Read the following sentences aloud. Then translate the sentences into English. Examples:

Kkinóⁿnoⁿge kʰe waṣnāthe tta tʰe: He should wax the car.

Wihé, wathíwiⁿ théwathe!: Friend, let's go shopping!

Wathíx̌u thix̌ú ga!: Draw a picture!

1. Wazhíⁿga oⁿgútta thoⁿkʰa tháwa ga!

2. Gátʰe sṇá wiwítta tʰe, wazéthe oⁿwóⁿppada egóⁿ.

3. Wathízha xǒⁿdethathe egóⁿ, thizhá a!

4. Wathíga níshtoⁿ i kki, watháthᵉ gí i ga ho!

5. Wasábe thiⁿ doⁿbá kki, mūhegazhi athá.

6. Waʔíⁿ ettá thoⁿ zhiⁿgá; waʔíⁿ wiwítta thoⁿ ttoⁿgá.

7. Môⁿde bixǒⁿ kʰe ppíʔoⁿ tte, wamāxu akʰa.

8. Wabthúga oⁿthátʰa, wikkóⁿ thiⁿkʰedi.

9. Núzhiⁿga shêhitʰoⁿ xtāatha mazhi; shóⁿshoⁿ wamóⁿthoⁿshtoⁿ.

10. Shénuzhiⁿga ama waskíthe, mikkáha, wanā moⁿthíⁿ noⁿ.

B. Translate the following sentences into Omaha.

1. I want to eat a ripe red tomato.

2. He can't fix it; he'll have to buy a new saw.

3. If you shoot an animal, once it's dead, hurry up and butcher it!

4. I don't play barefoot in the hay, because of the burrs.

5. When the killer showed up at the house, they say my grandmother had a rolling pin.

6. If you want to grease your shoes, take some bear fat.

7. You're good at drawing.

8. Say the number "nine."

9. My older brother always likes to polish his car.

10. It's good that he packed stuff to the house.

C. The instructor challenges each student with a base word, and the student responds with the corresponding wa- construction. While doing so, students should use an appropriate gesture. If the construction they envision is detransitivizing wa-, then they should wrap the right hand around the left fist to symbolize a verb governing an object noun. If it is nominalizing wa-, then they should place the left fist on top of the right hand cupped downward to symbolize a noun with a qualifying verb attached to it. Example:

Wagōⁿze: Moⁿthóⁿ. ("Steal.")

Grant: Wamóⁿthoⁿ. ("Steal.") [with right hand over left fist]

Wagōⁿze: Skíthe. ("Sweet.")

Cheryl: Waskíthe. ("Candy.") [with right hand under left fist]

D. The instructor asks each student a question that can be answered with a nominalizing or detransitivizing wa- word. The student responds appropriately, using a wa- noun or verb. Example:

Wagōⁿze: Shêhitʰe sábe tʰe thashtóⁿbe? ("Do you see that black thing over there?")

Will: Áoⁿ. Wasábe, ebthégoⁿ. ("Yes. I think it's a black bear.")

Wagōⁿze: Watʰé níwiⁿ a? ("Did you buy a skirt?")

Pam: Áⁿkkazhi, íⁿčʰoⁿ wabthíwiⁿ bthé. ("No, I'm just now going shopping.")

E. The students form small groups of about two or three and take turns asking each other questions that can be answered using a nominalizing or detransitivizing wa- word. Using the corresponding gestures with them is encouraged.

18.2 THE Ī- PREFIX

Ī- Before a Verb

bamóⁿ	*vt* file (it)	ī-bamoⁿ	*n* file
bethóⁿ	*vt* fold (it)	ī-betʰoⁿ	*n* wrapping, wrapper
díⁿdiⁿ	*vs* rigid	ī-diⁿdiⁿ	*n* brace
gaxáde	*vt* cover (it)	ī-gaxade	*n* cover, lid
nóⁿge	*va* roll	ī-nonge	*n* fare, ticket, gas money
thawá	*vt* count (them)	ī-thawa	*n* counter, chips
thibthóⁿ	*va* smell	ī-thibthoⁿ	*n* perfume, cologne, aftershave
thinóⁿge	*vt* roll (it)	ī-thinonge	*n* wheel
thizhá	*vt* wash (it)	ī-thizha	*n* washcloth, washrag, sponge, soap

- In English we can apply the suffix -er to the end of a verb to make a noun referring to a tool or piece of technology that we use to perform the action. Thus we would immediately understand the purpose of a tool called a pounder, a grinder, a cutter or a grabber. In Omaha we can apply the ī- *prefix* before a verb to get the same result. The ī- prefix can be understood as instrumentizing because it signals the instrument used to accomplish the verb's action, and it may allow the entire construct to be used as a noun. In contrast, the separate and distinct class of instrumental prefixes described in the previous chapter turn words indicating a condition into verbs of action. Instrumental prefixes tell of dynamic instrumentality, while the instrumentizing ī- prefix references the instrumentality of means.

- In the preceding table, bamóⁿ means to file, grind, or smooth something, while ībamoⁿ refers to a file in your toolset (for abbreviations see glossary, chapter 21). If something is díⁿdiⁿ, it is stiff or rigid, while īdiⁿdiⁿ is a brace, used to hold pieces in place while you work on them. To cover something up is gaxáde, but īgaxade is a lid. Thizhá is to wash something, while īthizha is any tool used in washing, whether the washcloth or the soap. Thinóⁿge is to roll something, and īthinoⁿge is the piece that lets you do it, the wheel. To count is thawá, and īthawa is a counter or token used for keeping count of things. If you want to smell nice like flowers, thibthóⁿ, then you may apply perfume or cologne, īthibthoⁿ. Nóⁿge is to roll, as perhaps in a car or a train, and if you want to roll away somewhere, your īnoⁿge, your fare, ticket or gas money, is your instrument for getting there.

- Note that in English -er is also commonly used to indicate the person who performs the action. Thus a worker or a writer is a person who works or writes, and a driver can be either a person who drives a car or an implement like a screwdriver, a piledriver, or a software driver on your computer. In Omaha the instrumentizing ī- prefix is used only for the instrument employed for the action, never for the person who performs it. To speak of the person who characteristically performs an action, you might use nominalizing wa-.

ī- Between a Noun and a Verb

íkki-ī-thidoⁿ	"chin puller"	rein
íkkihiⁿ-ī-gaskebe	"whisker scraper"	razor
iⁿdé-ī-gax̣ade	"face coverer"	veil
mí-ī-thawa	"sun counter"	calendar
ní-ī-thattoⁿ	"thing used to drink water"	cup, glass, dipper
noⁿbé-ī-bikʰa	"hand wiper"	hand towel
ttabé-ī-tʰiⁿ	"ball hitter"	baseball bat
ttāge-ī-gax̣ix̣e	"walnut cracker"	nutcracker
ttoⁿde-ī-noⁿse	"ground cutter"	spade
wazhíⁿga-ī-kkide	"bird shooter"	slingshot
x̌áde-ī-thize	"hay grabber"	pitchfork
zhoⁿbtháska-ī-biṣhnaha	"board smoother"	sandpaper

- Most of the time when instrumentizing ī- is used with a transitive verb, the noun that is the direct object of the verb is placed in front of the ī-. This is the same principle as "screw-driver" in English.

wa- with ī-

wēbamoⁿ (wa-ī-bamoⁿ)	*n* file
wēbax̣u (wa-ī-bax̣u)	*n* pen, pencil, marker, crayon
wēdiⁿdiⁿ (wa-ī-diⁿdiⁿ)	*n* brace
wēthawa (wa-ī-thawa)	*n* counter
wētʰiⁿ (wa-ī-tʰiⁿ)	*n* club, tomahawk, striker

- When instrumentizing ī- is preceded by the wa- prefix, the two prefixes contract to become wē-. Underlyingly, when you see a word beginning with wē-, that is actually the combination of wa- with ī-.

- Most of the time Omaha likes to have either an object noun or the wa- prefix before the instrumentizing ī-. The nine words listed in the first table in this chapter are among the few exceptions in which the ī- may stand bare, and some of these, like "file," "brace," and "counter," also use apparently synonymous alternative forms that have the wa-.

- The wa- prefix here can probably be considered detransitivizing wa-. It appears to replace the object noun for a transitive base verb when no particular object noun is specified.

Vocabulary: Active Verbs

bamóⁿ: file it, grind it, smooth it

betʰóⁿ: fold it

bikʰá: wipe it

biṣhnáha: sand it, make it smooth by rubbing

gaskébe: scrape it

gax̣íx̣e: crack it

gax̣áde: cover it

í ākkigthe: kiss ("put mouths together")

kkíde: shoot at it

nóⁿge: roll (like a cart)

FIG. 188. betʰóⁿ: fold it

FIG. 189. nóⁿge: roll (like a cart)

noⁿsé: cut it (down by your feet)

thattóⁿ: drink it

thawá: count them

thibthóⁿ: smell

thidóⁿ: pull

thinóⁿge: roll it

thizé: get, take, pick up, accept, receive

thizhá: wash it

ubéthoⁿ: wrap it

ugthóⁿ: contain

Vocabulary: Stative Verbs

díⁿdiⁿ: rigid, stiff

Vocabulary: Nouns

ībamoⁿ: file

ībethoⁿ: skin, cloth or paper to wrap
     something in

īdiⁿdiⁿ: brace

īgaxade: cover, lid

īnoⁿge: fare, ticket, gas money

īthawa: counter

īthibthoⁿ: perfume, cologne, aftershave

īthinoⁿge: wheel

īthizha: washcloth, washrag, sponge, soap

íkki: chin

íkki-īthidoⁿ: rein

íkkihiⁿ: chin-hair, whiskers, beard

íkkihiⁿ-īgaskebe: razor

iⁿdé: face

iⁿdé-īgaxade: veil

kkúge: box

mí: sun

mí-īdoⁿbe: clock, watch, o'clock

mí-īthawa: calendar

ní: water

ní-īthattoⁿ: cup, drinking glass

noⁿbé: hand

noⁿbé-ībikʰa: hand towel

ttabé: ball

ttabé-ītʰiⁿ: baseball bat

ttāge: walnut or chestnut

FIG. 190. ttāge: walnut

ttāge-īgax̌ixe: nutcracker

ttibútta: jail

ttōⁿde: ground

ttōⁿde-īnoⁿse: spade

wanóⁿshe: soldier,
     police, jailor, guard

FIG. 191. ttōⁿde-īnoⁿse: spade

wazhíⁿga: bird

wazhíⁿga-īkkide: slingshot

wēbamoⁿ: file

wēbaxu: pencil, pen, marker, crayon

wēdiⁿdiⁿ: brace

wēthawa: counter

wētʰiⁿ: club, tomahawk, striker

x̌áde: hay

x̌áde-īthize: pitchfork

zhoⁿbthaska: board

zhoⁿbthaska-ībishnaha: sandpaper

zhú: skin, flesh

Speaking Practice

A. Read the following sentences aloud.
Then translate the sentences into
English. Examples:

Īdiⁿdiⁿ gátʰedi itʰétha ga!: Set the
brace right there!

Ebé ttabéītʰiⁿ athíⁿ a?: Who has the
bat?

Wēbaxu kʰe oⁿʔí a!: Give me the pencil!

1. Íkki-īthidoⁿ kʰe māsa bi
ama, wat'éthe akʰa.

2. Sidādi mí-īdoⁿbe sháppe
tʰedi oⁿwóⁿthatʰa.

3. Wazhíⁿga-īkkide māgixa,
núzhiⁿga ittígoⁿ akʰa.

4. "Íⁿ! Iⁿdé xagá í āakkigthe
kkōⁿbtha mazhi. Íkkihiⁿ-īgaskebe
óⁿ a!" á, igáxthoⁿ akʰa.

5. Īthizha wiⁿ oⁿʔí a!

6. Wēbamoⁿ gōⁿtha, ittúshka
ttibútta ugthóⁿ akʰa.

7. Ībetʰoⁿ ítha egóⁿ, kkúge thoⁿ
ubétʰoⁿ, ittími akʰa.

8. Iⁿdé-īgaxade íⁿ athá; ttibútta
tʰedi wēbamoⁿ athíⁿ athá, ittími
akʰa.

9. Ittúshka akʰa mí-īthawa
dóⁿbe gthíⁿ bi ama, ttibútta
móⁿtʰadi.

10. Óⁿba thawá gthíⁿ; nóⁿdatta
wēthawa baxú gthíⁿ; íⁿčʰoⁿ
gthêboⁿhíⁿwiⁿ ahí bi ama.

B. Translate the following sentences
into Omaha.

1. His nephew wants a shovel.

2. He left with a pitchfork.

3. Does the carver use
sandpaper?

4. I'm going to buy a
nutcracker.

5. The warrior didn't find his
tomahawk, they say.

6. If they want to get there,
your nephews will have to ask for
gas money.

7. That woman always wears
pretty perfume.

8. The wheel is missing.

9. My sister-in-law won
seventeen chips.

10. Do you have a cup?

C. The instructor challenges each
student with a base verb, and the student
responds with the corresponding ī-
or wē- construction. While doing so,
students should use an appropriate
gesture. If the construction they are
using is simple ī- with no qualifying
argument, then they should make the
right hand into a fist except for the little
finger, which should be cocked back and
curved into a hook. If it is either a wē-
or a [noun]-ī-[verb] construction, then
they should wrap the right hand over the
left fist with the right little finger cocked

back in a hook, to show that the verb has caught its object noun. For the base verb, the instructor will show his cupped right hand. Example:

> Wagṓⁿze: Gaxáde. ("Cover it.") [said with cupped right hand]

> Lynn: Īgaxade. ("Lid.") [little finger cocked on right fist]

> Wagṓⁿze: Bamóⁿ. ("File it.") [said with cupped right hand]

> Ivy: Wēbamoⁿ. ("File.") [right holds left fist, pinky cocked]

> Wagṓⁿze: Thizé. ("Take it.") [said with cupped right hand]

> Anthony: Xáde-īthize. ("Pitchfork.") [right holds left, pinky cocked]

D. The instructor asks each student a question that can be answered with an ī- or wē- noun. The student responds appropriately, using one. Example:

> Wagṓⁿze: Ppáxu kkōⁿbtha. Eóⁿ? ("I want to write it. How?")

> Samantha: Wēbaxu óⁿ a! ("Use a pen/pencil!")

> Wagṓⁿze: Díⁿdiⁿ ppāxe kkōⁿbtha. Eóⁿ? ("I want to make it firm. How?")

> Jack: Īdiⁿdiⁿ óⁿ ga! ("Use a brace!")

E. The students form small groups of about two or three and take turns asking each other questions that can be answered using an ī- or wē- word. Using

the corresponding gestures with them is encouraged.

18.3 THE LOCATIVE U- PREFIX

Locative u- verbs: "into"

u-ʔé	dig into the soil for planting
u-báhiⁿ	insert, poke, get in where you're not supposed to be
u-bátti	plug a leak
u-gádoⁿ	pound in, as a nail into wood
u-gásʔiⁿ	peek in
u-mūbthiⁿ	penetrate, as water, snow or sand into your house
u-nóⁿzhiⁿ	fill in for someone, "stand in"
u-ppé	enter a house, crawl in
u-thíʔude	make a hole by boring or drilling
u-thíski	tighten; e.g., a lid
u-thísoⁿ	screw in, as a screw or a lid
u-zhí	put in, fill

- Many Omaha words use the *locative prefix* u-. This element is very old in Siouan, and it has developed a number of different meanings. One of the most common is the sense of "in" or "into," as an action in which one thing penetrates into another.

- As with the instrumental prefixes, the set of words using locative prefixes (u- and ā-) is probably fairly fixed in modern Omaha.

Locative u-: "within," "container,"
"together," "low spot," "downward"

u-bíso^{n}de	crowded, people packed together (*together*)
u-gá$^{\prime}$e	hang, sag, dangle (*downward*)
u-gáspe	depression or indentation, as on a bed you sat on (*low spot*)
u-gíppi	full, as a cup of water (*within a container*)
u-gthó^n	container (*container*)
u-hó^n	cook, broil (*within a container*)
u-mūbiχo^n	bloat (*within*)
u-nābiχo^n	rise, as yeast, bubble as beer, pop, or water about to boil (*within*)
u-núshka	small depression, low spot in the ground (*low spot*)
u-spé	valley (*low spot*); sink, as a boat (*downward*)
u-théwi^n	assemble as people or materials (*together*)
u-thízo^n	amongst, amid, in the center (*within*)
u-xthúχa	gully, gulch, trench, ditch, deep hole (*low spot*)
u-x̌páthe	fall, as from a height (*downward*)
u-x̌pé	dish, plate, pan, bowl (*container*)

- Besides "into," the u- prefix can simply mean "in," in the sense that the action is going on inside something. Bloating, or forming small bubbles when about to boil, take place on the inside, which is shown by the locative u- prefix. References to containers often include locative u-, because the interest is in one thing contained inside another. The common word for "cook," uhá^n, refers specifically to boiling, or cooking food within a container of water, as opposed to roasting it in open heat (zhégtho^n).

- The u- prefix can also suggest the *center* or motion toward the center. Gathering materials, or people coming together in assembly, or packing together in a crowd, is inward motion toward the center.

- *Holes* are commonly made by one thing penetrating into another. But this idea is extended to holes in the ground as well or any type of low spot. Words for dents, depressions, trenches, and valleys also seem to use the u- prefix.

- Finally, *downward* motion, as in falling, sinking, or dangling, may also use the u- prefix. The sense here, as with holes in the ground, may be movement *into* the earth under us.

Locative u-: "around"

u-bét^{h}o^n	wrap, as with a blanket or towel
u-gáṣno^n	lasso, throw a loop over something
u-gáshke	tie, as a horse
u-gátto^{n}the	tumble, roll over
u-mó^{n}thi^{n}kka	year, month, age
u-nó^{n}zhi^n	coat, jacket, shirt, cape, tunic
u-thíṣno^n	put on a necktie or a fanbelt
u-thíso^{n}the	turn over, flip over, as pancakes or frybread
u-thísho^n	go around the outside of something, or detour around an obstacle
u-thíx̌thax̌tha	loosen a rope or a knot
u-thíwi^{n}χe	spiral, like water down a drain, a tornado, or birds circling
u-thó^n	hold, grab, arrest
u-ttó^n	wear, as shirt, pants, shoes, hat, jewelry

- Other locative u- words seem to mean just the opposite. Instead of "into," they mean "around the outside of," or "spinning around." To be wrapped up in something, as clothing, or tied up with something, as a rope, or even months and years marked by the heavens turning around the earth, all take locative u-. The reason for this may become clearer if we think statively and do not prejudice the perspective of one "thing" over the other. "In" means that thing A is on the inside of thing B. "Around" means that thing B is on the outside of thing A. Viewed with stative objectivity, these are two ways of saying the same thing. Locative u- doesn't seem to discriminate.

Locative u-: "boundary"

u-báhe	edge, margin, boundary, border, as the edge of a table
u-bátʰe	lengthen cloth by sewing another piece on at the edge; exaggerate
u-hóⁿge	limit, boundary, end, as of a rope
u-hóⁿge-thiⁿge	endless, limitless, boundless

- Words referring to edges or borders may use locative u-, in a specialized sense of "around the outside."

Locative u-: "through"

u-gákkiba	split
u-shágthe	chops, serial cuts of meat that cut through the bone
u-thíṣnoⁿ	thread a needle

- The "into" sense of locative u- may also include one thing passing *through* another.

Locative u-: "path"

u-bíhe	line of gravel made by a grader
u-gáshoⁿ	travel, journey
u-hé	road, pass
u-héatʰoⁿ	bridge, ladder, stairway, viaduct
u-ttánoⁿ	path, aisle, walkway
u-zhóⁿge	road

- As an extension of "through," locative u- seems to cover paths, roads, and journeys, where one passes along a trail *through* the surrounding wilderness.

Locative u-verbs: "environment"

u-čʰízhe	weedy, thicket, brush, woods with lots of little trees
u-dá	icebound
u-gánoⁿppaze	darkness, pitch black
u-gáṣni	cool down, as in the evening
u-góⁿba	getting light out, dawn
u-nägoⁿbe	bright, glowing, as city lights from a distance, flash from a camera
u-óⁿze	shade, as from trees or an awning
u-ṣní	cold, as ambient temperature, not a person or an object
u-x̌thábe	bushes, forest, trees, timber, out in the woods

- Locative u- is often used to describe the surrounding *environment*. This again is an extension of "around."

Locative u-: "station"

u-gthíⁿ	spot where you sit or live
u-hítha-tti	bathroom, bath house, place where you bathe
u-kkóⁿ	an open place to put something
u-míⁿzhe	bed, place to lie down
u-néthe	stove, hearth, fireplace
u-nóⁿshtoⁿ	dock, port, station, depot, rest stop
u-stáppe	crash space, friendly household to stay with temporarily
u-shkáde	park, football field, soccer field, basketball court
u-shkóⁿ	place, site

- In contrast to the "environment" sense, locative u- is also used to refer to the *station* at which some activity takes place. This may represent the idea of a "center" for a particular specified activity within the general environment.

Nominalizing *wa-* with Locative *u-*

uhóⁿ	*vt* cook (it)	**ūhoⁿ**	*n* a cook
uthíṣne	*vt* slit (it)	**ūthiṣne**	*n* a slit

- Locative *u-* words can be either nouns or verbs. When they are verbs, they can be turned into nouns by adding a nominalizing *wa-* in front of them, just as with many other verbs.

- When *wa-* is added to a locative *u-* verb, it shows itself by pulling the accent forward onto the *u-* and making it canonically long.

- The reason for this is historical. The Omaha /u/ sound was originally pronounced /o/, as in most other Siouan languages. So locative *u-* was originally locative *o-*. A locative *o-* verb *o-háⁿ* could be turned into a noun by adding nominalizing *wa-*, *wa-ó-haⁿ*, which would pull the accent forward to the second syllable, *o-*. But the *a* and the *o* were hard to distinguish, so they blurred together into one long vowel *ō*, making the word *wō-haⁿ*. Then Omaha and Ponca raised the vowel /o/ to /u/. This theoretically made the word *wū-haⁿ*. But /w/ is a semi-vowel that is used as a consonant, but is really pronounced about the same way as the vowel /u/, and can't be distinguished from it here. So the *w* merged with the *u*, and the resulting noun ends up as *ūhaⁿ*.

- Any time a locative *u-* word has the accent on the first syllable as *ū-*, it means that there are actually two elements there, *wa-* + *u-*.

Vocabulary: Locative *u-* Words

u'é: plow, make holes for planting

ubáhe: edge, margin, border

ubáhiⁿ: insert, poke, get in where you shouldn't

ubátti: plug a leak

ubát^he: sew a piece on to lengthen cloth; exaggerate

ubét^hoⁿ: wrap, as with a blanket or towel

ubíhe: line of gravel left by a grader

ubísoⁿde: crowded, people pressed together

uč^hízhe: weedy, thicket, brush, forest with lots of little trees

udá: icebound

ugádoⁿ: pound in, as a nail

ugákkiba: split

ugánoⁿppaze: dark, pitch black, as from a blackout

ugás'iⁿ: peek in

ugáṣni: cool down, as in the evening

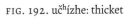

FIG. 192. uč^hízhe: thicket

ugáṣnoⁿ: lasso, throw a loop over something

ugáspe: depression, indentation, as on a bed where you sat

ugáshke: tie, as a horse

ugáshoⁿ: travel, journey

ugáttoⁿthe: tumble, roll over

ugíppi: full, as a cup of water

ugóⁿba: getting light out, dawn

FIG. 193. ugthíⁿ: spot where you sit or live

ugthíⁿ: spot where you sit or live

ugthóⁿ: container

uhé: road, pass

uhéatʰoⁿ: bridge, ladder, stairway, viaduct

uhíthatti: bathroom, bathhouse, place where you bathe

uháⁿ: cook, broil

ūhaⁿ: a cook

uhóⁿge: limit, boundary, end, as of a rope

uhóⁿgethiⁿge: endless, limitless, boundless

FIG. 194. uháⁿ: cook

ukkóⁿ: an open place to put something

umíⁿzhe: bed, place to lie down

umóⁿthiⁿkka: year, month, age

umūbixoⁿ: bloat

umūbthiⁿ: penetrate, as water, snow or sand into your house

unābixoⁿ: rise, as yeast; bubble as beer, pop, or water about to boil

unāgoⁿbe: bright, glowing, as city lights, or the flash of a camera

unéthe: stove, hearth, fireplace

unóⁿshtoⁿ: dock, port, station, depot, rest stop

unóⁿzhiⁿ: coat, jacket, shirt, cape, tunic

unóⁿzhiⁿ: fill in for someone, stand in

unúshka: small depression, low spot in the ground

uóⁿze: shade, as from trees or an awning

uppé: enter a house, crawl in

uṣní: cold (ambient temperature, not a person or object)

uspé: valley; sink, as a boat

ustáppe: crash space, friendly household to stay with temporarily

ushágthe: chops, serial cuts of meat that cut through the bone

ūshkade: park, football field, soccer field, basketball court

ushkóⁿ: place, site

uthéwiⁿ: assemble, as people or materials

uthíʔude: make a hole by boring or drilling

uthíski: tighten, as a lid

uthíṣne: make a slit

ūthiṣne: a slit

uthíṣnoⁿ: put on a necktie or fanbelt; thread a needle

uthísoⁿ: screw in, as a screw or lid

uthísoⁿthe: turn over, flip over, as pancakes or frybread

FIG. 195. uthísoⁿthe: flip over

uthíshoⁿ: go around the outside, or detour around an obstacle

uthíwiⁿχe: spiral, like water down a drain, a tornado, or birds circling

uthíχthaχtha: loosen a rope or knot

uthízoⁿ: among, amid, in the center

uthóⁿ: hold, grab, arrest

uttánoⁿ: path, aisle, walkway

uttóⁿ: wear, as shirt, pants, shoes, hat, jewelry

uχpáthe: fall, as from a height

uχpé: dish, plate, pan, bowl

uχthábe: bushes, forest, trees, timbers, out in the woods

uzhí: put in, fill

uzhóⁿge: road

Vocabulary: Nouns

ttadé: wind

wākku: awl

wākkuzhiⁿga: pin, needle ("little awl")

wākkuzhiⁿga gaʼúʼude: needle ("perforated pin")

Speaking Practice

A. Read the following sentences aloud. Then translate the sentences into English. Examples:

Ugásʼiⁿ azhi a!: Don't peek!

Ní-īthattoⁿ tʰe ugíppi a?: Is the cup full?

Áshiatta uṣní-atč: It's very cold outside.

1. Mí thoⁿ nāgoⁿbe. Gá!
   Ttōⁿde-īnoⁿse óⁿ uʼá!

2. Unúshka tʰe ttōⁿde uzhí gōⁿtha.

3. Umóⁿthiⁿkka ānoⁿ aníⁿ a?

4. Ttéskazhiⁿga ugáṣnoⁿ egóⁿ, ugáshka.

5. Thishtóⁿ egóⁿ, házhiⁿga kʰe uthíχthaχtha.

6. Wākkuzhiⁿga gaʼúʼude uthíṣnoⁿ, wiháⁿ akʰa.

7. Umóⁿthiⁿkka shêkʰe uṣní tʰe; moⁿdé kʰe udá bi ama.

8. Ugánoⁿppaze; mikkáʼe noⁿ dóⁿbewatha bazhi.

9. Umíⁿzhe kʰedi zhóⁿ bi ama, ithádi akʰa.

10. Zhóⁿ ūthiṣne ítha egóⁿ, ttíadi uppá bi ama, wēsʼa akʰa.

B. Translate the following sentences into Omaha.

1. Tighten the lid!

2. Since your mother will be away today, your elder sister will fill in for her.

3. Snow blowing in the wind might penetrate into the house.

4. Don't exaggerate!

5. There is a line of gravel made by a grader along the road.

6. While traveling, my nephew found a place to stay.

7. The park is crowded.

8. The stove is hot.

9. Last night the boat sank, they say.

10. At the bottom of the gully lay a dead buffalo bloating.

C. The instructor challenges the students with a base word, and the students respond with a corresponding u- word. While doing so, they should use the gesture of thrusting the right hand forward as they grasp the right wrist with the left hand. Example:

Wagōⁿze: Batʰé. ("Sew it.")

Ttáppuskazhiⁿga: Ubátʰe. ("Exaggerate.") [left hand grabs right wrist]

Wagōⁿze: Ṣní. ("Cold.")

Ttáppuskazhiⁿga: Uṣní. ("Cold out.") [left hand grabs right wrist]

D. The instructor says something to each student that can be answered with an u- or ū- word. The student responds appropriately. Example:

Wagōⁿze: Awádi ʾúde wiⁿ thêtʰe, zhoⁿbthāska kʰedi? ("Why is there a hole here in the board?")

Aubrey: Bob akʰa uthíʾuda i egóⁿ. ("Because Bob drilled it.")

Wagōⁿze: Azhōⁿ kkōⁿbtha. ("I want to lie down.")

Greta: Umíⁿzhe shêhikʰe óⁿ a! ("Use the bed over there!")

E. The students form small groups of about two or three and take turns asking each other questions that can be answered using an u- or ū- word. Using the corresponding gestures with them is encouraged.

18.4 CONJUGATION OF LOCATIVE U- VERBS

	u-hé	s/he passes him	u-hí	he wins
I-	u-áhe	I pass him	u-áhi	I win
you-	u-tháhe	you pass him	u-tháhi	you win
we-	oⁿgú-he	we pass him	oⁿgú-hi	we win
-me	oⁿwóⁿhe	he passes me	oⁿwóⁿhi	I lose
-you	u-thíhe	he passes you	u-thíhi	you lose
-us	u-wáhe	he passes us	u-wáhi	we lose
-them	u-wáhe	he passes them	u-wáhi	they lose
I-you	u-wíhe	I pass you	u-wíhi	I beat you
I-them	u-áwahe	I pass them	u-áwahi	I beat them
you-me	oⁿwóⁿthahe	you pass me	oⁿwóⁿthahi	you beat me
you-us	u-wāthahe	you pass us	u-wāthahi	you beat us
you-them	u-wáthahe	you pass them	u-wáthahi	you beat them
we-you	oⁿgú-thihe	we pass you	oⁿgú-thihi	we beat you
we-them	oⁿgú-wahe	we pass them	oⁿgú-wahi	we beat them

- Locative u- verbs generally conjugate by simply adding u- to the conjugated verb stem that follows it, as u-[affixed pronouns][verb stem].

- The exception to this is that the "we" affixed pronoun oⁿ(g)- attaches to the front of the locative u- instead, making the prefix oⁿgú- for "we [do locative u-verb]."

- When the "me" affixed pronoun oⁿ- follows the locative u- prefix as u-óⁿ-, the vowel quality of the oⁿ- bleeds back into the u-, and the u- becomes an epenthetic w (automatically occurring) to divide the syllables. If you try pronouncing u-óⁿ- somewhat lazily, it may come out sounding like oⁿwóⁿ-, which is how this sequence is usually pronounced in Omaha.

- Note that the "I" form is pronounced the same as the "us" and "them" forms, because the u- prefix automatically makes a w- sound anyway as it transitions into another vowel such as the "I" prefix a-: u-(w)-á- sounds just like u-wá-.

s/he-	**u-thóⁿ**	he grabs him	**u-gáshke**	he ties him
I-	**u-bthóⁿ**	I grab him	**u-áshke**	I tie him
you-	**u-nóⁿ**	you grab him	**u-tháshke**	you tie him
we-	**oⁿgú-thoⁿ**	we grab him	**oⁿgú-gashke**	we tie him
-me	**oⁿwóⁿthoⁿ**	he grabs me	**oⁿwóⁿgashke**	he ties me
-you	**u-thíthoⁿ**	he grabs you	**u-thígashke**	he ties you
-us	**u-wāthoⁿ**	he grabs us	**u-wāgashke**	he ties us
-them	**u-wáthoⁿ**	he grabs them	**u-wágashke**	he ties them
I-you	**u-wíbthoⁿ**	I grab you	**u-wíashke**	I tie you
I-them	**u-wábthoⁿ**	I grab them	**u-áwagashke**	I tie them
you-me	**oⁿwóⁿnoⁿ**	you grab me	**oⁿwóⁿthagashke**	you tie me
you-us	**u-wānoⁿ**	you grab us	**u-wāthashke**	you tie us
you-them	**u-wánoⁿ**	you grab them	**u-wáthashke**	you tie them
we-you	**oⁿgú-thithoⁿ**	we grab you	**oⁿgú-thigashke**	we tie you
we-them	**oⁿgú-wathoⁿ**	we grab them	**oⁿgú-wagashke**	we tie them

- Note that the special conjugation forms before certain consonants or prefixes still hold true when they are preceded by locative u-.

Vocabulary: Verbs

gattūbe: wrecked, as a totaled car

ugáshke: tie, as a horse

uhé: pass, as one car passes another

uhí: win, beat someone in a contest

uthóⁿ: hold, grab arrest

FIG. 196. ugáshke: tie, as a horse

Vocabulary: Nouns

banóⁿ: team, gang, flock, group of people or animals

nídeuthishi: pants

nīdushi: pants (contraction of nídeuthishi)

sí: seed(s)

wanóⁿshe: police, soldier, sheriff, guard

Speaking Practice

A. Read the following sentences aloud. Then translate the sentences into English. Examples:

Uwíhi tta miⁿkʰe: I will beat you.

Wazhíⁿga uwábthoⁿ bthíʼa: I couldn't grab the chickens.

Ttéskazhiⁿga utháske uthákkihi a?: Are you able to tie the calf?

1. Má kʰe umūbthiⁿ tʰedi uppátti tta miⁿkʰ'.

2. Wākkuzhiⁿga ubthíʼude tʰe ppóⁿzhiⁿga.

3. Uníski āttashoⁿ kki, mūthakkoⁿ íthagaskoⁿne tte.

4. Moⁿkkóⁿsabe tʰe ttéskamoⁿseni utházhi?

5. Banóⁿ wiwítta ma uwábthewiⁿ tta miⁿkʰ'.

6. Égithe uhéatʰoⁿ móⁿshiatta āthane kki, utháx̣pathe tte.

7. Ugáṣni tʰedi, shié kʰe waíⁿ ushpétʰoⁿ tta tʰe.

8. Uágashoⁿ bthé tta miⁿkʰe;
uxⁿthábe kʰedi kkáshi moⁿbthíⁿ
kkōⁿbtha.

9. Égithe nīdushi utháttoⁿ
thagísithazhi tte!

10. Kkinóⁿnoⁿge gattūbe
shêhikʰe uníshoⁿ tte. Égithe
wanóⁿshe ama uthíthoⁿ tte.

B. Translate the following sentences into
Omaha.

1. I put in the seeds.

2. I don't want to put on a
necktie.

3. *I'll* put it (the necktie) on you!

4. You might flip over the
cowboy bread.

5. Your mother is looking for
you.

6. Yes, I like to cook things like
that.

7. Don't grab me!

8. They say we lost.

9. We passed a red car on the
road.

10. Do you not know how to tie
your horse?

C. The instructor goes around the
class, challenging each student with a
u- verb and an emphatic pronoun. The
student responds with the appropriate
conjugation form. Note that "wí" and
"thí" will be reversed in the interaction.
Example:

Wagōⁿze: Uppé. Wí. ("Enter [house]. I.")

Rod: Utháppe. ("You entered.")

Wagōⁿze: Ugáshoⁿ. Oⁿgú. ("Travel.
We.")

Lucy: Oⁿgúgashoⁿ. ("We travel.")

Wagōⁿze: Uthíso. Thí. ("Screw it in.
You.")

Karen: Ubthíso. ("I screwed it in.")

D. The instructor goes around the class
again, challenging each student with a
transitive u- verb (such as uhé, uhí, uthóⁿ,
or ugáshke) and two emphatic pronouns.
The first pronoun is the object pronoun,
and the second is the subject pronoun.
A third person subject will be é. A third
person plural animate object, "them," will
be é ama. The student responds with the
appropriate conjugated form to have the
party indicated by the subject pronoun
inflict the verb's action upon the party of
the object pronoun. Again, "wí" and "thí"
will be reversed in the interaction.

E. The students form groups of about
four to six, with a deck of cards, and play
this as a game. One student is the dealer
and deals out five cards each. The person
to the dealer's left starts the game by
challenging another student as in exercise
D. In this game, the person challenged
may put the response in the negative,
in the future, or ask it as a question if
preferred. If that student answers with
the correct construction, the student gets
to put one card back in the deck, and the
turn passes to that student. Otherwise the
challenger must challenge someone else

with a different challenge. If all other students have failed on the challenger's turn, the challenger puts back a card and the turn passes to the person on the challenger's left. If the challenger gives a semantically unreasonable challenge, the victim may respond: Oⁿthóⁿwoⁿxazhi a/ga!, "Don't trick me!", in which case the challenger must accept a card from the undeceived challengee. The first player to lose all five cards is the winner.

18.5 THE LOCATIVE Ā- PREFIX

ā-ʾoⁿsi	jump onto; jump over; skip someone
ā-banoⁿ	gaze, watch, as a movie or a baseball game
ā-baxu	write on something
ā-bazu	point at
ā-bisṇathe	spread on, as in buttering bread
ā-bitte	touch, like a bannister walking downstairs
ā-doⁿbe	aim, focus on, view
ā-gaha	on top
ā-gasta	pile up, stack
ā-gashke	buckle, button, fasten one part of a garment to another
ā-gashoⁿ	spill something on someone
ā-gazhi	command, bid someone to do something
ā-gioⁿ	fly over, as a plane over a football game
ā-gthe	put on; set, e.g. a glass on a table
ā-gthiⁿ	chair; sit on; ride, as a horse
ā-he	walk on; walk along a path
ā-hoⁿ	lift onto
ā-kkippe	meet; greet
ā-kkoⁿ	leaning against
ā-moⁿx̌pi	cloudy, overcast
ā-ne	embrace, hug; climb
ā-noⁿʾoⁿ	listen to; heed; obey
ā-noⁿge	run over, as with a car
ā-oⁿthe	throw on top, stack; give someone a sickness, like a cold
ā-thade	recite, read aloud
ā-thaha	wear, as clothes; smear on, as makeup or warpaint
ā-thaskabe	adhere, stick to
ā-tʰoⁿ	porch
ā-x̌e	cry out, as an animal or a war-cry
ā-zhi	put on, as gravel on a road

Locative ā-: "on, onto, at, over, toward, against"

- The locative ā- prefix generally implies *on*, *onto*, *at*, *over*, or *against* something. Sometimes it means that the action of the verb is directed *toward* an object, as in the difference between noⁿʾóⁿ, "hear," and ānoⁿʾoⁿ, "listen to," or between dóⁿbe, "see," and ādoⁿbe, "look at" or "aim."

Vocabulary: Locative ā- Words

āʾoⁿsi: jump onto or over; skip someone

ābanoⁿ: gaze at, watch, as a movie or ball game

ābaxu: write on, as on a blackboard or a sheet of paper

ābazu: point at

ābisṇathe: spread on, as buttering bread

ābitte: touch, as a banister while walking downstairs

ādoⁿbe: aim, focus on, view

āgaha: on top

āgasta: pile up

āgashke: buckle, button, fasten, as one bit of clothing to another

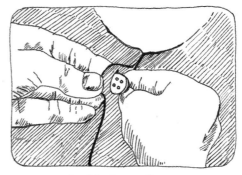

FIG. 197. āgashke: button, fasten, as one bit of clothing to another

āgashoⁿ: spill something on someone

āgazhi: command, bid someone to do something

āgioⁿ: fly over, as a plane over a football game

āgthe: put on, set, as a glass on the table

āgthiⁿ: chair; sit on, ride (a horse)

āhe: walk on; walk along a path

āhoⁿ: lift onto

ākkippe: meet, greet

ākkoⁿ: leaning against something

āmoⁿx̌pi: cloudy, overcast

āne: hug, embrace; climb

ānoⁿ'oⁿ: listen; heed; obey

ānoⁿge: run over, as with a car

āoⁿthe: throw on top, stack; give someone a cold or other illness

āthade: recite, read aloud

āthaha: wear (clothes); smear on (makeup or warpaint)

āthaskabe: adhere, stick to

ātʰoⁿ: porch

āx̣e: cry out, as an animal or a war cry

āzhi: put on, as gravel on a road

FIG. 198. ākkoⁿ: leaning against something

FIG. 199. ānoⁿge: run over, as with a car

Vocabulary: Nouns

bawēgthi: butter

ippíthage: belt

wamóske: bread

wamóske-nāx̌ude: toast

Speaking Practice

A. Read the following sentences aloud. Then translate the sentences into English. Examples:

Wabáx̣u kʰe ābax̣u ga!: Write down the letters!

Thiháⁿ ānoⁿ'oⁿ i a!: Listen to your mother!

X̌ithá wiⁿ āgioⁿ bi ama: They say an eagle flew overhead.

1. Wamóske-nāx̌ude shêtʰe āgasta tʰe bawēgthi ābiṣnatha (ga)!

2. Núzhiⁿga ābanoⁿ, mīzhiⁿga akʰa.

3. Nudóⁿhoⁿga wahúttoⁿthe uthóⁿ bi egóⁿ, ukkítte ādoⁿba bi ama.

4. Shêthoⁿ ttáx̌ti-ppa thoⁿ ābittazhi a/ga!

5. Zhóⁿ āgasta āgaha tʰe āgthiⁿ, iⁿgthóⁿge thiⁿkʰe.

6. Ukkóⁿ thêtʰedi ux̌pé tʰe āgasta āgtha!

7. Moⁿkkóⁿsabe nākkade tʰe iⁿdādi thiⁿkʰe āgashoⁿ akʰa, wí é bthíⁿ mazhi!

8. Wiháⁿ ak^ha wēohaⁿ ttaní ugíppi t^he unéthe āhoⁿ āgazhi, wisóⁿge thiⁿk^he.

9. Nú ak^ha nídushi ettá k^he uttóⁿ egóⁿ, ippíthage k^he āgashka.

9. Wizhíⁿthe ak^ha ippíthage ítha egóⁿ, nídushi ettá k^he uthíṣnoⁿ egóⁿ, āgashka.

10. Ikkáge thiⁿk^he ākkippa, wisóⁿge ak^ha, ugáshoⁿ k^hedi.

B. Translate the following sentences into Omaha.

1. The cat jumped up on the table.

2. They say the warrior rode a dappled horse.

3. The mother lifted the baby up onto the chair.

4. The girls walked along the boardwalk.

5. The niece hugged her aunt.

6. It will be overcast tomorrow.

7. They say his younger brother ran over a dog yesterday.

8. Recite the words!

9. Her nephew wore a striped shirt.

10. Don't point at your grandfather!

C. The instructor challenges the students with a base word, and the students respond with a corresponding ā- word. While doing so, they should use the gesture of placing the right hand flat on top of the back of the left hand. Example:

Wagōⁿze: Nóⁿge. ("Roll.")

Ttáppuskazhiⁿga: Ānoⁿge. ("Run over.") [right hand slaps onto left]

Wagōⁿze: Noⁿʼóⁿ. ("Hear.")

Ttáppuskazhiⁿga: Ānoⁿʼoⁿ. ("Listen to.") [right hand slaps onto left]

D. The instructor says something to each student that can be answered with an ā- word. The student responds appropriately. Example:

Wagōⁿze: Amy ak^ha águdix̌ti gthíⁿ a? ("Where is Amy sitting?")

Quincy: Shóⁿge thiⁿk^hedi āgthiⁿ. ("She's sitting on the horse.")

Wagōⁿze: Āshiatta eóⁿ a? ("How is it outside?")

Glenn: Āmoⁿx̌pi. ("It's overcast.")

E. The students form small groups of about two or three and take turns asking each other questions that can be answered using an ā- word. Using the corresponding gestures with them is encouraged.

18.6 CONJUGATION OF LOCATIVE Ā- VERBS

	āno^{n}ʔo^n	s/he heeds her
I-	ā-ano^{n}ʔo^n	I heed her
you-	ā-thano^{n}ʔo^n	you heed her
we-	o^{n}gāno^{n}ʔo^n	we heed her
-me	ā-o^{n}no^{n}ʔo^n	he heeds me
-you	ā-thino^{n}ʔo^n	he heeds you
-us	wāno^{n}ʔo^n	he heeds us
-them	wāno^{n}ʔo^n	he heeds them
I-you	ā-wino^{n}ʔo^n	I heed you
I-them	wāano^{n}ʔo^n	I heed them
you-me	ā-o^{n}thano^{n}ʔo^n	you heed me
you-us	wāthano^{n}ʔo^n	you heed us
you-them	wāthano^{n}ʔo^n	you heed them
we-you	o^{n}gāthino^{n}ʔo^n	we heed you
we-them	waó^{n}gano^{n}ʔo^n	we heed them

- The rules for conjugating locative ā-verbs are much like those for conjugating locative u- verbs. Again, affixed pronouns attach to the base verb, except for the "we" pronoun o^{n}g-, which attaches to the locative prefix. Note that for both prefixes, "we" is o^{n}g- rather than o^n-, since u- and ā- are both vowels.

- Unlike the u- locative prefix, ā- takes the accent. With a simple u- verb, the accent falls on the second syllable, following the prefix. For a simple verb with locative prefix ā-, the accent always falls on the ā-. This probably means that unlike u-, the ā- prefix was originally long. Here we write ā- with a macron to emphasize that fact, and in any case to help the reader pick out the very important ā- prefix when it appears as part of a word.

- The "I" affixed pronoun a- and the "me" affixed pronoun o^n- are so similar in sound to the locative prefix ā- that they merge with it when they follow ā-. When this happens, the sound is held a little longer. The combination ā-a- sounds like plain ā- or a-, but is held longer than either of these alone. The combination ā-o^n- may sound much like o^n- but held longer and taking the accent. We nevertheless write these as āa-[baseverb] and āo^n-[baseverb], respectively, to keep the parts clear.

- The affixed pronouns for "we," "us," and animate "them" are not as ancient as the ones for "I," "me," and "you," and they may not always appear in the same order with respect to the locative prefix ā-. For the "we" form of locative ā- verbs, the combined prefix may be either o^{n}gā- or ó^{n}ga-. For "us" and "them," it may be either wā- or āwa-. For "I-them," it might be either wāa- or āawa-. For "you-us" and "you-them," it might be either wātha- or āawatha-. For "we-you," it might be o^{n}gāthi- or ó^{n}gathi-, or even ó^{n}thi-, and for "we-them," we might have waó^{n}ga-, o^{n}gāwa-, or ó^{n}gawa. These forms have all been accepted at some time in elicitations, and it may be that the different forms represent nuances in what a speaker wants to emphasize in a given context. For the tables we have selected the version preferred by our speakers when offered alternatives and which also seem to have been used in the nineteenth century.

		ā banoⁿ	s/he watches her
I-		**ā-ppanoⁿ**	I gaze at her
you-		**ā-shpanoⁿ**	you gaze at her
we-		**oⁿgābanoⁿ**	we gaze at her
-me		**ā-oⁿbanoⁿ**	he gazes at me
-you		**ā-thibanoⁿ**	he gazes at you
-us		**wābanoⁿ**	he gazes at us
-them		**wābanoⁿ**	he gazes at them
I-you		**ā-wippanoⁿ**	I gaze at you
I-them		**wāppanoⁿ**	I gaze at them
you-me		**ā-oⁿshpanoⁿ**	you gaze at me
you-us		**wāshpanoⁿ**	you gaze at us
you-them		**wāshpanoⁿ**	you gaze at them
we-you		**oⁿgāthibanoⁿ**	we gaze at you
we-them		**waóⁿgabanoⁿ**	we gaze at them

- As with the u- verbs, "I" and "you" affixed pronouns take their special forms when they attach to ledh- verbs, simple stop consonants, and so forth.

Vocabulary: Locative ā- Words

āno'oⁿ: listen to, heed
ābanoⁿ: gaze at, watch

Vocabulary: Locative u- Words

ukkóⁿ: an open space to put something
uthíae: distribute something, like food

Vocabulary: Nouns

íⁿ'ezhiⁿga: gravel

Vocabulary: Question Words

awádi: why?

Speaking Practice

A. Read the following sentences aloud. Then translate the sentences into English. Examples:

Watháwa kʰe āppaxu: I wrote down the numbers.

Watʰé ānaha?: Did you wear a dress?

Xthabé tʰe oⁿgāna: We climbed the tree.

1. Ni-īthattoⁿ wāthatʰe āagthe itʰéathe, ukkóⁿ tʰedi.

2. Noⁿzhíⁿ tʰe āoⁿgazhi ga!

3. Íⁿezhiⁿga uzhóⁿge kʰe oⁿgāzhi tta oⁿgatʰoⁿ.

4. Āthaxe winóⁿʼoⁿ thoⁿzha, awádi thaxága?

5. Wathátʰe uthíae thoⁿzha, āoⁿʼoⁿsi.

6. Bawēgthi āshpiṣnathe tte, wamóske-nāxude kʰe.

7. Zhoⁿbtháska-uttánoⁿ oⁿgāhe oⁿgátha tta!

8. Nóⁿde tʰe āthakkoⁿ tʰe āwikkippe tte.

9. Zhū-nākkade wiwítta kʰe āwioⁿthe kkōⁿbtha mazhi.

10. Nídushi itháthe tʰegoⁿ, ippíthage āashke bthíkkuthe.

B. Translate the following sentences into Omaha.

    1. I'll meet you.

    2. You might hug your aunt.

    3. Don't touch me!

    4. I shall read.

    5. You spilled coffee on me.

    6. We lifted the bundle onto the table.

    7. You are good at riding a horse.

    8. You will wear a necklace.

    9. We didn't run over you.

    10. I want to fly over the football field.

C. The instructor goes around the class, challenging each student with an ā- verb and an emphatic pronoun. The student should respond with the appropriate conjugation form. Note that "wí" and "thí" will be reversed in the interaction. Example:

> Wagōⁿze: Ābiṣnathe. Thí. ("Butter it on. You.")
>
> Rod: Āppiṣnathe. ("I buttered it on.")
>
> Wagōⁿze: Āhoⁿ. Oⁿgú. ("Lift it onto. We.")
>
> Lucy: Oⁿgāhoⁿ. ("We lift it onto.")
>
> Wagōⁿze: Āzhi. Wí. ("Put it on. I.")
>
> Karen: Āthazhi. ("You put it on.")

D. The instructor goes around the class again, challenging each student with a transitive ā- verb (such as ānoⁿˀoⁿ, ābítte, ābanóⁿ, āgashoⁿ, āgazhi, āgioⁿ, āhoⁿ, ākkippe, āne, ānoⁿge, āoⁿthe, or āˀoⁿsi) and two emphatic pronouns. The first pronoun is the object pronoun, and the second is the subject pronoun. A third person subject will be é. A third person plural animate object, "them," will be é ama. The student should respond with the appropriate conjugated form to have the party indicated by the subject pronoun inflict the verb's action upon the party of the object pronoun. Again, "wí" and "thí" will be reversed in the interaction.

E. The students form groups of about four to six, with a deck of cards, and play this as a game. One student is the dealer and deals out five cards each. The person to the dealer's left starts the game by challenging another student with an ā- verb and a pronoun or two as in exercise D. The persons challenged may answer as they like, provided they put the verb in the correct conjugation. If they succeed, they get to put one of their cards back in the deck, and they become the challenger. Otherwise the challenger must challenge someone else with a different challenge. If all other students have failed on the challenger's turn, the challenger puts back a card and the turn passes to the person on the challenger's left. If the challenger gives a semantically unreasonable challenge, the victim may respond: Oⁿthóⁿwoⁿx̣azhi a/ga!, "Don't trick me!", in which case the challenger must accept a card from the undeceived challengee. The first player to lose all five cards is the winner.

18.7 THE TRANSITIVIZING Í- PREFIX

*Applicative í-: "directing the
action toward an object"*

í-ʔoⁿ	cultivate (a field)
í-bahoⁿ	know (someone or something)
í-gahi	mix in (an ingredient)
í-gaskoⁿthe	try, taste (something)
í-he	get through (an obstructed route)
í-husa	scold (someone)
í-kʰu	invite (someone)
í-moⁿthe	take revenge, lay for someone
í-moⁿxe	ask (someone) a question
í-niethe	injure (someone)
í-nitʰe	scold (someone)
í-noⁿhiⁿ	permit, allow, agree to (something)
í-noⁿxithe	chase (someone)
í-sabe	suffer (from something)
í-shte	be ashamed (of something or someone)
í-thade	read to someone
íthappe	wait for someone
í-the	find (something)
í-thibthoⁿ	scent, smell of (something)
í-thidoⁿdoⁿ	tug (something)
í-thise	cut (something)
í-thishi	feed (people or animals)
í-thizha	wash (something)
í-thizhoⁿzhoⁿ	jar, shake (someone)
í-tte	touch (something)
ítʰiⁿ	hit (someone)
itʔathe	dislike, loath (someone)
í-wakʰega	make (someone) sick
í-xaxa	ridicule (someone)

- *Valence* is the number of participants in the action of a verb. If we say: "The deer saw the hunter," then the valence is two, counting the deer and the hunter. If "John gave Suzie a bouquet," the valence is three: John, Suzie, and the bouquet. If "I walked away alone," then the valence is one: just myself. If "It's raining outside," then the valence is zero, since "it" doesn't count as a participant here.

- Omaha verbs may expect a certain number of participants. This number can be modified, in principle, by adding locative prefixes or detransitivizing wa-. Detransitivizing wa- stands in for an object participant and thereby reduces the valence of the verb by one.

- Locative prefixes, on the other hand, add a participant. Locative u- adds the participant inside of which or around which the action occurs, while locative ā- adds the participant upon or against which the action occurs.

- Two more prefixes, called *applicative* prefixes, also add a participant. One of these is the instrumentizing ī-, which adds the participant by means of which the action occurs.

- Our other applicative prefix is the *transitivizing* prefix í-. This prefix signals to the listener that the action is aimed at an object. The difference may be sensed by comparing āthade, "read," with íthade, "read to." The former may suggest a reciting action performed while hunched over the text you are attempting to decipher. The latter means that the action is done *to* someone, such as a child, who is the object to whom the action is directed.

- Note that transitivizing í- and instrumentizing ī- are pronounced almost identically, though their meanings are entirely different. The vowel of instrumentizing ī- is apparently held longer, which allows them to be distinguished.

Vocabulary: Transitivizing i- Verbs

í'oⁿ: cultivate; e.g., a field

íbahoⁿ: know (something or somebody)

ígahi: mix in (an ingredient)

ígaskoⁿthe: try or taste (something)

íhe: get through (an obstructed route)

íhusa: scold (somebody)

íkʰu: invite (somebody)

ímoⁿthe: avenge, take revenge on someone, lay for somebody

ímoⁿxe: ask (somebody) a question

íniethe: injure (somebody)

ínitʰe: scold (somebody)

ínoⁿhiⁿ: permit, allow, agree to (something)

ínoⁿxithe: chase (somebody)

ísabe: suffer (from something or for somebody)

íshte: be embarrassed or ashamed (of something or somebody)

íthade: read to (somebody)

íthappe: wait for (something or somebody)

íthe: find, discover (something or somebody)

íthibthoⁿ: scent, smell (something or somebody)

íthidoⁿdoⁿ: tug (on something)

íthise: cut (something)

íthishi: feed (people or animals)

íthizha: wash (something)

íthizhoⁿzhoⁿ: jar, shake (something or somebody)

ítte: touch (something or somebody)

ítʰiⁿ: hit (something or somebody)

ít'athe: loathe (somebody)

íwakʰega: make (somebody) sick

íxaxa: ridicule (somebody)

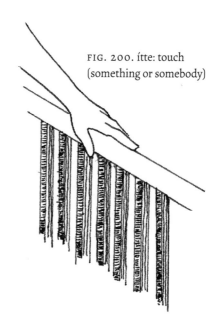

FIG. 200. ítte: touch (something or somebody)

Vocabulary: Stative Verbs

zóⁿsta: rotten, spoiled (meat or eggs)

zhōⁿttoⁿthiⁿge: nod off, go to sleep

Vocabulary: Nouns

niskíthe: salt

ūe: field

wakkóⁿdawaāthahoⁿtti: church ("house for worshiping God")

Speaking Practice

A. Read the following sentences aloud. Then translate the sentences into English. Examples:

Ikʰáge thiⁿkʰe íbahoⁿ: He recognized his friend.

Thikkóⁿ ímoⁿxa!: Ask your grandmother!

Iháⁿ thiⁿkʰe ítha bi ama: They say she found her mother.

1. Ūe ettá kʰe íʼoⁿ góⁿtha, wikkóⁿ akʰa.

2. Kki Moⁿshtíⁿge edí hí bi kki, Ppahé-Wāthahuni akʰa íbahoⁿ bi ama.

3. Niskíthe ígahi, wittími akʰa.

4. Uzhóⁿge bazhúzhu thoⁿzha, thiādi akʰa íhe ígaskoⁿtha.

5. Héga ítʼatha bi egóⁿ, ímoⁿtha bi ama, Ishtíthiⁿkʰe akʰa.

6. Wittóⁿshka idādoⁿshte íbahoⁿ azhi kki, ittígoⁿ ímoⁿxe tta tʰe.

7. Zhóⁿ gasé ígaskoⁿthe éde isóⁿge ínietha.

8. Kki ínitʰa, ithādi akʰa.

9. Shíⁿgazhiⁿga ābae zhūgthe athé tʰe ínoⁿhiⁿ bazhi, ithādi akʰa.

10. Wakkóⁿdawāthahoⁿtti tʰedi zhōⁿttoⁿthiⁿge gthíⁿ kki, íthizhoⁿzhoⁿ igáx̌thoⁿ akʰa.

B. Translate the following sentences into Omaha.

1. The boy was scolded by his mother.

2. That girl read to her father.

3. My elder brother has to wait for his grandmother.

4. Did my grandchild find the bread?

5. The dogs scented the raccoon.

6. The child tugged on the edge of his/her mother's dress.

7. He has to cut the rope.

8. My uncle didn't touch the snake.

9. The spoiled meat might make your child sick.

10. They say the black bears always ridiculed the human.

C. The instructor challenges the students with a base word, and the students respond with a corresponding í- word. While doing so, they should use the gesture of pointing at the left fist with the right forefinger. Example:

Wagōⁿze: Thizhá. ("Wash it.")

Ttáppuskazhiⁿga: Íthizha. ("Wash the particular thing.") [pointing at left fist]

Wagṓⁿze: Wakʰéga. ("Sick.")

Ttáppuskazhiⁿga: Íwakʰega. ("Make someone sick.") [pointing at left fist]

D. The instructor says something to each student that can be answered with an í- word. The student responds appropriately. Example:

Wagṓⁿze: Ann akʰa awádi shêtʰedi gthíⁿ a? ("Why is Ann sitting there?")

Bruce: Leslie íthappe gthíⁿ. ("She's waiting for Leslie.")

Wagṓⁿze: Awádi íshte gthíⁿ a, Ed akʰa? ("Why is Ed embarrassed?")

Phil: Núzhiⁿga ama íx̌ax̌a i tʰe. ("It seems the boys laughed at him.")

E. The students form small groups of about two or three and take turns asking each other questions that can be answered using an í- word. Using the corresponding gesture with them is encouraged.

18.8 CONJUGATION OF TRANSITIVIZING Í- VERBS

		í-bahoⁿ	s/he knows her
I-		itháppahoⁿ	I know her
you-		íthashpahoⁿ	you know her
we-		oⁿthóⁿbahoⁿ	we know her
-me		oⁿthóⁿbahoⁿ	he knows me
-you		í-thibahoⁿ	he knows you
-us		weábahoⁿ	he knows us
-them		wébahoⁿ	he knows them
I-you		í-wippahoⁿ	I know you
I-them		wéppahoⁿ	I know them
you-me		oⁿthóⁿshpahoⁿ	you know me
you-us		weáshpahoⁿ	you know us
you-them		wéshpahoⁿ	you know them
we-you		oⁿthóⁿthibahoⁿ	we know you
we-them		weóⁿbahoⁿ	we know them

- The conjugation of transitivizing í- verbs is rather complicated. The first rule to note is that all affixed pronouns except the wa- for "us" and "them" come after the í- prefix and before the verb stem. This may be hard to tell, however, because of serious phonetic changes affecting the í-.

- If an *i*-sound comes immediately before some other vowel with no break, the transition will automatically sound like *y*. Thus, if we say *i-a*, running the two vowels together, it will sound like *i-ya*. Omaha has no *y*-sound, however, so where this epenthetic (automatically occurring) -*y*- appeared is now transformed into Omaha -th-.

- The transitivizing prefix plus the "I" affixed pronoun is thus: í-a-, which sounded like i-ya-, and therefore became i-tha-. The transitivizing prefix plus the "you" affixed pronoun is of course í-tha-, which is about the same. The only way to distinguish the two is by switching up the accents. The "I" form is always pronounced with the accent on the second syllable, ithá-, while the "you" form leaves the accent on the first syllable, where it ought to be, given that transitivizing í- takes the accent: ítha-.

- The same thing happens when the transitivizing í- prefix comes before the affixed pronoun o^n-: í-o^n- became i-yo^n-. But in this case, the nasal vowel bleeds back to the i-, making this o^n-yo^n-, which gives us o^nthó^n-. Note that the accent shifts to the second syllable here.

- For the u- and ā- locative prefixes, the "we" affixed pronoun precedes them, giving us o^ngú- and o^ngā- for the "we" forms. But for the í- applicative prefix, the "we" pronoun follows it, giving us o^nthó^n-, just as for the "me" pronoun.

- When the "us" or "them" affixed pronoun wa- combines with transitivizing í-, it comes first, making wa-i-, which combine to become we-.

- In the case of "us," an extra -a- is added after we-, giving weá-.

Vocabulary: Transitivizing í- Verbs

íbaho^n: know

Vocabulary: Stative Verbs

gashétho^n: broken up, destroyed

no^{n}x̧íde-thi^{n}ge: naughty, disobedient ("no ears")

Vocabulary: Nouns

wagthí: maggot

Vocabulary: Adverbs

at^{h}ó^{n}shte: sometimes

shet^{h}ó^{n}na: still (as in "It's still your turn")

Speaking Practice

A. Read the following sentences aloud. Then translate the sentences into English. Examples:

Itháppaho^n mazhi: I don't know.

Íthathe?: Did you find it?

O^{n}thó^{n}no^{n}x̧ithazhi a!: Don't chase me!

1. "Negího, wa'úzhi^{n}ga ak^{h}a 'Thinégi thi^{n}k^{h}etta mo^{n}thí^n a!' á egó^n, o^{n}thó^{n}husa egó^n, ppí," á bi ama Mo^{n}shtí^{n}ge ak^{h}a.

2. Thihá^n ak^{h}a íthihusa tta.

3. Wētta thâbthi^n íthagahi tta ni^{n}kshe.

4. Ūha^n wiwítta t^{h}e íthiwak^{h}ega egó^n, iwíbthade tta mi^{n}k$^{h'}$.

5. Weániethe egó^n, o^{n}thó^{n}mo^{n}the gō^{n}tha.

6. Wittúshpa noⁿxíde-thiⁿge
egóⁿ, atʰóⁿshte weánoⁿxithe.

7. Wikkóⁿ akʰa oⁿtházhiⁿge
āzhi, oⁿthóⁿxaxa azhi.

8. "Íwishte noⁿ moⁿ!" á, thiháⁿ
akʰa, égoⁿ íthihusa tʰe anóⁿoⁿ.

9. "Uzhóⁿge kʰe gashéthoⁿ
thoⁿzha, wí itháhe itháppahoⁿ" á,
égthoⁿge wiwítta akʰa.

10. "Égoⁿ shetʰóⁿna thêthudi
ithábthappe agthíⁿ" á, igáxthoⁿ
akʰa.

B. Translate the following sentences
into Omaha.

1. They'll laugh at you.

2. I want to cultivate my field.

3. We will not permit it.

4. There is something I want to
ask you.

5. If they are hungry, we
should feed them.

6. I don't want you to be
ashamed of me.

7. Are you afraid to touch
maggots?

8. We know the people living
far away over there on the Missouri
River.

9. Are you able to cut the rope?

10. Don't dislike me!

C. The instructor goes around the
class, challenging each student with an

í- verb and an emphatic pronoun. The
student responds with the appropriate
conjugation form. Note that "wí" and
"thí" will be reversed in the interaction.
Example:

Wagōⁿze: Íthe. Wí. ("Find it. I.")

Tyler: Íthathe. ("You found it.")

Wagōⁿze: Íhusa. Oⁿgú. ("Scold him/
her. We.")

Victor: Oⁿthóⁿhusa. ("We scolded
him/her.")

Wagōⁿze: Íkʰu. Thí. ("Invite him/her.
You.")

Karen: Ithákʰu. ("I invited him/her.")

D. The instructor goes around the class
again, challenging each student with
a transitivizing í- verb and one or two
emphatic pronouns. If there are two,
the first pronoun is the object pronoun,
and the second is the subject pronoun.
A third person subject will be é. A third
person plural animate object, "them,"
will be é ama. A verb that takes no
personal object, such as ígaskoⁿthe, will
be presented with only one emphatic
pronoun. The student should respond
with the appropriate conjugated form.
Again, "wí" and "thí" will be reversed in
the interaction.

E. The students form groups of about
four to six, with a deck of cards, and play
this as a game using í- verbs, according to
the rules described in part E in 18.4 and
18.6.

18.9 COMBINATIONS OF APPLICATIVE Ī- AND Í- WITH LOCATIVE U- AND Ā- PREFIXES

Transitivizing í- plus Locative u- Verbs

uthúbido^n	í-ubído^n	push down, dunk
uthúdo^{n}be	í-udó^{n}be	watch out, caution, examine
uthúgahi	í-ugáhi	mix in, stir together
uthúgasho^n	í-ugásho^n	commute, shuttle back and forth
uthúhe	í-uhé	follow
uthúhi	í-uhí	reach
uthúkkikkie	í-ukkíkkie	discuss, converse
uthúkko^{n}the	í-ukkó^{n}the	bind together, cling, connect
uthúno^{n}zhi^n	í-unó^{n}zhi^n	depend upon, rely on, trust
uthúthe	í-uthe	ties, as to a person or place
uthút'athe	í-ut'áthe	dislike, envy, be jealous of
uthúxa	í-uxá	deceive, trick, fool

- When transitivizing í- comes before locative u-, the result is uthú-. The epenthetic "y" sound that comes between í- and u- turns to ledh, the "u" sound bleeds back to the first syllable, and the accent shifts to the second syllable. A number of verbs are formed in this pattern.

Conjugation of Transitivizing í- plus Locative u- Verbs

		follow him	examine her
	í-u-he	uthúhe	uthúdo^{n}be
I-	í-u-a-he	uthúahe	uthútto^{n}be
you-	í-u-tha-he	uthúthahe	uthúshto^{n}be
we-	í-o^{n}g-u-he	o^{n}thó^{n}guhe	o^{n}thó^{n}gudo^{n}be
-me	í-u-o^n-he	o^{n}thó^{n}wo^{n}he	o^{n}thó^{n}wo^{n}do^{n}be
-you	í-u-thi-he	uthúthihe	uthúthido^{n}be
-us	wa-í-a-(th)u-he	weáthuhe	weáthudo^{n}be
-them	wa-í-u-he	wiúhe	wiúdo^{n}be
I-you	í-u-wi-he	uthúwihe	uthúwitto^{n}be
I-them	wa-í-u-a-he	wiúahe	wiútto^{n}be
you-me	í-u-o^n-tha-he	o^{n}thó^{n}wo^{n}thahe	o^{n}thó^{n}wo^{n}shto^{n}be
you-us	wa-í-a-(th)u-tha-he	weáthuthahe	weáthushto^{n}be
you-them	wa-í-u-tha-he	wiúthahe	wiúshto^{n}be
we-you	í-o^{n}g-u-thi-he	o^{n}thó^{n}guthihe	o^{n}thó^{n}gudo^{n}be
we-them	wa-í-o^{n}g-u-he	wió^{n}guhe	wió^{n}gudo^{n}be

- If transitivizing í- comes before o^{n}g-, "we," or o^n-, "me," the result is o^{n}thó^n(g)-. Note that i- characteristically gives epenthetic th after it before another vowel, u- gives epethetic w, and all the vowels in the series adopt the value of the last one before a real consonant. Thus, i-u-o^n- becomes o^{n}tho^{n}wo^n-.

- The "us" forms do not break down quite as nicely as the others. Apparently these were secondarily reinterpreted as weá-, "transitivizing í- done to us," plus thu- in place of locative u- by analogy with the simpler forms of the verb, uthú-. This trick spared speakers from having to put a- in front of what was originally locative *o-, which might have been hard to distinguish (as earlier noted, the asterisk denotes words, sounds, or morphemes reconstructed for the ancestral language, before it developed into historical Omaha).

Instrumentizing ī- plus Locative u- Nouns

uthúga	ī-uga	material used in painting: coloring, paintbrush, paintstick
uthúgashke	ī-ugashke	hook, peg, something to hang things on

· When instrumentizing ī- comes before locative u-, the result is uthú-, just as for transitivizing í-.

Transitivizing í- plus Locative ā- Verbs

íthakkoⁿ	í-ākkoⁿ	lean on (something)
íthappe	í-āppe	wait for (someone)

· When transitivizing í- comes before locative ā-, the result is ítha-. Here, the initial í- retains both its accent and its sound value but still produces the epenthetic ledh between the two vowels.

Conjugation of Transitivizing í- plus Locative ā- Verbs

wait for	íthappe	
	wait for now	have waited for
I-	itháappe	itháthappe
you-	íthaappe	íthathappe
we-	oⁿthóⁿappe	oⁿthóⁿthappe
-me	oⁿthóⁿappe	oⁿthóⁿthappe
-you	íthiappe	íthithappe
-us	weáppe	weáthappe
-them	wéappe	wéthappe
I-you	íwiappe	íwithappe
I-them	weáwappe	weáwathappe
you-me	oⁿthóⁿthaappe	oⁿthóⁿthathappe
you-us	weáthaappe	weáthathappe
you-them	wéthaappe	wéthathappe
we-you	oⁿthóⁿthiappe	oⁿthóⁿthithappe
we-them	weóⁿappe	weóⁿthappe

· Our speakers seem to recognize two distinct, almost-complete conjugation patterns for the í-ā- verbs. One of them is used when the verb's salience is immediate and present; the other is used when the verb happened in the past or has been going on for a long time.

· The "present tense" pattern treats the original locative ā- as the beginning of the base word, and conjugates transitivizing í- with the affixed pronouns in front of it. The "past tense" pattern does the same thing, except that it treats the base word as beginning with the epenthetic ledh. Thus "wait" in the "present tense" is conjugated í-affixed to-appe, while "wait" in the "past tense" is conjugated í-affixed to-thappe. Similarly, for "lean on," íthakkoⁿ, the "present tense" is conjugated í-before-akkoⁿ, and the "past tense" is conjugated í-before-thakkoⁿ.

· The one exception to the pattern is the simple form of the verb itself. Íthappe, "wait for," is formed simply as í-ā-ppe, with clearly epenthetic ledh, and likewise for íthakkoⁿ, "lean on." These do not have a distinction between "present" and "past" tense. Yet their two distinct "tenses" for other conjugation forms are built on different interpretations of where the base word for their transitivizing í- begins.

Instrumentizing ī- plus Locative ā- Nouns

ithābaṣnu	ī-ābaṣnu	any tool used to cut off hair: scissors, shaver
ithāgaχade	ī-āgaχade	lid, cover

- When instrumentizing ī- comes before locative ā-, the result is ithā-. The phonological result is the same as for transitivizing í-, but the accent shifts to the second syllable where the locative ā- lives.

Vocabulary: í-u- Verbs

uthúbidon: push down, dunk

uthúdonbe: examine, look out, be careful

uthúgahi: mix in

uthúgashon: commute, shuttle back and forth

uthúhe: follow

uthúhi: reach

uthúhi-thi'áwathe: inaccessible

uthúkkikkie: discuss, converse

uthúkkonthe: bind together, cling, connect

uthúnonzhin: depend on, rely on, trust

uthúthe: ties, as to a person or place

uthúthe-thinge: have nobody left, nothing to hold you

uthút'athe: dislike, envy, be jealous of

uthúx̌e: deceive, trick, fool

Vocabulary: ī-u- Nouns

uthúga: coloring, paintbrush, paintstick

uthúgashke: hook, peg, something to hang things on

Vocabulary: í-ā- Verbs

íthakkon: lean on

íthappe: wait for

Vocabulary: ī-ā- Nouns

ithābaṣnu: scissors, shaver, any tool to cut off hair

ithāgax̌ade: cover, lid

Vocabulary: Nouns

wahónthishige: orphan

Vocabulary: Question Words

āgudi: where?

āgudix̌ti: where exactly?

Speaking Practice

A. Read the following sentences aloud. Then translate the sentences into English. Examples:

Nú x̌ubé uthúahe: I follow the holy man.

Ín'e thon uthúshtonbe a?: Did you examine the rock?

Onthónwonbidon bazhi i ga ho!: Don't push me under!

1. Thiādi akha wéahidex̌ti uthúgashon tta the.

2. Wétta thâbthin uthúgahi a/ga!

3. Uthúwix̌e kkōnbtha kki, onthónwonthat'athe tta ninkshe.

4. Égon onthóngukkikkie tta ongathon.

5. Uthúshtonbazhi kki, ppá thon uthúwishpidon tta minkh', nishúde khedi.

6. Wittóⁿshka akʰa thêthudi uthúthe athíⁿ egóⁿ, shóⁿshoⁿ uthúgashoⁿ moⁿthíⁿ.

7. Uthúdoⁿba! Égithe shínuda ama ttanúkka kʰe uthúhi tta.

8. Wikkóⁿ uthúanoⁿzhiⁿ éde, wí é shti oⁿthóⁿwoⁿnoⁿzhiⁿ.

9. Xáde xóⁿde ge házhiⁿga uthúkkoⁿtha i a/ga!

10. Ithābaṣnu utháne tʰe uthúgashke tʰedi íthathe tte.

B. Translate the following sentences into Omaha.

1. The stars are inaccessible.

2. My friend leaned against the tree.

3. Where exactly is the lid?

4. Be careful!

5. I depend on you.

6. They say that Ishtíthiⁿkʰe intended (wanted) to trick Rabbit.

7. My father should wait for my grandmother.

8. Don't follow me!

9. I can't reach it.

10. The old woman has nobody left.

C. The instructor goes around the class, challenging each student with an í- plus locative u- or ā- verb and an emphatic pronoun. The student responds with the

appropriate conjugation form. As usual, "wí" and "thí" will be reversed in the interaction. Example:

Wagōⁿze: Uthúhe. Oⁿgú. ("Follow him/ her. We.")

Megan: Oⁿthóⁿguhe. ("We follow him/ her.")

Wagōⁿze: Íthakkoⁿ. Thí. ("Lean on it. You.")

Oswald: Itháakkoⁿ/Itháthakkoⁿ. ("I lean/leaned on it.")

Wagōⁿze: Uthúhi. Wí. ("Reach it. I.")

Martha: Uthúthahi. ("You reached it.")

D. The instructor goes around the class again, challenging each student with a transitivizing í- plus locative u- or ā- verb and one or two emphatic pronouns. If there are two, the first pronoun is the object pronoun, and the second is the subject pronoun. A third person subject will be é. A third person plural animate object, "them," will be é ama. A verb that takes no personal object, such as ígaskoⁿthe, will be presented with only one emphatic pronoun. The student should respond with the appropriate conjugated form. Again, "wí" and "thí" will be reversed in the interaction.

E. The students form groups of about four to six, with a deck of cards, and play this as a game using í- plus locative u- and ā- verbs, according to the rules described in part E in 18.4 and 18.6.

18.10 COMBINATION OF WA- WITH LOCATIVE U- AND Ā-, AND Ī-, AND Í- VERBS

Combination of Detransitivizing or Nominalizing wa- Before u- Verbs

wa	+	u$^{\prime}$í	give, lend *vt.*	=	ū$^{\prime}$i		give, lend *vi.*
wa	+	uhóⁿ	cook *vt.*	=	ūhoⁿ		cook *vi., n.*

- When wa- comes before locative u-, the accent moves to the first syllable and we mark it as long. Here, the original wa- is absorbed into the u-, but its presence is shown by the fact that the ū- now takes the accent.

Combination of Detransitivizing or Nominalizing wa- Before ā- Verbs

wa	+	ābaxu	write on *vt.*	=	wābaxu		write on *vi.*
wa	+	āthatʰe	eat on *vt.*	=	wāthatʰe		table *n.*

- When wa- comes before locative ā-, its vowel merges with ā- to make wā-. If a word starting with wa- takes its accent on the first syllable, then it also contains locative ā-.

Combination of Detransitivizing or Nominalizing wa- Before Instrumentizing ī-

wa	+	ībamoⁿ	file *vt., n.*	=	wēbamoⁿ		file *n.*
wa	+	īthawa	counter	=	wēthawa		counter

- When wa- comes before instrumentizing ī-, the combination becomes wē-.

Combination of Detransitivizing or Nominalizing wa- Before í- Verbs

wa	+	íthade	read to *vt.*	=	wéthade		reader *n.*
wa	+	ítʰiⁿ	hit *vt.*	=	wétʰiⁿ		hit *vi.*

- When wa- comes before transitivizing í-, the combination becomes wé-.

Combination of wa- Before Instrumentizing ī- plus Locative u- (uthu-) Verbs

wa	+	ī-ubátti	plug with	=	wēobatti	cork *n.*
wa	+	ī-ubétʰoⁿ	wrap with	=	wēobetʰoⁿ	wrapping *n.*
wa	+	ī-ugá	color with	=	wēoga	paint, dye *n.*
wa	+	ī-ugáṣne	split with	=	wēogaṣne	wedge *n.*
wa	+	ī-ugóⁿba	illuminate with	=	wēogoⁿba	window *n.*
wa	+	ī-uhóⁿ	cook with	=	wēohoⁿ	cooking pot *n.*
wa	+	ī-uthá	tell with	=	wēotha	landmark, sign *n.*
wa	+	ī-uthí$^{\prime}$ude	make holes with	=	wēothi$^{\prime}$ude	drill, auger *n.*
wa	+	ī-uthídoⁿ	lock with	=	wēothidoⁿ	lock, latch *n.*
wa	+	ī-uthóⁿthe	hang up with	=	wēothoⁿthe	hanger *n.*

- When nominalizing wa- comes before the combination instrumentizing ī- with locative u-, the combination becomes wēo-.
- The wēo- combination may sometimes be seen written as wíu-, wiú-, or weó-. In fact, representing this in regular letters is problematic, because it is really the fusion of three separate elements, wa-, ī-, and u-, into a single prefix that behaves as a unit. The accent of a verb prefers to be on the second syllable if possible, which would be the o-/u- in the fully fused form, but historically it would be on the accent-drawing ī-, and hence on the wē-. Further, the combination developed from wē- + o- at a time

when Omaha u was still pronounced o. Since both e and o are mid-vowels, this meant that the combination became a diphthong glide from a front unround vowel to a back round vowel without the level of the jaw ever changing. When Omaha o became u, this produced a contradiction in the rules. Rule one said that mid-vowel o must be raised to become high-vowel u. Rule two said that mid-vowel e must remain e. Rule three said that the two vowels in wēo- must be pronounced at the same level. Rule three seems to win out, while rules one and two are still fighting. The result is a diphthong somewhere between weo- and wiu.

- Note that without the nominalizing wa-, the wēo- prefix would be the uthú- prefix we met in the previous lesson, from instrumentizing ī- + u-. When the wa- is added, it fuses first with ī- to become wē-, which does not produce epenthetic ledh before another vowel as plain ī- does.

Combination of wa- Before Instrumentizing ī- plus Locative ā- (ithā-) Verbs

wa	+	ī-ābax̌thade	fasten onto with	=	wēabax̌thade	hairpin *n.*
wa	+	ī-āgaspe	weigh down with	=	wēagaspe	paperweight *n.*
wa	+	ī-āthaskabe	stick to with	=	wēathaskabe	paste *n.*

- When nominalizing wa- comes before the combination instrumentizing ī- with locative ā-, the full series becomes wēa-.

- As with wēo-, wēa- acts as a unit in which the two vowels form a diphthong

in which either may be construed to take the accent. Unlike wēo-, there is no vowel shift to confuse matters.

- As with wēo-, removal of nominalizing wa- leaves the prefix instrumentizing ī- before the locative prefix. Here again, ī- alone produces epenthetic ledh before the next vowel, giving us the ithā- prefix met in 18.9. So wa- added to an ithā- word gets us a wēa- word.

Vocabulary: Plain Active Verbs

gaspé: settle out, like muddy water

thiṣhnúde: pry out, extract

Vocabulary: ā- Verbs

ābax̣u: write (something) on

āthaskabe: adhere, stick to

āthat^{h}e: eat on

Vocabulary: Transitivizing í- Verbs

íthade: read to

ít^{h}i^n: hit (something)

Vocabulary: ī- Words

ībamoⁿ: file with; a file

īthawa: count with; a counter

Vocabulary: u- Words

u'í: give, lend, loan (something)

ubátti: plug (a leak)

ubéthoⁿ: wrap

ugá: color, dye, paint (something)

ugáṣne: split, cracked

ugóⁿbe: bright, light out

uháⁿ: cook (something)

uthá: tell (the news)

uthí'ude: bore, drill, make holes

uthídoⁿ: lock, latch, pull shut or tight
   together (a door)

uthóⁿthe: hang up (clothes)

Vocabulary: wa-ā- Verbs

wābaxu: write (things) on

Vocabulary: wa-í- Verbs

wéthiⁿ: hit (things)

Vocabulary: wa-u- Verbs

ū'i: give, lend, loan (things)

ūhaⁿ: cook (things)

Vocabulary: Stative Verbs

ūmakka: easy

FIG. 201. wāthatʰe: table

Vocabulary: Nouns

iⁿdéugaxe: portrait, picture

móⁿze-wēogadoⁿ: nails

ūhaⁿ: (a) cook

wāgathe: gift

wāthatʰe: table

wēabax̌thade: hairpin

wēagaspe: paperweight

wēathaskabe: paste

wēbamoⁿ: a file

wēobatti: a cork

wēobetʰoⁿ: wrapping

wēoga: coloring, paint, dye

wēogaṣne: wedge

wēogoⁿba: window

wēohoⁿ: cooking pot

wēokkihoⁿ: pepper

wēotha: landmark, sign

wēothi'ude: drill, auger, corkscrew

wēothidoⁿ: lock, latch

wēothoⁿthe: hanger

wéthade: reader, a teacher

wēthawa: counter, cent

Speaking Practice

A. Read the following sentences aloud. Then translate the sentences into English. Examples:

Ūhaⁿ thiⁿkʰe thahídazhi ga!: Don't disrespect the cook!

Wāthatʰe kʰe wāshpax̣u tta tʰe: You should write on the table.

Wēotha uthíx̣ide noⁿzhíⁿ akʰa: He stood there looking for a landmark.

1. Hóⁿt'ega wiⁿ wēoga tʰe ubáhiⁿ.

2. Kkúge thêthoⁿ u'í kkōⁿbtha tʰe egoⁿ, wēobetʰoⁿ uáne.

3. Wēobatti tʰe thiṣhnúde gōⁿtha gthíⁿ.

4. Wēothi'ude athíⁿ kki, ūmakka.

5. Égithe wabthágase thithítta tʰe gahíthe tta. Gá! wēagaspe óⁿ a!

6. Wizhíⁿge akʰa iⁿdéugax̣e tʰe nóⁿdatta wēathaskabe uthúthoⁿtha.

7. Wahóⁿthishige egóⁿ, uthúthe-thiⁿge gthíⁿ.

8. Ūhaⁿ gōⁿtha, wizhóⁿge akʰa.

9. Ttibútta móⁿtʰadi agthíⁿ thoⁿdi, wēbamoⁿ kkōⁿbtha noⁿ moⁿ.

10. Zhóⁿ kʰe uthúgaṣne shkōⁿna kki, móⁿze-wēogaṣne óⁿ ga!

B. Translate the following sentences into Omaha.

1. If you're giving things away, give me five cents!

2. The reader stood in front of the church, reading aloud.

3. They say she peeped in through the window.

4. Do you have paint?

5. The lock on the door is broken.

6. Then use nails!

7. Put away the hanger on the hook!

8. Do you see the sign?

9. I'm going to put the pepper in the pot.

10. My older sister has a new hairpin.

C. The instructor goes around the class, challenging each student with a possible base word from this lesson but with the initial wa- removed. The student needs to say the word properly with the wa- restored. Example:

Wagōⁿze: Ítʰiⁿ. ("Hit it.")

Ivan: Wétʰiⁿ. ("Hit.")

Wagōⁿze: Ībamoⁿ. ("File.")

Holly: Wēbamoⁿ. ("File.")

Wagōⁿze: Āthatʰe. ("Eat on it.")

Francine: Wāthatʰe. ("Table.")

D. The instructor goes around the class
   again, challenging each student with a
   base word from this lesson, plus gestures
   for leading locatives and applicatives
   either on the base word or to be attached
   to it. The student has to add wa- to the
   front of the series and say the whole
   word. Example:

> Wagṓⁿze: Uháⁿ. ("Cook it.") [makes the
> u- gesture]

> Pat: Ūhaⁿ. ("Cook.")

> Wagṓⁿze: Uháⁿ. ("Cook it.") [makes the
> u- and ī- gestures]

> Leonard: Wēohaⁿ. ("Cooking pot.")

> Wagṓⁿze: Gaspé. ("Settle out.") [makes
> the ā- and ī- gestures]

> Kevin: Wēagaspe. ("Paperweight.")

E. The students form groups of about
   four to six, with a deck of cards, and play
   the challenge and response game in part
   D according to the rules described in
   part E in 18.4 and 18.6.

Self Affixes and Datives

19.1 THE POSSESSIVE GI- PREFIX

Transitive Verbs and the Possessive gi- Prefix

ʔį́ⁿ	pack on one's back	gi-ʔį́ⁿ	pack one's own	
dóⁿbe	see	gi-ttóⁿbe	see one's own	
í-the	find	í-gi-the	find one's own	
nā	ask for	gi-nā	ask for one's own back	
ōⁿthe	abandon	gi-ōⁿthe	abandon ones' own	
ṣnāthe	paint, smear, polish	gi-ṣnāthe	paint, smear, polish one's own	
thatʰé	eat	gthátʰe	eat one's own	
thizé	take	gthíze	take one's own	
tʔé-the	kill	tʔé-gi-the	kill one's own	
u-né	seek	u-gi-ne	seek one's own	
zhū-gthe	accompany	zhū-gi-gthe	accompany one's own	

- The possessive prefix gi- before a transitive verb implies that the verb affects an object that is the possession of the subject. Thus the subject is acting on his or her *own* thing or relative.

- Possessive gi- does not draw the accent. It takes the accent only if it is the second syllable and the first syllable doesn't draw the accent either.

- In conjugation, possessive gi- comes between the affixed pronoun and the main verb. When the affixed pronoun is infixed within the verb, so is the gi-.

- Possessive gi- verbs conjugate in the common way, with a-gi- for "I do it to my own" and tha-gi- for "You do it to your own."

- When possessive gi- precedes a ledh- verb, it loses its own vowel and merges as gth-. Note that the lost vowel was originally there, because it draws the accent forward to the new "first" syllable. Thus thatʰé becomes gthátʰe, and thizé becomes gthíze.

- When possessive gi- precedes a verb beginning with the instrumental prefix ga-, the combination becomes gtha-, just as with the instrumental prefix tha-.

- When possessive gi- precedes a simple stop verb, the following stop becomes tense. Thus, dóⁿbe becomes gittóⁿbe.

- A common use of possessive gi- is in reference to one's relatives. Thus agíttoⁿbe could mean either "I see my own (comb)," or "I see my own (kinsperson)."

Vocabulary: Transitive Verbs

ʔį́ⁿ: pack on one's back

dóⁿbe: see

giʔį́ⁿ: pack one's own on one's back

ginā: ask for one's own back

giōⁿthe: abandon one's own

giṣnāthe: paint, smear, polish one's own

gthátʰe: eat one's own

gthíze: take or grab one's own

ígithe: find one's own

íthe: find

nā: ask for, beg, request

ōⁿthe: abandon, throw away

ṣnāthe: paint, smear, polish

thatʰé: eat

thizé: take, grab

t'égithe: kill one's own

t'éthe: kill

ugíne: seek one's own

uné: seek

zhūgigthe: accompany one's own

zhūgthe: accompany

Vocabulary: Stative Verbs

skīge: heavy

Vocabulary: Nouns

ppéttoⁿ: crane (the bird)

sígthe: footprints, track, trail

uthízoⁿ: among, midst, amid, in the middle of a group

ǩádeīnoⁿse: mower

FIG. 202. ppéttoⁿ: crane

Vocabulary: Miscellaneous

hôⁿde: last night

Speaking Practice

A. Read the following sentences aloud. Then translate the sentences into English. Examples:

Wizhíⁿge agíttoⁿbe kkōⁿbtha: I want to see my own son.

Ikkóⁿ thiⁿkʰe zhūgigthe gthíⁿ: He lived together with his grandmother.

Môⁿde kʰe gthíza, nudóⁿ akʰa: The warrior grabbed his bow.

1. Kʰagého! Ūzhiha thithítta kʰe skīge. Ppahé shêhithoⁿttatʰoⁿ thagí'iⁿ a?

2. Kkáshi Moⁿshtíⁿge kʰe ígitha bi ama, ikkóⁿ akʰa.

3. Iⁿdādi akʰa ǩáde-īnoⁿse ettá kʰe ginā tta tʰe.

4. Shíⁿgazhiⁿga wiwítta ma agíoⁿtha mazhi tta miⁿkʰe.

5. Wa'úzhiⁿga ppiāzhi akʰa nudóⁿ thiⁿkʰe t'éthe gōⁿtha éde, izhóⁿge thiⁿkʰe t'égitha bi ama.

6. Iⁿdé thoⁿ gişnātha bi egóⁿ, igáǩthoⁿ ugíne athá bi ama, nudóⁿ akʰa.

7. Igáǩthoⁿ iⁿdé shi gittóⁿbe gōⁿtha bi ama; wa'ú thiⁿkʰe giōⁿthe gōⁿtha bazhi bi ama.

8. Sígthe kʰe uthúha bi egóⁿ, ígitha bi ama, igáǩthoⁿ thiⁿkʰe, ukkítte uthízoⁿ gthíⁿ thiⁿkʰe.

9. Móⁿde kʰe gthíza bi egóⁿ,
ukkítte ímoⁿthe íthappe gthíⁿ bi
ama, uzhóⁿge kʰedi.

10. Igáx̌thoⁿ zhūgigthe hátheza
agthí bi ama, nudóⁿ akʰa.

B. Translate the following sentences into Omaha.

1. Rabbit set out together with his grandmother, they say.

2. Husband! Ask your uncle for your gun back!

3. I'm going to go searching for my brother.

4. Did you eat your own food last night?

5. I want to go with my father when he leaves on his commute.

6. I'm going to go to war. So I'm smearing my face with paint.

7. Even though it is heavy, I will bear my own pack.

8. That bellowing calf is looking for its mother.

9. Beware that if you touch the crane's chick, its mother may abandon it.

10. "Sister! I've searched for you so long, and now that I've found you I can see your face!" said my older sister.

C. The instructor goes around the class, challenging each student with a base verb. The student responds by giving the possessive gi- form, along with a gesture of crossing arms with each hand grasping the opposite upper arm, as if hugging a relative. Example:

Wagōⁿze: Nā. ("Ask for it.")

Gina: Ginā. ("Ask for one's own.")
[makes gi- gesture]

Wagōⁿze: Dóⁿbe. ("See it.")

Frank: Gittóⁿbe. ("See one's own.")
[makes gi- gesture]

Wagōⁿze: Thatʰé. ("Eat it.")

Wallace: Gthátʰe. ("Eat one's own.")
[makes gi- gesture]

Wagōⁿze: Íthe. ("Find it.")

Pepper: Ígithe. ("Find one's own.")
[makes gi- gesture]

D. The instructor goes around the class again, challenging each student with a base verb and one or two emphatic pronouns. If there are two, the first pronoun is the object pronoun, and the second is the subject pronoun. A third person subject will be é. A third person plural animate object, "them," will be é ama. The student should respond with the gi- form of the word, appropriately conjugated, along with the possessive gi- gesture. Again, "wí" and "thí" will be reversed in the interaction.

E. The students form groups of about four to six, with a deck of cards, and play this as a game using the gi- form of verbs, according to the rules described in part E in 18.4 and 18.6.

19.2 THE SUUS GI- PREFIX

The Suus Prefix

baxú	write	gippáxu	sign up, enlist
-gthé	place upright	gigthé	take after (mom or dad)
-ni	live, breathe ?	giní	recover, get well
-noⁿkkúwiⁿxe	go around in circles on foot	ginóⁿkkuwiⁿxe	run around trying to get things done
-sithe	recollect ?	gisíthe	remember
-siⁿ	be aware ?	gisíⁿ	revive, recover consciousness

- The prefix gi- can also be used intransitively to indicate a moving or self-transforming action done by oneself. In a moving sense, it suggests to "betake oneself." Otherwise, it means to come into the state indicated by the root.

- Some of these roots are too old to remain as separate words.

- The word "suus" is from Latin, in reference to the self. Here it is used to mean that the verb state or action is operative on the subject him- or herself.

- The suus gi- forms generally combine and conjugate the same as possessive gi-. Note that when suus gi- combines with a simple stop verb such as baxú, the initial stop becomes tense, as with possessive gi-.

Vertitive: Suus for Verbs of Motion

hí	arrive there	kʰí	arrive back there
í	come	gí	come back
moⁿthíⁿ	go, walk	moⁿgthíⁿ	go, walk back
thé	go	gthé	go back
tʰí	arrive here	gthí	arrive back here

- The vertitive forms of the verbs of motion may be considered special cases of suus gi-. In these cases the verbs and their suus forms are old and tightly fused. Nevertheless, each vertitive "back" form is really just gi- plus the plain form.

- The vertitive forms indicate not only "betake oneself" but also the sense that the motion is back to the original position. Many of the other suus forms, such as giní, gisíthe, and gisíⁿ, also indicate return to the normal state.

The Suus Form with Ledh and ga- Verbs

gáthe	give away	gigtháthe	volunteer, offer to give of oneself
-gazú	bearings	gigtházu	recover, wake from a coma
thaxúbe	praise	gigtháxube	boast, praise oneself
thiwãgazu	set straight	gigthíwagazu	settle one's own affairs (write a will)

- For verbs other than the verbs of motion, however, suus gi- before a ledh verb or a that starts with ga- usually seems to combine as gigth-. This may represent two separate gi- prefixes, perhaps suus gi- added onto possessive gi-.

Vocabulary: Verbs

baxú: write

gáthe: give, give away, donate

gí: come back

gigtháthe: volunteer, offer to give of oneself

gigtháx̌ube: boast, praise oneself

gigtházu: recover, wake from a coma

gigthé: take after

gigthíwagazu: settle one's own affairs, as in writing a will

giní: recover, get well

ginón̖kkuwin̖x̌e: run around trying to get things done

gippáx̌u: sign up, enlist (in the army)

gisíthe: remember

gisín̄: revive, recover consciousness

gthé: go back

gthí: arrive back here

hí: arrive there

í: come

kʰí: arrive back there

mon̄gthín̄: go back, walk back

mon̄thín̄: go, walk

thax̌úbe: praise

thé: go

thiwágazu: set straight

Vocabulary: Nouns

wanón̄she: police, soldier

Speaking Practice

A. Read the following sentences aloud. Then translate the sentences into English. Examples:

Agísitha mazhi: I don't remember.

Mon̄gthín̄ i ga ho!: Go back where you all came from!

Gigtháx̌ubazhi a!: Don't boast!

1. Thittínu akʰa wanón̄she gippáx̌u tʰe thagísithe?

2. Wathágigthathe non̄ zhon̄; égon̄ shón̄shon̄ thagínon̄kkuwin̄x̌e mon̄nín̄.

3. Shín̄gazhin̄ga ama ihán̄ thin̄kʰe gigthá.

4. Ón̄bathe on̄wón̄kʰega éde, gasón̄thin̄ agíni tta min̄kʰe. Égon̄ shón̄shon̄ mon̄bthín̄.

5. Wittígon̄ akʰa gigthíwagazu thishtón̄ egón̄, giní bi am'.

6. T'á bi ethégon̄ thon̄zha, gigtházu.

7. Agígtháx̌ube kki, ón̄ačʰakki ga!

8. Winégi gisín̄ thon̄zha, ón̄gisitha bazhi.

9. Mon̄kkón̄sabe tʰe, wétta tʰe, hin̄bthín̄ge tʰe agísitha mazhi; égon̄ agínon̄kkuwin̄x̌e mon̄bthín̄.

10. Sidādi agísin̄ egón̄, gasón̄thin̄ ttíadi akʰí tta min̄kʰe.

B. Translate the following sentences into Omaha.

1. My son will enlist in the army.

2. My son takes after his father.

3. Today my mother needs to run around getting things done.

4. Did your aunt get better?

5. Yes. They say she recovered consciousness last night.

6. When she woke up, they say she remembered all her grandchildren.

7. She always offers to give of herself.

8. Since I have become an old man, I'm going to put my affairs in order.

9. I don't like that boy because he's boastful.

10. If she recovers, she may return home.

C. The instructor goes around the class, challenging each student with a suus gi- verb and an emphatic pronoun. The student should respond with the appropriate conjugation form, along with the suus gi- gesture of forearms planted on the table, lifted, thrust forward a few inches, and planted again. Note that "wí" and "thí" will be reversed in the interaction. Example:

Wagōⁿze: Giní. Thí. ("Get well. You.")

Rose: Agíni. ("I got well.") [with suus gi- gesture]

Wagōⁿze: Gigthé. Oⁿgú. ("Take after him/her. We.")

Leif: Oⁿgígtha. ("We take after him/her.") [with suus gi- gesture]

Wagōⁿze: Gippáx̣u. Wí. ("Enlist. I.")

Sanna: Thagíppax̣u. ("You enlisted.") [with suus gi- gesture]

D. The instructor goes around the class again, challenging each student with either a suus or a possessive gi- verb and

one or two emphatic pronouns. If there are two, the first pronoun is the object pronoun, and the second is the subject pronoun. A third person subject will be é. A third person plural animate object, "them," will be é ama. A verb that takes no personal object will be presented with only one emphatic pronoun. The student should respond with the appropriate conjugated form, along with the correct gi- gesture. Again, "wí" and "thí" will be reversed in the interaction.

E. The students form groups of about four to six, with a deck of cards, and play this as a game using suus and possessive gi- verbs, according to the rules described in part E in 18.4 and 18.6.

19.3 THE REFLEXIVE KKI- PREFIX

Verbs Using the Reflexive or Reciprocal Prefix kki-

āni	fan	kkigthāni	fan oneself
bakkúwiⁿx̣e	push around in a circle	kkippákkuwiⁿx̣e	turn themselves around
gāx̣e	make	kkikkāx̣e	make for oneself
-hoⁿ	lift	kkihóⁿ	lift oneself up
noⁿsé	cut, as grass	kkinóⁿse	trip, stumble, fall
-óⁿhe	move away	kkióⁿhe	flee
ōⁿthe	throw	kkiōⁿthe	throw oneself at
thiāzhi	make different	kkigthíauzhi	transform oneself
thisóⁿthe	turn over	kkigthísoⁿthe	swap ends
-thishkóⁿ	make move	kkigthishkoⁿshkoⁿ	squirm, wriggle
thizhá	wash	kkigthízha	wash up
ūdazhi	not good, bad	kkiūdazhi	they don't get along
uné	seek	ukkíne	seek for oneself

- The reflexive kki- prefix indicates that the action is done either *to* or *for* oneself.

- As with possessive and suus gi-, reflexive kki- combined with a simple stop verb makes the simple stop become tense. Thus gāxe, "make," becomes kkikkāxe, "make for oneself."

- Conjugated, kkikkāxe becomes akkíppaxe for the I-form, and thakkíshkaxe for the you-form.
- Combined with a ledh verb, reflexive kki- becomes kkigth-.
- Combined with locative prefix ā-, reflexive kki- becomes kkigthā-.
- Reflexive kki- also seems to be used for *reciprocal* cases, when two parties are doing something to each other.

Vocabulary: Verbs

āni: fan

bakkúwi^{n}xe: push around in a circle

kkigthāni: fan oneself

kkigthíauzhi: transform oneself, as a shapeshifter

kkigthíso^{n}the: swap ends, as a buffalo

kkigthíshko^{n}shko^n: squirm, wriggle, like puppies

kkigthízha: wash up, as for dinner

kkihó^n: lift oneself up

kkikkāxe: make for oneself

kkikkína: fight, brawl with each other

kkinó^{n}se: trip, stumble, fall

kkiō^{n}the: throw oneself at

kkippákkuwi^{n}xe: turn themselves around, as a stampeding herd

kkiūdazhi: they don't get along with each other

no^{n}sé: cut something low down, like grass

ō^{n}the: throw

thiāzhi: change, make different

thisó^{n}the: turn over, as a pancake

thizhá: wash

ūdazhi: not good, bad situation

ukkíne: seek for oneself

uné: seek

xeáthe: fall down

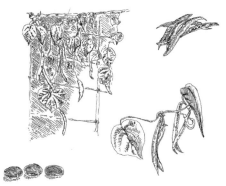

FIG. 203. hi^{n}bthí^{n}ge: beans

Vocabulary: Nouns

hi^{n}bthí^{n}ge: beans

shó^{n}tto^{n}ga: wolf

Vocabulary: Miscellaneous

sabázhi: suddenly, unexpectedly

uppáhadi: beside

FIG. 204. shó^{n}tto^{n}ga: wolf

Speaking Practice

A. Read the following sentences aloud. Then translate the sentences into English. Examples:

Hiⁿbthíⁿge uákkine: I'm trying to find me some beans.

Kkiūda bazhi, winísi ama: My children don't get along with each other.

Tushpahá, kkigthízha a!: Grandchild, wash up!

1. Thakkígthizha egóⁿ, sakkáid' thoⁿ oⁿtháthe tta oⁿgathoⁿ.

2. Híde khedi athá bi ama, niáshiⁿga xubé ama, wanítta, wazhíⁿga kkigthíauzhi thegóⁿ.

3. Shínuja ama kkigthíshkoⁿshkoⁿ zhōⁿ khe, iháⁿ uppáhadi.

4. Winísi akha ttoⁿthiⁿ kkinóⁿse xeátha thoⁿzha, shí kkihóⁿ.

5. Móⁿshoⁿ uákkine; môⁿde akkíppaxe kkōⁿbtha.

6. Ttáxti kkióⁿhe thiⁿ kkiōⁿtha bi ama, shóⁿttoⁿga nugá akha.

7. Uthúdoⁿba ga! Sabázhi kkigthísoⁿthe tta, ttenúga shêthiⁿ!

8. Nākkade kki, oⁿkkígthane oⁿgthíⁿ.

9. Thakkíudazhi thoⁿzha, kkikkína bazhi i a!

10. Nudóⁿ akha āgthiⁿ kkióⁿhe agthá bi kki, shóⁿge ettá ama kkinóⁿsa bi ama.

B. Translate the following sentences into Omaha.

1. It's hot. I'm fanning myself.

2. Are you making yourself a bow?

3. My grandmother fell, but she lifted herself up.

4. The running buffalos were turning themselves around in a circle.

5. When I saw the black bear, I ran away.

6. They say the buffalo swapped ends.

7. If I stumble, I'll lift myself up.

8. They say the warrior threw himself on the enemy.

9. Are you able to turn yourself into a wolf?

10. My sister-in-law is sitting at home fanning herself.

C. The instructor goes around the class, challenging the students with a base verb. The students respond by giving the reflexive kki- form, along with a gesture of lightly slapping themselves on the upper chest to indicate that the action is done to or for themselves. Example:

Wagōⁿze: Uné. ("Search for it.")

Ttáppuskazhiⁿga: Ukkíne. ("Seek for oneself.") [making kki- gesture]

Wagōⁿze: Gāxe. ("Make it.")

Ttáppuskazhiⁿga: Kkikkáx̣e. ("Make for oneself.") [making kki- gesture]

Wagōⁿze: Thizhá. ("Wash it.")

Ttáppuskazhiⁿga: Kkigthízha. ("Wash oneself.") [making kki- gesture]

Wagōⁿze: Āni. ("Fan it.")

Ttáppuskazhiⁿga: Kkigthāni. ("Fan one's own.") [making kki- gesture]

D. The instructor goes around the class again, challenging each student with a reflexive kki- verb and one or two emphatic pronouns. If there are two, the first pronoun is the object pronoun, and the second is the subject pronoun. A third person subject will be é. A third person plural animate object, "them," will be é ama. The student should respond with the appropriately conjugated form of the kki- word, along with the reflexive kki- gesture. Again, "wí" and "thí" will be reversed in the interaction.

E. The students form groups of about four to six, with a deck of cards, and play this as a game using reflexive kki- verbs, according to the rules described in part E in 18.4 and 18.6.

19.4 THE VICTIMIZED KKE- PREFIX AND EVIDENTIAL T^HE

The Victimized Prefix kke-

ít^hiⁿ	bump something	íkket^hiⁿ	bump oneself
uthá	tell	ukkégtha	get told on
uthíske	arms folded over chest	ukkégthiske	straitjacketed
uthíspe	restrain someone	ukkégthispe	be restrained

- The prefix kke- is much like kki-. But where kki- allows that the action was intentional, kke- implies that it happened accidentally or against the subject's will, with unfortunate consequences. In English we might say that someone "got beat up" or "got in a wreck" or "bumped their head" (not intentionally) to give the sense of Omaha kke-. In cases like this, the point is that the subject is the *victim* of the action.

Evidential t^he

Nudóⁿ ak^ha kkída i t^he.	The warrior (evidently) has shot it.
Nudóⁿ ak^ha kkída bi t^he ama.	The warrior (evidently) had shot it.

- The evidential particle t^he coming after a verb may be an entirely different word from the common positional t^he. Evidential t^he seems to imply that the action was completed prior to the stream of the narrative and that it may simply be deduced from evidence discovered within the stream. Thus it combines the functions of present and past perfect in English (has done it, had done it) with an acknowledgment of possible doubt, in that the action claimed is reconstructed (evidently) rather than known directly.

- Evidential t^he comes after i or bi but before any final particle. Thus it splits the common sequence bi ama, showing that these are originally two separate words. In the nineteenth century, narrative action statements normally ended in [verb] i ha (for a male speaker) or [verb] i he (for a female speaker) when the speaker was making the statement on their own authority. When reporting hearsay, the speaker used [verb] bi ama, and [verb] bi tʰe ama for something that *had* happened, or had *evidently* happened, prior to the current stage of the narrative. For an evidential statement on their own authority, speakers ended the sentence with [verb] i tʰe, dropping the emphatic ha or he. In the early twentieth century the ha and he particles were dropped altogether, along with the preceding i. This seems to have left the i before tʰe, and before clause conjunctions like kki and egóⁿ, somewhat in limbo as well.

- Evidential tʰe is normally used only in statements and only in the third person. It doesn't usually make sense to publish deductions about the actions of people who are party to the conversation.

Vocabulary: Active Verbs

íkketʰiⁿ: bump oneself

ní-thaẋthude: drown

ukkégtha: get told on, be gossiped about

ukkégthaspe: get restrained from talking or eating

ukkégthiske: straitjacketed, arms folded involuntarily

ukkégthispe: get restrained from doing something

uthá: tell

utháspe: restrain someone from talking or eating

uthíske: arms folded over the chest, as pharaohs or spiders

uthíspe: restrain someone from doing something

Vocabulary: Stative Verbs

gthóⁿthiⁿ: crazy

Vocabulary: Nouns

astúhi: elbow

hizhū: gums

kkúkkusi: pig, hog

neúthishoⁿ: lake

noⁿshkí: the cranial part of the head

ppāhiⁿ: porcupine

thióⁿba: lightning

tteníẋa-ugthezhe: mushroom, morel

zhū: skin, flesh

FIG. 205. kkúkkusi: pig

FIG. 206. ppāhiⁿ: porcupine

FIG. 207. tteníẋa-ugthezhe: mushroom, morel

Vocabulary: Question Words

awádi?: why?

Vocabulary: Miscellaneous

akkíthitta: across

ónthinoⁿ: almost

tʰe: evidential particle

wāspa (ga)!: Behave!

Speaking Practice

A. Read the following sentences aloud.
Then translate the sentences into
English. Examples:

Noⁿshkí ithákketʰiⁿ: I bumped my
head.

Mīzhiⁿga shêhithiⁿkʰe ukkégtha: That
girl over there got told on.

Ābae athá bi tʰe ama: Evidently he had
gone hunting.

1. Niáshiⁿga xubé wiⁿ
akkíkkina éde, tteníxa-ugthezhe
uákkegthiauzhi.

2. Iⁿdādi akʰa núzhiⁿga kʰedi
neúthishoⁿ móⁿtʰadi niúoⁿ bi
ama, ikʰáge zhūwagigthe. Sabāzhi
thióⁿba kʰe unāgoⁿba bi ama.
Gashíbe ahí bi kki, núzhiⁿga
wôⁿgithe ama zhū kkegthígtheza bi
tʰe ama, sóⁿ, ní gahá kʰedi.

3. Núzhiⁿga kikkína góⁿtha
thoⁿzha, ukkégthispa bi ama;
ikʰáge ame, é uthíspa bi tʰe ama.

4. Nú gthóⁿthiⁿ wiⁿ
ukkégthiske gthíⁿ.

5. Shínuda oⁿgútta akʰa ppāhiⁿ
ítha i tʰe. Ppá kʰedi, í kʰedi, hizhū
kʰedi kkeppáxthu thêthudí xthíⁿ
gthíⁿ thiⁿkʰe. Iⁿdādi akʰa ppahīⁿ
thishnúde tta tʰe.

6. Tteníxa-ugthezhe
íthashpahoⁿ azhi kki, thatʰá bazhi i
a! Égithe íwathakkekʰega tte.

7. Uzhóⁿge uppáhadi, ppāhiⁿ
wiⁿ kkigthíshkoⁿshkoⁿ zhōⁿ kʰe
ākkenoⁿga i tʰe.

8. Neúthishoⁿ akkíthitta
niúwoⁿ moⁿthíⁿ bi tʰe ama.
Ōⁿthinoⁿ ní-kkegtháxthuda bi ama.

9. Astúhi íthakketʰiⁿ a?

10. Kkúkkusi ama gashíbe
kkimūgthoⁿ athá i tʰe. Ūe kʰe
noⁿshéthoⁿ kʰe.

B. Translate the following sentences
into Omaha.

1. That (aforementioned) pig
got eaten.

2. "We got branded," the cattle
supposedly said.

3. You got singed.

4. I don't want to be
straightjacketed.

5. Watch out! You'll bump your
head!

6. Behave! You might get
gossiped about.

7. Why are you crying? Did you get hit?

8. Evidently, the enemy has seen us.

9. Evidently, the ice has melted.

10. The trees evidently had burned all around the boy.

C. The instructor goes around the class, challenging the students with a base verb. The students respond by giving the victimized kke- form, along with a gesture of lightly slapping themselves on the side of the head. Example:

Wagōⁿze: Ítʰiⁿ. ("Hit it.")

Ttáppuskazhiⁿga: Íkketʰiⁿ. ("Bump oneself.") [making kke- gesture]

Wagōⁿze: Uthíspe. ("Restrain him/her.")

Ttáppuskazhiⁿga: Ukkégthispe. ("Be restrained.") [making kke- gesture]

Wagōⁿze: Uthá. ("Tell it.")

Ttáppuskazhiⁿga: Ukkégtha. ("Get told on.") [making kke- gesture]

Wagōⁿze: Uthíske. ("Arms folded over chest.")

Ttáppuskazhiⁿga: Ukkégthiske. ("Straitjacketed.") [making kke-gesture]

D. The instructor goes around the class again, challenging each student with either a reflexive kki- verb or a victimized kke- verb and one or two emphatic pronouns. If there are two, the first pronoun is the object pronoun, and the second is the subject pronoun. A third person subject will be é. A third person plural animate object, "them," will be é ama. The student should respond with the appropriately conjugated form of the kki- or kke- word, along with the appropriate kki- or kke- gesture. Again, "wí" and "thí" will be reversed in the interaction.

E. The students form groups of about four to six, with a deck of cards, and play this as a game using reflexive kki- and victimized kke- verbs, according to the rules described in part E in 18.4 and 18.6.

19.5 THE DATIVE GĪ- AND -Ī-

Active Dative Verbs Using the Prefix gī-

bóⁿ	call, yell	gīboⁿ	call someone over
dóⁿbe	see	gídoⁿbe	look at for someone's benefit
gáҳe	make	giáҳe	make for someone's benefit
-gōⁿze	measure	gióⁿze	teach someone
kkíde	shoot	gíkkide	shoot for someone's benefit
-kʰú	invite	gíkʰu	invite someone (to a feast)
nã	ask for	gína	collect (a debt) from
-noⁿshe	take away?	gínoⁿshe	take away, confiscate from
ōⁿtha	throw	gíoⁿtha	throw something at someone
-shi	favor?	gíshi	ask someone to do something
thikkúthe	hurry	gíthikkuthe	hurry for someone's benefit
-zha	?	gízha	deny, doubt an allegation

- The dative prefix gī- indicates that the action is performed for someone else's *benefit*, or sometimes the reverse. The emphasis is on the party who is the indirect object of the action.

- Dative gī- can be distinguished from possessive or suus gi- by the fact that it draws the accent and that its vowel is generally held rather long.

· Unlike possessive or suus gi-, dative gī- does not become gth- before a ledh verb, as seen by gīthikkuthe.

· Unlike possessive or suus gi-, dative gī- does not cause a simple stop at the beginning of the following verb to become tense, as seen by gīdo^{n}be.

· When the following verb begins with the simple stop g-, however, the simple stop g- may be lost and the dative gī- prefix loses its accent to the following vowel. Thus gī- + gāx̣e becomes giāx̣e, and gī- + gō^{n}ze becomes giō^{n}ze.

The Dative -ī- Affix Following a Locative Prefix

u-hé	follow (a path)	u-ī-he	follow or join someone
-u-kkó^n	help ?	u-ī-kko^n	help someone
u-thá	tell	u-ī-tha	tell to someone
u-zhí	fill	u-ī-zhi	fill for someone's benefit

· When the dative prefix gī- comes after the locative prefix u-, it loses its initial g- to appear as -ī-.

Stative Dative Verbs Using the Prefix gī-

gīsho^n	pleased, happy, approves
gīthe	happy, blissful
gīttex̣i	suffering difficulties, hard times
gītto^{n}ga	conceited, boastful
gīudo^n	like something, feel good, as when you hear good news
gīwazhi^{n}ska	sober, sane
gīzhu	lucky

· When the dative prefix gī- is used in a stative sense, the subject is the indirect object affected by the verb. Stative use generally implies something about the subject's mental state or well-being.

Vocabulary: Verbs

FIG. 208. bó^n: yell

bó^n: call, yell

dó^{n}be: see

gāx̣e: make

giāx̣e: make for someone

gībo^n: call someone over

gīdo^{n}be: look at for someone's benefit

gīkkide: shoot for someone

gīk^{h}u: invite someone, as to a feast

gīna: collect a debt or a loan

gīno^{n}she: confiscate, take something away from someone

gīo^{n}tha: throw something at someone

giō^{n}ze: teach someone

gīshi: ask someone to do something

gīsho^n: pleased, happy, approves of something

gīthe: happy, blissful

gīthikkuthe: hurry for someone's benefit

gīttex̣i: suffering difficulties, hard times

gītto^{n}ga: conceited, boastful

gīudo^n: like something, feel good, glad

gīwazhi^{n}ska: sober, sane

gīzha: deny or doubt an allegation

gīzhu: lucky

kkíde: shoot

nā: ask for, beg, request

ōⁿtha: throw

thikkúthe: hurry

uhé: follow, as a path

uháⁿ: cook

uīhe: follow or join someone

uīhaⁿ: cook for someone

uīkkoⁿ: help someone

uītha: tell someone

uīzhi: fill for someone

uthá: tell

uzhí: fill

FIG. 209. uhé: follow, as a path

Vocabulary: Stative Verbs

dāthiⁿ: drunk, intoxicated

dāthiⁿ-giudoⁿ: drunkard, alcoholic

noⁿppéhiⁿ: hungry

Vocabulary: Nouns

iⁿdéugaxe: picture, portrait

mōⁿzeska: silver, money, dollar

ppashtóⁿga: moose, or Rocky Mountain sheep

Vocabulary: Adverbs

é-nóⁿx̌či: alone, by him- or herself

moⁿttánoⁿha: wild, like kids running through the woods barefoot

si-thúkkathiⁿ: barefoot

Speaking Practice

A. Read the following sentences aloud. Then translate the sentences into English. Examples:

Thikʰáge gīboⁿ ga!: Call your friend over!

Thiādi akʰa winégi uīkkoⁿ noⁿzhíⁿ: Your father stands helping my uncle.

Wittóⁿge akʰa gīttex̌i moⁿthíⁿ: My sister is going through hard times.

1. Núzhiⁿga iⁿdéugaxe thix̌ú tʰe gīdoⁿba, iháⁿ akʰa.

2. Moⁿshtíⁿge akʰa ppashtóⁿga- ppa gīoⁿtha bi ama, Uṣní thiⁿkʰe.

3. Mīzhiⁿga uthá i tʰe gīzha bi ama, núzhiⁿga akʰa.

4. Mōⁿzeska ettá tʰe gīna ahí, iⁿsh'áge akʰa.

5. Gátʰe moⁿkkóⁿsabe. Thikkóⁿ niīthattoⁿ tʰe uīzhi ga!

6. Thittóⁿde dāthiⁿ-
giudoⁿ thóⁿshti thoⁿzha, íⁿčʰoⁿ
gīwazhiⁿska noⁿ gthíⁿ.

7. Uītha tʰedi, gītha bazhi.

8. Wittóⁿde akʰa shóⁿshoⁿ
uǧthábe kʰedi enóⁿǧči gīthe
moⁿttánoⁿha ugáshoⁿ moⁿthíⁿ.

9. Igáǧthoⁿ ittínu uīkkoⁿ gīshi,
iⁿshʼáge akʰa.

10. Waʼúzhiⁿga akʰa gītteǧi
thoⁿzha, ittínu akʰa uīkkoⁿ tʰe
uītha tʰedi, gītha.

B. Translate the following sentences
into Omaha.

1. The boys followed the holy
person, they say.

2. My father approves of my
husband.

3. My grandfather should
teach my child Omaha.

4. The police took the children
away from their mother.

5. Tell your mother!

6. That man over there acts
conceited.

7. Invite your aunt, and your
sister-in-law as well!

8. I think your nephew is
hungry. Hurry up and cook for
him!

9. Make your niece a dress!

10. Shoot a rabbit for your
sister-in-law!

C. The instructor goes around the class,
challenging the students with a base
verb. The students respond by giving
the dative gī- form, along with a gesture
of pointing up with the forefinger of
the right hand while simultaneously
pointing to the left fist with the right
thumb. Example:

Wagōⁿze: Bóⁿ. ("Yell.")

Ttáppuskazhiⁿga: Gīboⁿ. ("Call over.")
[making gī- gesture]

Wagōⁿze: Dóⁿbe. ("See it.")

Ttáppuskazhiⁿga: Gīdoⁿbe. ("Look at
for.") [making gī- gesture]

Wagōⁿze: Uthá. ("Tell it.")

Ttáppuskazhiⁿga: Uītha. ("Tell it to.")
[making gī- gesture]

Wagōⁿze: Ūdaⁿ. ("It's good.")

Ttáppuskazhiⁿga: Gīudoⁿ. ("It's good
for him/her.") [making gī- gesture]

D. The instructor says something to
each student that can be answered
with a gī- word. The student responds
appropriately. Example:

Wagōⁿze: Ittúshka noⁿppéhiⁿ gthíⁿ
egóⁿ, uháⁿ thikkútha. ("Since her
nephew was hungry, she hurried to
cook.")

Amber: Ittúshka gīthikkutha. ("She
hurried for her nephew.")

Wagōⁿze: Ittúshpa akʰa môⁿde gōⁿtha
bi egóⁿ, iⁿshʼáge akʰa wiⁿ gáǧa bi
ama. ("Since his grandchild wanted
a bow, the old man made one.")

Laura: Môⁿde wiⁿ giāǧa bi ama. ("He
made a bow for him.")

E. The students form small groups of about two or three and take turns asking each other questions that can be answered using a dative gī- word. Using the corresponding gesture with the sentences is encouraged.

19.6 CONJUGATION OF THE DATIVE

Conjugation of Dative gī-

Subject	Object	Affix	**gī-kʰu**	'to invite'
3ʳᵈ	3ʳᵈ		**gī-kʰu**	s/he invites him/her
I	3ʳᵈ	-ē-	**ē-kʰu**	I invite him/her
you	3ʳᵈ	-thē-	**thē-kʰu**	you invite him/her
we	3ʳᵈ	-oⁿ-	**oⁿ-gī-kʰu**	we invite him/her
3ʳᵈ	me	-īⁿ-	**īⁿ-kʰu**	s/he invites me
3ʳᵈ	you	-thī-	**thī-kʰu**	s/he invites you
3ʳᵈ	us	-wē-	**wē-kʰu**	s/he invites us
3ʳᵈ	them	-wē-	**wē-kʰu**	s/he invites them
I	you	-wī-	**wī-kʰu**	I invite you
I	them	-ē-wē-	**e-wē-kʰu**	I invite them
you	me	-īⁿ-thē-	**iⁿ-thē-kʰu**	you invite me
you	us	-wē-thē-	**we-thē-kʰu**	you invite us
you	them	-wē-thē-	**we-thē-kʰu**	you invite them
we	you	-oⁿ-thī-	**oⁿ-thī-kʰu**	we invite you
we	them	-oⁿ-wē-	**oⁿ-wē-kʰu**	we invite them

- Conjugation of the dative appears entirely different from the regular conjugation paradigm. Many of the differences can be explained as the result of flavoring the vowel of the regular affixed pronoun with an extra i, as if the gī- turns to ī- and the affixed pronoun is attached in front of it. This way, a- becomes e-, oⁿ becomes iⁿ, and i stays i. So the a-, tha-, and wa- affixes become e-,

the-, and we-, respectively; oⁿ- becomes iⁿ-; and thi- and wi- remain thi- and wi-.

- The regular affixed pronouns always come before the dative prefix gī-/ī-. This "i" quality then affects the entire string of a- and oⁿ- vowels preceding it, so long as they are not separated by any consonants other than w and th.

Subject	Object	Affix	**u-ī-kkoⁿ**	'to help someone'
3ʳᵈ	3ʳᵈ		**u-ī-kkoⁿ**	s/he helps him/her
I	3ʳᵈ	-ē-	**u-ē-kkoⁿ**	I help him/her
you	3ʳᵈ	-thē-	**u-thē-kkoⁿ**	you help him/her
we	3ʳᵈ	-oⁿ-	**oⁿgú-i-kkoⁿ**	we help him/her
3ʳᵈ	me	-īⁿ-	**iⁿwīⁿ-kkoⁿ**	s/he helps me
3ʳᵈ	you	-thī-	**u-thī-kkoⁿ**	s/he helps you
3ʳᵈ	us	-wē-	**u-wē-kkoⁿ**	s/he helps us
3ʳᵈ	them	-wē-	**u-wē-kkoⁿ**	s/he helps them
I	you	-wī-	**u-wī-kkoⁿ**	I help you
I	them	-ē-wē-	**u-ē-we-kkoⁿ**	I help them
you	me	-īⁿ-thē-	**iⁿwīⁿ-the-kkoⁿ**	you help me
you	us	-wē-thē-	**u-wē-the-kkoⁿ**	you help us
you	them	-wē-thē-	**u-wē-the-kkoⁿ**	you help them
we	you	-oⁿg-thī-	**oⁿgú-thi-kkoⁿ**	we help you
we	us	-oⁿg-wē-	**oⁿgú-we-kkoⁿ**	we help each other
we	them	-oⁿg-wē-	**oⁿgú-we-kkoⁿ**	we help them

- Apart from the change from gī- to ī- in the third person after a locative prefix, all other members of the conjugation are the same for either case.

- In working out this conjugation paradigm, our speakers have indicated that there is a slot for "we do it to us," in the sense of "we do it to each other." This holds for both oⁿgúwekkoⁿ, "we help each other," and oⁿgúwetha, "we tell each other," at least.

- Researchers working with other speakers have found different patterns in some cases than the ones we have listed here. The differences are mainly in conjugation forms involving "us" and "them." Interestingly, these alternative forms seem to be uncontracted sequences showing wagi- in places where we have recorded we-, or wathagi- where we have recorded wethe-. These indicate the same underlying sequence, which suggests that two valid alternative forms have been preserved, possibly from a very long time ago, just as in English we still use both "can't" and "cannot."

Subject	Object	Affix	**gī-the**	'be happy'
3rd	3rd		**gī-the**	s/he is happy
3rd	me	-ī^n-	**ī^n-the**	I am happy
3rd	you	-thī-	**thī-the**	you are happy
3rd	us	-wē-	**wē-the**	we are happy
3rd	them	-wē-	**wē-the**	they are happy

- As with the direct object conjugation, stative verbs formed from dative gī- use only the object affixed pronouns of the dative conjugation.

Vocabulary: Verbs

gīk^{h}u: invite

u'é: plow, hoe, make holes for planting

Vocabulary: Stative Verbs

si-thúkkathi^n: barefoot

FIG. 210. u'é: plow, hoe, make holes for planting

Vocabulary: Nouns

ttō^{n}de-thittūbe: plow

Vocabulary: Names

Ppāthi^n: Pawnee

Ppáx̌ude: Ioway

Vocabulary: Miscellaneous

kkúde tte: ought to, should

wí-nó^{n}x̌či: I alone, by myself

Speaking Practice

A. Read the following sentences aloud. Then translate the sentences into English. Examples:

I^{n}wí^{n}kko^n ga!: Help me!

Mô^{n}de thiāx̌e tta, thinégi ak^{h}a: Your uncle may make you a bow.

Wēzhu kki, o^{n}gúhi tta: We might win if we are lucky.

1. "Awádi thax̌áge a?" á bi ama, ik^{h}ágetha i ama. "Áo^n, wisó^{n}ge t'éo^{n}githe t^{h}e, égo^n ī^{n}the mazhi agthí^n," á bi ama, Mikká ak^{h}a.

2. Dāthi^n thīudo^n mo^{n}ní^n kki, wīsho^n mazhi tta mi^{n}k^{h}e.

3. Wagthábaze āppax̌u thêk^{h}e ī^{n}do^{n}ba ga!

4. Ūe thêk^{h}e uá'e bthí'a. Wittó^{n}de ma ttō^{n}de-thittūbe ó^n u'é i^{n}wí^{n}kko^n ewēbo^n tta mi^{n}k^{h}e.

5. Wagthábaze ābthade wí-nóⁿx̌či īⁿthe agthíⁿ noⁿ moⁿ.

6. Wittími akʰa wabátʰe iⁿgōⁿze tta akʰa.

7. Íⁿʼe thoⁿ wēoⁿtha, núzhiⁿga akʰa.

8. Gahíge uēhe thiⁿkʰe ēbthikkuthe tta tʰe.

9. Thiādi thiⁿkʰe môⁿde thigāx̌e tʰe thēshi kkúde tte.

10. Sithúkkathiⁿ ux̌thabe kʰedi moⁿttánoⁿha moⁿbthíⁿ īⁿudoⁿ.

B. Translate the following sentences into Omaha.

1. Why did you call me over?

2. My son-in-law shot a pig for us.

3. The chief invited the Pawnees and the Ioways as well.

4. Do you doubt that your brother-in-law took my mower?

5. Okay, I'll tell you.

6. I don't approve of my son-in-law.

7. Thank you for filling my cup.

8. Now I am sober.

9. You should help the chief you follow.

10. Mom! Your sister-in-law is here to collect her money from you.

C. The instructor goes around the class, challenging each student with a dative gī- verb and an emphatic pronoun. The student should respond with the appropriate conjugation form. Note that "wí" and "thí" will be reversed in the interaction. Example:

Wagōⁿze: Gīkʰu. Oⁿgú. ("Invite him/her. We.")

Jessica: Oⁿgīkʰu. ("We invited him/her.")

Wagōⁿze: Gīshi. Thí. ("Ask to do something. You.")

Rick: Ēshi. ("I asked him/her to do it.")

Wagōⁿze: Uīkkoⁿ. Wí. ("Help him/her. I.")

John: Uthēkkoⁿ. ("You helped him/her.")

D. The instructor goes around the class again, challenging each student with a dative í- verb and one or two emphatic pronouns. If there are two, the first pronoun is the object pronoun, and the second is the subject pronoun. A third person subject will be é. A third person plural animate object, "them," will be é ama. A verb that takes no personal object will be presented with only one emphatic pronoun. The student should respond with the appropriate conjugated form. Again, "wí" and "thí" will be reversed in the interaction.

E. The students form groups of about four to six, with a deck of cards, and play this as a game using gī- verbs, according to the rules described in part E in 18.4 and 18.6.

12.1 COMMANDS:

THE PARTICLES A AND GA

A.

1. **Gthíⁿ a!:** Sit! (woman speaking)

2. **Gí a!:** Come here! (woman speaking)

3. **Moⁿthíⁿ ga!:** Go! (man speaking casually)

4. **Noⁿzhíⁿ a!:** Stand! (woman speaking)

5. **Gthíⁿ ga ho!:** Sit! (man speaking formally)

6. **Gí ga!:** Come here! (man speaking formally)

7. **Noⁿzhíⁿ ga ho!:** Stand! (man speaking formally)

8. **Gthíⁿ ga!:** Sit! (man speaking casually)

9. **Moⁿthíⁿ a!:** Go! (woman speaking)

10. **Moⁿthíⁿ ga ho!:** Go! (man speaking formally)

12.2 COMMANDS: ABLAUT

A.

1. **Á!:** Say it! (woman speaking)

2. **Dóⁿba ga ho!:** Look! (man speaking formally)

3. **Thatʰá ga!:** Eat it! (man speaking casually)

4. **Gą̄xa!:** Make it! / Do it! (woman speaking)

5. **Uná!:** Look for it! (woman speaking)

6. **Ígaskoⁿtha ga!:** Try it! (man speaking casually)

7. **Uthíxida ga!:** Look around! (man speaking casually)

8. **Thizá!:** Take it! / Pick it up! (woman speaking)

9. **Āshiatta shkāda!:** Go play outside! (woman speaking)

10. **Wagthábaze itʰétha ga ho!:** Put away the books/notes/papers! (man speaking formally)

12.3 PLURAL COMMANDS: I AND ABLAUT

A.

1. **Gą̄xa i a!:** Make it! / Do it! (woman speaking to a group)

2. **Gthíⁿ i ga!:** Sit! (man speaking casually to a group)

3. **Thizá!:** Take it! / Pick it up! (woman speaking to one person)

4. **"Wíbthahoⁿ" á i ga ho!:** Say "thank you"! (man speaking formally to a group)

5. **Uthíxida i a!:** Look around for it! (woman speaking to a group)

6. **Ĭe tʰe é ígaskoⁿtha i ga!:** Try to speak the language! (man speaking casually to a group)

7. **Ní tʰe thattóⁿ ga!:** Drink the water! (man speaking casually to one person)

8. **Gióⁿ moⁿthíⁿ i a!:** Go fly! (woman speaking to a group)

9. **Wabáxu kʰe āthada i a!:** Spell it! (woman speaking to a group)

10. **Wagthábaze itʰétha i ga ho!:** Put away the books/notes/papers! (man speaking formally to a group)

B.

1. Try it!: **Ígaskonⁿtha (ga)!**

2. Eat it!: **Thatʰá (ga)!**

3. Look for it!: **Uná (ga)!**

4. Stand up!: **Nonⁿzhíⁿ a/ga!**

5. Lie down!: **Zhōⁿ a/ga!**

6. Take the water!: **Ní tʰe thizá (ga)!**

7. Write the word!: **Īe tʰe baxú a/ga!**

8. Look at the blackboard!: **Zhonⁿbtháskasabe dónⁿba (ga)!**

9. Go play outside!: **Āshiatta shkāde monⁿthíⁿ a/ga!**

10. Try to read it!: **Āthade ígaskonⁿtha (ga)!**

C.

1. **Ígaskonⁿtha i a/ga!**

2. **Thatʰá i a/ga!**

3. **Uná i a/ga!**

4. **Nonⁿzhíⁿ i a/ga!**

5. **Zhōⁿ i a/ga!**

6. **Ní tʰe thizá i a/ga!**

7. **Īe tʰe baxú i a/ga!**

8. **Zhonⁿbtháskasabe dónⁿba i a/ga!**

9. **Āshiatta shkāde monⁿthíⁿ i a/ga!**

10. **Āthade ígaskonⁿtha i a/ga!**

12.4 QUESTIONS: A WITH NO ABLAUT

A.

1. **Uthíxide a?:** Did s/he look around? Is s/he looking around?

2. **Nonⁿzhíⁿ a?:** Did s/he stand? Is s/he standing?

3. **Ttí gāxe a?:** Did s/he make believe? Is s/he pretending?

4. **Ttí tʰe dónⁿbe a?:** Did s/he look at/see the house? Is s/he looking at the house/building?

5. **Wēbaxu uné a?:** Did s/he look for the pen/pencil? Is s/he looking for the pen/pencil?

6. **Īe tʰe é a?:** Does s/he speak the language? Is s/he speaking the language? Did s/he say the word? Is s/he saying the word?

7. **Ūdaⁿ monⁿthíⁿ a?:** Is s/he getting along well?

8. **Umóⁿhoⁿ ie tʰe íbahoⁿ a?:** Does s/he know the Omaha language?

9. **Ttóⁿthiⁿ nonⁿshtóⁿ a?:** Did s/he stop running? Is s/he stopping running?

10. **Ūzhiha thoⁿ itʰéthe a?:** Did s/he put away the bag? Is s/he putting away the bag?

B.

1. Does she hear it?: **No'óⁿ a?**

2. Does he want it?: **Gōⁿtha a?**

3. Did he try it?: **Ígaskonⁿthe a?**

4. Is she sitting?: **Gthíⁿ a?**

5. Did he sleep well?: **Ūdaⁿ zhōⁿ a?**

6. Is he playing outside?: **Āshiatta shkāde a?**

7. Does he love her?: **X̌tāthe a?**

8. Does she know Omaha?: **Umóⁿhoⁿ īe tʰe íbahoⁿ a?**

9. Is he good at writing Omaha?: **Umóⁿhoⁿ īe tʰe bax̣ú thippí a?**

10. Did she refuse to do it?: **Uthí'age a?**

12.5 THIRD-PERSON STATEMENT OF ACTION: ABLAUT FOR DECLARATION

A.

1. **Gthíⁿ:** S/he sat. S/he is sitting.

2. **Noⁿóⁿ:** S/he heard. S/he is hearing.

3. **Thi'á:** S/he is unable/failed. S/he was unable/failed.

4. **X̌tātha:** S/he loves him/her/it/them.

5. **Thizá:** S/he is picking it up. S/he picked it up. S/he is taking it. S/he took it.

6. **Uthíx̣ida:** S/he is looking around. S/he was looking around.

7. **Wēbax̣u tʰe thawá:** S/he is counting the pencils/pens. S/he counted the pencils/pens.

8. **Āshiatta shkāda:** S/he is playing outside. S/he played outside.

9. **Ūdaⁿ moⁿthíⁿ:** S/he is doing well.

10. **Zhoⁿbtháskasabe dóⁿbe ígaskoⁿthe gthíⁿ:** S/he is sitting, trying to look at/ see the blackboard. S/he sat, trying to look at/see the blackboard.

B.

1. He wants it: **Gōⁿtha.**

2. He stopped walking: **Moⁿthíⁿ noⁿshtóⁿ.**

3. She's looking for the pen: **Wēbax̣u kʰe uná.**

4. She bit the apple: **Shé thoⁿ thax̌tá.**

5. He asked for the book: **Wagthábaze tʰe nā.**

6. She said the word: **Īe tʰe á.**

7. He refused to put away the backpack: **Ūzhiha thoⁿ itʰéthe uthí'aga.**

8. She knows how to spell the word: **Īe tʰe wabáx̣u kʰe íbahoⁿ.**

9. They're drinking the coffee: **Moⁿkkóⁿsabe tʰe thattóⁿ.**

10. She can't make cowboy bread: **Wamóskeshuga gāx̣e thi'á.**

12.6 NEGATION: ABLAUT BEFORE "NOT"

A.

1. **Uthíx̣idá bazhi:** S/he didn't look around.

2. **Gthíⁿ bazhi:** S/he didn't sit.

3. **Thippí bazhi:** S/he isn't good at it.

4. **Thax̌tá azhi a!:** Don't bite it! (woman speaking to one person)

5. **Īe tʰe á azhi ga!:** Don't say the word! (man speaking to one person)

6. **Wāthatʰe kʰe badóⁿ azhi a!:** Don't push the table! (woman speaking to one person)

7. **Wāx̣e īe tʰe iá bazhi i ga ho!:** Don't speak English! (man speaking formally to a group)

8. **Uóⁿsisi āgazhi bazhi i a!:** Don't command someone to jump! (woman speaking to a group)

9. **Izházhe tʰe ímoⁿx̣a bazhi i a!:** Don't ask his/her name! (woman speaking to a group)

10. **Izházhe tʰe íbahoⁿ bazhi:** S/he doesn't know his/her name.

B.

1. Don't say it!: **Á azhi a/ga!**

2. She didn't want it: **Gōⁿtha bazhi.**

3. He didn't refuse: **Uthíʼaga bazhi.**

4. Don't sleep!: **Zhōⁿ azhi a/ga!**

5. Don't go running!: **Ttóⁿthiⁿ moⁿthíⁿ azhi a/ga!**

6. He didn't try to speak Omaha: **Umóⁿhoⁿ īe ígaskoⁿtha bazhi.**

7. She didn't like him: **X̌tátha bazhi.**

8. Don't lift the table!: **Wāthatʰe kʰe thihóⁿ azhi a!**

9. He didn't speak English well: **Wāx̌e īe tʰe íe thippí bazhi.**

10. Don't touch it!: **Ābitta azhi a!**

12.7 THE POTENTIAL PARTICLE TTE

A.

1. **Thippí tte:** S/he might be an expert.

2. **Thiʼá tte:** S/he might be unable/ might fail.

3. **Wēbax̣u thizé tte:** S/he might pick up the pencil.

4. **Ní tʰe thattóⁿ tta akʰa:** S/he'll probably drink the water.

5. **Ímoⁿx̣e tta akʰa:** S/he'll probably ask.

6. **Izházhe tʰe uthá tte:** S/he might tell the name.

7. **Uóⁿsisi āgazhi tta akʰa:** S/he'll probably command it to jump.

8. **Wāx̌e īe tʰe ié tta akʰa:** S/he'll probably speak English.

9. **Wāthatʰe kʰe badóⁿ tte:** S/he might push the table.

10. **Móⁿgasiⁿde kʰe thidóⁿ tta akʰa:** S/he'll probably pull the skunk's tail.

B.

1. He might take it: **Thizé tte.**

2. She will probably eat it: **Thatʰé tta akʰa.**

3. He might look for it: **Uné tte.**

4. She will probably say it: **É tta akʰa.**

5. He will probably fail: **Thiʼá tta akʰa.**

6. He will probably drink the coffee: **Moⁿkkóⁿsabe tʰe thattóⁿ tta akʰa.**

7. She may order him to speak English: **Wāx̌e īe tʰe ié āgazhi tte.**

8. He will probably put the backpack away: **Ūzhiha thoⁿ itʰéthe tta akʰa.**

9. He may try to make a house: **Ttí gāx̣e ígaskoⁿthe tte.**

10. She might be able to pick up the table: **Wāthatʰe kʰe thihóⁿ ukkíhi tte.**

12.8 THE HEARSAY PARTICLE SET BI AMA

A.

1. **Āshiatta gthíⁿ bi ama:** Supposedly s/he sat outside.

2. **Noⁿzhíⁿ bi ama:** Supposedly s/he is standing.

3. **Ié thippí bi ama:** Supposedly s/he is good at speaking.

4. **Ní tʰe thattóⁿ bi ama:** It is said that s/he drank the water.

5. **Ímoⁿχa bi ama:** S/he asked, they say.

6. **Ígaskoⁿtha bazhi āgazhi bi ama:** Supposedly s/he commanded him/her to not try.

7. **Āshka bi ama:** In a little while, they say.

8. **Wagthábaze kʰe itʰétha bazhi bi ama:** Supposedly s/he didn't put away the book.

9. **Izházhe tʰe uthá bazhi bi ama:** Supposedly s/he didn't tell the name.

10. **Móⁿgasiⁿde kʰe thidóⁿ ígaskoⁿtha bi ama:** Supposedly s/he tried to pull the skunk's tail.

B.

1. He supposedly bit it: **Thaχtá bi ama.**

2. She supposedly knew: **Íbahoⁿ bi ama.**

3. They were playing, they say: **Shkāda bi ama.**

4. She didn't say it, they say: **Á bazhi bi ama.**

5. Everyone wrote it, they say: **Wôⁿgithe baχú bi ama.**

6. He couldn't lift the table, they say: **Wāthatʰe kʰe thihóⁿ ukkíhi bazhi bi ama. / Wāthatʰe kʰe thihóⁿ thiʼá bi ama.**

7. It is said she wanted to speak Winnebago: **Húttoⁿga īe tʰe ié gōⁿtha bi ama.**

8. He supposedly saw the black backpack: **Ūzhiha sábe thoⁿ dóⁿba bi ama.**

9. He didn't count the trees, they say: **Χthabé tʰe thawá bazhi bi ama.**

10. It is said she wanted to be able to make cowboy bread: **Wamóskeshuga gāχe ukkíhi gōⁿtha bi ama.**

12.9 SIGNALING DEMAND IN ENGLISH AND OMAHA

A.

1. **Umóⁿhoⁿ ié thippí gōⁿtha bi ama:** Supposedly, s/he wants to be good at speaking Omaha. (statement—hearsay)

2. **Umóⁿhoⁿ īe tʰe baχú ígaskoⁿthe a?:** Is s/he trying to write the Omaha language? (question)

3. **Áⁿkkazhi, thiʼá. Wēbaχu shóⁿshoⁿ uná:** No, s/he cannot. S/he is still looking for a pencil. (statement)

4. **Wabáχu kʰe āthade tte:** S/he might read the letters. S/he might spell it. (statement—potential)

5. **Umóⁿhoⁿ wabáχu kʰe íbahoⁿ bazhi:** S/he doesn't know the Omaha letters. (statement)

6. **Wāχe wagthábaze āthade ukkíhi:** S/he can read the English book. (statement)

7. **Āshka Umóⁿhoⁿ ié thippí tta akʰa:** S/he will probably be good at speaking Omaha in a little while. (statement—potential)

8. **Wēbax̣u wiwítta kʰe thizá ga!:** Pick up/ take my pencil! (male commanding a single person)

9. **Izházhe tʰe uthá i a!:** Tell the name! (female commanding a group of people)

10. **Wāthatʰe kʰe badóⁿ bazhi i ga ho!:** Don't push the table! (male formally commanding a group of people)

B.

1. Is he running?: **Ttóⁿthiⁿ a?**

2. She knows the name: **Izházhe tʰe íbahoⁿ.**

3. Tomorrow it will likely rain: **Gasóⁿthiⁿ noⁿzhīⁿ tta akʰa.**

4. They say she refused: **Uthíʔaga bi ama.**

5. Take the coffee!: **Moⁿkkóⁿsabe tʰe thizá a/ga!**

6. She might play outside: **Āshiatta shkāde tte.**

7. Ask for the watch!: **Miīdoⁿbe tʰe nā a/ga!**

8. Is she able to lift the blue bag?: **Ūzhiha ttú thoⁿ thihóⁿ ukkíhi a?**

9. Don't tell him to jump!: **Uóⁿsi āgazhi azhi a!**

10. They say she was making cowboy bread: **Wamóskeshuga gāxa bi ama.**

A.

1. **Āgthiⁿ tʰe thagthíⁿ:** You are sitting on the chair.

2. **Aníuoⁿ:** I am swimming.

3. **Anóⁿtʰe anóⁿshtoⁿ:** I stopped kicking.

4. **Ní tʰe thanóⁿʔoⁿ a?:** Do you hear the water?

5. **Āshiatta thashkāde:** You are playing outside.

6. **Ttéska kʰe ax̌é:** I buried the cow.

7. **Maⁿčʰú egoⁿ thax̌thíⁿ:** You growl like a grizzly bear.

8. **Wanóⁿx̣e egoⁿ thazúde:** You whistle like a ghost.

9. **Móⁿzeska attóⁿ:** I am wealthy.

10. **Anúzoⁿ kkōⁿbtha:** I want to skate or sled.

B.

1. Do you hear it?: **Thanóⁿʔoⁿ a?**

2. I hear it: **Anóⁿʔoⁿ.**

3. Are you standing outside?: **Āshiatta thanóⁿzhiⁿ a?**

4. Did you stop running?: **Thattóⁿthiⁿ thanóⁿshtoⁿ a?**

5. Are you sleeping?: **Thazhō̄ⁿ a?**

6. I am sleeping well: **Ūdaⁿ azhōⁿ.**

7. Did you bury the skunk?: **Móⁿga kʰe thax̌é a?**

8. No, I buried the rabbit: **Áⁿkkazhi, moⁿshtíⁿge kʰe áx̌e.**

9. Today I am playing: **Óⁿbathe ashkāde.**

10. I am whistling: **Azúde.**

13.2 AFFIXED PRONOUNS: I AND YOU FOR LEDH VERBS

A.

1. **Bthíze:** I take it.

2. **Nátʰe a?:** Did you eat it? Are you eating?

3. **Náwa níppi:** You are good at counting.

4. **Nástube tte:** You might lick it.

5. **Ūdaⁿ moⁿbthíⁿ:** I am doing well.

6. **Wēbax̱u kʰe ubthíx̱ide:** I am looking for the pencil.

7. **Maⁿč̣ʰú síⁿde kʰe náx̌ta tte:** You might bite the grizzly bear's tail.

8. **Áⁿkkazhi, btháx̌ta ubthíʔage:** No, I refuse to bite it.

9. **Nú níⁿ a? Waʔú níⁿ a?:** Are you a man? Are you a woman?

10. **Móⁿzeska sáttoⁿ abthíⁿ:** I have five dollars.

B.

1. I licked it: **Bthástube.**

2. You pulled it: **Nídoⁿ.**

3. Are you looking around?: **Uníx̱ide a?**

4. You should go to the board: **Zhoⁿbtháskaska tʰe moⁿíⁿ tta akʰa.**

5. I'm good at skating: **Anúzoⁿ bthíppi.**

6. I can't count the stars: **Mikkáʔe btháwa bthíʔa.**

7. I refuse to look for the cat: **Iⁿgthóⁿga akʰa uáne ubthíʔage.**

8. Do you have a pencil?: **Wēbax̱u kʰe aníⁿ a?**

9. Can you whistle?: **Thazúde uthákkihi a?**

10. I can swim: **Aníuoⁿ uákkihi.**

13.3 AFFIXED PRONOUNS: I AND YOU FOR VERBS BEGINNING WITH SIMPLE STOPS

A.

1. **Shóⁿ ppāx̱e:** I make it stop.

2. **Īe tʰe shpáx̱u tte:** You might write the word.

3. **Attóⁿba mazhi:** I didn't see it.

4. **Dūba shkōⁿna?:** Do you want some?

5. **Má kʰe íⁿč̣ʰoⁿ ppádi:** I just pushed off the snow.

6. **Zūde wiwítta tʰe attóⁿba mazhi:** I don't see my whistle.

7. **Móⁿga kʰe thashtóⁿbe (a)?:** Do you see the (dead) skunk?

8. **Áoⁿ. Móⁿga kʰe āshiatta ppádoⁿ:** Yes. I'm pushing the (dead) skunk outside.

9. **Wāthatʰe tʰe shpádoⁿ tte:** You might push the table.

10. **Ttízhiⁿga tʰe āshiatta shkāx̌e tte:** You might make/build the outhouse/small house outside.

B.

1. Do you see the badger?: **X̌úga thashtóⁿbe (a)?**

2. Do you see the board?: **Zhoⁿbláska tʰe thashtóⁿbe (a)?**

3. Did you make some coffee?: **Moⁿkkóⁿsabe dūba shkā̧x̧e (a)?**

4. Yesterday I pushed a grizzly bear: **Sidādi, maⁿčʰú wiⁿ ppádoⁿ.**

5. Are you writing/did you write your name?: **Izházhe thithítta tʰe shpáx̧u (a)?**

6. They say he wrote a book: **Wagthábaze bax̧ú bi ama.**

7. Kathleen, did you push off the snow?: **Kathleen, má kʰe shpádi (a)?**

8. I might build an outhouse: **Ttízhiⁿga ppā̧x̧e tte.**

9. Today I am making cowboy bread: **Óⁿbathe wamóskeshuga ppā̧x̧e.**

10. Did you write a book?: **Wagthábaze shpáx̧u (a)?**

13.4 AFFIXED PRONOUNS: I AND YOU FOR VERBS BEGINNING WITH SIMPLE STOP G-

A.

1. **Agíoⁿ bthíppi kkō̧ⁿbtha:** I want to be good at flying.

2. **Wamóskeshuga ppā̧x̧e agísithe kkō̧ⁿbtha:** I want to remember how to make cowboy bread.

3. **Hūttoⁿga īe tʰe shpáx̧u shkóⁿzhiⁿga (a)?:** Don't you know how to write the Winnebago language?

4. **Óⁿpʰaⁿ kʰe thagísithe (a)?:** Do you remember the (dead or lying down) elk?

5. **Wēbax̧u náwa shkóⁿna (a)?:** Do you want to count the pens/pencils?

6. **Umóⁿhoⁿ īe tʰe ppáx̧u ppóⁿzhiⁿga:** I don't know how to write the Omaha language.

7. **Má wasábe ppā̧x̧e tʰe nástube shkōⁿna (a)?:** Do you want to lick the snowbear I made?

8. **Thiháⁿ izházhe tʰe thagísitha azhi:** You don't remember your mother's name.

9. **Thagíoⁿ shkōⁿna (a)?:** Do you want to fly?

10. **Hiⁿbé ppā̧x̧e ppóⁿzhiⁿga:** I don't know how to make moccasins.

B.

1. I want to fly: **Agíoⁿ kkō̧ⁿbtha.**

2. You pushed the chair: **Āgthiⁿ tʰe shpádoⁿ.**

3. I remember my school: **Ttáppu̧ska wiwítta agísithe.**

4. She doesn't know how to make cherry juice: **Nóⁿppa ní gā̧x̧e góⁿzhiⁿga.**

5. I don't want to kick the door: **Ttizhébe tʰe anóⁿtʰe kkō̧ⁿbtha mazhi.**

6. I don't know how to whistle: **Azúde ppóⁿzhiⁿga.**

7. Do you remember it?: **Thagísithe (a)?**

8. Do you not know how to swim?: **Thaníuoⁿ shkóⁿzhiⁿga (a)?**

9. She remembers flying: **Gióⁿ gisíthe.**

10. Do you remember swimming?: **Thaníuoⁿ thagísithe (a)?**

13.5 AFFIXED PRONOUNS: I AND YOU FOR OLD GLOTTAL STOP VERBS AND "SAY"

A.

1. **"Maⁿčʰúska ú tʰe íbahoⁿ," eshé:** "S/he knows that s/he shot at the polar bear," you said/say.

2. **Watʰé zhíⁿ noⁿ zhóⁿ:** You habitually wear the skirt/dress.

3. **Unóⁿzhiⁿshtoⁿga tʰe míⁿ:** I wear/am wearing the jacket.

4. **Mīzhiⁿga thiⁿkʰe watʰé zhīde íⁿ thiⁿkʰe thashtóⁿbe a?:** Do you see the girl wearing the red dress?

5. **"Mōⁿzeska kkúge wiⁿ bthíze." Edépʰe a?:** "I took one thousand dollars." What did I say?

6. **Hiⁿbé sábe tʰe zhíⁿ tʰe oⁿʔí ga!:** Give me the black shoe you are wearing!

7. **Watháge zhiégoⁿ íⁿ noⁿ:** S/he regularly wears the pink hat.

8. **Edéshe?:** What did you say?

9. **Iⁿshʼáge akʰa wasábe thiⁿkʰe ú:** The old man shoots the sleeping bear.

10. **"Shóⁿge tʼé wiwítta kʰe shpádoⁿ íthagaskoⁿne tte," ehé:** "You might try to push my dead horse," I said.

B.

1. I want to wear a snake-skin jacket: **Wésʼa há unóⁿzhiⁿshtoⁿga míⁿ kkōⁿbtha.**

2. Did he wound the dog?: **Shínuda thiⁿkʰe ú (a)?**

3. What did I say?: **Edépʰe?**

4. "Go to the board!" I said: **"Zhoⁿbtháskaska tʰe moⁿthíⁿ a!" ehé.**

5. I am trying to wear the long jacket: **Unóⁿzhiⁿshtoⁿga snéde tʰe míⁿ ithágaskoⁿbthe.**

6. She said, "I want to slap his dirty face": **"Iⁿdé shnábe ú kkōⁿbtha," á.**

7. That's baloney!: **Eē-shtoⁿna!**

8. Yesterday, you tried to take the pair of white shoes: **Sidādi, hiⁿbé ská tʰe níze íthagaskoⁿne.**

9. Today, you are wearing them: **Óⁿbathe zhíⁿ.**

10. Oh! What did you say?: **Íⁿ!/Ba! Edéshe?**

13.6 AFFIXED PRONOUNS: WE

A.

1. **Ūdaⁿ oⁿmóⁿthiⁿ:** We are doing well.

2. **Īe tʰe oⁿbáx̣u tte:** We might write the word.

3. **Shé ge oⁿtháwa:** We counted the apples.

4. **Āshka oⁿshkāde tte:** We might play in a little while.

5. **Oⁿnóⁿzhiⁿ oⁿgóⁿtha:** We want to stand.

6. **Umóⁿhoⁿ īe tʰe oⁿthíppi kkōⁿbtha:** I want us to be experts at the Omaha language.

7. **Oⁿthástube oⁿgúthiʼaga:** We are unwilling to lick it.

8. **Kkinóⁿnoⁿge kʰe shpádoⁿ oⁿgóⁿtha:** We want you to push the car.

9. **Sidādi x̌ithámoⁿshoⁿ wiⁿ oⁿthíza:** Yesterday, we took one eagle feather.

10. **Wôⁿgithe wamóskeshuga oⁿgāx̌a:** We all made cowboy bread.

B.

1. We all see it: **Wôⁿgithe oⁿdóⁿba.**

2. We two bit it: **Wôⁿdoⁿ oⁿtháx̌ta.**

3. We pushed the car: **Kkinóⁿnoⁿge kʰe oⁿbádoⁿ.**

4. We might sleep: **Oⁿzhōⁿ tte.**

5. We want to drink coffee: **Moⁿkkóⁿsabe oⁿtháttoⁿ oⁿgóⁿtha.**

6. We lifted the bag: **Ūzhiha thoⁿ oⁿthíhoⁿ.**

7. We couldn't lift the car: **Kkinóⁿnoⁿge kʰe oⁿthíhoⁿ oⁿthíʼa.**

8. We are expert at swimming: **Oⁿníuoⁿ oⁿthíppi.**

9. We don't know how to write it in Omaha: **Umóⁿhoⁿ īe tʰe oⁿbáx̌u oⁿgóⁿzhiⁿga.**

10. In a little while, we'll stop walking: **Áshka oⁿmóⁿthiⁿ oⁿnóⁿshtoⁿ tte.**

13.7 PERSON AND NUMBER OF THE SUBJECT

A.

1. **Níppi:** You are an expert.

2. **Thashkāda:** You (plural) are playing.

3. **Utháne:** You (singular) are seeking it.

4. **Ppāx̌e tte:** I might do it.

5. **Bax̌ú:** S/he is writing.

6. **Ní tʰe náttoⁿ tte:** You might drink the water.

7. **Wagthábaze ūzhiha oⁿthíza:** We took the paper bag.

8. **Kkinóⁿnoⁿge kʰe shpádoⁿ thanóⁿshtoⁿ tte:** You might stop pushing the car.

9. **Moⁿx̌pí thashtóⁿbe thagthíⁿ:** You are sitting, watching the clouds.

10. **Wabáx̌u kʰe oⁿgáthade oⁿgúkkihi:** We can spell the words.

B.

1. You bit it: **Nax̌tá.**

2. You all refused: **Uníʼaga i.**

3. They made cowboy bread: **Wamóskeshuga gāx̌a.**

4. We drank it yesterday: **Sidádi oⁿtháttoⁿ.**

5. You (sing.) refused: **Uníʼage.**

6. I am able to lift a horse: **Shóⁿge bthíhoⁿ uákkihi.**

7. You couldn't push the car: **Kkinóⁿnoⁿge kʰe shpádoⁿ níʼa.**

8. She wants to take the card: **Wathíbaba kʰe thizé gōⁿtha.**

9. Did he look for a chair yesterday?: **Sidādi āgthiⁿ wiⁿ uné a?**

10. Try to speak Omaha! (to one/to a group): **Umóⁿhoⁿ ié ígaskoⁿtha a!/Umóⁿhoⁿ ié ígaskoⁿtha i a!**

13.8 PERSON AND NUMBER: NEGATION

A.

1. **Thaxtá bazhi:** S/he didn't bite it.

2. **Ashkāda mazhi:** I didn't play.

3. **Thanóⁿzhiⁿ azhi:** You (sing.) didn't stand.

4. **Wéathatʰe oⁿnā bazhi:** We didn't ask for food.

5. **Thazhōⁿ bazhi:** You (pl.) aren't sleeping/ didn't sleep.

6. **Umóⁿhoⁿ ié āagazhi mazhi:** I didn't command him/her to speak Omaha.

7. **Ūzhiha thoⁿ oⁿthíhoⁿ oⁿthíʔa bazhi:** We are not unable to lift the bag. / We did not fail to lift the bag.

8. **Āshiatta uáne moⁿbthíⁿ mazhi:** I can't go searching outside.

9. **Wabáxu kʰe āshpaxu shkóⁿzhiⁿga bazhi:** You (pl.) don't not know how to write the letters/word.

10. **Umóⁿhoⁿ īe tʰe itháppahoⁿ mazhi:** I don't know the Omaha language.

B.

1. Don't you want it?: **Shkōⁿnazhi a?**

2. We are not able to make it: **Oⁿgāxe oⁿgúkkihi bazhi. / Oⁿgāxe oⁿthíʔa.**

3. I didn't stop walking: **Moⁿbthíⁿ anóⁿshtoⁿ mazhi.**

4. We are not sitting outside: **Āshiatta oⁿgthíⁿ bazhi.**

5. You (sing.) didn't try: **Íthagaskoⁿnazhi.**

6. I wasn't able to push the car: **Kkinóⁿnoⁿge kʰe ppádoⁿ uákkihi mazhi.**

7. We don't want to swim: **Oⁿníuoⁿ oⁿgōⁿtha bazhi.**

8. You are not expert at skating: **Thanúzoⁿ níppi azhi.**

9. We didn't tell him to write it down: **Ābaxu oⁿgágazhi bazhi.**

10. I didn't see the red car: **Kkinóⁿnoⁿge zhīde kʰe attóⁿba mazhi.**

13.9 PATIENT-AFFIXED PRONOUNS

A.

1. **Oⁿtháxtazhi a!:** Don't bite me!

2. **Óⁿthatʰe tte:** S/he might eat me.

3. **Wāthihoⁿ:** They lift us.

4. **Wanóⁿʔoⁿ a?:** Does s/he hear them?

5. **Thaxáge thinóⁿʔoⁿ a?:** Does he hear you crying?

6. **Ttáxti akʰa wādoⁿbe a?:** Does the deer see us?

7. **Égithe wanóⁿtʰe tte:** Beware, they might kick them.

8. **Gasóⁿthiⁿ, thithíze tte:** Tomorrow, s/he might take you.

9. **Égithe manč̣ʰú wāthatʰe tte:** It might happen that the grizzly bear might eat me.

10. **Égithe shínuda akʰa ónthax̌ta tte:** It might happen that the dog might bite me.

B.

1. He didn't hear you: **Thinóⁿ'oⁿ bazhi.**

2. Yesterday, she saw me: **Sidādi, óⁿdoⁿba.**

3. The horse bit you: **Shóⁿge akʰa thitháx̌ta.**

4. He doesn't know how to push you: **Thibádoⁿ góⁿzhiⁿga.**

5. He is able to lift you: **Thithího ukkíhi.**

6. He kicked me: **Óⁿnoⁿtʰa.**

7. Beware! He might see you: **Égithe, thidóⁿbe tte.**

8. Today, the car pulled us: **Óⁿbathe, kkinóⁿnoⁿge kʰe wāthidoⁿ.**

9. Did she take him?: **Thizé a?**

10. I think he wants to eat them: **Wathátʰe gōⁿtha, ebthégoⁿ.**

13.10 PATIENT-AFFIXED PRONOUNS FOR Ā-, Í, AND U- VERBS

A.

1. **Āthibitte, íthibahoⁿ gōⁿtha, móⁿga akʰa:** The skunk wants to know and touch you.

2. **Uthíne tte:** He might seek you.

3. **Uthítʰiⁿ kki, uthíhi:** If s/he hits you, s/he beats you.

4. **Iⁿdé thastúbe íthimoⁿx̌e:** S/he asked you if it licks faces.

5. **Oⁿwóⁿtʰiⁿ bazhi:** S/he didn't hit me.

6. **Ttáx̌ti uníx̌ide āthigazhi a?:** Did s/he command you to look around for the deer?

7. **Égithe uthího thithátʰe tte:** It might happen that s/he might cook you and eat you.

8. **Wôⁿgithe oⁿthóⁿbahoⁿ bazhi:** Everyone doesn't know me.

9. **Íthashpahoⁿ shkōⁿna kki, íwamoⁿx̌a ga!:** If you want to know it, ask us/them about it!

10. **Huhú dūba athíⁿ kki, uwáhoⁿ tte:** If s/he has some fish, s/he might cook them.

B.

1. If they touch you, scream!: **Āthibitte kki, bóⁿ a!**

2. They're looking for me: **Oⁿwóⁿna (i). / Uóⁿthix̌ida (i).**

3. Did the mouse touch you?: **Iⁿcʰóⁿga akʰa āthibitte a?**

4. They want to hit us: **Uwātʰíⁿ gōⁿtha.**

5. Did she tell you to sit down?: **Thagthíⁿ āthigazhi a?**

6. They don't know how to beat us: **Uwāhi góⁿzhiⁿga (i).**

7. After a little while, she went looking for them: **Áshka uwáne/uwáthix̌ide moⁿthíⁿ.**

8. If he knows, he might hit me: **Íbahoⁿ kki, oⁿwóⁿtʰiⁿ tte.**

9. If he commands you, do it!: **Āthigazhi kki, gāx̣a a!**

10. Yesterday, she tried to ask us: **Sidādi, íwamoⁿx̣e ígaskoⁿtha.**

13.11 AGENT-TO-PATIENT AFFIXED PRONOUN COMBINATIONS

A.

1. **Āwippitta mazhi:** I didn't touch you.

2. **Oⁿthánoⁿʔoⁿ a?:** Did you hear me?

3. **Oⁿthíthihoⁿ:** We lifted you.

4. **Oⁿtháshtoⁿbe (a)?:** Did you see me?

5. **Kkáshi x̣agá (i) oⁿwóʔnoⁿʔoⁿ:** For a long time, we heard them crying.

6. **Umóⁿhoⁿ oⁿthóⁿe wāthanoⁿʔoⁿ a?:** Did you hear us speaking Omaha?

7. **Égithe, oⁿnáx̣ta kki wippádoⁿ tte:** It might happen that if you bite me, I might push you.

8. **X̌tāwithe:** I like you.

9. **Eáttoⁿ wāthanoⁿtʰeʔ?:** Why did you kick us?

10. **Nóⁿzhiⁿ (i) kki watháshtoⁿbe tte:** If they stand, you might see them.

B.

1. I am able to hear you: **Winóⁿʔoⁿ uákkihi.**

2. You were unable to lift us: **Wāthathihoⁿ níʔa.**

3. You tried to kick me: **Oⁿthánoⁿtʰe íthagaskoⁿne.**

4. We didn't bite you: **Oⁿthíthax̣ta bazhi.**

5. I wanted to hear them: **Awánoⁿʔoⁿ kkōⁿbtha.**

6. We don't know how to see them: **Oⁿwóⁿdoⁿbe góⁿzhiⁿga.**

7. I want to look for them: **Uáwane kkōⁿbtha.**

8. Do you want to eat them?: **Watháthatʰe shkōⁿna a?**

9. Are you trying to pull me outside?: **Āshiatta oⁿtháthidoⁿ íthagaskoⁿne a?**

10. If I see you, I may know you: **Wittóⁿbe kki, íwippahoⁿ tte.**

13.12 SUBJECT-AFFIXED PRONOUN FOR STATIVE VERBS

A.

1. **Thinóⁿkka:** You are hurt or injured.

2. **Oⁿníe:** I am hurting or in pain.

3. **Wôⁿgithe waṣní:** We/they are all cold.

4. **Móⁿzeska oⁿthíⁿge:** I don't have money.

5. **Iⁿdé thoⁿ thibútta:** Your face is round.

6. **Oⁿtʔé shkoⁿna kki, atʔé kkōⁿbtha:** If you want me to die, I want to die.

7. **Oⁿnítta moⁿbthíⁿ:** I'm alive/living.

8. **Wathátʰe thithíⁿge kki, thatʔé tte:** If you don't have food, you might die.

9. **Ishtá thoⁿ wattóⁿga, sháge tʰe waṣnéde:** We/they have big eyes and long nails.

10. **Noⁿshkí thoⁿ oⁿsági tʰe ūdaⁿ:** It's good I have a hard head.

B.

1. Don't you have any money?: **Mó^{n}zeska aní^n a? / Mó^{n}zeska thithí^{n}ge a?**

2. My arms are long: **Á t^{h}e o^{n}ṣnéde.**

3. I have a big nose: **Ppá k^{h}e o^{n}ttó^{n}ga.**

4. Are your ears cold?: **Nittá thiṣní a?**

5. Are you tired?: **Uthízhetha a?**

6. I want to live: **O^{n}nítta kkō^{n}btha.**

7. We don't have water: **Ní wathí^{n}ge. / Ní o^{n}gáthi^n bazhi.**

8. If I'm injured, I might die: **O^{n}nó^{n}kka kki, at'é tte.**

9. Do your teeth hurt?: **Hí k^{h}e thiníe a?**

10. My eye has been hurting for a long time: **Kkáshi, ishtá tho^n o^{n}níe.**

14.1 INANIMATE POSITIONALS

A.

1. **Mó^{n}zemo^n t^{h}e o^n'í ga!:** Give me the bullets!

2. **Wétta tho^n thasní^n:** S/he swallowed the egg.

3. **Ttí t^{h}e tto^{n}gá:** The house is big.

4. **Wēbaxú k^{h}e itháthe:** I found the pen/pencil.

5. **Ppahé ge o^{n}gúha:** We went along past the (scattered) hills.

6. **Zhó^n k^{h}e shpáhi kki, ppéde ppax̱e uákkihi tte:** If you pick up the wood, I might be able to make a fire.

7. **X̌thabé t^{h}e āane kkō^{n}btha mazhi. Ubthí'age:** I don't want to climb the tree. I'm unwilling to. / I refuse.

8. **Ttabé tho^n wi'í kki, thizá i ga ho!:** If I give you the ball, you all take it!

9. **Wahútto^{n}the k^{h}e āo^{n}bazu azhi ga!:** Don't point the gun at me!

10. **Wāi^n zhīde tho^n thashtó^{n}be a?:** Do you see the red blanket/shawl?

B.

1. I have the bullets: **Mó^{n}zemo^n t^{h}e abthí^n.**

2. He gave me the gun: **Wahútto^{n}the k^{h}e o^n'í.**

3. Follow the line of hills!: **Ppahé k^{h}e uhá a!**

4. He climbed the rope: **Házhi^{n}ga k^{h}e āna.**

5. We gathered up the arrows: **Mô^n ge o^{n}báhi.**

6. Did you find the standing rock?: **Í^n'e t^{h}e íthathe a?**

7. What? Did you swallow the potato?: **Edādo^n? Nú tho^n násni a?**

8. I passed over the land for a long time: **Kkáshi, mo^{n}zhó^n k^{h}e uáhe.**

9. He took the stick and hit me: **Zhó^{n}zhi^{n}ga k^{h}e thizé o^{n}wó^{n}t^{h}i^n.**

10. If the path is long, I may not find the tree: **Uzhó^{n}ge k^{h}e snéde kki, x̌thabé t^{h}e itháthe mazhi tte.**

14.2 ACTIVE SUBJECT POSITIONALS

A.

1. **Núzhiⁿga akʰá x̣agé tte:** The boy might cry.

2. **Nú ttóⁿga akʰá uzhóⁿge kʰe uhá:** The big man followed the road.

3. **Waʔú amá wamóskeshuga gāx̣e tta ama:** The women might make cowboy bread.

4. **Mīzhiⁿga akʰá uthá bi ama:** The girl told, they say.

5. **Waíⁿ gōⁿtha, waʔúzhiⁿga akʰá:** The woman wants a blanket/shawl.

6. **Núzhiⁿga akʰá ttabé thoⁿ thizá i egóⁿ, óⁿtha thétha:** The boy took the ball, and then threw it.

7. **Wéathatʰe thiⁿgé kki, shíⁿgazhiⁿga amá tʔé tta:** If the baby doesn't have food, it might die. / If the food's gone, the baby might die.

8. **Nudóⁿhoⁿga amá gí bi ama:** The war chief/leader came back, they say.

9. **Iⁿshʔáge akʰá moⁿkkóⁿsabe gōⁿtha kki, ʔí i ga ho!:** If the old man wants coffee, you all give it to him!

10. **Núzhiⁿga akʰá moⁿthíⁿ kki, moⁿshtíⁿge amá uóⁿsisi athá:** If/when the boy walks, the rabbit goes (or the rabbits go) jumping.

B.

1. The buzzard saw it: **Héga akʰá dóⁿba.**

2. The boys gathered rocks: **Núzhiⁿga amá íⁿʔe bahí.**

3. The rabbit tried to jump: **Moⁿshtíⁿge akʰá uóⁿsi ígaskoⁿtha.**

4. "Yes," said Tom: **"Áoⁿ," á, Tom akʰá.**

5. The child ate the egg: **Shíⁿgazhiⁿga akʰá wétta thoⁿ thatʰá.**

6. When the boy saw the rope, he climbed the tree: **Núzhiⁿga akʰá házhiⁿga kʰe dóⁿba i egóⁿ, x̣thabé tʰe āna.**

7. Having drunk the water, the man lay down: **Ní tʰe thattóⁿ egóⁿ, nú akʰá zhōⁿ.**

8. The women want to gather plums tomorrow: **Gasóⁿthiⁿ waʔú amá kkóⁿde bahí gōⁿtha.**

9. The three girls pointed at the feather: **Mīzhiⁿga thâbthiⁿ akʰá móⁿshoⁿ kʰe ābazu.**

10. The teachers tried to find the markers: **Wagōⁿze amá wēbax̣u ge íthe ígaskoⁿtha.**

14.3 ANIMATE POSITIONALS

A.

1. **Huhú kʰe ttóⁿ:** S/he has fish (characteristically). / S/he is a fisherman.

2. **Wazhíⁿga thiⁿkʰé oⁿgúhoⁿ oⁿthátʰe shkōⁿna?:** Do you want us to cook and eat the chicken?

3. **Iⁿgthóⁿga akʰá iⁿx̌čʰóⁿga ma doⁿbá i kki, wiⁿ thiⁿkʰé thix̣á:** When the cat saw the mice, it chased one.

4. **Mīzhiⁿga thiⁿkʰé utʰíⁿ bi ama, núzhiⁿga akʰá:** The boy hit the girl, they say.

5. **Íthashpahoⁿ shkōⁿna kki, waʔúzhiⁿga thiⁿkʰé ímaχa a!:** If you want to know, ask the old woman.

6. **Nú akʰá núzhiⁿga thiⁿkʰé ttabé thoⁿ ʔí:** The man gave the boy the ball.

7. **Wésʔa kʰe kkáshi tʔé. Ābitta bazhí i a!:** The snake has been dead a long time. Don't touch it! (woman speaking to multiple people)

8. **Iⁿshʔáge zhōⁿtʔe kʰe ítha i kki, ithádi thiⁿkʰé thiχí, mízhiⁿga akʰá:** When the girl found the sleeping old man, she woke up her father.

9. **Gasóⁿthiⁿ núzhiⁿga shóⁿge tʰoⁿ āgthiⁿ ígaskoⁿthe tta akʰa:** Tomorrow the boy might try to ride the horse.

10. **Shaóⁿ níkkashiⁿga ma wadóⁿba i egóⁿ, nudóⁿ amá gí:** The warriors came back after they saw the Sioux.

B.

1. I saw the buzzards: **Héga ma attóⁿbe.**

2. The girl lifted the cat: **Mīzhiⁿga akʰá iⁿgthóⁿga thiⁿkʰé thihóⁿ.**

3. The boy pushed the two girls: **Núzhiⁿga akʰá mīzhiⁿga noⁿbá thoⁿká badóⁿ.**

4. They all laughed at the old man: **Iⁿshʔáge thiⁿkʰé íχaχa, wôⁿgithe.**

5. Did you swallow the fly?: **Hóⁿtʔega thiⁿkʰé násniⁿ a?**

6. She wanted to know the old woman: **Waʔúzhiⁿga thiⁿkʰé íbahoⁿ góⁿtha.**

7. If you see the deer, give me the gun: **Ttáχti thiⁿkʰé thashtóⁿbe kki, wahúttoⁿthe kʰe oⁿʔí a/ga!**

8. We pulled the (dead) cow: **Ttéska kʰe oⁿthídoⁿ.**

9. Give the teacher the marker!: **Wēbaχu kʰe, wagōⁿze thiⁿkʰé ʔí a/ga!**

10. Don't point at the person!: **Niáshiⁿga thiⁿkʰé ābaxu azhi a/ga! / Niáshiⁿga thiⁿkʰé ābaxu bazhi i a/ga!**

14.4 ARTICLES

A.

1. **Ttáχti thashtóⁿbe kki, thawá a!:** If/when you see deer, count them!

2. **Āshiatta ttáχti dūba awáttoⁿbe:** I see some deer outside.

3. **Ttáχti thoⁿkʰá doⁿbá bi ama:** S/he or they saw the deer, they say.

4. **Mīzhiⁿga utʰíⁿ tte, núzhiⁿga akʰá:** The boy might hit a (any) girl.

5. **Shínuda wíⁿ uátʰiⁿ ithágaskoⁿbthe kki, oⁿtháχta:** If/when I try to hit a dog, it bites me.

6. **Shóⁿge thiⁿkʰé utʰíⁿ bi ama, niáshiⁿga wíⁿ:** A person hit the horse, they say.

7. **Iⁿshʔáge wíⁿ ttabé thoⁿ ítha:** An old man found the ball.

8. **Iⁿshʔáge akʰá ttabé wíⁿ ítha:** The old man found a ball.

9. **Núzhiⁿga wíⁿ amá ttabé íthe gōⁿtha bi ama:** A particular group of boys wanted to find a (any) ball, they say.

10. **Núzhiⁿga ttabé thinā kki, wíⁿ ʔí a!:** If/when a (any) boy asks you for a (any) ball, give it to him!

B.

1. Do you want a (any) plum?: **Kkóⁿde shkōⁿna?**

2. We rode a (particular) horse: **Shóⁿge wíⁿ oⁿgāgthiⁿ.**

3. I saw some horses: **Shóⁿge dūba awáttoⁿbe.**

4. The rabbit kicked the ball, they say: **Moⁿshtíⁿge akʰá ttabé thoⁿ noⁿtʰá, bi ama.**

5. The dogs bit the rabbit: **Shínuda amá moⁿshtíⁿge thiⁿkʰé thaxtá.**

6. She tried to see a (any) warrior: **Nudóⁿ dóⁿbe ígaskoⁿtha.**

7. The cat chased a (particular) fly: **Iⁿgthóⁿga akʰá hóⁿtʼega wíⁿ thixá.**

8. Give me an (any) arrow!: **Môⁿ oⁿʼí a/ga!**

9. I don't know how to make a (any) bow: **Môⁿde ppāxe ppóⁿzhiⁿga.**

10. The person looked around for deer: **Niáshiⁿga akʰá ttáxti uwána.**

14.5 FUTURE

A.

1. **Uwítʰiⁿ tta miⁿkʰe:** I will hit you.

2. **Íthaxa tta niⁿkshe:** You will laugh.

3. **Ttáxti wíⁿ thixé tta i tʰe:** They must/should chase a deer.

4. **Waʼúzhiⁿga amá thidóⁿbe kki, thithíxe tta ama:** If/when the old women see you, they will chase you.

5. **Shóⁿge tʰoⁿ ní ʼí tta tʰe, núzhiⁿga akʰá:** The boy should give the horse water.

6. **Āshiatta áshka bthé tta miⁿkʰe:** I will go outside in a little while.

7. **Wéathatʰe bthúga náṣniⁿ tta niⁿkshe:** You will swallow all the food.

8. **Hīga oⁿgútha tta oⁿgatʰoⁿ:** We will tell the legends/stories.

9. **Môⁿ ge íthe tta i tʰe:** They must/should find the (scattered) arrows.

10. **Wôⁿgithe ishtá thipʼíⁿze tta i tʰe:** They should all close their eyes.

B.

1. You are going to win: **Utháhi tta niⁿkshe.**

2. We are going to write it: **Oⁿbáxu tta oⁿgatʰoⁿ.**

3. The old man should make a house: **Iⁿshʼáge akʰá tti gāxe tta tʰe.**

4. I am going to pull the car: **Kkinóⁿnoⁿge kʰe bthídoⁿ tta miⁿkʰe.**

5. The rabbits have to jump: **Moⁿshtíⁿge amá uóⁿsi tta i tʰe.**

6. She will point at it: **Ābazu tta akʰa.**

7. You will cook it: **Utháhoⁿ tta niⁿkshe.**

8. We are going to know Omaha: **Umóⁿhoⁿ oⁿthóⁿbahoⁿ tta oⁿgatʰoⁿ.**

9. Tomorrow I will be able to lift the deer: **Gasóⁿthiⁿ, ttáxti kʰe bthíhoⁿ uákkihi tta miⁿkʰe.**

10. The girls have to gather eggs: **Mīzhiⁿga amá wétta bahí tta i tʰe.**

14.6 DEMONSTRATIVES: THIS AND THAT

A.

1. **Mⁿzhóⁿ thêthudi ūdaⁿ ebthégoⁿ:** I think the land around here is good.

2. **Shêhi tʰe noⁿzhíⁿ amá hátheze gí tta i tʰe:** The soldiers must come back safely.

3. **Dúda! Shíⁿgazhiⁿga dúde gí i a!:** Hey! You small children all come back this way!

4. **Shêhi tʰe gthíⁿ amá nudóⁿ wiⁿ atʰí:** A warrior arrived here from the people (living elsewhere).

5. **Thêthudi thé tʰe noⁿzhíⁿ:** Around here is where s/he stood.

6. **Maⁿčʰú akʰá dúdiha moⁿthíⁿ tta akʰá:** The grizzly bear will walk/go over here.

7. **Eshóⁿ thagthíⁿ. Gúde moⁿníⁿ tte:** You are sitting very close. You might go/move away.

8. **Thêthudi hīga uthá tta akʰa, wagōⁿze akʰá:** The teacher will tell the story around here.

9. **Wāthatʰe thashtóⁿbe tʰe thê gthíⁿ:** The table you see is where s/he sat.

10. **Thê hóⁿtʼega akʰá gióⁿ bi ama:** This fly flew, they say.

B.

1. I have the card. Here, take it: **Wathíbaba kʰe abthíⁿ. Gá, thizá a/ga!**

2. I don't want it. Get out of here!: **Kkōⁿbtha mazhi. Gúdiha moⁿthíⁿ a/ga!**

3. The people over there (in another land) might die: **Shêhi tʰe gthíⁿ amá tʼé tte.**

4. Teacher, come over here!: **Wagōⁿze, dúdiha gí a/ga!**

5. This girl (that I mentioned) lifted the doll: **Thê mīzhiⁿga akʰá shíⁿgazhiⁿga kʰe thihóⁿ.**

6. The bird will fly over there: **Wazhíⁿga akʰá dúdiha gióⁿ tta akʰa.**

7. Did you see the people living over there?: **Shêhi tʰe gthíⁿ thoⁿkʰá watháshtoⁿbe a?**

8. He was over there (in another land) for a long time: **Kkáshi shêhi tʰe noⁿzhíⁿ.**

9. This boy (mentioned in 8) came back safely: **Thê núzhiⁿga akʰá hátheza.**

10. Come closer! This is where he lay: **Eshóⁿ gí a/ga!/ Dúde gí a/ga! Eshóⁿ, dúde gí a/ga! Thê tʰe zhōⁿ. / Gátʰedi zhōⁿ.**

14.7 DEMONSTRATIVE PRONOUNS

A.

1. **Gátʰoⁿ āgthiⁿ ga!:** Sit on that! Ride that (standing) one!

2. **Shêama waʼú amá shé bahí tta ama:** Those women will gather apples.

3. **Shêhige wiⁿ shkōⁿna kki, thizá a!:** If you want one of those things scattered over there, take it!

4. **Núzhiⁿga dúakʰa thêthudi niúoⁿ gōⁿtha:** This boy wants to swim in this area/here.

5. **Shêhitʰe xthabé tʰe thashtóⁿbe a?:** Do you see that tree over yonder?

6. **Wéttaugthe shêtho^n athí^n āne gí mo^{n}thí^n ga!:** Go climb it and get that nest!

7. **Égo^n x̌thabé t^{h}e āna bi ama, thêak^{h}a núzhi^{n}ga ak^{h}á:** They say that for that reason this (here) boy climbed the tree.

8. **Wa'úzhi^{n}ga shêak^{h}a dúdiha mo^{n}thí^n tta t^{h}e:** That old woman should go/move over here.

9. **Wathíbaba gák^{h}e bthíze tta mi^{n}k^{h}e:** I will take that (particular) card.

10. **Duátho^n ūzhiha x̌uí^n tho^n gúdiha athí^n mo^{n}thí^n a!:** Take away this stinky bag!

B.

1. Here, take this arrow!: **Gá, mô^n duák^{h}e thizá a/ga!**

2. Point it at that bird!: **Wazhí^{n}ga shêthi^{n}k^{h}e ābazu a/ga!**

3. The aforementioned boy took the arrow, they say: **Mô^n k^{h}e thizé bi ama, núzhi^{n}ga thêak^{h}a.**

4. If you do not know how to shoot, you will not be able to hit that deer: **Kkíde shkó^{n}zhi^{n}ga kki, ttáx̌ti shêthi^{n}k^{h}e ú ní'a tta ni^{n}kshe.**

5. This bear wants to eat you: **Wasábe dúak^{h}a thithát^{h}e gō^{n}tha.**

6. Those buzzards over there are circling: **Héga shêhiama gakkúwi^{n}x̌e.**

7. Do you remember that old man?: **I^{n}sh'áge shêthi^{n}k^{h}e thagísithe a?**

8. Those (boys) shouldn't whistle: **Núzhi^{n}ga thêama zúda bazhi tta i t^{h}e.**

9. We're going to push this car: **Kkinó^{n}no^{n}ge duák^{h}e o^{n}bádo^n tta o^{n}gat^{h}o^n.**

10. This (girl) wants that doll: **Mīzhi^{n}ga dúak^{h}a shí^{n}gazhi^{n}ga shêt^{h}e gō^{n}tha.**

14.8 EMPHATIC PRONOUNS

A.

1. **O^{n}gú o^{n}gúhi tta o^{n}gat^{h}o^n:** *We* will win.

2. **É shti ttanúkka that^{h}é gō^{n}tha:** *S/he* also wants to eat meat.

3. **Thí é ní^n:** It is *you*.

4. **Wí shti anúzo^n ithágasko^{n}bthe tta mi^{n}k^{h}e:** *I* also will try to skate.

5. **É niúo^n bazhi. O^{n}gú o^{n}níuo^n:** *S/he / they* aren't swimming. *We* are swimming.

6. **Wéttaugthe shêt^{h}e wí itháthe:** *I* found that nest.

7. **Wathíbaba gák^{h}e shkō^{n}na azhi kki, wí bthíze tta mi^{n}k^{h}e:** If you don't want that card over there, *I* will take it.

8. **Égo^n uná t^{h}e, é wí^{n}k^{h}a bazhi:** What you said, *it* is not true.

9. **O^{n}gú shti wagthábaze shêk^{h}e o^{n}gáthade o^{n}gó^{n}zhi^{n}ga:** *We* also don't know how to read that book.

10. **Thêak^{h}a niáshi^{n}ga ak^{h}á thí é ní^n a?:** Are *you* him/her (this person we've been talking about)?

B.

1. *I* am the one who saw the buzzards: **Héga ma wadónbe akʰa wí é bthíⁿ.**

2. *I* didn't do it; *you* did: **Wí ppaχa mazhi; thí shkaχa.**

3. *It* was the gun that the aforementioned man took, they say: **Wahúttoⁿthe kʰe, é nú thêakʰa thizá bi ama.**

4. They were the ones who shot at it; *we* didn't have a gun: **É kkída; oⁿgú wahúttoⁿthe oⁿgáthiⁿ bazhi.**

5. That man over there is the one who must do it: **Nú shêhiakʰa é gaχe tta tʰe.**

6. That is the dog that bit him: **Shínuda shêakʰa é thaχtá.**

7. I am the only one who remembers that old man. *Those* (people) don't know him: **Iⁿsh'áge thêthiⁿkʰe wí noⁿ agísithe. Shêama íbahoⁿ bazhi.**

8. *We* will make cowboy bread; *you* will give them this meat: **Wamóskeshuga kʰe oⁿgú oⁿgaχe tta oⁿgatʰoⁿ; ttanúkka duátʰe thí wathá'i tta niⁿkshe.**

9. *You* too can speak Omaha!: **Thí shti Umóⁿhoⁿ íthae uthákkihi.**

10. The one who wrote that is *I*: **Shêkʰe baχú akʰa wí é bthíⁿ.**

14.9 POSSESSIVE PRONOUNS

A.

1. **Ttí oⁿgútta tʰe ttoⁿgá:** Our house is big.

2. **Iⁿgthóⁿga wiwítta thiⁿkʰé uáne:** I'm looking for my cat.

3. **Wagōⁿze thithítta thiⁿkʰé, wí é bthíⁿ:** *I'm* the one who is your teacher.

4. **Dúakʰa shóⁿge akʰá wiwítta; shêhitʰoⁿ thithítta:** This horse right here is mine; that one over there is yours.

5. **Gá! Wēbaχu wiwítta kʰe wi'í:** Here! I give you my pencil.

6. **Ttabé duáthoⁿ ebé ettá?:** Whose ball is this?

7. **Thí noⁿ shóⁿge thithítta tʰoⁿ āthagthiⁿ uthákkihi:** You are the only one able to ride your horse.

8. **Mōⁿzeska oⁿgútta tʰe níze kki, níde thithítta kʰe anóⁿtʰe tta miⁿkʰe:** If you take our money, I will kick your butt.

9. **Wéathatʰe thithítta tʰe wí shti hébe winā tte:** I too might ask you for a piece of your food.

10. **Shóⁿge shêhiakʰa wiwítta kki, é āagthiⁿ tta miⁿkʰe:** If that's my horse, I will ride it.

B.

1. This car is mine; that one is yours: **Kkinóⁿnoⁿge duákʰe wiwítta; shêkʰe thithítta.**

2. Now it is our turn: **Íⁿčʰoⁿ oⁿgútta.**

3. It was my gun that the man took: **Wahúttoⁿthe wiwítta kʰe é nú akʰá thizá.**

4. Did you find your money?: **Móⁿzeska thithítta tʰe íthathe a?**

5. She's looking for her dog: **Shínuda ettá thiⁿkʰé uná.**

6. My name is _____. What is your name?: **Izházhe wiwítta t^{h}e_____. Izházhe thithítta t^{h}e i^{n}dádo^n a?**

7. Your hands are pretty: **No^{n}bé thithítta t^{h}e ûja^n.**

8. I want some of your cowboy bread too: **Wamóskeshuga thithítta k^{h}e wí shti dūba kkō^{n}btha.**

9. I am the only one who saw your horse: **Shó^{n}ge thithítta t^{h}o^n wí no^n attó^{n}be.**

10. This is my knife. I'm looking for my spoon: **Duák^{h}e mô^{n}hi k^{h}e wiwítta. Ttehé wiwítta k^{h}e uáne.**

15.1 POSTPOSITIONS

A.

1. **Ttó^{n}dadi zhō^n:** S/he lay down on the ground.

2. **Wazhí^{n}ga ama mó^{n}xadi thanó'o^n a?:** Do you hear the birds in the sky?

3. **"Ettát^{h}o^n gí i a!" á bi ama ihá^n ak^{h}á:** "Come back from there!" said their mother, supposedly.

4. **Núzhi^{n}ga ak^{h}á edí no^n'ó^n azhi gthí^n bi ama:** They say the boy sat there not listening.

5. **Ttó^{n}datta dó^{n}ba i ga ho!:** Look at the ground!

6. **Mó^{n}xadit^{h}o^n uxpátha bi ama:** They say she fell from the sky.

7. **Wēbaxu thithítta k^{h}e gát^{h}edi íthathe tte:** You might find your pencil at that particular place/right there.

8. **Thí shti thé:thudi gthí^n a!:** You also sit here!

9. **Ttíat^{h}o^n ttó^{n}datta uó^{n}si:** S/he jumped from the house toward the ground.

10. **Xithá ak^{h}a mó^{n}xatta kkúwi^{n}xe gió^n mo^{n}thí^n:** The eagle is flying, circling skyward. / The eagle went flying, circling toward the sky.

B.

1. Stand next to that (vertical thing)!: **Shêt^{h}edi no^{n}zhí^n a/ga!**

2. It arrived here from the sky: **Mó^{n}xadit^{h}o^n at^{h}í.**

3. It arrived here from the ground: **Ttó^{n}dat^{h}o^n at^{h}í.**

4. The mouse runs inside the house: **I^{n}c^{h}ó^{n}ga ak^{h}a ttíadi ttó^{n}thi^n mo^{n}thí^n.**

5. Are you able to pull that tree branch toward the ground?: **Gāxa k^{h}e ttó^{n}datta nído^n uthákkihi a?**

6. The children will play there (at the aforementioned location): **Shí^{n}gazhi^{n}ga amá edí shkāde tta ama.**

7. The snake moves into the house: **Wés'a ak^{h}a ttíadi uppé mo^{n}thí^n.**

8. They say she sits in the sky: **Mó^{n}xadi gthí^n bi ama.**

9. You too might look around for something here, in this area: **Thí shti théthudi uníxide tte.**

10. Do you see the airplane that is flying, circling skyward?: **Mo^{n}dégio^n mó^{n}xatta kkúwi^{n}xe gió^n mo^{n}thí^n k^{h}e thashtó^{n}be a?**

15.2 POSITIONALS AND POSTPOSITIONS

A.

1. **Mīzhiⁿga akʰa wahúttoⁿthe kʰetʰoⁿ ttóⁿthiⁿ moⁿthíⁿ**: The girl ran from the gun.

2. **Ttabé thoⁿtta uóⁿsisi**: S/he jumped toward the ball.

3. **Wathíbaba geditʰoⁿ wiⁿ thizá ga!**: Pick one of the scattered cards!

4. **Izházhe thithítta tʰe thêkʰedi baχú ga!**: Write your name right here on this line!

5. **Inégi thiⁿkʰédi gthíⁿ bi ama**: They say s/he sat/resided/was at his/her uncle's.

6. **X̌thabé tʰedi āna bi ama, núzhiⁿga akʰa**: At the tree, the boy climbed, they say.

7. **X̌thabé tʰetʰoⁿ ttóⁿdatta uχpátha bi ama**: They say s/he fell from the tree toward the ground.

8. **Héga amá shóⁿge kʰetta gióⁿ tta ama**: The buzzards will probably fly toward the horse.

9. **Nóⁿde kʰetta thashtóⁿbe kki, miĩdoⁿbe gátʰedi thashtóⁿbe tta niⁿkshe**: If you look toward the wall, you will see the clock right there.

10. **Ttizhébe shêhitʰetta moⁿthíⁿ a!**: Go toward the door over yonder there!

B.

1. The otter swam toward the turtle: **Kké thiⁿkʰétta niúoⁿ, nushnáⁿ akʰá.**

2. What is in your bag?: **Ūzhiha thithítta thoⁿdi idādoⁿ a?**

3. She stood by the door, they say: **Ttizhébe tʰedi noⁿzhíⁿ bi ama.**

4. Do you want to drink from the cup?: **Niĩthattoⁿ tʰetʰoⁿ náttoⁿ shkōⁿna?**

5. The card passes to the instructor: **Wagōⁿze thiⁿkʰétta wathíbaba kʰe uhé.**

6. Put the seed in the earth!: **Sí tʰe moⁿthíⁿkka kʰedi itʰétha a/ga!**

7. Rabbit will walk toward the soup, they say: **Moⁿshtíⁿge akʰa ttaní thoⁿtta móⁿthiⁿ tta akʰa, á bi ama.**

8. They sat at the table: **Wôⁿgithe wāthatʰe kʰedi gthíⁿ.**

9. He went running over the land: **Moⁿzhóⁿ kʰedi uhé ttóⁿthiⁿ moⁿthíⁿ.**

10. Go get a knife from the pack!: **Ūzhiha thoⁿditʰoⁿ môⁿhiⁿ athíⁿ gí moⁿthíⁿ a/ga!**

15.3 LOCATION NOUNS AND ADVERBS

A.

1. **Gúdiha moⁿthíⁿ i ga! Eshóⁿ āttashoⁿ thagthíⁿ**: Go away! (plural command, male speaker) You are sitting very/too close.

2. **Wāthatʰe égaχe gthíⁿ i ga ho!**: Sit surrounding the table! (plural command, male speaker, formal)

3. **Ittóⁿthiⁿatta moⁿthíⁿ bi ama, núzhiⁿga akʰá**: The boy went ahead, they say.

4. **Mīzhiⁿga akʰa kkinóⁿnoⁿge móⁿtʰadi gthíⁿ**: The girl is sitting in the car.

5. **"Shíⁿgazhiⁿga athíⁿ gashíbe gí a!" á bi ama, iháⁿ akʰá:** They say his mother said, "Bring the child out!"

6. **X̌thabé ppaháshiatta āane kki, wéahidex̌ti attóⁿbe uákkihi tte:** If I climb toward the top of the tree, I might be able to see very far away.

7. **Níshude móⁿtʰadi niúoⁿ kki, moⁿsóⁿthiⁿatta hí ígaskoⁿthe tta akʰa:** If/when s/he swims in the river, s/he will try to arrive at the far side.

8. **Ppahóⁿgax̌tidi Wakkóⁿda akʰa móⁿx̌e kʰe, moⁿthíⁿkka kʰe gāx̌a bi ama:** At the very beginning, the Creator/God made the sky (heavens) and the earth, they say.

9. **Ppahé hídatta ní wiⁿ ítha bi ama, nú akʰá:** The man found water toward the bottom of the hill, they say.

10. **Kkóⁿgatta moⁿthíⁿ bi ama, nudóⁿ akʰá:** The warrior was approaching, they say.

B.

1. Stand up front (facing the class)!: **Uthúshiadi noⁿzhíⁿ a/ga!**

2. The girl walked behind: **Háshiatta moⁿthíⁿ, mīzhiⁿga akʰá.**

3. They say he stood in the center (of the circle), speaking Omaha: **Ídabe noⁿzhíⁿ bi ama, Umóⁿhoⁿ iá bi ama.**

4. He looked behind him: **Názatta dóⁿba.**

5. He threw the ball up high: **Ttabé thoⁿ móⁿshiatta/móⁿshiadi thétha.**

6. Omaha is spoken here: **Thêthudi Umóⁿhoⁿ ié noⁿ.**

7. They live on the other side: **Moⁿsóⁿthiadi gthíⁿ.**

8. Please look for my knife in that bag!: **Ūzhiha shêthoⁿ móⁿtʰadi môⁿhiⁿ wiwítta tʰe utháne tte.**

9. She reached across the table and picked up the card: **Wāthátʰe akkíwatta wathíbaba kʰe thizá.**

10. The leader should walk at the head of the line. Warriors should walk behind: **Gahíge akʰá ppahóⁿgatta moⁿthíⁿ tta tʰe. Nudóⁿ amá háshiatta moⁿthíⁿ tta i tʰe.**

15.4 VERBS OF MOTION

A.

1. **Ppahóⁿgatta thé gōntha, núzhiⁿga akʰa:** The boy wants to go toward the front.

2. **Ettátʰoⁿ í ukkíhi bazhi bi ama, nudóⁿ ama:** The warriors were not able to come from that direction, they say.

3. **Ppahé ppiâzhi kʰe edí tháazhi a!:** Don't go to the bad hill there!

4. **Niáshiⁿga ama edí hí noⁿ thoⁿdi watháhuni noⁿ i he:** Whenever people went there they were devoured.

5. **Edí hí kki, "Ppahé-watháhuni, óⁿthahuni ga!" á bi ama, Moⁿshtíⁿge akʰa:** They say that when he arrived there, Rabbit said, "Devouring Hill, gobble me up!"

6. **Ppahé-watháhuni níx̌a móⁿtʰatta hí kki, Moⁿshtíⁿge ígtheba bi ama:** After

he went inside the Devouring Hill's stomach, it vomited Rabbit up, they say.

7. **Égithe níkkashiⁿga ppahóⁿga hí ma t'é ma, wahí kʰe sóⁿ kʰé ama:** It came to pass that the people who arrived there first were dead; their bones were lying there white.

8. **Ttí ppaháshiatta hí ígaskoⁿtha i kki, thi'á:** When s/he tried to get on top of the house, s/he failed.

9. **Wagōⁿze akʰa tʰí noⁿ thoⁿdi, uthúshiadi noⁿzhíⁿ noⁿ:** Whenever the teacher arrived here, he always stood in front.

10. **Wahí kʰedi thé kki, Moⁿshtíⁿge Ppahé-watháhuni akʰa thahúni tta akʰa:** If he goes to where the bones lie, the Devouring Hill will gobble Rabbit up.

B.

1. Did he try to go?: **Athé ígaskoⁿthe a?**

2. Whenever the old men used to arrive there, the Devouring Hill would gobble them up: **Iⁿsh'áge ama edí hí noⁿ thoⁿdi, Ppahé-watháhuni akʰa thahúni noⁿ.**

3. When your uncle gets here, we will eat: **Thinégi akʰa tʰí kki, oⁿthátʰe tta oⁿgatʰoⁿ.**

4. Don't go to where the pale white bones are lying!: **Wahí sóⁿ kʰedi tháazhi a/ga!**

5. When the people arrived, the Devouring Hill said, "Come here!": **Niáshiⁿga ama hí kki, "Gí i ga!" á, Ppahé-wáthahuni akʰa.**

6. When he got ahead, he screamed, "I win!": **Ittóⁿthiⁿatta hí kki, "Bthíze!" bóⁿ.**

7. When she got to the base of the hill, she saw the deer: **Ppahé hídatta hí kki, ttáx̌ti dóⁿba.**

8. He wanted to get here yesterday: **Thêthudi sidādi tʰí gōⁿtha.**

9. When the Rabbit got inside the Devouring Hill's belly, he saw its heart: **Ppahé-watháhuni níx̌a móⁿtʰatta hí kki, nôⁿde ettá dóⁿba, Moⁿshtíⁿge akʰa.**

10. The boy didn't want to come: **Núzhiⁿga akʰa í gōⁿtha bazhi.**

15.5 VERBS OF MOTION WITH THE A- PREFIX

A.

1. **Ppamú athá bi ama, Moⁿshtíⁿge akʰa:** Rabbit went downhill, they say.

2. **Ettátʰoⁿ aí bi ama, nudóⁿ ama:** The warriors were coming from that direction, they say.

3. **Ittóⁿthiⁿatta athá bi ama, núzhiⁿga akʰa:** The boy went ahead, they say.

4. **X̌ithá akʰa mōⁿshiatta athé tta akʰa:** The eagle will go toward above. / The eagle will go higher.

5. **Shíⁿgazhiⁿga ama hátheze atʰí:** The children have safely arrived here.

6. **X̌thabé tʰedi ahí i egóⁿ, uthíx̌ida:** Having arrived at the tree, she/he / they looked around.

7. **Níshude mõⁿtʰadi niúoⁿ akʰa moⁿsóⁿthiⁿadi hátheze atʰí:** The one swimming in the river arrived safely on the far side.

8. **Wéahidatta athá bi ama, nudóⁿ akʰa:** The warrior went far away, they say.

9. **Ppahé hídatta ppamú aí:** S/he came down the hill toward the bottom.

10. **Nudóⁿ akʰa kkóⁿgatta ahí:** The warrior arrived near there.

B.

1. He went to the end of the line: **Uhóⁿgatta athá.**

2. The old man arrived there: **Iⁿshʼáge akʰa ahí.**

3. Your grandmother has arrived (here): **Thikkóⁿ akʰa atʰí.**

4. They say that Ishtíthiⁿkʰe was coming: **Ishtíthiⁿkʰe akʰa aí bi ama.**

5. The girls left: **Mīzhiⁿga ama athá.**

6. He reached the other side: **Moⁿsóⁿthiⁿadi ahí.**

7. It went up toward the sky: **Móⁿxatta athá.**

8. He got here yesterday: **Sidādi théthudi atʰí.**

9. That one should leave tomorrow: **Gasóⁿthiⁿ shêakʰa athé tta tʰe.**

10. The Rabbit got to the bottom of the hill: **Moⁿshtíⁿge akʰa ppahé hídatta ahí.**

15.6 RETURN VERBS OF MOTION

A.

1. **"Uthá moⁿgthíⁿ i ga!" á bi ama, Ppóⁿkka ama:** They say the Ponca said, "Go home and tell the news!" / "You all go back and tell it!"

2. **Umóⁿhoⁿ ama edí athá bi ama, Ppóⁿkka ttí i thóⁿdi:** The Omaha supposedly departed to go the place where the Ponca were dwelling. / Supposedly the Omaha went to the Ponca encampment.

3. **Moⁿzhóⁿ ūdaⁿ gāx̣e niníba athíⁿ agí bi ama:** Supposedly he came back with a pipe to make peace.

4. **Atʰí bi ama, āhigi ama:** Many arrived here, they say.

5. **Edí kkóⁿgex̌či ahí gōⁿtha bi ama:** S/he wanted to arrive very close to there, they say.

6. **Waíⁿ, ttíha, wéathatʰe gthūbax̌ti, ʼíⁿ agí bi ama:** They say s/he / they set out to return, carrying all of the robes, tipi covers, and food.

7. **Kki dūba agthí ama wéathatʰe gōⁿtha bi ama:** And it so happened that some of those arriving back here wanted food, they say. / And supposedly some of them arrived back here wanting to eat.

8. **"Moⁿshíattahá moⁿgthíⁿ i ga!" á bi ama:** "You all go back further up!" he supposedly said.

9. **Ppáthiⁿ iⁿshʼáge ʼíthe akʰí bi ama:** The old Pawnee man arrived back there to discuss it, they say.

10. **Níkkashiⁿga athíⁿ akʰí bi ama, Ppáthiⁿ ama:** The Pawnees arrived back there with a person, they say. / The Pawnees arrived bringing a person, they say.

B.

1. Has she come back?: **Agthí a?**

2. Go back where you came from!: **Moⁿgthíⁿ a/ga!**

3. The old Ponca woman got home: **Póⁿkka waʼúzhiⁿga akʰa akʰí.**

4. The buzzards went back to the dead horse: **Héga ama shóⁿge kʰetta agthá.**

5. When he finishes, he will come back: **Shóⁿ gāx̱e kki, agí tta akʰa.**

6. Having swum to the other side, he started back: **Moⁿsóⁿthiⁿadi niúoⁿ ahí i egóⁿ, agí.**

7. On his way back, the enemy were shooting at him: **Agí kki, ukkítte kkída.**

8. They didn't hit him, and he arrived back here safely: **Ú bazhi egóⁿ, hátheze agthí.**

9. When the warriors showed up, the enemy retreated: **Nudóⁿ ama atʰí kki, ukkítte ama agthá.**

10. All of the warriors arrived home safely: **Nudóⁿ wôⁿgithe ama hátheze akʰí.**

15.7 CONJUGATING VERBS OF MOTION

A.

1. **Edí shóⁿge uáwane pʰí:** I arrived there, seeking horses.

2. **Thagthé a?:** Did you go back? / Did you go home?

3. **Moⁿzhóⁿ údaⁿ ppāx̱e niníba abthíⁿ bthé kkōⁿbtha:** I want to go with the peace pipe to make peace.

4. **Né shkōⁿna thóⁿzha, hátheze shkí tte enégoⁿ?:** Although you want to go, do you think you might come back safely?

5. **Āshka oⁿgákʰi tta, ebthégoⁿ:** In a little while we might arrive back there, I think.

6. **Waíⁿ, ttíha, wéathatʰe gthūbax̱ti, thaʼíⁿ shkí wíttoⁿbe tʰe, údaⁿx̌ti:** I'm glad to see you coming back, carrying all of the robes, tipi covers, and food.

7. **Ppí kki, oⁿthóⁿshpahoⁿ tta niⁿkshe:** When I come (back), you will know me.

8. **Né kki, moⁿkkóⁿsabe, zhoⁿní dūba aníⁿ shkí moⁿníⁿ tte:** If/when you go, you might bring back some candy/sugar and coffee.

9. **Wasékkoⁿ moⁿbthíⁿ ppahóⁿgadi pʰí kki, iⁿshʼáge oⁿwóⁿkkie egóⁿ, háshiadi ppí:** When I arrived at the front walking fast, an old man talked to me, and I came back to the end of the line.

10. **Kkáshi wíttoⁿba mazhi egóⁿ, hátheze thagthí tʰe údaⁿ:** Not having seen you for a long time, it's good that you arrived here safely.

B.

1. Are you coming back tomorrow?: **Sidádi shkí a?**

2. We will get there soon: **Áshka oⁿgáhi tta oⁿgatʰoⁿ.**

3. Do you want to go home?: **Thagthé shkōⁿna a?**

4. We just left (coming back): **Íⁿčʰoⁿ oⁿgági.**

5. I will get there before you do: **Shí kki, ppahóⁿga pʰí tta miⁿkʰe.**

6. On our way back, we saw one elk (as said by a person who has just come home): **Oⁿgági kki, óⁿpʰaⁿ wiⁿáx̌či oⁿdóⁿba.**

7. We are coming to pick grapes: **Hāzi oⁿbáhi oⁿgági.**

8. I got there, but I didn't see the Pawnees: **Pʰí thóⁿzha, Ppáthiⁿ awáttoⁿba mazhi.**

9. Whenever you get home, look around for the turtle!: **Atʰóⁿkki thakʰí kki, kké thiⁿkʰe uthíx̌ida (ga)!**

10. Try to swim to the other side!: **Moⁿsóⁿthiⁿaditta niúoⁿ hí ígaskoⁿtha a/ga!**

15.8 VERB CHAINING AND CONTINUATIVES

A.

1. **Wazhíⁿ ppíazhi gthíⁿ:** He's in a bad mood. / He sits in a bad mood.

2. **Umóⁿhoⁿ ama wanóⁿse gthíⁿ bi ama:** The Omaha were camped to surround the herd, they say.

3. **Unúshkadi ttezhíⁿga wiⁿ tʼétha bi ama; ppáde noⁿzhíⁿ bi ama:** Supposedly (they say) they killed a buffalo calf in the valley; they butchered it, they say.

4. **Shaóⁿ ama wagtháde aí bi ama, shóⁿge āgthiⁿ sháppex̌ti égoⁿ:** They say the Sioux came sneaking, riding exactly six horses.

5. **Wahúttoⁿthiⁿ uzhíazhi noⁿzhíⁿ bi ama, wizhíⁿthe tʰoⁿ:** They say my elder brother was standing with an empty gun.

6. **Wénoⁿx̌itha i de, kkuʼé aí bi ama, Shaóⁿ ama:** Supposedly when the Sioux attacked they came rushing forward headlong.

7. **Kkuʼé aí bi egóⁿ, tʼéwatha bi ama, wappé thiⁿgé egóⁿ:** Charging headlong, the Sioux supposedly killed them, because they had no weapons.

8. **Égithe uthá agthí. "Umóⁿhoⁿ noⁿbá tʼéwatha í," é uthá agthí:** They came back to tell the news. "Two Omahas were killed," that is what they came back to tell.

9. **Shaóⁿ ama ʼóⁿhe agthá bi ama, watʼéthe ama:** They say the Sioux, the killers, fled back home.

10. **Edí ahí égoⁿ, waʼíⁿ agthí:** Having arrived there, they (the Omahas) carried them back.

B.

1. He's whistling: **Zudé noⁿzhíⁿ.**

2. He came running: **Ttóⁿthiⁿ aí.**

3. She's always in a bad temper: **Wazhíⁿ ppíazhi moⁿthíⁿ/gthíⁿ noⁿ.**

4. My older brother was butchering the buffalo: **Wizhíⁿthe akʰa tté kʰe ppáde noⁿzhíⁿ.**

5. The warriors were charging forward to attack them: **Nudóⁿ ama wénoⁿx̣ithe kku'é athá.**

6. A person arrived there to tell the news: **Niáshiⁿga wíⁿ uthá ahí.**

7. You're sitting pretty: **Ûjaⁿ thagthíⁿ.**

8. They came back carrying the three dead men: **Nú t'é thâbthiⁿ kʰe wa'íⁿ aí.**

9. The eagle is looking around: **X̌ithá akʰa uthíx̣ide gthíⁿ. / X̌ithá akʰa uthíx̣ide gióⁿ moⁿthíⁿ.**

10. They say the Sioux were camped in a valley to surround the buffalo herd: **Shaóⁿ ama unúshkadi wanóⁿse gthíⁿ bi ama.**

15.9 POSITIONALS AS CONTINUATIVES

A.

1. **Uthíx̣ida bazhi gthíⁿ thoⁿkʰa:** They were sitting, not looking around for it.

2. **Óⁿpʰaⁿ wiⁿ ahóⁿbthe; óⁿpʰaⁿ nugá ttoⁿgáx̌či edí noⁿzhíⁿ akʰa:** I dreamed of an elk; it was a very large bull elk standing there.

3. **Óⁿpʰaⁿ shêhiama ppahé hídex̌ti uhé ama ama:** They say there were elk over yonder passing along the very bottom of a hill.

4. **Nudóⁿ hoⁿga wénoⁿx̣ithe wégazhi akʰa éde, nudóⁿ wiⁿ uthí'age tʰoⁿ:** The leader commanded them to charge; one warrior stood refusing.

5. **Wahúttoⁿthiⁿ uzhíazhi kʰe; égoⁿ 'óⁿhe agthé tta miⁿkʰe:** The gun was not loaded; therefore, I will run away back home.

6. **Ttéska t'é kʰe. Héga dūba gakkúwiⁿx̣e gióⁿ ama:** The cow is lying dead. Some buzzards are flying in spirals.

7. **Ttáppuskazhiⁿga shêthiⁿkʰe wathíbaba uhí noⁿ gthíⁿ thiⁿkʰe:** That student regularly wins at cards.

8. **Góⁿkki ttezhíⁿga ídatha bi kki, skáx̌či tʰoⁿ ama:** It came to pass that a buffalo calf was born and it stood very white, they say.

9. **"Míkkasi akʰé" á bi ama niáshiⁿga ama:** Supposedly the people said, "That is Coyote."

10. **Má zhīdex̌ti kʰe, Moⁿshtíⁿge wamí éwoⁿ:** The snow lay very red due to Rabbit's blood.

B.

1. The warrior is lying dead: **Nudóⁿ akʰa t'é kʰe.**

2. They say the people were going around in circles: **Niáshiⁿga ama gakkúwiⁿx̣e moⁿthíⁿ ama ama.**

3. She's sitting in the house: **Ttíadi gthíⁿ thiⁿkʰe. / Ttí tʰe móⁿtʰadi gthíⁿ thiⁿkʰe.**

4. A valley is on the other side of this mountain: **Ppahé ttóⁿga duátʰe moⁿsóⁿthiⁿadi unúshka wiⁿ edí kʰe.**

5. That mountain lion is about to make its move: **Iⁿgthóⁿsiⁿṣnede shêakʰa shkóⁿ tte gthíⁿ thiⁿkʰe.**

6. They killed him, they say. His gun was lying there empty: **Tʼétha bi ama. Wahúttoⁿthe/Wahúttoⁿthiⁿ ettá uzhíazhi kʰe.**

7. The buffalo was standing there, very dark: **Tté akʰa shéthudi noⁿzhíⁿ, shabéx̌či tʰoⁿ.**

8. A woman is sitting there weeping: **Waʼú wiⁿ edí x̠agé gthíⁿ akʰa.**

9. A boy was going about playing with a ball: **Núzhiⁿga wiⁿ ttabé shkāde moⁿthíⁿ akʰa.**

10. The moon was very pale: **Nióⁿba sóⁿx̌či thoⁿ.**

15.10 DECLARATION OF EXISTENCE USING POSITIONALS

A.

1. **Wagōⁿze akʰa edí akʰa:** There is a teacher.

2. **Ttabé thoⁿ ededí thoⁿ:** There is a ball (right there).

3. **Unúshka shêhíkʰedi óⁿpʰaⁿ dūba ededí ma:** There are some elk (right there) in that valley over there.

4. **Shaóⁿ nudóⁿ wiⁿ ededí thiⁿ:** There is one Sioux warrior (right there).

5. **Wahúttoⁿthiⁿ uzhí kʰe edí kʰe ama:** Supposedly there was a loaded gun.

6. **Ttáppuskazhiⁿga wôⁿgithe edí thoⁿkʰa:** There are all the students.

7. **Shóⁿge tʼé kʰe ededí kʰe:** There is a dead horse (right there).

8. **Égithe "Ttáx̌tigikkidabi" izházhe athíⁿ akʰa ededí akʰa ama:** It so happened that there was one with the name "For Whom They Shoot the Deer."

9. **Kki ukkítte ma shínuda shti wathátʰe noⁿ ma edí ma ama:** Supposedly there are tribes that even eat dogs.

10. **Égoⁿ shínuda waṣníde gáthudi edí bazhi ama:** Therefore there are no slow dogs there.

B.

1. There's a mouse in the house: **Ttíadi iⁿcʰóⁿga wiⁿ edí akʰa.**

2. There is food on the table: **Wāthatʰe gahádi wéathatʰe edí kʰe.**

3. There is a book in the bag: **Ūzhiha móⁿtʰadi wagthábaze shúga edí kʰe.**

4. There was a boy running away: **Núzhiⁿga wiⁿ ʼóⁿhe edí akʰa/thiⁿ.**

5. There is a house over there: **Ttí wiⁿ shêhitʰe ededí tʰe.**

6. There is a person sitting there whistling: **Niáshiⁿga wiⁿ zudé gthíⁿ ededí akʰa.**

7. There is a marker by the whiteboard: **Zhoⁿbtháska ská kʰedi wēbax̠u wiⁿ edí kʰe.**

8. There is a rock at the foot of the hill: **Ppahé hídadi íⁿʼe wiⁿ edí kʰe.**

9. There are buzzards circling around above the dead horse: **Shóⁿge tʼé kʰe héga ama móⁿx̠atta gakkúwiⁿx̠e edí ama.**

10. They say there were people camped in a valley to surround buffalo: **Níkkashiⁿga ama unúshkadi wanóⁿse gthíⁿ edí ama ama.**

16.1 GRANDPARENTS AND GRANDCHILDREN

A.

1. **Wamóskeshuga gā̱xa, thikkó^n ak^{h}a:** Your grandmother makes cowboy bread.

2. **"Umó^{n}ho^n ié thippí, wittúshpa ak^{h}a," á, ittígo^n ak^{h}a:** "My grandchild is expert at speaking Omaha," the grandfather said.

3. **Ittúshpa thanó'o^n?:** Do you hear his grandchild?

4. **Ttigó^{n}ho! Mo^{n}kkó^{n}sabe dūba shkō^{n}na?:** Grandfather! Would you like some coffee?

5. **Thittígo^n thi^{n}k^{h}e dó^{n}be ukkíhi, wittígo^n ak^{h}a:** My grandfather is able to see your grandfather.

6. **Shó^{n}ge ma sidādi thi̱xá bi ama, thittúshpa ak^{h}a:** They say your grandchild chased the horses yesterday.

7. **Ttéskamo^{n}zéni thattó^n gō^{n}tha, wikkó^n ak^{h}a:** My grandmother wanted to drink milk.

8. **Kko^{n}há! Thazhō^n a?:** Grandmother! Are you sleeping?

9. **"Ttushpahá! Āno^n'o^n a!" á, ikkó^n ak^{h}a:** "Grandchild! Listen!" said the grandmother.

10. **Ttushpáho! Ttanúkka tho^n thizá ga ho!:** Grandchild! Take the meat!

B.

1. Grandchild! Do you know how to swim?: **Ttushpahá!/Ttushpáho! Thaníuo^n íthashpaho^n a?**

2. His grandchild doesn't want to play outside: **Āshiatta shkāda gō^{n}tha bazhi, ittúshpa ak^{h}a.**

3. Is your grandmother looking for the coat?: **Thikkó^n ak^{h}a unó^{n}zhi^{n}tto^{n}ga t^{h}e uthí̱xide a?**

4. Grandfather! It is good that you are here: **Ttigó^{n}ho! That^{h}í t^{h}e ūda^n.**

5. Do you remember my grandchild?: **Wittúshpa thi^{n}k^{h}e thagísithe a?**

6. The grandmother might eat the plum: **Ikkó^n ak^{h}a kkó^{n}de tho^n that^{h}á tte.**

7. Your grandmother will come back tomorrow: **Gasó^{n}thi^n gí tta ak^{h}a, thikkó^n ak^{h}a.**

8. My grandfather is going on the summer buffalo hunt: **Wittígo^n ak^{h}a núgetteūne ttó^{n}de áhe athá.**

9. Grandmother! I don't see your dog!: **Kko^{n}há!/Kko^{n}hó! Shínuda thithítta thi^{n}k^{h}e attó^{n}ba mazhi!**

10. How is your grandchild doing?: **Thittúshpa ak^{h}a eó^n a?**

16.2 PARENTS AND CHILDREN

A.

1. **Dadihá! É zudé ak^{h}a thí e ní^n a?:** Father! Is that *you* whistling? (female speaking)

2. **Uzhéthe gthí^n, izhó^{n}ge thi^{n}k^{h}e:** The daughter sits tired.

3. **Wasékko^n ittó^{n}thi^n athá, thinísi ak^{h}a:** Your son quickly goes ahead.

4. **Mo^{n}só^{n}thi^{n}adi ahí, wihá^n ak^{h}a:** My mother reached the other side.

5. **Thiādi kʰe hóⁿbthe zhō:** Your father sleeps and dreams.

6. **Nisího! Moⁿgthíⁿ ga ho!:** Daughter! Go home! (male speaking)

7. **Nisího! Wittóⁿbe:** Son! I see you. (male speaking)

8. **Winísi akʰa shínudattí gāx̣e tta tʰe:** My son/daughter should build a dog house. (male speaking)

9. **Wizhíⁿge akʰa shóⁿge shêhithiⁿ thix̣é akʰa é thiⁿ kki, uthóⁿ tta akʰa:** If my son is the one who chases the horse, he will catch it. (female speaking)

10. **Ithādi akʰa móⁿzeska ttóⁿ bi ama:** His/her father is wealthy, they say.

B.

1. Mother! I'm going to go (female speaking): **Naⁿhá! Bthé tta miⁿkʰe.**

2. Father! We are unable to push the big black car (male speaking): **Dadího! Kkinóⁿnoⁿge sábe ttóⁿga kʰe oⁿbádoⁿ oⁿthíʼa.**

3. In a little while my father came laughing: **Áshka íx̣a aí, iⁿdādi akʰa.**

4. Your daughter will probably pull the skunk's tail (addressing a female): **Móⁿgasiⁿde kʰe thidóⁿ tta akʰa, thizhóⁿge akʰa.**

5. Who is your son? (addressing a female): **Thizhíⁿge ebé a?**

6. Son! What did I say? (female speaking): **Zhiⁿgehá! Edépʰe?**

7. My daughter is trying to speak Spanish: **Heshpaiúni ié ígaskoⁿthe, wizhóⁿge akʰa.**

8. "Do well!" the mother told her son: **Iháⁿ akʰa: "Washkóⁿ a!" āgazhi, izhíⁿge thiⁿkʰe.**

9. Your mother counted twelve (scattered) cherry trees: **Nóⁿppahí ge sháppa noⁿbá thawá, thiháⁿ akʰa.**

10. Mother! You might drink a little bit of water (male speaking): **Naⁿhó! Ní jūba náttoⁿ tte.**

16.3 SIBLINGS

A.

1. **Núzhiⁿga akʰa ittóⁿge zhūgthe athá bi ama, wēahidatta:** They say the boy and his sister were going far away.

2. **Soⁿgehá! Maⁿčʰúska ānoⁿ a?:** Younger brother! How many polar bears are there? (female addressing)

3. **Ttigóⁿho! Thizhíⁿthe ama nishúde kkóⁿgadi noⁿzhíⁿ a?:** Grandfather! Is your elder brother near by the river?

4. **"Wittóⁿge akʰa x̣thabé tʰe āna. Égoⁿ ppāx̣e ubthíʼage," á, núzhiⁿga akʰa:** "My younger sister is climbing the tree. I'm unwilling to," said the boy.

5. **Zhoⁿthehá! Wamóskex̣ude noⁿbé noⁿbá ttaní tʰe uázhi tta miⁿkʰe:** Elder sister! I will put two handfuls of flour into the soup. (female addressing)

6. **Ttoⁿgého! Thêak^ha at^hí bi ama:** Sister! Supposedly that fellow we were talking about arrived. (male addressing)

7. **Égithe, isóⁿge ak^ha thinóⁿt^he tte:** Beware, the younger brother might kick you.

8. **Thisóⁿge ak^ha wathát^ha bazhi:** Your younger brother didn't eat.

9. **"Wittóⁿge ak^ha ux̌pé thoⁿ it^hétha," á, ikkóⁿ ak^ha:** "My younger sister put away the dish," said the grandmother.

10. **Ittínu ak^ha ābae nóⁿ, ebthégoⁿ:** I think her elder brother hunts regularly.

B.

1. Younger brother! What is it like outdoors today? (male addressing): **Soⁿgého! Óⁿbathe āshiatta eóⁿ a?**

2. "My elder brother asked for the book," said the girl: **Wittínu ak^ha wagthábaze t^he nā," á, mīzhiⁿga ak^ha.**

3. My younger sister has a puppy in her backpack: **Wittóⁿge ak^ha ūzhiha móⁿt^hadi shínuja zhíⁿga wiⁿ athíⁿ.**

4. His elder brother took the (round) ball: **Izhíⁿthe ak^ha ttabé thoⁿ thizá.**

5. "My elder sister was following the trail," said the woman: **"Wizhóⁿthe ak^ha uzhóⁿge k^he uhá," a, wa'ú ak^ha.**

6. Younger brother! How do you say "Superman" in Omaha? (female addressing): **Soⁿgehá! "Superman," Umóⁿhoⁿ īe t^he awat^hégoⁿ?**

7. Grandfather! Tell your elder sister to stand up!: **Ttigóⁿho!/Ttigoⁿhá! Thittóⁿge noⁿzhiⁿ āgazhi ga/a!**

8. Younger sister! Write your name! (male addressing): **Ttoⁿgého! Izházhe thithítta t^he ābax̧u ga!**

9. The baby was carried by her elder sister: **Shié thiⁿk^hé 'íⁿ, izhóⁿthe ak^ha.**

10. My elder brother gathers the scattered bullets (female speaking): **Wittínu ak^ha mōⁿzemoⁿ ge bahí.**

16.4 UNCLES AND AUNTS, NIECES AND NEPHEWS

A.

1. **Íⁿč^hoⁿ shóⁿge wiwítta duáthiⁿk^he moⁿthóⁿ, thittízhoⁿ ak^ha:** Just now, your niece is stealing my horse right here.

2. **Dadího! Wahúttoⁿthiⁿ wiwítta k^he uné moⁿthíⁿ ga ho!:** Father! Go seek my gun!

3. **Naⁿhá! Ppáhoⁿ a!:** Mother! Get up!

4. **Wiháⁿ ak^ha x̌thabé t^he thawá:** My mother counted the trees.

5. **Iⁿč^hóⁿgawathat^he dūba aníⁿ kki, wittízhoⁿ ak^ha égoⁿ íbahoⁿ gōⁿtha:** If you have some cheese, my niece wants to know about it.

6. **Ithādi ak^ha thippí tte:** His/her father might be an expert.

7. **Thittóⁿshka thiⁿk^he uníx̧ide a?:** Are you looking around for your nephew?

8. **Thiháⁿ wamóske ettá gāx̧e égoⁿ, ppóⁿzhiⁿga:** I don't know how your mother's sister makes her bread.

9. **Ttimího! Wétta ánoⁿ shpáhiⁿ a?**: Aunt (father's sister)! How many eggs did you gather?

10. **Negihá! Hīga wiⁿ uthá i a!**: Uncles! Tell us a story!

B.

1. How is your aunt, your father's sister?: **Thittími akʰa eóⁿ a?**

2. Nephew! Come here! (uncle speaking): **Ttoⁿshkáho! Gí ga!**

3. My mother's brother refuses to take his cup: **Niīthattoⁿ ettá tʰe thizé uthí'aga, winégi akʰa.**

4. Niece! Go fish for a card! (aunt speaking): **Ttúzhoⁿgehá! Wathíbaba wiⁿ hugási moⁿthíⁿ a!**

5. The aunt's niece went fishing. "I did not get it," she said. "It's your turn": **Hugási moⁿthíⁿ, ittúzhoⁿge akʰa. "Bthíza mazhi. Thithítta," á.**

6. "I win!" said the aunt, the mother's sister: **"Uáhi!" á, iháⁿ akʰa.**

7. Aunt (father's sister)! Do you see that airplane far over there?: **Ttimihá/ ttimího! Moⁿdégioⁿ shêhitʰe thashtóⁿbe a?**

8. "I don't see it," said the aunt. "Where is it?": **"Attóⁿbe mazhi," á ittími akʰa. "Águdi a?"**

9. Tomorrow we both might see it: **Gasóⁿthiⁿ wôⁿdoⁿ oⁿdóⁿbe tte.**

10. "I want to sleep for a little while," said my father's brother: **"Áshka azhóⁿ kkōⁿbtha," á, iⁿdādi akʰa.**

16.5 SPOUSES AND IN-LAWS

A.

1. **Égthoⁿge wiwítta akʰa ābae athá**: My husband went hunting.

2. **Awíⁿoⁿwatta thé a, thittígoⁿ akʰa?**: Where is your father-in-law going?

3. **Ihóⁿga akʰa atʰí**: His sister-in-law has arrived here.

4. **Wigáx̌thoⁿ akʰa uzhóⁿge kʰe uhá**: My wife followed the path.

5. **Shikkoⁿhá! Izházhe thithítta tʰe wabáx̌u kʰe āthada!**: Sister-in-law! Spell your name! (woman speaking)

6. **Thittóⁿde akʰa wagthábaze shúga bax̌ú a?**: Is your son-in-law writing a book?

7. **Nudóⁿ akʰa gí kki, ikkóⁿ thiⁿkʰe ttanúkka thoⁿ 'í**: When the warrior comes back, he gives his mother-in-law meat.

8. **Ttinihá! Kkinóⁿnoⁿge kʰe nóⁿgethe shkōⁿna?**: Daughter-in-law! Do you want to start the car? (woman speaking)

9. **Wittáhoⁿ akʰa uīkkoⁿ ukkíhi tte**: My brother-in-law might be able to help. (man speaking)

10. **Ishí'e akʰa íⁿ'utʰíⁿ nudóⁿhoⁿga thíⁿ tte**: Her brother-in-law might be the Man in Charge for the handgame.

B.

1. I know her sister-in-law: **Ishíkkoⁿ thiⁿkʰe itháppahoⁿ.**

2. Is that your mother-in-law, wearing the green shawl?: **É akʰa waíⁿ ppēzhittu íⁿ akʰa thikkóⁿ é thíⁿ a?**

3. My sister-in-law is wearing the brown jacket (male speaking): **Wihóⁿga akʰa unóⁿzhiⁿttoⁿga zíshabe thoⁿ íⁿ.**

4. Husband! Chase the rabbit!: **Iⁿsh'áge! Moⁿshtíⁿge thiⁿkʰe thiǧá!**

5. His wife will return in a little while: **Igáǧthoⁿ akʰa góⁿčʰēgoⁿ agthí tta akʰá.**

6. My father-in-law sang: **Wittígoⁿ akʰa waóⁿ.**

7. Brother-in-law! Is it you arriving here? (male speaking): **Ttahóⁿho! É théthudi atʰí akʰa thí é níⁿ a?**

8. It's me, your son-in-law: **Wí é bthíⁿ, thittóⁿde akʰa.**

9. Daughter-in-law! Make soup!: **Ttinihá! Ttaní gáǧa!**

10. Her brother-in-law keeps eating it: **Ishí'e akʰa shóⁿshoⁿ thatʰá.**

16.6 CAUSATIVES: THE BASIC CONSTRUCTION WITH -THE

A.

1. **Nudóⁿ akʰa tté thiⁿ t'étha:** The warrior killed the buffalo.

2. **Ukkítte thiⁿkʰé nóⁿkkatha, Póⁿkka nú akʰa:** The Ponca man injured the enemy.

3. **Shínuja thiⁿkʰé tha'étha:** She feels pity for the puppy.

4. **Kkinóⁿnoⁿge zhīde kʰe nóⁿga:** The red car is running.

5. **Nihóⁿga shêhi bīzethe:** The spring of water over there is going dry.

6. **Nibtháska nishúde kʰe bīzetha bazhi i ga ho!:** Don't cause the Platte River to dry out!

7. **Niskíthettóⁿwoⁿgthoⁿtta eshóⁿ mátha:** It's snowing near Lincoln.

8. **Moⁿzhóⁿ bīze kʰe águdi a?:** Where is the dry land?

9. **Wiháⁿ akʰa gāǧa ge ǧóⁿdethe thizá:** My mother picked up the scattered branches and gathered them into a bunch.

10. **Ebé ppāshudethe a?:** Who caused the nosebleed? / Who has the nosebleed?

B.

1. Rabbit acquired some money: **Móⁿzeska dūba ttóⁿtha, Moⁿshtíⁿge akʰa.**

2. Did your mother dry your shirt?: **Thiháⁿ akʰa unóⁿzhiⁿ thithítta bīzethe a?**

3. The clouds piled up in the sky: **Moⁿǧpí tʰe móⁿǧadi ǧóⁿdetha.**

4. Don't pity the bad man!: **Nú ppiâzhi tha'éthazhi a/ga!**

5. The pile of acorns dwindled away: **Ttáshka ǧóⁿde tʰe zhiⁿgátha.**

6. It was the squirrels eating that reduced the pile of acorns: **Síⁿga thatʰá ama é ttáshka ǧóⁿde tʰe zhiⁿgátha.**

7. Don't hit your younger brother and make his nose bleed!: **Thisóⁿge thiⁿkʰe ppāshudethe utʰíⁿ azhi a/ga!**

8. If my elder sister is injured, he will feel pity for her: **Wizhóⁿthe akʰa nóⁿkka kki, thaʔéthe tta akʰá.**

9. Where exactly did it snow yesterday?: **Sidādi máthe águdix̌ti a?**

10. Since it snowed, he is running the snowplow: **Máthe egóⁿ, mábadi nóⁿgetha.**

16.7 CONJUGATION OF THE CAUSATIVE

A.

1. **Thaʔéoⁿthathe:** You feel pity for me.

2. **Ppāshudeathe mazhi:** I didn't give her a bloody nose.

3. **Thittígoⁿ akʰa théthudi théthithe a?:** Did your grandfather send you here?

4. **Nóⁿkkaoⁿthithe tte:** We might injure you.

5. **Thaʔéawathe tta miⁿkʰe:** I will feel pity for them.

6. **"X̌tāwithe noⁿ," waóⁿ waʔú akʰa:** "I will always like you," the woman sang.

7. **Ttéskamoⁿzéni sʔáthe tʰe oⁿshóⁿtha:** We spilled the sour milk.

8. **Móⁿga thiⁿkʰe tʔéthathe a?:** Did you kill the skunk?

9. **Noⁿʔóⁿawathe kkóⁿbtha mazhi:** I don't want him to hear us.

10. **Hāthe ge x̌óⁿdeathe ubthóⁿ bīzeatha:** I gathered the clothes into a pile and hung them up to dry.

B.

1. We let them be heard: **Noⁿʔóⁿoⁿwatha.**

2. She feels pity for me: **Thaʔéoⁿthe.**

3. You injured them: **Nóⁿkkawathathe.**

4. You are unable to injure me: **Nóⁿkkaoⁿthathe níʔa.**

5. Rabbit spilled cherry juice, they say: **Moⁿshtíⁿge akʰa nóⁿppa nískithe shóⁿtha bi ama.**

6. We sent him toward the house: **Ttíatta théoⁿtha.**

7. You sent us toward your uncle's place: **Thinégi thiⁿkʰétta théwathatha.**

8. The whole family likes you: **Ttíuzhi ama wôⁿgithe x̌tāthitha.**

9. I see your younger sister drying her hair: **Thittóⁿge thiⁿkʰe noⁿzhīⁿha ettá kʰe bīzethe attóⁿbe.**

10. He will like them: **X̌tāwathe tta akʰa.**

16.8 THE DATIVE CAUSATIVE: -KʰITHE

A.

1. **Thizhóⁿthe noⁿʔóⁿ-thakʰithe:** You (female) let your elder sister hear it.

2. **Izhíⁿge é-kʰitha:** S/he let her/his son say it.

3. **Núzhiⁿga thoⁿkʰa wakkóⁿdagi dóⁿbe-wakʰitha bi ama, niáshiⁿga x̌ubé akʰa:** The holy person let the boys see the water monster, they say.

4. **Unóⁿzhiⁿ bīzeathe-oⁿkʰitha:** S/he let me dry my shirt.

5. **Nóⁿkkathathe-thikʰithe:** S/he lets you harm her/him/it.

6. **Ppāshudeathe-oⁿthakʰithe:** You let me give him a bloody nose.

7. **Ttanúkka thatʰé-wakʰitha, shínuda thoⁿkʰa:** S/he lets the meat go rancid.

8. **Wagōⁿze akʰa ttáppuskazhiⁿga thiⁿkʰe wagthábaze shúga tʰe dóⁿbekʰitha:** The teacher let the student see the book.

9. **Shíⁿgazhiⁿga thiⁿkʰe moⁿshtíⁿgeha thoⁿ ābitte-akʰithe:** I let the child touch the rabbit pelt.

10. **Égthoⁿge wiwítta thiⁿkʰe thaʼéthe-kʰithe:** S/he lets my husband pity her/him/it.

B.

1. She lets us go: **Thé-awakʰithe.**

2. He is letting the leader die: **Nudóⁿhoⁿga thiⁿkʰe tʼé-kʰithe.**

3. The woman is letting her husband practice his mysterious powers: **Waʼú akʰa égthoⁿge ettá thiⁿkʰe xubékkithe-kʰithe.**

4. She lets him love her: **Xtāthe-kʰithe.**

5. Let it dwindle away!: **Zhiⁿgáthe-kʰitha (ga)!**

6. Don't let him eat it!: **Thatʰé-kʰitha azhi a/ga!**

7. I let you take the card: **Wathíbaba tʰe níze-wikʰithe.**

8. You let her read it: **Āthade-thakʰitha.**

9. She wants to let her son hear Omaha: **Izhíⁿge thiⁿkʰe Umóⁿhoⁿ noⁿʼóⁿ-kʰithe gōⁿtha.**

10. My grandchild will not let the pile of leaves dwindle away: **Wittúshpa akʰa zhóⁿabe xōⁿde thoⁿ zhiⁿgáthe-kʰitha bazhi tta akʰa.**

16.9 THE CAUSATIVE OF POTENTIALITY: -WATHE

A.

1. **Maⁿčʰú akʰa nóⁿppewathe:** The grizzly bear is scary or dangerous.

2. **Thinégi akʰa íxawathe:** Your uncle is funny or comical.

3. **Thinégi íxawathe akʰa uóⁿsisi:** Your funny uncle is jumping.

4. **Tté shêhiama dóⁿbewatha:** Those bison over there are visible.

5. **Dóⁿbewatha bazhi:** S/he or it isn't visible.

6. **Nóⁿwappewathe:** We are scary.

7. **Nóⁿppamoⁿttānoⁿha thatʰéwatha:** Chokecherries are edible.

8. **Wamóskeskithe ettá thoⁿ thatʰéwatha bazhi:** Her cookies are not edible.

9. **Nóⁿppewathe bthíⁿ:** I am scary.

10. **Thí nóⁿppewathe:** You are scary.

B.

1. Is this egg edible?: **Wétta duáthoⁿ thatʰéwathe a?**

2. That (egg we have been talking about) is not edible: **Thêthoⁿ thatʰéwatha bazhi.**

3. You are visible: **Thidóⁿbewathe.**

4. The stars in the sky are visible: **Mikkáʼe ge móⁿxadi dóⁿbewatha.**

5. The warriors are scary: **Nudóⁿ ama nóⁿppewatha.**

6. He is not funny: **Íxawatha bazhi.**

7. Don't laugh! The story is scary: **Íxa bazhi i a/ga! Hīga nóⁿppewathe.**

8. If you eat it, it is edible: **Nátʰe kki, thatʰéwathe.**

9. The black bear is comical: **Wasábe akʰa íxawathe.**

10. Is that whistling one a scary ghost?: **É akʰa zudé akʰa wanóⁿxe nóⁿppewathe é thíⁿ a?**

16.10 CAUSATIVES AND KINSHIP

A.

1. **Ikʰágeawathe:** He has us as friends.

2. **Iⁿshʼáge ikʰágethe akʰa gthíⁿ:** The old man's friend sat.

3. **Ittóⁿgewithe:** I have you as a younger sister.

4. **Wikʰáge akʰa moⁿkkóⁿsabe dūba gōⁿtha tte:** My friend might want some coffee.

5. **Kʰagého! Águdi thágthiⁿ a?:** Friend! Where are you sitting?/Where do you live?

6. **Ithāditha i ama ittígoⁿtha i thiⁿkʰe āwakkippe athá bi ama, Wazhíⁿdathiⁿ etta:** The Indian agents went to Washington D C to meet the president, they say.

7. **Ikʰágewathathe nā ga!:** Ask your friends for it!

8. **"Ppáthiⁿ āhigi ikʰágeoⁿwatha," á bi ama, Umóⁿhoⁿ gahíge akʰa:** "We have many Pawnee friends," said the Omaha chief, they say.

9. **Ikʰágewathathe ama hátheza atʰí bi ama:** Those whom you have as friends just arrived safely, they say.

10. **Ikʰágewithe tʰe ūdaⁿ:** It is good that I have you as a friend.

B.

1. Friends! Bring the soup!: **Kʰagého! Ttaní athíⁿ gí i ga ho!**

2. Are you my friend?: **Ikʰágewithe a?**

3. We have you as a father: **Ithādioⁿthithe.**

4. Do you have her as a grandmother?: **Ikkóⁿthathe a?**

5. Supposedly the Indian agents counted the money: **Ithāditha i ama móⁿzeska thawá bi ama.**

6. The president will talk about it: **Ittígoⁿtha i akʰa ʼíthe tta akʰa.**

7. His friends felt pity for Rabbit, they say: **Ikʰáge ama Moⁿshtíⁿge thiⁿkʰe thaʔétha bi ama.**

8. Is he your friend?: **Ikʰágethathe a?**

9. You might tell me the name of your new friend: **Thikʰáge ttéga izházhe ettá tʰe oⁿwóⁿthatha tte.**

10. "You have me as a friend," said the Ponca man, they say: "**Ikʰágeoⁿthatha,**" **á bi ama, Ppóⁿka nú akʰa.**

17.1 THI- "BY HAND"

A.

1. **Waʔú akʰa hiⁿbé tʰe thigthéza:** The woman makes stripes or stitches lines in the moccasin.

2. **Watʰé thithítta tʰe thiská a?:** Did she bleach your dress?

3. **Zizíkka kʰe thiṣhná a!:** Pluck the turkey!

4. **Wizhóⁿge akʰa wāthiχoⁿ tʰe thiχóⁿ:** My daughter broke the toy.

5. **Thizhíⁿge akʰa ttabé thoⁿ thibtháska:** Your son deflated the ball.

6. **Ttaní uháⁿ tʰe thibthóⁿ:** He smells soup cooking.

7. **Niáshiⁿga χubé akʰa noⁿbé wôⁿdoⁿ etta tʰe thimōⁿshi:** The holy man raises both his hands up in the air.

8. **Thithúttoⁿ bi ama:** S/he straightened it, they say.

9. **Móⁿhiⁿ tʰe thippái i ga ho!:** Sharpen the knives!

10. **Izhóⁿthe akʰa wāiⁿ kʰe thizhá kki, thiskí thibīze tta tʰe:** If her older sister washes the blanket, then she should wring it out and dry it.

B.

1. Pull the chair!: **Āgthiⁿ thidóⁿ a/ga!**

2. His friend released the eagle: **Ikʰáge akʰa χithá thiⁿkʰe thishtóⁿ.**

3. She is skilled at cutting hair, they say: **Noⁿzhīⁿha thisé thippí bi ama.**

4. The dog may scare away the skunk: **Shínuda akʰa mōⁿga thiⁿkʰe thihí tte.**

5. Don't open your eyes! (addressing one person): **Íshta thithítta thibthá azhi a/ga!**

6. Your mother may turn down the light: **Thiháⁿ akʰa wanākkoⁿthe tʰe thinūshi tte.**

7. His father should clean up the house: **Ithādi akʰa ttí thisíhi tta tʰe.**

8. When the warrior fortifies a door, the leader tears down a wall: **Nudóⁿ akʰa ttizhébe thisági kki, nudóⁿhoⁿga akʰa nóⁿde thithíⁿge.**

9. My grandchild is unable to sweep the leaves into a pile: **Wittúshpa akʰa zhoⁿábe ge thibéχi χōⁿdethe thiʔá.**

10. The old man made a sketch, then tore the page: **Iⁿshʔáge akʰa iⁿdéugaχe thiχú tʰegoⁿ, wagthábaze tʰe thibthāze.**

17.2 THA- "BY MOUTH"

A.

1. **Wôⁿdoⁿ oⁿtháoⁿba:** We two/both talked all night.

2. **Umóⁿhoⁿ btháppi:** I am fluent in speaking Omaha.

3. **Mīkkasi akʰa wahí kʰe hébe thaṣhpá i egóⁿ, thasníⁿ ígaskoⁿtha:** After Coyote bit off a piece of the bone, he tried to swallow.

4. **Égoⁿ thaẋthúda bi ama:** Then he choked, they say.

5. **Mīkkasi akʰa tha'á:** Coyote failed at eating.

6. **Thahūni bazhi i ga!:** Don't gobble it all up! (addressing a group)

7. **Nátʰe shkōⁿna kki, óⁿnahoⁿ tte:** If you want to eat, you might thank me.

8. **Wíbthahoⁿ:** I thank you.

9. **Oⁿthíthaẋuba:** We praise you.

10. **Wittúshpa thiⁿkʰe btházhiⁿge mazhi:** I don't belittle my grandchild.

B.

1. The funny uncle teases his nephew: **Inégi íẋawathe akʰa ittóⁿshka thiⁿkʰe thahíde.**

2. Rabbit was nibbling some meat, they say: **Moⁿshtíⁿge akʰa ttanúkka dūba thaẋthí, á bi ama.**

3. "Stop eating the food!" his grandmother told him: **"Wathátʰe tʰe thashtóⁿ a!" á, ikkóⁿ akʰa.**

4. It so happened that Rabbit sucked many of the bones: **Kki Moⁿshtíⁿge akʰa wahí āhigi thadóⁿ.**

5. He must drink all of the milk: **Ttéskamoⁿzéni bthūga thattóⁿ tta tʰe.**

6. If he drinks it dry, he will see the bottom of the cup: **Thabīze kki, niīthattoⁿ híde tʰe dóⁿbe tta akʰa.**

7. If the dog bites you, you might cuss: **Shínuda akʰa thitháẋta kki, nágthoⁿ tte.**

8. What do you want to drink?: **Náttoⁿ shkōⁿna tʰe idādoⁿ?/Idādoⁿ náttoⁿ shkōⁿna?**

9. Don't pinch it off! Bite it off!: **Thishpá azhi a/ga! Thashpá a/ga!**

10. We fluent speakers might talk all night: **Īe oⁿtháppi oⁿtháoⁿba tte.**

17.3 NOⁿ- "BY FOOT"

A.

1. **Wačʰígaẋe noⁿóⁿba bazhi i a!:** Don't dance all night! (female addressing a group)

2. **Thanóⁿṣhnaha a?:** Did you slip?

3. **Moⁿhíⁿ kʰe noⁿsá ga!:** Mow the grass!

4. **Ttóⁿthiⁿ noⁿshtóⁿ ga!:** Stop running! (male addressing one person)

5. **Máthe kki, uhé oⁿnóⁿsagi tta oⁿgatʰoⁿ:** When it snows, we will make a path through.

6. **Uhé kʰedi noⁿthíⁿge kʰe:** The path here is eroded/has ruts.

7. **Móⁿzemoⁿ thoⁿ noⁿttóⁿza:** The bullet bounced off.

8. **Ttabé ettá thoⁿ thanóⁿtʰe íthagaskoⁿne kki, thanóⁿʾa tta niⁿkshe:** If you try to kick her ball, you will fail.

9. **Ux̌pé noⁿx̌óⁿ kʰe thiháⁿ thiⁿkʰe dóⁿbe kkōⁿbtha mazhi:** I don't want your mother to see the broken dish.

10. **Ttaní thithítta thoⁿ thanóⁿx̌toⁿ kki, thiūdaⁿ tte:** If you strain your soup, it might be improved.

B.

1. He stood, shaded: **Noⁿshábe noⁿzhíⁿ akʰa.**

2. Grind up the corn!: **Wahába noⁿttúba (ga)!**

3. The car tire is flat: **Kkinóⁿnoⁿgehazízige noⁿbtháze kʰe.**

4. All the horses pranced: **Shóⁿge wôⁿgithe noⁿstáppi.**

5. You might shade the child: **Shíⁿgazhiⁿga thiⁿkʰe thanóⁿshabe tte.**

6. He bumped into the table and knocked it down: **Wāthatʰe tʰe noⁿx̌pátha.**

7. She knocked her younger sister down: **Ittóⁿge thiⁿkʰe noⁿbthízha.**

8. She gathered the scattered shelled corn into a pile: **Wahába noⁿshpí ge x̌óⁿdetha.**

9. Her friends danced all night until daybreak: **Ikʰágethe ama wačʰígax̌e noⁿóⁿba.**

10. Don't stomp on my balloon! Deflate it by hand!: **Ttadé ubíx̌e/hazizíge ubíx̌oⁿ wiwítta thoⁿ noⁿbtháska azhi a/ga! Thibtháska a/ga!**

17.4 BA- "BY PUSHING"

A.

1. **Nídushi ettá kʰe basáde ígaskoⁿtha:** He tried to iron his pants.

2. **Bazú azhi a!:** Don't point!

3. **Íⁿʾutʰiⁿ baṣnú:** They rescheduled the handgame.

4. **Winégi akʰa wagáx̌e bashéthoⁿ:** My uncle paid off the debt.

5. **Ttáx̌tihe bax̌óⁿ bi ama:** The deer's antlers broke off, they say.

6. **Āshiatta ní tʰe bashóⁿtha ga!:** Dump the water outside!

7. **Hax̌úde ma basé akʰa wí é bthíⁿ:** I am the one who shears the sheep.

8. **Íⁿʾe thoⁿ oⁿbánoⁿga, ppamú:** We rolled the rock down the hill.

9. **Nú ama ttéska thoⁿkʰa basí ukkíhi éde, tté ma bax̌té ukkíhi bazhi:** The men are able to herd the cows; they are not able to corral the bison.

10. **Iⁿshʾáge akʰa noⁿzhíⁿha ettá tʰe bashná azhi, ppá ettá kʰe bax̌thu azhi tta tʰe:** The old man should not shave off his hair or pierce his nose.

B.

1. Did the baby burp?: **Shié kʰe baʼú a?**

2. Don't pull! Push!: **Thidóⁿ azhi a/ga! Badóⁿ a/ga!**

3. The little boy poked his elder sister: **Shénuzhiⁿga akʰa ittóⁿge thiⁿkʰe bazhíba.**

4. Her sister-in-law sews beautiful shawls: **Ishíkkoⁿ akʰa waíⁿ ûjaⁿ batʰá.**

5. She might show one of her shawls: **Waíⁿ ettá wiⁿ bahá tte.**

6. It's your turn to deal the cards: **Shpáṣnide tʰe thithítta.**

7. If you sweep it, I will mop it: **Níbex̣iⁿ kki, ppábize tta miⁿkʰe.**

8. I think someone punctured the car tire: **Kkinóⁿnoⁿgehazizige baʼúde, ebthégoⁿ.**

9. Pour the coffee!: **Moⁿkkóⁿsabe tʰe bax̌tóⁿ a/ga!**

10. Are you the one who is hiccuping?: **Baníuski akʰa thí é níⁿ a?**

17.5 BI- "BY PRESSURE" OR "BY BLOWING"

A.

1. **Āgthiⁿ tʰe bibéniⁿ azhi ga!:** Don't bend the chair!

2. **Wamóskebimóⁿthishtoⁿ thoⁿ bimóⁿ egóⁿ, bibída:** After she kneaded the dough, she molded it.

3. **Weógoⁿbanoⁿx̣e tʰe shpíbize tte:** You might dry the window glass.

4. **Ppíbthaska bthíʼa:** I am unable to smash it.

5. **Bix̌tóⁿ ígaskoⁿtha!:** Try to turn on the water!

6. **Thittúshpa ama uzhóⁿ kʰe uóⁿsi bix̌óⁿ a?:** Did your grandchildren jump and break the bed?

7. **Aóⁿ, bishéthoⁿ:** Yes, they destroyed it.

8. **Wanākkoⁿgthe tʰe ppíx̣oⁿ:** I blew out the candle.

9. **Shúde kʰe bihītha ga!:** Blow away the smoke!

10. **Bigīze akʰa thí é níⁿ a?:** Are you the one who caused that creak?

B.

1. Wring it out!: **Bishkí a/ga!**

2. I know how to knead dough: **Wamóskebimóⁿthishtoⁿ ppímoⁿ bthíppi.**

3. Did your blister bust?: **Noⁿdáze thithítta tʰe bibtháze a?**

4. They say his grandfather felled the tree by leaning on it: **Ittígoⁿ akʰa x̌thabé tʰe bibthízha bi ama.**

5. I smoothed out the blue blanket: **Wāiⁿ ttú kʰe ppísada.**

6. You might wipe that (table nearby): **Shêkʰe shpíkʰa tte.**

7. The warriors rubbed their bows smooth: **Nudóⁿ ama mōⁿde ettá tʰe biṣhnáha.**

8. Should they flatten the cookie dough into circular patties?: **Wamóskeskithebimóⁿthishtoⁿ thoⁿ bibthúga tta i tʰe a?**

9. No, they should make it into round balls: **Áⁿkkazhi. Bibútta tta i tʰe.**

10. Did he blow the flute?: **Nisūde kʰe bihūttoⁿ a?**

17.6 GA- "BY FORCE"

A.

1. **Niáshiⁿga x̌ubé akʰa gasáthu:** The holy man shook the rattle.

2. **Zhóⁿabe ge gahītha:** The scattered leaves blew in the wind.

3. **Ábthoⁿ:** I made a stink by moving something spoiled through the air.

4. **Mé kʰedi wax̌tá gabthá:** In spring the flowers bloom.

5. **Ttenúga ttóⁿga akʰa gappāmoⁿgtha bi ama:** They say the big male buffalo lowered his head to charge.

6. **Gashūde kʰedi attóⁿba mazhi:** I couldn't see in the blizzard.

7. **Zhóⁿ gasé ígaskoⁿthe éde ga'á:** He tried to chop wood but he failed.

8. **Tháwakʰega a?:** Are you nauseous (carsick or seasick)?

9. **Shíⁿgazhiⁿga ama zhoⁿní gthūba thatʰé kki, ga'óⁿsisi:** After the children ate all the candy, they were bouncing.

10. **Wa'úzhiⁿga akʰa gaīⁿx̌e moⁿthíⁿ bi ama:** The old woman wheezed as she walked, they say.

B.

1. The boy wanted to dig a hole, they say: **Núzhiⁿga akʰa ga'é gōⁿtha bi ama.**

2. Did that aforementioned boy make a hole?: **Núzhiⁿga thêakʰa ga'úde a?**

3. Don't blink your eyes!: **Ishtá thithítta tʰe gabízhazhi a/ga!**

4. The water is sloshing: **Ní kʰe gathúzhe.**

5. She is pruning the apple tree: **Shéhi tʰe gasúde.**

6. We all lifted something heavy: **Wôⁿgithe oⁿgáhoⁿ.**

7. I didn't slap you: **Wiáčʰakki mazhi.**

8. Did you scrape your knee?: **Shinôⁿde thithítta tʰe tháx̣abe a?**

9. I combed my hair: **Noⁿzhíⁿha wiwítta kʰe áha.**

10. The drum fell with a thump: **Kkúge thoⁿ gakkúge ux̌pátha.**

17.7 NĀ- "BY FIRE"

A.

1. **Mí thoⁿ nāgoⁿbe:** The sun is bright. / The sun is shining.

2. **Wamóskeshuga thithítta kʰe nāx̌uda:** Your cowboy bread was scorched.

3. **"Nāwax̣u," á bi ama, ttéska ama:** "We got branded," the cattle supposedly said.

4. **"Nāwathaxu shkóⁿzhiⁿga," á bi ama, tté ama:** "You do not know how to brand us," the buffalo supposedly said.

5. **Shêhithudi bashté ge nāzhide:** Over yonder there the scattered strawberries are ripe.

6. **Nātha'a:** You failed at trying to burn it.

7. **Mōⁿze kʰe nāasagi:** I hardened the metal by heat.

8. **Mikká'e ge móⁿxadi nāttaze:** The stars scattered in the sky are shining.

9. **Nāoⁿthazi azhi:** You didn't singe me.

10. **Ttanúkka shêthoⁿ nāsage a? Nāttube a? Awíⁿoⁿwoⁿ?:** Is that meat hardened by heat? Or is it cooked tender?

B.

1. The fire is spreading fast: **Ppéde thoⁿ nāhegazhi.**

2. It (this aforementioned fire) might burn all night until daylight: **Thêthoⁿ nāoⁿba tte.**

3. The land might be burnt black: **Moⁿzhóⁿ kʰe nāsabe tte.**

4. Around here is the smell of fire: **Thêthudi shúde nābthoⁿ.**

5. I see the light right there, at that spot: **Nākkoⁿ gátʰe attóⁿbe.**

6. The cooking pot exploded: **Wēuhoⁿ thoⁿ nābthaza.**

7. This plastic toy is warped: **Hazízige wāthixoⁿ duáthoⁿ nāttubthiⁿ.**

8. It's hot outside: **Āshiatta nākkade.**

9. Since the ice melted, the water has warmed. Swim!: **Núxe thoⁿ nāskoⁿ egóⁿ, ní thoⁿ nāshta. Niúoⁿ a/ga!**

10. All around the boy the trees were burning: **Núzhiⁿga égaxe xthabé tʰe nāxthiⁿ bi ama.**

17.8 MĀ- "BY CUTTING"

A.

1. **Sákkathide/sakkáid' thoⁿ māxoⁿ a!:** Cut up the watermelon!

2. **Sidādi māoⁿxoⁿ:** We cut it up yesterday.

3. **Thittízhoⁿ māxu:** Your niece engraved it.

4. **Nudóⁿ akʰa móⁿde ettá kʰe māski māxu gisítha bi ama:** The warrior remembered to notch the end of his bow, they say.

5. **Māthaxu kki, xthabé tʰe t'é tte:** If you notch it, the tree might die.

6. **Hébe wiⁿ māse a?:** Did s/he cut a piece?

7. **Māttube thoⁿ athíⁿ gí ga!:** Bring back the ground meat!

8. **Shé dúba thizhá, māgixa:** She washed and sliced some apples.

9. **Māse gōⁿtha kki, môⁿhiⁿ íthe tta tʰe:** If s/he wants to cut it, s/he must find a knife.

10. **Watʰóⁿ thoⁿdi iⁿdé māthaxu a?:** Did you carve a face in the pumpkin?

B.

1. My father whittled a flute: **Iⁿdādi akʰa nisūde māgixa.**

2. My younger sister engraved it: **Ittóⁿge akʰa māxu.**

3. Don't cut the cheese!: **Iⁿčʰóⁿgawathatʰe thoⁿ māsazhi a/ga!**

4. She found the ground meat: **Māttube thoⁿ ítha.**

5. I didn't slice the bread: **Wamóske thoⁿ māaxoⁿ mazhi.**

6. Your mother's brother (uncle) should slice the meat: **Thinégi akʰa ttanúkka thoⁿ māʼe tta tʰe.**

7. Do you know how to whittle wood?: **Zhóⁿ māthagixe níppi a?**

8. Since you sliced the meat, we ate it: **Ttanúkka thoⁿ māthaʼe egóⁿ, oⁿthátʰa.**

9. Notch the stick!: **Zhóⁿzhiⁿga māski a/ga!**

10. She is cutting up the edible ripe strawberries: **Bashté nāzhide thatʰéwathe tʰe māʼe.**

17.9 MŪ- "BY SHOOTING"

A.

1. **Kkíde mūṣhnoⁿ:** S/he shot and missed the mark.

2. **Ní kʰedi mūxa, mīxa ma:** The ducks were standing up (on the water).

3. **Ppáthiⁿ nudóⁿ akʰa mūhatheza bi ama:** The Pawnee warrior came back safely from being shot at, they say.

4. **Ttúska akʰa xthabé tʰe mūxtaxta:** The woodpecker was pecking the tree.

5. **Shíⁿgazhiⁿga akʰa mūgthoⁿ bazhi:** The child didn't wander off.

6. **Iⁿkʰéde kʰe mūoⁿdada:** I have aching pain in my shoulder.

7. **Mūoⁿgixa:** We made a furrow by shooting.

8. **Kkída bi ama, mūhegazhi:** He fired a gun with a loud bang, they say.

9. **Moⁿkkóⁿsabe mūppa dūba shkāxe tte:** You might make some strong coffee.

10. **Sidādi mūazhoⁿ éde, mūahitha mazhi:** Yesterday I sifted it out, but I didn't blow it away.

B.

1. The old man wounded Rabbit slightly when he shot him: **Iⁿshʼáge akʰa Moⁿshtíⁿge thiⁿkʰe mūhega.**

2. I will make it rumble (by shooting an arrow at it): **Mūakkuge tta miⁿkʰe.**

3. I heard you shoot until nightfall: **Mūthahoⁿ winóʼoⁿ.**

4. The gun (barrel) exploded, they say: **Wahúttoⁿthe kʰe mūbthaza bi ama.**

5. The bushy-haired cat jumped: **Iⁿgthóⁿga mūxadoⁿ akʰa uóⁿsi.**

6. Now water is flowing: **Íⁿčʰoⁿ ní mūxtoⁿ.**

7. You blew forcefully: **Mūthabixoⁿ.**

8. I'm going to plant fenceposts: **Mūza bthé.**

9. Tap lightly right here!: **Gátʰedi mūkkoⁿ a/ga!**

10. They have aching pain in their hands: **Noⁿbé tʰe mūwadada.**

18.1 THE WA- PREFIX

A.

1. **Wazhíⁿga oⁿgútta thoⁿkʰa tháwa ga!:** Count our chickens!

2. **Gátʰe sṇá wiwítta tʰe, wazéthe oⁿwóⁿppada egóⁿ:** That's my scar, from surgery.

3. **Wathízha x̌óⁿdethathe egóⁿ, thizhá a!:** When you've gathered all the laundry into a pile, wash it!

4. **Wathíga níshtoⁿ i kki, wathátʰe gí i ga ho!:** If you're done shucking corn, come eat!

5. **Wasábe thiⁿ doⁿbá kki, mūhegazhi athá:** When he saw the black bear, he took off like a shot.

6. **Waʔíⁿ ettá thoⁿ zhiⁿgá; waʔíⁿ wiwítta thoⁿ ttoⁿgá:** His bundle is small; my bundle is big.

7. **Môⁿde bix̌óⁿ kʰe ppíʔoⁿ tte, wamáx̌u akʰa:** The carver might fix the broken bow.

8. **Wabthúga oⁿthátʰa, wikkóⁿ thiⁿkʰedi:** We ate Indian porridge at my grandmother's.

9. **Núzhiⁿga shêhitʰoⁿ x̌tāatha mazhi; shóⁿshoⁿ wamóⁿthoⁿshtoⁿ:** I don't like that boy standing over there; he's always stealing things.

10. **Shénuzhiⁿga ama waskíthe, mikkáha, wanā moⁿthíⁿ noⁿ:** The little boys were always going around begging for candy or quarters.

B.

1. I want to eat a ripe red tomato: **Wazhīde zhīde nāzhide bthátʰe kkōⁿbtha.**

2. He can't fix it; he'll have to buy a new saw: **Ppíʔoⁿ ukkíhi bazhi; wabáse ttéga thiwíⁿ tta tʰe.**

3. If you shoot an animal, once it's dead, hurry up and butcher it!: **Wanītta wiⁿ thakkíde kki, tʔé kʰe egóⁿ, ppáde thikkútha (ga)!**

4. I don't play barefoot in the hay, because of the burrs: **Sithúkkathiⁿ x̌áde kʰedi ashkāda mazhi, wax̌ága egóⁿ.**

5. When the killer showed up at the house, they say my grandmother had a rolling pin: **Watʔéthe ttíadi atʰí egóⁿ, wabíbthuga wiⁿ athíⁿ bi ama, wikkóⁿ akʰa.**

6. If you want to grease your shoes, take some bear fat: **Hiⁿbé tʰe watháṣnathe shkōⁿna kki, wasábewashíⁿ dūba thizá (ga).**

7. You're good at drawing: **Wathíx̣u tʰe níppi.**

8. Say the number "nine": **Watháwa "shóⁿkka" á (ga)!**

9. My older brother always likes to polish his car: **Kkinóⁿnoⁿge ettá kʰe shóⁿshoⁿ wasṇáthe x̌táthe noⁿ, wizhíⁿthe/ wittínu akʰa.**

10. It's good that he packed stuff to the house: **Ttíatta waʔíⁿ tʰe ūdaⁿ.**

18.2 THE Ī- PREFIX

A.

1. **Íkki-īthidoⁿ kʰe māsa bi ama, watʼéthe akʰa:** The killer cut the reins, they say.

2. **Sidādi mí-īdoⁿbe sháppe tʰedi oⁿwóⁿthatʰa:** We ate at six o'clock yesterday.

3. **Wazhíⁿga-īkkide māgiχa, núzhiⁿga ittígoⁿ akʰa:** The boy's grandfather carved a slingshot.

4. **"Íⁿ! Iⁿdé χagá í āakkigthe kkōⁿbtha mazhi. Íkkihiⁿ-īgaskebe óⁿ a!" á, igáχthoⁿ akʰa:** "Ee! I don't want to kiss a prickly face. Use a razor!" said his wife.

5. **Īthizha wiⁿ oⁿʼí a!:** Give me a washcloth!

6. **Wēbamoⁿ gōⁿtha, ittúshka ttibútta ugthóⁿ akʰa:** Her nephew in jail wanted a file.

7. **Ībetʰoⁿ ítha egóⁿ, kkúge thoⁿ ubétʰoⁿ, ittími akʰa:** Having found some wrapping, his aunt wrapped the box.

8. **Iⁿdé-īgaχade íⁿ athá; ttibútta tʰedi wēbamoⁿ athíⁿ athá, ittími akʰa:** She set out wearing a veil; his aunt went to the jail with the file.

9. **Ittúshka akʰa mí-īthawa dóⁿbe gthíⁿ bi ama, ttibútta móⁿtʰadi:** Her nephew sat in jail, looking at the calendar.

10. **Óⁿba thawá gthíⁿ; nóⁿdatta wēthawa baχú gthíⁿ; íⁿčʰoⁿ gthêboⁿhíⁿwiⁿ ahí bi ama:** He sat counting the days, marking counters on the wall. Now he had reached a hundred, they say.

B.

1. His nephew wants a shovel: **Ittóⁿshka akʰa ttōⁿde-īnoⁿse gōⁿtha.**

2. He left with a pitchfork: **X̌áde-īthize athíⁿ athá.**

3. Does the carver use sandpaper?: **Zhoⁿbtháska-ībiṣhnaha óⁿ a, wamāχu akʰa?**

4. I'm going to buy a nutcracker: **Ttāge-īgaχiχe bthíwiⁿ tta miⁿkʰe.**

5. The warrior didn't find his tomahawk, they say: **Nudóⁿ akʰa wētʼiⁿ ettá kʰe ítha bazhi bi ama.**

6. If they want to get there, your nephews will have to ask for gas money: **Édi ahí gōⁿtha kki, īnoⁿge nā tta i tʰe, thittóⁿshka ama.**

7. That woman always wears pretty perfume: **Waʼú shêthiⁿkʰe shóⁿshoⁿ īthibthoⁿ ûjaⁿ íⁿ.**

8. The wheel is missing: **Īthinoⁿge thoⁿ thiⁿgé.**

9. My sister-in-law won seventeen chips: **Īthawa agthíⁿppethoⁿba uhí, wishíkkoⁿ akʰa.**

10. Do you have a cup?: **Niīthattoⁿ aníⁿ a?**

18.3 THE U- PREFIX

A.

1. **Mí thoⁿ nāgoⁿbe. Gá! Ttōⁿde-īnoⁿse óⁿ uʼá!:** The sun is shining. Here! Dig for planting with a spade!

2. **Unúshka t^he ttōⁿde uzhí gōⁿtha:** She wanted to fill the low spot with soil.

3. **Umóⁿthiⁿkka ānoⁿ aní a?:** How many years old are you?

4. **Ttéskazhiⁿga ugáṣnoⁿ egóⁿ, ugáshka:** Having lassoed the calf, he tied it.

5. **Thishtóⁿ egóⁿ, házhiⁿga k^he uthíx̌thax̌tha:** When he was done, he loosened the rope.

6. **Wākkuzhiⁿga ga'ú'ude uthíṣnoⁿ, wiháⁿ ak^ha:** My mother threaded a needle.

7. **Umóⁿthiⁿkka shêk^he uṣní t^he; moⁿdé k^he udá bi ama:** That year was cold; the boats were icebound.

8. **Ugánoⁿppaze; mikká'e noⁿ dóⁿbewatha bazhi:** It was pitch dark; not even the stars could be seen.

9. **Umíⁿzhe k^hedi zhóⁿ bi ama, itházhi ak^ha:** His father was lying in the bed, they say.

10. **Zhóⁿ ūthiṣne ítha egóⁿ, ttíadi uppá bi ama, wēs'a ak^ha:** Having found a slit in the wood, the snake crawled into the house.

B.

1. Tighten the lid!: **Īgax̌ade t^he uthíski a/ga!**

2. Since your mother will be away today, your elder sister will fill in for her: **Thiháⁿ óⁿbathe aíatha t^hegóⁿ, thizhóⁿthe/thittóⁿge unóⁿzhiⁿ tta t^he.**

3. Snow blowing in the wind might penetrate into the house: **Má gahíthe k^he ttíadi umūbthiⁿ tte.**

4. Don't exaggerate!: **Ubát^hazhi a/ga!**

5. There is a line of gravel made by a grader along the road: **Uzhóⁿge k^hedi ubíhe k^he.**

6. While traveling, my nephew found a place to stay: **Ugáshoⁿ moⁿthíⁿ t^hedi, ustáppe wiⁿ ítha, wittúshpa/wittóⁿshka ak^ha.**

7. The park is crowded: **Ūshkade thoⁿ ubísoⁿde.**

8. The stove is hot: **Unéthe t^he nākkade.**

9. Last night the boat sank, they say: **Hôⁿde moⁿdé k^he uspá bi ama.**

10. At the bottom of the gully lay a dead buffalo bloating: **Ux̌thúx̌a híde t^hedi, tté t'é wiⁿ umūbix̌oⁿ k^he.**

18.4 CONJUGATION OF LOCATIVE U- VERBS

A.

1. **Má k^he umūbthiⁿ t^hedi uppátti tta miⁿk^h:** I'll plug the spot where the snow is getting in.

2. **Wākkuzhiⁿga ubthí'ude t^he ppóⁿzhiⁿga:** I don't know how to make a hole in a pin.

3. **Uníski āttashoⁿ kki, mūthakkoⁿ íthagaskoⁿne tte:** If you tightened it too much, you might try tapping it lightly to loosen it.

4. **Moⁿkkóⁿsabe t^he ttéskamoⁿzeni utházhi?:** Do you put milk in your coffee?

5. **Banóⁿ wiwítta ma uwábthewiⁿ tta miⁿk^h:** I'll get my gang together.

6. **Égithe uhéat^hoⁿ móⁿshiatta āthane kki, utháx̌pathe tte:** Beware of climbing high up the ladder, lest you fall.

7. **Ugáṣni tʰedi, shié kʰe waíⁿ ushpétʰoⁿ tta tʰe:** When it cools down, you should wrap the baby in a blanket.

8. **Uágashoⁿ bthé tta miⁿkʰe; uẋthábe kʰedi kkáshi moⁿbthíⁿ kkōⁿbtha:** I'm going to go on a journey; I want to walk for a long time out in the woods.

9. **Égithe nīdushi utháttoⁿ thagísithazhi tte!:** Be careful that you don't forget to wear pants!

10. **Kkinóⁿnoⁿge gattūbe shêhikʰe uníshoⁿ tte. Égithe wanóⁿshe ama uthíthoⁿ tte:** You might go around that wrecked car over there. Be careful lest the police arrest you.

B.

1. I put in the seeds: **Sí tʰe uázhi.**

2. I don't want to put on a necktie: **Wãẋe-wanóⁿpʼiⁿ ubthíṣnoⁿ kkōⁿbtha mazhi.**

3. *I'll* put it (the necktie) on you!: **Wí uwíbthiṣnoⁿ tta miⁿkʰʼ!**

4. You might flip over the cowboy bread: **Wamóskeshuga kʰe unísoⁿthe tte.**

5. Your mother is looking for you: **Thiháⁿ akʰa uthína.**

6. Yes, I like to cook things like that: **Áoⁿ, égoⁿ uáhoⁿ ẋtāathe noⁿ moⁿ.**

7. Don't grab me!: **Oⁿwóⁿthoⁿ azhi a/ga!**

8. They say we lost: **Uwáhi bi am'.**

9. We passed a red car on the road: **Kkinóⁿnoⁿge zhīde kʰe oⁿgúha, uzhóⁿge kʰedi.**

10. Do you not know how to tie your horse?: **Shóⁿge thithítta uthāshke shkóⁿzhiⁿga?**

18.5 THE Ā- PREFIX

A.

1. **Wamóske-nāẋude shêtʰe āgasta tʰe bawēgthi ābiṣnatha (ga)!:** Butter that stack of toast!

2. **Núzhiⁿga ābanoⁿ, mīzhiⁿga akʰa:** The girl gazed at the boy.

3. **Nudóⁿhoⁿga wahúttoⁿthe uthóⁿ bi egóⁿ, ukkítte ādoⁿba bi ama:** Grabbing his gun, the war leader took aim at the enemy.

4. **Shêthoⁿ ttáẋti-ppa thoⁿ ābittazhi a/ga!:** Don't touch that deerhead!

5. **Zhóⁿ āgasta āgaha tʰe āgthiⁿ, iⁿgthóⁿge thiⁿkʰe:** The cat sat on top of the pile of wood.

6. **Ukkóⁿ thêtʰedi uẋpé tʰe āgasta āgtha!:** Stack the dishes up here in this open spot!

7. **Moⁿkkóⁿsabe nākkade tʰe iⁿdādi thiⁿkʰe āgashoⁿ akʰa, wí é bthíⁿ mazhi!:** *I am not the one who spilled hot coffee on Dad!*

8. **Wiháⁿ akʰa wēuhoⁿ ttaní ugíppi tʰe unéthe āho āgazhi, wisóⁿge thiⁿkʰe:** My mother told my younger brother to lift the pot full of soup onto the stove.

9. **Nú akʰa nídushi ettá kʰe uttóⁿ egóⁿ, ippíthage kʰe āgashka:** Having put on his pants, the man buckled his belt.

9. **Wizhíⁿthe ak^ha ippíthage ítha egóⁿ, nídushi ettá k^he uthíṣnoⁿ egóⁿ, āgashka:** Having found a belt, my elder brother threaded it through his pants and buckled it.

10. **Ikkáge thiⁿk^he ākkippa, wisóⁿge ak^ha, ugáshoⁿ k^hedi:** My younger brother met his friend while he was traveling.

B.

1. The cat jumped up on the table: **Iⁿgthóⁿga ak^ha wāthat^he k^he ā'oⁿsi.**

2. They say the warrior rode a dappled horse: **Shóⁿge gthézhe āgthiⁿ bi ama, nudóⁿ ak^ha.**

3. The mother lifted the baby up onto the chair: **Shié k^he āgthiⁿ āgaha t^he āhoⁿ, iháⁿ ak^ha.**

4. The girls walked along the boardwalk: **Zhoⁿbtháska uttánoⁿ k^he āha moⁿthíⁿ, mīzhiⁿga ama.**

5. The niece hugged her aunt: **Ittími āna bi ama, ittúzhoⁿge ak^ha.**

6. It will be overcast tomorrow: **Gasóⁿthiⁿ āmoⁿx̌pi tta ak^ha.**

7. They say his younger brother ran over a dog yesterday: **Sidādi shínuda ānoⁿga bi ama, isóⁿge ak^ha.**

8. Recite the words!: **Īe k^he āthada (ga)!**

9. Her nephew wore a striped shirt: **Unóⁿzhiⁿ gthéze āthaha, ittúshka ak^ha.**

10. Don't point at your grandfather!: **Thittígoⁿ ābazu azhi a/ga!**

18.6 CONJUGATION OF Ā- VERBS

A.

1. **Niīthattoⁿ wāthat^he āagthe it^héathe, ukkóⁿ t^hedi:** I put the cup away on the table, in an open spot.

2. **Noⁿzhíⁿ t^he āoⁿgazhi ga!:** Tell me to stand up!

3. **Íⁿ'ezhiⁿga uzhóⁿge k^he oⁿgāzhi tta oⁿgat^hoⁿ:** We're going to put gravel on the road.

4. **Āthax̌e winóⁿ'oⁿ thoⁿzha, awádi thax̌ága?:** I heard you cry out. Why are you crying?

5. **Wathát^he uthíae thoⁿzha, āoⁿ'oⁿsi:** They were distributing food, but skipped me.

6. **Bawēgthi āshpiṣnathe tte, wamóske-nāx̌ude k^he:** You might butter the toast.

7. **Zhoⁿbtháska-uttánoⁿ oⁿgāhe oⁿgátha tta!:** Let's go walking on the boardwalk!

8. **Nóⁿde t^he āthakkoⁿ t^he āwikkippe tte:** I might meet you leaning against the wall.

9. **Zhū-nākkade wiwítta k^he āwioⁿthe kkōⁿbtha mazhi:** I don't want to give you my sickness.

10. **Nídushi itháthe t^hegoⁿ, ippíthage āashke bthíkkuthe:** Now that I've found my pants, I'm hurrying to buckle my belt.

B.

1. I'll meet you: **Āwikkippe tta miⁿk^he.**

2. You might hug your aunt: **Thittími āthane tte.**

3. Don't touch me!: **Āoⁿbittazhi a/ga!**

4. I shall read: **Ābthade tta mi^{n}k^{h}e.**

5. You spilled coffee on me: **Mo^{n}kkó^{n}sabe āo^{n}thasho^n.**

6. We lifted the bundle onto the table: **Wa'í^n tho^n wāthat^{h}e k^{h}e o^{n}gāho^n.**

7. You are good at riding a horse: **Shó^{n}ge āthagthi^n t^{h}e níppi.**

8. You will wear a necklace: **Wanó^{n}p'i^n ānaha tta ni^{n}kshe.**

9. We didn't run over you: **O^{n}gāthino^{n}ga bazhi.**

10. I want to fly over the football field: **Ūshkade āagio^n kkō^{n}btha.**

18.7 THE TRANSITIVIZING Í- PREFIX

A.

1. **Ūe ettá k^{h}e í'o^n gō^{n}tha, wikkó^n ak^{h}a:** My grandmother wants to cultivate her field.

2. **Kki Mo^{n}shtí^{n}ge edí hí bi kki, Ppahé-Wāthahuni ak^{h}a íbaho^n bi ama:** And when Rabbit got there, the Devouring Hill recognized him, they say.

3. **Niskíthe ígahi, wittími ak^{h}a:** My aunt mixed in some salt.

4. **Uzhó^{n}ge bazhúzhu tho^{n}zha, thiādi ak^{h}a íhe ígasko^{n}tha:** Even though the road was rough, your father tried to get through.

5. **Héga it'atha bi egó^n, ímo^{n}tha bi ama, Ishtíthi^{n}k^{h}e ak^{h}a:** They say that Ishtíthi^{n}k^{h}e, hating the Buzzard, laid for him.

6. **Wittó^{n}shka idādo^{n}shte íbaho^n azhi kki, ittígo^n ímo^{n}xe tta t^{h}e:** If there is

anything my nephew doesn't know, he should ask his grandfather.

7. **Zhó^n gasé ígasko^{n}the éde isó^{n}ge ínietha:** He tried to chop wood but he injured his younger brother.

8. **Kki ínit^{h}a, ithādi ak^{h}a:** And his father reproved him.

9. **Shí^{n}gazhi^{n}ga ābae zhūgthe athé t^{h}e íno^{n}hi^n bazhi, ithādi ak^{h}a:** The father did not allow the child to go along on the hunt.

10. **Wakkó^{n}dawāthaho^{n}tti t^{h}edi zhō^{n}tto^{n}thi^{n}ge gthí^n kki, íthizho^{n}zho^n igáx̌tho^n ak^{h}a:** When he started to nod off in church, his wife shook him.

B.

1. The boy was scolded by his mother: **Núzhi^{n}ga thi^{n}k^{h}e íhusa, ihá^n ak^{h}a.**

2. That girl read to her father: **Ithādi íthada, mīzhi^{n}ga shêak^{h}a.**

3. My elder brother has to wait for his grandmother: **Wizhí^{n}the ak^{h}a ikkó^n íthappe tta t^{h}e.**

4. Did my grandchild find the bread?: **Wamóske t^{h}e íthe a, wittúshpa ak^{h}a?**

5. The dogs scented the raccoon: **Mikká thi^{n}k^{h}e íthibtho^n, shínuda ama.**

6. The child tugged on the edge of his/her mother's dress: **Shí^{n}gazhi^{n}ga ak^{h}a ihá^n wat^{h}é ubáhe íthido^{n}do^n.**

7. He has to cut the rope: **Házhi^{n}ga íthise tta t^{h}e.**

8. My uncle didn't touch the snake: **Winégi akʰa wés'a kʰe ítta bazhi.**

9. The spoiled meat might make your child sick: **Thinísi íwakʰega tte, ttanúkka zóⁿsta tʰe.**

10. They say the black bears always ridiculed the human: **Níkkashiⁿga íxaxa noⁿ óⁿ bi ama, wasábe ama.**

18.8 CONJUGATION OF TRANSITIVIZING Í- VERBS

A.

1. **"Negího, wa'úzhiⁿga akʰa 'Thinégi thiⁿkʰetta moⁿthíⁿ a!' á egóⁿ, oⁿthóⁿhusa egóⁿ, ppí," á bi ama Moⁿshtíⁿge akʰa:** "Uncle, the old woman said, 'Go to your uncle's!', and scolded me, so I have come," said the Rabbit, they say.

2. **Thiháⁿ akʰa íthihusa tta:** Your mother will scold you.

3. **Wētta thâbthiⁿ íthagahi tta niⁿkshe:** You will mix in three eggs.

4. **Ūhaⁿ wiwítta tʰe íthiwakʰega egóⁿ, iwíbthade tta miⁿkʰ:** Since my cooking made you sick, I'll read to you.

5. **Weániethe egóⁿ, oⁿthóⁿmoⁿthe gōⁿtha:** Since I injured them, they want to take revenge on me.

6. **Wittúshpa noⁿxíde-thiⁿge egóⁿ, atʰóⁿshte weánoⁿxithe:** Since my grandkids are disobedient, sometimes I chase them.

7. **Wikkóⁿ akʰa oⁿtházhiⁿge āzhi, oⁿthóⁿxaxa azhi:** My grandmother doesn't belittle me or ridicule me.

8. **"Íwishte noⁿ moⁿ!" á, thiháⁿ akʰa, égoⁿ íthihusa tʰe anóⁿ'oⁿ:** I heard your mother scolding you, saying "I'm always ashamed of you!"

9. **"Uzhóⁿge kʰe gashéthoⁿ thoⁿzha, wí itháhe itháppahoⁿ" á, égthoⁿge wiwítta akʰa:** "Even though the road is destroyed, I know how to get through," said my husband.

10. **"Égoⁿ shetʰóⁿna thêthudi ithábthappe agthíⁿ" á, igáxthoⁿ akʰa:** "Therefore I'm still sitting here waiting for him," said his wife.

B.

1. They'll laugh at you: **Íthixaxa tta.**

2. I want to cultivate my field: **Ūe wiwítta kʰe ithá'oⁿ kkóⁿbtha.**

3. We will not permit it: **Oⁿthóⁿnoⁿhiⁿ bazhi tta oⁿgatʰoⁿ.**

4. There is something I want to ask you: **Idādoⁿshte íwimoⁿxe kkōⁿbtha.**

5. If they are hungry, we should feed them: **Noⁿppéhiⁿ kki, weóⁿthishi tta i tʰe.**

6. I don't want you to be ashamed of me: **Oⁿthóⁿthashta tʰe kkōⁿbtha mazhi.**

7. Are you afraid to touch maggots?: **Wagthí íthatte nóⁿthappe a?**

8. We know the people living far away over there on the Missouri River: **Shêhitʰe gthíⁿ ma Nishúde kʰedi weóⁿbahoⁿ.**

9. Are you able to cut the rope?: **Házhiⁿga k^he ínise uthákkihi a?**

10. Don't dislike me!: **Oⁿthóⁿt'athazhi a/ga!**

10. **Ithābaṣnu utháne t^he uthúgashke t^hedi íthathe tte:** You might find the scissors you are looking for on the peg.

18.9 COMBINATIONS OF APPLICATIVE Ī AND Í- WITH U- AND Ā- PREFIXES

A.

1. **Thiādi ak^ha wéahidexti uthúgashoⁿ tta t^he:** Your father has to commute very far.

2. **Wétta thâbthiⁿ uthúgahi a/ga!:** Mix in three eggs!

3. **Uthúwixe kkōⁿbtha kki, oⁿthóⁿwoⁿthat'athe tta niⁿkshe:** If I seek to fool you, you will dislike me.

4. **Égoⁿ oⁿthóⁿgukkikkie tta oⁿgat^hoⁿ:** We'll discuss that.

5. **Uthúshtoⁿbazhi kki, ppá thoⁿ uthúwishpidoⁿ tta miⁿk^{h'}, nishúde k^hedi:** If you don't watch out, I'll dunk your head in the river.

6. **Wittóⁿshka ak^ha thêthudi uthúthe athíⁿ egóⁿ, shóⁿshoⁿ uthúgashoⁿ moⁿthíⁿ:** Since my nephew has ties here, he's always shuttling back and forth.

7. **Uthúdoⁿba! Égithe shínuda ama ttanúkka k^he uthúhi tta:** Be careful! The dogs might get to the meat.

8. **Wikkóⁿ uthúanoⁿzhiⁿ éde, wí é shti oⁿthóⁿwoⁿnoⁿzhiⁿ:** I depend on my grandmother, and she depends on me.

9. **Xáde xóⁿde ge házhiⁿga uthúkkoⁿtha i a/ga!:** Bind the scattered piles of hay together with string!

B.

1. The stars are inaccessible: **Mikká'e ge uthúhi-thi'áwathe.**

2. My friend leaned against the tree: **Wik^háge ak^ha xthabé t^he íthakkoⁿ.**

3. Where exactly is the lid?: **Ithāgaxade t^he āgudixti?**

4. Be careful!: **Uthúdoⁿba (ga)!**

5. I depend on you: **Uthúwinoⁿzhiⁿ.**

6. They say that Ishtíthiⁿk^he intended (wanted) to trick Rabbit: **Moⁿshtíⁿge uthúxa gōⁿtha bi ama, Ishtíthiⁿk^he ak^ha.**

7. My father should wait for my grandmother: **Wikkóⁿ íthappe tta t^he, iⁿdādi ak^ha.**

8. Don't follow me!: **Oⁿthóⁿwoⁿhazhi a/ga!**

9. I can't reach it: **Uthúahi bthí'a.**

10. The old woman has nobody left: **Wa'úzhiⁿga thiⁿk^he uthúthe thiⁿge.**

18.10 COMBINATION OF WA- WITH U- AND Ā-, AND Ī- AND Í- VERBS

A.

1. **Hóⁿt'ega wiⁿ wēoga t^he ubáhiⁿ:** A fly got into the paint.

2. **Kkúge thêthoⁿ u'í kkōⁿbtha t^he egoⁿ, wēobet^hoⁿ uáne:** I want to donate this box, so I'm looking for wrapping.

3. **Wēobatti t^{h}e thiṣhnúde gō^{n}tha gthí^n:** He is trying to get the cork out.

4. **Wēothi'ude athí^n kki, ūmakka:** It would be easy if he had a corkscrew.

5. **Égithe wabthágase thithítta t^{h}e gahíthe tta. Gá! wēagaspe ó^n a!:** Your papers might blow away. Here! Use a paperweight!

6. **Wizhí^{n}ge ak^{h}a i^{n}déugaxe t^{h}e nó^{n}datta wēathaskabe uthútho^{n}tha:** My son hung up the picture on the wall with paste.

7. **Wahó^{n}thishige egó^n, uthúthe-thi^{n}ge gthí^n:** Since he is an orphan, he has no ties to hold him.

8. **Ūha^n gō^{n}tha, wizhó^{n}ge ak^{h}a:** My daughter wants to cook.

9. **Ttibútta mó^{n}t^{h}adi agthí^n tho^{n}di, wēbamo^n kkō^{n}btha no^n mo^n:** Back when I was in jail, I always wanted a file.

10. **Zhó^n k^{h}e uthúgaṣne shkō^{n}na kki, mó^{n}ze-wēogaṣne ó^n ga!:** If you want to split the wood, use an iron wedge!

B.

1. If you're giving things away, give me five cents!: **Ūtha'i kki, wēthawa sátto^n o^n'í ga!**

2. The reader stood in front of the church, reading aloud: **Wéthade ak^{h}a uthúshiatta āthade no^{n}zhí^n, wakkó^{n}da-wāthaho^n tti t^{h}edi.**

3. They say she peeped in through the window: **Wēogo^{n}ba t^{h}e ugás'i^n bi ama.**

4. Do you have paint?: **Wēoga aní^n a?**

5. The lock on the door is broken: **Ttizhébe wēothido^n t^{h}e x̌ó^n.**

6. Then use nails!: **Égo^n mó^{n}zeugado^n ó^n a/ga!**

7. Put away the hanger on the hook!: **Wēotho^{n}the k^{h}e uthúgashke t^{h}edi it^{h}étha (ga)!**

8. Do you see the sign?: **Wēotha t^{h}e thashtó^{n}be a?**

9. I'm going to put the pepper in the pot: **Wēokkiho^n t^{h}e wēoho^n uázhi tta mi^{n}k^{h}e.**

10. My older sister has a new hairpin: **Wēabax̌thade wi^n ttéga athí^n, wizhó^{n}the ak^{h}a.**

19.1 THE POSSESSIVE GI- PREFIX

A.

1. **K^{h}agého! Ūzhiha thithítta k^{h}e skīge. Ppahé shêhitho^{n}ttat^{h}o^n thagí'i^n a?:** Friend! Your backpack is heavy. Did you pack it from yonder roundish hill?

2. **Kkáshi Mo^{n}shtí^{n}ge k^{h}e ígitha bi ama, ikkó^n ak^{h}a:** After a long time, Rabbit's grandmother found him, they say.

3. **I^{n}dādi ak^{h}a x̌áde-īno^{n}se ettá k^{h}e ginā tta t^{h}e:** My father should ask for his mower back.

4. **Shí^{n}gazhi^{n}ga wiwítta ma agío^{n}tha mazhi tta mi^{n}k^{h}e:** I will not abandon my own children.

5. **Wa'úzhi^{n}ga ppiāzhi ak^{h}a nudó^n thi^{n}k^{h}e t'éthe gō^{n}tha éde, izhó^{n}ge thi^{n}k^{h}e t'égitha bi ama:** The bad woman wanted

to kill the warrior, but she killed her own daughter, they say.

6. **Iⁿdé thoⁿ gisṇátha bi egóⁿ, igáx̌thoⁿ ugíne athá bi ama, nudóⁿ akʰa:** Having painted his face, the warrior set out in search of his wife, they say.

7. **Igáx̌thoⁿ iⁿdé shi gittóⁿbe gōⁿtha bi ama; waʼú thiⁿkʰe giōⁿthe gōⁿtha bazhi bi ama:** He wanted to see his wife's face again; he did not want to abandon his own woman, they say.

8. **Sígthe kʰe uthúha bi egóⁿ, ígitha bi ama, igáx̌thoⁿ thiⁿkʰe, ukkítte uthízoⁿ gthíⁿ thiⁿkʰe:** Having followed the trail, he found his wife, they say, sitting among the enemy.

9. **Móⁿde kʰe gthíza bi egóⁿ, ukkítte ímoⁿthe íthappe gthíⁿ bi ama, uzhóⁿge kʰedi:** Grabbing his bow, he sat waiting by the road, they say, laying for the enemy.

10. **Igáx̌thoⁿ zhūgigthe hátheza agthí bi ama, nudóⁿ akʰa:** The warrior returned home safely with his wife.

B.

1. Rabbit set out together with his grandmother, they say: **Moⁿshtíⁿge akʰa ikkóⁿ zhūgigthe athá bi ama.**

2. Husband! Ask your uncle for your gun back!: **Iⁿshʼáge! Thinégi thiⁿkʰe wahúttoⁿthiⁿ thithítta kʰe ginā a!**

3. I'm going to go searching for my brother: **Wisóⁿge uágine bthé tta miⁿkʰe.**

4. Did you eat your own food last night?: **Watháthe hôⁿde thagtháthe a?**

5. I want to go with my father when he leaves on his commute: **Iⁿdādi uthúgashoⁿ athé tʰedi, zhūagigthe kkōⁿbtha.**

6. I'm going to go to war. So I'm smearing my face with paint: **Nudóⁿ bthé tta miⁿkʰe. Égoⁿ wēoga agísṇathe, iⁿdé thoⁿ.**

7. Even though it is heavy, I will bear my own pack: **Skīge thoⁿzha, ūzhiha wiwítta thoⁿ agíʼiⁿ tta miⁿkʰe.**

8. That bellowing calf is looking for its mother: **Ttéskazhiⁿga bóⁿ shêakʰa iháⁿ ugína.**

9. Beware that if you touch the crane's chick, its mother may abandon it: **Égithe ppéttoⁿ izhíⁿga íthatte kki, iháⁿ akʰa giōⁿthe tta.**

10. "Sister! I've searched for you so long, and now that I've found you I can see your face!" said my older sister: **Ttoⁿgehá! Kkáshi uwígine éde, íⁿčʰoⁿ íwigithe tʰe iⁿdé thoⁿ agíttoⁿbe!" á, wizhóⁿthe akʰa.**

19.2 THE SUUS GI- PREFIX

A.

1. **Thittínu akʰa wanóⁿshe gippáx̌u tʰe thagísithe?:** Do you remember when your older brother enlisted in the military?

2. **Wathágigthathe noⁿ zhoⁿ; égoⁿ shóⁿshoⁿ thagínoⁿkkuwiⁿx̌e moⁿníⁿ:** You always volunteer for things; that's

why you're always running around trying to get things done.

3. **Shíⁿgazhiⁿga ama iháⁿ thiⁿkʰe gigthá:** The children take after their mother.

4. **Óⁿbathe oⁿwóⁿkʰega éde, gasóⁿthiⁿ agíni tta miⁿkʰe. Égoⁿ shóⁿshoⁿ moⁿbthíⁿ:** Today I'm sick, but tomorrow I'll be better. That's how it always is with me.

5. **Wittígoⁿ akʰa gigthíwagazu thishtóⁿ egóⁿ, giní bi am':** My grandfather, having made out his will, recovered, they say.

6. **T'á bi ethégoⁿ thoⁿzha, gigtházu:** Though they thought he would die, he recovered.

7. **Agígthaxube kki, óⁿačʰakki ga!:** If I boast, slap me!

8. **Winégi gisíⁿ thoⁿzha, óⁿgisitha bazhi:** Though my uncle recovered consciousness, he did not remember me.

9. **Moⁿkkóⁿsabe tʰe, wétta tʰe, hiⁿbthíⁿge tʰe agísitha mazhi; égoⁿ agínoⁿkkuwiⁿxe moⁿbthíⁿ:** I forgot the coffee, the eggs and the beans, so I'm running around all over the place.

10. **Sidādi agísiⁿ egóⁿ, gasóⁿthiⁿ ttíadi akʰí tta miⁿkʰe:** Yesterday I revived, so tomorrow I'll go home.

B.

1. My son will enlist in the army: **Wanóⁿshe gippáxu tta akʰa, winísi akʰa.**

2. My son takes after his father: **Ithādi gigthá, wizhíⁿge akʰa.**

3. Today my mother needs to run around getting things done: **Óⁿbathe wiháⁿ akʰa ginóⁿkkuwiⁿxe tta tʰe.**

4. Did your aunt get better?: **Thittími akʰa giní a?**

5. Yes. They say she recovered consciousness last night: **Áoⁿ. Hôⁿde gisíⁿ bi am'.**

6. When she woke up, they say she remembered all her grandchildren: **Gigtházu kki, ittúshpa wôⁿgithe wagísitha bi am'.**

7. She always offers to give of herself: **Shóⁿshoⁿ gigtháthe noⁿ.**

8. Since I have become an old man, I'm going to put my affairs in order: **Iⁿsh'áge ahí tʰe egóⁿ, agígthiwagazu tta miⁿkʰe.**

9. I don't like that boy because he's boastful: **Shê núzhiⁿga akʰa gigtháxube egóⁿ, ithát'abthe.**

10. If she recovers, she may return home: **Giní kki, ttíadi agthí tta.**

19.3 THE REFLEXIVE KKI- PREFIX

A.

1. **Thakkígthizha egóⁿ, sakkáid' thoⁿ oⁿtháтʰe tta oⁿgatʰoⁿ:** When you've washed up, we'll eat the watermelon.

2. **Híde kʰedi athá bi ama, niáshiⁿga χubé ama, wanítta, wazhíⁿga kkigthíauzhi tʰegóⁿ:** The holy men went down to the bottoms, they say, to turn themselves into animals or birds.

3. **Shínuja ama kkigthíshkoⁿshkoⁿ zhō̄ⁿ kʰe, iháⁿ uppáhadi:** The puppies lay squirming beside their mother.

4. **Winísi akʰa ttōⁿthiⁿ kkinóⁿse χeátha thoⁿzha, shí kkihóⁿ:** My son/daughter tripped and fell down while running, but lifted him/herself up again.

5. **Móⁿshoⁿ uákkine; mônde akkíppaχe kkōⁿbtha:** I'm looking for feathers. I want to make myself a bow.

6. **Ttáχti kkióⁿhe thiⁿ kkiōⁿtha bi ama, shóⁿttoⁿga nugá akʰa:** The male wolf threw itself at the fleeing deer.

7. **Uthúdoⁿba ga! Sabázhi kkigthísoⁿthe tta, ttenúga shêthiⁿ!:** Watch out! That running buffalo bull might turn on you!

8. **Nākkade kki, oⁿkkígthane oⁿgthíⁿ:** When it is hot, we sit fanning ourselves.

9. **Thakkíudazhi thoⁿzha, kkikkína bazhi i a!:** Even though you don't get along, don't fight!

10. **Nudóⁿ akʰa āgthiⁿ kkióⁿhe agthá bi kki, shóⁿge ettá ama kkinóⁿsa bi ama:** When the warrior rode back in retreat, his horse stumbled, they say.

B.

1. It's hot. I'm fanning myself: **Nākkad'atč. Akkígthani.**

2. Are you making yourself a bow?: **Mônde thakkíkkaχe?**

3. My grandmother fell, but she lifted herself up: **Wikkóⁿ akʰa χeátha éde, kkihóⁿ.**

4. The running buffalos were turning themselves around in a circle: **Tté ttóⁿthiⁿ ama kkippákkuwiⁿχe moⁿthíⁿ ama.**

5. When I saw the black bear, I ran away: **Wasábe attóⁿbe kki, akkíoⁿhe.**

6. They say the buffalo swapped ends: **Tté akʰa kkigthísoⁿtha bi ama.**

7. If I stumble, I'll lift myself up: **Akkínoⁿse kki, akkíhoⁿ tta miⁿkʰe.**

8. They say the warrior threw himself on the enemy: **Ukkítte kkióⁿtha bi ama, nudóⁿ akʰa.**

9. Are you able to turn yourself into a wolf?: **Shóⁿttoⁿga thakkígthiauzhi uthákkihi a?**

10. My sister-in-law is sitting at home fanning herself: **Ttíadi kkigthāni gthíⁿ, wihóⁿga/wishíkkoⁿ akʰa.**

19.4 THE VICTIMIZED KKE- PREFIX
AND EVIDENTIAL T^{h}E

A.

1. **Niáshi^{n}ga x̌ubé wi^n akkíkkina éde, tteníx̌a-ugthezhe uákkegthiauzhi:** I fought with a holy person, but I got turned into a mushroom.

2. **I^{n}dādi ak^{h}a núzhi^{n}ga k^{h}edi neúthisho^n mó^{n}t^{h}adi niúwo^n bi ama, ik^{h}áge zhūwagigthe. Sabāzhi thió^{n}ba k^{h}e unāgo^{n}ba bi ama. Gashíbe ahí bi kki, núzhi^{n}ga wô^{n}githe ama zhū kkegthígtheza bi t^{h}e ama, só^n, ní gahá k^{h}edi:** When he was a boy, my father went swimming in a lake with his friends. Suddenly, there was a great flash of lightning. When they got out, all the boys had got white stripes on their skin, where the surface of the water had been.

3. **Núzhi^{n}ga kikkína gō^{n}tha tho^{n}zha, ukkégthispa bi ama; ik^{h}áge ame, é uthíspa bi t^{h}e ama:** Though the boy wanted to fight, he was restrained; it was his friends, they evidently held him back.

4. **Nú gthó^{n}thi^n wi^n ukkégthiske gthí^n:** A crazy man sat straightjacketed.

5. **Shínuda o^{n}gútta ak^{h}a ppāhi^n ítha i t^{h}e. Ppá k^{h}edi, í k^{h}edi, hizhū k^{h}edi kkeppáx̌thu thêthudí x̌thí^n gthí^n thi^{n}k^{h}e. I^{n}dādi ak^{h}a ppahī^n thiṣhnúde tta t^{h}e:** Our dog evidently found a porcupine. It's sitting here growling, pierced in its nose, mouth and gums. My father has to pull the quills out.

6. **Tteníx̌a-ugthezhe íthashpaho^n azhi kki, that^{h}á bazhi i a! Égithe íwathakkek^{h}ega**

tte: If you don't know a mushroom, don't eat it. You might make yourself sick.

7. **Uzhó^{n}ge uppáhadi, ppāhi^n wi^n kkigthíshko^{n}shko^n zhō^n k^{h}e ākkeno^{n}ga i t^{h}e:** Beside the road, a porcupine lay twitching, evidently having been run over.

8. **Neúthisho^n akkíthitta niúwo^n mo^{n}thí^n bi t^{h}e ama. Ō^{n}thino^n ní-kkegtháx̌thuda bi ama:** Evidently he swam across the lake, they say. They say he almost drowned himself.

9. **Astúhi íthakket^{h}i^n a?:** Did you bump your elbow?

10. **Kkúkkusi ama gashíbe kkimūgtho^n athá i t^{h}e. Ūe k^{h}e no^{n}shétho^n k^{h}e:** Evidently the pigs got out. The field is trampled and destroyed.

B.

1. That (aforementioned) pig got eaten: **Kkúkkusi thêthi^{n}k^{h}e kkegthát^{h}a.**

2. "We got branded," the cattle supposedly said: **"Nāwakkex̣u," á bi ama, ttéska ama.**

3. You got singed: **Nāthakkezi.**

4. I don't want to be straightjacketed: **Uákkegthiske kkō^{n}btha mazhi.**

5. Watch out! You'll bump your head!: **Uthúdo^{n}ba ga! Sabāzhi no^{n}shkí tho^n íthakket^{h}i^n tta ni^{n}kshe!**

6. Behave! You might get gossiped about: **Wáspa! Égithe uthákkegtha tte.**

7. Why are you crying? Did you get hit?: **Awádi thaxáge? Uthákketʰiⁿ a?**

8. Evidently, the enemy has seen us: **Wadóⁿba i tʰe, ukkítte ama.**

9. Evidently, the ice has melted: **Núxe thoⁿ nāskoⁿ i tʰe.**

10. The trees evidently had burned all around the boy: **Núzhiⁿga égaxe xthabé tʰe nāxthiⁿ bi tʰe ama.**

19.5 THE DATIVE GĪ- AND -Ī-

A.

1. **Núzhiⁿga iⁿdéugaxe thixú tʰe gīdoⁿba, ihaⁿ akʰa:** His mother looked at the picture for him, which the boy had drawn.

2. **Moⁿshtíⁿge akʰa ppashtóⁿga-ppa gīoⁿtha bi ama, Uṣní thiⁿkʰe:** Rabbit threw a bighorn sheep/moose head at Old Man Winter.

3. **Mīzhiⁿga uthá i tʰe gīzha bi ama, núzhiⁿga akʰa:** The boy denied what the girl had reported.

4. **Mōⁿzeska ettá tʰe gīna ahí, iⁿshʼáge akʰa:** The old man arrived there to collect his debt/ask for his money back.

5. **Gátʰe moⁿkkóⁿsabe. Thikkóⁿ niīthattoⁿ tʰe uīzhi ga!:** There's coffee. Fill your grandmother's cup for her!

6. **Thittóⁿde dāthiⁿ-giudoⁿ thóⁿshti thoⁿzha, íⁿčʰoⁿ gīwazhiⁿska noⁿ gthíⁿ:** Your son-in-law used to be a drunkard, but now he's always sober.

7. **Uītha tʰedi, gītha bazhi:** When they told him, he wasn't happy.

8. **Wittóⁿde akʰa shóⁿshoⁿ uxthábe kʰedi é-nóⁿxči gīthe moⁿttánoⁿha ugáshoⁿ moⁿthíⁿ:** My brother-in-law is always wandering wild through the woods, happy by himself.

9. **Igáxthoⁿ ittínu uīkkoⁿ gīshi, iⁿshʼáge akʰa:** The old man asked his wife to help his daughter-in-law.

10. **Waʼúzhiⁿga akʰa gīttexi thoⁿzha, ittínu akʰa uīkkoⁿ tʰe uītha tʰedi, gītha:** Although the old woman was going through hard times, she rejoiced when they told her that her daughter-in-law would help her.

B.

1. The boys followed the holy person, they say: **Niáshiⁿga xubé uíha biama, shénuzhiⁿga ama.**

2. My father approves of my husband: **Iⁿdādi akʰa égthoⁿge wiwítta thiⁿkʰe gīshoⁿ gthíⁿ.**

3. My grandfather should teach my child Omaha: **Wittígoⁿ akʰa winísi Umóⁿhoⁿ ie tʰe gīoⁿze tta tʰe.**

4. The police took the children away from their mother: **Shíⁿgazhiⁿga thoⁿkʰa ihaⁿ thiⁿkʰe gīnoⁿsha, wanóⁿshe ama.**

5. Tell your mother!: **Thihaⁿ uītha a/ga!**

6. That man over there acts conceited: **Nú shêhiakʰa gīttoⁿga moⁿthíⁿ.**

7. Invite your aunt, and your sister-in-law as well!: **Thittími, thihóⁿga megoⁿ, gīkʰu a/ga! / Thittími, thishíkkoⁿ megoⁿ, gīkʰu a/ga!**

8. I think your nephew is hungry. Hurry up and cook for him!: **Thittúshka noⁿppéhiⁿ, ebthégoⁿ. Uíhoⁿ gíthikkutha (ga)!**

9. Make your niece a dress!: **Thittúzhoⁿge watʰé giãxa (ga)!**

10. Shoot a rabbit for your sister-in-law!: **Thihóⁿga moⁿshtíⁿge gíkkida (ga)! / Thishíkkoⁿ moⁿshtíⁿge gíkkida (ga)!**

7. **Íⁿʔe thoⁿ wēoⁿtha, núzhiⁿga akʰa:** The boy threw the rock at them.

8. **Gahíge uëhe thiⁿkʰe ēbthikkuthe tta tʰe:** I have to hurry for the chief I follow.

9. **Thiãdi thiⁿkʰe môⁿde thigãxe tʰe thēshi kkúde tte:** You should ask your father to make a bow for you.

10. **Sithúkkathiⁿ ux̌thábe kʰedi moⁿttánoⁿha moⁿbthíⁿ íⁿudoⁿ:** I like running wild in the woods, barefoot.

19.6 CONJUGATION OF THE DATIVE

A.

1. **"Awádi thaxáge a?" á bi ama, ikʰágetha i ama. "Áoⁿ, wisóⁿge tʔéoⁿgithe tʰe, égoⁿ íⁿthe mazhi agthíⁿ," á bi ama, Mikká akʰa:** "Why are you crying?" asked his friends. "Yes, my own younger brother has died on me, so I am unhappy," replied the Raccoon.

2. **Dāthiⁿ thiudoⁿ moⁿníⁿ kki, wīshoⁿ mazhi tta miⁿkʰe:** If you like to go around drunk, I won't approve of you.

3. **Wagthábaze āppaxu thêkʰe íⁿdoⁿba ga!:** Look over what I've written down on this paper for me!

4. **Ūe thêkʰe uáʔe bthíʔa. Wittóⁿde ma ttōⁿde-thittūbe óⁿ uʔé iⁿwíⁿkkoⁿ ewēboⁿ tta miⁿkʰe:** I can't plow this field. I'll call over my sons-in-law to help me plow it with a plow.

5. **Wagthábaze ābthade wí-nóⁿx̌či íⁿthe agthíⁿ noⁿ moⁿ:** I'm happy by myself, reading books.

6. **Wittími akʰa wabátʰe íⁿgoⁿze tta akʰa:** My aunt is going to teach me how to sew.

B.

1. Why did you call me over?: **Awádi iⁿthēboⁿ a?**

2. My son-in-law shot a pig for us: **Kkúkkusi wiⁿ wēkkida, wittóⁿde akʰa.**

3. The chief invited the Pawnees and the Ioways as well: **Ppāthiⁿ ma shti, Ppáx̌ude ma shti, wēkʰu bi ama, gahíge akʰa.**

4. Do you doubt that your brother-in-law took my mower?: **Thishíʔe akʰa x̌ade-īnoⁿse wiwítta tʰe thizé tʰe thēzha?**

5. Okay, I'll tell you: **Há/Hó, uwíbtha tta miⁿkʰe.**

6. I don't approve of my son-in-law: **Wittóⁿde íⁿshoⁿ mazhi.**

7. Thank you for filling my cup: **Niīthattoⁿ wiwítta iⁿwíⁿthezhi tʰe, wíbthahoⁿ.**

8. Now I am sober: **Íⁿčʰoⁿ íⁿwazhiⁿska.**

9. You should help the chief you follow: **Gahíge uthēhe thiⁿkʰe uthēkkoⁿ tta i tʰe.**

10. Mom! Your sister-in-law is here to collect her money from you: **Naⁿhá! Mōⁿzeska ettá tʰe thīna atʰí, thishíkkoⁿ akʰa.**

21.1 UMÓⁿHOⁿ ORTHOGRAPHY

SYMBOL	UMÓⁿHOⁿ EXAMPLE	NOTES
○○	ččéshka	Held long or tense unaspirated consonant
○ʰ○	óⁿpʰoⁿ	Aspirated consonant (Unicode 02B0) - All capitals version ○ᴴ (Unicode 1D34)
○̣	x̣agé	Muted consonant (Underdot, Unicode 0323)
○̆	ttáx̌ti	Harsh consonant (Hacek, Unicode 030C)
○ⁿ○	óⁿba	Nasalized vowel (Unicode 207F) - All capitals version ○ᴺ (Unicode 1D3A) IPA suggests that a superscript "n" be used but there have been troubles with superscript format being lost when changing versions of editors so we use a Unicode symbol.
ó	wétta	Accented syllable, pitch rising (Acute, unicode 0301)
ô	shêthu	Accented vowel in which the pitch rises and falls (Circumflex, unicode 0302)
ō	āthada	Accented syllable with a moderately long vowel (Macron, Unicode 0304)
○ʔ○	tʔé	Glottal stop (unicode 02C0) (capital ʔUʔúde)
ɛ	hóⁿɛⁿgoⁿče	only used nasalized (Unicode 025B)

21.2 UMÓᴺHOᴺ ALPHABET

LETTER	NAME	UMÓᴺHOᴺ EXAMPLES	AMERICAN ENGLISH EXAMPLES	NOTES
ʔ◯	ʔáʔa	ʔíthe	uh-oh	glottal stop
a	a	ská	Lisa, father	unround low or mid central vowel
aⁿ	aⁿ	iháⁿ	uhunh	nasalized mid central vowel, like the vowel sound in English "under," "Monday," or "nun"
oⁿ	oⁿ	óⁿba, zhōⁿ, zhóⁿ	bon in French	nasalized mid back vowel or diphthong, similar to aⁿ, but sounding more o-like. It has little or no rounding. In most orthographies, aⁿ and oⁿ are not distinguished, with Dorsey and the Ponca tribe using aⁿ for both, while La Flesche and the Omaha tribe use oⁿ for both.
b	be	bimóⁿ	boy	
č	če	é-nóⁿx̌či	church	un-aspirated ch, has been marked as ch
čč	če-díⁿdiⁿ	ččéshka	gotcha	tense ch, has been marked as ch
čʰ	če-ha	iⁿčʰóⁿga	church	aspirated ch, has been marked as chʰ
d	de	dūba, dúba	dog	
e	e	shé, tʰe	weight, Las Vegas, pet	unround mid front vowel
εⁿ	εⁿ	hóⁿεⁿgoⁿče		vowel like ε, the sound in "pet", but nasalized as in "men"
g	ge	égoⁿ	girl	
h	ha	huhú	high	
i	i	sí	feet, radiant	high front vowel
iⁿ	iⁿ	wíⁿ	mean, machine, injury	high front vowel, nasalized i; without a fully pronounced n. This sound may be more central than i, more like the nasalized vowel in "fin" or "dim".
j	jútta	júba	judge	
k	ka	ččéshka	skate	simple un-aspirated k found in consonant clusters only
kk	ka-díⁿdiⁿ	kké		tense, un-aspirated k, held extra long. Marked as k in Macy orthography.
kʰ	ka-ha	akʰí	kettle, kite	aspirated k
m	mi	mí	man	

n	ni	nú	no	
o	o	hó	hold, go	o-diphthong, used in modern Omaha primarily for the male emphatic hó. Also used to represent the second part of the common prefix that may be written either weo- or wiu-
p	pe	noⁿshpí	spit	simple un-aspirated p found in consonant clusters only
pp	pe-díⁿdiⁿ	ppá		tense, un-aspirated p, held extra long. Marked as p in Macy orthography.
pʰ	pe-ha	óⁿpʰoⁿ	pit	aspirated p
pʼ	pe-ʼáʼa	thipʼíⁿze	uh-oh	glottal stop released right after p
s	sa	sábe	sun	
ṣ	sa-shtóⁿga	baṣnú		like s but muted by early nasalization before the following n
sʼ	sa-ʼáʼa	ugásʼiⁿ	uh-oh	glottal stop released right after s
sh	she	shé	ship	(linguists might use š)
ṣh	she-shtóⁿga	biṣhnáha		like sh but muted by early nasalization before the following n
shʼ	she-ʼáʼa	iⁿshʼáge	uh-oh	glottal stop released right after sh
t	te	ttáx̌ti	stop	simple un-aspirated t found in consonant clusters only
tt	te-díⁿdiⁿ	ttehé	libretto in Italian, wakatta in Japanese	tense, un-aspirated t, held extra long. Marked as t in Macy orthography.
tʰ	te-ha	atʰí	top	aspirated t
tʼ	te-ʼáʼa	tʼé	uh-oh	glottal stop released right after t
th	tha	watháwa		not in English; ledh, a sound transitioning from l to th (linguists might use r) (IPA approximation l͡ð)
u	u	ttú	blue, loot	high back round vowel
w	wau	waʼú	wing	
x̣	x̣a	x̣agé	sagen in German	soft or voiced x; may be marked as gh in Macy orthography or ǧ in Lakota orthography. Dorsey uses x.
x̌	x̌u	ttáx̌ti	Bach in German	harsh, voiceless x; marked as x in Macy orthography or ȟ in Lakota orthography. Dorsey uses q.
z	ze	zí	zoo	
zh	zhu	mīzhiⁿga	beige, vision	(linguists might use ž, Dorsey uses j)

21.3 GLOSSARY: UMÓⁿHOⁿ TO ENGLISH

GLOSSARY ABBREVIATIONS

adj.	adjective	*state*	word referring to a state or condition
adv	adverb		
art.	article	*sv.*	stative verb
aug.	augment (bi or i)	*time*	adverb of time
conj.	conjunction	*uu.*	unitary utterance (a single word orexpression, like *ouch!, hello!,* or *yes*)
dem.	demonstrative		
demand	demand particle		
epron.	emphatic pronoun	*v.*	verb
kin.	kinship term	*va.*	active verb
n.	noun	*vdat.*	dative verb
nloc.	noun of location	*vi.*	intransitive verb
nom.	proper name	*vm.*	verb of motion
num.	number	*vmodal.*	modal verb
part.	partitive	*vrecip.*	reciprocal verb
particle	particle (a small grammatical word)	*vrefl.*	reflexive verb
		vs.	stative verb
pos.	positional	*vsdat.*	dative verb used statively
possessive	possessive term	*vsuus.*	suus verb, for verbs of self action beginning with the gi- or g- prefix
pp.	postpositional phrase		
qw.	question word (like *who?* or *what?*)	*vt.*	transitive verb
sound	word referring to a sound	*vvict.*	verb of victimhood, for verbs beginning with the kke- prefix

The numbers included in each entry refer to the ULCC and UNL lesson number(s) in this textbook in which the word is introduced or used.

ʼí *va.* give   14.1

ʼíthe *va.* talk about something   15.6

ʼíⁿ *vt.* bear, pack or carry on one's back   18.1, 19.1

ʼóⁿhe *va.* flee   15.8

ʼuʼúde *vs.* holes, tattered, full of holes   10.9

á *n.* arm   10.3, 13.12

áʼoⁿsi *va.* jump onto, as a cat onto the table; jump over, skip someone, as when serving food   18.5

ābae *va.* hunting, hunt   16.2

ābanoⁿ *va.* gaze, watch, as a movie or a baseball game   18.5, 18.6

ābax̣u *va.* write down, write on   12.6, 18.5, 18.10

ābazu *va.* point at   14.1, 18.5

ābiṣnathe *va.* spread on, as buttering bread   18.5

ābitte *va.* touch, as a bannister while walking downstairs   12.6, 13.10, 18.5

ādoⁿbe *vt.* look at, aim, focus on, view 16.4, 18.5

āgaha *nloc.* on top, outside 18.5

āgasta *va.* pile up 18.5

āgashke *va.* buckle, button, fasten one bit of clothing to another 18.5

āgashoⁿ *va.* spill something on someone 18.5

āgazhi *va.* command, tell someone to do something 12.1, 13.10, 18.5

agí *va.* come back 15.6

āgioⁿ *va.* fly over, as a plane over a football game 18.5

agthé *va.* go back 14.2, 15.6

āgthe *vt.* put on, set, as putting a glass on the table; bother, annoy, blame 16.9, 18.5

āgthewathe *vs.* bothersome, annoying, troublesome 16.9

agthí *va.* arrive back here 15.6

āgthiⁿ *n.* chair, seat 10.11, 11.1, 14.3, 18.5

āgthiⁿ *va.* sit on, ride, as a horse 14.3, 18.5

agthíⁿwiⁿ *num.* eleven 11.4

āgudi *qw.* where? 18.9

āgudix̌ti *qw.* where exactly? 18.9

āhe *va.* walk on, walk along a path 18.5

ahí *va.* arrive there 15.5

āhigi *adj.* many, numerous, a lot 15.6

áhiⁿ *n.* wing 10.4

Ahó! *uu.* Hello! (used only by men) 11.5

āhoⁿ *va.* lift onto 18.5

aí *va.* come 15.5

aíathe *va.* leave, be gone away 16.2

ākkippe *va.* meet, greet 18.5

akkíthitta *pp.* across 19.4

akkíwatta *adv.* across, as in reaching across the table 15.3

ākkoⁿ *va.* lean on or against 18.5

akʰa *pos.* article/positional: the (active subject) 14.2

akʰí *va.* arrive back there 15.6

ama *pos.* article/positional: the (active plural subject) 14.2

āmoⁿx̌pi *vs.* cloudy, overcast 18.5

āne *va.* climb, hug, embrace 14.1, 15.1, 18.5

āni *vt.* fan 19.3

Áⁿkkazhi *uu.* no 11.5

ānoⁿ *qw.* how many? 11.4

ānoⁿʼoⁿ *vt.* listen to, listen, heed, obey 16.4, 18.5, 18.6

ānoⁿge *va.* run over, as with a car 18.5

áoⁿ *n.* yes 10.4, 11.5

āoⁿthe *va.* stack, throw on top, give, as a cold 18.5

astúhi *n.* elbow 19.4

āshi *nloc.* outdoors, outside 15.3

āshiatta *adv.* outside 12.2

āshka *adv.* in a little while 12.8

āthade *va.* read, recite, call 10.11, 12.2, 18.5

āthaha *va.* wear, as clothing, smear on, as makeup or warpaint 18.5

āthaskabe *v.* adhere, stick to, like wallpaper to a wall 18.5

āthatʰe *va.* eat on 18.10

athé *va.* go 14.2, 15.5

athíⁿ *va.* have, have something at hand 13.2, 14.7

athíⁿ gí *vt.* bring ("come back having") 14.7

athíⁿ moⁿthíⁿ *vt.* take ("go having") 14.7

āttashoⁿ *adv.* very, extremely, too much, an intensifier 15.3

atʰí *vi.* arrive here, he or she arrived here 14.6, 15.5

ātʰoⁿ *n.* porch 18.5

atʰóⁿshte *adv.* sometimes 18.8

awádi *qw.* why? 13.1, 18.6, 19.4

awatʰégoⁿ *qw.* how? explain this, what does it mean?, how?, explain this 11.1

āx̌e *va.* cry out, as an animal or a war cry 18.5

āzhi *adv.* other, different   17.1

āzhi *va.* put on, as gravel on a road   18.5

Bá! *uu.* male exclamation made when
   startled, as if by a sudden sound   11.5

baʼú *va.* belch, burp   17.4

baʼúde *vt.* puncture (a tire or a balloon),
   drill a hole (in wood)   17.4

babéxiⁿ *va.* sweep   17.4

babīze *va.* mop, make a floor dry   17.4

badí *va.* push off, as snow with a shovel   13.3

badóⁿ *va.* push   12.6, 13.3, 13.9, 17.4

bahá *va.* show, display   11.9, 17.4

bahé *vt.* push or shove; e.g., a person   17.4

bahí *va.* gather, pick up, collecting   14.1

bakkúwiⁿxe *vt.* push around in a circle   19.3

bamóⁿ *vt.* file, grind, smooth   17.4, 18.2

baníuski *va.* hiccup, burp   17.4

banóⁿ *n.* team, gang, flock   18.4

banóⁿge *vt.* roll something by pushing it   17.4

basáde *vt.* iron clothes, press clothes
   into a suitcase   17.4

basé *vt.* saw (wood), shear (sheep)   17.4, 18.1

basí *vt.* shoo, herd or drive animals   17.4

baṣníde *va.* shuffle or deal out (cards),
   squirt (diarrhea)   17.4

baṣnú *vt.* slide by pushing (furniture),
   reschedule   17.4

baspóⁿ *vt.* poke, nudge   17.4

bashéthoⁿ *vt.* wipe out, eliminate, write off,
   pay off a debt; in cards, lay down one's
   hand to win   17.4

baṣhná *vt.* shave, shave off, give a real close
   haircut, buzz somebody   17.4

bashóⁿthe *vt.* dump, pour out; e.g., your dirty
   dishwater outside   17.4

bashté *n.* strawberry   17.7, 17.8

bathóⁿ *va.* thrust up; e.g., with a broomstick
   to get those spider webs   17.4

batʰé *va.* sew, stitch   17.4

bawēgthi *n.* butter   18.5

baxóⁿ *va.* break off; e.g., an antler   17.4

baxthú *vt.* pierce; e.g., ears, nose, tongue,
   or belly button   17.4

baxté *vt.* shove into a bundle or bale,
   corral an animal   17.4

baxtóⁿ *vt.* pour out (water) intentionally   17.4

baxú *va.* write   10.6, 12.1, 13.3, 17.4, 19.2

bazú *va.* point (with a finger)   17.4

bazhíbe *vt.* poke; e.g., someone
   in the side   17.4

betʰóⁿ *vt.* fold   18.2

bibéniⁿ *vt.* bend by weight or pressure   17.5

bibíde *vt.* shape or mold clay, dough or
   caulk (but not snow, wood or metal)   17.5

bibīze *vt.* dry, mop, wipe   17.5

bibthāska *vt.* flatten, smash, deflate   17.5

bibtháze *vt.* bust (a water balloon
   or a blister)   17.5

bibthízhe *vt.* fell by weight, as a tree
   by leaning against it   17.5

bibthúga *vt.* flatten (dough) into a circular
   patty between one's hands   17.5, 18.1

bibútta *vt.* make a round ball (of dough)
   between one's hands   17.5

bigíze *va.* creak   17.5

bihíthe *vt.* blow away, as a person
   blowing on something   17.5

bihūttoⁿ *vt.* blow (a horn)   17.5

bikʰá *vt.* wipe   17.5, 18.2

bimóⁿ *vt.* knead (bread)   17.5

bisáde *vt.* shake out, smooth out,
   straighten out; e.g., a sheet   17.5

bishéthoⁿ *vt.* destroy by weight; e.g.,
   breaking a chair by sitting on it   17.5

bishkí *vt.* wring out (water); e.g., by
   kneading on a washboard   17.5

biṣhnáha *vt.* sand, make smooth
by rubbing   17.5, 18.2

bixǒⁿ *v.* break, broken   17.5

bixtóⁿ *vt.* get fluid from a dispensing
machine   17.5

bixǭⁿ *vt.* blow up (balloon or mattress),
blow out (candle)   17.5

bīze *vs.* dry (the state of being dry)
16.6, 17.1, 17.2

bīzethe *va.* dry out, cause to dry   16.6

bóⁿ *va.* scream, yell, call   10.5, 19.5

btháska *sv.* flat   11.8, 17.1

bthé *vi.* I go   14.5

bthóⁿ *n.* smell, odor, odoriferous   10.10, 17.1

bthúga *vs.* round and flat   18.1

Bushéam! *uu.* male exclamation of surprise:
Wow! Check this out!   11.5

bútta *vs.* round   13.12

Būu-hūu-! *uu.* male exclamation of
direct surprise, or on hearing
surprising news   11.5

ččéshka *vs.* short   10.7, 13.12

dáthiⁿ *vs.* drunk, intoxicated   19.5

dáthiⁿ-giudoⁿ *vs.* drunkard, alcoholic   19.5

de *conj.* but, when   15.8

díⁿdiⁿ *vs.* rigid, stiff   18.2

dóⁿbe *va.* see   12.2, 13.3, 16.9, 19.1, 19.5

dóⁿbewathe *vs.* visible   16.9

dúba *num.* four   10.5, 11.4

dūba *adj.* some   15.6

Dúda *uu.* directed utterance for getting
attention (both sexes): Hey!, Hey
there!   11.5, 14.6

dúde *adv.* this way   14.6

dúdiha *adv.* over here, as a place
to move   14.6

é *va.* say   12.2, 13.5

é *epron.* he, she, it, they, him, her, them;
generic third person emphatic
pronoun   14.8

ebé *qw.* who?   11.1

edādoⁿ *qw.* what? (specifically)   14.1, 14.3

edéshe *qw.* what did you say?   13.5

edí *adv.* there, in the aforementioned
location, there exist   15.1

Eē-! *uu.* female directed utterance: Are you
kidding me?!   11.5

Eē-shtoⁿna! *uu.* Baloney!, directed utterance,
humorously accusing someone of pulling
your leg (both sexes)   11.5

égaxe *adv.* around, surrounding, around the
periphery   15.3

égithe *conj.* beware!, it might happen,
after a while   13.9, 15.8, 15.10

égoⁿ *adv.* like, like that   14.2, 14.3

egóⁿ *conj.* having, the foregoing
having happened . . .   14.2

égoⁿ *conj.* so, therefore, thereupon, for that
reason; yes, I agree, it is so, mmhm   14.7

égthoⁿge *kin.* husband   16.5

é-nóⁿxči *adv.* alone, by him- or herself   19.5

eóⁿ *qw.* how?   11.3

eshóⁿ *adv.* close, near, close together,
very close   14.6, 15.3

ethégoⁿ *va.* think   13.2

ettá *possessive* his, her, hers, its, their,
theirs   14.9

ettá *adv.* that way, in that direction   15.1

Éwoⁿ *uu.* that's why, that's the reason,
he's to blame   15.9

gá *dem.* that exact one   14.6

Gá! *uu.* Here!, as when giving something
to someone   14.6

ga'á *va.* fail, as at chopping wood   17.6

ga'é *va.* dig a hole, as to put your tomato plant in   17.6

ga'óⁿsi *va.* bounce, as on a trampoline (not bounce a ball)   17.6

ga'úde *va.* make a hole   17.6

gabīze *vt.* dry something in the open air, as laundry   17.6

gabízhe *vt.* snap, shake out (a washrag), blink (an eye)   17.6

gabthá *va.* open up, spread out (a bedsheet); bloom (a flower)   17.6

gabtháze *va.* bust by falling, like a ceramic cat's head   17.6

gabthóⁿ *va.* make a stink, as by moving something spoiled through the air   17.6

gačʰákki *vt.* smack, clap, slap someone up   17.6

gahá *nloc.* on, upon   15.3

gahé *vt.* comb someone's hair   17.6

gahíge *n.* chief   11.8

gahīthe *vs.* blowing or drifting in the wind, like leaves, grass or cottonwood down   17.6

gahóⁿ *vt.* lift something heavy, like furniture or a boat   17.6

gaīⁿxe *va.* wheeze, trying to draw breath   17.6

gakkúge *v.* thump, the sound of something hollow falling   17.6

gakkúwiⁿxe *v.* circling, spinning, moving in a spiral, going around in circles   14.7, 15.1

gappāmoⁿgthe *v.* lower the head to charge, like a bull   17.6

gasáppi *v.* lash, whip, snap a towel   17.6

gasáthu *vt.* rattle, shake a gourd   17.6

gasé *vt.* chop, cut, as a deck of cards   17.6

gaskébe *vt.* scrape   18.2

gaṣné *vs.* frayed   17.6

gasóⁿthiⁿ *adv.* tomorrow   12.7

gaspé *v.* settle out, like muddy water   17.6, 18.10

gasúde *vt.* trim, prune   17.6

gashéthoⁿ *vs.* broken up, destroyed   18.8

gashíbe *adv.* out, emerging from anything but a house   15.3

gashūde *vs.* whiteout, blizzard, snowstorm, muddy water   17.6

gáthe *vt.* give, donate, give away

gáthu *adv.* there, that specified area   15.3

gathúzhe *v.* slosh   17.6

gattūbe *n.* wrecked   18.4

gawákʰega *vs.* seasick, carsick, nauseous from the environment   17.6

gawíⁿxe *va.* tilt, swerve, bank, as a bird or airplane   17.6

gāx̌á *n.* branch, tree branch   15.1

gax̌íxe *vt.* crack   18.2

gax̌óⁿ *vt.* break by striking   17.6

-gax̌thoⁿ *kin.* wife   16.5

gax̌ábe *v.* scrape, skin; e.g., a knee or an elbow from falling   17.6

gax̌áde *vt.* cover   18.2

gāx̌e *va.* make, do   11.9, 12.2, 13.3, 13.4, 19.5

ge *pos.* article/positional: the (scattered)   14.1

gí *va.* come, come back   12.1, 14.2, 14.3, 15.6, 19.2

gi'íⁿ *vt.* pack one's own on one's back   19.1

giāx̌e *vdat.* make for someone   19.5

gīboⁿ *vdat.* call someone over   19.5

gīdoⁿbe *vdat.* look at for someone's benefit   19.5

gigtháthe *vsuus.* volunteer, offer to give of oneself   19.2

gigtháx̌ube *vsuus.* boast, praise oneself   19.2

gigtházu *vsuus.* recover, wake from a coma   19.2

gigthé *vsuus.* take after, as mom or dad   19.2

gigthíwagazu *vsuus.* settle one's own affairs, as in writing a will   19.2

gíkkide *vdat.* shoot for someone   19.5

gíkʰu *vdat.* invite someone   19.5, 19.6

ginā *vt.* ask for one's own back   19.1

gīna *vdat.* ask for, collect a debt   19.5

giní *vsuus.* recover, get well   19.2

ginóⁿkkuwiⁿx̣e *vsuus.* run around trying to get things done   19.2

gīnoⁿshe *vdat.* confiscate, take something away from someone   19.5

gióⁿ *va.* fly   10.5, 11.2, 11.9, 13.4

gīoⁿtha *vdat.* throw something at someone   19.5

gīōⁿthe *vt.* abandon one's own   19.1

gīōⁿze *vdat.* teach someone   19.5

gippáx̣u *vsuus.* sign up, enlist   19.2

gisíthe *va.* remember   13.4, 19.2

gisíⁿ *vsuus.* revive, recover consciousness   19.2

gis̟nāthe *vt.* paint one's own, smear one's own, polish one's own   19.1

gīshi *vdat.* ask someone to do something   19.5

gīshoⁿ *vsdat.* pleased, happy, approving   19.5

gīthe *vsdat.* happy, blissful   19.5

gīthikkuthe *vdat.* hurry for someone's benefit   19.5

gīttex̣i *vsdat.* suffering difficulties, hard times   19.5

gīttoⁿga *vsdat.* conceited, boastful   19.5

gīudoⁿ *vsdat.* glad, like something, feel good   19.5

gīwazhiⁿska *vsdat.* sober, sane   19.5

gīzha *vdat.* deny or doubt an allegation   19.5

gīzhu *vsdat.* lucky   19.5

gōⁿtha *va.* want, want to   11.10, 13.4, 16.9

gōⁿthawathe *vs.* desirable   16.9

góⁿzhiⁿga *va.* not know how   13.4

gthátʰe *vt.* eat one's own   19.1

gthé *va.* go back   15.6, 19.2

gthêboⁿ *num.* ten   10.10, 11.4

gthêboⁿhíⁿwiⁿ *num.* hundred   11.4

gthedóⁿ *n.* hawk   10.10, 11.8, 11.9, 15.1

gthéze *vs.* striped   11.3, 17.1

gthézhe *vs.* spotted   11.3

gthí *va.* arrive back here   15.6, 19.2

gthíze *vt.* take one's own, grab one's own   19.1

gthíⁿ *va.* sit, sit down   10.10, 11.2, 12.1, 13.1

gthóⁿ *v.* bad language, name-calling   17.2

gthóⁿthiⁿ *vs.* crazy   19.4

gthūba *adj.* all of it   15.6

gúdiha *adv.* away, over there, as a place to move   14.6

há *n.* leather, hide, skin   10.3, 11.7

Há *uu.* female response to being hailed: Yes? What?   11.5

háshi *nloc.* behind, last   15.3

hāthe *n.* clothes, clothing   16.7

hátheze *vi.* survive, come back safely from a place of danger   14.6

hāzi *n.* grapes   15.7

hazízige *n.* rubber, balloon; bandage, stretchy fabric   17.7

házhiⁿga *n.* rope, strap, cord   14.1

-háⁿ *kin.* mother   16.2

hé *n.* horn, antler   10.3, 11.7, 11.8

hébe *n.* part, piece, portion   14.9, 17.1

héga *n.* buzzard, vulture   14.2, 14.7

Heshpaiúni *nom.* Spanish, Hispanic, Mexican   11.1

hethúbazhoⁿ *n.* swing   14.1

hí *n.* tooth, teeth   10.3, 13.12

hí *n.* stalk, stem, trunk, tree, plant   11.7

hí *va.* arrive there   15.3, 15.4, 19.2

híde *nloc.* down bottom, base,
   low down   15.3, 17.1, 17.2

hīga *n.* legend, traditional tale   14.5

híⁿ *n.* body hair, animal hair   10.4

hiⁿbé *n.* shoe, moccasin   10.5, 11.1, 13.5

hiⁿbthíⁿge *n.* beans   19.3

Híⁿiⁿ-! *uu.* female exclamation at
   hearing surprising news   11.5

Hīⁿiⁿ-thāa-! *uu.* female exclamation
   of direct surprise   11.5

Hó *uu.* male response to being hailed:
   Yes? What?   11.5

hôⁿ *n.* night   10.4

hôⁿbthe *va.* dream   15.9

hôⁿde *n.* last night   10.11, 19.1

-hoⁿga *kin.* man's sister-in-law   16.5

hóⁿt'ega *n.* fly   14.3

hôⁿwidetʰoⁿ *time* midnight   17.2

hú *n.* voice   10.3

huhú *n.* fish   10.3

Húttoⁿga *nom.* Winnebago, Hochunk   11.1

í *n.* mouth   10.3, 13.12

í *vi.* come   14.3, 15.4, 19.2

i *aug.* augment: plural or action   14.3

í ākkigthe *vr.* kiss   18.2

i'oⁿ *vt.* cultivate   18.7

íbahoⁿ *va.* know   12.4, 13.3, 13.10, 18.7, 18.8

ībamoⁿ *n.* file, file with it   18.2, 18.10

ībetʰoⁿ *n.* wrapper, skin, cloth or paper
   to wrap something in   18.2

ídabe *adv.* in the middle; e.g., of a
   tribal circle   15.3

idādoⁿ *qw.* what?   11.1

ídathe *v.* be born   15.9

īdiⁿdiⁿ *n.* brace   18.2

īe *n.* word, language, speech   11.1, 12.1

ié *va.* speak   12.6

ígahi *vt.* mix in   18.7

ígaskoⁿthe *va.* try, attempt, taste
   11.10, 12.2, 13.4, 18.7

īgaxade *n.* cover, lid   18.2

ígithe *vt.* find one's own   19.1

ígthebe *va.* vomit up   15.4

íha *n.* lips   10.3, 13.12

iháⁿ *n.* mother, his or her mother   10.4, 15.3

íhe *vt.* pass, get through an obstructed
   route   16.9, 18.7

íhethi'awathe *vs.* impassable   16.9

íhusa *vt.* scold   18.7

Í-jí-jí-! *uu.* a cry when burned:
   Ouch-ouch-ouch!   11.5

íkketʰiⁿ *vvict.* bump oneself   19.4

íkki *n.* chin   18.2

íkkihiⁿ *n.* whiskers, beard, chin hair   18.2

íkkihiⁿīgaskebe *n.* razor   18.2

íkkiīthidoⁿ *n.* rein   18.2

íkʰu *vt.* invite   18.7

ímoⁿthe *vt.* avenge, take revenge on,
   lay for someone   18.7

ímoⁿxe *va.* ask, inquire, ask a question
   12.4, 13.10, 18.7

inégi *kin.* uncle, his or her uncle   15.2

íniethe *vt.* injure   18.7

ínitʰe *vt.* scold   18.7

īnoⁿge *n.* fare, ticket, gas money   18.2

ínoⁿhiⁿ *vt.* permit, allow, agree to   18.7

ínoⁿxithe *vt.* chase   18.7

ísabe *vt.* suffer   18.7

íshkoⁿ *vt.* move something   16.9

íshkoⁿazhiwathe *vs.* immovable   16.9

ishtá *n.* eye   11.8, 13.12

íshte *vt.* embarrassed, ashamed of something
   or someone   16.9, 18.7

íshtewathe *vs.* embarrassing, shameful   16.9

Ishtíthiⁿkʰe *n.* Trickster   14.2

ishtíthi^{n}k^{h}e *n.* monkey 14.2

ithābaṣnu *n.* scissors, shaver, any tool to cut off hair 18.9

íthade *vt.* read to 18.7, 18.10

ithádi *n.* father, his or her father 14.3, 16.2

ithāditha-i *n.* Indian agent 16.10

ithāgaxade *n.* lid, cover 18.9

íthakko^{n} *vt.* lean on 18.9

íthappe *vt.* wait for 18.7, 18.9

īthawa *n.* counter, count with 18.2, 18.10

íthe *va.* find, discover 14.1, 14.9, 15.3, 18.7, 19.1

īthibtho^{n} *n.* perfume, cologne, aftershave 18.2

íthibtho^{n} *vt.* scent, smell 18.7

íthido^{n}do^{n} *vt.* jar, shake 18.7

īthino^{n}ge *n.* wheel 18.2

íthise *vt.* cut 18.7

íthishi *vt.* feed 18.7

īthizha *n.* washcloth, washrag, sponge, soap 18.2

íthizha *vt.* wash 18.7

íthizho^{n}zho^{n} *vt.* jar, shake, as a spray can 18.7

ítte *vt.* touch 18.7

ittígo^{n}tha-i *n.* president of the United States 16.10

ittígo^{n}the *n.* grandfather, president of the United States 16.10

ittó^{n}thi^{n} *nloc.* ahead, as in a race 15.3

it^{h}éthe *va.* set, place, or put away standing 12.2

it^{h}i^{n} *vt.* hit 18.7, 18.10

ít'athe *vt.* detest, loathe, dislike 16.9, 18.7

ít'athewathe *vs.* detestable, despicable, loathsome 16.9

íwakhega *vt.* sicken, make someone sick 18.7

íxa *vi.* laugh, ridicule, laugh at

íxawathe *vs.* comical, funny 16.9

íxaxa *v.* laughing, ridicule, laugh at 14.3, 18.7

izházhe *n.* name 10.6, 12.6

í^{n} *va.* wear 13.5

Í^{n}! *uu.* female cry of startled fright: Yikes! Eek! 11.5

í^{n}'e *n.* rock, stone 14.1

í^{n}'ezhi^{n}ga *n.* gravel 18.6

í^{n}'ut^{h}i^{n} *n.* handgame 9.13

í^{n}č^{h}o^{n} *adv.* now, just now 10.7, 14.9

i^{n}č^{h}ó^{n}ga *n.* mouse 10.7

i^{n}č^{h}ó^{n}gawathat^{h}e *n.* cheese 16.4, 17.8

i^{n}dé *n.* face 10.5, 13.12, 18.2

i^{n}déīgaxade *n.* veil 18.2

i^{n}déugaxe *n.* portrait, picture 18.10, 19.5

i^{n}gthó^{n}ga *n.* cat 10.10

i^{n}gthó^{n}si^{n}ṣnede *n.* mountain lion, cougar, puma, panther 15.9

i^{n}k^{h}éde *n.* shoulder 13.12

i^{n}sh'áge *n.* old man; in cards, the king 10.9, 11.2, 14.2

kkáshi *adv.* for a long time 13.11

kkāxe *n.* crow, bustle 11.8, 11.9

kké *n.* turtle 10.5, 11.7, 11.8, 11.9

kképpa *n.* turtle head; the playing card suit of diamonds 11.7

kki *conj.* if, when 13.9, 14.2, 14.3

kki *conj.* and it so happened that... 15.6

kkíde *v.* shoot, shoot at, shoot cards 14.7, 18.2, 19.5

kkigthāni *vrefl.* fan oneself 19.3

kkigthíauzhi *vrefl.* change, transform oneself, as a shapeshifter 19.3

kkigthíso^{n}the *vrefl.* turn around, wheel, swap ends, as a buffalo 19.3

kkigthíshko^{n}shko^{n} *vrefl.* wriggle, squirm 19.3

kkigthízha *vrefl.* wash up, as for dinner, wash oneself 19.3

kkihóⁿ *vrefl.* lift oneself up   19.3

kkikkáꭕe *vrefl.* make for oneself   19.3

kkikkína *vrecip.* fight or brawl with each other   19.3

kkinóⁿnoⁿge *n.* car, automobile   13.6

kkinóⁿse *vrefl.* trip, stumble, fall   19.3

kkióⁿhe *vrefl.* flee, run away   19.3

kkiōⁿthe *vrefl.* throw oneself at   19.3

kkippákkuwiⁿꭕe *vrefl.* turn themselves around, as a stampeding herd   19.3

kkiūdazhi *vrefl.* they don't get along well together   19.3

-kkoⁿ *kin.* grandmother, mother-in-law   16.1, 16.5

kkóⁿde *n.* plum   11.7, 14.4

kkóⁿdehi *n.* plum tree   11.7

kkóⁿdeni *n.* plum juice   11.7

kkóⁿge *nloc.* near   15.3

kku'é *va.* rushing forward, headlong   15.8

kkúge *n., num.* box, thousand   11.4, 16.2, 18.2

kkúkkusi *n.* pig, hog, swine   19.4

kʰagé *n.* friend   16.10

kʰe *pos.* article/positional: the (lying)   14.1

kʰí *va.* arrive back there   10.5, 15.6, 19.2

ma *pos.* article/positional: the (non-subject distributive plural)   14.3

má *n.* snow   10.4, 15.9, 16.6

mā'é *vt.* slice thin, whittle, carve   17.8

mábadi *n.* snowplow   16.6

māgiꭕe *vt.* carve, whittle, cut meat, fruit, or other food   17.8

māse *vt.* cut   17.8

māski *n.* notch, notches at the end of a bow for attachment of the string   17.8

máthe *vi.* snow, snowing   16.6

māttube *n.* ground meat   17.8

māꭓoⁿ *vt.* cut with a knife; e.g., watermelon or bread   17.8

māꭓu *vt.* engrave, carve, notch   17.8, 18.1

maⁿčʰú *n.* grizzly bear   10.7, 11.8, 11.9

mé *n.* spring (the season)   10.4

mégoⁿ *conj.* also, as well as, in addition; used for including a party besides the first one mentioned   16.1

mí *n.* sun, month, moon   10.4, 11.9, 18.2

migá *vs.* female (animal only)   10.5

miīdoⁿbe *n.* clock, watch, time, o'clock   11.1, 18.2

miīthawa *n.* calendar   18.2

mikká *n.* raccoon   11.7, 11.9

mikká'e *n.* star   10.9

mikkáha *n.* raccoon skin, quarter dollar, the price of a raccoon skin   11.7

miīwathiꭓe *kin.* daughter-in-law   16.5

míꭓa *n.* duck, goose   10.6

miīzhiⁿga *n.* girl   11.2, 14.2

môⁿ *n.* arrow   14.1

môⁿde *n.* bow   10.11, 14.1

moⁿdé *n.* boat   11.9

móⁿga *n.* skunk; in cards, a skunk hand   10.5

mōⁿge *n.* chest (anat.)   11.8

moⁿgthíⁿ *vm.* go back, walk back   19.2

moⁿhíⁿ *n.* grass   17.3

móⁿhiⁿ *n.* knife   10.4

moⁿkkóⁿsabe *n.* coffee   12.5

moⁿsóⁿthiⁿ *nloc.* across, side, on the far side   15.3

móⁿshi *nloc.* above, high, up, overhead, high up   15.3, 17.1

moⁿshíattaha *adv.* further off   15.6

móⁿshoⁿ *n.* feather, plume   10.6, 13.6

moⁿshtíⁿge *n.* rabbit   10.10, 14.2

moⁿthíⁿ *va.* walk, go   10.8, 11.2, 11.9, 12.1, 13.2, 19.2

moⁿthíⁿkka *n.* earth, soil   11.9, 15.2, 15.3

moⁿthóⁿ *v.* steal   14.9, 18.1

moⁿttánoⁿha *adv.* wild, like kids running around the woods barefoot   19.5

móⁿtʰe *nloc.* in, inside   15.3

moⁿx̌pí *n.* cloud, clouds   11.9, 13.7

móⁿx̌e *n.* sky   15.1

móⁿze *n.* metal, iron   10.6, 11.8, 11.9

moⁿzé *n.* breast, udder   11.7

móⁿzemoⁿ *n.* bullet, shot   14.1, 17.3

moⁿzéni *n.* milk   10.6, 11.7

mõⁿzeska *n.* silver, money, dollar   19.5

móⁿze-wēogadoⁿ *n.* nails   18.10

moⁿzhóⁿ *n.* land   14.1

moⁿzhóⁿ ūdoⁿ gáx̌e *v.* make peace   15.6

mūbix̌oⁿ *va.* blow forcefully, as with a bellows   17.9

mūbthaze *va.* explode, as a gun when fired   17.9

mūdada *vs.* ache, aching pain   17.9

mūgix̌e *va.* make a furrow by shooting   17.9

mūgthoⁿ *va.* wander away, stray off   17.9

mūhatheza *va.* come away safe from being shot at   17.9

mūhega *vt.* wound slightly by shooting   17.9

mūhegazhi *v.* loud gunshot, kill many or wound badly by shooting   17.9

mūhithe *vt.* blow away, as with a fan   17.9

mūhoⁿ *va.* shoot all day until nightfall   17.9

mūkkoⁿ *vt.* fillip, tap to loosen something   17.9

mūkkuge *v.* make rumble by shooting against something hollow   17.9

mūppa *vs.* strong (coffee or cider), as when oversteeped   17.9

mūsisi *v.* shooting pain   17.9

mūshnoⁿ *vt.* miss the mark when shooting   17.9

mūx̌pa *va.* peck with the head, as a woodpecker   17.9

mūx̌toⁿ *va.* flow, like water from a water faucet   17.9

mūx̌a *vs.* standing up, like ducks on the water, or unruly hair   17.9

mūx̌adoⁿ *vs.* bushy haired, as a person, sheep, or scared cat   17.9

mūza *vs.* stick up, protrude, plant (fenceposts)   17.9

mūzhoⁿ *vt.* winnow, sift, strain out   17.9

nā *va.* ask for, beg, request   12.5, 13.8, 18.1, 19.1, 19.5

nāʼa *v.* fail at burning or freezing   17.7

nābize *v.* dry something by heat   17.7

nābthaze *v.* explode   17.7

nābthoⁿ *v.* smell of fire, incense, or cooking   17.7

nādaze *v.* sparks, as from a car battery, flint, or cinders   17.7

nāgoⁿbe *vs.* bright, shining   17.7

nāhegazhi *vs.* flare, spreading fire, burning well, all lit up   17.7

nākkade *vs.* hot, heat   17.7

nākkoⁿ *vs.* light   17.7

nāoⁿba *v.* burn all night till dawn   17.7

nāsabe *vs.* scorched, burnt black   17.7

nāsade *vs.* ironed (clothes)   17.7

nāsage *vs.* crisp, hardened by heat   17.7

nāsagi *vt.* harden by heat   17.7

nāskoⁿ *v.* melt, thaw   17.7

nāshta *vs.* warm (water)   17.7

nāttaze *vs.* shiny in little spots, like stars in a planetarium, or lights from the chinks in a woodstove at night   17.7

nāttube *vs.* tender, cooked so tender the meat just falls off the bones   17.7

nāttûbthiⁿ *vs.* warped, crinkly, as the packages you left in the back seat of your car on a hot day   17.7

nāt'e *vs.* sunburn; die by electrocution 17.7

nāx̌thiⁿ *v.* fire, flame, burn 17.7

nāx̌ude *vs.* scorched 17.7

nāx̌u *v.* brand (cattle) 17.7

náze *nloc.* behind, in back of 15.3

nāzi *v.* singe 17.7

nāzhide *vs.* red hot (in a fire), ripe fruit turned red in the sun 17.7

naⁿ- *kin.* mother (addressing only) 16.2

-negi *kin.* uncle, mother's brother 16.4

neúthishoⁿ *n.* lake 19.4

ní *n.* water, liquid 10.4, 11.7, 11.8, 14.1

níabix̌e *n.* beer 16.8

niáshiⁿga *n.* person 14.2, 14.3

nîde *vs.* ripe, cooked, done 10.11

níde *n.* buttocks 10.11

níde-ūthishi *n.* pants, trousers 18.4

nídushi *n.* pants, trousers 18.4

nié *vs.* hurting, in pain 13.12

niīthattoⁿ *n.* cup 15.2

níkkashiⁿga *n.* people 14.3

niníba *n.* pipe, peace pipe 15.6

-nisi *kin.* son or daughter (father speaking) 16.2

niskíthe *n.* salt 18.7

Niskíthettoⁿwoⁿgthoⁿ *nom.* Lincoln, Nebraska 16.6

nítta *vs.* alive, live, living 13.12, 18.1

nittá *n.* ear, external ear 13.12

niúoⁿ *va.* swim 13.1, 14.8

níx̌a *n.* stomach, belly 15.4

noⁿ *adv.* regularly, routinely, habitually 13.5, 15.4

nóⁿ *vs.* adult, grown up, mature 10.4

noⁿ *adv.* only 14.8

noⁿ'á *va.* fail at kicking; e.g., a soccer ball 17.3

noⁿ'óⁿ *va.* hear 13.1, 13.9, 16.6

noⁿ'óⁿ-kʰithe *vd.* allow to hear 16.8

noⁿ'óⁿthe *vt.* cause to hear 16.6

noⁿbá *num.* two 10.5, 11.4

noⁿbé *n.* hand 10.5, 11.8, 13.12, 18.2

noⁿbéhi *n.* finger 13.12

noⁿbéībikʰa *n.* hand towel, napkin, handkerchief 18.2

noⁿbtháska *vt.* flatten by trampling or stomping, as an aluminum can 17.3

noⁿbtháze *v.* explode underfoot (a balloon, a milk carton), flat tire 17.3

noⁿbthízhe *vt.* push someone down 17.3

noⁿdáze *n.* blister 17.5

nôⁿde *n.* heart, the suit of hearts 10.11

nóⁿde *n.* wall 10.11, 11.1

nóⁿge *vi.* roll, like a cart; run, as a car or machine 16.6, 17.1, 18.2

nóⁿgethe *vt.* operate, run a machine or an event 16.6

nóⁿkka *n.* back (anat.) 11.8

nóⁿkka *vs.* hurt, injured 13.12, 14.7, 16.6

nóⁿkkathe *vt.* injure, cause injury 16.6

noⁿkkúwiⁿx̌e *va.* go around in circles on foot 19.2

noⁿóⁿba *va.* walk, run, or dance all night until daybreak 17.3

nóⁿppa *n.* chokecherry, cherry 11.7

nóⁿppahi *n.* cherry tree 11.7

nóⁿppani *n.* cherry juice 11.7

nóⁿppe *va.* fear an immediate threat 16.9

noⁿppéhi *vs.* hungry 16.4, 19.5

nóⁿppewathe *vs.* scary, dangerous 16.9

noⁿsági *va.* harden by walking; e.g., a path to school through the snow 17.3

noⁿsé *vt.* mow, cut something low to the ground, like grass or sod 17.3

noⁿstáppi *va.* prance (horses), march (cheerleaders), lifting one's knees high 17.3

noⁿshábe *vs.* shade, shaded 17.3

no^{n}shkí *n.* the cranial part of the head, as opposed to the face 13.12

no^{n}ṣhnáha *va.* slip (while walking) 17.3

no^{n}shpí *va.* shell corn 17.3

no^{n}shtó^n *va.* stop running, walking, dancing or kicking 12.4, 17.3

no^{n}thí^{n}ge *v.* erode (ruts in a gravel road, or roadkill that is run over until it is gone) 17.3

no^{n}ttó^{n}ze *va.* bounce off of something hard, like a shield, or hail off a roof 17.3

no^{n}ttūbe *v.* grind, grind up, milled, mealy 17.3

no^{n}t^{h}é *va.* kick 13.1, 17.3, 13.9

no^{n}x̌ó^n *v.* break, broken 17.3

no^{n}x̌páthe *vt.* knock over by kicking or by bumping into it while walking 17.3

no^{n}x̌tó^n *vt.* strain, pour out water against a ladle so the rice remains 17.3

no^{n}x̣íde *n.* ear, hearing, internal ear 13.12

no^{n}x̣íde-thi^{n}ge *vs.* naughty, disobedient 18.8

no^{n}zhí^n *va.* stand, stand up 10.6, 11.2, 11.9, 12.1, 13.1, 17.3

no^{n}zhī^n *n.* rain 11.9, 12.9

no^{n}zhí^{n}ha *n.* hair of the head, scalp 10.6, 13.12

nú *n.* man 10.4, 11.2, 14.2

nú *n.* potato 14.1

núde *n.* throat, neck 10.5, 13.12

nudó^n *n.* warrior 14.3, 15.5

nudó^{n}ho^{n}ga *n.* war chief, leader, boss 14.2

nugá *vs.* male (animal only) 10.5

nuṣhná^n *n.* otter 10.6

núx̣e *n.* ice 17.7

nuzó^n *va.* skate, sled 13.1, 14.8

núzhi^{n}ga *n.* boy, young man 11.2, 14.2

ó^n *va.* do, behave habitually 13.5

ó^n *vt.* use 16.9

ó^{n}ba *n.* day, daylight 10.5, 17.2

ó^{n}bathe *adv.* today 12.7

o^{n}gú *epron.* we, us, emphatic pronoun, we or me 14.8

o^{n}gútta *possessive* our, ours 14.9

Ó^{n}ho^n *uu.* yes (nineteenth century) 11.5

Ō^{n}o^n-hō^{n}o^n-hō^{n}o^n-! *uu.* groan of internal pain 11.5

Ō^{n}o^n-nō^{n}o^n-nō^{n}o^n-! *uu.* groan of pain due to external injury 11.5

ó^{n}p^{h}a^n *n.* elk 10.5, 11.8, 11.9

ó^{n}tha thétha *va.* throw, throw away 14.2

ō^{n}the *vt.* throw, throw away, abandon, discard 19.1

ō^{n}thino^n *adv.* almost 19.4

ó^{n}wathe *vs.* usable 16.9

ppá *n.* nose 10.5, 13.12

ppá *n.* head, whole head including the face 10.5, 13.12

ppáde *va.* cut up, butcher, slaughter, do surgery 15.8, 18.1

ppaháshi *nloc.* above, on top 15.3

ppahé *n.* hill 14.1, 15.3, 15.4

Ppáhe-wáthahuni *nom.* Devouring Hill 15.4

ppāhi^n *n.* porcupine, quillwork 19.4

ppáho^n *vi.* arise, get up 14.3

ppahó^{n}ga *nloc.* before, ahead, first, in front 15.3

ppaí *vs.* sharp 17.1

ppamú *adv.* downhill 15.3

ppasó^n *n.* bald eagle 11.9

ppashtó^{n}ga *n.* moose, Rocky Mountain sheep 19.5

ppāshude *vs.* bloody nose 16.6

ppāshudethe *va.* cause a nosebleed 16.6

Ppāthi^n *nom.* Pawnee 19.6

Ppáx̌ude *nom.* Ioway 19.6

ppāze *n.* evening, twilight 17.1

ppé *n.* forehead 10.5, 13.12

ppéde *n.* fire, match 11.7, 14.1

ppedéni *n.* firewater, whisky, hard liquor 11.7

ppethâbthiⁿ *num.* eight 11.4

ppéthoⁿ**ba** *num.* seven 11.4

ppéttoⁿ *n.* crane 19.1

ppí *n.* liver 10.5

ppí'oⁿ *vt.* fix, repair 18.1

ppiâzhi *vs.* bad, ugly, evil, rancid 11.3, 16.6

ppiâzhithe *vi.* go rancid 16.6

s'áthe *vs.* sour 10.9, 16.7

Sabá! *uu.* Beware! (woman's command) 17.2

sabázhi *adv.* suddenly, unexpectedly 19.3

sábe *vs.* black 10.6, 11.3, 18.1

sagí *vs.* hard 10.6, 13.12, 17.1

sakkáid *n.* watermelon 17.8

sákkathide *n.* watermelon 17.8

sáttoⁿ *num.* five 11.4

sí *n.* foot 10.6, 11.8, 13.12

sí *n.* seed 18.4

sidādi *adv.* yesterday 12.7

sígthe *n.* footprints, trail, track 19.1

sithúkkathiⁿ *vs.* barefoot 18.1, 19.5, 19.6

síⁿ**de** *n.* tail 10.6, 11.7, 11.9

ská *vs.* white, vanilla (ice cream) 10.10, 11.3, 11.8, 17.1

skīge *vs.* heavy 19.1

skíthe *vs.* sweet 10.10, 16.7, 18.1

ṣná *n.* scar 18.1

ṣnáthe *vt.* smear, spread, paint, polish, butter 18.1, 19.1

ṣnéde *sv.* long, tall 11.8, 13.12

ṣní *vs.* cold (an object) 10.6, 10.10, 13.12

sóⁿ *vs.* pale, white, distant white 10.6, 11.3, 11.8

-soⁿ**ga** *kin.* younger brother 16.3

shábe *vs.* dark, chocolate (ice cream) 10.6, 11.3, 11.8

sháge *n.* nail (anat.), claw, hoof, talon, fingernail, toenail 10.6, 11.8, 13.12

Shaóⁿ *nom.* Sioux 11.1

sháppe *num.* six 11.4

sháppenoⁿ**ba** *num.* twelve 11.4

shé *n.* apple 10.6, 11.7, 14.1

shê *dem.* that 14.6

shêhi *dem.* that yonder 14.6

shéhi *n.* apple tree 11.7

shêhi tʰ**e gthí**ⁿ *n.* people living somewhere else far away 14.6

shêhi tʰ**e no**ⁿ**zhí**ⁿ *n.* soldier or traveler in other lands far away 14.6

shêhithu *adv.* that area over yonder 15.3

shémizhiⁿ**ga** *n.* girl, little girl 11.2

shéni *n.* apple cider 11.7

Shénoⁿ *uu.* directed utterance indicating that one is finished speaking 11.5

shénuzhiⁿ**ga** *n.* boy, little boy 11.2

shêthu *adv.* that area 15.3

shetʰ**ó**ⁿ**na** *adv.* still, yet 18.8

-shie *kin.* woman's brother-in-law 16.5

-shikkoⁿ *kin.* woman's sister-in-law 16.5

shínuda *n.* dog 10.6, 14.4

shínuja *n.* puppy 10.7

shíⁿ *vs.* fat, chubby 17.1, 18.1

shíⁿ**gazhi**ⁿ**ga** *n.* child, baby, toddler, doll, small child 11.2, 14.2

shkāde *va.* play 12.2, 13.1

ṣhná *vs.* bald 17.1

ṣhnábe *vs.* dirty 10.6, 10.10

Shóⁿ**!** *uu.* done, directed utterance indicating that we are done with an activity 11.5

shóⁿ**ge** *n.* horse 10.6, 14.4

shóⁿ**kka** *num.* nine 11.4

shóⁿ**sho**ⁿ *adv.* still, continually, always 12.9

shóⁿ**the** *va.* spill 16.7

shóⁿ**tto**ⁿ**ga** *n.* wolf 19.3

-shte *adv.* at all; -ever, as in whatever 16.1

shti *adv.* too, also 14.8, 15.1

shtóⁿ**ga** *vs.* soft 10.10, 11.8, 13.12, 17.1

shúde *n.* smoke 17.5, 17.7

shugá *vs.* thick 10.6

tha'á *va.* fail at eating; e.g., spit out something too hot 17.2

tha'é *vs.* miserable, wretched, pitiable, pitiful 16.6

tha'éthe *vt.* pity, feel pity for 16.6

thabīze *vt.* absorb, drink dry 17.2

thâbthiⁿ *num.* three 10.11, 11.4

thadóⁿ *va.* suck 17.2

thagthóⁿ *va.* cuss, say bad things 17.2

thahíde *vt.* taunt, tease, give someone a hard time, mess around with 17.2

thahóⁿ *va.* thank, thank someone, give thanks 17.2

thahúni *va.* devour, gobble up, gobble it all up, leaving no leftovers 15.4, 17.2

thaóⁿba *va.* talk all night, talk till daybreak, talk the night away 17.2

thappí *vs.* fluent, skilled at speaking 17.2

thaṣníⁿ *va.* swallow, devour 14.1

thastúbe *va.* lick, taste 12.7, 13.2

thashpé *va.* bite off a piece 17.2

thashtóⁿ *va.* stop talking, singing, eating, or drinking 17.2

thattóⁿ *va.* drink 10.8, 11.2, 12.1, 13.2, 17.2, 18.2

thatʰé *va.* eat, chew 10.8, 12.2, 13.2, 13.9, 16.9, 17.2, 18.1, 19.1

thatʰéwathe *vs.* edible 16.9

thawá *va.* count 12.5, 13.2, 18.1, 18.2

thax̌thí *va.* nibble, as picking off meat from a chicken neck 17.2

thax̌thúde *va.* choke on food 17.2

thax̌tá *va.* bite 12.4, 13.2, 13.9, 17.2

thax̌úbe *vt.* praise 17.2, 19.2

thazhíⁿga *vt.* belittle 17.2

thé *va.* go 15.4, 16.6, 16.9, 19.2

thê *dem.* this, the one we were talking about, not present 14.6

théthe *va.* send, throw, cause to go 15.3, 16.6

théthi'awathe *vs.* untraversable 16.9

thêthu *adv.* here, in this area 15.3

thêthudi *adv.* here, around here, in this area 14.6, 15.2

théwathe *demand* Let's go! 18.1

théze *n.* tongue 13.12

thí *epron.* you, thou, thee; second person emphatic pronoun 14.8

thi'á *va.* fail, be unable, can't do it 11.10, 12.5, 13.2, 17.1

thiāzhi *v.* change, transform, make different 17.1

thibéx̌iⁿ *vt.* sweep, rake 17.1

thibīze *vt.* make dry, as a family drinking all the water from a bucket 17.1

thibthá *va.* spread open (a board game or door cover), unfold (a blanket); open (eyes or mouth) 14.1, 17.1

thibthāska *vt.* flatten, deflate, let the air out 17.1

thibthāze *vt.* tear (a page from a Sears catalog for toilet paper) 17.1

thibthóⁿ *vt.* smell, sniff (a rose) 17.1, 18.2

thidóⁿ *va.* pull 12.6, 13.2, 13.9, 17.1, 18.2

thigá *vt.* take apart, as in undoing braids or shucking corn 17.1, 18.1

thigthéze *vt.* streak, make stripes, stitch lines 17.1

thihébe *vt.* decrease volume or speed 17.1

thihí *vt.* scare, scare up (game), scare away 11.9

thihíde *vt.* lower (a bucket or a shade); put someone down, tease, taunt, seduce 17.1

thihóⁿ *vt.* lift something easily handled 11.9, 12.6, 13.2, 17.1

thikkúwiⁿx̣e *vt.* turn (a doorknob or a faucet handle), spin (a wheel) 17.1

thikʰúthe *va.* hurry 16.4, 19.5

thimōⁿshi *vt.* elevate, raise up into the air, lift, as a weight 17.1

thinóⁿge *vt.* roll by hand, like a hoop or a beachball; turn on, as water or a machine 17.1, 18.2

thinūshi *vt.* turn down (the volume), dim (a lamp) 17.1

thióⁿba *n.* lightning, lightning flash 19.4

thippái *vt.* sharpen (a knife) 17.1

thippāze *vt.* darken like evening, as with a smudge fire for mosquitoes 17.1

thippí *vs.* expert, skilled, good at doing something 11.10, 12.4, 13.2, 17.1

thip'íⁿze *va.* close (eyes) 14.1

thisági *vt.* harden, fortify 17.1

thisé *vt.* cut, clip (hair) 17.1

thisíhi *vt.* clean, straighten up (the house) 17.1

thiská *vt.* whiten, bleach out 17.1

thiskí *vt.* wring out (socks) 17.1

thiṣnú *vt.* drag, pull, tow, move, as a piece on a boardgame 17.1

thisóⁿde *vt.* tighten (a washer) 17.1

thisóⁿthe *vt.* turn over, as a pancake or a card, twist, as a rope 19.3

thishíⁿ *vt.* fatten (a pigeon) 17.1

thiṣhná *vt.* pluck (a chicken) 17.1

thiṣhnúde *vt.* pry out, extract 18.10

thishpé *vt.* pinch off a piece 17.1

thishtóⁿ *vt.* done, finished, release (a prisoner), let (a bird) go 17.1

thishtóⁿge *vt.* soften 17.1

thithítta *possessive* your, yours, thy, thine 14.9

thithíⁿge *vt.* demolish, tear down 17.1

thithúttoⁿ *vt.* straighten (an arrow or a wire) 17.1

thītta *n.* pigeon, dove 17.1

thittéga *vt.* renew 17.1

thittóⁿga *vt.* enlarge, expand, increase, dilate 17.1

thiūdoⁿ *vt.* improve, make better 17.1

thiûjoⁿ *vt.* decorate 17.1

thiwágazu *vt.* set straight, recognize, examine, look hard 19.2

thiwíⁿ *vt.* buy, purchase 18.1

thix̌í *vt.* wake up 14.3

thix̌óⁿ *vt.* break 17.1

thix̣é *vt.* chase 14.3

thix̣ú *vt.* draw, sketch, mark 17.1, 18.1

thizé *va.* take, pick up, get, accept, receive, take it 13.2, 13.9, 17.1

thizhá *vt.* wash 17.1

thiⁿ *pos.* article/positional: the (non-subject moving) 14.3

thíⁿ *va.* be, be a member of 13.2

thiⁿgé *vs.* lacking, none, gone, there is none 13.12, 15.8, 17.1

thiⁿkʰe *pos.* article/positional: the (passive singular) 14.3

thoⁿ *pos.* article/positional: the (globular) 14.1

thoⁿdi *conj.* when in the past 15.4

thoⁿkʰa *pos.* article/positional: the (passive collective plural) 14.3

thoⁿzha *conj.* but, however, nevertheless 15.7

thúkkathiⁿ *vs.* bare skin, naked 18.1

thúttoⁿ *vs.* straight 17.1

ttá *n.* meat, dried meat 11.7

ttabé *n.* ball 14.1, 18.2

ttabéītʰiⁿ *n.* baseball bat 18.2

ttadé *n.* wind 18.3

ttāge *n.* walnut, chestnut 18.2

ttāgeīgax̣ix̣e *n.* nutcracker 18.2

-ttahoⁿ *kin.* man's brother-in-law 16.5

ttaní *n.* soup, broth 15.2

ttanúkka *n.* meat, fresh meat 14.8

ttáppuskazhiⁿga *n.* student, pupil 11.2, 15.9

ttáx̌ti *n.* deer 14.4

tté *n.* buffalo, bison 10.5, 11.7

ttébi'a *n.* frog 10.9

ttéga *vs.* new 17.1

ttehé *n.* buffalo horn, spoon 11.7

Ttená! *uu.* male exclamation of startled fright: Yikes! Eek! 11.5

tteníx̌a-ugthezhe *n.* mushroom, morel 19.4

ttesíⁿde *n.* buffalo tail 11.7

ttéska *n.* cow, cattle 11.7, 15.9

ttéskamoⁿzéni *n.* cow's milk 11.7

ttí *n.* house, building 10.5, 14.1, 15.1

ttibútta *n.* jail 18.2

-ttigoⁿ *kin.* grandfather, father-in-law 16.1, 16.5

-ttimi *kin.* aunt, father's sister 16.4

-ttini *kin.* daughter-in-law 16.5

-ttinu *kin.* elder brother of a female 16.3

ttíuzhi *n.* family, household 16.7

ttizhébe *n.* door 11.1

ttízhiⁿga *n.* bathroom, outhouse, potty 13.3

-ttizhoⁿ *kin.* uncle's niece 16.4

ttóⁿ *va.* have, possess, have characteristically 13.1, 16.6

ttóⁿde *n.* ground 14.1, 15.1, 18.2

-ttoⁿde *kin.* son-in-law 16.5

ttōⁿdeīnoⁿse *n.* spade 18.2

ttōⁿde-thittūbe *n.* plow 19.6

ttoⁿgá *vs.* big, large, great 11.3, 11.8, 13.12, 17.1

-ttoⁿge *kin.* any sister of a male or younger sister of a female 16.3

-ttoⁿshka *kin.* uncle's nephew 16.4

ttóⁿthe *vt.* acquire 16.6

ttóⁿthiⁿ *va.* run 10.8, 13.1

ttóⁿwoⁿ *n.* town, village 11.9

ttú *vs.* blue 10.5, 11.3

ttúska *n.* woodpecker 17.9

-ttushka *kin.* aunt's nephew 16.4

-ttushpa *kin.* grandchild 16.1

-ttuzhoⁿge *kin.* aunt's niece 16.4

tʰe *pos.* article/positional: the (inanimate standing) 14.1

tʰe *particle* evidential particle 19.4

tʰí *va.* arrive here 10.5, 15.3, 15.4

tʰoⁿ *pos.* article/positional: the (animate standing) 14.3

t'é *v.* dead, die 10.9, 13.12, 16.6

t'égithe *vt.* kill one's own 19.1

t'éthe *va.* kill, cause to die 15.8, 16.6

ú *va.* hit with a shot, wound 13.5, 14.7

u'é *v.* plow, make holes or furrows for planting 18.3, 19.6

u'í *vt.* give, lend or loan (something) 18.10

ū'i *vi.* give, lend or loan (things) 18.10

ubáhe *n.* edge, margin, border 18.3

ubáhiⁿ *va.* insert, poke, put something in where it shouldn't be, like a finger in hot soup 18.3

ubátti *va.* plug, as a leak, or cork a bottle 18.3

ubátʰe *va.* lengthen cloth by sewing a piece on, exaggerate 18.3

ubétʰoⁿ *vt.* wrap, fold; wrap, as with a towel or blanket 18.2, 18.3, 18.10

ubíhe *n.* line of gravel left by a grader 18.3

ubísoⁿde *vs.* crowded, crowded in, squeezed close together, people pressed together 18.3

učʰízhe *vs.* weedy, thicket, brush, forest with lots of little trees 18.3

udá *vs.* icebound 18.3

ūdazhi *vs.* bad, not good, grim situation 19.3

ūdaⁿ *vs.* good 10.11, 11.3, 17.1

ūe *n.* field 18.7

ugá *vt.* color, dye, paint 18.10

ugádoⁿ *va.* pound, as a nail into wood 18.3

ugákkiba *vs.* split 18.3

ugánoⁿppaze *vs.* dark, pitch black, as from a blackout 18.3

ugás'iⁿ *va.* peek in 18.3

ugáṣne *vs.* split, cracked 18.10

ugáṣni *vs.* cool down, as in the evening 18.3

ugáṣnoⁿ *va.* lasso, throw a loop over something, make a basket 18.3

ugáspe *vs.* depression or indentation, as on a bed where someone sat 18.3

ugáshke *v.* tie, as a horse, hang from 18.3, 18.4

ugáshoⁿ *va.* travel, journey 18.3

ugáttoⁿthe *va.* tumble, roll over 18.3

ūgaxe *n.* picture 13.4

ugíne *vt.* seek one's own 19.1

ugíppi *vs.* full, as a cup of water 18.3

ugóⁿba *vs.* dawn, getting light out 18.3

ugóⁿbe *vs.* bright, light out 18.10

ugthíⁿ *n.* place where you sit or live 18.3

ugthóⁿ *vt.* contain, put into 18.2

ugthóⁿ *n.* container 18.3

uháⁿ *va.* cook, broil, boil, cook (something) 10.4, 16.4, 18.3, 18.3, 18.10, 19.5

ūhaⁿ *vi.* cook (things) 18.10

uhé *va.* pass, go along, road, follow, as a path 14.1, 15.2, 18.3, 18.4, 19.5

uhéatʰoⁿ *n.* bridge, ladder, stairway, viaduct 18.3

uhí *va.* beat, win, beat someone in a contest 13.10, 18.4

uhíthatti *n.* bathroom, bathhouse, place where you bathe 18.3

uhóⁿge *n.* limit, boundary, end, as of a rope, goal, as in a football game 18.3

uhóⁿgethiⁿge *vs.* endless, limitless, boundless 18.3

uīhaⁿ *vdat.* cook for someone 19.5

uīhe *vdat.* follow or join someone, attend, as a particular school 19.5

uīkkoⁿ *vdat.* help someone, help someone 16.5, 19.5

uītha *vdat.* tell someone 19.5

uīzhi *vdat.* fill for someone 19.5

ûjaⁿ *vs.* pretty 10.11, 14.9, 17.1

ukkégtha *vvict.* get told on, be gossiped about, hear something about yourself through the grapevine 19.4

ukkégthaspe *vvict.* get restrained from talking or eating 19.4

ukkégthiske *vvict.* straitjacketed, arms folded involuntarily 19.4

ukkégthispe *vvict.* get restrained from doing something 19.4

ukkíhi *va.* can, able to do something 11.10, 12.9

ukkíne *vrefl.* seek for oneself 19.3

ukkítte *n.* tribe, nation, foreigner, enemy 15.6

ukkóⁿ *n.* place, spot, an open space to put something 18.3

ūmakka *vs.* easy, cheap 18.10

umíⁿzhe *n.* bed, place to lie down 18.3

Umóⁿhoⁿ *nom.* Omaha 11.1

umóⁿthiⁿkka *n.* year, month, age 16.3, 18.3

umūbixoⁿ *vs.* bloat 18.3

umūbthiⁿ *v.* penetrate, as water, sand or snow into your house 18.3

unābixoⁿ *vs.* rise, as yeast, bubble as beer, pop, or water about to boil 18.3

unāgoⁿbe *vs.* bright or glowing, like city lights in the distance, or the flash of a camera 18.3

uné *va.* look for, seek, search for 12.2, 13.2, 13.10

unéthe *n.* stove, hearth, fireplace 18.3

unóⁿshtoⁿ *n.* dock, port, station, depot, rest stop, parking 18.3

unóⁿzhiⁿ *n.* shirt, jacket, coat, cape, tunic 13.5, 18.3

unóⁿzhiⁿ *va.* stand in, fill in for someone 18.3

unóⁿzhiⁿshtoⁿga *n.* jacket 13.5

unóⁿzhiⁿttoⁿga *n.* coat 13.5

unúshka *vs.* valley, small depression, or low spot in the ground 15.8, 18.3

uóⁿsisi *va.* jumping 11.2

uóⁿze *vs.* shade, as from trees or an awning 18.3

uppáhadi *pp.* beside 19.3

uppé *va.* crawl into or enter, as a house 15.1, 15.3, 18.3

uṣní *vs.* winter, cold (ambient temperature) 10.6, 18.3

uspé *n. v.* valley, sink, as a boat 18.3

ustáppe *n.* crash space, friendly household to stay with temporarily, as when traveling 18.3

ushágthe *n.* chops, serial cuts of meat that cut through the bone 18.3

ūshkade *n.* park, playing field, football or soccer field, or basketball court 18.3

ushkóⁿ *n.* ways, customs, habits, characteristics 9.3

ushkóⁿ *n.* place, site 18.3

uthá *va.* tell (the news) 12.7, 14.1, 14.4, 18.10, 19.4, 19.5

utháspe *vt.* restrain from doing something involving the mouth, such as talking or eating 19.4

ūthashte *n.* leftovers; food taken home from a doings or feast, which has been prayed over 9.11

uthéwiⁿ *v.* gather or assemble, as people or materials 18.3

uthí'age *va.* refuse to do it, unwilling, be reluctant to do something 11.10, 12.4, 13.2

uthí'ude *vt.* bore, drill, make a hole by boring or drilling 18.3

uthíae *v.* distribute something, such as food 18.6

uthídoⁿ *vt.* lock, latch; in use, as a bathroom 18.10

uthíske *vs.* arms folded over the chest, as pharoahs in their coffins, or spiders 19.4

uthíski *va.* tighten, as a lid 18.3

ūthiṣne *n.* slit, make a slit 18.3, 18.3

uthíṣnoⁿ *va.* put on a necktie or a fanbelt, or thread a needle 18.3

uthísoⁿ *va.* screw in, as a screw or lid 18.3

uthísoⁿthe *va.* turn over or flip over, as pancakes or frybread 18.3

uthíspe *vt.* restrain someone from doing something, as pulling back the reins on runaway horses 19.4

uthíshoⁿ *va.* go around the outside of something, like a powwow circle, or detour around an obstacle 18.3

uthíwiⁿxe *v.* spiral, like water down a drain, a tornado, or birds circling 18.3

uthíx̌thax̌tha *v.* loosen a rope or a knot 18.3

uthíx̣ide *va.* look around 12.2, 13.2

uthízoⁿ *nloc.* among, amid, midst, in the center, down the middle, in the middle of a group of people or animals 18.3, 19.1

uthóⁿ *va.* catch, hold, grab, arrest 18.3, 18.4

uthóⁿthe *vt.* hang up, as clothing 18.10

uthúbidoⁿ *vt.* push down, dip or dunk, as a piece of bread into sauce or gravy, or someone's head into the water 18.9

uthúdoⁿbe *v.* examine, watch out, be careful 18.9

uthúga *n.* coloring, paintbrush, paintstick; any tool or material used for coloring 18.9

uthúgahi *vt.* mix in, stir 18.9

uthúgashke *n.* hook, peg, something to hang things on 18.9

uthúgashoⁿ *v.* commute, travel back and forth 18.9

uthúhe *vt.* follow 18.9

uthúhi *vt.* reach 16.9, 18.9

uthúhithi'awathe *vs.* inaccessible 16.9, 18.9

uthúkkikkie *v.* discuss, converse 18.9

uthúkkoⁿthe *vt.* bind together, cling, connect 18.9

uthúnoⁿzhiⁿ *vt.* depend on, rely on, trust 18.9

uthúshi *nloc.* in front, facing a crowd, between (players) 15.3

uthúthe *n.* ties, as to a person or place 18.9

uthúthe-thiⁿge *vs.* have nobody left, nothing to hold you 18.9

uthút'athe *vt.* dislike, envy, be jealous of 18.9

uthúxa *vt.* deceive, trick, fool 18.9

uttánoⁿ *n.* path, aisle, walkway 18.3

uttóⁿ *v.* wear, as shirt, pants, shoes, hat, jewelry 18.3

utʰíⁿ *va.* hit 13.10

uxpáthe *va.* fall, as from a height 15.1, 18.3

uxpé *n.* dish, plate, pan, bowl 10.10, 18.3

uxthábe *vs.* bushes, forest, trees, timbers, out in the woods 18.3

uzhétha *vs.* tired, weary 13.12

uzhí *v.* put in, fill, full, loaded 15.8, 18.3, 19.5

ūzhiha *n.* bag, pack, backpack, purse 12.4

uzhóⁿ *n.* bed, bedroom 17.5

uzhóⁿge *n.* road, path 10.6, 14.1, 18.3

wa'íⁿ *n.* backpack, pack, load 18.1

wa'ú *n.* woman 10.9, 11.2, 14.2

wa'úzhiⁿga *n.* old woman 11.2, 14.2

waáthixoⁿ *n.* toy 17.7

wabáse *n.* saw (the tool) 18.1

wabátʰe *vt.* sewing 16.3

wābaxu *vi.* write (things) on 18.10

wabáxu kʰe *n.* the letters (in a word or sentence) 12.2

wabíbthuga *n.* rolling pin 18.1

wabthúga *n.* hominy 18.1

wāgathe *n.* gift 18.10

wagáxthoⁿ *n.* assistant 11.2

wagōⁿze *n.* teacher 11.2

wagthábaze *n.* book, paper, notes, papers 11.1, 12.2

wagtháde *va.* creep up 15.8

wagthí *n.* maggot 18.8

wahába *n.* corn 17.3

wahí *n.* bone 15.4

wahúttoⁿthe *n.* gun 14.1, 14.8

waíⁿ *n.* robe, blanket, shawl 14.1

Wakkóⁿda *nom.* God 15.3

wakkóⁿdagi *n.* water monster 16.8

wakkóⁿda-waāthahoⁿ-tti *n.* church 18.7

wākku *n.* awl, fork 18.3

wākkuzhiⁿga *n.* pin, needle 18.3

wākkuzhiⁿga ga'ú'ude *n.* needle 18.3

wamāxu *n.* carver 18.1

wamí *n.* blood 15.9

wamóske *n.* bread 18.5

wamóskebimóⁿthishtoⁿ *n.* dough 17.5

wamóske-nāxude *n.* toast 18.5

wamóskeshuga *n.* cowboy bread 12.5

wamóskexude *n.* flour 14.3

wanākkoⁿgthe *n.* candle, lamp 17.5

wanītta *n.* animal, four-legged animal 18.1

wanóⁿp'iⁿ *n.* necklace, choker 10.9

wanóⁿse *va.* surround, cut off, or control a herd 15.8

wanóⁿshe *n.* police, soldier 18.4

wanóⁿxe *n.* ghost 13.1

wappáde *n.* incision 18.1

wappé *n.* weapon 15.8

wasábe *n.* black bear 11.8, 18.1

wasékkoⁿ *vs.* fast, speedy 15.7

waskíthe *n.* sweets, fruit, berries, melon, dessert, pudding, jello 18.1

wasṇíde *vs.* slow, late 15.10

wāspe *v.* behave properly 19.4

washíⁿ *n.* fat, as for cooking 18.1

watháge *n.* cap, hat, headdress 13.5

watháthe *n.* food, meal 18.1

wāthathe *n.* table 11.1

wāthathe *vi.* eat (things) on 18.10

watháwa *n.* numbers 18.1

wathíbaba *n.* card, playing card 15.2

wāthixoⁿ *n.* toy 17.1

wathíxu *n.* drawing or painting (the picture) 18.1

wathízha *n.* laundry 18.1

watʰé *n.* skirt, dress 13.5

watʰóⁿ *n.* pumpkin, squash, melon 17.8

wat'éthe *n.* killer 15.8, 18.1

waxága *n.* burr 18.1

Wāxe *nom.* white person, non-Indian, non-Indian 10.8, 11.1

waxthí *v.* frightened, scared, afraid, phobic fear, as of snakes, spiders, heights, the dark, or ghosts 16.9

waxthíwathe *vs.* scary, potentially dangerous, as when looking down from a height 16.9

wazéthe *n.* doctor 18.1

wazhíde *n.* tomato, ketchup, buffalo berry 18.1

wazhíⁿ ppíazhi *vs.* angry, in a bad mood 15.8

Wazhíⁿ-dathiⁿ *nom.* Washington DC 16.10

wazhíⁿga *n.* bird, fowl, chicken 10.8, 18.1

wazhíⁿgaīkkide *n.* slingshot 18.2

wēabaxthade *n.* hairpin 18.10

wēagaspe *n.* paperweight 18.10

wéahide *nloc.* far away 15.3

wēathaskabe *n.* paste, tape 18.10

wéathathe *n.* food 13.7

wēbamoⁿ *n.* file 18.2, 18.10

wēbaxu *n.* pen, pencil, crayon, chalk, marker; any writing implement 11.1, 14.1, 18.2

wēdiⁿdiⁿ *n.* brace 18.2

wégazhi *va.* command them 15.9

wénoⁿxithe *va.* attack them 15.8

wēobatti *n.* cork 18.10

wēobetʰoⁿ *n.* wrapping 18.10

wēoga *n.* paint, dye, coloring 18.10

wēogaṣne *n.* wedge 18.10

wēogoⁿba *n.* window 18.10

wēogoⁿbanoⁿxe *n.* window glass 17.5

wēohoⁿ *n.* cooking pot, pan, cake pan 18.10

wēokkihoⁿ *n.* pepper 18.10

wēotha *n.* landmark, sign 18.10

wēothi'ude *n.* drill, auger, gimlet, corkscrew, brace and bit 18.10

wēothidoⁿ *n.* lock, latch 18.10

wēothoⁿthe *n.* hanger 18.10

wés'a *n.* snake 10.9

wéthade *n.* reader, teacher 18.10

wēthawa *n.* counter, nickel, cent 18.2, 18.10

wétta *n.* egg 14.1

wéttaugthe *n.* nest (for eggs) 14.7

wētʰiⁿ *n.* club, tomahawk, striker, hatchet; the suit of clubs 18.2

wétʰiⁿ *vi* hit (things) 18.10

wēuhoⁿ *n.* cooking pot 17.7

wí *epron.* I or me (emphatic pronoun) 14.8

wihé *n.* friend (female), female's little sister 16.10

wíkʰe *v.* true, tell the truth 14.8

wí-nóⁿxči *adv.* alone, by him- or herself 19.6

wiwítta *possessive* my, mine 14.9

wíⁿ *art.* one, a, an 10.8, 11.4, 13.6

wiⁿáxči *num.* one 11.4

wôⁿdoⁿ *part.* both 13.6

wôⁿgithe *n.* all, everyone, everybody 12.3, 13.6

Wúx̌! *uu.* Baloney!, male exclamation indicating that what the other person has said is nonsense 11.5

X̌āa-īi-! *uu.* male exclamation of exasperation (nineteenth century) 11.5

x̌áde *n.* hay, fodder 10.6, 18.2

x̌ádeīnoⁿse *n.* mower 19.1

x̌ádeīthize *n.* pitchfork 18.2

x̌ága *vs.* prickly, twisted, gnarled 18.1

x̌čǎthe *vt.* love 8.1

x̌é *va.* bury 10.6, 13.1

x̌eáthe *va.* fall down, as a person or animal while walking, or off a chair 19.3

x̌ithá *n.* eagle, golden eagle 10.8, 11.9, 13.6

x̌óⁿ *vs.* broken, broke, out of money 17.1

x̌óⁿde *n.* bunch, pile, heap 16.6

x̌óⁿdethe *vt.* rake together, gather into a bunch 16.6

x̌thá *vs.* skinny, thin 10.10

x̌thabé *n.* tree 14.1, 15.5

x̌thíⁿ *va.* growl 13.1

x̌tā *vs.* loved, liked 16.6

x̌tāthazhiwathe *vs.* unlikable 16.9

x̌tāthe *va.* love, like 12.4, 16.6

x̌ti *adv.* very, really, real, an intensifier 15.3

x̌ubé *vs.* holy, sacred, mysterious power 10.6, 16.8, 17.2

x̌ubékkithe *va.* practice one's mysterious powers 16.8

x̌úde *vs.* gray 10.6, 11.3, 11.8

x̌úga *n.* badger 10.6

x̌uíⁿ *vs.* smelly, stinky 14.7

x̣agé *va.* cry, weep 10.6, 11.9, 13.1

zéthe *vt.* doctor, treat a patient 18.1

zí *vs.* yellow 10.6, 11.3

zóⁿsta *vs.* spoiled or rotten, as meat or eggs 18.7

zúde *va.* whistle 13.1

zhábe *n.* beaver 10.6

zhíbe *n.* leg (esp. the lower leg), leg, thigh 10.6, 13.12

zhíde *vs.* red 11.3, 11.8, 18.1

zhiⁿgá *vs.* small, little, young 10.6, 11.3, 11.8, 13.12, 16.6, 17.2, 18.1

zhiⁿgáthe *va.* dwindle, reduce 16.6

-zhíⁿge *kin.* son 16.2

-zhiⁿthe *kin.* elder brother of a male 16.3

zhōⁿ *va.* lie, sleep, lie down 11.2, 13.1

zhóⁿ *n.* wood 10.6, 11.7, 11.8, 14.1

zhoⁿbtháska *n.* board, floor 12.3, 18.2

zhoⁿbtháskaībiṣhnaha *n.* sandpaper 18.2

zhoⁿbtháskasabe *n.* blackboard 12.3

zhoⁿbtháskaska *n.* whiteboard 12.3

-zhóⁿge *kin.* daughter 16.2

zhoⁿní *n.* maple syrup, sugar, candy 11.7

-zhoⁿthe *kin.* elder sister of a female 16.3

zhōⁿttoⁿthiⁿge *vs.* nod off, go to sleep 18.7

zhōⁿt'e *vs.* sound asleep 14.3

zhóⁿzhiⁿga *n.* stick 14.1

zhú *n.* skin, flesh 18.2, 19.4

zhūgigthe *vt.* accompany one's own 19.1

zhūgthe *vt.* accompany, together 16.3

zizíkka *n.* turkey 17.1

21.4 GLOSSARY: ENGLISH TO UMÓⁿHOⁿ

a	wíⁿ	aisle	uttánoⁿ
abandon	ōⁿthe	alcoholic	dāthiⁿ-giudoⁿ
abandon one's own	giōⁿthe	alive	nítta
		all	gthūba; bthūga; wôⁿgithe
able	ukkíhi		
above	móⁿshi; ppaháshi	allow	ínoⁿhiⁿ
absorb	thabīze	almost	ōⁿthinoⁿ
accept	thizé	alone	é-nóⁿx̌či
accompany	zhūgthe	alone (I alone)	wí-nóⁿx̌či
accompany one's own	zhūgigthe		
		also	mégoⁿ; shti
ache	mūdada	always	shóⁿshoⁿ
acorn	óⁿzhiⁿga	amid	uthízoⁿ
acquire	ttóⁿthe	among	uthízoⁿ
across	akkíthitta; akkíwatta; moⁿsóⁿthiⁿ	an	wíⁿ
		and	kki
adhere	āthaskabe	angry	wazhíⁿ ppíazhi; wazhíⁿshte
adjust	ubázhiⁿ		
adult	nóⁿ	animal	wanītta
afraid	wax̌thí	ankle	sikkóⁿ
again	shi	annoy	āgthe
age	umóⁿthiⁿkka	annoying	āgthewathe
agree to	ínoⁿhiⁿ	antler	hé
ahead	ppahóⁿga	appearance	udóⁿbe
aim	ādoⁿbe	apple	shé

apple cider	shéni	auger	wēothiʔude
apple tree	shéhi	augment: plural or action	i
approves	gīshoⁿ		
arise	ppáhoⁿ	aunt	-ttimi
arm	á	automobile	kkinóⁿnoⁿge
around	égaxe; kkúwiⁿxe	avenge	ímoⁿthe
arrest	uthóⁿ	await	íthappe
arrive back here	agthí; gthí	away	gúdiha
		awl	wākku
arrive back there	akʰí; kʰí	baby	shíⁿgazhiⁿga
		back (anat.)	nóⁿkka
arrive here	atʰí; tʰí	backpack	ūzhiha; waʔíⁿ
arrive there	ahí; hí	bad	ppiâzhi; ūdazhi
arrow	môⁿ	badger	xúga
ashamed	íshte	bag	ūzhiha
ask	ímoⁿxe	bald	shná
ask for	gīna; nā	bald eagle	ppasóⁿ
ask for one's own back	ginā	ball	ttabé
		Baloney!	Eē-shtoⁿna!; Wúx̌!
assemble	uthéwiⁿ; uthéwiⁿthe	bank (tilt)	gawíⁿxe
assistant	wagáx̌thoⁿ	barefoot	sithúkkathiⁿ
attack them	wénoⁿxithe	bare skin	thúkkathiⁿ
attempt	ígaskoⁿthe	base	híde
attend	uīhe	bathroom	ttízhiⁿga
attention getting word: Hey!	Dúda	be	thíⁿ
		beans	hiⁿbthíⁿge

bear (carry)	ʾíⁿ	bind together	uthúkkoⁿthe
bear: black bear	wasábe	bird	wazhíⁿga
		bison	tté
bear: grizzly bear	maⁿčʰú	bite	thaχtá
		bitter	mūppa
beard	íkkihiⁿ	black	sábe
beat (win)	uhí	black bear	wasábe
beaver	zhábe	blackboard	zhoⁿbtháskasabe
bed	umíⁿzhe; uzhóⁿ	blame	āgthe
bedroom	uzhóⁿ	blanket	waíⁿ
beer	níabiχe	bleach out	thiská
before	ppahóⁿga	blink	gabízhe
beg	nā	blink (eyes)	thipʾíⁿpʾiⁿze
behave properly	wāspe	blissful	gīthe
behind	háshi; náze	blister	noⁿdáze
belch	baʾú	blizzard	gashūde
belittle	thazhíⁿga	bloat	umūbiχoⁿ
belly	níχa	blood	wamí
bend	bibéniⁿ	bloody nose	ppāshude
berries	waskíthe	bloom	gabthá
beside	uppáhadi	blow	bihūttoⁿ; gahīthe; mūbiχoⁿ
Beware!	Sabá!	blow away	bihíthe; mūhithe
beware!	égithe	blow out	biχōⁿ
bid	āgazhi	blow up	biχōⁿ
big	ttoⁿgá	blue	ttú

board	zhon btháska	break	bixǒ́n; gaxǒ́n; non xǒ́n; thixǒ́n
boast	gigtháxube	break off	baxǒ́n
boastful	gītton ga	breast	mon zé
boat	mon dé	bridge	uhéath on
boil (cook)	uhá n	bright	nāgon be; ugón be; unāgon be
bone	wahí		
book	wagthábaze	bring	athín gí
border	ubáhe	broil	uhá n
bore	uthí'ude	broke	xǒ́n
boss	nudón hon ga	broken	bixǒ́n; non xǒ́n; xǒ́n
both	wôn don	broken up	gashétho n
bother	āgthe	broom	wēbabexin
bothersome	āgthewathe	broth	ttaní
bottom	híde	brother	kh agézhin ga
bounce	ga'ón si	brother-in-law: man's brother-in-law	-ttaho n
bounce off	non ttón ze		
boundary	uhón ge		
boundless	uhón gethin ge	brother-in-law: woman's brother-in-law	-shie
bow	môn de		
bowl	uxpé		
box	kkúge	brother: elder brother of a female	-ttinu
boy	núzhin ga; shénuzhin ga		
brace	īdin din; wēdin din		
branch	gāxǎ	brother: elder brother of a male	-zhin the
brand	nāxu		
brawl	kkikkína	brother: younger brother	-son ga
bread	wamóske		

brown	zíshabe	buzzard	héga
brush (thicket)	učʰízhe	calico	waxíⁿha
brush (broom)	wēbabexiⁿ	call	āthade; bóⁿ
bubble	unābixoⁿ	can (able)	ukkíhi
buckle	āgashke	candle	wanākkoⁿgthe
buffalo	tté	candy	zhoⁿní
buffalo berry	wazhīde	cannot do it	thiʾá
buffalo horn	ttehé	cap	watháge
buffalo tail	ttesíⁿde	cape	unóⁿzhiⁿ
building	ttí	car	kkinóⁿnoⁿge
bullet	móⁿzemoⁿ	card	wathíbaba
bunch	xóⁿde	carsick	gawákʰega
burn	nāxthiⁿ	cart	zhoⁿmóⁿthiⁿ
burp	baʾú; baníuski; banúski	carve	māʾé; māgixe; māxu
burr	waxága	carver	wamāxu
bury	xé	cat	iⁿgthóⁿga
bushes	uxthábe	catch	uthóⁿ
bushy haired	mūxadoⁿ	cattle	ttéska
		cent	wēthawa
bust	bibtháze; gabtháze	chair	āgthiⁿ
but	de; ede; thoⁿzha	chalk	wēbaxu
butcher	ppáde	change	kkigthíauzhi; thiāzhi
butt	níde	changed	thiāzhi
butter	bawēgthi; ṣnáthe	characteristics	ūshkoⁿ
button (verb)	āgashke	chase	ínoⁿxithe; thixé
		cheap	ūmakka
buy	thiwíⁿ	cheese	iⁿčʰóⁿgawathatʰe

cherry	nóⁿppa	clock	miīdoⁿbe
cherry juice	nóⁿppani	close (near)	eshóⁿ
cherry tree	nóⁿppahi	close (eyes)	thip'íⁿze
chest (anat.)	mōⁿge	cloth	waxíⁿha
chestnut	ttāge	clothes	hāthe
chew	thatʰé	cloud	moⁿx̌pí
chewing gum	zháppe	clouds	moⁿx̌pí
chicken	wazhíⁿga	cloudy	āmoⁿx̌pi
chief	gahíge; níkkagahi	club	wētʰiⁿ
child	shíⁿgazhiⁿga	clubs (suit)	wētʰiⁿ
chimney	ttíhukkoⁿ	coat	unóⁿzhiⁿ;
chin	íkki		unóⁿzhiⁿttoⁿga
choke	thax̌thúde	coffee	moⁿkkóⁿsabe
chokecherry	nóⁿppa	cold (ambient)	uṣní
chop	gasé	cold (an object)	ṣní
chops	ushágthe	collect a debt	gīna
chubby	shíⁿ	cologne	īthibthoⁿ
church	wakkóⁿda-wāthahoⁿ-tti	color	ugá; ūgax̌e
circling	gakkúwiⁿx̌e	coloring	uthúga; wēoga
clap	gačʰákki	comb	gahé
claw	sháge	come	aí; gí; í
clean	thisíhi	come back	agí; gí
clean up	thishúppa	comical	íx̌awathe
climb	āne	command	āgazhi
cling	uthúkkoⁿthe	common	ukkéthiⁿ
clip	thisé	commute	uthúgashoⁿ

conceited	gītto^{n}ga	cow	ttéska
confiscate	gīno^{n}she	cow's milk	ttéskamo^{n}zéni
connect	uthúkko^{n}the	cowboy bread	wamóskeshuga
contain	ugthó^n	crack	gax̌íx̣e
container	ugthó^n	cracked	ugáṣne
continually	shó^{n}sho^n	crane	ppétto^n
converse	uthúkkikkie	cranium	no^{n}shkí
cook (verb)	uhá^n	crash space	ustáppe
cook (person)	ūha^n	crawl into	uppé
cook for someone	uīha^n	crayon	wēbax̣u
cooked	nîde	crazy	gthó^{n}thi^n
cooking pot	wēoho^n	creak	bigíze
cool down	ugáṣni	creep up	wagtháde
cord	házhi^{n}ga	cricket	sí^{n}gthe
cork	wēobatti	crisp	nāsage
corkscrew	wēothi'ude	crow	kkāx̣e
corn	wahába	crowded	ubíso^{n}de
corner	ubázu	cry	x̣agé
cottonwood fluff	hi^{n}x̌pé	cry out	āx̣e
cougar	i^{n}gthó^{n}si^{n}ṣnede	cucumber	kkukkúmi
count	thawá	cultivate	i'o^n
count with	īthawa	cup	niīthatto^n
counter	īthawa; wēthawa	cuss	thagthó^n
cover	īgax̣ade; ithāgax̣ade	cut	gasé; íthise; māse; māx̌o^n; no^{n}sé; thisé
		cut off	íno^{n}se

cut up	ppáde	despicable	ít'athewathe
dangerous	nóⁿppewathe	dessert	waskíthe
dark	shábe; ugánoⁿppaze	destroyed	gashéthoⁿ
darken	thippāze	detest	ít'athe
daughter	-zhóⁿge	detestable	ít'athewathe
daughter (father speaking)	-nisi	detour	uthíshoⁿ
daughter-in-law	mīwathiǧe; -ttini	devour	thahúni; thaṣníⁿ
		Devouring Hill	Ppahé-wáthahuni
dawn	ugóⁿba	diamonds (suit)	kképpa
day	óⁿba	die	t'é
daylight	óⁿba	different	āzhi
dead	t'é	dig (a hole)	ga'é
deal out	baṣníde	dilate	thittóⁿga
deceive	uthúχa	dim	thinūshi
decorate	thiûjoⁿ	dip	uthúbidoⁿ
decrease	thihébe	dirty	ṣhnábe
deer	ttáǧti	discard	ōⁿthe
deflate	bibthāska; thibthāska	discover	íthe
demolish	thithíⁿge	discuss	uthúkkikkie
deny	gīzha	dish	uǧpé
depend on	uthúnoⁿzhiⁿ	dislike	ít'athe; uthút'athe
depot	unóⁿshtoⁿ	disobedient	noⁿǧíde-thiⁿge
depression	ugáspe; unúshka	display	bahá
deprive of	ínoⁿshe	distribute	uthíae
desirable	gōⁿthawathe	do	gāχe; óⁿ

dock	unóⁿshtoⁿ	drunk	dāthiⁿ
doctor (verb)	zéthe	drunkard	dāthiⁿ-giudoⁿ
doctor (person)	wazéthe	dry (adj.)	bīze
dog	shínuda	dry (verb)	bibīze; bīzethe; gabīze
doll	shíⁿgazhiⁿga	duck	míxa
dollar	mōⁿzeska	dump	bashóⁿthe
donate	gáthe	dunk	uthúbidoⁿ
done (finished)	Shóⁿ!; thishtóⁿ	dust devil	ttadóⁿhe
done (cooked)	nîde	dwindle	zhiⁿgáthe
door	ttizhébe	dye (verb)	ugá
doubt	gīzha	dye (noun)	wēoga
dough	wamóskebimóⁿthishtoⁿ	eagle: bald eagle	ppasóⁿ
dove	thītta	eagle: golden eagle	xithá
down	híde		
down feather	hiⁿxpé	ear (external)	nittá
downhill	ppamú	ear (internal)	noⁿxíde
drag	thiṣnú	earth	moⁿthíⁿkka
draw	thixú	easy	ūmakka
drawing	wathíxu	eat	thatʰé
dream	hôⁿbthe	eat on	āthatʰe; wāthatʰe
dress	watʰé	eat one's own	gthátʰe
drill (verb)	uthíʾude; baʾúde	edge	ubáhe
drill (tool)	wēothiʾude	edible	thatʰéwathe
drink	thattóⁿ	egg	wétta
drive	basí	eight	ppethâbthiⁿ

elbow	astúhi	explain this	awat^{h}égo^n
elevate	thimō^{n}shi	explode	mūbthaze; nābthaze; no^{n}btháze
eleven	agthí^{n}wi^n		
eliminate	bashétho^n	extended	thizú'e
elk	ó^{n}p^{h}a^n	extract	thiṣhnúde
embarrassed	íshte	extremely	āttasho^n
embarrassing	íshtewathe	eye	ishtá
embrace	āne	fabric	waxí^{n}ha
endless	uhó^{n}gethi^{n}ge	face	i^{n}dé
enemy	ukkítte	fail	thi'á
engrave	māxu	fall	kkinó^{n}se; uxpáthe
enlarge	thittó^{n}ga	fall down	xéáthe
enlist	gippáxu	family	ttíuzhi
enter	uppé	fan	āni
envy	uthút'athe	far	wéahide
erode	no^{n}thí^{n}ge	fare	īno^{n}ge
evening	ppāze	fast	wasékko^n
everybody	wô^{n}githe	fasten	āgashke
everyone	wô^{n}githe	fat	shí^n; washí^n
evidential particle	t^{h}e	father	ithádi
		father-in-law	-ttigo^n
evil	ppiâzhi	fatten	thishí^n
exaggerate	ubát^{h}e	fear	nó^{n}ppe
examine	thiwágazu; uthúdo^{n}be	feather	mó^{n}sho^n
expand	thittó^{n}ga	feed	íthishi
expert	thippí	fell	thabthízhe

female (animal only)	migá	flatten	bibthāska; noⁿbtháska; thibthāska
field	ūe	flee	ʾóⁿhe; kkióⁿhe
fight	kkikkína	flesh	zhú
file	bamóⁿ; ībamoⁿ; wēbamoⁿ	flip over	uthísoⁿthe
		flock	banóⁿ
file with	ībamoⁿ	floor	zhoⁿbtháska
fill	uzhí	flour	wamóskeẍude
fillip	mūkkoⁿ	flow	mūẍtoⁿ
find	íthe	fluent	thappí
find one's own	ígithe	fly (verb)	gióⁿ
finger	noⁿbéhi	fly (insect)	hóⁿtʾega
fingernail	sháge	fly over	āgioⁿ
finished	thishtóⁿ	focus on	ādoⁿbe
fire	nāẍthiⁿ; ppéde	fodder	ẍáde
fireplace	unéthe	fog	shúdemoⁿhoⁿ
firewater	ppedéni	fold	bet^hóⁿ; ubét^hoⁿ
first	ppahóⁿga	fold in	thippúẍe
fish	huhú	follow	uhé; uīhe; uthúhe
five	sáttoⁿ	food	wathát^he; wéathat^he
fix	ppíʾoⁿ	fool	uthúẍa
fizz	unābiẍoⁿ	foot	sí
flame	nāẍthiⁿ	football	ttabé-sippá
flare	nāhegazhi	footprints	sígthe
flat	btháska	forehead	ppé
		foreigner	ukkítte

forest	ux̌thábe	gift	wāgathe
fork	wākku	gimlet	wēothiʼude
forset	ux̌thábe	girl	mīzhiⁿga; shémizhiⁿga
fortify	thisági	give	ʼí; āoⁿthe; gáthe; uʼí; ūʼi
four	dúba		
fowl	wazhíⁿga	glad	gīudoⁿ
frayed	gaṣné	glowing	unāgoⁿbe
friend	kʰagé	gnarled	x̌ága
friend (female)	wihé	go	athé; moⁿthíⁿ; thé
frightened	wax̌thí	go along	uhé
frog	ttébiʼa	go back	agthé; gthé; moⁿgthíⁿ
front	ittóⁿthiⁿatta	go to sleep	zhōⁿttoⁿthiⁿge
fruit	waskíthe	gobble up	thahúni
fry	zhézhi	God	Wakkóⁿda
frying pan	wēzhezhi	golden eagle	x̌ithá
full	ugíppi; uzhí	gone	thiⁿgé
funny	íx̌awathe	gone away	aíathe
gang	banóⁿ	good	ūdaⁿ
gas money	īnoⁿge	good at	thippí
gather	bahí; uthéwiⁿ; x̌óⁿdethe	goose	míx̌a
		grab	uthóⁿ
gaze	ābanoⁿ	grab one's own	gthíze
get	thizé	grandchild	-ttushpa
get through	íhe	grandfather	ittígoⁿthe; -ttigoⁿ
get well	giní	grandmother	-kkoⁿ
ghost	wanóⁿxe	grapes	hāzi

grass	moⁿhíⁿ	hand towel	noⁿbéībikʰa
gravel	íⁿʾezhiⁿga	handgame	íⁿʾutʰiⁿ
gray	xúde	handkerchief	noⁿbéībikʰa
great	ttoⁿgá	hang	ugáshke
green	ppēzhittu	hang up	uthóⁿthe
greet	ākkippe	hanger	wēothoⁿthe
grind	bamóⁿ; noⁿttūbe	happy	gīshoⁿ; gīthe
grind up	noⁿttūbe	hard	sagí
grizzly bear	maⁿčʰú	harden	noⁿsági; thisági
ground	ttóⁿde	harden by heat	nāsagi
ground meat	māttube	hasten	hiⁿthéⁿkkithe
groundhog	moⁿthíⁿxude	hat	watháge
growl	xthíⁿ	hatchet	wētʰiⁿ
grown up	nóⁿ	hate	ítʾathe
gum	zháppe	have	athíⁿ; ttóⁿ
gun	wahúttoⁿthe	having	egóⁿ
habitually	noⁿ	hawk	gthedóⁿ
hair (of the head)	noⁿzhíⁿha	hay	xáde
		he	é
hair (body or animal)	híⁿ	head	noⁿshkí; ppá
		headdress	watháge
hairpin	wēabaxthade	headlong	kkuʾé
hairy	híⁿshkube	heap	xóⁿde
half	widétʰoⁿ	hear	noⁿʾóⁿ
hamburger	ttagáxthixthi	hearing	noⁿxíde
hand	noⁿbé		

heart	nônde	hold	uthóⁿ
hearth	unéthe	holes	ʾuʾúde
heat	nākkade	holy	xubé
heavy	skīge	hominy	wabthúga
heed	ānoⁿʾoⁿ	hoof	sháge
Hello! (men only)	Ahó!	hook	uthúgashke
		horn	hé
help (someone)	uīkkoⁿ	horse	shóⁿge
her	é; ettá	hot	nākkade
herd	basí	house	ttí
here	thêthu; thêthudi	household	ttíuzhi
Here!	Gá!	houseplant	waxtáhi
hers	ettá	how many?	ānoⁿ
Hey! Hey there!	Dúda	how?	awatʰégoⁿ; eóⁿ
hiccup	baníuski	how? explain this	awatʰégoⁿ
hide	há; íkkinoⁿxthe	however	thoⁿzha
high	móⁿshi	hug	āne
hill	ppahé	hundred	gthêboⁿhíⁿwiⁿ
him	é	hungry	noⁿppéhi
hips	síⁿdehi	hunt	ābae
his	ettá	hunting	ābae
Hispanic	Heshpaiúni	hurt	nóⁿkka
hit	ítʰiⁿ; utʰíⁿ; wétʰiⁿ	hurting	nié
hit with a shot	ú	husband	égthoⁿge
Hochunk	Húttoⁿga	I	wí
hog	kkúkkusi		

ice	núxe	jacket	unó^{n}zhi^n; unó^{n}zhi^{n}shto^{n}ga
icebound	udá	jail	ttibútta
if	at^{h}ó^{n}kkizhi; kki	jar	íthido^{n}do^n; íthizho^{n}zho^n
immovable	íshko^{n}azhiwathe	jello	waskíthe
impassable	íhethi'awathe	join	uīhe
improve	thiūdo^n	joker	wawéx̌ax̌a
in	mó^{n}t^{h}e	journey	ugásho^n
inaccessible	uthúhithi'awathe	jump onto	ā-'o^{n}si
incision	wappáde	jump over	ā-'o^{n}si
increase	thittó^{n}ga	jumping	uó^{n}sisi
indentation	ugáspe	just now	í^{n}č^{h}o^n
Indian agent	ithāditha-i	ketchup	wazhīde
injure	íniethe; nó^{n}kkathe	kick	no^{n}t^{h}é
injured	nó^{n}kka	kill	t'éthe
inquire	ímo^{n}x̣e	kill one's own	t'égithe
insert	ubáhi^n	killer	wat'éthe
inside	mó^{n}t^{h}e	kiss	í ākkigthe
intoxicated	dāthi^n	knead	bimó^n
invite	ík^{h}u	knife	mó^{n}hi^n
invite someone	gīk^{h}u	knock over	no^{n}x̌páthe
Ioway	Ppáx̌ude	know	íbaho^n
iron (metal)	mó^{n}ze	lacking	thi^{n}gé
iron (verb)	basáde; nāsade	ladder	uhéat^{h}o^n
it	é	lake	neúthisho^n
its	ettá		

lamp	wanākkoⁿgthe	lid	īgax̣ade; ithāgax̣ade
land	moⁿzhóⁿ	lie	zhōⁿ
language	īe	lift	gahóⁿ; thihóⁿ; thimōⁿshi
large	ttoⁿgá		
lash	gasáppi	lift onto	āhoⁿ
lasso	ugáṣnoⁿ	light	nākkoⁿ
last	háshi; íthishethoⁿ	lightning	thióⁿba
last night	hôⁿde	like	égoⁿ; x̌tāthe
latch (verb)	uthídoⁿ	liked	x̌tā
latch (noun)	wēothidoⁿ	limit	uhóⁿge
late	waṣníde	limitless	uhóⁿgethiⁿge
laugh	íx̌a	Lincoln, Nebraska	Niskíthettoⁿwoⁿgthoⁿ
laugh at	íx̌ax̌a		
laughing	íx̌ax̌a	lips	íha
laundry	wathízha	liquid	ní
lay	ihéthe	liquor	ppedéni
leader	nudóⁿhoⁿga	listen	ānoⁿʾoⁿ
lean on	ākkoⁿ; íthakkoⁿ	listen to	ānoⁿʾoⁿ
leather	há	little	zhiⁿgá
leave	aíathe	little toe	sippázhiⁿga
leg (esp. lower)	zhíbe	live	nítta
legend	hīga	liver	ppí
lend	uʾí; ūʾi	living	nítta
Let's go!	théwathe	load	waʾíⁿ
lick	thastúbe	loaded	uzhí
		loan	uʾí; ūʾi

loathe	ítʼathe	match	ppéde
loathsome	ítʼathewathe	material	waxíⁿha
lock (verb)	uthídoⁿ	me	wí
lock (noun)	wēothidoⁿ	meal	watháthᵉ
long	sṇéde	mealy	noⁿttūbe
look around	uthíx̣ide	meat	ttá; ttanúkka
look at	ādoⁿbe	meet	ākkippe
look for	uné	melon	waskíthe; watʰóⁿ
loosen	uthíx̌thax̌tha	melt	nāskoⁿ
love	x̌čāthe; x̌tāthe	metal	móⁿze
loved	x̌tā	Mexican	Heshpaiúni
low	híde	middle	ídabe
low spot	unúshka	midnight	hôⁿwidetʰoⁿ
lucky	gīzhu	midst	uthízoⁿ
maggot	wagthí	milk	moⁿzéni
make	gāx̣e	milk: cow's milk	ttéskamoⁿzéni
male (animal only)	nugá	milled	noⁿttūbe
man	nú	mine	wiwítta
man: old man	iⁿshʼáge	miserable	thaʼé
many	āhigi	miss	mūṣhnoⁿ
maple syrup	zhoⁿní	mix in	ígahi; uthúgahi
march	noⁿstáppi	moccasin	hiⁿbé; hiⁿbé-ukkéthiⁿ
margin	ubáhe	mold (verb)	bibíde
mark	thix̣ú	money	mōⁿzeska
marker	wēbax̣u	monkey	ishtíthiⁿkʰe

month	mí; umóⁿthiⁿkka	near	eshóⁿ; kkóⁿge
moon	mí	neck	núde; ppáhi
moose	ppashtóⁿga	necklace	wanóⁿp'iⁿ
mop (verb)	babīze; bibīze	needle	wākkuzhiⁿga;
morel	tteníxa-ugthezhe		wākkuzhiⁿga ga'ú'ude
mother	-háⁿ; iháⁿ	nephew: aunt's nephew	-ttushka
mother (addressing only)	naⁿ-	nephew: uncle's nephew	-ttoⁿshka
mother-in-law	-kkoⁿ	nest (for eggs)	wéttaugthe
mountain lion	iⁿgthóⁿsiⁿṣnede	nevertheless	thoⁿzha
mouse	iⁿčʰóⁿga	new	ttéga
mouth	í	nibble	thax̌thí
move	íshkoⁿ; thiṣnú; wahóⁿ	nickel	wēthawa
mow	noⁿsé	niece: aunt's niece	-ttuzhoⁿge
mower	x̌ádeīnoⁿse	niece: uncle's niece	-ttizhoⁿ
muddy water	gashūde	night	hôⁿ
mushroom	tteníx̌a-ugthezhe	nine	shóⁿkka
my	wiwítta	no	Áⁿkkazhi
nail (anat.)	sháge	nod off	zhōⁿttoⁿthiⁿge
nail (spike)	móⁿze-wēogadoⁿ	non-Indian	Wãx̌e
naked	thúkkathiⁿ	none	thiⁿgé
name	izházhe	normal	ukkéthiⁿ
napkin	noⁿbéībikʰa	nose	ppá
nation	ukkítte	notch	māski; māx̌u
naughty	noⁿx̌íde-thiⁿge		

notes	wagthábaze	ours	oⁿgútta
now	íⁿčʰoⁿ	out	gashíbe
nudge	baspóⁿ	outdoors	āshi
numbers	watháwa	outhouse	ttízhiⁿga
numerous	āhigi	outside	āgaha; āshi; āshiatta
nutcracker	ttāgeīgax̣ix̣e	overcast	āmoⁿx̌pi
o'clock	miīdoⁿbe	overhead	móⁿshi
obey	ānoⁿʾoⁿ	pack	ʾíⁿ; ūzhiha; waʾíⁿ
odor	bthóⁿ	pack on one's back	ʾíⁿ
odoriferous	bthóⁿ		
old man	iⁿshʾáge	pack one's own on one's back	giʾíⁿ
old woman	waʾúzhiⁿga		
Omaha	Umóⁿhoⁿ	pain	mūsisi
on	gahá	paint	ṣnáthe; ugá; wēoga
on top	āgaha	paint one's own	giṣnāthe
one	wíⁿ; wiⁿáx̌či	paintbrush	uthúga
only	noⁿ	painting	wathíx̣u
open	thibthá	paintstick	uthúga
open up	gabthá	pale	sóⁿ
operate	nóⁿgethe	pan	ux̌pé; wēohoⁿ
orange (fruit)	sézi	panther	iⁿgthóⁿsiⁿṣnede
orange (color)	sézi-egoⁿ	pants	níde-ūthishi; nídushi; nidūthishi
other	āzhi		
otter	nuṣhnáⁿ	paper	wagthábaze; wax̣íⁿha
our	oⁿgútta	papers	wagthábaze
		paperweight	wēagaspe

park	ūshkade	pick up collecting	bahí
parking	unóⁿshtoⁿ	pickle	kkukkúmi
part	hébe	pickle juice	kkukkúmi-ní
pass	íhe; uhé	picture	iⁿdéugaxe; ūgaxe; wathíxu
paste	wēathaskabe		
path	uttánoⁿ; uzhóⁿge	piece	hébe
Pawnee	Ppāthiⁿ	pierce	baxthú
pay off	bashéthoⁿ	pig	kkúkkusi
paycheck	wawéshi	pigeon	thītta
peace: make peace	moⁿzhóⁿ ūdoⁿ gāxe	pile	xóⁿde
		pile up	āgasta
peace pipe	niníba	pin	wākkuzhiⁿga
peanut	óⁿzhiⁿga	pink	zhí-egoⁿ
peck	mūxpa	pipe	niníba
peek in	ugás'iⁿ	pitchfork	xádeīthize
peg	uthúgashke	pitiable	tha'é
pelvic bone	siⁿdéhi-wahí	pitiful	tha'é
pen	wēbaxu	pity	tha'éthe
pencil	wēbaxu	place (verb)	ihéthe; ithóⁿthe; itʰéthe
penetrate	umūbthiⁿ		
people	níkkashiⁿga	place (noun)	ugthíⁿ; ukkóⁿ; ushkóⁿ
pepper	wēokkihoⁿ	plant (noun)	hí; waxtáhi
perfume	īthibthoⁿ; nubthóⁿ	plant (verb)	mūza
permit	ínoⁿhiⁿ	plate	uxpé
person	niáshiⁿga	play	shkāde
pick up	thizé		

playing field	ūshkade	potty	ttízhiⁿga
pleased	gīshoⁿ	pound	ugádoⁿ
plow	ttōⁿde-thittūbe; u'é	pour out	bashóⁿthe; baẋtóⁿ
pluck	thiṣhná	pouting	wazhíⁿshte
plug	ubátti	praise	thaẋúbe
plum	kkóⁿde	prance	noⁿstáppi
plum juice	kkóⁿdeni	President of the United States	ittígoⁿtha-i; ittígoⁿthe
plum tree	kkóⁿdehi		
plume	móⁿshoⁿ		
point	bazú	press	basáde
point at	ābazu	pretty	ûjaⁿ
poke	baspóⁿ; bazhíbe; ubáhiⁿ	prickly	ẋága
		protrude	mūza
police	wanóⁿshe	prune	gasúde
polish	ṣnáthe	pry out	thiṣhnúde
polish one's own	giṣnáthe	pudding	waskíthe
		pull	thidóⁿ; thiṣnú
pop	nígattushi	puma	iⁿgthóⁿsiⁿṣnede
porch	ātʰoⁿ	pumpkin	watʰóⁿ
porcupine	ppāhiⁿ	puncture	ba'úde
port	unóⁿshtoⁿ	pupil	ttáppuskazhiⁿga
portion	hébe	puppy	shínuja
portrait	iⁿdéugaẋe	purchase	thiwíⁿ
possess	ttóⁿ	purse	ūzhiha
pot	wēohoⁿ	push	badóⁿ; bahé
potato	nú	push down	uthúbidoⁿ

put	itʰéthe	recover	gigtházu; giní
put away	itʰéthe	red	zhīde
put in	uzhí	red hot	nāzhide
put into	ugthóⁿ	reduce	zhiⁿgáthe
put on	āgthe; āzhi; uthíṣnoⁿ	refuse	uthíʼage
quarter	mikkáha	refuse to do it	uthíʼage
quillwork	ppāhiⁿ	regularly	noⁿ
rabbit	moⁿshtíⁿge	rein	íkkiīthidoⁿ
raccoon	mikká	release	thishtóⁿ
raccoon skin	mikkáha	reluctant	uthíʼage
rain	noⁿzhīⁿ	rely on	uthúnoⁿzhiⁿ
raise	thimōⁿshi; uthéwiⁿthe	remaining	uīshte
rake	thibéẖiⁿ	remember	gisíthe
rancid	ppiâzhi	renew	thittéga
rattle	gasáthu; ppēẖe	repair	ppíʼoⁿ
razor	íkkihiⁿīgaskebe	request	nā
reach	uthúhi	reschedule	baṣnú
read	āthade	respect	gīthiezhuba
read to	íthade	rest stop	unóⁿshtoⁿ
reader	wéthade	restrain	utháspe; uthíspe
real	ẖti	revive	gisíⁿ
really	ẖti	ribbon	waẖíⁿha-nāgoⁿba
receive	thizé	ride	āgthiⁿ
recite	āthade	ridicule	íẖa; íẖaẖa
recognize	thiwágazu	rigid	díⁿdiⁿ

ripe	nāzhide; nîde	saw (verb)	basé
rise	unābixⁿ	saw (noun)	wabáse
road	uhé; uzhóⁿge	say	é
robe	waíⁿ	scalp	noⁿzhíⁿha
rock	íⁿʾe	scar	ṣná
Rocky Mountain sheep	ppashtóⁿga	scare	thihí
		scared	kkúhe; wax̌thí
roll	banóⁿge; nóⁿge; thinóⁿge	scary	nóⁿppewathe; wax̌thíwathe
rolling pin	wabíbthuga	scent	íthibthoⁿ
rope	házhiⁿga	scissors	ithābaṣnu
rotten	zóⁿsta	scold	íhusa; ínitʰe
round	bthúga; bútta	scorched	nāsabe; nax̌ude
round peak	bazú	scrape	gaskébe; gaxábe
routinely	noⁿ	scratch	thiʾú
rubber	hazízige	scream	bóⁿ
run	nóⁿge; ttóⁿthiⁿ	screw in	uthísoⁿ
run away	kkióⁿhe	search for	uné
run over	ānoⁿge	seasick	gawákʰega
rushing forward	kkuʾé	seat	āgthiⁿ
		seduce	thihíde
sacred	x̌ubé	see	dóⁿbe
salt	niskíthe	seed	sí
sand	biṣnáha	seek	uné
sandpaper	zhoⁿbtháskaībiṣnaha	seek one's own	ugíne
sane	gīwazhiⁿska		

send	théthe	shirt	unóⁿzhiⁿ
sense	ubéṣniⁿ	shoe	hiⁿbé
set	āgthe; itʰéthe	shoelaces	hiⁿbékkoⁿ
set straight	thiwágazu	shoo	basí
settle affairs	gigthíwagazu	shoot	kkíde
settle out	gaspé	short	ččéshka
seven	ppéthoⁿba	shot	móⁿzemoⁿ
sew	batʰé	shoulder	iⁿkʰéde
sew on	ubátʰe	shove	bahé
sewing	wabátʰe	shovel	basíhi
shade	noⁿshábe; uóⁿze	show	bahá
shaded	noⁿshábe	shuffle	baṣníde
shake	íthidoⁿdoⁿ; íthizhoⁿzhoⁿ	sicken	íwakhega
		side	moⁿsóⁿthiⁿ
shake out	bisáde; gabízhe	sift	mūzhoⁿ
shameful	íshtewathe	sign	wēotha
shape	bibíde	sign up	gippáχu
sharp	ppaí	silver	mōⁿzeska
sharpen	thippái	simple	ukkéthiⁿ
shave	baṣhná	singe	nāzi
shaver	ithābaṣnu	sink	uspé
shawl	waíⁿ	Sioux	Shaóⁿ
she	é	sister	wihé
shear	basé	sister-in-law: man's sister-in-law	-hoⁿga
shell corn	noⁿshpí		
shining	nāgoⁿbe		

sister-in-law: woman's sister-in-law	-shikkoⁿ
sister: any sister of a male or younger sister of a female	-ttoⁿge
sister: elder sister of a female	-zhoⁿthe
sit, sit down	gthíⁿ
sit on	āgthiⁿ
site	ushkóⁿ
six	sháppe
skate	nuzóⁿ
sketch	thixú
skilled	thippí
skillet	wēzhezhi
skin	gaxábe; há; zhú
skinny	xthá
skip	ā-ʾoⁿsi
skirt	watʰé
skull	noⁿshkí-wahí
skunk	móⁿga
sky	móⁿxe
slaughter	ppáde
sled	nuzóⁿ
sleep	zhōⁿ

slice thin	mā'é
slide	baṣnú
slingshot	wazhíⁿgaīkkide
slip	noⁿṣhnáha
slit	ūthiṣne
slosh	gathúzhe
slow	waṣníde
smack	gačʰákki
small	zhiⁿgá
smash	bibthāska
smear	ṣnáthe
smear on	āthaha
smear one's own	giṣnāthe
smell	bthóⁿ; íthibthoⁿ; thibthóⁿ
smelly	xuíⁿ
smile	íxazhiⁿga
smoke	shúde
smooth	bamóⁿ
smooth out	bisáde
snail	nihá
snake	wés'a
snap	gabízhe; gasáppi
sniff	thibthóⁿ
snow	má; máthe

snowing	máthe	spill on	āgashoⁿ
snowplow	mábadi	spin, spinning	gakkúwiⁿx̣e; thikkúwiⁿx̣e
snowstorm	gashūde	spiral	uthíwiⁿx̣e
so	égoⁿ	spit	baṣnóⁿ
soap	īthizha	split	ugákkiba; ugáṣne
sober	gīwazhiⁿska	spoiled	zóⁿsta
soft	shtóⁿga	sponge	īthizha
soften	thishtóⁿge	spooked	kkúhe
soil	moⁿthíⁿkka	spoon	ttehé
soldier	wanóⁿshe	spot	ukkóⁿ
some	dūba	spotted	gthézhe
sometimes	atʰóⁿshte	spread	ṣnáthe; thibthá
son	-zhíⁿge	spread on	ābiṣnathe
son (father speaking)	-nisi	spread open	thibthá
son-in-law	-ttoⁿde	spread out	gabthá
sound asleep	zhōⁿt'e	spring (the season)	mé
soup	ttaní	squash	watʰóⁿ
sour	s'áthe	squirm	kkigthíshkoⁿshkoⁿ
spade	ttōⁿdeīnoⁿse	squirrel	síⁿga
Spanish	Heshpaiúni	squirt	baṣníde
sparks	nādaze	stack	āoⁿthe
speak	ié	stairway	uhéatʰoⁿ
speech	īe	stalk	hí
speedy	wasékkoⁿ	stand	noⁿzhíⁿ
spill	shóⁿthe		

stand in	unóⁿzhiⁿ	strawberry	bashté
stand up	noⁿzhíⁿ	stray off	mūgthoⁿ
star	mikká'e	streak	thigthéze
station	unóⁿshtoⁿ	stretched out	thizú'e
steal	moⁿthóⁿ	stripe	thigthéze
stem	hí; zháhi	striped	gthéze
stick	zhóⁿzhiⁿga	strong	mūppa
stick to	āthaskabe	student	ttáppuskazhiⁿga
stick up	mūza	stuffing	wamóske-íkkigthahi
stiff	díⁿdiⁿ	stumble	kkinóⁿse
still	shetʰóⁿna; shóⁿshoⁿ	suck	thadóⁿ
stink	gabthóⁿ	suddenly	sabázhi
stinky	xuíⁿ	suffer	ísabe
stir	uthúgahi	sugar	zhoⁿní
stitch	batʰé	sun	mí
stomach	níxa	sunburn	nāt'e
stone	íⁿ'e	surround	wanóⁿse
story	íutha	surrounding	égaxe
stove	móⁿze-unéthe; unéthe	survive	hátheze
straight	thúttoⁿ	swallow	thaṣníⁿ
straighten	thithúttoⁿ	sweep	babéxiⁿ; thibéxiⁿ
strain	noⁿxtóⁿ	sweet	skíthe
strain out	mūzhoⁿ	sweets	waskíthe
straitjacketed	ukkégthiske	swerve	gawíⁿxe
strap	házhiⁿga	swim	niúoⁿ

swine	kkúkkusi	tell someone	uītha
swing	hethúbazhoⁿ	ten	gthêboⁿ
syrup	zhoⁿní-ṣnúṣnu	tender	nāttube
table	wāthatʰe	thank	thahón
tail	síⁿde	that	gá; shê
take	thizé	that yonder	shêhi
take ("go having")	athíⁿ moⁿthíⁿ	thaw	nāskoⁿ
take after	gigthé	the	akʰa; ama; ge; kʰe; ma; thiⁿ; thiⁿkʰe; thoⁿ; thoⁿkʰa; tʰe; tʰoⁿ
take apart	thigá	thee	thí
take away	ínoⁿshe	their, theirs	ettá
take one's own	gthíze	them	é
tall	ṣnéde	there	edí; gáthu; shêhithu; shêthu
talon	sháge	therefore	égoⁿ
tape	wēathaskabe	thereupon	égoⁿ
taste	ígaskoⁿthe; thastúbe	they	é
tattered	ʼuʼúde	thick	shugá
taunt	thahíde; thihíde	thicket	učʰízhe
tea	xádemoⁿkkoⁿ	thigh	zhíbe
teacher	wagōⁿze; wéthade	thin	xthá
team	banóⁿ	thine	thithítta
tear (verb)	thibthāze	think	ethégoⁿ
tear down	thithíⁿge	think about	síthe
tease	thahíde; thihíde	this	thê
teeth	hí		
tell (the news)	uthá		

thou	thí	tomato	wazhíde
thousand	kkúge	tomorrow	gasóⁿthiⁿ
thread	uthíṣnoⁿ	tongs	wēbaṣhnade
three	thâbthiⁿ	tongue	théze
throat	núde	too	shti
throw	óⁿtha thétha; ōⁿthe; théthe	too much	āttashoⁿ
		tooth	hí
throw away	óⁿtha thétha; ōⁿthe	tornado	ttadésagi-ttoⁿga; ttadóⁿhe-ttoⁿga
throw on	āoⁿthe		
thump	gakkúge	touch	ābitte; ítte
thy	thithítta	tow	thiṣnú
ticket	īnoⁿge	town	ttóⁿwoⁿ
tie (verb)	kkóⁿttoⁿ; ugáshke	toy	wāthiχoⁿ
ties	uthúthe	track	sígthe
tighten	thisóⁿde; uthíski	trail	sígthe
tilt	gawíⁿχe	transform	thiāzhi
timber	uχthábe	travel	ugáshoⁿ
time	miīdoⁿbe	treat	zéthe
tired	uzhétha	tree	hí; χthabé
toast	wamóske-nāχude	tree branch	gāχá
today	óⁿbathe	trees	uχthábe
toddler	shíⁿgazhiⁿga	tribal circle	húthuga
toe	sippá	tribe	ukkítte
toenail	sháge	trick	uthúχa
together	zhūgthe	Trickster	Ishtíthiⁿkʰe
tomahawk	wētʰiⁿ	trim	gasúde

trip	kkinóⁿse	unfold	thibthá
troublesome	āgthewathe	unlikable	x̌tāthazhiwathe
true	wíkʰe	untraversable	théthiʼawathe
trunk	hí	unwilling	uthíʼage
trust	uthúnoⁿzhiⁿ	up	móⁿshi
try	ígaskoⁿthe	upon	gahá
tumble	ugáttoⁿthe	us	oⁿgú
tunic	unóⁿzhiⁿ	usable	óⁿwathe
turkey	zizíkka	use	óⁿ
turn	thikkúwiⁿx̣e	valley	unúshka; uspé
turn around	kkigthísoⁿthe	veil	iⁿdéīgax̣ade
turn down	thinūshi	very	āttashoⁿ; x̌ti
turn on	thinóⁿge; umūttoⁿthiⁿ	viaduct	uhéatʰoⁿ
turn over	íbashoⁿthe; thisóⁿthe; uthísoⁿthe	view	ādoⁿbe
		village	ttóⁿwoⁿ
turtle	kké	visible	dóⁿbewathe
turtle head	kképpa	voice	hú
twelve	sháppenoⁿba	volunteer	gigtháthe
twilight	ppāze	vomit up	ígthebe
twist	thisóⁿthe	vulture	héga
twisted	x̌ága	wager	wéshi
two	noⁿbá	wagon	zhoⁿmóⁿthiⁿ
udder	moⁿzé	wait for	íthappe
ugly	ppiâzhi	wake up	thix̌í
uncle	inégi; -negi	walk	moⁿthíⁿ
unexpectedly	sabázhi		

walk back	moⁿgthíⁿ
walk on	āhe
walkway	uttánoⁿ
wall	nóⁿde
walnut	ttāge
wander away	mūgthoⁿ
want	gōⁿtha
want to	gōⁿtha
war chief	nudóⁿhoⁿga
warm	moⁿshté; nāshta
warped	nāttûbthiⁿ
warrior	nudóⁿ
wash	íthizha; thizhá
wash up	kkigthízha
washcloth	īthizha
Washington DC	Wazhíⁿ-dathiⁿ
washrag	īthizha
watch	ābanoⁿ; miīdoⁿbe
water	ní
water monster	wakkóⁿdagi
watermelon	sakkáid; sákkathide
wave to	wawégaχe
we	oⁿgú
weapon	wappé
wear	āthaha; íⁿ; uttóⁿ

weary	uzhétha
wedge	wēogaṣne
weedy	ucʰízhe
weep	χagé
weight	mōⁿzeskige
what (specific)	edādoⁿ
what does it mean?	awatʰégoⁿ
what?	idādoⁿ
wheel	īthinoⁿge
wheeze	gaīⁿχe
when	de; kki
where exactly?	āgudiχti
where?	āgudi
whip	gasáppi
whirlwind	ttadóⁿhe
whiskers	íkkihiⁿ
whisky	ppedéni
whistle	zúde
white	ská; sóⁿ
white person	Wāχe
white: distant white	sóⁿ
whiteboard	zhoⁿbtháskaska
whiten	thiská
whiteout	gashūde

whittle	mā'é; māgiẋe	wrapper	ībetʰoⁿ
who?	ebé	wrapping	wēobetʰoⁿ
why?	awádi	wrecked	gattūbe
wife	-gaẋthoⁿ	wretched	tha'é
wild	moⁿttánoⁿha	wriggle	kkigthíshkoⁿshkoⁿ
win	uhí	wring out	bishkí; thiskí
wind	ttadé	write	baẋú
window	wēogoⁿba	write down	ābaẋu
window glass	wēogoⁿbanoⁿẋe	write off	bashéthoⁿ
wing	áhiⁿ	write on	ābaẋu; wābaẋu
Winnebago	Húttoⁿga	writing implement	wēbaẋu
winnow	mūzhoⁿ		
winter	uṣní	year	umóⁿthiⁿkka
wipe	bibīze; bikʰá	yell	bóⁿ
wipe out	bashéthoⁿ	yellow	zí
wolf	shóⁿttoⁿga	yes	áoⁿ
woman	wa'ú	yes (nineteenth century)	óⁿhoⁿ
woman: old woman	wa'úzhiⁿga		
wood	zhóⁿ	yesterday	sidādi
woodpecker	ttúska	yet	shetʰóⁿna
word	īe	you	thí
wound	ú	young	zhiⁿgá
wrap	ubétʰoⁿ	young woman	mīzhiⁿga
		your, yours	thithítta

WORDS OF ENCOURAGEMENT

Wôⁿgithe washkóⁿ i a! Washkóⁿ i ga ho!
　　Everyone, good luck! Be strong and do well!

It is customary to mark the end of a class or lesson in Umóⁿhoⁿ by declaring, "Shóⁿ!"—"We are done (with this activity)!" However, this textbook's conclusion is not a final ending. We all continue to go on learning. We hope that your journey in speaking, listening to, reading, writing, appreciating, sharing, and living Umóⁿhoⁿ íye-tʰe, Umóⁿhoⁿ úshkoⁿ-tʰe continues. Thank you for joining us in this beautiful way.

Everyone, good luck! Be strong and do well!
　　Wôⁿgithe washkóⁿ i a! Washkóⁿ i ga ho!